Western European Party Systems

Western European Party Systems
Trends and Prospects

Peter H. Merkl, Editor

THE FREE PRESS
A Division of Macmillan Publishing Co., Inc.
NEW YORK

Collier Macmillan Publishers
LONDON

The Free Press
A Division of Macmillan Publishing Co., Inc.
866 Third Avenue, New York, N.Y. 10022

Collier Macmillan Canada, Ltd.

Library of Congress Catalog Card Number: 78-22783

Printed in the United States of America

printing number

1 2 3 4 5 6 7 8 9 10

Library of Congress Cataloging in Publication Data

Main entry under title:

Western European party systems.

  Based on papers given at a symposium held in Washington, D.C.
in the fall of 1977.
    Includes index.
    1. Political parties—Europe—Congresses.
I. Merkl, Peter H.
JN94.A979W47 1979   329'02'094   78-22783
ISBN 0-02-920060-1

CONTENTS

PREFACE AND
ACKNOWLEDGMENTS

IT IS NOT EASY to unravel the various antecedents and influences that led to the publication of this volume. A central source of inspiration has been the Seminar on Western European Politics which was held every winter for many years at the University of California, Santa Barbara. These seminars were always organized around one or two central subjects. Throughout most of the 1970s, the central topic was European party systems and elections, and it was he.e that the intellectual framework for this volume emerged. To fill in the spaces with authoritative accounts of each party system, Lowell G. Noonan, Raphael Zariski, and M. Donald Hancock—all three authors of works on comparative politics in Europe—were a logical choice for France, Italy, and Sweden respectively. Arthur Cyr agreed to write a chapter on Great Britain and I myself undertook to write on West German politics.

This still left most of the smaller European countries and special analytical topics to be covered. At this point, however, new talent and new lines of interest came into play, in particular an unrelated symposium on party factionalism directed by Frank Belloni and Dennis Beller. Some of the original and several new people then organized a round-table discussion on Western party systems at the American Political Science Association meeting in Washington, D.C., in 1977. This round table added, through the good offices of the association, Galen A. Irwin, Howard Wiarda, Sten Sparre Nilson, Lawrence Mayer, John C. Thomas, C. Neal Tate, Frank L. Wilson, Zelime Amen Ward, Jutta Helm, and Stephen Fisher to the original team.

In this fashion, the book took shape in an amazingly short period and under unusually favorable circumstances. Further contributors on the small countries were found in Pertti Suhonen and in Michael Carey, a graduate of the Santa Barbara Seminar. Margareta Mommsen-Reindl was known through her work for the *Politische Vierteljahresschrift.* Werner Kaltefleiter and his work were well-known for many years, and his contribution to this volume greatly enhances it.

My topical essay in Part Three and the concluding essay address the composition and political culture of the membership of various political movements. The essay in Part Three directs this interest at West German and Italian Socialists and Christian Democrats. It was part of a major interviewing project conducted in 1968/1969 and published in various places. The concluding essay, lacking interviewing data, compares such information on the composition of various major European parties as has become available now in a variety of places. This is a new and growing subject of sociological curiosity in which the nature of reality and the secular trends are just beginning to be recognized. Here I very much appreciated the advice and assistance of Sten Sparre Nilson.

This whole enterprise, as was said earlier, was favored by circumstances and by a cooperative attitude on the part of every single participant, including the prompt help and encouragement received at the hands of Colin Jones and Elly Dickason of The Free Press. Thanks are also due Pauline Mills who typed the manuscript with painstaking care. I can only wish that all joint publications were similarly favored with prompt cooperation and mutual regard.

LIST OF CONTRIBUTORS

MICHAEL CAREY, assistant professor, Loyola Marymount University, Los Angeles. Current research: bilingualism and local authorities in Ireland, food and agricultural policies in Europe.

ARTHUR CYR, program director, Chicago Council on Foreign Relations. Author of *Liberal Party Politics in Britain* and writings on British and West European politics and international relations.

STEPHEN L. FISHER, associate professor of political science, Emory and Henry College, Emory, Virginia. Author of *The Minor Parties of the Federal Republic in Germany: Toward a Comparative Theory of Minor Parties* (1974).

M. DONALD HANCOCK, director of the Center for European Studies and associate dean of the College of Liberal Arts at the University of Texas at Austin. Author of *Sweden: Politics of Postindustrial Change* (1972) and coeditor of *Politics in the Post-Welfare State: Responses to the New Individualism* (1972).

JUTTA A. HELM, assistant professor of political science at Western Illinois University, Macomb, Illinois. Author of articles on citizen roles in West Germany. Her current interests focus on environmental movements in Europe.

GALEN A. IRWIN, reader in political behavior and research methods at the University of Leiden, Netherlands. He was director of the 1977 Dutch National Election Study and coeditor of *De Nederlandse Kiezer '77*.

WERNER KALTEFLEITER, professor of political science and director of the Institute of Political Science, University of Kiel. Author of *Vorspiel zum*

ix

Wechsel: Eine Analyse zur Bundestagswahl 1976 (1977), *Zwischen Konsens und Krise—Analyse der Bundestagswahl 1972* (1973), and *Im Wechselspiel der Koalitionen—Analyse der Bundestagswahl 1969* (1970).

LAWRENCE C. MAYER, associate professor, Texas Technological University, Lubbock, Texas. Author of *Comparative Political Inquiry* (1972) and *Politics in Industrial Societies* (1977).

PETER H. MERKL, professor at University of California, Santa Barbara. Author of *Modern Comparative Politics* (2nd ed. 1977) and *Political Violence under the Swastika: 581 Early Nazis* (1975). Current research: local government reform in Bavaria and comparative economic growth policies in West Germany and Japan.

MARGARETA MOMMSEN-REINDL, assistant professor of political science at Bochum University, West Germany. Author of *Die Österreichische Proporzdemokratie und der Fall Habsburg* and articles on the Soviet system.

STEN SPARRE NILSON, associate professor of political science, University of Oslo, Norway. He has been a visiting fellow at the Center of International Studies, Princeton University, and a visiting professor at Louisiana State University and the University of Maryland. He has contributed to *Referendums* (1979); among his earlier publications are *Histoire et sciences politiques* and *Knut Hamsun und die Politik*.

LOWELL G. NOONAN, professor of political science, California State University, Northridge. Author of *France: the Politics of Continuity in Change* (1970), and other works.

C. NEAL TATE, associate professor of political science at North Texas State University. Author of a number of articles dealing with comparative electoral and judicial behavior and co-author of *The Supreme Court in American Politics: Policy through Law*.

JOHN CLAYTON THOMAS, assistant professor at the University of Cincinnati. Current research: articulation of policy demands by Western parties and American-based research on the intergovernmental implementation of minority employment policies.

PERTTI SUHONEN, docent in political science and research fellow at the Research Institute for Social Sciences at the University of Tampere, Finland. Lecturer in politics at the University of Jyväskylä and in sociology at the University of Tampere. Editor of *Sosiologia*.

ZELIME AMEN WARD, assistant professor at the University of Texas at Austin and researcher in West Germany, primarily in Bonn and at the Universities of Mannheim and Cologne. Her research focuses on European urban reform, European party systems, the women's movement in West Germany, nationalism in East Germany, and policy priorities in postindustrial societies.

HOWARD J. WIARDA, professor of political science and chairman of the Program in Latin American Studies at the University of Massachusetts. Author of *Dictatorship and Development, The Dominican Republic: Nation in Transition, The Brazilian Catholic Labor Movement, Politics and Social Change in Latin America, Corporatism and Development: The Portuguese Experience*, and *Latin American Politics and Development*. His present research focuses on the politics of population policy in Latin America, on the industrial relations systems of Southern Europe, and on state-society relations in Europe and the Americas.

FRANK L. WILSON, associate professor of political science at Purdue University. Author of *The French Democratic Left, 1963–1969: Toward a Modern Party System* (1971) and the co-author of *The Comparative Study of Politics* (1976).

RAPHAEL ZARISKI, professor of political science, University of Nebraska-Lincoln. Author of *Italy: The Politics of Uneven Development* (1972).

CHAPTER 1

INTRODUCTION: THE STUDY OF PARTY SYSTEMS

Peter H. Merkl

POLITICAL PARTIES AND PARTY SYSTEMS are among the most important political institutions of twentieth century societies. There are still countries, to be sure, in which parties may be suppressed altogether or may have to play second fiddle to such established forces as the army or the bureaucracy. But popular government in all its distinctive patterns has seemed to require parties to mobilize the people and to articulate their needs. Nowhere is this more true than in Western Europe where the recent fall of the last cryptofascist autocracies has removed the last barriers to the unrestrained operation of parties anywhere in the region.

European parties, of course, have been an important, even a classical object of academic study since the turn of the century and there has developed a research literature which in recent years has successfully tackled even such challenging subjects as the rise of mass politics and comparative party identification.[1] The purpose of this volume is at once more modest and more encompassing. We would like to survey Western European party systems as basic institutions somewhat in the manner in which the late Sigmund Neumann surveyed them in his *Modern Political Parties*[2] a quarter of a century ago, except for the addition of some crossnational comparisons. The shift from "parties" to "party systems," moreover, mirrors a macropolitical emphasis quite different from the preoccupation of the earlier literature with the definition and description of individual parties. To speak of party systems is to raise questions about the role of the parties in the political system, their

1

functions as Leon Epstein and Gabriel Almond each in his own way have described them,[3] and their numerical relationships and coalition behavior.[4] For lack of space and, in some cases, comparative material, we cannot deal with all their systemic properties here, nor need we do so when they have been treated elsewhere as thoroughly as, for example, the developmental aspects in Joseph La Palombara and Myron Weiner's *Political Parties and Political Development*[5] or Seymour M. Lipset and Stein Rokkan's *Party Systems and Voter Alignments.*[6]

Instead, we will concentrate on the five topics described in the following pages: (1) the role of parties in the political system, (2) the kinds of parties and party systems and their recent evolution, (3) their organizational features and political cultures, (4) the partisan cleavages in the electorate, and (5) the composition of the party membership, as far as it may be known, and its significance. The limitations of the available material and, sometimes, our own myopia may restrict this agenda still further. The geographical range of our treatment will, hopefully, make up for what it may lack in details.

The Role of Political Parties

Howard Wiarda in his contribution on Spain and Portugal draws a telling picture of the evolving role of the party systems there against the still dominant powers of the monarchy, the armed forces, and bureaucracy. He could just as well be speaking of the Third Republic of France or Imperial and Weimar Germany. His sensitive account of the antecedents of modern parties there in an earlier age, the personal and regional factions of *caciques* and men on horseback against a pervasive setting of clientelistic relationships, is another important aspect of the roles of the parties. Factionalism outside and inside the parties is a theme sounded in many of the country chapters, such as by Raphael Zariski on Italy, Peter Merkl on West Germany, Arthur Cyr on Great Britain, and, more broadly, in the literature on factions.[7]

Another aspect of the role of the parties are the antiparty feelings described by Werner Kaltefleiter in many Western European systems today. When people become dissatisfied with the existing parties—a familiar phenomenon in the United States today—they will not necessarily abstain or withdraw from politics. More often than not, they may turn to splinter groups or small parties that appear to be closer to their views. Stephen L. Fisher describes in this volume the strikingly different perspective we can get of a system when we take the small parties seriously rather than seeing in them only the splintering of the majority will. Citizens dissatisfied with the parties may also resort to the "citizen initiatives" described by Jutta Helm or to the other forms of direct action so pervasive in Western Europe that a recent statement of the Joint Committee on Western Europe of the Social Science Research Council and the American Council of Learned Societies suggested strongly that parties have been declining there while forms of direct action are on the ascendant.

Types of Party Systems

Numerical typologies of party systems have always been at the heart of serious studies of the macropolitics of parties, of elections, and of coalition behavior. They have ranged from elaborate attempts to explain away the third and further parties in "two-party systems" to the distinctions between "stable" or "moderate" and "unstable" or "extremely pluralistic" multiparty systems.[8] A look at a comparative table of recent election results (Tables 1–1 and 1–2) may remind us that much of the confusion is due to the fact that the popular classifications are related to the most visible function of a democratic party system, namely, the generation of a cohesive parliamentary majority for the purpose of governing the country. All Western European systems are variants of parliamentary government. It is not because of the actual distribution of the vote but of the need for a governing majority and a viable replacement for it that we tend to insist on calling the British, German and Austrian systems "two party" and the Scandinavian, Dutch, and Belgian multiparty systems "two-bloc" presumably different from the rest. Fortunately, we need not account here for the one hundred or more[9] diverse systems of the whole world, only for Western Europe.

When we "count" parties, to speak with Giovanni Sartori, therefore, we need to proceed by steps suggested by the access to power in the individual countries involved. First, we have to take into account the electoral system and other subterfuges favoring winners or incumbents. A brief glance at Tables 1–1 and 1–2 shows the extent to which the electoral systems of Great Britain, France, Spain, and Greece, to mention some of the more flagrant cases, help to create governing majorities where the voters have failed to do so. If it were up to the voters alone, in fact, only two of over 100 parties in 18 West European countries managed to poll a popular majority at the last elections: Austria's Socialists and Ireland's Fianna Fail. In many systems also, there are minority governments in office, as in Norway, Denmark, Italy, Spain, and Portugal, usually tolerated by the other parties in the absence of a good alternative. The effect is the same, although these minority governments may not be quite as capable of handling crises as might be a government with a parliamentary majority created solely by the electoral law.

Second, and this is Sartori's advice, we need not give equal weight to the size of parties at the fringes of the ideological spectrum because they are far less likely to be able to be included in government coalitions than even the smallest middle-of-the-road party. Sartori's point that a fringe party with 10% of the vote may have less capability for coalition than a party with 3% in the center

TABLE 1-1. Distribution of Popular Vote in Recent National Elections (Percent)

ELECTIONS	COMM.	SOC. LEFT	SOC. DEM. LABOUR	ONE ISSUE	REGIONAL	FARMER	LIBERAL	CHRIST. DEM.	CONSERV.	FAR RIGHT	TURNOUT
Major countries											
1974 (Oct.) Gr. Britain			39.3		6.5		18.3		35.8		72.8
1976 W. Germany			42.6				7.9	48.6			90.7
1978 France	18.6	30.7						23.2[a]	26.1		85.0
1976 Italy	35.9[b]	8.6	3.4	1.1[c]			3.1[d]	38.7	1.3[e]	6.1	90.0
Smaller countries											
1974 Belgium	3.2		26.7		21.3[f]		15.2	32.3	15.6		92.0
1974 Luxembourg	10.4	29.0	9.1				22.1	28.0	24.7		90.0
1977 Netherlands	1.7		33.8	6.1[g]		0.8	17.9	31.9	2.1[h]		80.0
1976 Sweden	4.7		42.7			24.1	11.1		15.6		91.7
1977 Norway	0.4	4.1	42.4	1.9		8.6	3.2	12.1	24.7		81.1
1977 Denmark	3.7	6.6	37.0	14.6		12.0[i]	3.6[j]	3.4	8.5		88.7
1975 Finland	18.9		24.9		5.0	21.5	4.4	3.3	18.4	1.6	73.8
1974 Iceland	18.3		9.1			4.6	24.9		42.7		91.4
1977 Ireland			11.5					29.0[k]	56.8		70.0
1975 Austria	1.2		50.4				5.4	42.9			91.8
1957 Switzerland	2.2	1.3	25.4	10.5[l]		10.1	22.4	20.6	3.0[m]	2.5	
1977 Spain	9.2		29.2		18.5			34.7[n]	8.4		
1976 Portugal	14.4		34.9					24.8[o]	16.0[p]		83.3
1977 Greece	9.3		25.3					11.9[q]	41.9	6.8	81.3

[a] Democratic Union (UDF).
[b] Incl. Dissident Socialists (PDUP).
[c] Radicals (PR).
[d] Republicans (PRI).
[e] Liberals (PLI).
[f] Both Flemish and Walloon parties.
[g] Both Democrats '66 and Social Democrats '70.
[h] State Reform party.
[i] Venstre.
[j] Radical Venstre.
[k] Fine Gael.
[l] Independents, etc.
[m] Republican Action.
[n] Democratic Union (UCD).
[o] Social Democrats/Democrats (SD/PD).
[p] Conservatives (CDS).
[q] Moderates (EDHK).

TABLE 1–2. Distribution of Parliamentary Seats after Recent Elections (Percent)

Elections	*Comm.*	*Soc. Left*	*Soc. Dem. Labour*	*One Issue*	*Regional*	*Farmer*	*Liberal*	*Christ. Dem.*	*Conserv.*	*Far Right*
Major countries										
1974 (Oct.) Gr. Britain			50.2		4.1		2.1		43.6	
1976 West Germany			42.9				7.9	49.2		
1978 France	17.5	23.0						27.9[a]	30.1	5.6
1976 Italy	37.1[b]	9.2	2.4	0.6[c]			2.2[d]	41.6	0.8[e]	
Smaller countries										
1974 Belgium	1.9		27.8		22.2[f]		14.2	34.0		
1974 Luxembourg	8.5	8.5	28.8				23.7	30.5		
1977 Netherlands	1.3		35.1	6.0[g]		0.7	18.5	32.5	2.0[h]	
1976 Sweden	4.9		43.5			24.6	11.2		15.8	
1977 Norway		1.3	49.2			7.7	1.3	14.2	26.5	
1977 Denmark	4.0	6.9	37.1	14.9		12.0[i]	3.4[j]	3.4	8.6	
1975 Finland	20.0		27.0		5.0	20.5	4.5	4.5	17.5	
1974 Iceland	18.3		8.3			3.3	28.3		41.7	
1977 Ireland		11.5					29.1[k]	56.8		
1975 Austria		50.8				5.5	43.7			
1975 Switzerland	2.1		29.3	5.9[l]		11.2	25.0	24.5	2.1[m]	
1977 Spain	5.7		33.7		6.3		47.1[n]		4.6	
1976 Portugal	15.3		40.5				27.9[o]		16.0[p]	
1977 Greece	3.7		31.2				5.0[q]		57.7	0.5

Note: Parties in government underscored.
[a] Democratic Union (UDF).
[b] Incl. Dissident Socialists (PDUP).
[c] Radicals (PR).
[d] Republicans (PRI).
[e] Liberals (PLI).
[f] Both Flemish and Walloon parties.
[g] Both Democrats '66 and Social Democrats '70.
[h] State Reform party.
[i] Venstre.
[j] Radical Venstre.
[k] Fine Gael.
[l] Independents, Liberals, Evangelics.
[m] Republican Action.
[n] Democratic Union (UCD).
[o] Social Democrats/Democrats (SD/PD).
[p] Conservatives (CDS).
[q] Moderates (EDHK).

range is well taken, as is his ancillary suggestion that from a certain size on even a fringe party may have major impact "by blackmail." However, size alone is not always sufficient to establish the influence of such a party. We need to account also for its revolutionary virulence, for crisis situations favoring its potential for sudden growth, and especially for changes in its fringe status. The seeming mellowing of the Communist parties of France and Italy in recent years provides an example of such changes in ideological distance, coalescibility, and reduction of isolated fringe status. Many party systems altogether lack an isolated fringe position on the right, and sometimes on the left as well. Still, a rough numerical formula would help to order the relationships at hand. Any threatening fringe party larger than 10% of the vote is sure to cast its shadow on the whole system. On the other hand, any small party capable of being included in a government has obvious possibilities of leverage. Its actual influence, however, may depend on its political skills and, most of all, on whether its small share is needed to form a majority. If its participation is badly enough needed, it can exact a price out of all proportion with its numbers. The current tax revolt movements in Denmark or Norway form an obvious exception to this rule of thumb, as do certain regional, ethnic, farmer, or ecological parties that cannot reconcile their *raison d'être* with the political consensus of the majority.

Our third step is to be as faithful to the numerical coalition arithmetic in each case exactly as the politicians of the country are likely to apply it, bearing in mind that the choice at any one time is always very narrow. To demonstrate this, we have put side by side in Table 1–3:

1. the number of parties that received 1% or more in the last elections,
2. the number of major parties that received 10.0–19.9%, 20.0–29.9%, 30.0–39.9%, or 40% and more of the parliamentary seats, with the total number of parties in parliament in brackets,
3. the number of parties in the government with similar gradations of their respective sizes, and

4–6. three indices of the size and state of the population.

The first column of Table 1–3 separates the "moderate" multiparty systems from the "extreme" ones. There are no real two-party systems. The moderate systems are

Great Britain   (5: Labour, Liberals, Conservatives, Scottish Nationalists, Plaid Cymru)
West Germany   (3: Christian Democrats, Social Democrats, Free
                          Democrats)
France   (5: Communists, Socialists, Left Radicals, Democratic Union, Gaullists)

Let us now examine the situation from the perspective of forming any majority at all. In theory, any two parties in the 20.0–29.9% range might suffice to form a governing coalition. In practice, however, workable coalitions are rarely formed by equal partners. More or less equal strength seems to make parties competitive rather than cooperative,[13] which may be another way of saying that a system of many smaller parties has little cohesion. A more plausible scenario for coalition building is the single large party, not unlike Sartori's "center" party, which strives to adopt one or more smaller parties to make a governing majority. Such a hegemonial system would have a numerical base in such countries as Sweden, Norway, Denmark, Iceland, Italy, and Portugal. At the same time, we have to remember that hegemony generates its own undoing. A hegemonial Socialist or Christian Democratic party which is not capable of surmounting the 50% barrier by itself will inevitably tempt all the others, small or medium, to form a counteralliance. Such an alliance may, as in Sweden, succeed momentarily in forming a government, unless there are uncooperative fringe parties whose size may foreclose this option. Short of the sting of hegemony, however, small parties rarely manage to form governing coalitions unless it is under the tutelage of a powerful president, as in Finland, or of similar nonpartisan domination.[14]

As compared with the proportions of the parliamentary parties, the number of parties in the government is less revealing of patterns. The hegemonial versus the counterhegemonial patterns explain many one-party cabinets as well as cabinets composed of three to five parties. They particularly apply to Sweden, Norway, Denmark, Ireland, and Portugal, but they hardly explain the multiparty cabinets of Finland and Switzerland, two countries with the most extreme kind of pluralism.

Can the population indices shed any light on the situation? A high degree of urbanization and low percentage of agriculturally employed males appear to characterize the large, centralized societies of Great Britain, West Germany, and the smaller Austria, the three countries of the seemingly strongest bipolarity. Of the others close to this group, the Netherlands still resembles the pattern, whereas Italy and agrarian Spain and Greece do not. The consociational democracies of Switzerland and the Benelux countries, in any case, vary as greatly in these indices as they do in their party systems. Among the Scandinavian democracies, also, agrarian Finland seems closer to Ireland and the Iberian countries in its patterns than to Sweden, Norway, and Denmark. This may also help to explain why Finland's party system differs so profoundly from those of the latter group of countries. It should be noted, however, that the newer party systems of the Iberian peninsula and Greece have by no means shown themselves to be any less capable of forming majorities than those of the older, more established, systems.

The longitudinal patterns of party systems in coalition formation would require more space than we have in this introduction. Suffice it to direct the attention of the reader to the contributions of Lawrence Mayer to this volume. For this introduction,we shall be content with a mere snapshot of the current reality for comparison.

TABLE 1–3. Number of Parties in Recent National Elections, in Parliament, and in Government (and population indices)[a]

	No. Over 1% in Elections	Number in Parliament					Number in Government					% Metro. Pop. (100,000+)	% Males in Agriculture	Pop. Size (Mil.)
		10.0–19.9%	20.0–29.9%	30.0–39.9%	40.0%+	All	10.0–19.9%	20.0–29.9%	30.0–39.9%	40.0%+	All			
Major countries														
1974 (Oct) Gr. Britain	5				2	(6)				1	1	71.6%	5%	54.6
1976 West Germany	3				2	(3)				1	2	51.5	8	59.0
1978 France	5	1	2	1		(4)		1	1		2	34.0	25	48.9
1976 Italy	8			1	1	(8)			1	1[a]	1	24.2	24	51.6
Smaller countries														
1974 Belgium	6	3	1	1		(6)		1	1		3	28.5	7	9.5
1974 Luxembourg	5	2	2			(5)		2			2	0.0	10	0.3
1977 Netherlands	7	1	2			(7)	1		1		2	38.0	13	12.3
1976 Sweden	5	2	1		1	(5)	2	1			3	25.1	18	7.7
1977 Norway	9	1	1		1	(6)				1	1	20.3	24	3.7
1977 Denmark	11	2		1		(11)			1		1	34.2	23	4.8
1975 Finland	10	1	3			(10)	3	1			5	20.1	38	4.6
1974 Iceland	5	1	1		1	(5)	1		1		2	0.0	37	0.2
1977 Ireland	3	1	1			(3)		1		1	2	23.3	42	2.9
1975 Austria	4	1		2		(3)			1		1	37.6	18	7.3

	1	3		1	3	4			
1975 Switzerland	11			(7)	1	3		15	29.1	5.9
1977 Spain	8	2	1	(8)	1	1	1	36	27.9	31.6
1976 Portugal	4		1	(5)	1	1	1	48	23.4	9.2
1977 Greece	6		1	(6)	1	1	1	48	27.5	8.6

[a] With the support of the constitutional parties including the PCI.

Source: Population statistics are from Charles L. Taylor and Michael C. Hudson, *World Handbook of Social Indicators*, second ed., New Haven, Conn.: Yale University Press, 1972.

9

Luxembourg   (5: Communists, Socialists, Democrats, Christian Socials, National Solidarity Party)

Sweden: (5: Communists, Social Democrats, Liberals, Center, Conservatives)

Iceland   (5: People's Alliance, Liberal Left, Social Democrats, Progressives, Independence)

Ireland   (3: Labour, Fine Gael, Fianna Fail)[10]

Austria   (4: Communists, Socialists, Liberals, People's Party)

Portugal   (4: Communists, Socialists, Democrats, Conservatives)

Examples of "extreme pluralism," according to Sartori, are

Italy   (8: Communists, Socialists, Social Democrats, Radicals, Republicans, Christian Democrats, Liberals, Neofascists)

Belgium   (6: Communists, Socialists, Liberals, Walloons, Flemish, Christian Socials)

Netherlands   (7: Communists, Labor, Democrats '66, Radicals, Liberals, Christian Democrats, Political Reform)[11]

Norway   (9: Communists, Socialist Left, Labor, Progress, Center, New People's Party, Liberals, Christian Democrats, Conservatives)

Denmark   (11: Communists, Left Socialists, Socialists, Social Democrats, Progress, Venstre, Center, Radicals, Christian People, Legal Justice, Conservatives)

Finland   (10: Democratic League, Socialists, Swedish People, Center, Rural, Liberals, Christians, National Coalition, Unification, Constitution)

Switzerland   (11: Communists, Autonomous Socialists, Socialists, Independents, Liberals, Evangelics, People's Party, Radical Democrats, Christian Democrats, Republican Action, National Action)

Spain   (8: Communists, Socialists, Christian Democrats, Regional groups, Democrats (UCD), Popular Alliance)

Greece   (6: Communists, Socialists, Progressives, Moderates, New Democracy, National Front)

Of these, seven have a fringe party under a size of 10%, but so do the moderate multiparty systems of Sweden and Austria. Two (Italy and Finland) have sizable Communist parties as do the moderate multiparty systems of France, Luxembourg, Iceland, and Portugal. The largest numbers of parties can be found in Norway, Denmark, Finland, and Switzerland.

The next sets of columns, the numbers of parties in parliament and in the government, tell a different story. Differentiating parliamentary parties by size permits us to see the extent of their dispersion. If we see the numerical aspects of coalition formation as a process of using building blocs of different size in order to achieve a working majority, the salient differences stand out. The party systems most closely conforming to a bipolar, potentially alternating, model have two parties of 40% or more of the seats in parliament: Great Britain, West Germany, and Austria. A second group composed of Italy (!), Spain, and Greece comes close to this model by having one party over 40% and another in the 30.0–39.9% range. Perhaps, we should add to this the Netherlands, which has two parties in the 30.0–39.9% range and thus also a basis for bipolarity if they choose to make use of it. So far we have looked at coalition formation from the angle of the potential for alternating coalitions.

Little needs to be said about the organizational features of the party systems of Western Europe. A long line of distinguished political scientists from Moisei Ostrogorski and Robert Michels to Maurice Duverger,[15] to mention only a few, have mined this lode so thoroughly as to leave little for us to do. It is worth emphasizing that there has been a steady increase in the regulation of political parties in most systems, especially in connection with campaign finance, the nomination of candidates for public office, and other aspects of intraparty democracy. On the other hand, the intensive organizational and social life of the great mass parties of Europe has visibly declined without necessarily bringing a reduction of their party bureaucracy. Even this trend, however, has always been subject to major fluctuations not unlike those recently diagnosed by Paul Allen Beck in American parties.[16] Periodically, whole party systems in Europe go through waves of ideological polarization and the mobilization of masses of voters and new members which may lead to a drastically simplified party system. These periods of contraction and polarization are followed, however, by periods of deideologization and rampant factionalism which may well herald fundamental realignments and the onset of the next wave of polarization.

The question of the wax and wane of ideological partisanship has also been addressed from a different angle in the research article by John Clayton Thomas in this volume. Thomas used the position on "traditional" and "postindustrial" issues of parties in six Western nations, including the United States, to test common hypotheses about the waning of ideology. From another perspective, again, C. Neal Tate examined the thesis of the decline of the centrality of party as a factor structuring the choice of the voters in five countries, again including the United States.

Our last two points, the partisan cleavages in the electorates and the membership of the parties will be discussed and compared in the concluding chapter of this volume. Rather than wanting to exhaust all the comparative perspectives, in any case, we would like to give the reader every opportunity to arrive at his (her) own comparative reflections as he contemplates the realities of Western European systems from Sicily and Cabo Vicente to the North Cape.

Notes

1. See Stein Rokkan, *Citizens, Elections, Parties,* New York: McKay, 1970; and Ian Budge, Ivor Crewe, and Dennis Farlie, *Party Identification and Beyond,* New York and London: Wiley, 1976.

2. Chicago: University of Chicago Press, 1954.

3. See Leon Epstein, *Political Parties in Western Democracies,* New York: Praeger, 1967, chaps. 7–12; and Gabriel A. Almond and G. Bingham Powell, Jr., *Comparative Politics: System, Process, and Policy,* 2nd ed., Boston: Little, Brown, 1978, pp. 97–99, 117, 123–130, 146–147, 180–181, 220–224.

4. See Sven Groennings et al., eds., *The Study of Coalition Behavior,* New York: Holt, Rinehart, 1970.

5. Princeton, N.J.: Princeton University Press, 1966.

6. New York: Free Press, 1967.

7. See esp. Frank Belloni and Dennis Beller, *Faction Politics: Political Parties and Factionalism in Comparative Perspective,* Santa Barbara, Calif.: Clio Press, 1978.

8. See esp. Giovanni Sartori's theory of extreme pluralism and the "center party," in his *Parties and Party Systems,* Cambridge: Cambridge University Press, 1976, vol. I, chap. 6. Moderate multipartyism, according to Sartori, involves three to five and extreme pluralism six or more parties.

9. Jean Blondel speaks of 102 party systems in 75 countries in *Comparing Political Systems,* New York: Praeger, 1972, p. 99. Kenneth Janda's International Comparative Political Parties Project, on the other hand, counted 250 parties with 5% or more representation in 90 national parliaments. See his *A Conceptual Framework for the Comparative Analysis of Political Parties,* Beverly Hills, Calif.: Sage, 1970.

10. Four more parties won one seat each.

11. Four more parties—the Reformed League, Pacifists, Farmers, and Democratic Socialists—won one seat each, not to mention other parties that did not gain representation.

12. The regional groups included the Democratic party for Catalonia and Basque Nationalist party. There were also the Socialist Union, Centre Independents, and four more that won one seat each.

13. The near equality of the Gaullists and the Union of French Democracy in France today might be a test case except that the threat of a united Left there is likely to force cooperation upon the divided right.

14. See also this writer's discussion of all-party coalitions under the postwar occupation (1947–1949) in the West German states, "Coalition Politics in West Germany," in Sven Groennings et al., eds., *The Study of Coalition Behavior,* pp. 15–17.

15. See esp. Seymour M. Lipset, "Ostrogorski and the Analytical Approach to the Comparative Study of Political Parties," reprinted from *Democracy and the Organization of Political Parties,* New York: Doubleday, 1964; and Maurice Duverger, *Political Parties,* London: Methuen, 1954.

16. In a lecture on cyclical trends in the American party system at the University of California, Santa Barbara, February 1978. See also his "Partisan Dealignment in the Postwar South," *American Political Science Review,* 71 (June 1977), 477ff.

Party Systems of Major Countries

INTRODUCTION TO PART ONE

Peter H. Merkl

THE FOUR LARGEST *of the Western European democracies are rather similar in size and, with the exception of Great Britain, share further background characteristics that have a bearing on their party systems. Great Britain differs mainly by its insularity and almost exclusive Protestantism both of which seem to have helped to simplify its political and constitutional history. Its monarchic heritage has also outlived the monarchies of France, Germany, and Italy, although it has not hampered partisan competition from holding sway, in marked contrast to the effect of monarchy on other countries. Britain again and again has tended toward two-party dominance and alternation, despite the presence of a third party, the Liberals, and, once again today, of regional parties of transitory strength. The three largest British parties, despite certain idiosyncratic features, are clearly analogous to the major continental parties: Conservative/Christian Democratic, Labour/Social Democratic, and Liberal.*

The three larger continental democracies, by way of contrast, have all gone through the purgatory of violent upheavals, intense ideological strife, and totalitarian dictatorship or occupation. All three lost their monarchies by a combination of revolution and involvement in major wars, and there have been distinctive republican traditions though they have varied significantly in strength and content. It can even be said that it took totalitarian dictatorship and occupation to convince the mass of Frenchmen, Germans, and Italians that democracy is the best way of operating an urban-industrial society. There is also in all three countries a strong laical tradition that evolved from intense and prolonged struggles

17

between the secular state and the Catholic church and that for many decades determined political alignments that had no parallel in British politics. Much as the British Conservatives and continental Christian Democrats, Labourites and Socialists, or Liberals in the two areas may seem to resemble each other today, here is a major difference in how the lines were drawn in the past.

Following from the republican rejection of aristocratic privileges and from the laïque *tradition of secular education, the three larger continental democracies furthermore have long adhered to a vision of meritocracy that has little regard for traditional social hierarchies and old-boy networks. This is not to say that these continental societies are any more equalitarian, but rather that there is less deference and more unabashed social conflict on the continent than in Great Britain. The organized class conflict reflected in the continental party systems, in spite of two decades of ideological moderation and "catch-all" parties on the left and right, consequently tends to center more nakedly on materialistic issues and the question of who controls industry than is the case in the British Isles.*

At first glance, the three larger continental party systems have appeared to be sufficiently different from each other to obscure any likenesses. A decade ago and more, in fact, only the common presence of several important political forces, such as the Socialists, Communists, Liberals, and Christian Democrats created some similarities to be contrasted to the obvious differences among the West German one-and-a-half party system, the Italian "imperfect two-party system" (Giorgio Galli), and the French systems of the Fourth and early Fifth republics. But we forget the considerable parallels in the evolution of these three systems, quite different from that of the British postwar party system: the immediate postwar years of dominant socialism/communism and of nationalizations as long as there was no American occupation to stop them; the marked turn toward conservative and especially Christian Democratic resurgence encouraged by the Cold War; the new mobilization of the late 1960s and early 1970s; and above all the emergence of competitive patterns that had long been familiar in Great Britain and the United States.

To be sure, Italy in 1948 had plenty of partisan conflict, in fact nearly civil war, rather than peaceful competition between evenly balanced major camps neither one of which would resort to dictatorial power if elected. France was virtually in a state of siege in the late 1950s and repeatedly in the first years of the Fifth republic, as President Charles de Gaulle wrestled with the diehards of a French Algeria. Again, this was quite unlike the peaceful competition between the consolidated right wing and the temporarily united left wing that has characterized recent French elections and their close outcomes.

The Federal Republic also began with a deeply divided multi-party system in 1949 that seemed no more promising than the multi-party

systems of the 1950s in France and Italy, or that of the Weimar Republic of
1919–1933. But then the consolidation of the Adenauer years created a
united right wing, which in turn induced the Social Democrats to make an
all-out effort to compete for a majority. They appealed successfully to new
masses of voters such as businessmen and professionals, rural Catholics,
and women whom they had always conceded to the Christian Democrats.
By 1961, the West German party system began to look like the British two-
and-a-half party system in spite of the German electoral law and use of
coalition government. In 1969, the opposition actually took its turn at the
helm of state, in coalition with the third party, and since that time the
Christian Democrats have been grooming themselves for their chance at
succession that must come one fine day. France and Italy are still hovering
at the threshold of complete alternation in power between the two camps,
but it too will come one day as surely as night follows day, now that the
conditions have been achieved to make alternation acceptable to a majority
of the people.

  Partisan competition thus has simplified the complex systems of the four
major Western European democracies in the direction of bipolarity. This
simplicity and trend toward bipolarity form a striking contrast, as will be
seen in Part Two, to most of the smaller Western European countries. It
may seem puzzling that size should have anything to do with it, although
one could argue that larger communities are less likely to maintain
consensual patterns that moderate conflict, as in the smaller democracies of
Part Two. Furthermore, the larger size of a political community raises the
stakes of power to a very high level. And, finally, the domestic and
international upheavals of the last hundred years, at least on the continent,
have tended to knock down much of the particularistic structures and
groups that once complicated the game of politics in these countries.

CHAPTER 2

WEST GERMANY

Peter H. Merkl

A PROFOUND PARADOX has characterized the role of the political parties in the West German political system from the very beginning. In the Weimar Republic of Germany (1919–1933), many Germans had viewed the extreme pluralism of interest groups and splinter parties and the multiparty system that was shakily governing Germany's first try at parliamentary government[1] with deep distrust. Instead of trusting in the parties, the Weimar Constitution set its hope in a strong, directly elected president and devices of direct democracy such as referenda, only to be overwhelmed in the end by a popular movement which claimed to be "above parties," National Socialism. After the totalitarian experience with the Third Reich, West German politicians pointedly rejected the Weimar legacy of plebiscites and a strong executive in their fear of the willful caprice of the people. Rather, they put their faith in British-style "party government" (with some modifications)[2] and even inserted an article (art. 21) in the West German Basic Law of 1949 recognizing the role of political parties in the formation of the political will of the state.[3]

This privileged role of the political parties has contributed remarkably to the stabilization of the Federal Republic over the three decades of its existence, although there has been a growing realization that the ensuing practical monopoly of the major parties on political power is not an unmixed blessing. Doubts about the wisdom of such oligopoly have arisen most notably in connection with three major issues over the years:

(1) In the 1960s, the introduction of public financing of election campaigns conjured up the image of incumbents perpetuating themselves in office with the help of tax monies and to the exclusion of new challengers.[4] (2) With the grand

21

coalition of 1966 between the two largest parties[5] and similar near-monopoly situations, there has been a growing concern about the waning role of opposition. Finally, (3) there has been an increase in organized attempts to represent local and especially environmental concerns, which none of the major parties cared to defend, by means of direct action or the "citizen initiatives" discussed elsewhere in this book. At times also, the latent dissatisfaction with the major parties has benefited dissident factions within them or protest movements such as the neofascist National Democratic party (NPD), or manifested itself in openly expressed disparagement.[6] But, on the whole, the relative monopoly position of the major parties has continued undiminished, in spite of the current criticisms, to this day.

The Metamorphosis of the Party System

In recent years, the West German party system has often been described as a two-and-a-half party system. The two largest parties, the Social Democratic party (SPD) and the Christian Democratic Union (CDU/CSU) have been rather evenly matched in size since 1961, and yet neither one has been capable of winning a majority by itself. To form a government they generally required a coalition with the third party, the Free Democratic party (FDP), which despite its small size could play the role of the balancer. But this was not always the configuration of the West German system that actually started with a multiparty format similar to that of the Weimar Republic.[7]

The first posttotalitarian state party systems under the occupation regime were multiparty systems composed of the Communists, the three Bonn parties (SPD, CDU/CSU, and FDP), and a number of smaller parties limited to only one region, including some regional parties.[8] These parties tended to form all-party coalitions, at least while the occupation lasted, and did not go over to a pattern of competitive politics until 1948 or even later.[9] There were ten parties in the first *Bundestag* (1949) even though the federal electoral law, a mixture of proportional representation and single-member districts, established a minimum of 5% of the popular vote or three directly elected representatives as the prerequisite for party representation. The two largest parties, the SPD with 29.2% and the CDU/CSU with 31.0%, together received less than two thirds of the popular vote. The smaller parties ranged from the Communists (KPD) with 5.7% to the German Reich party (DRP) with 1.8% on the extreme right. Five of the small parties had less than the 5% required, and there were four independent candidates. The leader of the CDU, Konrad Adenauer, moved swiftly to put together a shaky governing coalition of the CDU/CSU, the FDP, and the German party (DP, formerly Lower Saxonian Land party (NLP). This coalition still had to rely on compromises among the regional elements that had been dominant up until the foundation of the Federal Republic.[10]

The 1950s were a period of profound changes in West Germany's international position, in West German society, and in the party system. Favored by the circumstances, Adenauer's policies of economic recovery and West German integration into the Western alliance proved immensely popular among the voters. By 1957, his CDU/CSU had accomplished what no political party in German history had ever done: it received an absolute majority of the vote and in the Bundestag which made its continuation of coalition governments almost superfluous. This rise of the CDU/CSU was accompanied by the swallowing up of the smaller bourgeois parties one by one as they found themselves cornered between the 5% clause and the powerful embrace of the Christian Democrats. Even the new Refugee party (BHE), which many American observers viewed with great apprehension as a massive, irredentist threat in 1953, soon got sucked into the wake of Adenauer's bandwagon. Government credits and the new economic opportunities defused the potential for nationalism among the 12 million Eastern refugees in the Federal Republic while the BHE as a party lost its soul. The CDU/CSU alienated the BHE cabinet members from the rest of the party and sent the latter to the opposition benches. A similar fate befell the DP and, very nearly, the FPD as well.[11] The FDP was the only party to survive this ordeal while the other small parties disappeared from the political stage.

The rise and consolidation of Adenauer's powerful political machine was accompanied by a parallel consolidation of the interest group basis of German politics. The groups representing industry and the employers associations, retail, handicraft, refugees, and agiculture rallied to the commanding position of the CDU/CSU and its allies. They soon presented a common front behind the political scene which was rather inhospitable toward the continued autonomy of smaller bourgeois parties. So-called sponsor societies that raised campaign finances and furnished other assistance at election time for the right-of-center forces would not permit any group to challenge Adenauer's policies and often refused their support altogether. This great "catchall" rallying of political forces on the right, at least in comparison with Weimar, was facilitated by the evident demise of the deep ideological divisions that once accounted for much of the extreme pluralism of German politics.

The impact of the consolidation of the right and the accompanying changes in international alignments and in West German society were also felt on the left. At first, the KPD declined under the twin battering rams of the spectacle of the Communist takeover in East Germany and the Cold War sentiments of West Germans.[12] Then, the SPD underwent an agonizing reappraisal prompted by its electoral stagnation in the face of changes all around it and by the spectacular success of Adenauer's CDU/CSU. The party leaders decided to follow the example of their successful antagonists and to turn the SPD from a Marxist, class-bound party into a "people's party" ready to appeal to all parts of society. They laid down their new principles in the Bad Godesberg Program of 1959, eschewing socialist orthodoxy and pledging the overcoming of religious and especially Catholic resistance to them. Henceforth, they began to accept the government's foreign and defense policies and to redouble their efforts to appeal to farm and rural voters, Catholics, small business, and industry without necessarily abandoning their traditional working-class base. Their whole style of political campaigning changed from their traditional emphasis on ideological convictions to the marketing of candidates and concrete issues.[13]

This adaptation to the political and social realities of a prosperous and rearmed German society soon produced tangible results. In the elections of the 1960s, the SPD broke through the 35% barrier that had limited its growth in the 1940s and already in the Weimar Republic. In 1961 it achieved 36.2%, in 1965 39.3%, in 1969 42.7%, and in 1972 46.9% of the popular vote. Thus, SPD and CDU/CSU were now running neck to neck, and only the presence of the FPD marred what promised to be a fully operative, alternating two-party system.

At the beginning of the 1960s, the FDP was still tied firmly to the CDU/CSU, which gave Adenauer's successor Ludwig Erhard a coalition majority even though the CDU/CSU never recovered its singular majority of 1957–1961. But the tensions between the two coalition partners finally led to a complete break in 1966 that toppled Erhard and initiated a very controversial experiment in party government, the grand coalition of CDU/CSU and SPD, headed by Kurt Georg Kiesinger (CDU) and with Willy Brandt (SPD) as vice chancellor and foreign minister. Participating in the government helped to give the SPD the statesmanlike image that had eluded it in the past and enabled Willy Brandt in 1969 to reach for the chancellorship in coalition with a fundamentally changed FDP. The period of the grand coalition was characterized by the rise of the NPD on the right and of the extraparliamentary opposition and student rebellion on the left while the three major parties underwent considerable internal turmoil. For this reason some West German observers have viewed it as a crisis of legitimacy, or at least as an interregnum between the periods of CDU/CSU and SPD rule. Each period of partisan rule was preceded by an evident surge of strength shown by the dominant party-to-be in the state elections (Tables 2-1 and 2-2), whereas an upsurge of the opposition at this level usually signaled the decline of dominance.

Since 1969, the SPD and FDP have constituted the government of the Federal Republic, subject to the ups and downs of electoral fortune. In the 1972 elections, the SPD with 46.9% of the vote even surged ahead of the CDU/CSU with 44.8%, because of the hotly contested Eastern policies of Willy Brandt. But this apogee has since been followed by a string of electoral setbacks in the state elections, which gave the CDU/CSU an average of 51.4% (at the state level), and the bare survival of the government coalition (SPD 42.6%, FDP 7.9%) against a resurgent CDU/CSU (48.6%) in the 1976 elections. The reasons for the slump of the SPD vote are easy to see. Governmental responsibility has inevitably brought it disappointments along with the successes, spy scandals of major proportions, and new issues on which the

TABLE 2–1. West German Federal Election Results, 1949–1976 (Percent)

	1949	1953	1957	1961	1965	1969	1972	1976
Turnout	78.5	86.0	87.8	87.7	86.8	86.7	91.1	90.7
Christian Democrats	31.0	45.2	50.2	45.4	47.6	46.1	44.9	48.6
Social Democrats	29.2	28.8	31.8	36.2	39.3	42.7	45.8	42.6
Free Democrats	11.9	9.5	7.7	12.8	9.5	5.8	8.4	7.9
Communists	5.7	2.2	—	1.9	1.3	—	0.3	0.3
Neofascists	1.8	1.1	1.0	0.8	2.0	4.3	0.6	0.3
German party	4.0	3.3	3.4	—	—	—	—	—
Refugees	—	5.9	4.6	2.8	—	0.1	—	—
Center	3.1	0.8	0.3	—	—	—	—	—
Bavaria party	4.2	1.7	0.5	—	—	0.2	—	—
Others	9.1	1.5	0.5	0.1	0.3	0.8	—	0.3
	100.0	100.0	100.0	100.0	100.0	100.0	100.0	100.0

TABLE 2–2. Trends toward Bipolarity and Tripolarity in West German Elections, 1949–1976 (Percent)

	1949	1953	1957	1961	1965	1969	1972	1976
Christian Democratic and Social Democratic vote	60.2	74.0	82.0	81.5	86.9	88.8	90.7	91.2
Christian, Social, and Free Democratic vote	72.1	83.5	89.7	94.3	96.4	94.6	99.1	99.1

opposition gained an advantage. In the days of Adenauer's landslide elections of 1953 and 1957, already the state elections tended to favor those who were in the opposition at the federal level.[14] Beyond dealing with the routine problems of incumbency, the SPD was plagued by severe factional struggles stemming from the upheaval at German universities. Many student rebels joined the SPD and, as the dominant element of its Young Socialists (*Jusos*), challenged and embarrassed their elders at all levels. In big cities like Munich or Frankfurt, in particular, the internecine feuds led to substantial losses of support where the SPD had always been able to count on a clean sweep in the federal, state, and local elections of the past.[15]

The CDU/CSU has not been spared a resurgence of the factional disputes of past decades[16] either. The most recent factional crisis occurred in an aftermath conflict of the 1976 parliamentary elections when the Bavarian Christian Social Union (CSU), an autonomous affiliate of the CDU/CSU, temporarily severed its ties with the Christian Democratic Union. The cause of the acrimony was continuing disagreements between the chancellor candidate of the party, Helmut Kohl, and the CSU chairman Franz Josef Strauss, who had bitterly opposed Kohl's candidacy from the beginning.

Ideology and Centralization

Unlike the development of American parties, though with many parallels on the continent, German parties grew from curiously narrow and sectarian backgrounds, more like communities of faith than like modern associations. Shaped in the ideological confrontations of the 1789 and 1848 revolutions, their programmatic character antedated their organizational evolution, so to speak. Germany's late unification and the rapid course of industrialization and urbanization under the Empire may have further obstructed their attempts at building permanent national coalitions. Weimar politics, and even the early years of the Federal Republic, were still characterized more by sectarian and regional narrowness, including a narrow kind of ideological zealotry among interest groups, than they were by the politics of the open society. The early and very extensive development of party newspapers and periodicals gave expression to ideological interpretations and sectarian sentiments. The rise of the Nazi and Communist movements and the Third Reich constituted the climax of unrestrained sectarianism in its most tyrannical form.[17] The very excess of it eventually helped the Germans to overcome this legacy of doctrinaire, ideological thinking. But in the wake of World War II, when many Weimar groups reappeared with a vengeance, there was also a Catholic Center party that would have liked to have revived the spirit of the embattled German Catholic community dating back to Bismarck's anti-Catholic *Kulturkampf* of the 1870s. There was a successor organization of the Hanoveran party which under the Empire and Weimar had continued to represent the legacy of the long-dead state of Hanover and now called itself the Lower Saxonian Land party (DP). There have been many such stubborn survivors among the political forces on the right and not a few also inside the SPD and with the revived KPD. Fortunately, the attempt of the Christian Democrats to break out of "the tower" of Catholic sectarianism and to rally the faithful of Germany's other major religion, the Protestants, proved stronger than the resistance of the Center party. In the 1950s, the Christian Democrats achieved a modicum of unity among the various bourgeois, liberal, and conservative forces of pre-Hitler Germany, including the DP and other disparate groups such as the refugees. The integrating drive of Adenauer brought together a grand alliance of all the remaining non-Socialist and regional elements and thus buried for the time being the tendencies toward ideological fragmentation on the right in the pragmatic exercise of rebuilding government and the economy.

On the left, the demise of the early KPD and the steps of the SPD toward becoming a "people's party" were major strides away from the sectarian tendencies still present there and towards a deideologization of politics in the 1960s. In the meantime, however, a new Communist party, with close ties to the East German Socialist Unity party (SED) and the Soviet Communist party, the DKP,[18] a Maoist Communist party (KPD) and Communist/Marxist-Leninist party (KPD/ML), and small, activist Communist groups such as the Communist League West (KBW) have established themselves who are once again in the tradition of sectarian militancy. The spectrum of Young Socialist groups in the SPD[19] and many of the small groups of student militants at the universities likewise make any sweeping statement about the disappearance of political sectarianism in West German party politics seem premature even though the tenor of politics among the major parties has long been thoroughly pragmatic. It goes without saying that the secularization of ideological thinking contributed greatly to the legitimacy of the party system among a people long distrustful of party politics in itself.

A second feature at variance with the American experience is the bureaucratization and centralization of German parties. Because they are, generally speaking, an important part of the structure of representation of a nation-state, a centralization of internal authority in the hands of its parliamentary delegation may not seem unusual. The process of centralization we are concerned with, however, occurs outside of parliament among the apparatus of functionaries of a given party. Not content with founding a community of faith, most of these parties soon created a church with salaried priests as well and, eventually, a hierarchy of party bishops headed by a charismatic pope. To be sure, this is an overdrawn picture that in all its details applied only to a few Weimar parties, including in particular the Nazis and Communists. But it also makes plausible the distrust and alienation that even party members have felt on occasion toward unresponsive party bureaucracies[20] and the general concern about internal democracy in each party.

In 1911, the sociologist Robert Michels published a scathing attack on what he called the oligarchical tendencies in the SPD and the Socialist trade unions. Even the continental Socialist movements, the champions of democracy in his time, he insisted, could not escape the "iron law of oligarchy" by which elective elites in any organized context tend to perpetuate themselves.[21] The SPD was indeed the first German party to achieve such a state of organizational development, but by the 1920s its competitors followed not far behind. The most oligarchical were obviously the extremes of the right and left, in particular the National Socialist party (NSDAP) where Hitler had made himself a party dictator a dozen years before he became dictator of the whole country. In the KPD, it was rather a result of circumstances and of "democratic centralism" until, in the last years of the First Republic, the leadership cult of the right was taken over there as well. In each party, the question of internal democracy posed itself in a different way, depending on particular organizational features, personalities, and circumstances. It is, in fact, a different question, if raised from the point of view of the loyal party voter, the party member, a party leader competing with rivals in the same party, or the general public. And there is plenty of room for disagreement about such questions, for example, whether the extraparliamentary party ought to have a say about the decisions of the parliamentary party, what an elected deputy owes to his party—or to his partisan voters, and how the voters should participate in the nomination of candidates and in the policy decisions of a party.

The Basic Law of 1949 declared political parties to be an official part of the process of "forming the public will," guaranteed their right to form, and enjoined them to make their internal organization conform to democratic principles. It also empowered the Federal Constitutional Court in anticipation of a return of the totalitarian challenges of the early 1930s, to declare parties unconstitutional if they "seek to impair or destroy the free democratio basic order."[22] After several court decisions and protracted disputes, a Law on Parties (1967) spelled out some details regarding internal democracy and requiring parties to have written programs and statutes setting forth the conditions and rights of the card-carrying membership. It required party districts to have general meetings of the members or their delegates as the highest authority and prescribed plural leadership of no less than three and terms of office not exceeding two years for them. The voting for leaders and delegates as well as for the nomination of candidates for public office must be by secret ballots.[23] All this went far beyond the almost completely unregulated party situation in the Weimar Republic and yet fell short of the exhaustive legal regulation of parties in this country.

The great concern with organizational questions and internal democracy became pressing only with the evolution of political mass organizations and mass memberships in the party system. Since the 1890s, when labor unions, farmers' leagues, and Catholic associations began to play a major role in German party politics,[24] complex organization became a necessity and problems of representation inevitable. On the eve of World War I, the SPD topped out with a membership in excess of 1 million, the Center party's *Volksverein* had 800,000 and even the liberal parties could boast between 300,000 and 400,000. Salaried party functionaries, aside from the antecedent of the Progressive party of the late 1870s, generally began to replace honorary party officeholders in the 1890s. By the turn of the century, the liberal parties had all followed suit, replacing the parliamentary deputies who ran the party headquarters in their spare time with salaried functionaries and introducing bureaucratic record-keeping.[25] The problems of internal democracy, however, became most acute during the Weimar Republic when the greatly enhanced role of political parties, their remaining ideological sectarianism, and proportional representation intensified the general concern with centralized party bureaucracies unresponsive to popular wishes. Under proportional representation lists in particular, nominations of candidates for public office seemed to be more under the influence of the party apparatus than of the party voters or even the party members.

In the Federal Republic, the number of full-time party functionaries not on parliamentary payrolls is estimated to be in the neighborhood of 1,000 most of whom are county or district secretaries. Their salaries constitute a consider-

TABLE 2–3. West German Party Finance in 1975 (Percent)

	SOCIAL DEMOCRATS (SPD)	CHRISTIAN DEMOCRATS (CDU)	CHRISTIAN SOCIALS (CSU)	FREE DEMOCRATS (FDP)	COMMU- NISTS (DKP)
Members' fees	43	37	31	20	21
Public subsidies	31	32	48		1
Donations	10	26	17	38	43
Other	16	5	4	10	35
Totals	100	100	100	100	100
(Million DM)	130	113	20	22.8	12.2

able part of the annual expenditures of the political parties, which have been rising continuously from the modest beginnings of the republic to in excess of DM 400 million (see Table 2–3). Since 1959, public subsidies in one form or another have been authorized to assist with the work of "political education" and, since 1967, with the rising campaign expenditures of each party.[26] Aside from the salaried personnel, however, there are also large numbers of semi-salaried and honorary party functionaries, not to mention public officeholders who work as unpaid party officials but owe their offices to their party.

The Nomination of Candidates

In the Federal Republic, the Federal Electoral Law determines the basic outlines of the process of nominating candidates for the Bundestag[27] half of which is elected from single-member districts and half from *Land* lists presented by each party. The voters cast two ballots each. The candidates for the districts are selected by an assembly of party members or their delegates on recommendation of the electoral district committee.[28] Land or party district (SPD) functionaries often recommend a particular candidate, which some-times may be the kiss of death. Estimates at the time of the nominations to the 1969 elections suggest that only about 3.0% of the total membership of the major parties or 0.1% of the eligible voters of all parties participated in the selection of the candidates.[29] About one-fifth of these CDU/CSU and SPD candidates in 1969, including many prominent figures, were not even residents of their electoral districts. The vast majority of Bundestag candidates in the electoral districts contrived to have their names placed simultaneously on the Land lists from which the other half of the Bundestag is elected in accordance with the second (partisan) ballot cast by the voters on election day.[30] Thus, they may still get elected even if they failed to win a plurality in their district, provided that they can place their names high enough on the list. In a district usually captured by another party, or for the Free Democrats, this may be the only road to success.

The Land lists are the proportional representation element in West German electoral law that tends to predominate over the element of direct election. It permits the minority party in a Land, and especially the Free Democrats and smaller parties, to receive their due in Bundestag seats provided they can achieve 5% of the second ballot vote or three direct mandates. The smallest competitors thus are weeded out and barred from representation, a fate that since 1949 has usually befallen the neofascist and Communist parties.[31] Getting a promising spot on the Land list of one of the major parties is, understandably, the most contested achievement among would-be candidates. What is a promising spot can be determined from previous elections or by public opinion polls. The selection is made by the respective Land party convention and usually follows such criteria as seniority or prominence in the party or the representation of regions and special associations—youth, women, or refugees—within the party. The major interest groups of labor, business, handicraft, and farming also have enjoyed their share of nominations. In past decades, the CDU/CSU was reputed to favor certain interest groups, whereas the SPD more often nominated tried and trusted holders of lower party and trade union offices. In recent elections the Christian Democrats also have come around to a greater appreciation of candidates who served their way up through the ranks.[32]

The Christian Democrats

The largest West German party today, the CDU/CSU, only dates from the immediate post-World War II era, although its roots obviously go far into the Imperial period and even earlier.[33] Its main Catholic antecedent, the Center party of the Empire, grew from a broad tradition of Catholic resistance to the secular state and to a Prussian-led German national unification exclusive of Austria that made Catholics a besieged minority in Germany. This siege mentality was intensified in a lasting pattern by the hostility of the Prussian government and the liberal majorities in the 1870s so that Catholics lived in an encapsulated world of their beliefs and associations up until the end of the Weimar Republic. Unlike the other German parties of that period, the Center combined elements from all social classes united by the faith. Despite this sectarian exclusiveness, however, the Center party soon began to participate actively in governmental affairs, moving from the company of opposition ethnic and regional parties into the mainstream. It was so faithful to the main currents of German politics in fact, that it not only helped the National Liberals to write the Civil Code and supported the Kaiser's expansionism, but turned pacifist and republican after World War I, and eventually to the authoritarian right in the early 1930s.[34]

In 1945, former Center politicians shared the deep sense of shame of the German bourgeoisie about its entanglement with national socialism. Against the spiritual and institutional ravages of totalitarianism, only a broad religious revival of all nonsocialists of goodwill seemed to promise help.[35] Thus the first step was to reach out beyond the sectarian confines of political Catholicism to draw in responsible Protestant conservatives, many of whom had once been with the Weimar Nationalists (DNVP), People's party (DVP), Democrats (DDP), or the Christian Social People's Service (CSVD). The sweep of the "union" movement fell short of enveloping a number of small parties such as the predecessors of the FDP. The founders and leaders of the first few years ranged over a wide spectrum from resistance fighters and people persecuted by the Nazis to repentant minor Nazis. The second step was to overcome the barriers to party organization imposed by the Allied occupation and especially by the division of the country into occupation zones that had given the new movement strong regional colors. The consolidation of the Land parties into zonal parties, the unification of the British and American zones in 1947, and finally the establishment of the CDU/CSU of the Federal Republic were major landmarks of the history of the party that thereby acquired a rather decentralized structure.[36] The Bavarian affiliate, the CSU, to this day has jealously guarded its autonomy and different name, whereas in Lower Saxony, where the CDU was weak, a kind of symbiosis established itself with the conservative DP. Within the social gospel ideology of the "Christian" label[37] also there were pronounced regional differences ranging from the Christian socialism of the Catholic trade union tradition of the Rhineland to the archconservatism of Bavaria.

The political programs and manifestoes of the new CDU/CSU mirrored the sense of crisis and of the need for a new beginning of a whole generation and attempted to spell out the practical and political implications of Christian morality in a devastated and demoralized world. There were long lists of basic human rights and ethical principles that were believed to require emphatic reassertion, although here too, regional differences in the interpretation of Catholic or Protestant social philosophies played a role. This was most obvious in economic and institutional concerns where the progressive Rhineland obviously followed a different drummer than quasi-corporatist Bavaria. The 1946 (Neheim-Huesten) Program of the British zone CDU, for example, slyly suggested that

> The urgent question of socializing parts of the economy is not practical at this time since the German economy is not free [from occupation control].

Then it went on to "demand the socialization of the coal mines" as a sop to popular sentiment in those days of extreme scarcity.[38] A year later, the Ahlen Program of 1947 went much farther in charting an economic policy "between capitalism and Marxism" and between the "unrestrained rule of private capital," especially monopolies and large banks, and "state capitalism." It advocated a system of sharing economic control among public and private authority as well as planning and a scheme for labor codetermination[39] which soon became law in the coal and steel industry. The CSU Program of 1946, by way of contrast, equally rejected "economic liberalism" and a planned economy ("collectivistic thinking") and endorsed the rights of private property, especially of small enterprises against any "expropriation by collectivization or general socialization."[40]

Hence, when in 1948 Bizonal Economic Director Ludwig Erhard launched his neoliberal policy of "social market economics," he encountered at first a great deal of opposition from many people in the CDU/CSU, in particular from the labor-oriented Social Policy Committees of the party but also from the small business, handicraft, and farm groups and from Catholic conservatives who felt that his economic liberalism was a menace to good social order. An economist, Erhard had always been considered a liberal who had only recently joined the CDU. But the currency reform and the changed economic circumstances of the Marshall Plan soon won him the support of the economically most puissant elements in West German society and within the party. The "economic miracle" was off to a good start and progressively won over the CDU and CSU politicians as well as increasing numbers of voters. By the time of the 1953 CDU Program, the social market policy had become the new orthodoxy.[41] Christian socialism was a mere memory and to many of the party leaders not a pleasant one.[42] The CDU/CSU had become a conservative party dedicated to the economic prosperity of businessmen, industry, and agriculture, and its numerous blue- and white-collar supporters felt quite satisfied with their share of the newly generated wealth.

Political questions were also at issue among the regions of the CDU/CSU. To be sure, all the new Christian Democratic parties agreed on an antifascist and democratic course. But, beyond this, there were important differences. The CDU/CSU of the American zone of occupation, and especially the CSU, were far more bent on federalism and states rights than was the CDU of the British zone which possessed the greatest concentration of industry and population of West Germany. These issues of federal organization came to a head during the deliberations of the Parliamentary Council 1948–1949 and resulted not only in considerable modifications of the West German Basic Law, but in its failure to be ratified by the Bavarian diet.[43]

Konrad Adenauer, the sexagenarian former lord mayor of Cologne, had become the acknowledged leader of the heterogeneous movement by playing the role of the honest broker among the contending economic and political groupings of the party. In the area of foreign policy, however, especially of European integration and of the adherence of West Germany to the Western alliance, the "Old Man" had a very pronounced policy line of his own which was soon adopted by the entire party. The desire for European integration was motivated by the deep revulsion against the excesses of German nationalism and also because the Germans were very anxious to be accepted again by their neighbors who had learned to hate them during World War II. The creation of predominantly Catholic Little Europe in the 1950s and 1960s and Adenauer's close relationship with Charles de Gaulle eventually demonstrated both the achievements and the inherent limitations of this policy. That German reunification, the role of the former capital, Berlin, and a reconciliation with Germany's eastern neighbors would have to be sacrificed to adherence to the West was dictated by the unfolding of the Cold War. But this development was surely not unexpected by Adenauer who had predicted as early as May 1945 the postwar confrontation of the two superpowers and what the best course would be for Germany. There was considerable resistance to Adenauer's Western policies in the Berlin CDU where several leaders had claimed a leadership role in the new movement from the very beginning.[44] The strategic implications of the German division soon took away any leverage the Berliners may at first have had. Adenauer's cooperation with the United States on West German rearmament and integration in NATO in the 1950s was at once the key to Germany's reacceptance among Western nations and the basis of his and his party's resounding success at home.

Toward the end of the 1950s, as the international situation changed from the Cold War to the first signs of a thaw, and the impact of the economic miracle on the voters paled, Adenauer's grip began to loosen. A bitter struggle set in for succession and in some ways has continued to this day under the cover of various issues. At first, it was a matter of Adenauer trying to prevent the succession of Erhard. In the 1960s, it took the form of a foreign policy debate between "Atlanticists," such as the new Chancellor Erhard and his foreign minister, Gerhard Schroeder, and German "Gaullists" like the CSU leader, Franz Josef Strauss.[45] Later controversies over Willy Brandt's Eastern policies of reconciliation with Poland, the Soviet Union, and Czechoslovakia (1969–1972) have shown that the foreign policy posture of Strauss and other Christian Democratic hardliners represented a consistent conservative, anti-Communist position which had all along viewed European and Western defense integration as the defense of the occident against godless dialectical materialism.[46]

Being in the opposition since 1969, after 20 years in power, was not as disorienting to the CDU/CSU as many observers had predicted. The party did not disintegrate despite its continuing leadership squabbles and general heterogeneity. Instead, it concentrated on the *Laender* where it was strong and on the CDU/CSU-oriented Laender delegations in the Bundesrat, the second chamber of parliament. Under the leadership of several strong, conservative Laender chiefs, Bavaria's Strauss, Hesse's Alfred Dregger, Baden-Wuerttemberg's Josef Filbinger, and Schleswig-Holstein's Gerhard Stoltenberg, the party made deep inroads into SPD positions, especially on issues of education policy, which is under Laender jurisdiction. The SPD-FDP coalition was accused of changing the curriculum of public schools in a radical, even Communist, direction to permit radicals to get a foothold in the schools and in the public service.[47] The CDU/CSU also exploited the fears raised by the student upheaval of 1967–1969 and by the terrorist activist of the Baader-Meinhof group though neither of these could be clearly related to the governing parties.[48] The agitation of the Young Socialists (*Jusos*) in the big cities provided the party with an even better target, especially since, unlike the SPD itself, the Jusos frequently collaborated with the Communists and Communist groups at the local level.

In contrast to its considerable successes at the Laender level, the CDU/CSU notably failed in its national campaign against Brandt's *Ostpolitik* in 1972. It succeeded in weakening the government in the battle over ratification in the Bundestag to a point where Brandt was unable to pass the budget with the required majority. But in the electoral contest that followed, the governing coalition emerged with a far more comfortable margin than it had enjoyed in 1969. Still, the insinuations of government misconduct, of collusion with the Communist states involved, and of massive giveaways to the latter to purchase their cooperation with Brandt's Ostpolitik left considerable uneasiness in the wake of the ratified Eastern treaties. Later disappointments with the Ostpolitik and major spy scandals also lent themselves well to partisan propaganda.

Between the 1972 elections, in which they failed to stop the advance of Willy Brandt, and the 1976 elections, the CDU/CSU made a remarkable recovery which may well carry it back into power at the next opportunity. Over the grumbling of Strauss, the party in 1975 picked as a chancellor candidate Helmut Kohl, the minister president of Rhineland-Palatinate and the CDU chairman since 1973. In new programmatic departures, the party put into words the public feelings that the West German welfare state had passed its limits while at the same time promising a new deal to the underprivileged and unorganized of society, such as the elderly and mothers with children.[49] "Freedom instead of Socialism" became the CDU/CSU rallying cry in the 1976 elections, an effective slogan for mobilizing all kinds of conservative discontents against the SPD/FDP government in Bonn. Unlike earlier elections, the party had gained substantially in the self-confidence and militancy of its membership[50] which had also increased in numbers. From 380,000 members before the CDU/CSU lost office, the party had grown to 500,000 by the time of the 1972 elections and 740,000 by the spring of 1976, no longer far behind the mass membership (960,000) of the SPD. The CSU with 140,000 accounted for a substantial share of this growth and in the elections surpassed 62.1%, its previous majority in Bavaria, by a considerable margin (4.9%). On the nationwide level, however, the CDU/CSU again failed to deny a majority to the governing coalition of SPD and FDP, thus exposing itself to the ridicule of Franz Josef Strauss (CSU) who for a while even took his party out of the joint parliamentary caucus of a quarter century's standing. But soon the old leadership squabbles were smoothed over again, as the CDU/CSU resumed its waiting in the wings for the government to falter.

The Social Democrats

The other major party of the Federal Republic, the Social Democratic party of Germany, has been in existence as a party more than a hundred years.[51] It was founded in 1863 by Ferdinand Lassalle (1825–1864) whose philosophy placed the quest for universal suffrage and political power uppermost among the means to escape the "iron law of wages." Lassalle's General Association of German Labor followed in the footsteps of Louis Blanc and Napoleon III who favored an alliance of the authoritarian state with the workers against the bourgeoisie. In 1875, the General Association merged with the Social Democratic Workers Party (1869) of August Bebel and Wilhelm Liebknecht, the architects of the powerful organization to emerge in due course.[52] Within a few years the unified party already polled 9.1% of the popular vote (1877) and incurred the wrath of Bismarck.

Attempts on the life of the Kaiser in 1878 gave Bismarck the excuse to suppress the SPD as an organization, likewise its press and the socialist trade unions. The suppression was accompanied by arrests, exile, and jail sentences, and its effect on the growing labor movement was to demonstrate that this was indeed a state based on oppressive class domination. The Marxist interpretation of the worker's lot and revolutionary mission thus won the upper hand in the party during the 12 long years in the underground.[53] Only individuals campaigning for election to the legislatures and local union activity were permitted under the anti-Socialist laws of 1878–1890. The juxtaposition of the revolutionary, ideological, and utopian posture growing out of the period of suppression as against the earlier Lassallean and Progressive patterns of cooperating with the state, while trying to reform it, marks the opposite poles of the development of the SPD through nearly a hundred years of schisms since. The utopians from the Spartacists and Communists of Weimar to the *Stamokap*[54] faction of the Jusos of today have been waiting impatiently for the imminent collapse of the capitalist system, often ready to help it along by revolutionary action. The cooperative element, on the other hand, rallied to the cause of the patriotic war in 1914, defended the Weimar Republic by force against the revolutionary left, and has turned the SPD of the Bonn Republic from a Marxist class party into a New Dealish "people's party" since 1959. And, except for the schisms of the period between 1917 and 1919, these heterogeneous elements in the SPD have always been held together by a deeply ingrained sense of solidarity in adversity, the "organizational patriotism" of the simple, lifelong party member who is ever suspicious of the outside world and its hostile forces. A web of socialist mass associations ranging from the Friends of Children and workers' education societies to socialist sports and even funeral societies—from the cradle to the grave—made it easy for the faithful to shield themselves from the conflicts of the larger society.

The most important of these mass organizations were the Free Trade Unions (ADGB) of the socialist labor movement.[55] From rather ideological and politicized beginnings, the Free Trade Unions became a well-organized mass organization in the 1880s and rapidly grew to a membership of 2.5 million by 1913. Seasoned in countless strikes and labor battles with the similarly well-organized employers associations of German industry, they resembled an army as disciplined as the SPD itself. Given the bitter hostility and "master-of-the-house" attitude of many industrialists, they could hardly have been otherwise. The gathering waves of socialist and pacifist mobilization of 1917–1921 all over Europe raised the total German trade union membership to nearly 8 million by 1920 and 9 million in turbulent 1923, of whom the ADGB claimed the lion's share. The various trade unions, which ranged from Communist revolutionary units all the way to the *voelkisch* (and later Nazi) Retail Clerks Union (DHV), tended to stick together on most bread-and-butter issues despite their ideological and partisan differences. Their skillful collusion finally brought about the full-fledged welfare state just in time for its destruction by mass unemployment and fascist counterattack. The eight-hour day was born with the republic and the right to join a union even inscribed in the constitution (art. 159) which also placed labor "under the special protection of the Reich." An elaborate system of plant councils gave the workers a share in shaping their working conditions, while a system of labor courts at several levels adjudicated disputes arising from the specially sanctioned collective contracts that now covered labor-management relations. The Bismarckian scheme of social security, finally, was updated and expanded with the notable addition of unemployment insurance which, as fate would have it, soon became the Archimedean point to unhinge the whole glory of the labor movement. As rising mass unemployment in 1929 drove the Reich government to the edge of its ability to pay, labor movement plans to raise taxes clashed with the insistence of the business partners (DVP) in the grand coalition of 1928–1930 to cut the unemployment benefits instead.[56] Thus fell the last parliamentary cabinet of the Weimar Republic and gave way to the unrestrained warfare of the extreme right and left against the republic.

Compared to the success of the labor unions in the Weimar Republic, however short-lived, the SPD itself was far from the all-powerful position that its right-wing enemies liked to attribute to it. In the 1912 elections, its electoral triumph of 34.8% of the popular vote was still unmarred by the great schisms to follow.[57] The big division between the pacifist and revolutionary wing and the majority of the party was caused by the war and the Russian revolution and intensified by the violent confrontations between revolutionaries and troops, Freecorps, and police called in by SPD governments of the republic. In the end, the Weimar Social Democrats lost nearly a third of a potential share of 40–45% of the electorate to the Weimar Communists and still proved unable to hold the republic against the onslaught of the combined right-wing forces.

When the SPD reemerged after World War II and the fall of the Nazi regime, it did so with a mass membership, a spirit, and an organization that had no equal among the broken-down pillars of the German society of the day.

Even its ideological convictions, the mixture of doctrinaire Marxism and reformism adopted at the Heidelberg convention of 1925, seemed hardly in need of correction. Only in one respect did its charismatic chairman Kurt Schumacher (1895–1952), himself a concentration camp survivor of frail health, want to change the basic beliefs of the SPD. He wanted the SPD to be more nationalistic than it had been in the days when the Nazis were able to exploit national patriotism for their own ends and without any competition from the left. There were also some other developments that tended to reinforce the pride and self-sufficiency of the party. One was the painful break with the East German SPD that was forced by the Soviet occupation to merge with the KPD there. The other were the demonstrations and strikes against occupation policies such as the dismantling of German industry for reparations.[58] The SPD and the newly unified trade unions (DGB) were particularly favored by the British occupation authorities since the Labour party was in power in London. Under the circumstances, Schumacher fully expected that his party would take over West Germany as soon as the occupation period came to an end. However, as will be recalled, it was Adenauer and his mighty CDU/CSU coalition of bourgeois forces that dominated the first 20 years of the Federal Republic. All that remained for the SPD was an opposition role and an agonizing reappraisal of what had gone wrong with its proud ambitions.

The reappraisal took nearly a decade (1953–1959) during which the party also had to cope with the extraordinary changes then occurring in West German society and in the international role of the Federal Republic. There is a difference between initially opposing a policy such as German rearmament and continuing to oppose after the country has been rearmed and firmly integrated into NATO and while it faces a major military threat from the Soviet Union. Internally, the SPD was experiencing a drastic loss of membership from nearly 900,000 in 1946 to less than two-thirds of that number of the mid-1950s.[59] The party's resurrection in 1945–1946, to be sure, had not been merely the rising of the faithful of 1933. There were quite a few prominent new faces, liberal humanists like Professor Carlo Schmid, a smattering of Christian socialists, distinguished ex-Communists like Ernst Reuter, and many former nonsocialists from public and professional careers. Still, there obviously were far more members leaving every year than the 60,000–70,000 new joiners, and there was the same critical absence of youth that in the Weimar Republic had made the SPD an "old" party in contrast to the much younger Communists and Nazis. The death of its leader Schumacher on August 20, 1952 further disoriented the party and put it at a disadvantage against the charisma of Adenauer and Erhard.[60]

The "socialism of the first hour," the most obvious victim of the reappraisal, did not advocate state ownership of all German industry or, as a speaker put it at the first postwar convention in Hanover (1946), a "centralistic state capitalism without a market economy." The new socialist order promised to socialize the production of coal, iron and steel, energy, chemicals, basic building materials, and the large banks and insurance companies but presumably would maintain a free market among the processing and service industries with special safeguards against the reemergence of monopolies. The control of basic industries and monopoly was seen as a political necessity for the sake of ensuring democracy.[61] Other important positions of the Social Democrats in the 1950s were the opposition to German rearmament and integration into NATO and to economic absorption into the "conservative, clerical, capitalist, cartelist" Europe of the Six rather than the wider circle of Western—especially Northern and Northwestern—nations. Despite its obvious Western orientation, the stance of the SPD under and after Schumacher tended toward neutralist autonomy between the two blocs, with heavy emphasis on the quest for German reunification.[62] While the party mounted recurrent campaigns against various aspects of Adenauer's *Westpolitik* down to the massive antibomb demonstrations and the Germany Plan of 1959, which envisaged the two Germanies as a nonnuclear zone to be gradually reunified, the reconsideration of its basic positions was already under way, spurred on by a desire to overcome its poor showing at the 1953 and 1957 elections.[63]

The reappraisal began with the discarding of old party symbols and habits, for example, the use of the red flag and red color on the party posters, addressing each other with the fraternal "thou" (*Du*) and as "comrades" (*Genossen*), and, most of all, the doctrinaire habits of thinking and expression. As early as 1954 the SPD exchanged the conventional self-image of a class-based "workers party" for that of a "people's party" and stressed the ideological openness of the socialist faith. By 1958, the criticism of the old leadership had swept into the triumvirate of party chairmen[64] Herbert Wehner, a prominent ex-Communist, who soon became the mastermind behind the SPD strategies of the 1960s. In that year also, the party for the first time and in the face of the *fait accompli* of rearmament expressed support for a small volunteer army. The preparations for the revision of the last basic ideological program, that of Heidelberg (1925), began reluctantly in the mid-1950s but gathered reformist zeal by the end of the decade and led to the pivotal 1959 Bad Godesberg conference which laid the groundwork for the policies to follow.

At Bad Godesberg, all vestiges of ideological orthodoxy were dropped in favor of a statement of "basic values" that stressed individual freedom and democracy far more than socialist doctrine by any common definition. Democratic socialism was simply derived from "Christian ethics, humanism, and classical philosophy." Special efforts were made to reduce the aversion of Catholics, farmers, and people committed to national defense to the SPD by appropriate statements. The word "socialization" did not occur at all in the new basic program, although there were a few words defining public ownership as "a legitimate means of public control . . . of economic power." The new economic policy goal was defined ingeniously as "ever-growing prosperity and a just participation of all in the returns of the economy, a life in freedom without undignified dependency and exploitation." Indirect controls and modern planning were to guide the market economy, control monopolies, and ensure sufficient means for such public tastes as education and science.[65] The Godesberg Program completed a development that had begun with the absorption of the Imperial and Weimar SPD in pragmatic reform politics and manifested itself with the atrophy of the vast world of socialist associations after World War II which had always kept the socialist subculture sheltered and separate from the rest of German society. Now it was truly a "people's party."

The new style of SPD politics surfaced almost immediately with the sensational foreign policy speech of Wehner before the Bundestag of June 30, 1960, with which the SPD signaled its acceptance of Adenauer's basic foreign policies. All earlier and often acrimonious opposition statements were dropped, and there emerged a bipartisan foreign policy as the first harbinger of the new approach of "embracing the erstwhile enemy"—*amor vincit omnia*—just as the Catholics, churches, farmers, and military had been embraced in the Godesberg Program. A charismatic chancellor candidate, fighting Berlin mayor Willy Brandt, and a government "team" consisting of popular state and local politicians and national figures of nondoctrinaire reputation were then chosen for the 1961 parliamentary elections. The campaign was designed using every marketing trick of public relations managers and after careful observation of the Kennedy-Nixon campaign of 1961 in the United States.[66] The marketing of candidates and concrete issues rather than of ideological principles, in a way, had also been taken over from the practices of the CDU/CSU which had long employed political polls and professional campaign management. The results were impressive. The steady rise of the percentage of the popular vote went from 31.8% in 1957 to 36.2% in 1961 and on to 39.3% in 1965 and 42.7% in 1969.[67]

The SPD had succeeded in breaking out of its permanent minority position and becoming a real rival for the CDU/CSU, just as the latter began to reel from crisis to crisis. Adenauer's final stepping down (1963) and Erhard's failure in 1966 gave the SPD yet one more chance to embrace the CDU/CSU, the grand coalition of 1966–1969. Since the FDP refused to form another coalition with the Christian Democrats amid economic, foreign, and domestic political dangers, the CDU/CSU had little choice. For Brandt and Wehner, on the other hand, this was an opportunity to show what their "team" of competent leaders could do at the federal level if given half the chance. Brandt became foreign minister and vice chancellor under Kiesinger while eight other prominent SPD politicians occupied further cabinet seats, including the ministries of Economics (Karl Schiller), Justice, Traffic, and Health. To the many critics of this collaboration with the "old class enemy," Brandt replied characteristically that the SPD had now become too big to shun the responsibility for governing the country in its straits. It was worth the effort to try "to help Germany" and would earn the SPD additional public confidence for a creditable performance in key areas.[68]

With the benefit of hindsight we can now say, indeed, that this strategy smoothed the way into the era of SPD dominance that followed. But the strategy of embracing could not for long cover up fundamental disagreements between the major parties nor hold the emergence of divisions within the SPD at bay. The internal opposition, naturally, objected to coalition compromises and eventually drew the whole party back from its strategic collaboration with the CDU/CSU. The rise of the neofascist NPD on the right and the extraparliamentary opposition on the left created a climate of confrontations soon reinforced by massive student demonstrations at the universities. The great debate (1966–1968) over the emergency legislation, which was passed with the votes of the SPD, raised protest to levels not observed since the antirearmament and ban-the-bomb rallies of the 1950s.

As it soon turned out, this was only the beginning of the emerging internal dissent which coming to power with the FDP in 1969 could barely disguise. Some of the dissent had come throughout the 1960s from old Socialists unhappy about the tenor of the Godesberg Program and later decisions, such as joining the grand coalition.[69] There was even a noticeable slump in the membership and voting support of the party in 1967–1968, after an upward trend of 1960–1965 that was resumed in 1969 and peaked in 1972.[70] At the same time, an ever-growing share of public school and university students and recent graduates entered the party—two thirds of the new members by 1972 were under 35—and swelled there the ranks of the Young Socialists, that is, of all SPD members under 35. These new Socialists soon became a hotbed of radicalism, attracting the West German equivalent of the *gauchistes* of the restless youth of those years. Only a minority of the Young Socialists (Jusos) have been active in the Juso Working Committee which soon tackled the task of reestablishing the ideological foundations of the reluctant party.

The oppositional stance of the Jusos quickly spread in the years 1965 to 1969 from a regional base in Hesse, Schleswig-Holstein, and Bavaria to the rest of the country. There were no holy cows of official SPD policy that escaped Juso scrutiny. By 1967 they had tackled the question of recognition of the East German Republic (DDR), in 1968 the emergency legislation, and finally the "system" itself had to be "overcome." The debates of theoretical principles at the annual meetings rapidly took the Jusos farther and farther to the left, away from the party and, quite frequently, into all-out rejection of their own leadership of the previous year.[71] In their local campaigns of agitation and street mobilization which were the other aspect of their "double strategy" of influencing the establishment, they ignored the long-standing SPD taboo against cooperation with Communist organizations. Their clashes with well-established local SPD leaders became notorious embarrassments to the party while the right-wing parties had a field day of pointing to these Communist ties and to the "revolutionary character" of local housing or transport agitation of the Jusos.

Worse yet, their discussions of basic principles of socialism produced a proliferation of factions among the Jusos which was bound to diminish their prestige and effectiveness in the long run. At their 1971 meeting in Hanover, for example, four distinct factions emerged:

1. The Stamokap group, which was based on a core of members of the Socialist University Federation (SHB, expelled from the SPD in 1971–1972). Its theories define the enemy as "state monopoly capitalism"[72] and propose an "antimonopolistic alliance strategy."
2. The "nonrevisionists," whose members came especially from the New Left students of the universities of Goettingen and Hanover.
3. The ethical socialists, whose core were the Schleswig-Holstein Jusos and who were reputed to be the most likely to cooperate with the parent party.
4. The sizable faction gathered around the Juso chairman Wolfgang Roth and his predecessor Karsten Voigt. This group advocated political and social-psychological "structural reforms" such as democratization of schools and families to unhinge the depoliticized consciousness on which capitalist society is said to be based.[73]

This degree of factionalism and the conflicts with the party soon led to a relative decline of the importance of the Jusos. As electoral reverses in the Laender followed the triumph of 1972 and the establishment increasingly confronted the Jusos about the duplicity of their "double strategy" against the SPD itself, the Jusos came to adopt a lower profile. In many locations, they returned to patterns of cooperation with the party or at least refrained from seeking further confrontations. In the 1976 elections to the Bundestag, in particular, the Jusos participated quite faithfully, if in an autonomous manner, in the effort to reelect the SPD/FDP government in Bonn.

The Jusos have by no means been the only distinctive faction of the SPD. Since the 1950s, there has been a very large conservative backbencher group in the Bundestag known as the *Kanalarbeiter* (sewer workers) who have supported the Godesberg Program and most policies derived from it without necessarily forming a coherent ideological bloc themselves. Their controlling majority has always prevented any substantial inroads by the elements on the left. There are also small right-wing groups outside of the Bundestag.[74] Next to the Kanalarbeiter, there is the Left Center group, which often tries to mediate differences between the wings. On the left, there is the Leverkusen Circle, which receives additional extraparliamentary support from the Frankfurt and Tuebingen Circles. The left includes important Laender and district chairman as well as intellectuals eager to overhaul the theoretical base of the party. SPD leaders Willy Brandt and Herbert Wehner have expressed alarm at the increasing attempts to institutionalize these factions and branded them as first steps toward schisms. The Jusos, of course, had an institutional form to begin with and there is now also a Working Committee for Workers' Problems, which is expected to bring the ideological flights of fancy of new and old socialists down to the proletarian earth.[75]

Despite the dangers of factionalism, the SPD has been held together by the successes and failures of office. Its electoral triumphs have been as unifying as has been the bitter taste of defeat. The struggle to pass the Renunciation-of-Force Agreements with Moscow, Warsaw, and Prague, which constituted the heart of Brandt's Ostpolitik, had an electrifying effect on SPD members and sympathizers of every camp.[76] Domestic reforms, on the other hand, were noticeably more divisive, if successful, because they exacerbated the differences among the factions. On any reform issue, from abortion to the expansion of labor codetermination, there would always be a vanguard and a rearguard position to set the factions against each other. Because the essential completion of the foreign policies of Ostpolitik led the party back to its traditional stance of domestic social reforms, the *Modell Deutschland*, these divisions were impossible to avoid. With its electoral fortunes seemingly on the wane at all levels, on the other hand, the party can hardly afford to disagree. The resurgent CDU/CSU is already knocking at the gates of power.

The Free Democrats

West Germany's third party is the heir of a century and a half of liberal politics and thought, a history of disappointments as well as triumphs, stretching from before the abortive 1848 revolution of the liberal bourgeoisie to the erosion of liberal voting support by the rise of national socialism in the early 1930s. In the heyday of nineteenth century liberalism, its leaders tangled heroically with the old monarchies in 1848 and then with Otto von Bismarck in the Prussian constitutional dispute of the 1860s. Yet, ever divided into two mainstreams, the right-wing National Liberals soon joined Bismarck's bandwagon of national unification. The left-wing Progressives, throughout the Empire, remained in opposition until the early days of the Weimar Republic when they became one of the three large republican parties along with the SPD and the Center party.[77] With their passionate nationalism and the social crises of the German middle classes, the chief support of both Weimar liberal parties soon caused the bulk of their electorate to wander off to the right.

After the Third Reich came to an ignominious end, during the occupation years, the few liberals who had not succumbed to the appeal of the Christian Democratic rallying on the right or that of the SPD on the left, founded a new party, the West German FDP (also known as Liberal Democrats (LDP) and People's party (DVP) in some areas),[78] for people not religious enough for the CDU/CSU, nor socialistic enough for the SPD. The new FDP for the first time combined both the right- and the left-wing tendencies of its two Weimar predecessors. In addition to its older traditions, therefore, it has been characterized by considerable regional differences. In the South, for example, its brand of liberalism tends to emphasize personal and cultural freedoms, whereas in the industrialized West the stress is on *laissez-faire* economics. Such heterogeneity, naturally, produced factionalism and internal conflicts and affected, in particular, the inclination of the FDP to enter coalitions at the state or federal level with the CDU/CSU or the SPD.

The entire history of the FDP can be written in terms of the coalitions it formed at the federal level during most of the three decades of the Federal Republic. From 1949 until 1966 (except for the years 1956–1961), the party was part of the Adenauer government in which it formed simultaneously the right wing on economic and the left wing on cultural and foreign policies.[79] Its distinguished chairman, Theodor Heuss, was the first federal president of the new republic.

The FDP soon grew restless under Adenauer's dominance and resentful over his efforts to alienate a number of FDP cabinet ministers and their following. After a stint in the opposition, the Free Democrats, in 1961, even campaigned on a platform of ousting Adenauer while promising to rejoin the CDU/CSU in the government. They received their largest vote ever (Table 2–4) but were unable to force the Old Man into retirement for another two years.[80] Their participation in the coalition under Adenauer's successor Erhard (1963–1966) also ended in dissension, and they spent the years of the grand coalition (1966–1969) again in the opposition. Up until this time and despite the continual conflicts, the FDP had clearly been closer to the CDU/CSU and formed coalitions with the SPD only in a few Laender governments.[81] Under a new chairman, Walter Scheel (1968–1974), and besieged by inroads into its voting support on the part of the NPD that temporarily ousted the FDP from several representative assemblies,[83] the party now changed its course toward the left.[83] The new course was initiated with the rejection of the emergency legislation of 1968 and with the election of the new federal president, Gustav Heinemann (SPD) by a joint electoral college vote[84] of the SPD and FDP just prior to the 1969 Bundestag elections. Following the elections, the FDP joined the Brandt government. Scheel became its foreign minister and, in 1974, the next federal president. In 1971 a party convention in Freiburg confirmed the new course by enacting a program of "social liberalism."

The change from the old FDP course to the new was accompanied by wholesale changes in the membership and voters of the party. Large numbers of old middle-class elements such as farmers, professionals, and small businessmen dropped out and switched to the CDU/CSU, while new middle-

TABLE 2–4. The Free Democratic Party Vote in the Bundestag Elections, 1949–1976 (Percent)

1949	1953	1957	1961	1965	1969	1972	1976
11.9	9.5	7.7	12.8	9.5	5.8	8.4	7.9

class elements such as business executives and civil servants became dominant. The student movement also left an impact on the FDP, especially on the leftish Young Democrats, the autonomous youth organization of the party.[85] The general policy line of the FDP in the government since 1969 has been a judicious mixture of progressive initiatives and supports with a well-understood policy of moderating or balancing the left-wing tendencies in the SPD. On subjects such as abortion or the Eastern policies, the party has initiated or given its whole-hearted support to the government projects. On the policies of encouraging property holding (*Vermoegenspolitik*) and on the labor codetermination reform, on the other hand, the FDP played a strongly moderating role. Its Riemer model of labor codetermination, in fact, assigned to management executives on the factory councils a balancer role between the representatives of capital and labor not unlike the balancer role between CDU/CSU and SPD that the FDP has always sought to play.[86] The party has even told the voters time and again, "Vote for us so that the SPD government cannot go too far to the left," just as it used to present itself as a moderating influence in the government in its days with Adenauer.

The FDP as the third force in West German politics, and especially as a moderating factor or antidote to polarization, seems fragile indeed if we think of how close it often has come to falling below the 5% hurdle decreed by the electoral law. There have been recurrent threats by both major parties, moreover, to change the electoral law which even now permits the FDP only list mandates derived from the second ballot. As West German voters increasingly make use of ballot splitting, especially since the 1972 elections when many Social Democrats appear to have given the FDP their second vote, new patterns of dependency threaten the party.[87] The benefits of the balancer role between two parties so evenly matched that neither one can rule alone, on the other hand, are extraordinary. As a coalition partner of Adenauer and Erhard, or of the CDU/CSU at the Laender level, the FDP usually received more cabinet positions than its share of seats in the legislatures warranted.[88] This pattern has not changed one iota in its recent coalitions with the SPD. If anything, its influence on government policies since 1969 has been even greater than in the Adenauer and Erhard years and out of proportion with its actual size in the party system.

Smaller Parties

The seeming monopoly of the three major parties in the Bundestag during the last two decades has not precluded smaller regional or new parties from attempts to assert themselves at lower levels. In recent Laender elections, these other parties have polled combined totals between about 2% and 10% of the vote and, despite the minimal clauses of Land electoral laws, obtained a few seats for limited periods of time. At the local level, they have shown considerable strength in large cities and in certain regional pockets. Below a community size of about 3,000 to 5,000, moreover, nonpartisan politics has tended to prevail.[89] Let us take a closer look at the more important smaller parties.

The Communists are hardly a new party in Germany. Their antecedents include the powerful Weimar Communists and their postwar revivals in many big cities. In the Soviet zone and later the German Democratic Republic, the forced merger of KPD and SPD became the official Communist state party, with a monopoly of power.[90] In the Federal Republic, the revived KPD soon declined from an average of 9.6% of the vote in the Laender elections before 1949 (14.0% in 1947 in North Rhine Westphalia) to 2.2% in the federal elections of 1953. Following the outlawing of the neofascist Socialist Reich party (SRP), the KPD was suppressed in 1956 and went underground, working through front organizations and friendly groups, such as the German Peace Union (DFU) and parts of the trade unions. In 1968, the Communists were once more admitted as a legal party under the name DKP and began to participate in local campaigns with an intensity belying their small numbers of voters.[91] The DFU had polled no more than 1–2% in the 1960s. The DKP has not been able to attract more than 3% in any Land elections and polled a mere 0.3% in the Bundestag elections of 1972 and 1976.[92]

The DKP concentrates much of its efforts on its network of factory cells which is complemented by a string of factory newspapers with a total circulation of half a million copies. There is also a daily newspaper, *Unsere Zeit*, to spread the ideas of scientific socialism and a theoretical bimonthly journal. The DKP is one of the best financed political parties of the Federal Republic, with an annual income on a par with that of the FDP.[93] It also maintains a party functionary school and educational institutes of Marxism. The party organization is tightly knit along the lines of "democratic centralism" and, like the neo-Nazi NPD, frequently purges dissenters and whole groups whose cooperation may be less than perfect.[94] As in the Soviet Union and the DDR, the DKP also maintains a children's organization, the Young Pioneers, for the 6- to 14-year-olds, and a youth organization of about 13,000 which had to fight a continual rearguard action against the antiauthoritarian leftist trends that have motivated German youth since the late 1960s.

There are several dissident Communist groups which the DKP regards as "putschist" adventurers. Among these is the Maoist new KPD of 1971 which was built up from the Red Cells of universities in Berlin and acquired a reputation for street violence. The new KPD has less than 1,000 members and received 10,000 votes in West Berlin and perhaps twice that number in some Laender elections of the Federal Republic. A weekly, *Rote Fahne*, and other party publications and feeble mass organizations as well as several youth organizations including a university student group (KSV) given to spectacular and often violent actions in local campaigns flesh out the picture of a militant splinter group.[95] In some of these campaigns, the closest ally of the new KPD was the Communist League of West Germany (KBW) of 1973, another Maoist group of particular local strength at West German universities and in certain cities and industries. The KBW likewise has a reputation for political street violence and spectacular local campaigns. A third Maoist group, the KPD/ML, dates back to 1968 and has links to similar Maoist groups, as well as an interest in trade union activities.

At the other extreme of the political spectrum, where there had been an outpouring of dire warnings in the world press a few years ago, and a rash of scholarly studies as well,[96] few people pay much attention to the neofascist NPD today. The great ado about the alleged Nazi revival of 1966–1969, in any case, could impress only the uninformed, for it was neither the first nor the worst such resurgence in postwar Germany. It would have bordered on a miracle, had the many millions of card-carrying Nazis of 1945 and their families simply vanished without leaving behind a residue of incorrigibles and possibly attracting some new recruits. During the occupation years, of course, the occupying powers refused to license any persons or organizations suspect of Nazi leanings. As early as 1950–1951, however, a Socialist Reich party had absorbed most of the following of earlier ultraconservative groups.[97] Unlike its predecessors, the SRP was frankly neo-Nazi, although it was careful to hide its antisemitism and imperialism. As "national opposition" it opposed German rearmament and demanded German reunification. In 1951, when the SRP polled 7.7% of the vote in Bremen and 11.0% in Lower Saxony,[98] the still insecure Adenauer government decided to bring suit before the Federal Constitutional Court to have the SRP outlawed as a threat to the constitutional order. This action hit the ambitions of the far right in Germany like a bombshell and persuaded them to keep a low profile for the following decade.

By 1964, when even such potential reservoirs of right-wing recruits as the DP and the BHE had lost their place in the party system, and the climate of suspicion toward Nazi revivals had given way to indifference,[99] the time seemed ripe for another attempt to rally the scattered extreme right. Of several such efforts, the only one to succeed was the foundation of the NPD by remainders of the DP—under the leadership of Fritz Thielen, the DP chairman of Bremen—and of the DRP led by Adolf von Thadden and by leftovers of the Refugee party. The new party participated in a limited way in the federal elections of 1965, gathering 2% of the vote, and then had its most notable successes in the state elections of 1966, a year of recession, unemployment, and political crisis in Bonn.

In a string of Laender elections beginning with those of Hesse and Bavaria in late 1966, the NPD demonstrated its ability to rally the existing right-wing groups and to draw a protest vote from the FDP and other major parties (Table 2–5). Taking advantage of the electoral laws[100] and of the general crisis, the NPD won a number of Landtag seats only to lose them again in the following set of Laender elections. Thielen and von Thadden, moreover, became mortal

TABLE 2–5. Neofascist Gains and Other Parties' Losses in Laender Elections, 1966–1968[a]

LAND	NPD (%)	NPD SEATS	LOSERS (%)
Hamburg (1966)	3.9	—	Free Democrats: 2.8%, German Reich party (DRP): 0.9%
Hesse (1966)	7.9	8	Christian Democrats: 2.4%, Free Democrats: 1.1%, Refugees: 2%
Bavaria (1966)	7.4	15	Free Democrats: 0.8%, Bavaria party: 1.4%, Refugees: 5.0%
Schleswig-Holstein (1967)	5.8	4	Free Democrats: 2.0%, others: 0.7%
Rhineland-Palatinate (1967)	6.9	4	Social Democrats: 3.9%, Free Democrats: 1.8%
Lower Saxony (1967)	7.0	10	Refugees: 3.7%, German party: 2.7%, Free Democrats: 1.9%, Social Democrats: 1.8%, German Reich party: 1.5%
Bremen (1967)	8.8	8	Social Democrats: 8.7%, German party: 4.3%
Baden-Wuerttemberg (1968)	9.8	12	Social Democrats: 8.2%, Christian Democrats: 2.1%
Saar (1970)	3.4	—	Free Democrats: 3.9%, others: 4.8%

[a]The National Democrats chose not to compete in the 1966 elections of North Rhine Westphalia and the 1967 elections in West Berlin.

enemies and public opposition made it nearly impossible for the NPD to function like a normal political party. In the 1969 federal elections, the party with 4.3% fell just short of the 5% hurdle and has since sunk back into the *petit marais* of the right-wing fringe groups until the next revival, perhaps in another 10 or 15 years.

Partisan Cleavages in the Electorate

Political parties depend on the configurations of their support among the electorate as well as on the degree of political involvement of the people at large. Since the beginnings of their republic, West Germans have turned out to vote in larger and larger numbers, beginning with a rate of 78.5% of eligible voters in 1949 when many voters still felt a posttotalitarian revulsion toward politics. By the late 1950s, the turnout had risen to 87.8% (1957), although the *Civic Culture* study found the people to express very little pride in their political institutions and to show considerably less interest in politics than the British and the American electorate.[101] Since the late 1960s, however, a new attitude has developed toward political participation which appears to be related to generational change and, perhaps also, to the long-range effects of civic education in the schools and mass television use, as well as to the politicization of the years 1966–1972. Not only did the electoral turnout reach 91.2% in the 1972 elections, but the percentage of those expressing strong interest in politics outside the election campaigns rose from a level of about 30% up until 1965 to 43% in 1971 and 49% in 1973.[102] This rise in political interest would probably raise the Federal Republic in this respect at least to the level of the other Western democracies in a comparison today.

The West German party system rests on voting blocs that have shown remarkable stability over the years, even though their loyalty has been declining somewhat in the last ten years. At the outset, a UNESCO survey clearly showed the character of the two major blocs. The most loyal SPD following were Protestant skilled or semiskilled workers who belonged to the DGB; the core of the CDU/CSU following were regular churchgoers, especially Catholic and middle-class voters.[103] The social class division, however, was not as controlling as we might expect from the tradition of the SPD as a working-class party. Although the workers constituted three-fourths of the SPD electorate, they also made up two-fifths of the Christian Democratic voters (Table 2–6). White-collar voters were more evenly split between the two camps, and the independents and farmers were mostly in the CDU/CSU camp. This distribution does not appear to have changed much between 1953 and 1967 except for the losses of the FDP among the independents, a trend that became even stronger in 1968–1970,[105] when the FDP in turn attracted more of the volatile white-collar vote. Appearances, however, can be deceptive. A closer look at the distribution within each party (Table 2–6) shows that there was also a substantial shift in the SPD from the worker component to the white-collar supporters of the party in these 14 years. By today, this last-mentioned component of the SPD is likely to be even larger, as its share of the total population has grown further.

The trade union and churchgoer vote continued to be the mainstay of the two giant blocs, although the SPD in 1969 and, even more in 1972, attracted large numbers of the traditional Catholic clientele of the CDU/CSU, only to lose ground again in 1976. The SPD advances among Catholics, especially in metropolitan areas, and among white-collar voters actually have been going on since 1957, or since the Bad Godesberg Program.[106] By the same token, the CDU/CSU electorate has become more and more rural and small town, at least until the most recent successes of the party in some of the biggest metropoles. In 1972, the SPD even began to break into the rural preserves of

TABLE 2–6. Occupation of Respondent (or Head of Household) Identifying with Parties in 1953 and 1967 (Percent)

	WORKERS	*INDE-PENDENT*	*WHITE COLLAR (INCLUDING CIVIL SERVICE)*	*FARMERS (INCLUDING FARM LABOR)*
1953				
CDU/CSU-Z	32	49%	51%	58%
Bourgeois parties (FDP, DP, BP)	9	29	16	28
SPD–KPD	50	15	25	8
Others	9	7	8	6
	100	100	100	100
Group percentage	50.9	14.4	20	14.7 100%

	WORKERS	*INDE-PENDENT (INCLUDING FARMERS)*	*WHITE COLLAR (INCLUDING CIVIL SERVICE)*	*PENSIONERS*
1967				
CDU/CSU	33	58	45	45
FDP	1	8	4	2
SPD	49	14	34	36
Other	17	20	17	17
	100	100	100	100
Group percentage	37	16	28	19 100%

CDU/CSU strength and increased its hold on urban-industrial districts, whether Catholic or Protestant. Women constitute another group that used to vote heavily CDU/CSU until in 1969 and 1972 the SPD and FDP made great inroads possibly related to its abortion legislation. In 1976, the CDU/CSU claimed a return to the fold of substantial numbers of these wayward groups of voters. We must not forget that the CDU/CSU throughout these years of relative losses has remained a giant quite capable by itself of winning a majority of the West German vote.

These relationships and shifts finally have to be seen against the background of a gradually changing West German society recently described by David Conradt as follows: (1) a working-class bloc of 30% of the electorate voting mostly SPD; (2) a Catholic bloc of 20% spanning the social classes and voting mostly CDU/CSU; (3) a middle-class bloc of 23% whose independent, white-collar, and farm voters in the early and middle 1960s gave the majority of their vote to the CDU/CSU and FDP; and (4) a heterogeneous rest of 27%, composed, among others, of unionized civil servants and white-collar or upwardly mobile workers, of whom the SPD received nearly half the vote in those years.[107] In 1969 and 1972, the SPD succeeded in breaking into bloc 2 and taking over more of bloc 4, only to lose ground again in 1976. Long-range trends also make the political dissociation—that is, between CDU/CSU and FDP— of independents (farmers and business and professional people) from the new middle class (white collar) since the mid-1960s significant. Since 1925, the share of the independents has dropped from 36.8% to a mere 15% (20% in 1950), whereas white collar grew from 12.3% of the gainfully employed to about 30%.[108] Neither the share of workers (48%) nor that of civil servants (5%) have changed much. The long road toward a postindustrial society obviously generates its political consequences in the prevailing party system even if those consequences have not completely crystallized.[109]

Notes

1. Seventeen coalition governments followed each other in rapid succession during the 14 years of the First Republic, 14 of them prior to the emergency cabinet of Heinrich Bruening (1930), governing an average of 8 months each. In the decade from 1920 to 1930, no party won more than 30% of the seats, and the total number of parties in the *Reichstag* ranged between 10 and 17. See Bernhard Vogel et al., *Wahlen in Deutschland*, Berlin: De Gruyter, 1971, pp. 296–297.

2. See Merkl, "Party Government in the Bonn Republic," in Elke Frank, ed., *Lawmakers in a Changing World*, Englewood Cliffs, N.J.: Prentice-Hall, 1966, pp. 65–82.

3. This constitutional article also calls on Parliament to regulate the parties with legislation which, among other things, served as the basis for proceedings against subversive neofascist and Communist parties in the 1950s. The constitutional recognition of political parties forms a stark contrast to earlier liberal constitutions, including that of Weimar, which sought to safeguard the mandate of the individual parliamentary deputy against group pressures of all sorts including those of political parties. See esp. *Rechtliche Ordnung des Parteiwesens*, Probleme eines Parteiengesetzes, Bericht der Parteienrechtskommission, Frankfurt: Metzner, 1957, pp. 65–78 and 96–122.

4. On public campaign financing, see esp. the excerpts from "Party Law," in Louise W. Holborn et al., eds. *German Constitutional Documents Since 1871*, New York: Praeger, 1970, pp. 36–38, and Uwe Schleth and Michael Pinto-Duschinsky "Why Public Subsidies Have Become the Major Sources of Party Funds in West Germany, but not in Great Britain," in Arnold J. Heidenheimer, ed., *Comparative Political Finance*, Lexington, Ma.: Heath, 1970, pp. 25–49.

5. Together, the SPD and CDU/CSU commanded all but 9.9% of the seats in the *Bundestag*, leaving only the FDP and an extraparliamentary opposition movement (APO) to play the role of the opposition. See Kurt L. Shell,

"Extraparliamentary Opposition in Postwar Germany," *Comparative Politics*, 2 (July 1970), 653–680.

6. See the contribution by Werner Kaltefleiter to this volume.

7. The most important parties of the Weimar Republic were, from left to right, the Communist (KPD), Social Democratic (SPD), Democratic (DDP), People's (DVP), Catholic Center (Z), Nationalist (DNVP), and National Socialist (NSDAP) parties. At times, there were also farm and economic middle-class protest parties as well as regional and dissident groups on the left and right.

8. The smaller parties included a revived Center party to be found only in the Rhineland and an Economic Reconstruction party (WAV) limited to Bavaria. The regional parties were the Bavaria (BP) and Lower Saxonian Land (NLP) parties and the South Schleswig Voters Association (SSW) which tended to survive the early period in some form.

9. See Merkl, "Coalition Politics in West Germany," in Sven Groennings, E. W. Kelley, and Michael Leiserson, eds., *The Study of Coalition Behavior*, New York: Holt, Rinchart, 1970, pp. 15–17.

10. See, for example, Merkl, *The Origin of the West German Republic*, New York: Oxford University Press, 1963, pp. 165–172, and Arnold J. Heidenheimer, *Adenauer and the CDU: The Rise of the Leader and the Integration of the Party*, The Hague: Nijhoff, 1960.

11. See Merkl, *Germany: Yesterday and Tomorrow*, New York: Oxford University Press, 1965, pp. 280–281, and Heino Kaack, *Geschichte und Struktur des deutschen Parteiensystems*, Opladen: Westdeutscher Verlag, 1971, pp. 222–225 and 258–259.

12. Under the Soviet occupation, the East German SPD was forced to merge with the KPD there, which thus became the official state party, the Socialist Unity party (SED). This strong-arming and the subsequent style of Communist rule alienated much of the traditional Communist clientele in West Germany. The Cold War did the rest so that, by 1953, the KPD was down to a popular vote of 2.2% (from 5.7%). In 1956 it was outlawed as a party subversive of the constitution as was the Socialist Reich party (SRP), a neofascist revival, in 1952, after regional successes in 1951.

13. See also Merkl, "Comparative Study and Campaign Management: The Brandt Campaign in Western Germany," *Western Political Quarterly*, 15 (Dec. 1962), 681–704.

14. In the federal elections, an additional 10% of the voters have tended to turn out of whom the bulk have given their votes to the party in power. In the state elections, by way of contrast, a multiparty system of regionally strong forces lingered on that had long been overcome at the federal level.

15. In Munich, for example, the ouster of Lord Mayor Hans-Jochen Vogel by the Jusos and what was viewed as the public washing of the party's dirty linen so alienated old SPD voters that the SPD lost everyone of its traditional Landtag and Bundestag seats in that city. See also Joachim Raschke, *Innerparteiliche Opposition*, Hamburg: Hoffmann & Campe, 1974, on Berlin.

16. In the early years of the CDU/CSU, factionalism was based on regional or interest groups. Since the decline of Adenauer's leadership in the late 1950s, most

of the factions have been formed in conflicts over his successors and new leaders of the heterogeneous party. See also Merkl, "Equilibrium, Structure of Interests, and Leadership: Adenauer's Survival as Chancellor," *American Political Science Review*, 58 (Sept. 1962), 637–645, and Kaack's *Geschichte und Struktur*, pp. 266–270, 285, 300. See also Merkl, "The Limits of the West German Party State," in Frank Belloni and Dennis Beller, eds., *Faction Politics: Political Parties and Factionalism in Comparative Perspective*, Santa Barbara, Calif.: ABC-Clio Press, 1978, pp. 245–264.

17. The rise of National Socialism is quite appropriately contrasted with the historic failure of the German liberal bourgeoisie to develop constitutional democracy. The FDP as the sole heir, since the merger of 1948, of the several strands of German liberalism has been free of the sectarian tendencies of most of its historic antagonists and some of its antecedents.

18. For details, see Rolf Ebbighausen and Peter Kirchhoff, "Die DKP im Parteiensystem der Bundesrepublik," in Juergen Dittberner and Rolf Ebbighausen, eds., *Parteiensystem in der Legitimationskrise*, Opladen: Westdeutscher Verlag, pp. 427–466.

19. See esp. Volker Haese and Peter Mueller, "Die Jungsozialisten in der SPD," ibid., pp. 279–280 on the various schools and their views.

20. A telling example of such sentiments were the misgivings among the Nazi stormtroopers in 1930 about the party bureaucracy and its newly acquired and lavishly furnished Brown House in Munich. See Merkl, *The Making of Stormtroopers,* Princeton, N.J.: Princeton University Press, 1980.

21. See Robert Michels, *Political Parties: A Sociological Study of the Oligarchical Tendencies of Modern Democracy*, New York: Free Press, 1966, and the perceptive introduction to this book by Seymour Martin Lipset. See also the reappraisal of the "iron law" by Richard Willey, *Democracy in the West German Trade Unions*, Beverly Hills, Calif.: Sage, 1973.

22. Basic Law, art. 21.

23. A translation of the salient parts appears in Holborn et al. pp. 32–38. A major part of the law dealt with the financing and disclosure of sources of the parties.

24. The socialist trade unions, of course, date much farther back but achieved rapid growth and mass membership in the hundreds of thousands only after the lapse of the anti-Socialist laws of 1878–1890. See esp. Vernon L. Lidtke, *The Outlawed Party: Social Democracy in Germany, 1878–1890*, Princeton, N.J.: Princeton University Press, 1966. The agrarian-conservative *Bund der Landwirte* was founded 1893. The Catholic *Volksverein* of 1890 was the mass organization that completed the extant web of Kolping clubs, Christian trade unions, and farm organizations (*Bauernvereine*).

25. The National Liberals, who had kept no accounts or records before 1903, for example, by 1914 had 2 general secretaries and 17 employees at their Reich office and 50 salaried party secretaries in *Land* and provincial offices throughout the country. The SPD by that time employed 50 secretaries at the party district and 100 at the electoral district level. See *Rechtliche Ordnung*, pp. 19–20. For the Center and Conservative parties the Volksverein and Bund der Landwirte, respectively, took care of most of their bureaucratic functions.

26. According to the Law on Parties, each party that polled a certain percentage in the preceding election is entitled to DM 2.50 (now 3.50) for each ballot cast in its favor. At the rates of 1970/1971, a federal campaign cost 162 million marks, a set of Laender campaigns 85 million marks, and a local campaign throughout the country 65 million marks.

27. See Holborn et al., pp. 78–81, and Kaack, *Geschichte und Struktur*, pp. 595–620. Also Gerhard Loewenberg, *Parliament in the German Political System*, Ithaca: Cornell University Press, 1967, pp. 40–48, 63–84.

28. Delegate assemblies usually consist of holders of local party or public offices, and they tend to select persons of the same description. In metropolitan areas, nominating assemblies are sometimes joined together. The size of the assemblies varies from about 25 to 360 persons, or on the average about 60 for the CDU/CSU and 110 for the SPD.

29. Only about 15% of the card-carrying members of the major parties could be described as active members.

30. In recent elections, there has been an increasing amount of ticket-splitting whereby, for example, SPD voters in a "safe district" will give their second ballots to the FDP or another small party.

31. In every federal election, up to a dozen smaller parties usually fall victim to this clause. A few regionally strong small parties still survive in the state diets, although the state (Land) electoral laws impose similar and often even more demanding hurdles.

32. Kaack, *Geschichte und Struktur*, pp. 621–645. Persons already in the Bundestag generally enjoy the greatest likelihood of being renominated in a good place on the lists as long as they keep the discipline within the Land delegation.

33. The earliest antecedents are the Catholic political writers and active clergymen in the early nineteenth century state diets, in the Frankfurt Constituent Assembly of 1848/1849, and in the Prussian Diet of the 1850s and 1860s. See *Rechtliche Ordnung*, pp. 13–16, and Ludwig Bergstraesser, *Geschichte der politischen Parteien in Deutschland*, 10th ed. (Munich: Olzog, 1960), pp. 983–93, as well as the literature cited there.

34. See Bergstraesser, *Geschichte*, pp. 190–201, 209–211, 227–233, and 269–272.

35. For the political and constitutional implications of this reaction to totalitarianism, see Merkl, *The Origin of the West German Republic*, New York: Oxford University Press, 1963, chap. 2.

36. See Hans Georg Wieck, *Die Entstehung der CDU und die Wiedergruendung des Zentrums im Jahre 1945*, Duesseldorf: Droste, 1953, and Helmut Puetz, ed., *Konrad Adenauer und die CDU der britischen Besatzungszone*, Bonn: Eichholz-Verlag, 1975, pp. 3–24.

37. The Christian label of the CDU/CSU is easily misunderstood in countries like the United States where it has sometimes been adopted by extreme right-wing and antisemitic groups. To the West Germans of that period, it chiefly meant the desire to revive the humane values of religion and Christian humanism in place of the ungodly nihilism of national socialism. It also mirrored the high prestige and political prominence of both churches amid the collapse and disgrace of most public institutions in those days.

38. See Wolfgang Treue, ed., *Deutsche Parteiprogramme, 1861–1961*, 3rd ed., Goettingen: Musterschmidt, 1961, pp. 178–185.

39. See *Politisches Jahrbuch der CDU/CSU 1950*, p. 226. Codetermination involves the sharing of authority in the individual company or plant between representatives of management and labor on the plant councils (*Betriebsraete*). Depending on the list of competencies of these councils and the different ratios of their composition, including the possible representation of industrywide trade unions on them, codetermination plans may range from tokenism to what owners and managers may view as "cold socialization" or expropriation of their companies.

40. See Treue, *Parteiprogramme*, pp. 188–189. By the time of the 1949 elections, the CSU was willing to use the Duesseldorf Principles (1949) of the CDU as an election program, but only because they tended to gloss over the remaining disagreements.

41. For translated excerpts, see Holborn et al., *German Constitutional Documents*, pp. 46–49. The whole text is in Treue, *Parteiprogramme*, pp. 240–252.

42. This is not to say that the Social Policy Committees and Catholic labor groups have disappeared. See, for example, Norbert Bluem, *Reaktion oder Reform: Wohin geht die CDU?*, Hamburg: Rowohlt, 1972, and esp. Rolf Ebbighausen and Wilhelm Kaltenborn, "Arbeiterinteressen in der CDU? Zur Rolle der Sozialausschuesse," in Dittberner and Ebbighausen, *Parteiensystem*, pp. 172–199.

43. See Merkl, *Origin of the West German Republic*, pp. 148–161.

44. See Puetz, *Adenauer*, pp. 51–53, 57–64, 73–76. See also the many essays on Adenauer's *Westpolitik* in Dieter Blumenwitz et al., eds. *Konrad Adenauer und seine Zeit*, vol. 1, Stuttgart: DVA, 1976, and in Richard Loewenthal and Hans-Peter Schwarz, eds., *Die Zweite Republik: 25 Jahre BRD—Eine Bilanz*, Stuttgart: Seewald, 1974.

45. An Atlanticist policy placed primary emphasis on cooperation with the United States and Great Britain whereas "Gaullism" meant principal reliance on De Gaulle's France and European arrangements for defense. See Merkl, *German Foreign Policies, West and East*, Santa Barbara, Calif.: Clio Press, 1974, pp. 106–124. There were many voices in the CDU/CSU, including prominent Protestant and Catholic church leaders and Erhard's successor, Chancellor Kiesinger (1966–1969), who had avidly sought reconciliation with the Eastern nations back in the 1960s, until the Czechoslovak invasion of 1968 put an end to these antecedents of Ostpolitik for the time being.

46. On the CSU, see also Alf Mintzel, "Die CSU in Bayern," in Dittberner and Ebbighausen, eds., *Parteiensystem*, pp. 352–357.

47. The SPD-FDP government in 1972 responded with emergency measures barring Communists and former student radicals, the Radikalenerlass, which raised new controversies and criticism from the left.

48. Some of these fears, such as fear of crime and of political radicals were found to preoccupy 90% and more of West German voters in polls taken in May and June of 1976. They were topped only by concern about unemployment, inflated prices, excessive public spending, pollution, and vocational education. See Dieter

Oberndoerfer, *Umfrageergebnisse des SFK von Mai/Juni 1976 zu wichtigen politischen Fragen*, Sozialwissenschaftliches Forschungsinstitut Konrad-Adenauer-Stiftung (mimeographed), Tables 2, 3 and 4.

49. These were the formulation of the CDU convention of 1975 in Mannheim. Among upwardly mobile West Germans, in particular, there was widespread discontent about the increasingly larger bite taken by taxes as their income rose.

50. For the first time, large numbers of CDU/CSU partisans sported campaign buttons and bumper stickers to break what pollsters have sometimes called the "spiral of silence (Elisabeth Noelle-Neumann)," the spiraling diffidence that comes from party adherents afraid to speak up among the more outspoken Social Democrats.

51. Its antecedents go back to the 1848/1849 revolution when most of its spokesmen and local organizations were closely linked with the revolutionary liberal bourgeoisie. Although many of the revolutionaries had to flee abroad afterward, the 1850s and 1860s saw the foundation of local cooperative and workers educational associations, all still under the wing of left-wing liberalism.

52. The Eisenach Program (1869) of the Social Democratic Workers party had stressed both the democratic traditions of the Saxonian Progressives and Marxist internationalism and called for the abolition of class rule. The Gotha Program (1875) of unification drew negative criticisms from Karl Marx and Friedrich Engels who disliked in it both the Lassallean emphasis on welfare state measures and the Progressive stress on the democratization of state and society.

53. The chief popularizers of Marxism in those days were Karl Kautsky (1854–1938) and Eduard Bernstein (1850–1932) whose name later became associated particularly with the "evolutionary" reinterpretation of Marx (revisionism). The Erfurt Program of 1891 mirrored the extent to which Marxism had now become the exclusive theoretical basis of the SPD, although it also showed increasing preoccupation with pragmatic political concerns.

54. *Stamokap* stands for "state monopoly capitalism," which is the definition among members of this group and some neo-Marxist writers of the nature of present Western advanced industrial states.

55. The antecedents of trade unions in Germany also go back to 1848, although they began to be tolerated and eventually legalized only after the big strike wave of the 1860s. There were also Christian and Liberal (Hirsch-Duncker) unions of more modest size, numbering nearly half a million in 1913. The name *Allgemeiner Deutscher Gewerkschaftsbund* (ADGB) was the Weimar name and must be distinguished from the DGB of the Bonn Republic and the FDGB of East Germany.

56. Prevailing economic philosophy shied away from increasing the money supply as a way out of the dilemma. Throughout the worst years of unemployment, the emergency cabinets of the early 1930s adhered to a disastrous deflationary policy in the face of the spiraling crisis.

57. Under the prevailing majority electoral law this vote yielded 27.7% of the Reichstag seats, a far better representation than earlier elections when the SPD percentage of the seats was reduced by the *scrutin uninominal* to half (1898) or

even a third (1907) of its poll. This was an important reason for the SPD to advocate proportional representation which in 1919 became the law of the land.

58. Other confrontations were over the degree of decentralization of the Basic Law of 1949 on which the SPD still claims to have wrested significant concessions from the occupying powers. See, for example, Vorstand der SPD, *Sozialdemokraten in Deutschland, 1863–1976*, Cologne: Deutz, 1976, p. 61.

59. The younger generation of those years showed a pronounced reluctance to get involved in partisan politics. The CDU/CSU and FDP also lost a large part of their substantial membership of the more politicized, immediate postwar years, but they at least were in power. See Flechtheim, *Die Parteien in der BRD*, Hamburg: Hoffman & Campe, 1973, p. 398.

60. See esp. Susanne Miller, *Die SPD vor und nach Godesberg*, Bonn: Neue Gesellschaft, 1974, pp. 9–15.

61. There are some obvious parallels here with the Labour policies in Great Britain at the time, although the British occupation refused to entertain German demands of socializing the coal industry, Miller, *Die SPD*, pp. 15–17 and 75–80, and *SPD Jahrbuch 1948/49*, pp. 18–19.

62. Schumacher's anti-European policy had among its few prominent critics in the party such names as Ernst Reuter, Willy Brandt, and the Lord Mayors of Bremen and Hamburg. The DGB also favored the European Coal and Steel Community from the beginning. The recovery of the Oder-Neisse areas was a routine demand of SPD programs then as well as in the 1960s.

63. During these lean years of the party at the federal level, the SPD could boast of a large number of eminently successful and popular big-city mayors and Laender ministers president, although this did not seem to help it to generate public confidence in its "team" at federal elections.

64. The others were Schumacher's successor Erich Ollenhauer and the popular chairman of the Bavarian SPD, Waldemar von Knoeringen.

65. *Protokoll der Verhandlungen des Ausserordentlichen Parteitags der SPD vom 13.–15. Nov. 1959 in Bad Godesberg*, Bonn: Vorstand der SPD, 1960, pp. 9–30. Reprinted also in Miller, *Die SPD*, pp. 117–131. See also Douglas A. Chalmers, *The Social Democratic Party of Germany: From Working Class Movement to Modern Political Party*, New Haven, Conn.: Yale University Press, 1964, and Harold K. Schellenger, *The SPD in the Bonn Republic: A Socialist Party Modernizes*, The Hague: Mouton, 1968.

66. For details, see Merkl, "Comparative Study and Campaign Management: The Brandt Campaign in Western Germany," *Western Political Quarterly*, 15 (Dec. 1962), 681–704. Because of his role as the Lord Mayor of anti-Communist, beleaguered, Berlin, Brandt was a believable choice to make the new foreign policy plausible. See Abraham Ashkenasi, *Reformpartei und Aussenpolitik: Die Aussenpolitik der SPD*, Opladen: Westdeutscher Verlag, 1968, esp. p. 196.

67. By the end of the decade, the SPD had made inroads in most CDU/CSU strongholds. The 36.2% of 1961, as the party pointed out triumphantly, for the first time topped the percentage calculated as the West German share of the SPD vote of 1919, the year of the great socialist-pacifist wave, 35.4%. *SPD Jahrbuch 1960/61*, p. 321.

68. See esp. *Bestandsaufnahme 1966*, Bonn: Vorstand der SPD, 1966, pp. 61–62. The grand coalition can indeed be credited with having overcome the recession and special economic problems of 1966–1967.

69. See Peter Arend, *Die Innerparteiliche Entwicklung der SPD, 1966–1975*, Bonn: Eichholz, 1975, pp. 29–30. As early as 1960–1961, the SPD had begun to disavow and expel pacifistic and left-leaning groups and individuals. See *SPD Jahrbuch 1960/1961*, pp. 446, 451–452, 463–464, and 471–474. This included the Socialist Student Federation (SDS), the German Peace Union (DFU), and the Easter March (ban the bomb) participants.

70. See Arend, *Innerparteiliche Entwicklung*, pp. 34–38.

71. The ideological evolution of the Jusos at first had to overcome substantial loyalist elements in its own federal organs who were not eliminated completely until 1968–1969. See Arend, *Innerparteiliche Entwicklung*, pp. 46–54, and, for details on the individual issues, ibid., pp. 76–164. Their "double strategy" combines exercising pressure at the top of the party with mobilizing and agitation at the base and in the streets.

72. See esp. André Gorz, *Zur Strategie der Arbeiterbewegung im Neokapitalismus*, Frankfurt: Suhrkamp, 1967.

73. For details, see Volker Haese and Peter Mueller, "Die Jungsozialisten in der SPD," in Dittberner and Ebbighausen, eds., *Parteiensystem*, pp. 279–292, who also provide a balanced assessment of the limited impact of the Jusos during their strongest period from about 1969 to 1973, pp. 292–306.

74. They are often named after prominent SPD politicans of an earlier generation, such as the Fritz Erler Circle or the Kurt Schumacher Circle, which include many well-known politicians.

75. For details, see Arend, *Innerparteiliche Entwicklung*, pp. 54–61, and Horst W. Schmollinger, "Gewerkschafter in der SPD—Eine Fallstudie," in Dittberner and Ebbighausen, eds., *Parteiensystem*, pp. 229–274, which deals with an earlier working committee on the Trade Unions.

76. For details on the struggle over Ostpolitik, see Merkl, *German Foreign Policies*, chap. 5.

77. Under the name Democrats (DDP), they played a major role in framing the Weimar constitution and determining important Weimar policies until their voting support had dropped from 18.7% in 1919 to 1.0% in 1932. The right-wing liberal People's party (DVP), despite its more conservative and initially antirepublican course, suffered a similar fate.

78. In East Germany, its equivalent has been known as Liberal Democrats (LDP), a part of the multiparty facade of the Communist dictatorship. It had the same name in Hesse, whereas the southwestern liberals preferred People's party (DVP).

79. The FDP generally shared Adenauer's foreign policy goals but, in the 1950s, proved far more mindful of German reunification and of maintaining contacts with Eastern Germany than Christian Democratic orthodoxy would permit.

80. See Merkl, "Leadership, Equilibrium, and Structure of Interest: Adenauer's Survival as Chancellor," pp. 646–649.

81. See Merkl, "Coalition Politics in West Germany," pp. 19–25.

82. See below, p. 47.

83. See also Claus Montag, "FDP—Opposition ohne Alternative," *Deutsche Aussenpolitik*, 13 (July 1968), 862–870. The new course first appeared at the 1967 Party Conference in Hanover.

84. The Federal president is elected by the Federal Assembly, an electoral college composed of the members of the Bundestag and an equal number of Landtag deputies representative of the last Laender elections.

85. For details on the Young Democrats see Juergen Kunze, "Die Jungdemokraten zwischen Liberalismus und Sozialismus," in Dittberner und Ebbighausen, eds., *Parteiensystem*, pp. 307–326. The gains and losses of the FDP appeared to involve for the most part an exchange of members and voters with the CDU/CSU which lost much of its white-collar component in exchange for the self-employed former backers of the FDP. See esp. Lothar Albertin, "Intra-party Developments in the FDP," a paper delivered before the Conference Group on German Politics in Athens, Georgia, in 1973 and below, Table 25–2 and Table 25–5.

86. The executives have a part of the labor share on the councils. See also Wolfgang Mischnick, "Gesellschafts-und Sozialpolitik: Selbstbestimmung, Mitbestimmung, Solidaritaet," in Hans-Dietrich Genscher, ed., *Liberale in der Verantwortung*, Munich: Hanser, 1976, pp. 29–36, and "Bundesminister fuer Arbeit und Sozialordnung," *Mitbestimmung*, Bonn, 1976, pp. 11–34.

87. The FDP's reliance on attracting the floating vote was demonstrated once more in the 1976 election campaign when the party emphatically turned from issues to featuring the personalities of its leaders, headed by Vice Chancellor and Foreign Minister Hans-Dietrich Genscher.

88. See Merkl, "Coalition Politics in West Germany," pp. 39–40 and Tables 1–6 and 1–7.

89. The recent local territorial reform in most Laender, however, has left hardly any of the thousands of towns and villages of this size. See also Merkl, "The Limits of the West German Party State," in Belloni and Beller, eds., *Faction Politics*. Regional parties such as the Danish-German South Schleswig Voters Association or the Bavaria Party have declined in importance over the years, although they still win Landtag seats.

90. The SED received clear majorities in the communal elections of the immediate postwar period and later ruled through a multiparty facade of quotas of CDU, Liberal Democrats (LDP), National Democrats (NDP), and Farmers League (DBD) and other mass organizations in the National Front.

91. Their membership, too, had declined from an estimated 70,000 in the early 1950s to 7,000 in 1968. By 1976, it was believed to have grown again to a size of 40,000.

92. In the 1969 elections, the DKP participated through the Action Committee of Democratic Progress (ADF).

93. Well-informed government sources place the actual amount received at two-and-a-half times that level and surmise that the bulk of it comes from the East German SED. Helmut Bilstein et al., *Organisierter Kommunismus in der BRD*, Opladen: Leske, 1975, p. 20.

94. Bilstein, *Organisierter Kommunismus*, pp. 23–33.

95. The new KPD played a prominent role in the violent seizure of the Bonn City hall in 1973 and in street actions involving urban housing and transport in Frankfurt, Heidelberg, Mannheim, Cologne, and Stuttgart in 1974 and 1975. For details, see Helmut Bilstein et al., *Organisierter Kommunismus*, pp. 80–89 and the sources cited there.

96. For a partial list, see the bibliography of John D. Nagle, *The National Democratic Party: Right Radicalism in the Federal Republic of Germany*, Berkeley: University of California Press, 1970, pp. 212–215, or Lutz Niethammer, *Angepasster Faschismus*, Frankfurt: Suhrkamp, 1969.

97. This included especially the German Rightist (later Reich) party (DRP), which had six representatives in the first Bundestag, and smaller groups founded by prominent members of the Weimar DNVP or the German voelkisch movement (DVFP). The SRP was founded in 1949 and is said to be run on all levels by ex-Nazis. See Bergstraesser, *Geschichte*, pp. 332–333 and the sources mentioned there. More details also in Nagle, *The NDP*, pp. 16 30.

98. In Lower Saxony, the SRP profitted from former German party voters unhappy about the electoral alliance of the DP and CDU.

99. Other legal actions to suppress local neo-Nazi groups followed the outlawing of the SRP. At the level of smaller towns and cities, suspicion focused especially on the nonpartisan voters associations which were thought to be fronts for underground Nazis or Communists. See Merkl, "The Limits of the West German Party State," pp. 254–256.

100. In Bavaria, for example, the NPD ousted both the FDP and the Bavaria Party from the Landtag and inherited their 15 seats, even though these parties only lost 0.8% and 1.4%, respectively, of the popular vote in the state. The NPD succeeded in dislodging the FDP in Middle Franconia and the Bavaria party in Lower Bavaria, where they each had had the 10% of the regional vote required for representation in the Landtag. See esp. Willibald Fink, *Die NPD bei der bayerischen Landtagswahl, 1966*, Munich: Olzog, 1969, pp. 31–51.

101. Thirty-nine percent of West German respondents, as compared with 29% of Englishmen and 24% Americans, said they "never talk politics" with other people. Gabriel Almond and Sidney Verba, *The Civic Culture*, Princeton, N.J.: Princeton University Press, 1963, pp. 102, 116, 146. Only 35% (United States, 70%) of the Germans reported a sense of satisfaction when going to the polls.

102. Dieter Just and Lothar Romain, eds., *Auf der Suche nach dem muendigen Waehler*, Bonn: Bundeszentrale fuer politische Bildung no. 189, 1974, Table 26, citing polls of the Institut fuer Demoskopie, Allensbach. At the same time, those indicating no interest dropped from 25–35% to 11% in 1973.

103. The UNESCO survey of 1953 has been utilized and described by Juan J. Linz, "Cleavage and Consensus in West German Politics: The Early Fifties," in Seymour M. Lipset and Stein Rokkan, eds., *Party Systems and Voter Alignments*, New York: Free Press, 1967, pp. 283–321. In those days, the bourgeois parties (FDP, DP, and Bavaria party) received the bulk of the less religious middle-class vote.

104. Table 6 is derived from Linz, pp. 287–288 and from Derek W. Urwin, "Germany: Continuity and Change in Electoral Politics," in Richard Rose, ed., *Electoral Behavior: A Comparative Handbook*, New York: Free Press, 1974, p. 147, who reports INFAS data of 1967.

105. The total number of independents for 1953, it should be noted, also includes the DP and BP, two parties with strong rural and small town following. On the predicament of the FDP, see also Werner Kaltefleiter et al., *Im Wechselspiel der Koalitionen, Eine Analyse der Bundestagswahl 1969*, Verfassung und Verfassungswirklichkeit, Cologne: Heymanns, 1970, chapter 4. Between 1964 and 1974, according to the *Institut fuer Demoskopie*, the average FDP voter has become younger, more female, more educated, more white collar or civil servant (esp. executives), more skilled labor, and less independent middle class. See Elisabeth Noelle-Neumann in *Deutsche Zeitung*, October 24, 1975.

106. David P. Conradt's ecological analyses clearly show the inroads of the SPD since 1957 in predominantly Catholic and even Protestant districts as well as the relative CDU/CSU decline in the Catholic metropolitan and industrial areas. See his *The West German Party System: An Ecological Analysis of Social Structure and Voting Behavior, 1961–1969*, Beverly Hills, Calif.: Sage, 1972, pp. 20, 22, 23. The losses of the CDU/CSU were lowest in rural areas, whereas its losses in the industrial areas ranged between the metropolitan and the rural areas.

107. See his unpublished paper with Dwight Lambert, "The Legitimation of Competitive Politics in West Germany: An Ecological Analysis of the 1972 Federal Election." In the 1976 elections, observers in both parties agreed, upwardly mobile SPD voters dissatisfied with the welfare state and its high rates of taxation constituted an important part of the SPD losses.

108. The farm population alone declined from 15% in 1950 (30% in 1925) to 7% of the gainfully employed. Back in 1882, agriculture still accounted for 42.2% of the gainfully employed, white collar and the civil service was 7.2%, and the independents and their families made up 40.9% of German society. See Stephanie Muenke, *Die mobile Gesellschaft*, Stuttgart: Enke, 1967, pp. 127 and 141; *Statistisches Jahrbuch fuer das Deutsche Reich*, 1935, p. 14; and Statistisches Bundesamt, *Zahlenkompass 1977*, pp. 3–4.

109. The latest analysis of voting trends sees the two blocs of CDU/CSU and SPD/FDP evenly matched and contending for a floating vote. The FDP, however, has a steady clientele of only 3–4% of the popular vote, not enough to survive a downturn in electoral fortunes. Perceptions of the leading politicians and their ability to solve the most pressing problems govern the outcomes of elections. See Werner Kaltefleiter, "Der Gewinner hat nicht gesiegt," *Parlament*, suppl., December 11, 1976 and the 1977 issue of *Verfassung und Verfassungswirklichkeit*.

CHAPTER 3

GREAT BRITAIN

Arthur Cyr

CONFLICT AMIDST CONSENSUS is a fundamentally important characteristic of the British political system. This applies to relations among and within the political parties as it does to other sorts of associations of consequence to politics within that nation, both inside and outside the institutions of government. The purpose of this essay is to develop and refine this theme, with special attention to the manner in which the generalization applies to the present state of relations among the political parties. This will involve some considerable attention to the role of historical factors in the present-day functioning of the system. In Britain, as in other democracies, the parties serve as the pivotal source of communication between government and the governed. In Britain more than in most other countries, the forms of party action and competition have changed very gradually over time, with residual elements from the past strongly present in any particular period.

There are really two tasks which are preliminary to making conclusions about the role of the party system in Britain. First, one must describe the development of the parties as it relates to the current situation and to the historically significant past. As so many scholars and other analysts have observed, the British system is unusual in terms of the ability to combine traditional stability, deference to authority, and strong class consciousness with the capacity to support electoral democracy, representative institutions, and strong party competition. Britain has been described as a "traditionally modern" political system precisely because of the unusual combination of elements of continuity and the ability to reform. Very apparent consciousness of this quality of the British political system runs through a great deal of earlier political science literature. The balance between old and new elements, between conservative traditions and the desire for change, has customarily been praised by analysts of British politics. Some more recent scholars have also had this highly positive conception of British politics; it is present, for instance, in Samuel Beer's *British Politics in the Collectivist Age*. Nevertheless, in recent years there has been a tendency to take a much more restrained, if not critical, perspective on the British political system, as will be discussed in the following pages.[1]

Second, it is important to describe the current situation in terms of the empirical characteristics of the parties. This includes the features of their supporters, profiles of their structures, outlines of their policy positions, and other major qualities. Following that, it should be possible to generalize on the relationship between the parties and strengths and weaknesses of the British system in terms of party functioning and the definition and implementation of public policy. These perspectives are both developed in the essay that follows.

Political Culture and Party Development

The historical development of modern British political parties provides the overall background for and important insight into the current context, if not revealing the exact characteristics and features of the present situation. The British have had an effectively unified nation, with national public institutions, for a very long period of time, underscoring the point that the impact of those traditional institutions and attitudes has been especially great over time. The traditionalism so strongly embedded in British political culture and institutions means also that there is an automatic restraint, or brake, on the impetus toward reform.

The nature of British political culture has several major implications for this analysis. Most important perhaps is the recognition very early in British national life, and carried down to the present, that there are acceptable and legitimate restraints on monarchical, meaning executive, authority. This means that the traditionalism in British politics dictates not the absolutist perspective but rather the importance of restraint on authority. The early monarchs who established national unity in England were significant because they were strong-willed and authoritarian but not unbending or absolute dictators. The Tudor monarchy in the sixteenth century—Henry VII, Henry VIII, and Elizabeth I—established England as a unified nation, ruled from London, with itinerant justices the agents of the Crown to serve as practical reminders even to the hinterlands of the ruler's authority. However, the Tudors did not try to abolish Parliament or impose uncompromised dictatorship on the nation. The Tudors were stylistically disposed to treat the Parliament with considerable restraint. The Stuarts who followed did try to establish total absolute rule and did so ineptly; as a result they were deposed, their undoing ushering in the civil war, instability, radical socialism, Cromwellian dictatorship, and eventual reestablishment of the monarchy—but a limited monarchy to be sure—that characterized the latter part of the seventeenth century.

The restraint on the part of the monarchy permitted early establishment of the independent power of Parliament and, indeed, was responsible unintentionally for the generally separate legitimacy of the legislature. In the abstract hierarchy of the day, the monarch was the supreme empirical, earthly element in a partly metaphysical "great chain of being." But, if the Parliament was subordinate, it was also not totally dependent. The legislature had a separate, if related, identity and role. The taxing power of Parliament was a practical factor of very considerable consequence in the establishment of legislative independence and authority. The literature of English history understandably gives this dimension major emphasis. Once Parliament was clearly identified as the source of independent policy making and policy limitation, there was an automatic tendency to enhance parliamentary power as other sectors of the government expanded in size. A. L. Rowse's sympathetic description evokes the temper of those times well and is worth quoting at length:[2]

> The relations between Crown and Parliament were more like those between President and Congress than those that subsist in England today. The Queen's ministers—like the President's Cabinet—were responsible to her and not to Parliament; and it followed from that that government had to keep in touch by various means, direct and indirect, with the two Houses. The Lords offered no difficulty once the Acts of Supremacy and Uniformity were through, restoring the Edwardian settlement, and Mary's bishops were out. It was the Commons that mattered and that were difficult . . .
>
> Let us observe her for a little in action. Tact, tactical shrewdness, courtesy, consideration were keynotes of the government's behavior in relation to Parliament: one notices it in the Queen herself . . .

British court politics paved the way for the more elaborately structured, though not necessarily more elaborate, party politics of the seventeenth century and later. Conflicts in the Court were changeable and subtle, centering on personalities and the quest for influence rather than clashing organizations and the battle for policy victory. The goal was proximity to and the confidence of the Monarch rather than success of a particular doctrine or ideology. For our purposes, the important point is that the early establishment of the legitimacy of some degree of conflict and competition, including the clash of interest and view between Crown and Parliament, paved the way for the later formation of an independent legislature and the parties which took shape within it.

During the seventeenth century, the Tory party, the direct ancestor of the modern Conservative party, was formed. The Tories were generally comparatively strong supporters of the position of the Monarchy, though hardly inclined to surrender the independence of Parliament. On balance, the weight of the landed aristocracy was greater among the Tories than was the case with their opposite numbers in the Whigs. The striking feature of the Tories, however, not only in the seventeenth century but later, was their capacity to adjust, shift, and change with the demands of new circumstances and new political conditions. Informed by a general sense of the appropriateness of hierarchy and privilege, but not constrained by any tightly structured doctrine or ideology, the Tories were eminent pragmatists. Based in the landed aristocracy, they could adjust to accept new rising commercial classes as required for political success and survival. Strongly influenced by the force of tradition and the conservative's suspicion of change, they could not only accept reforms but could on occasion become themselves radical reformers, again as circumstances indicated.[3]

While these early Tories were a distinctive political formation, it should also be noted that politics was highly aristocratic across the board in the seventeenth and eighteenth centuries in England, with none of the democracy which has been characteristic of more recent periods. To be sure, members of Parliament in the Commons were representatives of their parliamentary constituencies, but electorates were very narrowly restricted. More important, M.P.s also represented strong family, land and commercial interests, which frequently transcended the particular boundaries of a local district. Beer describes the situation: "No less a man than the younger Pitt, for instance, upon being returned for one of Sir James Lowther's pocket boroughs in 1780, wrote of his relations with his patron that 'no kind of condition was mentioned but that if ever our lines of conduct should be opposite, I should give him the opportunity of choosing another member.' " Beer notes that "The House of Commons seems never to have been without members bearing some such relation to outside persons or bodies."[4] To be sure, this system involved corruption in the modern sense of prosperous individuals' and groups' bribing members of the very restricted electorate. At the same time, a broader tradition of the acceptability of close ties between representative and interests was established.

In short, both Parliamentary importance and a vigorous form of party politics were comparatively well established by the time the franchise was extended and a much more democratic form of politics developed in the nineteenth century. The dramatic, progressive broadening of the franchise successively in 1832 to much of the middle class, in 1867 to the smaller tradesmen and settled residents, in 1884 to virtually all the male working class, and finally in 1928 to women enormously enlarged the national pool of voters and, therefore, potential and actual party-political activists.[5] Party organization and structure, predictably, was transformed to accommodate a new electorate and quite a separate set of policy issues. Although the ultimate effect of the broadening of the franchise was to encourage encompassing popular membership structures, this was not the immediate result of the initial reform efforts. Rather, the extension of the franchise in 1832, the first and in some ways the most significant of the modern reform acts, led to greater freedom for

M.P.s from the limitations on their voting imposed by earlier interest group and constituency ties. The new voters broke into the existing, close, and comparatively closed relationships between representatives and patrons which had characterized Tory and Whig politics. During the period before the further reform of 1867 gave substantial impetus to large-scale popular organization by the major parties, M.P.s were able to operate very independently within the House of Commons.

There was, of course, party organization outside of Parliament, and it became very extensive after the 1832 act, but these nineteenth century constituency associations neither nominated candidates nor disciplined M.P.s who strayed from the party line. Rather, they were primarily practical mechanisms for the mobilization of popular support at election time. British electoral politics in this period was intensely fought, in the context of shifting structures and an expanding electorate. Bribery and corruption were not uncommon on the part of those seeking to sway voters at election time. H. J. Hanham, for instance, has noted in his comprehensive survey of later nineteenth century British politics, especially in the smaller towns and rural areas:[6]

> When the Reform League sent its agents to stir up the working men of Guilford to "assert their rights" and the dignity of labor, they met with a good-natured but negative response. J. B. Leno, a working-class poet, reported in some disgust that, election or no election, regular meetings were held at Tory public houses where punch costing ten shillings a bowl was dispensed to as many as cared to attend.

The comparatively weak party structures resulted in a highly individualistic form of Commons politics. Party labels were not as consequential as they had been, and not nearly as consequential as they would become later. Certainly nothing resembling modern party discipline, and the importance of partisan label to electoral success, was in existence. Discipline in the House ranged from loose to virtually nonexistent. Probably more closely than at any time before or since, issue politics dominated party politics. Coalitions would rise, shift, and collapse entirely on the basis of particular policy beliefs or disagreements. Because support was so uncertain, governments were insecure and required to be especially sensitive to shifting moods within the House. Cabinets and prime ministers had to be very conscious of Parliamentary sentiment, and M.P.s in turn were at least indirectly connected to the views and attitudes of their constituents. The balance was delicate but functional, and doubtless the manner in which the British political system operated during this period was an important factor in the quite positive and sympathetic evaluation of the nation's politics on the part of most analysts. Many Americans reflected Bagehot's view that "The English Premier being appointed by the selection, and being removable at the pleasure, of the preponderant Legislative Assembly, is sure to be able to rely on that Assembly. . . . But the American President has no similar security. He is elected in one way, at one time, and Congress (no matter which House) is elected in another way, at another time. The two have nothing to bind them together . . . they continually disagree."[7]

There were also important shifts in the party structures and alignments during the broad mid-nineteenth century period. Perhaps the most significant occurred during the controversy over the Corn laws, restrictions on the import of grains. Peel, the Conservative prime minister, finally succeeded in 1846 in repealing the Corn laws, which were strongly opposed as an intolerable restriction on free trade. The general result of these events was to usher in a period of party realignment, with a major segment of the Conservative party composed of free traders moving over into Liberal ranks. In a second, sizable popular shift later in the century, Joseph Chamberlain's Birmingham Caucus, often described as the first of the modern political machines, moved from the Liberal side of the aisle in the Commons to the Conservative over the issue of home rule for Ireland, which Chamberlain and his followers opposed. This change in the balance of forces, which occurred in 1886, was of great immediate benefit to the Conservatives and helped bring to an end a long period of Liberal party dominance. More generally, these events helped to illustrate the capacity of the party system to shift, even while the electorate and social bases of party were expanding, without overthrowing the political system.

This general period was one during which a great deal of energy was devoted to voluntary associations and reform movements, separate from the regular national party organizations. The principal force in the repeal of the Corn laws was the organizational effort of the Anti-Corn Law League. This was an especially dramatic instance of popular pressure group activity being employed successfully to change public policy. It was also representative of a broader phenomenon in an age when social service as well as reform associations were quite prominent and influential. The Anti-Corn Law League was part of a broader reform spirit which brought forward the antislavery societies, the Chartist groups, the national Reform League, the National Education League, and others. Along with the reform associations, the nineteenth century spawned a number of voluntary social service groups, whose activities both supplemented government programs and encouraged new reforms.

It was during this period of nineteenth century politics that a great many economic and social reforms were instituted, primarily by the Liberal party, thus paving the way for the modern welfare state and democratic politics of contemporary Britain. Showing their historic and strongly rooted flexibility, the Conservatives moved with the changing times to welcome much greater democratic reforms in the latter part of the nineteenth century. Led by Disraeli, an eminently calculating politician, the Conservatives after the Reform Act of 1867 proceeded successfully to organize a large number of workingmen's associations, thus ensuring the party would maintain a significant role despite a much enlarged electorate. As for the Liberals, while reluctance to accept the need for reform has often been cited as an explanation for their collapse from national political power early in the twentieth century, the record clearly indicates that they were in fact major reformers. This was especially true for the last period of Liberal government after the 1906 elections. The exceptional Liberal legislative achievements include the Trade Disputes Act of 1906, the Coal Mines Act of 1908, the Wages Boards Act of 1909, and the Labour Exchanges Act of 1909. The Liberal government was also responsible for a major education reform bill, four land bills, the taxation of land values, food tax reform, ending use of indentured Chinese, national health and unemployment insurance, and a minimum wages law.[8]

These many reforms, however, did not prevent the demise of the Liberal party as a national political force and one of the two main parties. While reforms were instituted, the party was undercut, and party politics was generally transformed, by important social and economic changes which were markedly altering the bases for defining public policy and conducting party competition. Politics was, along with government, becoming more disciplined, more organized, more firmly based on national issues and cleavages, and more clearly divided along social and economic class lines. The emerging political forms were very much out of tune with the individualism of Liberalism.

Rise of Party Government

Samuel Beer has employed the term *collectivist politics* to describe the modern state of affairs in British politics, meaning that party government and functional representation have become the basic features of political power and public policy in Britain. Party discipline has given cabinets a strong role vis-à-vis Parliament. Public policy has been formed as a result of very close consultation among government and interest representatives. Policy making has been highly centralized in large national ministries; interest groups are based on producer and consumer constituencies, generally national and industrywide in scope. Class-based cleavage has organized the electorate along fairly predictable class lines. This contrasts with the much more individualistic politics of nineteenth century Britain. At the same time, it must be remembered that the collectivist organizational ethos of modern Britain has been fully consistent with even older traditions and even earlier patterns of political behavior. Conceptions of inclusive and related social groupings were an important feature of Tory, Whig, and earlier Court politics.[9]

Naturally, collectivist politics has been reflected in the features of the parties. Structurally, there has been elaboration of organization and formalization within the two main parties, Conservative and Labour. Both operate with professional full-time staffs and large-scale organizations to handle record-keeping, fund raising, campaigning and publicity, and other tasks. In Parliament, party discipline has grown such that there is little deviation from the party line when formal positions are imposed. The party whips and leaders work closely in maintaining cohesion in the respective parties. There is in reality very little deviation from party positions when it has been decided in advance that members will be asked to vote the party line.[10]

Both main parties are mass membership organizations as well as parliamentary bodies. Of the two, the Conservatives have by far the simpler structure. Only individuals are formal members of the party, through local constituency associations. The National Union of Conservative and Unionist Associations normally gathers annually for the party conference. Between 3,000 and 4,000 representatives are involved. In the Labour party, individual members are complemented and, in many ways, compromised and limited by the affiliated members, which are in effect the memberships of the trade unions and certain other designated organizations. As a result of this situation, the affiliated representatives, who automatically carry the votes of their members in their pockets, heavily outnumber individual members. In the Labour Party conference, affiliated votes account usually for upwards of 90% of those cast.[11]

The discipline of the two main parties reflects as well the character of political cleavages within the electorate. With the growth of class conflict within the electorate in the twentieth century, there has been an increase in the intensity of sentiment and also the discipline within the electorate. The old well-worn Gilbert and Sullivan jibe to the effect that everyone in the nation was born either a Liberal or Conservative was obviously intended as an exaggeration but also one that did reflect the reality of the British party system.[12] A much more disciplined and regularly predictable party competition, at least in terms of where the vast majority of the voters place their loyalties, has operated in the twentieth century. It has not been absolutely certain whether the Conservative or Labour party would win a particular election; it has been clearly predictable, at least until very recent years, that the vast mass of the electorate would choose one of these two main parties. This uniformity of political preference has been one of the most striking characteristics of the British electorate, especially during the first two decades following the conclusion of World War II.

One defining characteristic of the modern period in British politics has been the small percentage of the electorate inclined to switch from one major party to the other. The vast majority not only has voted for one party or the alternative, it has been highly consistent in supporting its chosen vehicle. The large swings in the composition of parliamentary majorities reflected the first-past-the-post electoral system, in which only one candidate was returned for each district no matter how close the margin, rather than any regular sea changes in the public's sentiments.

The character of ideology and belief has reinforced the more empirical drives of sociology in creating two encompassing party coalitions. The Labour party, since the alignment of the Fabian intellectuals with the trade union movement during World War I, has been committed to a doctrinaire socialism that has included explicit policy prescriptions—industrial nationalization and a "socialist commonwealth," meaning thereby explicit recognition of the opposition between the classes and commitment to an end of the capitalist order. Ideological commitment has served to reinforce solidarity which has already been grounded in working-class consciousness within the electorate.[13]

Tory attitudes have been implicit in belief rather than explicit in ideological formulation, but they have nonetheless been most influential in guiding and forming the collective personality of the party. History is strongly represented in present attitudes within the party, in the sense that deference, respect for hierarchy, and faith in a ruling order or class are centrally apparent. Where the Labour party draws sustenance from a doctrine of class conflict and solidarity, the Tories have been influenced by more nebulous but no less important perspectives that are strongly rooted in British culture and traditions. Once again, as in the case of the Labour party, belief and sociology are reflected in one another. As described in more detail in the following paragraphs, the Conservatives have drawn strength not just from the bulk of the middle class, but also from a large minority of the working class which has been deferential rather than assertive in viewing authority.

For the Tories, the growth and development of collectivism has in a sense been a return to the past following a nineteenth century interlude of individualism and liberalism in British politics and economics. Modern class conflict and class-based politics has been much more congenial with old-fashioned organic and integrated conceptions of a social order than with the sort of atomism, decentralization, and faith in the market which characterized not only social thought but much of practical politics in the last century.[14]

Sociology of the Party System

British politics has reflected a marked tendency toward uniformity and regularity in the bases of party appeal within the electorate. The traditional conception of Britain as a highly stable nation politically has been reinforced by data from survey research indicating that there has in fact been considerable regularity to voting patterns. As noted earlier, collectivist party politics has been highly predictable in terms of both the directions of policy and the attitudes of electors. It is as if the abstract conceptual framework employed to describe and analyze contemporary politics in the nation has found a very concrete, practical, empirical reflection.

In the modern period, which can be identified as the period since the conclusion of World War I, there has not only been the powerful disposition to support Tory and Labour to the exclusion of other parties, the regularity in voting patterns noted above has been strongly correlated with socioeconomic class alignments, which is a different but related point. As the research of Robert Alford and others has indicated, British politics are highly stratified along class lines.[15] This becomes apparent when the electorate's attitudes and behavior is compared with those in other nations. The comprehensive analysis of David Butler and Donald Stokes has shown that British voters tend to think strongly in class terms, employing occupation as the primary indicator of one's class position, although it must be added that in the complex and subtle British social structure a variety of factors contribute to one's own and others' perceptions of position on the class scale. Electors generally regard the social structure as divided into two basic classes, middle and working.[16]

The two main parties have had markedly contrasting electorates, reflecting this overall situation. For decades, the Conservative party has regularly drawn the loyalty of approximately 90% of the middle class, plus about one-third of the working class. The latter group has provided the numbers which permit fairly equal competition with Labour on something resembling a basis of equality in national elections. One segment of the Tory working-class electorate is persuaded primarily by instrumental considerations, notably the belief that the Conservatives are by far the more able governing party. For the rest, traditional old-fashioned attitudes of deference to a superior ruling order explain their loyalty to a party controlled by the "other" class. Virtually all the rest of the electorate—meaning a small portion of the middle class plus the great bulk of the working class—has gone to the Labour party.

New Directions

Since the late 1950s, with progressive momentum, the collectivism which dominated twentieth century British politics in terms of political attitudes and behavior and government policy has given way to some extent to interesting new patterns of activism and policy issues. There has been growth in support for small parties, new attention to kinds of issues that had been important in the last century but submerged in collectivist politics, and forms of political activism which have moved entirely outside the party system. The regularity of British politics, which has been so much stressed by analysts, may be changing. The remainder of this essay will deal in explicit terms with these phenomena and discuss implications for the future of the British political system and, especially, the political parties. Is the system undergoing fundamental change and is British politics losing at least some of its predictability?

Although Britain remains a two-party system in the sense that the Conservative and Labour parties receive by far the majority of votes cast in general elections, and continue to hold most of the seats in the House of Commons, these parties no longer dominate either arena to the extent they previously did. In the two general elections of 1974, neither major party emerged as a really clear winner. To be sure, the first election was decisive in the sense that the Conservative government of Edward Heath, struggling vainly to overcome a crippling miners' strike, was removed from office. There was no overall Labour majority in the Commons, however, and the governments of that party have survived since coming to office only through support of the Liberals. The electorate was quite evenly divided with regard to the two main parties; more important, the elections resulted in dramatic gains for the small third parties, including most notably the Liberals, the Scottish National party (S.N.P.), and the Welsh National party (Plaid Cymru). This is in line with a trend of the past decade and a half. As Richard Scammon, the American elections analyst, observed, "In this kind of arithmetic analysis, only the Liberal party and the 'others' could claim any vote victory . . .". Table 3–1 shows the pattern of increasing support for these parties, and Table 3–2 recombines electoral data to illustrate the shrinking combined electoral base of Tory and Labour.[17]

TABLE 3–1. Nationalist and Liberal Parties in General Elections, Selected Years 1945–1974

Year	LIBERALS		PLAID CYMRU		SCOTTISH NATIONALISTS (S.N.P.)	
	% U.K. Vote	Candids.	% Welsh Vote	Candids.	% Scot. Vote	Candids.
1945	8.9	305	1.1	6	1.2	8
1950	9.1	475	1.2	7	0.4	3
1951	2.6	109	0.7	4	0.3	2
1955	2.7	110	3.1	11	0.5	2
1959	5.9	216	5.2	20	0.8	5
1964	11.2	365	4.8	23	2.4	15
1966	8.6	311	4.3	20	5.0	23
1970	7.5	332	11.5	36	11.4	65
1974 (Feb)	19.3	517	10.7	36	21.9	70
1974 (Oct)	18.3	619	10.8	36	30.0	70

TABLE 3–2. Combined Conservative/Labour Votes in General Elections, Selected Years 1950–1974

YEAR	UNITED KINGDOM	SCOTLAND
1950	88.1%	92.2%
1951	96.6	96.5
1955	96.1	96.8
1959	93.2	93.9
1964	87.4	89.3
1966	89.8	87.5
1970	89.3	82.5
1974 (Feb)	77.8	69.5
1974 (Oct)	75.4	61.0

Among the small parties, the Liberal advance has been the more long standing but also more uneven. During the late 1950s and early 1960s, there was a "revival" of the party under the lively leadership of Jo Grimond. The surge was visible in public opinion polls, which for a brief period in 1962 showed the Liberals were even with, and in one case leading, the two main parties; by-election returns; and, at least to some extent, in general election results. The Liberals did more than double their previous total popular vote in the general election of 1964 but were unable to overcome party-political and more structural electoral problems to emerge with a major role within the political system. This was followed by a slump and an even more dramatic revival in electoral terms during the early 1970s. In the two 1974 general elections, the Liberals more than tripled their 1970 poll and received approximately 20% of the total vote in each general election. Once again, however, a fairly large popular vote was only very partially reflected in the actual number of House of Commons seats secured for the party. Financial and other problems, including the ending of Jeremy Thorpe's tenure as party leader in the midst of some considerable controversy, have further hampered the party's efforts in more recent years.[18]

Both the Scottish and Welsh nationalists have made gains in their respective regions since the mid-1960s. Of the two, the S.N.P. has been by far the more impressive and in fact has had the most dramatic successes of any of the smaller parties. There are now 11 Scottish National M.P.s in Parliament at Westminster. The party has made steady progress with the Scottish electorate. This reached a crest of sorts, though there is no indication that this is the electoral ceiling of the party's support, in the 1974 general election. The S.N.P. pulled ahead of the Conservatives, traditionally the weaker of the two main parties in the region, and is in a very threatening position vis-à-vis Labour. A swing of less than 5% away from Labour in the next general election could give the nationalists a majority of the Scottish delegation of M.P.s.[19]

Related to the growth of small parties, there has been an increase in electoral volatility in Britain. Table 3–3 provides some evidence for the proposition that voters are much more inclined now than in the past to pick not only small parties, but also to move back and forth between the two major parties. The standard deviation indicates the extent to which measures of support have spread along the mathematical mean over time, when applied in the context of opinion poll data. In the early 1970s, there was an increase in measurable volatility in support of both major parties. The 1970 general election, in which an apparent last-minute swing in voter opinion handed victory to the Tory party, is a dramatic indication of how far this uncharacteristic instability has progressed within the British electorate.

Finally, in recent years there has been an increase in the amount of politically significant activism which has nevertheless been removed from regular parties and concentrated instead in voluntary reform and social service associations. To be sure, no recent period of British history has been without

TABLE 3–3.   Standard Deviations for British Gallup Polls, 1947–1973

YEAR	LABOUR	CONSERVATIVE
1947	6.86%	4.91%
1948	1.30	2.50
1949	2.33	4.07
1950	2.50	1.25
1951	6.02	2.27
1952	4.16	2.45
1953	1.25	1.45
1954	2.34	1.90
1955	0.74	2.24
1956	1.97	2.61
1957	2.36	11.34
1958	1.64	15.85
1959	1.46	6.47
1960	3.44	0.68
1961	1.80	4.72
1962	2.66	3.00
1963	1.81	1.35
1964	3.73	4.10
1965	8.04	6.24
1966	12.59	2.75
1967	14.48	6.39
1968	12.75	7.35
1969	14.90	4.53
1970	8.42	2.96
1971	6.97	10.35
1972	2.38	3.04
1973	3.90	5.60

Souroo: Britioh Gallup Pollo.

such voluntary groups. However, there are indications that these formations have proliferated markedly as the Collectivist Age has matured. The handbook and directory of the National Council of Social Services, *Voluntary Social Services*, lists figures that indicate that the rate at which national voluntary service associations are formed has accelerated since the last century. Before 1860, it has records for only 12 such organizations. Between the years 1860 and 1899, 31 were formed, a marked increase over the apparent tendency of previous years but not equal to the rate that followed: 46 groups were formed between 1900 and 1939 and 23 each during the two periods 1900–1919 and 1920–1939. The rate accelerated further after 1939, with 31 groups created between 1940 and 1959.[20]

In recent years, when the Liberal and Scottish and Welsh nationalist parties have enjoyed new energy and support, we have witnessed the birth of several large, very prominent national voluntary reform and service associations. The improvement in political support for these parties generally paralleled the growth in members and impact of the Campaign for Nuclear

Disarmament (CND, begun in 1958), the Child Poverty Action Group (CPAG, begun 1965), and Shelter (begun in 1966).[21]

There have also been significant increases in the number of small, local voluntary associations, of the type that is less easily quantified. Significantly, the start of their proliferation again generally correlates with the beginnings of the Liberal party's revival and proceeds through the growth in support for the nationalists. Perhaps the first of the new formations, notably ahead of the trend, were the Citizens' Advice Bureaux, local centers designed to handle inquiries from individuals concerning available public services and public assistance. Begun with government help by the National Council of Social Service in 1939, there were 430 such bureaux by the early 1960s. In the mid-1950s, the new forms of social and political energy directed themselves into the formation of the National Spastics Society, the Association of Mentally Handicapped Children, and the Muscular Dystrophy Group. Local branches of these, springing up across the country, were the vanguard of more of the same sort of neo-Liberal groups. In 1957, Duncan Sandys founded the Civic Trust, which led to the creation of the Civic and Amenity Societies, local planning groups. By 1966, there were 540 in operation. In 1960, the first Association for the Advancement of State Education was begun in Cambridge. Six years later, some 120 had been set up. In 1960, the Federation of Local Consumer Groups was formed, branches of which grew in the larger towns through the 1960s. Other groups, on the same model, were formed in connection with the hospital service. A very old form of the same type of organization, the Councils for Social Service, began to enjoy new life. By the middle of the 1960s, they had grown to 143 in the towns and 28 in the counties, all operating around the basic principle of serving as coordinating bodies linking other groups—the Citizens' Advice Bureaux, Marriage Guidance Councils, Arts Councils, and old people's welfare organizations.[22]

These groups, large and small, have grown to such an extent that some see them as the wave of the political future, replacing old-fashioned political parties. This may be an extreme prediction, especially as it relates to a political system and culture in which important change has been typified historically by slow motion and incrementalism. Yet the accretion of such neo-Liberal groups is striking. The Open Group, sponsored by the periodical *New Society*, published a pamphlet on social change in contemporary Britain which attempted to dramatize the potential policy importance of this style of activism:[23]

> government is now ringed by tens of thousands of organizations trying to influence it and each other. Civil rights were won in the eighteenth century, political rights in the nineteenth and in the twentieth economic rights. But change has throughout depended on exercising the right to free association and combination. It has become more crucial than ever in this century.

The significance of these developments should be evaluated accurately, without exaggeration or being overdrawn. In many ways, the dominant features and characteristics of the British political system remain what they have been for most of the Collectivist Age. The vast majority of the electorate is committed to one or the other of the two major parties, Conservative or Labour. Moreover, discipline within the parties remains comparatively strong. There have been some instances of individual M.P.s' moving from one party to the other, but the incidence of total independence from national or regional parties on the part of legislators has been very small, partly because party sentiment remains strong among politicians but primarily because it is still, despite changes in other areas, extraordinarily difficult to get elected to Parliament without a party label. Dick Taverne is the most striking recent example of such independence reaching success, and in his case the victory was only temporary. A leading proponent of the Common Market within the Labour Party at a time when the sentiment in that party was very much in the other direction, he was for this reason ousted as the official Labour candidate by his constituency association in Lincoln. Rejecting advice from friends that he seek another, more congenial Labour seat, he contested his old district as an independent and was returned, defeating the regular Labour candidate, in 1973 in a special by-election. The victory received considerable publicity because it was so unusual. In the second 1974 general election, he was defeated.[24]

The two main parties remain highly structured organizations. There is not only the importance of party label to provide discipline, there is also the continuing hold of ideology and belief, and a strong sense of hostile partisanship toward the other side, motivating both Tory and Labour activists. Again, the character of discipline within the Conservative and Labour parties should not be overestimated. There is, even in Tory ranks, consideration for the views of the rank-and-file on the part of the party leadership. As some academic analysis has indicated in recent years, there is in fact a good deal of informal consultation and give-and-take within the parliamentary parties, and party lines involve considerably more subtlety than simply the imposition of inflexible disciplinary whips from above. There is, along with pressure from the hierarchy, considerable internal consultation, bargaining, compromise, and emphasis on reconciliation. This point applies to the mass membership dimension as it does to the parliamentary party. Even the traditionally fractious Labour party has maintained overall unity and avoided sundering itself during even the bitterest internal quarrels, in part because of the dominant phalanx of conference votes provided by the trade union movement.[25]

Finally, national policy remains largely formed along national lines, concerning national issues and the intervention and influence of inclusive producer and consumer groups. In this sense, there has been comparatively little change in recent years in the dominant policy patterns associated with modern politics in Britain. To be sure, there have been proposals from the Conservative and, more notably, the Labour parties for the reform of regional government and administration, to provide some limited devolution of authority to Scotland and Wales. The Heath government was also active in trying to promote a more flexible, selective approach to welfare policy to reach the very poorest sectors of society that are often neglected by the welfare state. These have not, however, been the dominant policy patterns in Britain.[26]

Party Effectiveness

The most difficult task for such an analysis as this, and also the most significant, is to reach an accurate judgment concerning the effectiveness of the party system in Britain. Effectiveness can mean different things when evaluating democratic parties, depending upon the perspective of the analyst and the particular political context. In this case, we will try to relate the workings of the parties to those qualities that traditionally have been valued by students of the British political system. This includes the capacity to balance continuity with change, meaning innovation and reform married with lack of revolutionary or really drastic alteration in the system. The liberal political system within the conservative society, the ability to alter policy over time without overturning institutions, the reconciliation of democratic political representation with a very traditional, hierarchical and stratified social order: this difficult combination is what has been most often stressed by observers in this century and, more commonly, the last century who took a positive view of the British political system and government institutions.

For understandable reasons, the British political system is presently the target of a good deal of criticism, from journalistic, academic, and other quarters, and as a consequence British political parties are not regarded with the appreciation once afforded them and the system as a whole. During the nineteenth century and into the twentieth, Britain's comparatively prosperous economy, global empire, military power, and diplomatic prowess still kept the nation in a position of importance and special influence in the international system. When Britain was the dominant, or at least the major and pivotal, international power, there was a general and understandable tendency to assign particularly great virtue to the political institutions and practices of the nation. The two-party system in Britain was contrasted advantageously to the instability associated with the multiparty systems characteristic of France and other nations on the Continent.[27]

Britain's international position has changed and has been seen to have changed dramatically in recent years. There is at least a tendency to see some correlation between the strength of the nation and the effectiveness of the party system. The years since World War II have witnessed the abandonment of the global British empire, steady reduction in military resources, and the growth of very serious and persistent economic problems. Previously, British political institutions, including those of the government as well as the parties, were widely regarded as a model of effective combination of democracy and stability, the capacity for reform married with the advantages of continuity.

More recently, British public policy has been criticized for absence of imagination and innovation and the political system broadly for lack of ability to inspire, reform, and bring about changes necessary to spur the economy. This self-critical spirit has invaded popular commentary as well as more specialized work. In 1963, *Encounter* magazine devoted an entire issue to essays on the malaise and shortcomings of Britain.[28]

In this environment, there has been a predictable urge to focus not on the stability of British institutions and the moderation of British political practice but, rather, on the limitations and handicaps alleged to be present in the system. Consequently, because the nation has been seen to experience serious problems without drastic remedies being applied, there has been a tendency to see continuity as stagnation. The access of many different large-scale interest groups into the corridors of power is regarded as a source of concurrent veto over changes rather than effective representation of, and consequent sensitivity to, important orders within society. Frequently in the past, the long period of apprenticeship and gradual progress up the ladder of the party hierarchy was praised as a method whereby experienced leadership was guaranteed, in contrast to the more uncertain process of American presidential selection. In recent years, this British emphasis on long service and a regular pattern of recruitment and promotion has been viewed more as a principal factor in the lack of innovation and stimulating departures from the status quo that characterizes British public policy.

More broadly, the whole relationship within and between the parliamentary parties, and among them and the government, has been examined more skeptically and unfavorably than in the past. Earlier observers would often compare the British system overall with the American in a manner that clearly favored the former. The British approach was admired for a sensitive and effective coordination which combined yet also separated legislature, executive and the public at large. The cabinet was responsible to parliamentary opinion, which was in turn reflective of the public will. Democracy was present, but in indirect and stable form. History encouraged stability without stifling reform or popular representation. This was contrasted with the highly decentralized approach which pitted Congress against the president in a form of deadlock and made both institutions accountable to the public only every few years rather than continually through the possibility of parliamentary dissolution. To Bagehot as well as to American counterparts writing in the nineteenth century, the strength of Congress combined with the weakness of the presidency made the American system appear quite leaderless in comparison. In more recent periods, the growing strength of the presidency has seemed to underline the point that American power centers lack regular, orderly, popular accountability. Recently also, however, the operation of U.S. institutions and political practices, in which leadership selection is more free-wheeling, different sectors of government compete with one another, and parties are much more undisciplined, has been seen by many students to have the virtues of freshness and the capacity to change dramatically the policy directions being pursued. The British system, by contrast, has appeared to lack these very strengths, at the same time that growing central government power, the increasing importance of the prime minister's position, and party discipline has raised the image of very great power at the top and no real popular check through the possibility of an unpopular government being forced to call a general election.[29]

What is the most accurate conception of the effectiveness of British political parties, and by implication the national government, in the present period of general disillusionment and self-criticism, not only at home but among diverse observers abroad? Arguably, British politics has not performed nearly as badly as many observers believe. Related to this point, it is also possible to argue that the British system has never performed as smoothly, efficiently, and effectively as some former admirers have argued in the past. Several general observations can be made and developed to reinforce and elaborate this case. They relate to such matters as leadership selection, policy definition, implementation and change, and the broader functioning of the parties within the system.

LEADERSHIP SELECTION

Obviously, there are trade-offs in any system of national leadership selection. The British have had generally orderly progressions and successions in leadership but have lacked the broad range of leaders' backgrounds and experiences representative of the American situation. Several qualifying points, however, must be made concerning these two national environments. It is true that the British system, at least in recent times, has not had anyone comparable to an Eisenhower's or Willkie's securing party nomination and in the former case election by an enormous margin by moving laterally from a profession not directly related to elective politics. There has also, at least in this century, been no ready parallel to John F. Kennedy's example of plunging rapidly upward through party ranks to the top at a young age and following a career in the Senate and House of Representatives which did not involve important leadership posts or influence on the passage of legislation. There is also a price to be paid for the American approach, however. The other side of creativity and liveliness in policy is unpredictability of both leadership capacity and policy, lack of continuity, and at times considerable instability in policy. The distinction between the qualities which bring success in seeking the presidency within the party and among the electorate and those required to excel in securing a leadership post in the legislative branch has meant in practice that very few presidents have been effective in working their way with Congress. Eisenhower had a very good working relationship with the leaders of the House and Senate, Sam Rayburn and Lyndon Johnson, respectively, but this is at least partly explained by the absence of an ambitious presidential legislative program. Johnson as president for a time was enormously successful in moving legislation through Congress, but there were special circumstances involved, including the large Democratic margin in the 1964 election and the atmosphere following President Kennedy's assassination. Johnson's widely recognized talents in managing the Senate had not been helpful in his unsuccessful campaign against Kennedy to secure the Democratic nomination in 1960.[30] By contrast, British prime ministers have been cautioned and restrained by the need to consult first in their own governments, then more widely in Parliament, before legislation is proposed, but their proposals arguably are more likely to be passed. Harold Wilson's reformist legislative program of the mid-1960s may be described as more modest than the Democrats' in the United States during the same period but also more assured of passage. The regional policy of this period in many ways epitomizes both the style and substance of the approach. It involved significant changes in administrative and economic planning structures while skirting complex political issues associated with devolution of political power.

From a somewhat different viewpoint, the American process has not been so unlike the British. Among the postwar presidents, only Eisenhower did not have significant practical party-political experience, and even he was a product of years of both government service and high-level working contact with the civilian political and governmental leadership in Washington. Virtually all the others had significant experience in the vice presidency, House of Representatives, or Senate, except for the especially unusual case of President Carter.

The relationship among president and prime minister and the cabinet is another important area where, again, it is not clear that the British system is distinctively inferior to the American. In both British parties, senior office is a necessary condition before becoming a senior government minister. Again, this is a factor that encourages uniformity of view within the cabinet; yet, at the same time, the requirement that major party factions be represented also ensures some diversity of perspective on policy. The political influence of the cabinet in Britain serves as a partial check on and balance of prime ministerial power in a period when the authority and public visibility of that office have been growing. Cabinet ministers also serve as effective and influential advocates in Parliament, as they are members with significant prestige.[31] Thus, significant factions within each of the parties are provided representation in a comparatively collegial government.

The American cabinet does not have any meaningful political independence from the president and, as a consequence, is not in a position to provide the same sort of political check on presidential power or political influence within the Congress. This has not been the situation throughout the history of the Republic. During the first decades of its existence, the comparatively small U.S. presidential cabinet was made up of prominent figures who had established their reputations and individual political support during the years of the Revolutionary War and the early period of independence immediately thereafter. As a result, a process of discussion, bargaining, and compromise characterized executive branch decision-making at the top. Over time, this situation has changed. More specifically, with the elaboration of the powers of the presidency in recent decades and the granting of a staff to the president with the Reorganization Act of 1939, dependence on cabinet officers for practical assistance has waned. The much more centralized American executive office has not been noticeably superior. During the Johnson and Nixon administrations, the growing power of the presidency vis-à-vis other parts of the government, including the cabinet, reached a pinnacle of sorts. This meant, among other things, that dissent at senior levels of the government in both foreign and domestic affairs was discouraged, a point that bears directly on the political excesses and ultimate demise of both these administrations.[32]

These observations relate very clearly and directly to the role of party in the two countries, and American experience may be used to highlight and evaluate important features of the British situation. The significance of party in government in Britain is obvious and has consequences that are positively as well as negatively impressive. Party leadership selection encourages uniformity of view and outlook, as many have recently observed, but the ways in which party hierarchy is represented in government also fosters some diversity and balance to prime ministerial power while ensuring that the government will carry considerable weight in Parliament.

POLICY CHANGE AND IMPLEMENTATION

British government is often accused of stagnation and inability to change, as discussed earlier, and this is at least partially laid at the door, again, of a party system that encourages a status quo perspective and puts partisanship above the smooth implementation of public policy. Once again, it can be argued that this sort of perspective is a serious distortion of the political and governmental reality. While abrupt departures from the status quo are not characteristic of the British government, arguably such a policy style is not typical of any large-scale political systems given the character of modern bureaucracy. Moreover, once decisions have been taken, the British governmental system does have some unusual strengths in the area of policy implementation.

The problem of implementing policy once it has been decided upon is the bane of modern government and administration, not a peculiarly British phenomenon. Harry Truman's remark, on departing from the presidency, that Eisenhower would find the White House considerably different from the military, that he would give orders and suffer the frustration of nothing happening, is quoted so frequently because the point is often made that government has strong inertia. The only problem with the statement is that bureaucratic inertia and the barriers placed in the way of change are handicaps from which the military is hardly immune.[33] Not only in Britain and the United States, but in modern states generally, the range and complexity of issues and topics which fall under the general rubric of public policy has expanded enormously. Democratic Western governments currently are responsible for a wide range of social welfare and service programs, economic planning and management tasks, and other functions which were generally not part of the public domain in the nineteenth or even early twentieth centuries. Moreover, the growth of science and technology as a force in modern life has enormously complicated policy making in the public and also private sectors.[34]

In this environment, the British system once again has strengths as well as weaknesses that influence policy. On the one hand, the powerful force of tradition and historically based social and political attitudes, the veto power of large-scale national interest groups, and the characteristics of leadership selection work to encourage continuity and loyalty to the status quo. Again, the Collectivist Age has brought elaborate structures into existence which mesh with social and institutional predispositions deeply rooted in history. On the other hand, once decisions have clearly been made, the British system has a capacity to implement them very quickly and generally smoothly. This is in contrast to the American system and relates directly to the strong integration of the British system and the corresponding lack of decentralization and barriers within administrative sectors of the government. The civil service world of London is a small and intensive one, where news, including news of important decisions, travels remarkably quickly. Hugh Heclo and Aaron Wildavsky, two American political scientists who have conducted a recent analysis of public policy in Britain, were impressed by the efficiency of this network of communication, and this theme is featured in their published study. In another context, a senior British foreign policy official remarked in the course of an interview that he was startled to come from a cabinet meeting in which he had scored a major personal victory to discover that his staff was already breaking out the champagne when he arrived back at his own office.[35]

Regional policy is one of a number of specific areas from which examples can be drawn of the manner in which public policy has responded to perceptions of need and expressed political demands. This is a particularly important subject, given the pressures exerted by the nationalists, especially the S.N.P., in recent years and widespread complaints that the central government has been highly deficient in responding to the problems of the regions. Attention is frequently focused on the slow motion with which London has moved in granting any sort of political devolution to the regions. Within the last three years, proposals have been made by both the Conservative and Labour parties for forms of administrative devolution in Scotland and Wales. The Labour party has been somewhat more ambitious than the Tory, proposing new legislative assemblies for both regions. The Conservatives have restricted themselves to a Scottish assembly. Powers of the assemblies proposed by both parties would be restricted to certain specific policy areas, including education, housing, some local services, and some economic planning. Grants would be received from the central government, with no independent taxation power to be granted to the assemblies. The caution and conservatism of these proposals, and the fact that a lot of time was required for them to be proposed at all, have been emphasized by numerous critics of the two major parties on this issue.[36]

From another perspective, however, the records of both Tory and Labour parties have been much more impressive on the regional issue. There has been no effort to grant anything resembling true political independence to Wales, or even Scotland, from the central government in London, and given the unitary traditions in Britain it would be surprising if the situation were otherwise. However, both major parties have been active, not only recently but for a number of years reaching back before World War II, in promoting regional economic development and aid policies in an effort to remedy the comparatively serious economic problems of these areas. High unemployment, slow growth, a large proportion of aged and declining industries, and other related difficulties have been stressed by both the nationalist parties in their quests for votes. The two main parties, when in government, have responded forcefully to these economic problems. Beginning in the 1930s, the Conservative-dominated national government began a comprehensive regional economic planning and development program. Annual regional aid was increased regularly following World War II. In the 1950s, it stood at £10 million annually. By 1967–1968, the annual grant had grown to £250 million for Scotland alone. Regional policy indicates the rapidity with which government institutions can be established and changed once consensus has been reached on policy. Regionalism was a central theme of Harold Wilson's government, and almost immediately after Labour returned to power in 1964 a new comprehensive regional development ministry, under George Brown, was established. In this connection, one student of the Wilson government has noted that, " 'Regionalism' was the great rage of the early years of the Labour government."[37]

Two points can be made concerning the role of political party in this process of policy making and implementation. First, party research and publications have played a major role in defining policy not only toward the regions but across the board on major issues. Those familiar with American political parties, which lack extensive professional research staffs and treat election platforms in casual and often cynical fashion, find a strong contrast in a British system where election manifestoes reflect ideology and fervor to be sure, but also policies which are based on extensive research and analysis efforts. These are witnessed in the many pamphlets and more sizable documents produced by party research arms. Second, although party discipline even in Tory ranks is a complex process involving far more than simple imposition of rule from above, once a position has been decided upon, that discipline does ensure that the ruling party's parliamentary majority will carry through in passing the appropriate legislation. Just as civil service coordination facilitates smooth and often very rapid implementation of policy, so does party coordination facilitate comparatively efficient passage of enabling legislation.

PARTY COMPETITION

In earlier periods, Britain was praised as a model of stable two-party democratic political competition and alternation, in contrast to the more unstable and disorderly Continental systems; in more recent times, the British have been criticized for having two major parties which monopolize politics and elections without responding to important public demands or defining novel policy departures, especially in the troubled economic sphere. Important internal characteristics of the parties, including the nature of leadership selection and policy definition as well as discipline in Parliament, have already been touched on. Related to these is the subject of competition among parties and the extent to which the party system may be termed effective because broadly responsive to public demands and public problems.

There have also been strong factions within each of the two major parties. Of the two, the Labour party has known the more serious internal strife. Within that party, there has been a continuing general division between a moderate coalition, which normally has had majority support within the national conference and, especially, the parliamentary party, and a left-wing group, which has usually not been able to have its views formally adopted as party policy. Until recent years, the large trade union associations within the party were clearly opposed to the left wing, thus ensuring the moderates of victory in the party assembly. Since the late 1960s, this situation has been more ambiguous, with two large union organizations, the Transport and General Workers Union and the Amalgamated Engineering and Foundryworkers Union, moving to the left under the leadership of Jack Jones and Hugh Scanlon. During the late 1940s and the 1950s, the union alliance could be counted on to oppose doctrinaire commitment to nationalization and unilateral nuclear disarmament. The 1960 Labour conference, when unilateralism was formally though temporarily adopted as party policy, was a dramatic exception to this trend. In the latter part of the 1960s and into the 1970s, left-wing union leaders have played a central role in forestalling Labour party and Labour government adoption of statutory wage control policies desired by other sectors of the leadership. The situation has been more ambiguous in the Conservative party, with lines between internal groups being less explicit and more likely to shift over particular issues. There have been significant victories for persistent groups within the party opposing established party policy over a period of time. Perhaps the most notable instance in the 1960s was the eventual abandonment of the minimum pricing policy known as *resale price maintenance*. At the same time, the Conservative party has not developed the clearly defined, continuing factions characteristic of Labour. Enoch Powell's opposition to the broad thrust of Tory policy, in race relations and in other areas, resulted in speculation that he might carve out a right-wing faction within the party. The actual course of events, however, led to his growing isolation within and ultimate departure from the Conservative party, providing current evidence that the party remains resistant to strong factions.

Viewed and analyzed in total, the British party system, and the public sentiment that influences the parties, may be described as reflecting both continuity and change. There has been growth in the volatility of public sentiment in terms of attachment to the two main parties. There has been an increase in the support for third parties and, outside the boundaries of the party system, for voluntary reform and social service associations. These specific shifts, along with the broader perception that the political system is not as effective as once was believed to be the case, has resulted in questioning of the traditional assumption that Britain represents an unusually impressive and effective combination of democracy and authority, of conservatism and reformism. In a very broad context, the international decline of Britain as a world power has been accompanied by growth of skepticism concerning the workability and strength of national political institutions.

This essay has attempted to develop themes and related conclusions that address this point of view. First, the changes that have occurred in the axes of political competition and the sociology of the electorate are to some extent not sharp breaks with the nation's past but rather continuous with earlier patterns. Specifically, a number of parallels may be drawn between electoral volatility and growth of third parties and voluntary groups in the current period and patterns of behavior associated with nineteenth century Liberal politics. Thus, in the present time as in the past, the importance of traditionalism and the slowness of significant shifts in British politics is underlined. Second, the distinctions often made between Britain and the United States, frequently to the detriment of the latter in the past and of the former currently, may be accurately termed overdrawn. Among other considerations, the British system has successfully blended the scope for political reform, albeit normally of a cautious variety, with a strong sense of the importance of traditionalism. In short, even if earlier tendencies to emphasize the effectiveness of British institutions resulted in exaggeration, the party system has maintained the capacity to merge conservatism and change, stability and reform, in the current period as well as historically.

Notes

1. Samuel H. Beer, *British Politics in the Collectivist Age*, New York: Alfred A. Knopf, 1967, passim. and especially the closing remarks on p. 390; hereafter cited as Beer.

2. A. L. Rowse, *The England of Elizabeth*, New York: Macmillan, 1961, pp. 294–295.

3. Beer, op. cit., chapter 1.

4. Ibid., p. 23.

5. "The old Radical political ideals also won ever wider acceptance, and democracy was continually broadened in a series of acts between 1918 and 1969 that abolished the last restrictions on manhood suffrage, extended the vote to women on the same basis as it was held by men, abolished the plural votes that some property owners had retained, reduced still further the powers of the Lords, and finally, in 1969, gave the vote to eighteen-year-olds." Samuel H. Beer, "The British Political System," in Beer and Ulam, eds., *Patterns of Government*, 2nd ed., New York: Random House, 1973, p. 272; hereafter cited as *Patterns*.

6. H. J. Hanham, *Elections and Party Management*, London: Longmans, Green, 1959, p. 65.

7. The quotation is from Walter Bagehot, *The English Constitution*, London: Collins, 1963, p. 300. On the individualism of Commons politics during this period, see Beer, op. cit., pp. 50–51; Hanham, pp. 347 ff.

8. Arthur Cyr, *Liberal Party Politics in Britain*, London: John Calder Ltd., 1977, pp. 62–63.

9. Beer, op. cit., pp. 94 ff.

10. *Patterns*, op. cit., pp. 206 ff.

11. Ibid., p. 297.

12. David Thomson, *England in the Nineteenth Century*, Harmondsworth: Penguin Books, 1950, p. 119.

13. Beer, op. cit., Chapter 3.

14. See Ibid., p. 71.

15. Robert Alford, *Party and Society*, London: John Murray, 1964, p. 133 and *passim*.

16. Patterns, op. cit., p. 308.

17. Richard Scammon, "The Election and the Future of British Electoral Reform," in Howard R. Penniman, ed., *Britain at the Polls—the Parliamentary Elections of 1974*, Washington, D.C.: The American Enterprise Institute for Public Policy Research, 1975, p. 163.

18. Cyr, op. cit., especially the Foreword by Michael Steed, pp. 11–35 and also pp. 97–114. Material in this section is adopted from this volume.

19. See *The Economist*, October 19, 1974, pp. 36–38.

20. "A central link between different voluntary organizations and official bodies concerned with social welfare is provided by the National Council of Social Services." From the British Information Service, *Social Services in Britain*, ID 780 (revised), HMSO, 1963, p. 90; Kathleen Slack, "Voluntary Effort," in James Farndale, ed., *Trends in Social Welfare*, Oxford: Pergamon Press, 1965, pp. 36–37.

21. On the CND, see Norman Birnbaum, "Great Britain: The Reactive Revolt," in Morton Kaplan, ed., *The Revolution in World Politics*, New York: John Wiley, 1962, pp. 34–68.

22. L. J. Sharpe, "Leadership and Representation in Local Government," *Political Quarterly*, 37 (April–June 1966), 156.

23. "Social Reform in the Centrifugal Society," *New Society*: London, 1969, p. 19.

24. Dick Taverne, *The Future of the Left: Lincoln and After*, London: Jonathan Cape, 1974, passim.

25. On this general point concerning the parties, see Robert Jackson, *Rebels and Whips*, London: Macmillan, 1968, pp. 202–227 and passim.

26. See Cyr, op. cit., Chapter 5.

27. See Kenneth Waltz, *Foreign Policy and Democratic Politics*, Boston: Little, Brown and Co., 1967, pp. 298 ff.

28. *Encounter*, 21 (July 1963), passim.

29. The case for a lack of balance in the British system is made in various places, including R. H. S. Crossman, *The Myths of Cabinet Government*, Cambridge: Harvard University Press, 1972.

30. A range of personal parallels can be and have been drawn between British political features and characteristics of the American presidents of recent years: Eisenhower's efforts to emphasize cabinet government, Kennedy's personal style, and Johnson's background as legislative leader.

31. The relationship between prime minister and cabinet is analyzed at length by Hugh Heclo and Aaron Wildavsky, *The Private Government of Public Money*, Berkeley and Los Angeles: University of California Press, 1974, chapter 4 and passim.

32. Doris Kearns, *Lyndon Johnson and the American Dream*, New York: New American Library, 1976, pp. 253–256.

33. Elie Abel, *The Missile Crisis*, New York: Bantam Books, 1968, pp. 169, 173; Arthur Schlesinger Jr., *A Thousand Days*, Boston: Houghton Mifflin Co., 1965, pp. 794–830.

34. *Patterns*, op. cit., pp. 5–7.

35. Author's interviews in London, summer 1975.

36. On devolution proposals, see, for example, *The Economist*, September 28, 1974, p. 33.

37. Brian Lapping, *The Labour Government, 1964–70*, Harmondsworth: Penguin Books, 1970, pp. 198–200.

CHAPTER 4

FRANCE

Lowell G. Noonan

Competing Interpretations of the Party System[1]

Georges Lavau notes that the French have had little experience with collective responsibilities, that they have fewer associations than many other Western societies, and that those associations that do exist operate less intensively than their counterparts elsewhere.[2] He states that, during part of the Second Empire, worker's clubs were active, bourgeois political "circles" existed, and rural life was characterized by some organizational activities but that group activities subsequently gravitated toward a "style of bourgeois life" turned toward the "inside" and the exercise of "family virtues."[3] The result was what Lavau describes as a "legendary individualism." Why, asks Lavau, did the Frenchman—in searching for guarantees for individual liberty— exclude himself from groups? Why did he emerge with this version of "isolated individualism"? Why is his allegiance to groups or even to a social class so weak? Why does he show so little need to adhere to a political party or a political movement?

Lavau states that for Frenchmen "party is . . . first a doctrine, a system, or sometimes simply a state of spirit, never a social group playing a precise role in economic progress or social life."[4] Lavau describes this outlook as "unrealistic." He is of the opinion that the lack of realism in French political life is the consequence of nonparticipation in groups and lack of exercise of responsibility within them. The one area that could provide the very best source of political training, says Lavau, is infrequently resorted to and used. "Deprived of their education," the French are consequently led to the abstract and in politics tend to be moralistic. Lacking prior training in problems of the concrete, and without prior exposure to the "politics of the concrete," the Frenchman tends to be ignorant of the concrete. He forgets the "worldliness of politics" and "makes a morality of the absolute." His options hinge on ideas.[5] This "unrealism"—which has its origins in the poverty of community life— results in a chapel-like image of party.

Maurice Duverger describes the French multiparty system as the result of the "noncoincidences of the main cleavages in opinion."[6] The system arises, he says, from the mutual independence of sets of antitheses, and it presupposes different sectors of political activity to be relatively isolated and sealed off from each other. The two-party system, says Duverger, is "natural." Whenever the factions within both parties no longer can find common ground, the tendency toward dualism is defeated and the transition to multipartyism is made. Unlike Duverger, Leon Epstein views multipartyism as perhaps "more natural" in a modern pluralist society.[7] He argues that, if one begins not with two sides but rather with the existence of a variety of interests and opinions, then one would expect multipartyism "unless unusual circumstances channeled the variety into only two parties."[8] He asks, very plausibly, why "should all the inevitable cleavages coincide with respect to such diverse issues as welfare, civil rights, foreign policy, religious education and the nature of government authority?"[9] There is, indeed, no reason why they should, and it is not often that they do. On the other hand, as Raymond Aron says, the multiplicity of ideological families, various electoral laws, and economic and social diversities certainly do not raise an insurmountable barrier to a system of few parties.[10]

Development of the System

The party system postdates by many years the evolution of French political development along multifactional lines; nevertheless, the system has absorbed many of these elements. The system operates within a country where different regions have evolved differently, where the vote is dominated by different traditions and interests, and where, as Raymond Aron says, people entertain different "politico-metaphysical" convictions.[11] The system has been shaped and transformed by, and in the backwash of, numerous historical phenomena, among them the Revolution of 1789, the Industrial Revolution of the last century, the Russian Revolution of 1917, and the Gaullist seizure of power in 1958. The system has been shaped by republicanism and its history of ups and downs. The system was for many years relatively open—that is, new parties had little difficulty breaking into it, and until recently the system was not hard on smaller parties, affording them for a variety of reasons conditions that enabled them to hang on in the party arena. The system appeared until 1968 to be completely unreceptive to one party's obtaining a unified and homogeneous legislative majority—until that was achieved that year by the Gaullists. The system comprised under the Fourth Republic parties that failed generally to recruit members and supporters on a mass basis (exceptions were the Communist and Socialist parties), and, consequently, parties such as the Radical Socialists and the Independents operated for many years as cadre organizations with large executive heads and miniscule membership bodies. The discipline of these parties in Parliament was ineffective, and various of their deputies often voted with other undisciplined deputies for the purpose of bringing down cabinets. Such deputies had little to fear, knowing that the strength that they enjoyed in their own fieflike electoral districts would protect them against their own political organizations. Today, the system is different, for the number of deputies who can operate without real dependence upon a national political party has declined and now candidates for legislative seats run generally under the banners of a national political organization.

The system did give government in most eras the means to govern, for, as Duverger says, ". . . all of this did not work as badly as we have been told. . . . Between 1875 and 1920, the Third Republic was one of the best political systems of Europe."[12] In some eras, however, the system contributed to governmental instability, or inhibited governments from entering into some vital areas of policy making, as for example, during the Fourth Republic, when the poison of the Algerian conflict spread throughout French society and often governments abandoned the making of policies relative to it. A "good" party system maintains conditions for effective governance—during times good and bad, in crisis and noncrisis; the system during the Fourth Republic frequently was inadequate for this task.

The system contains parties that have adopted recently some of the modern techniques of political persuasion applied effectively by political parties in other countries. In 1966 the Gaullist party implemented local polls in approximately 50 electoral districts prior to the meeting of its national council in Poitiers, and the public relations firm *Services et méthodes* helped centrist Jean Lecanuet create on television an image that was both persuasive and amiable during the presidential campaign of 1965.[13] In 1967, for the Gaullist party, the same organization conducted seminars in which it taught the party how to make the most of its appeal. The system contains parties that have discovered that political clubs serve purposes of recruiting, organizing, and carrying through on political campaigns (although the Communist party offers great resistance to this innovation, being gravely suspicious of such unorthodox ventures).[14] Giscard d'Estaing's political groups *Perspectives et réalités* were created to bolster support for his kind of thought.

The system contains parties that participate generally in federations. The late Federation of the Left (FG) included, for example, the former Socialist party (SFIO) and the Radical Socialist party (PRS) and the participants foresaw electoral, parliamentary, and eventually governmental collaboration (although the participating parties did not lose their identities in the federation, preserving in it their organic uniqueness). Early in 1968 the FG signed electoral agreements with the Communist party (PCF) which did not go as far as the parliamentary and governmental stages of collaboration. Dissolved in 1968, the FG was succeeded in 1972 by the Union of the Left, a federation in which the PCF and Socialist (PS) parties, and the Radicals of the Left (MRG) retain their separate identities while looking forward to electoral, parliamentary, and governmental collaboration during a previously specified period of time. Finally, the Center of Social Democrats (CDS) and the Republican party (PR) now participate together in a federation, having realized agreements that are electoral, parliamentary, and governmental.[15]

The system contains parties that De Gaulle sought to bar from access to the "conversion processes" during his 11-year reign, to whom he attributed inadequacies that ranged from responsibility for the fall of the Third Republic to blame for the destruction of the Fourth Republic. De Gaulle, in fact, did all that he could to keep from real governance during those years even the party that is Gaullist and that claimed in 1968 for the first time in French legislative history command in the National Assembly of a unified and homogeneous majority. Today, after the departure of De Gaulle, the political parties continue to play in the operation of the political system roles that are less than dominant, and Giscard d'Estaing, leader of the PR and president of the Republic, tells the French with pride that he is not a party man, as does his academician-turned-premier, Raymond Barre.[16]

Cleavages and Clienteles

To which political parties do the diverse social categories of the nation give their support? How is this support distributed among the parties?[17] The PCF electorate is predominantly male (58%). Its electorate is among the youngest of party electorates, only 16% being more than 65 years of age and 60% being less than 50 years of age. About 52% of the party's supporters derive from the working class and about one-fourth from the middle class. The membership composition does not differ greatly from that of its supporters in the country. Communist voters usually earn more than Radical Socialist, Socialist, Center of Social Democrats, and Republican party voters. It is not, as Duhamel says, "the bottom of the working class but its aristocracy" that often votes Communist.

The voting clientele of the Unified Socialist party (PSU) is exceptionally young, about 45% being 21–34 years of age, with approximately 19% in the category of 50 years or more. Some 24% are liberal professions and upper management, and, although the party truly is socialist, its worker vote may be as low as 22% (according to the public opinion agency SOFRES), whereas the

French Institute of Public Opinion (IFOP) places it as high as 34%. The PS's electorate is predominantly male (53%), 58% of whom are under 50 years of age. Though called sometimes the "party of civil servants," the party, nevertheless, draws support from all social categories. Workers supply about 35% of its votes and retirees about 26%. Voters comprise salaried employees (21%), persons in middle management (7%), and people in agriculture (only 5%). Electors are divided between large and middle-sized cities; generally they tend not to be rural or Parisian.

The PRS electorate is predominantly male, aged, and rural. Workers comprise about a fourth of its voters. No longer is agriculture heavily represented among its supporters. The party's strength is greater among rural *communes* than in large cities. The Rally for the Republic (RPR) draws its strength from all social categories. Its clientele comprises more females than males. Only 24% of its voters are under 35 years of age, and 24% are over 65. This party refers to the opposition parties as the "old parties," but, in terms of the ages of its own supporters, this party is truly "old." Its clientele includes 22% workers. Approximately 17% of its supporters are in agriculture. The party's occupational group support includes employees, persons in middle management, and the liberal professions, industrialists, merchants, and others. Its voters tend to be better off financially, being outdone in earnings only by Independent party electors. Its electorate is more urban than rural and is well distributed geographically. The CDS electorate is more female than male. Youth is not greatly attracted to it. Approximately 16% of its voters are in agriculture; another 21% are workers. Employees and middle-management persons are well represented in its electorate. Representation is greater in the provinces and smaller cities than in the Paris region. Earnings of its electors tend to be slight.

In the PR electorate there is about equal distribution of males and females. More than 50% of its voters are under 50 years of age. Industrialists, merchants, employees, and middle-management persons are well represented in it. People in agriculture support the party, but it is not a rural party, being well represented in the large cities. The party's electorate is not rich. The Independent party's (CNIP) electorate is more masculine than female and of elevated age. The party comprises among its electors people who are self-employed and members of the liberal professions. Twenty percent of its electorate is in agriculture, and 20% are workers.

The Political Parties and the Electoral Law

The PCF wishes to substitute for the present mode of election proportional representation.[18] The party's electoral preference is understandable,[19] for in the legislative elections of 1958, the PCF received on the first ballot 18.9% of the votes cast, and after completion of the second ballot the party ended up with but 2.1% of the parliamentary seats. In 1962 the PCF received 21.8% of the votes cast on the first ballot and only 8.6% of the seats after the second ballot. In 1967 the party received 22.4% of the vote and 15.3% of the seats on the first ballot; and in 1968 the party won 20% of the vote and came away with 7% of the seats on the first ballot. In turn, the single-member constituency with two ballotings has done well by the Gaullists and their party affiliates. In 1962 that bloc received 55.0% of the seats in the assembly and 35.5% of the votes cast. In 1967 the allocation of seats was nearly 50.0% with 37.8% of the votes cast, and in 1968 74.3% of the seats and 43.7% of the vote. The Gaullist bloc of parties received in the country in 1973 fewer votes than the left opposition parties, and yet it emerged in the National Assembly with a majority of 99 seats.

Abandonment of the single-member constituency and adoption of proportional representation is unlikely as long as the Gaullists (RPR) have anything to do with reconsideration of the electoral law, for the hostility of the Gaullist party to proportional representation appears to be absolute—particularly when Michel Debré argues that "Proportional representation leads to anarchy and to the end of the Republic" and Olivier Guichard states that it will lead to the destruction of the majority.[20] However, despite such representations, the attitude of the Gaullists relative to the electoral law presently has much to do with the ability of the different parties that make up the Gaullist bloc to maintain unity; fragmentation or destruction of that unity could lead subsequently to a possible revision in the Gaullists' outlook relative to the electoral law, for the strength of a political party resides not only in the number of its deputies but also in its alliances with other parties. As these alliances weaken, adjustments in electoral law often come in for serious consideration, for even the most "profoundly committed" of political parties find ways to reconsider whenever new transformations dictate readaptation. In a few words, political parties favor naturally those electoral laws that favor themselves. In recent months, some centrist elements presently in support of the Gaullist bloc, and some Republican (PR) members have suggested that there is merit in the opposition's plea for the adoption of proportional representation, and rumors continue to circulate that President Giscard d'Estaing wishes to "proportionalize" the electoral system.[21] If true, his position may have much to do with the idea that a return to proportional representation during a period of left ascendancy might lead possibly in the legislature to realization of an array of forces with the balance still in the hands of the center and the right.[22]

The Elections to the National Assembly

The legislative elections of 1958, the first held under the new Fifth Republic, constituted the first in a series of defeats administered the classical political parties, representing for some the beginning of the end (the CNIP, the sole exception, began its electoral decline some years later, in the legislative elections of 1962). In 1958 it was difficult to realize that the old party system was permanently injured and that its electorate would be reduced drastically in coming years. Yet, by the time of the legislative elections of 1962, the new Gaullist Union for a New Republic/Union for Democratic Labor (UNR-UDT), although still lacking a unified and homogeneous majority in the National Assembly, had become the largest group ever to be seated in any national legislative body under any republic. That election signaled yet another step in the evolution of the Fifth Republic, burying still deeper some of the classical formations held over from the Fourth.

The legislative elections of 1967 were conducted in an atmosphere different from that of preceding legislative elections. The Algerian war had been terminated. A recession took place in the UNR-UDT segment of the Gaullist formation; nevertheless, those elections increased the size of Giscard d'Estaing's segment of the Gaullist coalition, the Independent republicans, entrusting him and his party in the National Assembly with the "keys to the majority." In turn, the PCF and SFIO also were able to conclude on the second ballot enough electoral agreements to bolster their strength in the National Assembly. The 1967 legislative elections—instead of comprising innumerable political parties of varying sizes—included four great formations, and, when the voting had been completed, the number had been reduced from four to three, causing observers to wonder if a trend toward bipolarization was in progress?

The legislative elections of 1968 occurred under unusual circumstances, following by only a month the great demonstrations of May 1968. The campaign was attended by frequent Gaullist warnings of an impending "Red totalitarianism." The elections produced a huge Gaullist victory, a unified and homogeneous majority for the Gaullist formation in the National Assembly, and for the left one of the heaviest electoral defeats in all of French history. Left unity was missing from this election. The left, moreover, was unable to claim from the center too many votes. The election transformed Gaullism from predominantly an urban phenomenon to one both urban and rural. Finally, the Gaullist UDR having attained in the National Assembly a majority of its own, succeeded in divesting Giscard d'Estaing and his CNIP of the "keys to the majority."

The majority won by the Gaullist coalition in the legislative elections of March 1973 differed considerably from the Gaullist majority that existed previously, for now the new majority was no longer the property of its Gaullist component, the UDR. Moreover, the UDR was in the country in numerical decline, and that decline would have been greater if in numerous departments centrists (then the Réformateurs) had not withdrawn so as to enable the majority to avoid further losses.[23] Second, the left increased its parliamentary representation in the National Assembly, and yet the additional seats acquired did not secure for the left greater influence in Parliament. Third, the centrist Réformateurs—in the words of Jacques Fauvet—were in the elections both the artisans and the victims of the success of the majority.[24] The Réformateurs had hoped that they would detract from the majority enough votes to enable them to gather enough seats to complete the majority and arrange subsequently for its more liberal transformation. While contributing to the Gaullist victory by their deferrals to Gaullist candidates on the second ballot, the Réformateurs still fell short, however, of winning the number of seats that they had hoped to gain for themselves. Consequently, with only 31 seats, they failed in their effort to attain the position assumed previously by Giscard d'Estaing and his Independent Republicans after the legislative elections of 1967, when Giscard had held the "keys to the majority" with but 50 seats. They soon abandoned their position in the opposition. Some of the Réformateurs' principal leaders were rewarded with cabinet posts and the formation joined the majority bloc. Fourth, the PS—while increasing its position in the country from that of 1968[25]—was still short of Mitterand's goal of "rebalancing the French left." Within another year, however, the Socialist party bolstered considerably its strength and succeeded in becoming the dominant party of the left.[26] Fifth, any step after the election by other organizations of the majority to exclude the UDR from the coalition was unfeasible. Consequently, components of an "unhappy" majority appeared condemned to live with each other until expiration of the legislative mandate in 1978. Sixth, the legislative elections did not lead to an institutional crisis, for defeat of the left at the polls precluded possible appointment by the president of the Republic of a minority Gaullist government.[27] And the elections, moreover, did not weaken demonstrably the hand of the president, assuring him continuity in his approach to the cabinet and legislature. The second ballot was considered by the majority to be a step in the direction of a presidential election that was expected to be held in 1976. Pompidou's hold on the presidency appeared not to have been substantially damaged by the results of the legislative elections, providing during his occupancy that he could avoid involvement in future adventures. That hold was relinquished, however, with his passing in 1974; when his successor, Giscard d'Estaing, came to the post, the scenario again was transformed, and weaker relations emerged among the UDR and other components of the legislative majority.

The Legislative Elections of March 1978[28]

In the parliamentary elections of 1978, the left parties won 48.6% of the vote on the first ballot (Tables 4–1 and 4–2). The result was particularly galling for the PS, the self-proclaimed "leading party of France," which claimed 22.6% of the ballots cast, exactly the percentage won by its rival, the Gaullist

TABLE 4–1. French Legislative Elections in the Fifth Republic, 1958–1978 (Percent)[a]

	1958	1962	1967	1968	1973	1978
Gaullists[b]	28.1	40.5	42.6	48.8	46.3	26.1
National Center of Independents	15.4	7.4	—	—	—	—
Popular Republican Movement	7.3	5.3	—	—	—	—
Democratic Center, Reform	—	—	7.1	8.1	6.1	—
Union for French Democracy	—	—	—	—	—	23.2
Radicals, Moderates, Left Republicans	11.2	7.0	—	—	—	—
Socialists	13.8	15.2	—	—	—	—
Federation of the Left	—	—	25.0	21.6	26.4	30.6
Communists	20.5	21.3	21.4	19.9	20.6	18.6

[a]Second ballot.
[b]Union for the New Republic, Union for a Democratic Republic, Rally for the Republic.

TABLE 4–2. Voting Strength and Seats in the Legislative Elections of March 1978

PARTY	FIRST BALLOT		SECOND BALLOT		TOTAL SEATS	GAINS OR LOSSES
	Per-cent	Seats	Per-cent	Seats		
Opposition						
Communists	20.6	4	18.6	82	86	+12
Socialist	22.6	1	28.3	103	104	+9
Radical Left	2.1	—	2.3	10	10	−3
Other	6.1	—	0.2	1	1	—
Majority						
Gaullists	22.6[a]	30	26.1	123	153	−20
Republicans		16		53	69	+8
Center Soc. Dem.	21.5[b]	6	23.2	29	35	+7
Radicals		1		8	9	+2
Others		10		13	23	−2
Total		68		423	491	

RPR. The PCF, with 20.6% of the vote, ran at least 0.4% behind the strength predicted for it in the polls. The MRG received 2.1%, the extreme left 3.3%. The Union for French Democracy (UDF), an electoral coalition consisting of Giscard's PR, as well as the CDS and the PRS, claimed 21.5%; other center right factions supported it with an additional 2.4%. The government parties registered a total of 46.5% (which includes the RPR's 22.6%).[29] Only sixty-eight of the 491 seats at stake were won on the first ballot; 63 were either UDF or RPR.[30] On the second ballot, 423 seats remained to be filled, and that ballot was more polarized than ever. Of the total, 408, or 96.5%, of the contests were "duels" between the majority and its opposition, surpassing the record attained June 30, 1968, when on the second ballot two-way "duels" reached 85.1%[31]

The left concluded between the two ballots agreements to support, on the second ballot, the candidate of the left arithmetically best placed. The government parties also closed ranks between ballots, and Chirac, Lecanuet, and Motte confirmed their prior agreement of September 14, 1977 to run in each electoral district only one center-right candidate, the one favored arithmetically by the results of the first ballot.[32]

The center-right coalition of government parties won on the second ballot 50.5% of the vote and 291 seats in the National Assembly. The left parties captured 49.3% of the vote and 199 seats.[33] The PCF's performance on the second ballot ran behind expectations, falling to 18.6% of the vote and 86 seats, whereas the PS rose to 28.3% and 104 seats. The MRG held fast at 2.3% and 10 seats. The RPR continued its decline within the majority, falling to 26.1% of the vote and 153 seats, whereas the UDF and other of its affiliates accounted for 23.2% and 137 seats. Within the UDF, the respective party returns were 69 PR, 35 CDS, 16 majorité présidentielle, 9 PRS, 7 CNIP, and 1 Mouvement démocrate socialiste de France (MDSF).

When the candidate of the left on the second ballot was in various departments a Communist rather than a Socialist or a Radical of the Left, abstentions tended to increase and the PCF candidates did not fare as well as their partners, showing that the anti-Communist reflex remained strong. However, in 11 of 30 districts when the only candidate of the left on the second ballot was either a Socialist or a Radical of the Left, the rate of abstentions declined.[34]

The electoral campaign, according to Pierre Viansson-Ponté, was at best mediocre and relatively free from serious debate over such vital issues as a choice of society, different conceptions of the State, the role of France in the world, and the confrontation of two styles of management of society. All these appeared to Viansson-Ponté to have been phenomena that were eclipsed by dogmatism and polemics.[35]

During the campaign the right emphasized the dangers of an impending Communism. Chirac, for example, announced that half the ministerial portfolios in a future government of the left would go to the PCF, and Raymond Barre called to public attention the likelihood of a PCF demand for control of the ministries of Defense and Foreign Affairs.[36] In addition to capitalizing on the anti-Communist reflex, the leaders of the majority also were able to play in the campaign roles that were different, complementary (although in some instances temporary), and seemingly effective. Barre fell back on his professional image and told the voters with sophistication about the economic risks of a victory of the left and the hollowness of various left promises, Chirac emphasized the weakness and ambivalence of the Socialist party relative to its partner—the PCF, and the president of the Republic described both the political and economic risks posed by the Common Program.[37]

The defeat of the left appears also to have been affected by disagreements between the PCF and PS relative to the evolution of the Common Program and by the numerous attacks by the PCF on the PS that appear to have had the effect of cutting into the Common Front theme and that probably provoked on the first ballot some losses and that sometimes inhibited on the second ballot the transfer of votes from one party to another.[38] Nevertheless, left disunity, magnification by the right of a threat of an impending communism, the inequity of the electoral law, etc., etc., seemingly all fell short of explaining the defeat of the left and the success of the majority.[39]

The left at present is farther than ever from power, although it can be argued also that a portion of it now is potentially closer to it than it has been for years, for Giscard would like to extend a hand of welcome to those conservative Socialists who remain apprehensive of participating with the Communists in a Common Program and bring them into his coalition. Perhaps some will make the transition, giving Giscard thereby some house Socialists to unveil before the nation for purposes of public relations. Nevertheless, it is questionable whether Giscard will be able to rearrange things so as to terminate his dependence upon Jacques Chirac and his RPR. And it also appears unlikely that Chirac—who could precipitate a parliamentary crisis at any time—will open such a crisis, for now his strategy appears to be one of watchful waiting, hoping that Giscard will make the kind of mistake that will enable him to make a decisive move in the direction of the presidency.[40] Consequently, Chirac holds the keys to the majority, and it is unlikely that he will allow Giscard to forget where they are. Finally, defeat of the left in the legislative elections of March 1978 signaled at least temporarily the end of the Common Program.[41]

The Presidential Elections

The presidential electoral system offers on the second ballot a choice between only two candidates (no candidate has ever won office on the first ballot). Consequently, the political parties are compelled to endorse on the second ballot one of the two remaining candidates or—as was the case in 1969 with the Communist party—urge on it massive abstentions. Therefore, a political party infrequently is in a position to endorse on the second ballot a candidate of its first choice. Moreover, the size of a political party sometimes is secondary to its alliances insofar as advancing its candidate on the second ballot is concerned. When Giscard d'Estaing won the presidency in 1974, his second ballot victory was achieved despite the fact that he was the leader of a relatively small and not so significant party, whereas Chaban-Delmas, his vanquished opponent, had on the first ballot (he did not make it to the second ballot) the support of a large segment of France's largest political party, the

UDR (although not the support of the UDR's Jacques Chirac, who threw his weight to Giscard).

Only recently have political parties played a larger role in presidential politics. The election in December 1958 of Charles de Gaulle by an electoral college was in the immediate backwash of June 13 and the Gaullist seizure of power and the creation shortly afterward of the Gaullist Fifth Republic.[42] Consequently, the political parties—operating in what was for them a demoralized political environment—had little impact on the course of events. This was not the case, however, after the constitutional referendum of 1962, which provided for the direct election of the president. The presidential election of 1965, therefore, raised great hopes for a renovation of the left.

Nevertheless, Gaston Defferre's left candidacy for the presidency did not come initially as the result of a party nomination. In fact, his selection was unique in French politics, for the Socialist mayor of Marseilles was presented first to the public by the weekly *l'Express* as "M. X.," the ideal candidate of the opposition. During his campaign, Defferre remained aloof from the political parties (although he eventually solicited and received grudgingly from his own party the nomination), placing himself above party and seeking to ride into the presidency on the shoulders of a great wave of public opinion; his project failed, his candidacy disintegrated, and he was replaced by François Mitterrand who, unlike Defferre, negotiated first with the traditional parties of the left and their apparatus before participating in the race. Although Mitterrand was supported by the PCF and PS, his treatment of parties was in appearance at times almost antiparty—for example, "I wish to create some psychological conditions which are free from thought patterns and discussions of parties. I have no apparatus. I am almost alone." He explained further, "I am not a man of party, I am not a man of a coalition of parties. I am a candidate of all the Left."[43] Mitterrand's opponent, Charles de Gaulle, did not tie his candidacy to his own party, rejecting parties both theoretically and practically and approaching the electors like an understanding father. De Gaulle won on the first ballot approximately 44% of the vote, Mitterrand 32% (Lecanuet's candidacy by the MRP prevented De Gaulle from winning a majority on the first ballot). De Gaulle received on the second ballot 55% of the vote cast and Mitterrand 45%. The IFOP noted that 13% of the electors who voted habitually for the three parties of the left voted for De Gaulle. The floating vote was estimated to have been at times as great as 29%, meaning that up to the last minute the fluidity of the electoral body injected in the elections elements of uncertainty.

The presidential election of June 1969 was the consequence of a resignation by a De Gaulle who had staked and lost his political life unnecessarily on the outcome of the referendum of April 29, 1969. Left disunity in this election was particularly apparent, and the parties of the left were unable to unite behind one presidential candidate. Consequently, they each presented (with the exception of the Radicals) their own candidates. The disasters experienced previously by the left in the legislative elections of 1968 thus continued into the presidential election of 1969. Seven candidates appeared on the first ballot, including the PCF's Jacques Duclos and the PS's Defferre. Mitterrand was not a candidate. The candidate of the right, Georges Pompidou, followed a strategy calculated to capture a good portion of the centrist electorate, whereas Alain Poher, the centrist president of the Senate, sought to carry the left and a good portion of the right. In that election Poher said that he accepted political parties, although he claimed no particular affiliation with any one of them.

Pompidou and Poher faced each other on the second ballot, and Pompidou won with 58% of the votes cast. Poher's 42% of the vote was bolstered by approximately one-fourth of the PCF electorate who cast for him perhaps 1,200,000 votes, despite the call by the PCF for a massive abstention. Moreover, the *gauchisation* of Poher's campaign between the first and second ballots appears to have driven towards Pompidou on the second ballot perhaps 7% of moderate first ballot Poher voters. The center, still weak in 1969, was stronger, nonetheless, than it had been in 1965 when Lecanuet was presented as its candidate. Finally, the PCF's recommendation for a massive abstention on the second ballot assured the victory of Pompidou and the defeat on the second ballot of the centrist Poher.

The presidential election of 1974 took place during growing energy and financial crises. Although Pompidou had indicated before his death a vague preference for Giscard d'Estaing as his successor, his choice was not definitive. Giscard d'Estaing's candidacy was put forth by his relatively small FNRI, whereas Chaban-Delmas was presented by the Gaullist UDR. There was yet another candidate of the right, the late Jean Royer. Prior to the election, the right appeared hopelessly divided and so were the center parties. The parties of the left had met previously and agreed to support François Mitterrand.

Giscard appealed also to the centrist vote, whereas his opponents concentrated less on enlarging their electoral bases. When the race was over and Giscard was the victor, it was apparent that the electorate of the parties of the left had given to Mitterrand less than full support. A number of his own PS electors wavered on the first ballot and voted for other candidates, as did various PCF electors, losses that were not compensated for by gains from centrist and rightist voters. Chaban-Delmas had little success with his own party's electorate. Giscard and Mitterrand thus faced each other on the second ballot. During the race, Giscard received from the Gaullist UDR weak support in funds and speakers, whereas Mitterrand in turn received the full support of the PCF in meetings and publicity. Giscard won the 1974 presidential election on the second ballot because of his ability to carry both the center and the right and approximately 3% of the left vote. The distribution of votes was 50.7% to 49.3% and Giscard won the day by fewer than 400,000 ballots.

The Union of the Left and the Common Program

Socialist and Communist parties entered in 1972 (and subsequently the MRG) into a Common Program for the realization of short- and long-term objectives, limited to the duration of the next legislature (to be seated in 1978 at the latest). By the terms of the agreement, the parties retained during its application their own identities and no merger of the two was suggested. Following are the Common Program's main outlines:[44]

1. Adoption of a higher monthly minimum wage, revised periodically to keep abreast of inflation; retirement at 60 for males, 55 for females; adoption of a 40-hour week; the right to professional training.
2. Freedom of unions from both the state and political parties; the freedom to form unions.
3. Adoption of methods to restrict speculation in lands and buildings; construction of 700,000 dwellings per year.
4. Adoption of measures to end social segregation. Free studies, books, and transportation for students. Compulsory education until the age of 18. Social aid to families.
5. Granting of divorce by mutual consent; maternity leave of 16 weeks.
6. Compulsory military service but reduction of term to 6 months.
7. "Economic democracy and political democracy are inseparable." Extension of the rights of workers in all sectors of the economy by the mechanism of collective bargaining contracts.
8. Democratization, reorganization, and extension of the public sector to banking, financial, and industrial groups with dominant and strategic positions that perform a public service, dominate production, and control essential branches for development of the national economy. Involved are subsoil resources and industries dealing with arms, space, aeronautics, nuclear power, pharmaceuticals, and a large part of the electronic and chemical industries.
9. Creation of democratic planning, with "the greatest participation of workers and population."
10. All foreign investments must be useful to the economy.
11. A "fair deal" for agriculture; alteration of the policy of the European Economic Community in matters of price support and the organization of markets.
12. Institution of *habeas corpus* and the end of administrative deprivations of freedom.
13. Creation of a supreme court of nine members with nine-year non-renewable terms—three elected by the National Assembly (two by majority, one by minority), three elected by Senate (two by majority, one minority), one appointed by the president of the Republic, and two by the *Conseil superièur de la magistrature*.

14. Adoption of proportional representation for National Assembly elections.
15. Abolition of Article 16 of the Constitution.
16. Reduction of presidential term from seven to five years and limitation of presidential power without countersignature to designation of premier, sending messages to Parliament, relations with the Supreme Court, and dissolution of National Assembly.
17. Strengthening of Parliament, modification of Article 38, and the *vote bloquée*. Determination by each house of its own rules. Elimination of incompatibility between ministerial and parliamentary mandates.
18. In case of crisis, if the president of the Republic does not dissolve the National Assembly, he names the premier and members of a new government which then commits before the National Assembly its responsibility. If approval is not secured, the president of the Republic will be required to dissolve the National Assembly.
19. Communal autonomy.
20. Support for regionalism—each region to have a directly elected assembly.
21. General, universal and controlled disarmament. End of the *force de frappe* in its present form and conversion to peaceful nuclear industry.
22. No reintegration in NATO but adoption of defense and nonaggression force. Simultaneous dissolution of the North Atlantic and Warsaw pacts and participation by the United States and Canada in a confederation for security and cooperation in Europe.
23. Independence from military blocs.
24. Continued participation in European Economic Community (EEC) but liberation of the organization from *grand capital*, democratization of its institutions, and support in it for demands of workers. Preservation within EEC of French liberty of action for realization of its own political, economic, and social program. French governments reserve the right to extend the public sector of the economy within French territory. France reserves the right to its own "democratic planning."
25. Right of Israel and the Arab states to exist. More aid for the African states.

Despite the PCF's declared adherence to the Common Program, the agreement—in the eyes of PCF leader Georges Marchais—did not go as far as a socialism defined as "the collective ownership of the principal methods of production and distribution, and the power of the working class and its allies."[45] Consequently, a left victory in the legislative elections of 1973 would have been interpreted by the PCF not as socialism but as *démocratie avancée*, as a step in the direction of a possible transition toward socialism. For Marchais, moreover, "the union was not a merger in one party. Communists, Socialists, and Radicals do not have the same conception of the world, the same organization of party, the same views on a number of questions. We do not intend to renounce a single one of our convictions and we know very well that our allies are attached to theirs. Our alliance does not put an end to our differences. Inversely, these differences, as we see it, must not be contrary to our alliance."[46] In 1977 and 1978, the Communist party demanded certain transformations in the Common Program—that is, an increase in nationalizations and retention of the independent nuclear deterrent; consequently, negotiations with the Socialist party have reached an apparent impasse.[47]

The PS's position on relations with the PCF after its adherence to the Common Program appears to be accurately reflected in the report presented in 1976 to the executive committee of the PS by M. Jospin.[48] The report states that (1) although PCF polemics take diverse forms, the PCF seeks always to maintain pressure on the Socialist party as it searches for political control of the working class; (2) even if the PCF did condemn initially entry of Soviet troops into Czechoslovakia and the presence of forced labor camps in the Soviet Union, the party has since yielded to silence on the "normalization" of Czechoslovakia, and it continues to defend in Portugal the same themes as those defended by the Communist party of the Soviet Union; (3) the compatibility of the union of the people of France with the union of the left is strategically still far from evident; (4) if there is going to be a real turnabout in PCF policy and behavior, the answer is probably too soon to determine and nothing must be done to harm the existing Socialist-Communist dialogue.[49]

The Eternal Problem of the Left

Communist and Socialist party relationships over the span of three republics have ranged periodically from no relationship whatsoever to some form of collaboration in a union of the left. These unions may be primarily electoral, that is, ones in which the two parties advance certain candidates and retire others between ballots to avoid elimination at the polls, or they may be electoral and legislative, looking forward ultimately to a program of government.

Unions of the left are collaborative frameworks within which both the PCF and PS compete for leadership of the venture, for within them each participant hopes to get out in front of the other as the interpreter and leader in the country of left unity. If this competition is sometimes vituperative and pejorative, it is, nonetheless, normal.

The rationale for a union of the left is simple enough; both the PCF and PS lack individually enough votes in the country to establish their own legislative and presidential majorities. Consequently, if a left majority is in the country at all possible, that majority can only be the result of collaboration between the two major components of the French left, the Communist left and the non-Communist left.

Results of legislative contests in the Fifth Republic generally testify to the desirability of electoral agreements by the PS and PCF for seats in the National Assembly. When the left unites, each of its components generally profits numerically in terms of the number of seats won. When in legislative contests the left is disunited, both the Communist and non-Communist left generally suffer loss of a considerable number of seats. A disunited left in the legislative contests of 1958 produced, for example, only 10 seats for the PCF and for the non-Communist left a meager 107 seats. However, in 1962, when in a given number of electoral constituencies the Communist and non-Communist left collaborated, left representation in the National Assembly increased by 31 PCF, 21 PS, and 19 MRG. In 1967, in yet another year of left unity, the PCF increased its representation in the National Assembly 31 seats and the PS by 11 (the MRG dropped 2). However, in 1968, in a year of grave left disunity, the PCF dropped 38 seats, and PS and MRG representation in the National Assembly declined from 116 to 57 (in the Federation of the Socialist and Democratic Left). Finally, Mitterrand's 1965 campaign for the presidency, which was waged with the support of a united left, brought to him considerable votes and prepared the way for the legislative elections of 1967. In fact, the legislative elections of 1967 were regarded by some people as but the final ballot of the 1965 presidential election. However, in the presidential election of 1969, a divided left assured the defeat of the centrist Poher and the victory of the Gaullist Pompidou.

If the non-Communist left stands to gain legislative seats as a consequence of its electoral collaboration with the Communist left, why, then, is this strategy at times resisted so avidly by some leaders of the non-Communist left? There is to this question no single answer. First, the non-Communist left must always be heedful of not allowing its collaboration with the PCF to drive into the hands of the right too many of those centrist voters who are attracted to and vote periodically to the left. The non-Communist left knows that most legislative and presidential elections are made or unmade by the center, that component of the French electorate capable of giving either to the left or the right a majority in the National Assembly or to the country a president of the Republic. If there are times during the life of a republic when centrist voters support the left in greater proportions than normally is the case, there also are times—as, for example, in 1968—when the spectre of communism (whether real or imaginary) drives many centrists into support of the right. In other words, a political environment that will give those centrists sympathetic to the non-Communist left reasonable assurances of the improbability of a significant Communist advance (e.g., a unified and homogeneous Communist legislative majority/or domination by Communists of a cabinet) is at the polls probably more conducive to greater turnouts by centrists in support of the left. Consequently, an electoral union in which the PCF is clearly a secondary force will probably win more centrist votes than one in which the PCF is or promises to be a primary force.

Tactically, the alternative to PS collaboration with the PCF is for the PS to stand alone electorally or to enter with the center into some type of electoral collaboration. Although standing alone in legislative contests usually is less than rewarding, nevertheless, the price demanded by the center for PS collaboration with it may be considerable, meaning for the PS abandonment in the country generally of any real application of socialism. Second, some non-Communist left leaders fear collaboration with a vehicle with so strong an organization as the PCF, for a party with a mediocre organization can, under some circumstances, be taken in tow by it. In other words, resistance offered by some PS leaders to unity with the PCF sometimes has little to do with communism per se, or the differences between it and socialism, but with fear of suffering at the hands of one whose organization is superior. When the late Guy Mollet talked, for example, about the Soviet seizure of Czechoslovakia and why it prevented an opening to the left and French Socialists from working with the PCF, it probably was Mollet's way of saying that that was not an appropriate time for unity, for in times such as those such unity could have set back French socialism even farther behind communism. Such doctrinal expositions often are calculated to protect the organization. Sometime later, though, when Czechoslovakia still was under Soviet occupation—but after the disastrous defeat of Defferre and Poher in the presidential campaign of 1969—Mollet changed his tune and asked in the Congress of the Socialist party in Issy-les-Molineaux for an *overture à gauche.*[50] Mollet's new policy was the result of an agreement with Pierre Mauroy and Alain Savary, even though earlier Mauroy had called in the presidential election of 1969 for a vote on the second ballot for the centrist Poher, whose success would "guarantee the democratic order only in which socialist combat can develop." For Mauroy, Poher was at that time the instrumentality by which the socialists could continue their struggle. Several months after the second ballot, Mauroy was, however, for a rapprochement with the PCF.

In 1969 in its congress in Issy-les-Moulineaux the Socialist party voted by a strong majority (2,025 of 3,074) for an *ouverture à gauche.* That decision came only a little more than a month after the party had voted on the second ballot support to Alain Poher in the presidential election of 1969.[51] Consequently, the party now repudiated "all alliance with the political forces representative of capitalism, including those who search for centrist combinations."[52] The party now proclaimed that the "union of the left constitutes the normal axis of socialist strategy."[53] The new policy was a reversal of the party's decision of May 4, 1969, at Alfortville, to abandon the policy of collaboration followed with the Communist party since 1965.[54] The new policy meant defeat for conventional elements of the party that had always had their eyes more toward the center than to the left and that could not bear the thought of an alliance with the Communist party.

When an entirely new Socialist party was created at the Congress of

Epinay-sur-Seine in June 1971,[55] the new organization was more clearly oriented to the left than its predecessor, and, consequently, the idea of a program of government with the PCF no longer remained remote. Delegates to the congress excluded "all third force strategy" and prescribed the getting of a program of government that could be discussed with the Communists.[56]

The Identity Crisis of the Communist Party

The PCF at present seems to be afflicted with an identity crisis, a condition due in part to changes in the international situation—that is, the passing of the cold war, the coming of *détente*, the rise of Eurocommunism—and also to recent domestic transformations within the French left. The PCF, the leading party of the French left after the Liberation, was also the leading party of the left after the advent of the Gaullist republic. Nonetheless, the presidential election of 1974 and recent legislative by-elections have since displaced the PCF as the first party of the French left. Now various formations of the left are regrouping around the Socialist party. This is frightening to the PCF, and leader Georges Marchais does not hesitate to remind his listeners that, if the PS dominates the left, that association will not miss a chance to ditch the PCF and "return to a policy of class collaboration with the grande bourgeoisie."[57] The PCF, says Marchais, cannot risk creation in the country of a combination of forces that will allow the PS to abandon its alliance with the left. Here Marchais is very much aware of Mitterrand's well-known statement articulated in Vienna, June 28, 1972, "I made an alliance with the Communists because I couldn't do otherwise" and "The reconstitution of this historical bloc ... this is the only tactical method available to us."[58]

Jean Elleinstein, a member of the PCF and author of the much publicized book, *Le P.C.*, argues that the evolution of the PCF has been under way for many years; in 1964 the thesis of the *parti unique* was abandoned, and, then, in 1967, the theme of a democratic road to socialism was adopted. In fact, says Elleinstein, the party affirmed very clearly that no other road is possible in France, for the problem of the state today is very different from the problem during the time of Marx and Lenin. The state now can be conquered only by something other than a frontal attack. The conquest only can operate democratically, by the "*guerre de positions*"; it can be carried out only by a long historical process, involving a series of modifications, transformations, and changes in structures. To undo the state—in the sense in which Lenin used the word years ago in *The State and Revolution*—makes little sense in the France of today.

Elleinstein has little use for the Soviet conception of *internationalisme prolétarien*, which presents the Soviet Union as "the model of socialism and the pilot-state." Elleinstein states[59]

I know very few Communists in France who would live under the conditions of the Soviet Union or other countries where there's no liberty of the press, freedom of expression, etc. It is contrary to all the historical practice of French Communists.

The PCF attempted during the late 1960s to give itself more of a "new look," transforming various of its meetings into debates, exposing its leaders to questions—many of them indiscreet—and inviting the attendance of various non-communists. *L'Humanité* began to reproduce accounts of the debates of the party's central committee, not just its resolutions.[60] People began to ask publicly if the new image was in reality with the PCF itself? Others argued that the party had been compelled to change its image because publicly it had changed already its strategy, having supported Mitterrand in 1965, showing that it wished to come to power by a legal path, and having condemned publicly in 1968 the Soviet Union for its military intervention in Czechoslovakia. Attempts were made by the party to show that its version of socialism is really a socialism *à la française*, and Georges Marchais told the country that "The idea that we will do in France what was done in Belgrade, in Sofia, in Prague, or in Moscow is absurd. The situation is no longer the same as it was in 1917 for the workers' movement; the democratic traditions of France are different." And, he added, "I don't have a good meal with vodka, but with wine, because I'm French."[61]

The November 1975 meeting of the central committee of the Communist party was marked by the party's first attempt to define a method of coming to power and arriving at socialism according to the realities of French society.[62] This was followed in 1976 by Marchais's renunciation of the "dictatorship of the proletariat," a step that had been initiated earlier, in 1964, when in the 17th Congress of the PCF reference was made by PCF leaders to the "temporary character of this revolutionary phrase."[63] Although Waldeck-Rochet had said then that it is possible to envisage in France some forms of dictatorship that are less violent and briefer in the passage to socialism, the term itself simply fell into disuse after 1968. The word dictatorship simply was out of tune with the times—and, for that matter, that was true also of the word proletariat.[64] Finally, in the 22nd Congress of the PCF in Saint-Ouen in February 1976, the PCF affirmed its *évolution à l'italienne*. In what was described by Marchais as a historic congress, the party presented the passage to socialism as a continuing process of democratization and not as a rupture of a revolutionary character. The *voie démocratique* dear to PCF leader Georges Marchais had apparently been adopted.[65]

If the PCF has succeeded in forgetting its past, can the French succeed in doing so too—at least on a broad basis? The *légende noire* of the PCF appears in recent years to have softened considerably, as some people concede that the PCF plays in French politics a role that is considered occasionally useful, expressing various social demands and representing disprivileged categories.[66]

Yet, if people are willing to see the party exercise in government certain technical responsibilities, not too many are willing to give the organization direction of national policy, for suspicions remain relative to its intentions.[67]

The Parties of the Left and the Labor Unions

Implementation by the left of a Common Program will be affected in no small way by (1) the ability of the labor unions[68]—primarily the General Federation of Labor (CGT) and the Democratic Federation of Labor (CFDT)— to arrive at a common program of their own and (2) the ability of the labor unions to coordinate their own common program with a Common Program of the left—and at the time of this writing these unions have not worked out this relationship with each other and with the political parties of the left. CFDT leaders Descamps and Jeanson argue that union action involves the responsibility of the unions, not the political parties, that unionism must be the master of its own commitments, and that distinctions must be maintained between unions and political parties "without subordination of one to the other."[69] On the other hand, CGT leader Georges Séguy argues that the union movement—under the pretext of apoliticism—has descended into a paralyzing kind of neutrality and become conservative relative to some of the great contemporary political problems.[70]

The CGT acts for the PCF as a "transmission belt" for a considerable segment of public opinion.[71] Positions adopted publicly by both organizations seldom differ when the questions relate to the economy or, for example, Czechoslovakia or Poland. Conceptions of *rassemblement* advanced by both of these forces tend to be strikingly similar. The CGT's attitude relative to *les gauchistes* is like that of the PCF, a number having been dismissed already from both of their ranks.[72]

Although the CGT and the CFDT both pledge themselves to the acquisition of socialism, both organizations see themselves as having embarked on different roads to it. Edmond Maire, secretary general of the CFDT, is convinced that the CGT follows too closely the PCF, to which the CGT replies that this is but a rhetorical tactic by one overly interested in intervening in its internal affairs.[73] Moreover, the CFDT has posed to the CGT such questions as, Does the CGT foresee effective direction of enterprise by workers, does it endorse economic decentralization, will it support political decentralization, should the defense of socialism lead to reevaluation of certain fundamental liberties, etc., etc.? Both organizations see these areas in dissimilar ways, and they remain from each other still some distance insofar as common action is concerned.[74]

The Center Parties' Flight to the Right

In 1969 Jean-Jacques Servan-Schreiber, or JJSS, as he is commonly known, was installed in the post of secretary general of the PRS and given three months to elaborate a new political platform. Initially, he sought creation of a great center-left force outside the PCF, one positioned between communism and Gaullism, comprising the PRS, the PS, and the centrist parties. That effort failed, as did his subsequent challenge to the majority when he carried his movement into the second district of Bordeaux and ran for the National Assembly as a candidate against Jacques Chaban-Delmas, mayor of Bordeaux and at that time prime minister of France. JJSS's next maneuver consisted of entering with his PRS before and during the legislative elections of 1973 into a working relationship with Jean Lecanuet's CD in a *Mouvement réformateur*, an effort that failed to recruit the large *rassemblement* for which both men had hoped. Before long, JJSS abandoned the opposition and affiliated his party with the majority, supporting Giscard d'Estaing in the presidential election of 1974.

The positioning of Jean Lecanuet and his CD occurred around the same time as that of JJSS and his PRS. Lecanuet's CD maintained its position in the opposition until 1973, when it made its peace with the majority and gave it its support in the country. This maneuver brought both major centrist organizations to a position on the right, and yet it was not until 1976 that representatives of the CD and of the late Jacques Duhamel's CDP met in Rennes for the purpose of merging the two parties in a new organization called the CDS.[75] Jean Lecanuet was elected president of the organization. This latest creation brings back together in one organization two groups that exhibit certain similarities and dissimilarities. Both are supporters of Christian democracy, anti-Communist, pro-Atlantic alliance, and convinced Europeans. Both are reformist, open to dialogue and conciliation, yet there is disagreement between them relative to two related areas. The former CD includes many partisans of proportional representation (although Lecanuet has reservations about it), who argue that the single-member constituency favors bipolarization of the party system. Finally, a number of the former CD people want preelectoral agreements and a strategy based on an agreement between the CDS and the Giscardiens, while many of the supporters of the late Jacques Duhamel are reserved about working with Giscard's Republican party. Nevertheless, the CDS works presently with the majority, even if some members of the Gaullist RPR feel that the CDS may be directed against them eventually.[76]

The Right

Many years ago Charles de Gaulle asked André Malraux the question, "It was you who invented the word Gaullism, wasn't it? What did you mean by it, in the beginning?" Malraux replied, "For the majority of those who followed you, it does not seem to me that your ideology was the major element. The most important thing was something else: during the war, obviously, it was the national will; afterward, and especially since 1958, it was the feeling that your motives, good or bad, were not the motives of the politicians."[77] Gaullism was tied originally in one way or another to outright or partial rejection of the motives of the political class of the Fourth Republic and to resistance to the political institutions associated with that class. After 1958 Gaullism developed its own political class and its own political institutions, and, then, with the passage of time, that new political class was enlarged, comprising many individuals who came from traditional social *milieux* and who were invested with traditional notions. As this happened, Gaullism became more and more of a traditional thing.[78]

The Gaullist organization that was created in 1958 called itself a party. It tried to look like one, and yet at first it was more of a giant formation called into existence because of De Gaulle's presence. The first Gaullist parliamentary party included many people who took time along the way to be elected to the legislature, and the organization was given by De Gaulle only a very limited hand in implementing "conversion processes." Nonetheless, in subsequent years the party succeeded in shaping up internal cohesiveness; it developed greatly its own organization, it survived the departure of De Gaulle, and it evolved internal mechanisms that allowed it to function as a true party. The General was gone, and no longer could the party depend on "signals" from him.

The Gaullist party, the UDR, was reorganized in 1976, primarily at the insistence of its new leader Jacques Chirac, and its name was changed to the Rally for the Republic, RPR.[79] The manifesto of the newly created RPR clearly is antiparty, attributing to the political parties "bad reasons" and "false responses."[80] Revived by the manifesto directly is the theme of opposition to the "regime of parties" and indirectly the idea that a victory of the left in the legislative elections will herald the return of parties and the dominance of the regime of assembly.[81]

Jacques Chirac, leader of the RPR, is among those persons who made it possible for Giscard d'Estaing to become in 1974 president of the French Republic. Chirac—in an effort to head off his Gaullist colleague Chaban-Delmas—threw his weight to Giscard and received for his reward the premiership, which he held for approximately two years. After he was dropped from the post, Chirac contested the dismissal publicly, and since then he has been critical of Giscard, attacking his hesitation and his willingness to compromise. Chirac was joined by Debré and Guéna, and the conflict between the Rally for the Republic parliamentary party and the president of the Republic deepened. The Rally for the Republic parliamentary group swung over to a strategy of "conditional, measured and selective support" for Raymond Barre, Giscard's prime minister, a policy initiated by Chirac and endorsed by the political council of the Rally for the Republic. Chirac then told Barre that he had saved the government for the last time.[82] Moreover, in announcing January 19, 1977, his candidacy for the mayorship of Paris, Chirac challenged Giscard directly, for previously the president of the Republic had nominated for the post M. d'Ornano, his minister of industry and research.[83]

Chirac's strategy is apparent—in his eyes Giscard has lost all credibility, and Premier Barre is weak and no longer the "best" economist in France. Barre's government is portrayed as "mediocre," and his parliamentary support is ill organized. Giscard can no longer be salvaged, and the real leader of the majority, the man truly capable of leading it to victory in 1981 in the presidential elections (earlier if, for example, Giscard could be induced to resign), is Jacques Chirac. There is in other words still a majority, but the atmosphere within it is more than just competitive, bordering on the internecine. The president of the Republic is all but isolated, and within the majority his closest competitor would settle seemingly for nothing less than his banishment. And that competitor appears to have at his disposal virtually unlimited funds (some rumored to be of Middle Eastern origin) in carrying on his contest with the president of the Republic.[84]

Chirac and Giscard remain with each other in competition; nonetheless, they have not terminated the loose collaboration that exists between their respective political parties—for no other combination is for them presently likely. Consequently, the two parties maintain a relationship that is both collaborative and competitive. Giscard's PR asserts its own personality within the majority, declaring that "Nobody will speak in our name nor define our position."[85] Secretary General Jacques Dominati describes most RPR leaders as Chiraquiens who understand nothing and are closed to new ideas; for Dominati, the RPR is "too arrogant" and its leaders—who represent a "page of the past"—merely "want to save their former power."[86] In the meanwhile, the PR likes to inform the public that it is involved seriously in the business of really becoming something and that its membership is growing all the time,[87] even if it is recognized generally that the party was created primarily for the purpose of furthering Giscard's political career and that prospects appear dim for increasing greatly the size of its parliamentary party.

The France of the Future

During the era of De Gaulle the record of the left was that of a long string of tactical errors and frequently impractical recommendations. Left efforts early in the history of the Fifth Republic to return to "government by assembly" involved defense of a system that had demonstrated previously its ineffectiveness and from which public opinion generally had been alienated. The left's campaign in 1962 against De Gaulle's questionably "constitutional" referendum was confused and mismanaged. De Gaulle's regime was riddled with faults, and yet his left opposition was unable to devise an alternative program capable of appealing to the needs of the country and incapable of offering the society the promise of stable government. For years a majority of public opinion appeared unwilling to believe in the opposition's ability to implement an operable order.

Presidents of the Fifth Republic have exercised for years authority that has ranged seemingly from that which is royal to that which is semiroyal (not even premiers have been informed in advance of some decisions taken by some presidents), and presidential declarations have ranged from claims of personal superiority to political parties to milder assertions of nondependence upon them. Recently, however, segments of public opinion have been turning away from this style of leadership and to its opposition, to a left that has made lately much of parties and numerous representations in their behalf. If these parties become the principal actors on the political scene, will they be able to wield successfully the functions expected generally of them? Will they become part of a modern political party system, one that will go in hand with a modern French republic?

The strengthening of French political parties depends seemingly on the implementation of a variety of conditions. First, parties will have to develop further their ability to bring to the front more leaders who inspire public trust as has been done, for example, in the case of the leader of the left, François Mitterrand, for it was not so long ago that those who had reservations about him were almost as numerous as those who supported him. Mitterrand's brain trust brought him along quietly and judiciously, helping him win for himself growing popular support. It remains to be seen whether this can be accomplished with the present leader of the RPR, Jacques Chirac. Second, if parties are going to attract the populace, it would seem that they will have to develop closer ties with it. Continuing loud declarations by the parties in behalf of pluralist democracy are likely to continue to ring hollow if the designation of important party candidates continues to be the result of manipulations by small numbers of influential people, as was the case in 1965 with presidential candidates Defferre, Lecanuet, and Mitterrand and in 1974 with Giscard. Third, the parties will have to show their willingness to allow youthful leaders to come to the fore and contend seriously for important posts in them. Handing candidacies to those politically dead is not going to win the support of the young. Fourth, the parties will have to search out the support of as many social categories as prove to be accessible and not flinch when they are accused of trying to act as "catchall" parties.[88] Any party, either of the left or the right, will have slight chance for its candidate to win the presidency on the basis of its own electorate; consequently, increasing dependence by parties on multiple and overlapping electorates generally will serve as a condition of future success in presidential contests. Fifth, further strengthening of parties may depend more on future successes of the left than on victories of the right, for, during the brief history of the Fifth Republic, the relationship between party and the left has been closer than between party and the right; that is, the latter has shown only too frequently a preference for movements that resemble party but that fall short of it (although this is not to say that all men of the left have always been party men consistently, for who could say that entirely about Defferre's first presidential candidacy or, for that matter, Mitterrand's?). Finally, persistent left failures in future electoral contests could contribute possibly to a growing sense of hopelessness on the part of left electors and detract from revitalization of the political parties, contributing to their further devastation and placing on a less solid footing French republicanism.

Notes

1. The political party system includes the Communist party (*Parti communiste français*), the Unified Socialist party (*Parti socialiste unifié*), the Socialist party (*Parti socialiste*), the Radicals of the Left (*Mouvement des Radicaux de gauche*), the Radical Socialist party (*Parti radical-socialiste*), the Center of Social Democrats (*Centre des démocrates-sociaux*), the Rally for the Republic (*Rassemblement pour la République*), the Republican party (*Parti républicain*), and the Independent party (*Centre national des indépendants*). Excluded from this list are a number of smaller parties too insignificant to mention here. The Communist party was formed in the schism in 1920 at the Congress of Tours when the old unified socialists (SFIO) broke into several parts. As an upshot of this rupture, a new rump party, SFIO (*Section française d'Internationale Ouvrière*), was created during the same year and lasted until 1971, when it was replaced by the present Socialist party (PS). The Unified Socialist party (PSU) was created in 1958, in reaction to the SFIO's policy on Algeria and the treatment extended to the association's minority by its late leader Secretary General Guy Mollet. The Radicals of the Left (MRG) are an offshoot of the Radical Socialist party (PRS) consisting of individuals who until 1978 subscribed to the Common Program of the Left, adhered to also by the Socialist and Communist parties. The PRS, created late in the nineteenth century, was once France's largest and most influential parties. The Center of Social Democrats (CDS) is a new creation that absorbed in 1977 both the Center for Democracy and Progress (*Centre de la démocratie et du progrès*) and the Democratic Center (*Centre démocrate*), associations that had acted as successors to the old Popular Republican party, MRP (*Mouvement républicain populaire*). The Rally for the Republic (RPR) is the name adopted in 1976 by the Gaullist party, an organization that has undergone ten name changes. The Republican party (PR) is the name, adopted in 1977 by the former Independent Republican party, FNRI (*Fédération nationale des républicains indépendents*), of President Giscard d'Estaing. The Independent party, one of the major associations of the Fourth Republic, is important today only because of the number of mayorships it holds; approximate membership claims are PC, 600,000; PS, 160,000; CDS, 30,000; PRS, 60,000; and RPR, 270,000.
2. Georges Lavau, *Partis politiques et réalités sociales*, Paris: Colin, 1953, p. 155.
3. Lavau, p. 156.
4. Lavau, p. 157.

5. Lavau, p. 157.

6. Maurice Duverger, *Political Parties*, New York: Wiley, 1954, p. 234.

7. Leon D. Epstein, *Political Parties in Western Democracies*, New York: Praeger, 1967, p. 70.

8. Epstein, p. 70.

9. Epstein, p. 70.

10. Raymond Aron, *Immuable et changeante*, Paris: Calmann-Lévy, 1959, p. 67.

11. Aron, p. 67.

12. Maurice Duverger, "The Development of Democracy in France," in Henry W. Ehrmann, ed., *Democracy in a Changing Society*, New York: Praeger, 1964, p. 71. As Duverger explains, ". . . it was a republic which . . . was able to create a State, to dispose of an opposition that originated in the struggles of the previous century, and to preserve great internal freedom."

13. Pierre Viansson-Ponté, "Prélude à la campagne. II. Le nouveau parti," *Le Monde*, July 7, 1966, p. 6.

14. It should be noted that political clubs have not attained the popularity predicted of them by some observers. As Georges Lavau says, the clubs risk living perpetually at the side of and in the margin of the political system. See Janine Mossuz, *Les clubs et la politique en France*, Dossiers U2, Paris: Colin, 1970, p. 54 for Lavau's comments.

15. Despite, at the time of this writing, some antagonisms between the two.

16. See, for example, *Le Monde*, October 12, 1971, p. 8 for an address of Giscard three years before he became president of the Republic in which he told his Independent Republican party delegates assembled in the annual congress that he was not a "political man," that his movement was based not on a political machine, professionals or "old foxes," and that it was more of an expression of civic spirit than a political party. See also *Le Monde*, December 23, 1976, p. 6 and Giscard's statement that "the President of the Republic is above parties: the President of the Republic is not a party leader," and his denouncement of "the excessive influence" of the political party movement. See *Le Monde*, May 11, 1977, p. 7 and Giscard's statement that he wishes "*éviter que la France retombe dans le regime des partis*" See also *Le Monde*, November 19, 1971, p. 1 for views of Giscard's predecessor, the late Georges Pompidou, expressed in the 1971 Strasbourg meeting of the Union of Democrats for the Fifth Republic (UDR) where he stated that the UDR should remain a "movement" and guard against becoming a "party."

17. All data appearing in this section are drawn from the following sources: "Les élections législatives des 4 et 11 mars 1973," *Sondages*, no. 1, 1973, pp. 15–19; "Les forces politiques et les élections de mars 1973," *Un dossier du Monde*. Supplément aux "Dossiers et Documents du Monde," March 1973; Alain Duhamel, "La structure sociologique de l'électorate," in "La vie politique de novembre 1964 à avril 1966," *Sondages*, no. 2, 1966, pp. 3–9.

18. The 1958 electoral law is a Gaullist creation modeled on that of the Third Republic. Voting is confined to single-member constituencies, two ballots required if no candidate is elected by a majority on the first, a plurality sufficing on the second. Numerical discrepancies among the electoral districts are considerable; also great is the range of discrepancies between the least and more populated

districts. Twenty-six of the 491 districts contain fewer than 40,000 voters each, whereas 43 comprise more than 85,000 voters each. Twelve districts contain more than 100,000 voters each. Fifteen of the least densely populated constituencies—situated in Paris—are in a state of continuing population decline. Electoral districts comprising fewer than 40,000 registered voters each exist within the four least populated departments of France—the Alpes-de-haute Provence, Hautes-Alpes, Lozère, and the territory of Belfort—all areas of continuing population decline. The largest electoral districts of France, however, are in areas of ascending population, with new influxes taking place in them each year. The 20 smallest districts had 705,147 registered voters in 1967, 694,849 in 1968, and 676,835 in 1973. The 20 largest districts comprised 1,840,046 voters in 1967, 1,842,914 in 1968, and 2,097,409 in 1973. In fact, between 1968 and 1973 the electoral population of the third district of the Essone acquired an additional 29,409 voters—a gain superior to the number of voters in each electoral district of the Lozère, in the second district of the territory of Belfort, and in the second district of the Hautes-Alpes. In the entire department of the Essone, 431,440 registered voters were entitled in 1973 to four deputies, whereas in the department of the Allier 243,648 registered voters also were represented by the same number of deputies. In other words, France—despite the existence in it of notions of equality which are both juridical and social—is clearly not a country of "one person, one vote." For additional data, see the article by Michel Belinski and Frédéric Bon, "Un homme, une voix. II. Les inégalités," *Le Monde*, December 27, 1974, p. 5.

19. Proportional representation is favored also by the PS and the MRG.

20. *Le Monde*, December 25, 1976, p. 5.

21. See Maurice Duverger's discussion of this in "La loi de la majorité," *Le Monde*, July 11–12, 1971, pp. 1, 4. See also *Le Monde*, April 22, 1977, and premier Barre's statement that he does not exclude modification of the electoral law.

22. Maurice Duverger suggests this in his "Le gadget électoral," *Le Monde*, April 19, 1977, pp. 1, 10.

23. See *Le Monde*, March 14, 1973, p. 1. The Gaullist forces established in the assembly a majority of 99 seats, although the total number of votes realized in the country by the left on the second ballot exceeded that of the "majority." Left formations received on the second ballot 46.0% of the vote cast, whereas the Gaullist formation obtained 46.3%.

24. Jacques Fauvet, "Equité," *Le Monde*, March 13, 1973, pp. 1, 4.

25. See *Le Monde*, March 8, 1973, p. 6. According to first-ballot analyses conducted by Frédéric Bon, Jerome Jaffre, and Colette Ysmal in behalf of the *Société d'information appliquée*, an expanding non-Communist left took away from the Communist left votes in traditional strongholds of the conservative right—that is, Britanny, Loire, and Lorraine. The Socialists also blocked the Communists in the Paris region, although in areas where the Socialists traditionally have been a force, Socialist-Communist competition was to the advantage of the Communists—in Acquitaine, Languedoc-Roussillon, Provence-Cote-d'Azur, and Nord. Loss by the Socialist party of traditional votes was accompanied, however, by gains in regions considered previously by the Socialists as *terres de mission*, places where left influence had been weak—in Haute-Normandie, Basse-Normandie, Bretagne, Lorraine, and the Paris region. The majority of these votes appear to have been derived from the center.

26. In the municipal elections of March 13 and 20, 1977, the PS took 27 new cities, including Montpellier, Nantes, and Rennes, and the PCF took 12 more including Bourges, Le Mans and Saint-Etienne. In all, Socialists passed in cities of more than 30,000 inhabitants from 46 to control of 81, and the Communists from 50 to 72. The opposition now controls 159 of the 221 cities of more than 30,000 inhabitants in place of 103 previously. Fifty-five of these cities went from the majority to the opposition, whereas 3 went from the opposition to the majority. Public response to the majority was clearly negative, although it retained control of such important cities as Paris, Bordeaux, Rouen, Strasbourg, Lyon, Nice, and Toulouse. For results of both ballotings, see *Le Monde*, March 15 and 22, 1977, and Jacques Fauvet, "Un phénomène de rejet," *Le Monde*, March 22, 1977, p. 1, who states that the victory by the left was too extensive, geographically and demographically, not to be interpreted as a strong desire for change. He also states that the left success in the provinces and Chirac's victory in Paris in winning the mayorship constituted a double defeat for Giscard.

27. Had the left parties won the elections and returned to the National Assembly a left majority, a political crisis involving the presidential office would not have been unlikely—for the late President Pompidou had announced just prior to the elections that he was not a "slave" of the National Assembly and that he was not compelled by the constitution to appoint a prime minister from the left if the latter won a majority in the National Assembly. Fortunately for him, the Gaullist coalition claimed in the elections a majority, and a political crisis was thereby averted. Nevertheless, if in the years to come, France elects presidents of the Republic and majorities in the National Assembly that are of different and opposed political persuasions, will this impair the system to the point where the presidential office is incapable of functioning, or will presidents learn to accommodate hostile party majorities in the National Assembly and pick their cabinets—however reluctantly—from them? Whatever the turn of events, it is unlikely that French presidents yielding to a hostile majority can become simply inactive and virtually "retire" while continuing to remain in office, for since 1962 presidents of the Fifth Republic have been elected by universal suffrage and are expected, consequently, to fill a political role.

28. Under the law of July 19, 1976, candidates were eligible to appear on the second ballot if they had at least 12.5% of the registered vote obtained on the first ballot. In cases in which only one candidate satisfied these conditions, the candidate obtaining on the first ballot the greatest number of votes as runner-up could run on the second ballot. If all candidates failed to satisfy these conditions, the two leading candidates on the first ballot were eligible to appear on the second ballot.

29. See *Le Monde*, March 15, 1978, p. 13 for results of the first ballot supplied by the Ministry of the Interior; see the study of 1,719 candidates invested on the first ballot by seven major parties (RPR, PR, CDS, PRS, MRG, PS, PCF) authored by Gilles Fabre-Rosane and Alain Guède, "Une sociologie des candidats des grandes formations," *Le Monde*, March 17, 1978, p. 13. Females constituted 6.34% of the candidates, the PCF leading all parties with 13.2%. "Young" candidates were those of the left, PS candidates averaging 43 years, 5 months, PCF 44 years, MRG 45 years, 3 months. The PRS were an exception, averaging 43 years. Within the majority, the CDS averaged 46 years, 8 months, the PR 47 years, the RPR 48 years. The party with the greatest percentage of high civil servants was the PR, with 10%, the PCF the lowest, with zero. The party with the greatest percentage of

graduates of the National School of Administration was the PR with 5.6%. The party with the greatest percentage of leaders of enterprise and high executives was the PRS, whereas the MRG appeared as the party with the greatest percentage in the liberal professions. Teachers constituted 38.7% of the PS candidates, workers 32.3% of the PCF candidates. The PR led in the percentage of candidates belonging to well-to-do categories (i.e., high civil servants, leaders of enterprise, high executives, liberal professions).

30. *Le Monde*, March 19–20, 1978, p. 8. They were 30 RPR, 16 PR, 7 presidential majority, 6 CDS, 4 PCF, 3 CNIP, 1 PRS, and 1 accredited to the PS.

31. See *Le Monde*, March 16, 1978, p. 12 for details of the "duels." The RPR put up 217 of its candidates against 84 PCF, 21 PS, 10 MRG, and 1 *divers* opposition. The PR ran 93 of its candidates against 25 PCF, 63 PS, and 5 MRG. The CDS ran 16 candidates against the PCF, 28 against the PS, and managed to be on hand in 47 districts. Twenty-six candidates of the *majorité présidentielle* went against 9 PCF, 16 PS, and 1 MRG, while 16 PRS went against 8 PCF, 7 PS, and 1 MRG. The CNIP presented itself only in 9 districts, against 3 PCF and 6 PS. The PS presented candidates in 241 districts, whereas the PCF was present in 145—contesting in 11 departments all of the districts. Finally, in some districts some candidates of the majority combatted each other—that is, 2 PR versus 2 RPR, 1 UDR versus 1 RPR, and 2 CDS versus 2 RPR.

32. *Le Monde*, March 16, 1978, p. 10.

33. *Le Monde*, March 21, 1978, p. 3. Fifty-seven deputies elected carried over their adversaries by one percentage point.

34. See *Le Monde*, March 21, 1978, p. 2 for list of these districts.

35. *Le Monde*, March 21, 1978, p. 5.

36. *Le Monde*, March 16, 1978, p. 10. The PCF had suggested between the first and second ballots that a future cabinet of the left be staffed on the basis of the respective strengths of the left parties, an offer that was rejected by both the PS and the MRG—a fact that probably was unknown to many electors. See also *Le Monde*, March 9, 1978, p. 7 for remarks by Raymond Barre that Mitterrand is not Paul Ramadier or Jules Moch and therefore unable to provide a barrier against Communism.

37. See the description of the roles played by all three in Denis Lindon and Pierre Weill, "Pourquoi la gauche a-t-elle perdu?," *Le Monde*, March 31, 1978, p. 10.

38. Jacques Fauvet, "Un vainqueur," *Le Monde*, March 21, 1978, pp. 1, 5. Ibid., p. 5. Fauvet minimizes the significance of economic crisis within some regions and argues that it is less severe or less resented than was thought previously.

39. Ibid., p. 5. Fauvet minimizes the significance of economic crisis within some regions and argues that it is less severe or less resented than was thought previously.

40. *Le Monde*, March 21, 1978, p. 6. Jean-Pierre Soisson, secretary general of the Republican party, says that "Jacques Chirac suivra, Jacques Chirac suivra" ("Jacques Chirac will follow, Jacques Chirac will follow").

41. *Le Monde*, March 22, 1978, p. 8. See the bitter statements made by the PS against the PCF after the defeat. Some accuse Marchais of having served the right; that it was not the union of the left but its disunion that caused the defeat—a disunion

deliberately provoked by the leadership of the PCF which was determined to arrest the progress of the PS, etc., etc. It should be said here, however, that a portion of the left wing of the PS—particularly CERES—remains an ardent defender of the Common Program and argues that it is not terminated.

42. Two methods have been employed in the Fifth Republic for electing a president; the first in 1958, was indirect, restricted to an electoral college of approximately 80,000 voters, whereas the second—adopted in 1962 as the result of a constitutional amendment—is direct and universal.

43. *Le nouvel observateur*, September 25, 1965, p. 4.

44. For official text of the Common Program, see *Programme commun de gouvernement du parti communiste et du parti socialiste*, Paris: Editions sociales, 1972. For lengthy resumé of the agreement, see *Le Monde*, June 29, 1972, pp. 6, 7. The brief outline contained above is based on the initial agreement of 1972 and not on modifications made of it subsequently; the Common Program is without precedent in French history, bearing no analogy to the Popular Front agreements of 1936. The program of the Popular Front was designed specifically for common acceptance by diverse groups and prior agreement was obtained on adoption of a nonsocialist program. The program was considerably diffused, containing a series of broad prescriptions relative to domestic and foreign problems. The PCF demanded that the program remain free from socialism, despite pleas to the contrary by some PS leaders. When the Popular Front government came to office in 1936, Premier Léon Blum explained to the country that "our's is not a socialist government, and we do not seek either directly or insiduously to institute a socialist program, but we are working with entire loyalty within the framework of existing society and legal institutions under the present regime of property. . . . We must work within the capitalistic regime as long as we do not have a clear majority." See Léon Blum, *L'exercice du pouvoir; discours prononcés de mai 1963 à 1937*, 7e éd., Paris: Gallimard, 1937, pp. 67, 70–71, 347–348.

45. See the interview with Marchais, "Ce qui fait peur aux français," *Le nouvel observateur*, no. 43, February 12–18, 1973, pp. 32–33.

46. *Le Monde*, December 3–4, 1972, p. 5.

47. This is in spite of the fact that determination of the details was two-thirds completed as of July 1977, according to *L'express*, August 7, 1977, pp. 28–29.

48. See *Le Monde*, January 29, 1976, p. 8 for report on the Jospin *rapport*. Various members of the PS described the piece as the *Rapport sur l'état de l'Union*.

49. *Le Monde*, January 29, 1976, p. 8.

50. See, however, Mollet's statement in *Le Monde*, January 16, 1971, p. 8 and his reasons for his common list with the Communists in the municipal elections: "It's a normal evolution for reasons of a local character as well as national. After 1965 a fruitful dialogue existed between the PCF and the SFIO, followed by the common candidacy of François Mitterrand in the presidential elections of 1965 and by the recovery of the left in the legislative elections of 1967. The evolution has been rapid since 1968, thanks in particular to Waldeck Rochet who is somewhat the 'John XXIII' of the Communist party. . . . The birth of the new Socialist party marks a certain radicalization of positions in the search for an opening to the left. Inside the party, I have become one of the defenders of the opening to the left and of its existence."

51. *Le Monde*, July 15, 1969, p. 1.

52. *Le Monde*, July 15, 1969, p. 1.

53. *Le Monde*, July 15, 1969, p. 1.

54. The PS had abandoned at the Congress of Alfortville the policy of collaboration with the PCF followed between 1965 and early 1968. The party returned during the presidential election of 1969 to a policy of centrism setting the stage for Alain Poher to run second on the first ballot in order to win on the second ballot and present the country with a third-force majority.

55. *Le Monde*, June 13–14, 1971, p. 22.

56. See *Le Monde*, June 15, 1971, p. 1 for address of Mitterrand to Congress and his request that the new PS (1) regain the ground lost already to the PCF and (2) engage in a public dialogue with the PCF on concrete action, dates, and program, thought that dialogue should not be ideological: "There will be no electoral alliance, there will be no electoral program, there will be no common majority if there is not a contract of the majority, if there is not a government of the left, if there is no contract of government. In order to know what we are going to do, it is precisely that we must discuss it." The observer should notice that in the congress the majority and minority motions were supported by almost the same number of delegates. Mitterrand's received 43,926 and Savary's 41,757, with 3,925 abstentions.

57. See *Le Monde*, November 13, 1975, pp. 1, 13 for remarks by Marchais; see also *Le Monde*, July 18, 1975, p. 1 for a report of Mitterrand's comments in the Socialist party publication *Unité* on the report presented by Marchais on June 23, 1972 to the central committee of the Communist party. Marchais questioned Socialist sincerity of commitment to left unity and Socialist ideology, which he describes as strictly reformist. Mitterrand, in turn, commented caustically on a strategy that consists of constructing an alliance with Socialist partners who are "so doubtful."

58. *Le Monde*, March 20, 1975, p. 9.

59. "Un communiste juge les communistes," *Le nouvel observateur*, no. 617, September 6–12, 1976, pp. 60–74.

60. *L'Express*, no. 1047, August 2–8, 1971, pp. 14, 15.

61. *L'Express*, no. 1047, August 2–8, 1971, pp. 14, 15.

62. *Le Monde*, November 13, 1975, pp. 1, 13.

63. *Le Monde*, January 9, 1976, p. 1.

64. See, however, Georges Many and his interview with Louis Althusser, "De bon usage des contradictions," *Le nouvel observateur*, February 28–March 6, 1977, no. 642, p. 25. Althusser referred to the XXII Congress of the PCF as "an event without precedent in the history of the party, because of its elimination of the theme of the dictatorship of the proletariat." Nevertheless, Althusser says, "If I had been a delegate I never would have voted the amendment for suppression of this notion." The great innovation of the congress, says Althusser, has been to affirm that the strategy called the "Common Program" must lead to socialism and must be democratic and peaceful. He says that Marchais may see a *bonne voie* and a global approach to the crisis in the system of the domination of *grand capital*, but Althusser sees perhaps a chaotic transition.

65. *Le Monde*, February 10, 1976, p. 6.

66. See discussion of this in Georges Lavau, "Le parti communiste dans le systeme francais," in *Le communisme en France* (Paris: Colin, 1969), pp. 7–81. Lavau says that the party's role has been generally that of a critic of government, whose criticism prevented for years the system from functioning in "excessive security and sterile conformity."

67. See "L'opinion d'aout 1975 à aout 1976," *Sondages*, nos. 3–4, 1976, pp. 28–29. In this survey, 44% of respondents are favorable, 19% opposed. Nevertheless, apprehension about a PCF role in the government is expressed by respondents in certain sensitive areas. See, for example, "L'opinion d'aout 1974 à juillet 1975," *Sondages*, nos. 3–4, 1975, p. 51: good for individual liberties 25%, bad 43%, no opinion 32%; good for national independence 23%, bad 40%, no opinion 37%.

68. *Le Monde*, January 26, 1977, p. 35. Union membership claims (including retirees) are CGT (*Confédération générale du travail*) 2,300,000; CFDT (*Confédération francaise démocratique du travail*) 820,490; FO (*Force Ouvrière*) 900,000; CFTC (*Confédération francaise de travailleurs chrétiens*) 225,000; CGC (*Confédération générale des cadres*) 250,000; FEN (*Fédération d'éducation nationale*) 550,000.

69. See André Jeanson, "La CFDT à pied d'oeuvre," *Le Monde*, June 14–15, 1970, p. 7. See in the same issue a report on the three questions asked in 1970 of CGT leader Séguy and CFDT leader Descamps relative to relationships between labor unions and political parties in a socialist society.

70. See *Le Monde*, October 26, 1976, p. 33. Séguy says that the CGT supports the Common Program of the left, "And there's no point or need of preliminary negotiations between the unions and the left in order to define the future social and economic program of the government. That's been done already with the Common Program. It's simply a case of applying it. . . ."

71. See *Le Monde*, November 23–24, 1969, pp. 1, 28. Although Séguy says that the CGT "has no need of political tutelage," CGT leaders show no inclination to renounce their responsibilities within the PCF. Séguy insists, however, that CGT members have outside their organization free choice in political activities, although they may not be elected to posts in political organizations. Séguy states that "The experiences of the CGT demonstrate the evidence that union independence can perfectly accommodate liberty, leaving to union militants to occupy the functions that their party judges useful to confide in them." He asks that party militants abstain from interference in the affairs of the union and that they respect its free determination, its statutes, its programs, and its rules. He concludes that the CGT does want some alliances with left parties based on the working class, although he says that he refuses to any the status of a "privileged partner." See also Georges Séguy, *Lutter* (Paris: Stock, 1976). Séguy places the number of CGT members who belong to the PCF at 250,000–300,000, leaving more than 2 million members who do not belong to the PCF. See *Le Monde*, April 30, 1975, p. 36. Séguy states that nothing in the statutes of the CGT prevents him from belonging to the PCF.

72. *Le Monde*, April 14, 1972, p. 33.

73. *Le Monde*, March 9, 1972, pp. 1, 8.

74. See *Sondages*, no. 3, 1972, pp. 104, 109, 110, 133. As of June 1971, respondents

interrogated by the IFOP were receptive to strong unionism, but one that is limited, nonetheless, in its objectives. There appeared a preference for merger of the different unions in one great organization. Fear was expressed among respondents other than PCF voters that the unions are too political. The strength and the style of the CGT was viewed as in excess of the CFDT and regarded as more left, more militant, and closer to the workers. Finally, respondents estimated that union wage demands play less of a role in social progress than economic expansion or government decisions, although union negotiations à chaud of the Matignon or Grenelle type, supported by economic expansion, was considered one of the surest promoters of social progress.

75. For the Congress of Rennes, see Le Monde, May 25, 1976, pp. 1, 8.

76. See statements at Congress of Rennes, Le Monde, May 25, 1976, pp. 1, 8.

77. See André Malraux, Felled Oaks: Conversation with de Gaulle, New York: Holt, Rinehart, 1971, p. 82.

78. Works on Gaullology have become so numerous that no attempt is made to list them here.

79. Chirac had argued in 1971 that the political parties—because of their organization— are incapable of responding to citizens' demands and that they are more like screens between citizens and government. His statements, made when he was ministre délégué chargé des relations avec le Parlement, are reproduced in Le Monde, November 25, 1971. Consequently, some deputies began to refer to him as ministre chargé de la liquidation de Parlement. See Maurice Duverger, "M. Chirac et l'héritage gaulliste," Le Monde, December 18, 1976, p. 1. Commenting on the reorganization, Duverger states, "No democratic party is organized on so autocratic a model. . . . It's not normal to introduce in a democratic party procedures of a conseil du roi"; the reorganization was opposed by Gaullist and former premier Jacques Chaban-Delmas who states that now there is danger that the organization may represent only one of two camps. For comments, see Le Monde, December 5–6, 1976, pp. 1, 12–13, and André Passeron, "L'Élysee et les initiatives de M. Chirac," Le Monde, December 5–6, 1976, pp. 1, 12.

80. For a copy of the manifesto, see Le Monde, December 1, 1976, p. 8. The manifesto urges defense of national independence, support for national defense and the force de frappe, construction of Europe (although the word used to describe Europe is ensemble), rigorous management of public funds, development of science and technology, pursuance of contractual policies for labor, development of worker participation in enterprise, fiscal reform, support for local government, support for the family, and support for the institutions of the Fifth Republic. These themes were repeated by Chirac in his address to the RPR in Verseilles, reported in Le Monde, December 9, 1976, p. 9.

81. Expression of this theme appeared also in Giscardian Poniatowski's address to the 3rd Congress of the GSL (Mouvement génération sociale et liberale), the young Giscardians, reported in Le Monde, December 14, 1976, p. 9.

82. Le Monde, May 3, 1977, p. 1.

83. Le Monde, January 30–31, 1977, pp. 1, 6–7. Premier Barre states that Chirac announced his nomination for the Paris mayorship without consultation with the majority and Giscard. See for reproduction of the letters exchanged between Chirac and Barre in which Chirac complains of "mediocre attitudes," "Florentine

combinations," and the "aggressive attitudes and bad will" of some government ministers. Barre's reply emphasized that Chirac's mayorship campaign would divide the majority.

84. Chirac's press has been recently on the upswing, for it was not long ago that Duverger wrote in *Le Monde*, December 18, 1974, p. 10, that Chirac should not let his "authoritarian temperament" push him toward a "kind of fascism." See, however, *Le Figaro* January 28, 1977, p. 1, where its former writer Raymond Aron argues that there are understandable aspects of Chirac's recent behavior—for example, the Rally for the Republic is the largest party of the majority and yet it lost the presidency in 1974, then the Rally for the Republic lost the premiership to an academician from outside the parties, and, finally, the Rally for the Republic was threatened with the loss of Paris' mayorship, after the "arbitration," it is said, of premier Barre.

85. *Le Monde*, May 5, 1971, p. 10.

86. *Le Monde*, April 16–17, 1975, p. 1.

87. *Le Monde*, July 29, 1975, p. 11. Dominati states that the PR had as of this date more than 25,000 members and that it expected to gain within three months at least 50,000 members!

88. See, for example, the article much resented by some elements of the PS, Roland Cayrol and Jerome Jaffre, "Y a-t-il plusieurs électorats socialistes?," *Le Monde*, March 22, 1977, p. 10. The authors question whether the growing strength of the Socialist party will change the party. They state that 19% of the Socialist electorate consists of people who—on the second ballot in the presidential election of 1974— voted for Giscard. Inasmuch as those Socialist electors who voted Giscard in 1974 clearly are more conservative than those Socialist electors who voted Mitterrand, they ask whether there are two Socialist electorates and whether the party will become a "catch-all" party, and a party of government, without seriously modifying its political attitudes?

CHAPTER 5

ITALY

Raphael Zariski

THE ITALIAN PARTY SYSTEM, as with the party system of any Western democracy, can be viewed from a variety of perspectives. Giovanni Sartori sees the Italian party system as being characterized by extreme pluralism, possessing at least five "relevant" parties. It is also marked by a high degree of polarization; that is, there are right and left extreme poles of the system, each represented by a powerful extremist party, and these poles are separated by a great ideological distance. And, finally, the extreme pluralist system displays strong centrifugal tendencies—the extremist parties tend to gain at the expense of the center.[1]

A second approach to the Italian party system is that of Giorgio Galli. He sees the Italian party system as an "imperfect two-party system," with the Communist party (PCI) and the Christian Democratic party (DC) getting the lion's share of the votes, while the other parties—consigned to the status of permanent satellites of the two major parties—can only hope to be junior partners in a cabinet coalition. Given their mass memberships, their financial strength, their close ties with affiliated pressure groups and (in the case of the Christian Democrats) with certain public enterprises, and their well-articulated grass-roots party organizations, these two giant parties have simply not been in the same league with their smaller competitors.[2]

A third approach, which appears in the writings of many students of Italian politics, is the stability thesis. According to this view, the Italian party system is remarkably stable and immobile. Elections tend to have a minimal effect on party strength in Parliament, for parties tend to make only marginal gains or suffer only marginal losses. Voters display an amazing fidelity to their respective political subcultures—Barnes uses the term "tradition" to embrace

122

ideology and organization as well as subculture[3]—and, when they *do* shift from one party to another, it is usually *within* the left or *within* the center or *within* the right. Among the reasons given for the stable voting habits of the Italian electorate are (1) the very high degree of party identification in Italy, reenforced by the strong socializing influence of such one-party regional milieus, as is seen by leftist Emilia or the Catholic Veneto, and (2) the very high turnout in Italian elections (close to 90%), which has the effect of reducing the number of "floating voters" who do so much to inject the element of unpredictability into British and French elections.[4]

These are only a few of a potentially large number of perspectives from which Italian parties may be observed. A complex and crisis-ridden party system has elicited a heterogeneous body of scholarly literature. In this chapter we shall describe briefly (1) the component elements of the party system, (2) the main features of the party system, (3) the role of party factions, (4) the emergence of the parties in the late nineteenth and early twentieth centuries, (5) the characteristics and goals of the various parties, (6) the more significant aspects of party organization and party functions in Italy, (7) the membership and leadership composition of the main parties, (8) the major sources of party voting strength, (9) the electoral system, (10) the main campaign techniques, and (11) the role of Italian parties in the larger political system of which they form a part.

The Party System: A Preliminary Overview

Italy has a multiparty system, which is to say that more than two relevant parties exist. The dominant party on the extreme left is the PCI, which received 34.4% of the votes cast in the elections for the Chamber of Deputies in 1976. To the left of the PCI is a small militant splinter party of left-wing Marxists, the Democratic Party of Proletarian Unity (PDUP), which polled a scanty 1.5% of the votes in 1976. Another small and intransigent party of the left, particularly concerned about such life-style issues as abortion and women's liberation, is the Radical party (PR): in 1976, it garnered 1.1% of the votes. Finally, there are *two* democratic Socialist parties, the Italian Socialist party (PSI) and the somewhat more moderate Italian Social Democratic party (PSDI). Their respective shares of the total vote in 1976 were 9.6% and 3.4%. If we exclude the PSDI which is perhaps more centrist than leftist, the left vote in 1976 was 46.6% of the total number of valid votes.

Moving to the center of the political spectrum, we have already noted the PSDI with its 3.4% of the votes. A rather progressive party of the center is the Republican party (PRI) with 3.1% of the votes in 1976. On the moderate right, acting as a democratic opposition party and once representing the views of a significant segment of the Northern big business community, is the Italian

Liberal party (PLI), which received only 1.5% of the votes in 1976. Finally, ranging across a large portion of the Italian political spectrum from the moderate left to the moderate right, is the DC, the dominant party in the Italian system, with 38.7% of the votes in 1976. Because the DC is generally, despite its great variety of internal factions and tendencies, considered to be a party of the center, we may conclude that the center parties in Italy obtained a 46.9% share of the total vote.

The extreme right of the political spectrum has been sharply reduced in recent years. The declining Monarchist party (PDIUM) merged with the Neo-Fascist party, whose official title is Italian Social Movement (MSI), several years ago. And the MSI share of the total vote in 1976 was only 6.1%.[5] Even this relatively weak party has been further divided since the June 1976 elections, however. In December 1976, half the MSI deputies and a majority of the MSI senators seceded to form a new right-wing party, National Democracy (DN), which renounced any association with the fascist past.

As Sartori has pointed out, the Italian party system has been characterized by "polarized pluralism."[6] It has an extreme left pole (the PCI), an extreme right pole (the MSI), and a dominant center pole (the DC). Also there has been a marked centrifugal tendency, with the DC and the other center parties losing some ground over the past 20 years and the Communists steadily gaining strength. The PCI has steadily expanded its share of the total vote: 22.6% in 1953, 22.7% in 1958, 25.3% in 1963, 26.9% in 1968, 27.2% in 1972, and—in a great leap forward—34.4% in 1976.[7]

On the other end of the political spectrum, the MSI shows a much less consistent pattern: 5.8% in 1953, 4.8% in 1958, 5.1% in 1963, 4.4% in 1968, 8.7% in 1972, and 6.1% in 1976. There is fluctuation here rather than steady progress, so that Sartori's centrifugal effect appears to hold true only for the extreme left pole.

Another way to measure centrifugal tendencies, however, is to take the combined vote of the PCI and MSI. And here we see a pattern of steady almost unbroken forward progress: 28.4% in 1953, 27.5% in 1958, 30.4% in 1963, 31.3% in 1968, 35.9% in 1972, and 40.5% in 1976. Of course, it must be pointed out that the gains being made by the combined extremes are really reflections of Communist progress. Also, some scholars would argue with Sartori's view of the PCI as an antisystem or extremist party and would suggest that the PCI has moved closer to the center of the political spectrum and has developed a vested interest in the status quo. With these provisos, we can still conclude that the Sartori thesis has so far been partly confirmed.

In Italy's pluralist party system, the dominant DC can never be fully ousted from office. With almost 40% of the seats in the Chamber of Deputies, its support is indispensable for the survival of any cabinet coalition that does not include the PCI. A setback for the DC in a general election would, at the most, induce it to change allies. Sartori refers to this process as "peripheral turnover."[8] Because alternation in power is out of the question, the Communists are fully aware of the fact that they will not be called on to take primary responsibility for governing the country and delivering on their promises. This painful truth is even more evident to the PSI and the minor center parties, which can only aspire to be junior partners of the DC. A sense of impotence breeds petulance and irresponsibility. Meanwhile, faced with no credible challenge to its rule, the DC can safely put off vital decisions that might hurt the party's interclass image. In the light of Sartori's and Di Palma's analysis, the immobilism of the Italian political system becomes understandable.[9] But one recent development may be heralding a new era in Italian politics: since 1976, the PCI has become a credible alternative to the DC. Peripheral turnover may be replaced by alternation in office.

We may refer briefly to some other striking characteristics of the Italian party system. First, there is the presence of a dominant party, the DC, which has headed every Italian cabinet since December 1945. The DC appeals to virtually all segments of Italy's electorate and is primarily interested in winning elections and staying in office. Consequently, its programs are deliberately vague. Second, the PCI is the second largest party in the system in terms of voting strength and is posing an increasingly credible challenge to the supremacy of the DC. Third, Italian socialism is chronically divided with two and sometimes three socialist parties competing against each other. And, finally, we should point to the disproportionate weight exerted by *two* of the parties in Italy's multiparty system. For, if we compute the combined PCI-DC vote since 1953, we obtain 62.7% in 1953, 65.1% in 1958, 63.5% in 1963, 66.0% in 1968, 66.0% in 1972, and 73.1% in 1976. These figures appear to lend support to Galli's thesis that Italy has an "imperfect two-party system."[10]—imperfect in the sense that there is no clear alternation in office between government and opposition and that elections have a minimal effect.

The Role of Factions

In addition to the hegemony of two dominant parties, the existence of extreme pluralism and of a high degree of polarization, and the development of "catchall" parties, the Italian party system is also characterized by a high degree of factionalism. Before describing the emergence and development of the Italian party system, we shall deal briefly with one of its most striking features: the presence in most Italian parties of highly organized competing factions.

Factionalism, to be sure, is not a uniquely Italian phenomenon, but the Italian variety is marked by a very superior stage of organization and cohesion. In a number of Italian parties, factions have their own newspapers or journals, their own parliamentary subgroups, their own sources of income, and their own share of party patronage. Also, they have their own factional leader or leaders, who are empowered to negotiate with other factional leaders within the party, or even in allied parties, so that a settlement of outstanding disputes may be reached. The relationship between contending factions has much in common with the fierce competition that is carried on by the parties in an extremely polarized multiparty system.

Factionalism plays a key role in the process of nominating parliamentary candidates and party officials, the formation of cabinets and of regional and local executive organs, and the distribution of patronage. In all these cases, each faction within a party demands its share of representation. As a result, most party politicians affiliate with a faction, so as not to be left out of the picture when spoils are to be divided.

The importance of factions has greatly complicated the nature of the Italian multiparty system. For what may appear to be a coalition cabinet composed of parties commanding a firm majority in Parliament may turn out to be a slender reed when one or more of the component parties contains a powerful faction that views the cabinet formula with hostility. Several times DC-led cabinets have had to resign because of the opposition, not of one of the parties allied with the DC, but of a faction within the DC itself. True, the parties are centralized and disciplined, and the parties in Parliament generally vote as cohesive blocs. But the threat of an intraparty revolt resulting from factional disaffection can cause the leadership of a party to abandon or postpone a sensitive policy decision. It is thus not too difficult to understand the immobilism of Italian government policy: intraparty politics, as much as interparty politics, represents a major barrier to innovation.

Although even the PCI is known to include covert factions, it is the democratic parties that are torn by the most violent and public factional conflicts. And this applies particularly to the two largest democratic parties: the DC and the PSI. The bases of factional division in these parties have tended to vary. Ideological or policy questions have played a major role, to be sure. What allies along the political spectrum should the PSI, or the DC, cultivate? In the DC, for example, the more conservative factions would press for an alliance with the PSDI or even with the PLI, whereas the left-wing factions regard the PSI, and more recently even the PCI, as potential allies.

However, in addition to ideological and party views, personal motivations such as the careerist ambitions of factional leaders are of great importance in explaining factional behavior.[11] There are far more factions in the PSI and the DC than ideological or policy distinctions would justify. To an increasing degree, intraparty politics has come to be based on clashes between leading personalities rather than on principles and/or grand strategy. It is becoming difficult to distinguish between certain major DC and PSI factions, with regard to their concrete objectives. And some factional leaders display remarkable ideological volatility. The recent Italian prime minister, Giulio Andreotti, is a case in point. In the 1950s and early 1960s Andreotti led the Primavera faction that sought an alliance with the rightist parties; in the summer of 1970

Andreotti's efforts to form a cabinet failed, partly because the PSDI feared he was overly leftist in his sympathies.

It is to be noted that the prevalence of careerist or patronage motivations in party factionalism seems to be closely related to access to public office. Such motivations were evident in the DC, Italy's dominant party, even in the 1950s; they mushroomed in the PSI *after* 1963, the year that the PSI finally entered the cabinet after 15 years in opposition.[12]

The Emergence and Development of the System

In the years immediately following unification, Italy had a rather peculiar kind of party system. With a very restricted electorate, parties were mere parliamentary factions consisting of "liberal" local notables, each with his own personal clientele in his home constituency. Some of these liberal groupings were designated as belonging to the right (especially those elements connected with landed property), some as belonging to the left (especially commercial interests and professional men), but the difference between rightist and leftist positions was often hard to discern.

In 1876, the left came to power under Prime Minister Agostino Depretis. Depretis was credited by many writers with originating the practice of *trasformismo*, of building a parliamentary majority based on special favors for legislators who agreed to support the government, of rigging elections to ensure the victory of the government's legislative supporters, and of carefully cultivating local notables and their clienteles. This practice prevented the crystallization of an organized opposition, as many of the ablest potential opposition leaders were simply co-opted into the government coalition.

With the electoral law of 1882—which had the effect of enfranchising part of the lower middle class and the more skilled and educated artisans—and with the beginnings of industrialization, new parties, characterized by more sharply delineated policy postures and ideological commitments, began to appear. The PR (a progressive democratic party appealing to the lower middle class) was formed as early as 1878; the PRI (followers of Giuseppe Mazzini, who wanted a republic based on universal suffrage and on a network of voluntary associations) emerged as an organized political party in the 1890s; and in 1892 the PSI was founded. All these groupings operated at a considerable disadvantage because the suffrage was still narrowly restricted.

With the electoral laws of 1912 and 1919, which established universal manhood suffrage, the Socialists became the largest party in Italy. At the same time, devout Catholics who had abstained from participating in national politics in protest against the forcible Italian annexation of the papal city of Rome in 1870, began—with tacit papal approval—to play a more active role. After helping proclerical candidates in 1904 and 1913, Catholics formed a full-fledged party of their own at the close of World War I: the Italian Popular party (PPI), led by Don Sturzo. Socialism and political Catholicism thus emerged as the two dominant forces in the post-World War I political prospectus. Meanwhile, the PR and the PRI benefited rather little from the extension of the suffrage and remained virtual splinter parties.

The new Italian mass parties had powerful extraparliamentary party organizations at the national and provincial levels, thus contrasting sharply with the loose coalitions of PLI notables. But they shared one distinctive characteristic in common with the PLI: an intense factionalism, which often made it extremely difficult for a party to act as a cohesive unit and which constantly posed the threat of schism. It was a schism in the PSI in 1921 that led to the formation of the PCI.

The rise of the Fascist party (PNF) after World War I represented, to a considerable degree, a middle-class backlash against the long-delayed and suddenly consummated entry of the masses into national politics. Unlike the British Conservatives, who had promptly appealed to the newly enfranchised workers after the passage of the Reform Act of 1867, the PLI lacked either the time or the inclination to absorb the new voters. Only Prime Minister Giolitti, who had been responsible for the 1912 electoral law and who had attempted unsuccessfully to induce the PSI to enter his cabinet coalition, made some efforts in this direction. Lacking the flexibility of their British counterparts, the Italian middle classes reacted with fear and outrage to the rise of disciplined mass parties like the PSI and therefore showed considerable tolerance for the violent repressive methods employed by the Fascist action squads. In the years 1920–1922, an armed Fascist minority, financed by PLI industrialists and large landowners and supported by the police, reduced the PSI to complete impotence and set the stage for Mussolini's March on Rome. During this period, the two mass parties were too torn by internal factional conflict to join forces against the Fascist threat. The tenuous Catholic-PSI alliance of the 1960s and early 1970s (the so-called left-center coalition or opening to the left) was in part an effort to avoid a recurrence of the extremist upsurge that overpowered the nation in 1922. And many of those non-Communists who favor admitting the PCI to the cabinet today are similarly affected by the memory of the historical events we have just cited and by fear of a possible right-wing uprising.

It is interesting to observe that, after the fall of the Fascist regime in World War II, the pre-1922 parties emerged from their years of exile and resumed their activities as if fascism had been only a momentary interruption of an established routine. The PLI reformed their much-diminished ranks (at first representing themselves to the voters as the NDU) as did the Republican party. The DC inherited the tradition, cadres, and electorate of the old Popular party of 1919–1922 but was able to appeal to a larger share of the electorate. Because of its role in the underground movement and the Resistance, the PCI loomed as a major force on the left, while the PSI were soon engaged in their all-too-familiar internal factional disputes. Even the Fascist party was revived in the guise of the MSI. The only major newcomer to the political scene was the PDIUM, which—after a gradual decline to the status of a splinter movement—eventually vanished through merger with the MSI.

But what exists today is more than a mere reproduction of the pre-1922 party system. For one thing there has been a considerable alteration in the respective strength of the various parties within the system. The PCI are now stronger than the PSI; the DC are the dominant party, with a plurality in every election since 1946; and the Liberals, once the dominant force in Italian politics, are now a mere fringe group. And, second, *all* Italian parties today are centralized and disciplined and maintain cohesive ranks in Parliament. Bitter factional conflict continues, but within clearly understood limits: violations of party discipline can, and sometimes do, lead to expulsion or to a party split. So, although traditional political practices of the nineteenth and early twentieth centuries survive in a somewhat altered form, the Italian party system has acquired some modern organizational features.

The Parties and Their Goals

Following is a brief descriptive analysis of the more influential political parties in Italy. As a reference, it may be helpful to study Tables 5–1 and 5–2, both of which provide general pictures of the Italian party strengths.

THE COMMUNIST PARTY

The PCI was founded in 1921 at Leghorn by a group of secessionists from the PSI. After 1926, the PCI (as well as all other nonfascist parties) was outlawed; its leader, Antonio Gramsci, was arrested in 1927 and died in prison a decade later. During the period between 1926 and 1943, the PCI had to operate as a clandestine organization on Italian soil, while the leadership of the PCI outside of Italy was exercised by Palmiro Togliatti, who was living in the Soviet Union. It was Togliatti who, on his return to Italy in March 1944, took over the leadership of the PCI and transformed it into the largest party in Italy in terms of members and the second largest in terms of votes.

The underground struggle against the fascist regime and later against the Nazi occupation of 1943–1945 reaped copious benefits for the PCI. By virtue of its organization and of its membership's zeal, it was better prepared than other parties to play a leading role in the Resistance movement. It was the brilliant and heroic performance of the Communists in the Resistance that enabled them to sink deep roots among the masses and to attract many idealistic intellectuals to their cause. After the war, the PCI emerged as one of

TABLE 5–1.   Percentages of the Total Vote Polled by Italian Parties in Elections for the Constituent Assembly in 1946 and for the Chamber of Deputies from 1948 through 1976[a]

	1946	1948	1953	1958	1963	1968	1972	1976
Communists	19.0		22.6	22.7	25.3	26.9	27.1	34.4
Proletarian Democrats	—	31[c]	—	—	—	4.5	1.9	1.5[b]
Radicals	—		—	—	—	—	—	1.1
Socialists	20.7[d]		12.7	14.2	13.8	14.5[e]	9.6	9.6
Social Democrats	—	7.1	4.5	4.5	6.1		5.1	3.4
Republicans	4.4	2.5	1.6	1.4	1.4	2.0	2.8	3.1
Christian Democrats	35.2	48.5	40.0	42.4	38.3	39.1	38.7	38.7
Liberals	6.8[f]	3.8	3.0	3.5	7.0	5.8	3.9	1.3
Qualunquists (extreme right)	5.3	—	—	—	—	—	—	—
Monarchists	2.8	2.8	6.8	4.8[f]	1.7	1.3	—	—
Neo-Fascists	—	2.0	5.9	4.8	5.1	4.5	8.7	6.1[h]
Others	5.8[i]	2.3	2.9	1.7	1.3	1.4	2.1	0.7

[a]Data for this table are drawn from sources cited in note 7.
[b]The PDUP was the successor of the Italian Socialist Party of Proletarian Unity (PSIUP), which ran in 1968 and 1972 and then merged with the Communists.
[c]In 1948, the PCI and PSI formed a single electoral bloc, the People's Democratic Front. The experiment was not repeated.
[d]In 1946, the PSI and PSDI were united in a single party. The party split in 1947.
[e]In 1968, the PSI and PSDI ran together as a unified party: the Unified Socialist party. In 1969, this party split up.
[f]The PLI list in 1946 was known as the National Democratic Union (UDN).
[g]There were two Monarchist parties in 1958, polling 2.2% and 2.6% of the votes, respectively.
[h]In December 1976, the MSI split, with about half of its deputies joining a new rightist party—the DN.
[i]This category in 1946 included the short-lived Action party, many of whose members joined the PSI or the PRI.

the leading parties in Italy. And although it ranked behind the Socialists in the June 1946 elections to the Constituent Assembly, the great schism that split the PSI in January 1947 gave the PCI the opportunity to pull ahead of its ally. Ever since 1947, the PCI has been the leading party on the left wing of the Italian political spectrum.

The PCI's goals are characterized by a kind of equivocal moderation, as befits a party that must take into account both the Italian domestic situation and the international Communist movement. Even under Togliatti, before the accession to party leadership of the present incumbent, Enrico Berlinguer, the PCI had indicated that its conception of "The Italian Way to Socialism" included a legal and peaceful accession to power, the preservation of a multiparty system, and continuing respect for constitutional guarantees. In fact, the PCI has always been most vociferous in demanding that the provisions of the Italian Constitution be enforced with despatch. Yet, the PCI has continued to support Leninist principles, which are virtually impossible to reconcile with democratic norms.[13] For this and other similar reasons, friends

TABLE 5–2. Seats Won by the Various Italian Parties in the Italian Constituent Assembly in 1946 and in the Italian Chamber of Deputies from 1948 through 1976[a]

	1946	1948	1953	1958	1963	1968	1972	1976
Communists	104		143	140	166	171	179	228
Proletarian Democrats	—	183[c]	—	—	—	23	0	6[b]
Radicals	—		—	—	—	—	—	4
Socialists	115[d]		75	84	87	91[e]	61	58
Social Democrats	—	33	19	22	33		29	15
Republicans	23	9	5	6	6	9	15	14
Christian Democrats	207	305	262	273	260	265	266	262
Liberals	41[f]	19	14	17	39	31	20	5
Qualunquists (extreme right)	30	—	—	—	—	—	—	—
Monarchists	0	14	40	25[g]	8	6	—	—
Neo-Fascists	—	6	29	15	27	24	56	35[h]
Others	35[i]	5	3	5	4	10	4	3

NOTE: See Table 5–1 for explanatory notes.

of Italian democracy have tended to be rather skeptical about Communist intentions, despite the fact that the PCI *appears* to be firmly committed to democratic methods and goals. This skepticism has been reenforced by the relative lack of intraparty democracy in the PCI.

This appearance of moderation is also evident with regard to the PCI's stand on specific policy issues.[14] For example, the PCI does not seem to be pressing for further nationalizations which would expand the already swollen public sector of the economy. In fact, its policy goals are disarmingly modest and somewhat orthodox: the tightening of tax loopholes, a credit policy designed to help small businessmen, greater financial autonomy for local authorities, government spending in various social fields designed as a job-generating, pump-priming device, the maintenance of law and order, and honesty in government. Moreover, the PCI has attempted, not too success-fully, to curb the wage demands of organized labor. And it has soft-pedalled its attacks on the Catholic church, despite the anticlerical prejudices of so many of its supporters.

Generally, the PCI tries to project an image of a solid, mature opposition party, imbued with a sober sense of responsibility, but it must also try to appear in the eyes of its supporters as a party of protest. And, finally, as with other Italian parties, it must try to defend the established privileges of its members and supporters through the dispensation of jobs and favors and through the passage of minor legislation that aids only restricted sectors of the society.[15] These conflicting missions are very hard to fulfill simultaneously.

In the area of foreign affairs, the PCI has repeatedly asserted its independence of Soviet control. It sharply criticized the Soviet Union for its invasion of Czechoslovakia; it resisted Soviet efforts to arrange for international Communist conferences for the purpose of denouncing the Chinese Communist party; it defended the Spanish Communist leader, Carrillo, against Soviet criticism. Today, it accepts Italy's membership in NATO, though there are those who are less than totally convinced of the PCI's fidelity to the Western alliance.

The image of moderation is reflected also in the PCI's attitude vis-à-vis the proper formula for constructing a cabinet coalition. Impressed by what happened in Chile, where a Popular Front government composed entirely of leftist parties succeeded only in provoking a rightist revolt, the leaders of the PCI have rejected a Popular Front "left alternative" in favor of what it calls the "historic compromise"—a formula for a coalition of PCI, PSI, *and* DC. When the DC rejected this formula, the Communists proceeded to propose an "emergency" cabinet including all "democratic" parties and excluding only the MSI. And after the elections of 1976, since the DC leadership was not prepared to buy the formula of an "emergency government" either, the PCI agreed to abstain on votes of confidence in Parliament (thus permitting Andreotti's minority all-DC cabinet to survive) in exchange for regular consultation with the government on proposed legislation.

Since 1976, the PCI has been on the horns of a dilemma. It governs (with PSI support) 6 of Italy's 20 regions and most of her big cities. Elsewhere at the regional and local level, it is consulted by the left-center executive juntas, even when its members do not actually form part of the governing majority. And, at the national level, as we have seen, the cabinet remains in office through its tacit consent, expressed in the form of abstention on key votes and in cooperation in standing committees. But how long can the PCI be satisfied with this role? The party rank-and-file is bound to exert pressure for more than a mere consultative presence in the national decision-making process, for the achievement of either the "historic compromise" or the "emergency government" formula. And how long can the PCI collaborate with the establishment without losing its appeal for voters who wish to express a protest? There are signs that the PCI has alienated radical groups among the students. And finally, even admission to the cabinet might prove to be a two-edged sword: since Italy's problems may well be insoluble, the PCI might stand to lose its reputation for efficiency and effectiveness if it entered the government. (To illustrate, the Communist mayor of Naples has not been able to make much of a dent in that hapless city's problems.) In short, the PCI may face a Hobson's choice: whether it enters the cabinet or not, it may undergo serious damage in either event.

THE TWO SOCIALIST PARTIES

Italian socialism has always been a sorely divided movement, ever since the PSI was founded in 1892. On the one hand, the so-called Maximalists, or orthodox Marxists, have insisted that the PSI refuse to take part in coalition cabinets dominated by bourgeois forces and have also demanded that the party either remain in glorious isolation or cement alliances only with the PCI. On the other hand, the Reformist elements have sought to establish ties with other democratic parties, have spurned collaboration with the Communists, and have advocated that Italian socialism bear its share of responsibility for governing the country, even at the price of collaboration with bourgeois democratic parties.

As a result of these internal tensions, the PSI has been subject to a series of major splits. On a number of occasions, the outnumbered Reformists have withdrawn from the party and have formed a PSDI under a variety of different labels. This happened shortly after World War I. It happened again in 1947, when Giuseppe Saragat, fearing imminent fusion between the PSI and the PCI, led his followers out of the PSI and founded the PSDI. After 1947, the PSI collaborated closely with the PCI, while the PSDI formed part of a DC-dominated center coalition.

By 1956, Pietro Nenni, the leader of the PSI, was ready to move away from the close alliance with the PCI. In only seven years, he was able, by gradual stages, to loosen the ties that bound the PSI to the PCI and to lead his party into an alliance with the DC and other center parties. In 1963, the PSI finally entered a DC-led cabinet. And in 1966, after a divorce of 19 years, the Socialists and Social Democrats achieved reunification. It was hoped that this would result in Italian socialism's replacing communism as the leading leftist force in the country.

However, the Socialist reunification and the PSI's entry into a left-center cabinet did not lead to the political renaissance so many observers had expected. For one thing, a direct result of the PSI's entry into the cabinet in 1963 was the secession of its left-wing factions, which formed the PSIUP in 1964. Moreover, Socialist dissatisfaction was soon aroused by the economic recession of 1963–1965, by the DC's chronic slowness in adopting reforms that had been agreed on at the time the PSI entered the cabinet and by the reunified PSI's disappointing showing in the elections of 1968. The upshot of all this was that the PSDI seceded again in 1969. PSI reunification had lasted less than three years.

Since 1969, the two main socialist parties have suffered a steady decline. Their combined vote in 1972 was 14.7% of the total valid votes cast; by 1976, their combined vote was down to 13.0%. To be sure, the PSDI had accounted for the entire percentage loss between 1972 and 1976, sinking from 5.1% to 3.4%, while the PSI stood pat with 9.6%. But it is worthwhile noting that 1976 marked the lowest voting percentage either one of these two parties had polled in the past 30 years. Just as collaboration in a DC-dominated center coalition hurt the PSDI, similarly the PSI has emerged badly battered from its 15 years as a junior partner in left-center coalitions.

With regard to policy goals, both parties have supported the left-center coalition formula since 1963. But the PSI has demanded (but usually failed to get) more vigorous prosecution of reformist goals by the DC, which has been the dominant party in the left center. The PSI has favored a somewhat greater emphasis on public enterprise and direct regulation of industry by the government, whereas the Social Democrats have tended to favor more freedom for private enterprise and a socialism confined largely to public works and social welfare. In foreign affairs, both parties support the North Atlantic Treaty, but the PSDI are unreservedly pro-Atlantic, whereas the PSI's orientation toward the Third World and pacifist tradition have raised some doubts about its allegiance to NATO.

The main distinction between the two parties lies in their attitude toward the PCI. The PSDI has consistently refused to enter regional, provincial, and local executive organs if the PCI is allowed to enter. And this attitude has been adopted also at the national level. Instead the PSI not only entered left-center regional juntas in 1970, but also entered two left regional juntas in that same year—juntas that were PCI dominated. And in 1976 and 1977 the PSI made it quite clear that it would not back a national cabinet from which the PCI was totally excluded. This strong disagreement between the PSI and the PSDI over the proper role of the PCI in the Italian system helps to nourish the mutual suspicion that has kept these two parties apart.

THE CHRISTIAN DEMOCRATIC PARTY

The DC is a relative newcomer on the Italian political scene. It was founded in September 1943, on the heels of the armistice with the Western allies. However, the DC is not the first political force to represent the Catholic outlook in Italy. The Popular party of Don Luigi Sturzo was founded in 1919 and dissolved under Fascist pressure in 1926. And long before the establishment of the Popular party, political Catholicism had manifested itself through the widespread activities of a multiplicity of Catholic organizations: rural savings banks, workingmen's associations, peasant leagues, and parochial and diocesan committees. Since the Holy See had issued an admonition (the *non expedit*) to the Catholic masses against either voting or running for office in the secular state which had seized Rome by force of arms, Catholic organizations did not actually play an independent role in Italian elections until the early twentieth century. It was only then that the papacy began to relax its policy against Catholic participation in elections.

Founded in 1919, the Popular party soon became a progressive and innovative force in Italian politics. It supported decentralization of government functions, women's suffrage, land reform, and the strengthening of local authority. It managed to poll slightly over 20% of the votes in the general election of 1920 and 1921. However, like the DC today, it was afflicted by factional conflict between its moderate and progressive elements. And once the

Fascists came to power, the Popular party was abandoned by the Vatican, which had decided to encourage cooperation with the Fascist regime.

When the DC was formed in 1943, just after the fall of Mussolini, the PLI and the business community as well were under suspicion because of their earlier collaboration with fascism. With the forces of the left seemingly on the verge of seizing power, the DC seemed to be the only real hope for Italian conservatives. Given this situation and given the inspiring leadership of De Gasperi, the DC was able to attain unprecedented electoral strength. Since World War II, the DC has never failed to obtain a plurality in any general election and has never polled less than 35% of the vote. This performance, spectacular by Italian standards, was based partly on the traditional Catholic strongholds of Northern and Northeastern Italy. But it was also based on the penetration of Southern Italy, where the Popular party had been weak but where the DC was successful in attracting the vaguely "liberal" local notables and their clienteles.

Since 1946, the DC has dominated every Italian cabinet, and every Italian prime minister has been a DC. But the DC has never, except in 1948–1953, had an absolute majority in either house of the Italian Parliament. To govern, it has needed allies, either inside or outside the cabinet. And this has raised the obvious question, and the source of endless factional controversy in DC intraparty politics. Which allies is the DC to select?

From 1947 to 1953, the DC pursued a centrist coalition policy, based on an alliance with the three minor center parties: the PSDI, the PRI, and the PLI. However, antagonisms between the PSDI and PRI, on the one hand, and the business-oriented PLI on the other, soon rendered that alternative impracticable. Another formula, occasionally employed between 1954 and 1962 but abandoned because unacceptable to the DC left and to two of the minor center parties, was the right-center coalition between the DC and the PLI with PDIUM and MSI support. A limited left-center solution (DC, PSDI, and PRI, excluding the PSI) simply lacked enough parliamentary support to ensure a stable cabinet. Over the long run, to safeguard democratic stability, it was necessary to have an expanded left-center coalition including the PSI. And in 1962 this giant step forward (the opening to the left) was finally completed. From 1962, the left-center solution (DC, PSDI, PRI, and PSI) was the standard norm in the Italian political system. Occasional breakdowns in the alliance were usually patched over by having an all-DC minority cabinet preside during a prolonged cooling-off period.

In recent years, the left-center formula has become increasingly discredited, partly because of Italy's growing social and economic difficulties, partly because of PSI dissatisfaction with the role of junior partner. Moreover recent gains by the PCI have given rise to demands that the PCI be admitted to the cabinet, to have a grand coalition of all the pro-constitution parties (i.e., excluding only the MSI) to cope with the emergency situation. Since 1976, the left-center parties no longer have a majority in Parliament and need PCI support or abstention to govern. And, as we have seen, there has been an informal agreement between the DC and the PCI for the DC to consult the PCI on major legislation in return for PCI abstention on parliamentary votes involving major bills submitted by the all-DC Andreotti cabinet. By the winter of 1978 this solution, too, was outdated. Under pressure from their own rank and file, the PCI was demanding further steps toward the "historic compromise." And the PSI and PRI were showing support for these claims.

During these years of uncertainty over the cabinet formula, the DC's main problems have been internal, for virtually every conceivable cabinet solution has its proponents among one or more of the DC factions. And virtually every Italian party (not excluding the PCI and MSI) has would-be allies within the DC. The question of cabinet alliances has been one of the main themes of factional conflict within the DC. But the factional picture has been further complicated by the tendency of factions to be based largely on conflicts between leading personalities, many of whom show a disconcerting ideological volatility. It is not uncommon to see a factional leader be a strong advocate of, say, a left-center coalition one year and become an equally impassioned advocate of a center or right-center coalition two years hence.

Since the DC is something of a catchall party, its policy goals are not easy to pin down. It has naturally been quite pro-clerical in its policy stance, supporting government aid to parochial schools and seeking to maintain the ban on divorce (the MSI and the DC were the only two parties backing a referendum proposal in 1974 to repeal a recently passed divorce law). However, even on the divorce question, the DC was by no means unanimous.

In domestic affairs, the more welfare-oriented elements in the DC have gradually gained the upper hand, passing land reform and low-cost housing laws and pushing for tax reform. And the DC has taken a clear line in favor of the expansion of the public sector of the Italian economy. Ever since the nationalization of the electric power industry in 1964, the public corporations have grown in scope and power. This development has, in fact, contributed to Italy's economic crisis; for the public sector has become a patronage hunting-ground for the DC and many of its directors are patronage appointees with close political ties to the DC. Wasteful politically motivated investments by public sector industries are widely believed to have contributed to Italy's economic difficulties.

In the field of foreign affairs, the DC has generally taken a "European" position, favoring Italy's cooperation in NATO and the Common Market and supporting a close Italian alignment with U.S. foreign policy leadership. But there is some element of discord within the DC on foreign policy. Some top-echelon leaders have advocated a more independent foreign policy, a more neutral attitude toward East-West issues, and an Italian effort to serve as a bridge between the West and the Arab world.

When we consider the goals of Italian Christian Democracy, we must bear in mind that those goals are rendered uncertain and ambiguous by the heterogeneity, accentuated factionalism, and exaggerated pragmatism that characterize the DC. With its variegated electorate—businessmen, farmers, industrial workers, pensioners, housewives—the DC is compelled to try to be all things to all men. So, while the dominant forces in the DC have been moderately committed to economic and social reforms, they have always had to water down their solutions to domestic problems to placate powerful minority factions and safeguard party unity. Besides, given the DC's permanent status as a governing party dispensing loaves and fishes, reformist impulses have often been overshadowed by patronage considerations, so that even the more progressive factions in the DC often give the impression of being primarily interested in empire building—that is, in gaining control over public agencies and public corporations and using them to reward their friends and expand their influence. Moreover, given the DC's diversity and its inability to agree on a coherent set of policies, it often appears that a policy of petty favors, of subsidies and concessions to special interests, serves as the lowest common denominator that best defines the party's stance. The myriads of *leggine* (laws of minor importance serving narrowly defined interests) that are passed by the Italian Parliament are a symptom of the DC's propensity for putting off major decisions and concentrating on a politics of uncoordinated handouts.[16]

OTHER NATIONAL PARTIES

The remaining five national parties accounted for only 13.1% of the votes cast in 1976. They include two parties of the left—the PDUP and the PR, two center parties—the PRI and the PLI, and the Neo-Fascist party—MSI. In December 1976, about half the MSI seceded to form a nonfascist ultra-conservative party, DN, whose prowess has yet to be tested at the polls.

The PR dates back to the late nineteenth century, but it has never been successful in competing with the mass parties. It has generally been a party of elites, of forward-looking intellectuals, except in a few central Italian provinces where it has been able to command substantial peasant support based on certain historical traditions. Yet, so complex is the Italian multiparty system that the PRI's handful of votes in Parliament have frequently been crucial to the survival of a cabinet.

The Republican program is moderately left of center, but not Marxist. It involves a rather anticlerical posture of hostility toward the special privileges enjoyed by the Catholic church, a firm attachment to democratic institutions, a belief in state intervention in economic life through economic planning rather than nationalization, and support for NATO and European integration. Formerly opposed to any collaboration with the PCI, the PRI in early 1978 was demanding that the Communists be either admitted to the cabinet or be recognized as external supporters of the cabinet, so that the government would have more authority to cope with the crisis facing Italy.

The PRI's appeal is limited but growing. It polled only 3.1% of the votes in 1976, but this was its best performance since 1946. It was the only nonleftist party to gain ground in the 1976 elections.

The other minor center party, the PLI, used to be a dominant force in Italian politics before the advent of fascism, even though it was a collection of independent factions and tendencies rather than a cohesive party. In 1912 and 1919, its supremacy was fatally undermined by the expansion of the suffrage. And in 1919–1922, Liberals utterly failed to check the advance of fascism. In fact, a number of Liberal industrialists and landowners had given some measure of economic and moral support to the vigilante activities of the fascist action squads.

After World War II, the DC was able to mobilize most of those middle-class voters who had backed various PLI groupings in prefascist days, for the DC was a party of order, which appealed to all social classes including the business community, and had a much more honorable record than the PLI with respect to earlier resistance against fascism. Only in 1963 did resentment against the "opening to the left" by the DC cause a temporary PLI upsurge to a postwar high of 7.0% of the total vote. Since then, the PLI's decline has been steady. In 1976, it polled only 1.3% of the vote.

Apart from its questionable record with regard to the fascist experience, the PLI's chief weakness is that it is almost exclusively recruited from the rural and urban upper middle classes: landowners and businessmen, for the most part. As a result, it suffers from a rightist bias which has ruled out its participation in the same cabinet with the PRI and the PSDI, to say nothing of the PSI. For this reason a center coalition, which the PLI wants, would be rejected by the other center parties and by the left-wing factions of the DC. On the other hand, the PLI's attachment to democratic institutions renders an alliance with the MSI unpalatable for most of the party's leaders. With so many alternative possibilities foreclosed, the PLI has become increasingly isolated.

In the field of domestic affairs, PLI goals have been quite different from those of the PRI. The PLI regarded the "opening to the left" in 1962 with great skepticism. It has opposed the growth of the public sector of the economy and has argued against extensive government regulation of the private sector. While the PRI seems to be a kind of Italian New Deal party, the PLI might better be compared to the conservative wing of the GOP.

Where the PLI and the PRI tend to agree is in the spheres of church-state relations and foreign policy. Like the PRI, the PLI favor a secular state, the elimination of special privileges for the Catholic church, and a ban on discrimination against Protestant religious minorities. They have also aligned themselves with the PRI (as well as with the PSI and PCI, in this instance) behind the passage of the divorce bill in 1970 and against the referendum proposal to repeal the divorce law in 1974. And, in foreign affairs, they have shared the PRI's views in backing European integration and Italian coopera-tion with the U.S. line in NATO.

The two leftist parties we have not yet dealt with are of relatively minor significance. The PDUP and the PR together polled 2.6% of the votes in 1976. We mention them after the PRI and PLI, not only because they are weaker, but also because they are normally not included in national or regional cabinet coalitions. The PDUP is actually to the left of the PCI; it opposed the "historic compromise" because it does not believe any nonleftist party (in this case, the DC) should be in the cabinet. It seeks to appeal to those who believe the present leaders of the PCI are too ready to cooperate with bourgeois-dominated regimes. The PR is bitterly anticlerical and committed to women's rights. Although not Marxist like the PDUP, it professes an extreme form of civil libertarian outlook and appeals to the public to reject traditional parties. Both parties derive their strength, such as it is, mostly from middle-class voters and students. They cater to the protest voter, but they have failed to generate mass support even among those social categories most receptive to their message.

Finally, let us dwell briefly on the MSI, a party of nostalgia which mourns the vanished glories of Mussolini's Fascist empire. This party has fluctuated in strength, drawing from 4.5% to 8.7% of the total vote. With 6.1% of the votes in 1976 (a decline from the 8.7% of 1972), it ranked fourth among Italian parties. And the violent methods frequently used by its adherents give it an importance out of proportion to its numbers.

The MSI, like the PCI, denies any intention of setting up a totalitarian state and piously proclaims its allegiance to democratic methods. Many of its issue stands appear, on the surface, to be simply rightist positions such as any conservative party could defend. It favors a right-center cabinet coalition, it is opposed to the kind of national economic planning advocated by the parties of the left, it sought the repeal of the divorce law, and it is hostile to detente. But the MSI is more than just a conventional party of the right. It *does* favor a national corporate state based on functional representation and this goal—along with the MSI's symbolism and political style—conjures up disturbing memories of the fascist past.

Organizational Features and Functional Roles

In the previous section, we discussed developmental and policy distinctions among the Italian parties; in this section, we shall touch on certain common features that tend to hold true for all or most Italian parties. These include their internal organization and the roles they perform in the political system.

Italian parties are characterized by a high degree of centralization, cohesion, and discipline. The central party organization has a qualified veto power over parliamentary nominees, whose candidacies are submitted to central headquarters by provincial and interprovincial party organs. Cohesion is evident when members of the party in Parliament vote together as a solid bloc. And in all Italian parties, breaches of party discipline are frequently—but not always—punished by suspension or expulsion from the party.

Cohesion and discipline prevail, not only in classic branch-type parties like the PSI and DC, but also in a predominantly middle-class party such as the PLI. Although Duverger has implied that middle-class parties do not respond well to cohesion and discipline,[17] this implication does not seem to be borne out by the Italian party system. The most plausible explanation for the cohesion and discipline of Italian parties may be the great strength of the extreme left in Italy. Before 1956, the PSI was allied with the PCI, and their combined vote was about 40% of the total votes cast in parliamentary elections. With a relatively slim anti-Communist majority in Parliament and in the country, Italian deputies of centrist and rightist persuasion may have viewed any breach of party discipline as a possible weakening of the anti-Communist front at a time when a Communist takeover was a distinct possibility.[18]

In discussing party cohesion and discipline, one possibility should not be excluded. Cohesion may be a mere facade of unity, whereas intraparty opposition manifests itself behind closed doors. As a result many a new initiative will be abandoned, usually by being unaccountably bogged down in committee.

A second organizational feature of most Italian parties is the major role played by the extraparliamentary party organizations in influencing the decisions adopted by the parties in Parliament. Directorates (executive committees) and secretaries will take a very active part in the negotiations over the formation of a new coalition cabinet. In fact, it has been pointed out that almost all Italian cabinet crises have been extraparliamentary in origin—a decision taken at a meeting of a party directorate or even a statement issued by a party secretary may cause the fall of a cabinet.[19] But we should bear in mind that party secretaries are themselves usually members of Parliament, as are over 50% of the members of party directorates.[20] With so much intermeshing between the party directorate and the party parliamentary group, it is wrong to assume that two distinct and separate entities are involved. Still, it must be conceded that the *locale* of decision making in an Italian cabinet crisis gives the public the partly erroneous sensation that its political destinies are being decided by faceless party bureaucrats.

Generally speaking, all Italian parties share the same organizational structures. They are organized by communes (the communal section), provinces (the provincial federation), and regions (the regional committee or federation), with power centered at the national and—to a much lesser degree—at the regional and provincial levels. Each party has a system of representative assemblies—usually referred to as the sectional assembly at the strictly local level, the congress at all other levels—which meet periodically to elect the party executive organs at each level. These executive organs usually include, at the national level, a quasi-legislative body (known as the National

Council in the DC and PLI, whereas the PCI, the PSI, and the PSDI have a Central Committee); an executive organ (referred to, in most parties, as the Directorate), and an administrative organ (the Secretariat), whereas the leader of the extraparliamentary party is known as the Secretary. Similar organs exist at the regional and provincial levels and, in more rudimentary form, at the local level.

A few structural differences should be cited, however. For one, the leftist parties have tried to supplement their local sections with a system of workplace organizations: the Communist "cells" and the Socialist "shop nuclei." Second, centralization is far more rigidly enforced in the PCI than in other Italian parties. And, finally, the smaller parties—because of their lack of funds and membership—have a more skeletal organization and much fewer full-time employees than the mass parties.

One function performed by Italian political parties is that of political socialization. Such parties as the PCI, PSI, and DC provide their members with a set of values and goals and a sense of belonging acquired through integration in a mass organization.[21] But even the smaller parties try to transmit certain values and attitudes to their members. Yet, party membership alone does not necessarily imply exposure to political socialization. Many party members, particularly those who have joined mainly in search of patronage, are rather inactive and are therefore unlikely to expose themselves to the socializing process. Others—like the Southern peasants who migrate to the industrial Northwest—may join a party to achieve social integration with their environment; that is, they may seek to blend in with the leftist (or Catholic) atmosphere of their workplace and neighborhood or to win fuller acceptance by their friends or colleagues.

There is some ground for believing that Italian parties are playing an ever less effective role in the performance of their socialization function. A case in point is the growing loss of Communist control over the protest movement. Neither the student rebellion of 1968 nor the wildcat strikes of the "hot autumn" of 1970 were initiated, organized, or even desired by the PCI, although the Communists *did* belatedly give some support to these movements to avoid being left behind.

A second major function performed by all Italian political parties is political recruitment. This is most evident in the process of nominating candidates for the Senate and for the Chamber of Deputies. Candidates are nominated by provincial party committees, and winnowed out by inter-provincial or regional party committees. The central party organization in Rome retains a veto power and also the power to propose one or two candidates of its own for each electoral circumscription of two to four provinces. There is, then, nothing corresponding to the American direct primary. A local notable may seek to bypass this process by placing himself at the head of an independent local list. But, given the nature of Italian voting habits, his chances of being elected without the label of one of the national parties are virtually nil.

The nominating function is controlled by Italy's highly centralized, cohesive, and disciplined parties.

To be sure, there are some additional influences on the recruitment process. The requests of intraparty factions and of friendly pressure groups are given a respectful hearing during the early stages of drawing up party slates. Political friendships also play an important role. Prominent party leaders often arrange to have youthful protegés included in the lists (Andreotti began his career this way in 1946 under the protective wing of the DC leader, Alcide De Gasperi). And, finally, the voter in elections for the Chamber of Deputies has the right to indicate his preference for up to four candidates on his party's list, thus helping to determine which individuals within his party are actually elected.

Party Personnel: Membership and Leadership

We know that a remarkably high number of Italians join political parties, either on their own initiative or through the purchase of a party card on their behalf by some party official. About 4 million Italians are party members, with about 1½ million belonging to the DC, another 1½ million to the PCI, about half a million to the PSI, and the remaining half million scattered among the other parties.[22]

In its membership composition, the PCI is more of a working-class party than is the case with the DC. Over 40% of its members were industrial workers in 1973, as compared with 13.6% of the DC membership in 1971.[23] The PSI is more oriented toward the working class than the DC but less than the PCI: 35.2% of its members in 1970 were industrial workers.[24]

The PCI used to have a larger proportion of peasants and farm workers than the DC, but this has changed with the exodus from the rural areas that has affected the PCI more than the DC. In 1973, 13.3% of the PCI's membership were employed on the land, whereas 15.2% of the DC's membership in 1971 worked in agriculture. But most of the peasant Communists are sharecroppers or farm laborers, whereas most of the Christian Democratic peasant members are small landowning farmers. The proportion of peasant members is declining in both parties as more and more people leave the rural areas.[25]

Housewives (25.0% of DC membership in 1971 as compared with 12.3% of PCI membership in 1973) are the largest single occupational group in the ranks of Christian Democracy. The DC also contains a sizable proportion of civil servants (12.7%) and white-collar employees of various types. The PCI has been successful in recent years in broadening its appeal, so that, in 1973, 8.4% of its members belonged to the category of "artisans, shopkeepers, small businessmen" and 16.7% were pensioners.[26] Both the PCI and the DC have made substantial gains in recruiting members by virtue of their roles in dispensing patronage at the national, regional, and local levels. The PCI's greatest membership strength is in North Central Italy where the party has many public jobs and perquisites to distribute, as well as nonmaterial rewards. The DC has been remarkably successful in recruiting new members in the underdeveloped South, where a DC card is believed to be a passport to priority consideration in the allocation of government jobs and favors.[27]

In addition to relying on patronage and perquisites, the DC also appeals to conservatively oriented middle-class people in highly industrialized regions. Galli can thus aptly describe the DC as a kind of hybrid: a Catholic party, an urban middle-class party, and a peasant party, all in one.[28] In short, whereas the PCI is largely a working-class party (but with a growing middle-class component) in its social composition, the DC is an interclass party.

The leadership strata of the various Italian parties have a middle-class character. And the percentage of middle-class leaders tends to increase in magnitude as one moves from the lower to the upper echelons of the party hierarchy. This is true even of the PCI, the only party in which a large percentage of the members of local executive committees (40%) is composed of persons of proletarian origin but in which far smaller proportions of cadres of working-class occupational origin are to be found at the provincial, regional, and national headquarters levels. In both mass parties, the proportion of working-class leaders diminishes sharply south of Rome.

Supposedly, executive committee members at all levels are chosen by the section meeting (local level) or by an elected party congress (provincial, regional, and national levels). But in reality, the executive committees tend to play a dominant role in these gatherings, and the election of new executive committee members is normally a process of co-optation. To the extent that contests *do* take place, they are channeled and managed from above by highly organized factions. And once leaders are entrenched in power, especially at the national level, they are singularly hard to displace. Even if a party secretary is forced to resign his post, he will still remain a member of the Directorate and the Central Committee. Usually, only death or senility removes Italian political leaders from positions of prominence.

One major trend is becoming increasingly evident with regard to the composition of party leadership strata. The top echelons of the party leadership, especially in the mass parties such as the PCI and DC, are being colonized increasingly by men who have risen through the ranks of the party bureaucracy. The "great notables" of the immediate postwar years—the illustrious lawyers and other professional men who had acquired a strong personal following—are vanishing as more and more political professionals come to the fore. The vast patronage possibilities opened up by the expansion of the public corporate sector throughout Italy, and by the creation of new public and semipublic agencies and credit institutions, have rendered the political profession more attractive for rising young men on the make.[29]

Voting Cleavages

To what degree are social, economic, and regional cleavages in Italian society reflected in election returns? One politically relevant cleavage divides devout Catholics from anticlericals. In regions such as the Veneto, where the church is strong and popular, traditional attachment to the Catholic church has been translated into a steadfast allegiance to the Christian Democratic party. In North-Central Italy, on the other hand, the traditional anticlericalism of Emilia, Tuscany, Umbria, and the Marches helped to make these regions hotbeds of political unrest as early as the beginning of the twentieth century and helps to account for the strength of the extreme left today.[30]

But certain social cleavages should also be emphasized in accounting for the strength of the various parties. For instance, PCI and PSI successes in North-Central Italy could be partly attributed to the presence in that area of great masses of sharecroppers and farm laborers, who suffered very acutely under the violence unleashed by Fascist action squads during the Fascist rise to power in 1919–1922.[31] To be sure, the rural exodus has reduced the ranks of these two social categories. But the established leftist voting traditions persist.

As for other agricultural voters, the large landowners have tended to support the parties of the right (the PLI, the now-defunct PDIUM, and the MSI). The medium and small landowners, on the other hand, have been overwhelmingly DC. The allegiance of even marginal small farmers to Italian Christian Democracy has in all likelihood been related to the small farmers' dependence on the semipublic Federation of Agricultural Consortiums (Federconsorzi) for credit, low-cost seed, and other assistance. The Federconsorzi, in turn, has been thoroughly controlled by the DC-dominated small farmers' organization, the National Confederation of Direct Cultivators.[32]

Among industrial workers, the Communists have been estimated to receive about 40% of the working-class vote in the 1960s, with almost 30% going to the PSI and PSDI and about 25% to the DC. There seems to be some evidence that the PCI have been more successful among unskilled and/or illiterate workers, whereas the PSI and PSDI have been strongest among skilled workers in the large industrial communes and in zones where illiteracy rates are particularly low.[33] Some Italian scholars have therefore concluded that the electorate of the non-Communist left "better reflects industrial society in the course of development"—more so than the Communist electorate in fact.[34] But elections held in the 1970s seem to indicate significant gains by the PCI in working-class areas—gains made at the expense of the DC, the PSI, and the PSDI.[35] The PSI losses in the Northwest Industrial Triangle have been indicative of an apparent major shift in the working-class vote.[36]

The urban middle class constitutes about one-third of the electorate. And here it would appear that the parties of the Left have been most successful in seeking the votes of white-collar workers and lower-level civil servants, about 40% of whom have voted for the PCI, the PSI, and the PSDI. On the other hand, shopkeepers and artisans—the *self-employed* lower middle classes—have given about half their votes to the DC and about 25% to the extreme right. Between these two extremes, the so-called middle bourgeoisie (army officers, high school teachers, engineers, medium-sized shopkeepers) and the upper bourgeoisie (bankers, industrialists, and so on) have tended to support the PLI and the DC and to have given much less support to the extreme right. So the only segment of the bourgeoisie that has given a sizable proportion of its national votes to the extreme right has been the self-employed petty bourgeoisie, which might have the most to gain from an alliance with the working class and the landless peasantry but which is obsessed with its inability to compete effectively in a modern capitalist society. But once again we must modify our description of middle-class voting behavior in the light of recent developments. Just as the PCI has been gaining at the expense of the PSI, the PSDI, and the DC, similarly the DC has been gaining at the expense of the PSI, the PLI, and the MSI. There appears to be a sort of class polarization, with the PCI increasing its already massive share of working-class votes and the DC making further gains among the middle-class voters.[37] The debacle of the minor parties in 1976—particularly striking in the case of the PSI and PLI—seems to lend some credence to this interpretation.

Before outlining some recent changes in voting patterns, we should touch briefly on a few additional features of postwar Italian voting behavior. First, the electoral fortunes of the various parties fluctuate from region to region. As we have seen, the DC, powerful everywhere, is especially strong in the Northeast; the PCI, powerful everywhere, is particularly strong in North-Central Italy. The minor center parties are somewhat stronger in the Northwest Triangle than elsewhere in the country; and the MSI commands its highest voting percentages south of Rome. It must be stressed, however, that neither the minor center parties nor the MSI actually dominate any region.

It should also be pointed out that the PCI has been able to obtain a sizable minority of the middle-class vote in the Red Belt of North-Central Italy simply by virtue of being the party in power.[38] It is natural, in such a milieu, for local businessmen to want to stay in favor with the incumbents and to become accustomed to a certain type of administration to the point of resisting change.

Finally, some students of Italian politics have placed more emphasis on "social networks" than on social status or region in explaining voting behavior in Italy.[39] Two networks in particular—active church-going Catholics and members of the Italian General Confederation of Labor (CGIL)—influence the behavior of a majority of the Italian people. Religious practice and union membership, predisposing voters in right and left directions, respectively, are the most important independent variables in affecting Italian voting preferences.

Let us now look at the major changes that have taken place in Italian elections since 1972 and especially in the regional elections of 1975 and the general elections of 1976. We may note the great leap forward of the PCI in

1976 (already visible in 1975), the PSI's drop below the 10% mark in 1972 and 1976, the terrible losses suffered by the PSI and PLI, and the somewhat less conspicuous setback of the MSI in 1976 after their 1972 triumph. These developments call into question the thesis that the Italian party system is basically stable.

What factors seem to underlie these shifts? In the case of the PSI, PLI, and even MSI losses, several observers suggest that the DC has attracted large numbers of middle-class voters from the center and from the extreme right by virtue of its anti-Communist posture during the 1976 campaign at a time when many voters, fearing a PCI victory, might regard the smaller parties as too weak to offer effective resistance against the PCI.[40] In short, there was an instinctive middle-class reaction in favor of the "party of order."

The weak performance of the PSI may be attributed partly to the presence of two splinter parties—the PDUP and the PR—which appealed largely to leftist voters and which garnered 2.6% of the votes. Also notable were gains by the PCI in working-class districts at the expense of the PSI and DC. The factional conflict which has divided the PSI, the embarrassing role assigned the PSI as a junior partner in DC-led coalitions, and the PSI's campaign blunder of advocating a Leftist alternative (an all-left Cabinet), as contrasted to the more moderate Communist proposal of a cabinet coalition open to all progressive parties, including the DC, all played a role in the PSI's unimpressive showing.[41]

But the most important phenomenon of the 1976 elections was the heavy gain made by the PCI. One reason for this appears to have been the entry of new age cohorts into the electorate and the lowering of the voting age to 18. Younger voters tend to be predominantly leftist in Italy, and 4.5 million new voters have entered the electorate since 1972.[42] Another reason appears to be the continuing process of urbanization. There is evidence that rural voters moving to the cities have been prone to drop their former partisan traditions and affiliations and become receptive to the PCI's appeal.[43] A third factor is the success of the PCI in impressing Italian voters—over half of whom were not of voting age in 1946, when Stalinism posed a mortal threat to the West—with its moderate image.[44] And finally, the PCI has had some modest measure of success in increasing its voting percentages among the middle classes.[45]

Closely connected with the strengthening of the PCI has been the weakening of Italian Christian Democracy as a force barring the progress of communism. First, the church and its lay organizations have suffered heavy losses in both members and cadres.[46] Also, neither the church nor the Catholic lay organizations are giving the DC the all-out support it used to receive. In fact, the attitude of Catholic Action and of the Christian Association of Italian Workers during the 1976 campaign was quite ambiguous.[47] And some members of the hierarchy are known to be not entirely opposed to the "historic compromise." The mass media, both Catholic and business oriented, have begun to reflect this ambivalence toward the Communists. All this has apparently affected the public.[48] If the PCI is no longer beyond the pale, why not vote for it on occasion?

One last point refers to the role of the referendum of 1974 (the unsuccessful attempt to repeal the divorce law) in weakening traditional loyalties and blurring left-right distinctions.[49] The DC and the MSI were the only two parties in favor of repeal; the center parties were wholly against repeal. And on this occasion the PCI was on the side of the center parties. The divorce referendum brought about a split in the Catholic vote (many DC voters apparently opposed repeal) and also enabled the PCI to acquire a halo of respectability by allying itself with the center bloc. It thus helped to strengthen Italian communism.

The Electoral System and Campaign Techniques

In electing members of the lower house of Parliament, the Chamber of Deputies, Italy relies on a list system of proportional representation, with large multimember districts (circumscriptions) embracing from two to four provinces each and with a system of preference votes to give voters some choice among the names on their party's list. The system employed in electing senators is more complex. Each of the 20 regions is divided into single-member districts. Those few candidates who receive over 65% of the votes in their districts are elected; the rest have to pool their votes with all the other votes cast for their party in the region. The remaining seats are distributed among the parties in each region on the basis of proportional representation, after counting the pooled votes, using the system of the highest average. These electoral systems help to keep splinter parties alive by guaranteeing them at least a few seats. And the system of preference votes encourages factionalism, pressure group interference in party affairs, and the creation of impregnable personal fiefs by deputies who are particularly adept in nursing their constituencies.

Some basic changes have taken place in Italian political campaigns since 1946. Whereas in 1946 and 1947 the party leaders used to address mammoth Sunday rallies in the principal squares of Italian cities, in the 1960s and 1970s such rallies were much more sparsely attended. It is now forbidden to use streamers and billboards for campaign advertising, though wall posters are still legal. The use of sound trucks and the distribution of flyers are still permissible but only under stringent regulation. Generally speaking, the campaigns are placing less emphasis on issues and ideas and are communicating with the voters largely with brief, catchy slogans.[50] In place of the old-style party rally, we have letters and pamphlets mailed to members of specific categories of citizens, word-of-mouth communication by party activists, and allotted time on television. In any event, these changes may be of minor significance. There is little evidence that Italian political campaigns have a major impact on election results.

Conclusions

The foregoing discussion has largely confirmed Sartori's thesis that the Italian party system is centrifugal, polarized, and multipolar, and is rendered immobile and unresponsive by peripheral turnover. Galli's view that Italy has an imperfect two-party system, in which both the overweening strength of the giants and the feebleness of the pygmies are self-perpetuating, also appears to be bolstered by recent events.

But what *has* been seriously shaken has been the thesis that the Italian party system is basically stable and immobile. The increasing volatility of voting behavior; the erosion of the DC's monopoly of power, as the dying off of older voters and the exodus from the rural areas thin the ranks of political Catholicism; the capture by the left of two of the three regions in the Northwest Industrial Triangle; the polarization of class voting, as the PCI and DC capture larger proportions of working-class and middle-class voters, respectively—all these are changes of great magnitude. The tacit collaboration given by the PCI to the Andreotti cabinet in 1976–1978 and the habitual exchange of favors and courtesies among cadres of opposing parties at the grass roots[51] are signs that a breakthrough like the "historic compromise" is not altogether inconceivable.

But even the "historic compromise"—which might cost the PCI its present status as a protest party and lead to the emergence of a new mass party on the extreme left—would not resolve the more basic defects of the Italian party system. The absence of even the *appearance* of turnover deprives the voters of any real sense of efficacy. And the domination of the parties by seemingly irremovable elites causes apathy among some voters, bitter alienation among others. Even if a kind of "grand coalition" were formed, these problems would remain. Voters would still lack that sense of participation and ultimate control that makes for a positive affect toward democratic institutions.

The problems confronting the system as a whole are very grave. But even more severe are the dilemmas facing the two giant parties. On the one hand, the PCI faces a harsh choice between a policy of collaboration with the DC and the other center parties and a policy of all-out opposition. The first alternative involves sharing the blame for the inevitable hardships Italian society must undergo in the near future, deluding the expectations of the young, running the risk of being co-opted by the bourgeois parties. The second alternative poses the danger of a "Chilean solution."

And the DC, too, must make unpalatable choices, for it is a polyglot, heterogeneous party which could select any one of a variety of paths. It has a strong Catholic component, involving more or less close ties with the church; it has a laic component, based on the anti-Communist middle classes; it has a set of progressive factions (symbolized by Secretary Zaccagnini); and it has strongly conservative elements (rallying around ex-Secretary Fanfani). And its class composition is just as varied: conservative members of the petty bourgeoisie, white-collar workers, farmers, industrial workers, and progressive intellectuals all co-exist in this vast catchall party. Which vector is to prevail?

Whatever road the DC takes, it faces unfavorable odds. For its strongest bases of support—the older-age cohorts, the rural areas, the small towns—are all suffering a demographic decline. And this decline far outweighs the limited reservoir of middle-class voters the DC can lure away from the minor center parties and the right as it did in 1976. So, if existing trends continue and if the two chief protagonists cannot resolve their respective dilemmas, Italian democracy faces a time of trouble.

Notes

Much of this chapter is drawn from Raphael Zariski, *Italy: The Politics of Uneven Development*, Hinsdale, Ill.: Dryden Press, 1972, pp. 30–33, 68–71, 75–90, 140–200.

1. See Giovanni Sartori, "European Political Parties: The Case of Polarized Pluralism," in Joseph La Palombara and Myron Weiner, eds., *Political Parties and Political Development*, Princeton, N.J.: Princeton University Press, 1966, chap. 5; and Giovanni Sartori, *Parties and Party Systems: A Framework for Analysis*, Cambridge and New York: Cambridge University Press, 1976: vol. I, pp. 131–145.

2. See Giorgio Galli, *Il bipartitismo imperfetto*, Bologna: Il Mulino, 1966.

3. See Samuel H. Barnes, *Representation in Italy: Institutionalized Tradition and Electoral Choice*, Chicago: University of Chicago Press, 1977, pp. 18, 19, 23–25.

4. See Raphael Zariski, *Italy: The Politics of Uneven Development*, Hinsdale, Ill.: Dryden Press, 1972, pp. 146–147; Giacomo Sani, "Le elezioni degli anni settanta: terremoto o evoluzione?," *Rivista Italiana di Scienze Politica*, 6 (August 1976), 271–274; and Giacomo Sani, "Secular Trends and Party Realignments in Italy: The 1975 Elections," paper delivered at the 1975 annual meeting of the American Political Science Association, San Francisco, September 2–5, 1975, pp. 1–2 and n. 3.

5. Election results for 1976 were drawn from "Results of the Italian General Elections Held in June 1976," *Italy: Documents and Notes*, 25 (May–June 1976), 196.

6. See Sartori, *Political Parties*, pp. 26–27, 131–145.

7. For election statistics for the years 1946–1976, see "Results of the Italian General Elections Held in June 1976," which also contains the 1972 results; "General

Elections 1968: Official Results," *Italy: Documents and Notes*, 17 (May–June 1968), 200; "The General Election: Italy's Fourth Republican Parliament," *Italian Affairs: Documents and Notes*, 12 (1963), 67; "The General Elections," *Italian Affairs*, 7 (September–October 1958), 38; and "The Italian General Election," *Italian Affairs*, 2 (June 1953), 10, which includes the 1946, 1948, and 1953 figures.

8. See Sartori, *Political Parties*, p. 139.

9. Ibid., pp. 131–145. See also Giuseppe Di Palma, *Surviving Without Governing: The Italian Parties in Parliament*, Berkeley: University of California Press, 1977, chap. 6.

10. See Galli, op. cit.

11. See Di Palma, pp. 268–271, and Alan Zuckerman, *Political Clienteles in Power: Party Factions and Cabinet Coalitions in Italy*, Beverly Hills, Calif.: Sage Professional Papers in Comparative Politics, 1975, pp. 20–45.

12. See Di Palma, op. cit., pp. 268–271.

13. See Galli, op. cit., pp. 83–87.

14. For a discussion of the programs of the various Italian parties, see Orazio Maria Petracca, "Tattica e strategia nei programmi elettorali," in Mattei Dogan and Orazio Maria Petracca, *Partiti politici e strutture sociali in Italia*, Milano: Comunità, 1968, pp. 51–120. On Communist programs in particular, see "Italy's Communists," *The Economist*, March 5, 1976, pp. 57–58. See also the chapters by Donald L. M. Blackmer, Stephen Hellman, Peter Weitz, and Sidney Tarrow, in Donald L. M. Blackmer and Sidney Tarrow, eds., *Communism in Italy and France*, Princeton, N.J.: Princeton University Press, 1975, chaps. 1, 10, 14, 15.

15. See Di Palma, pp. 260–262.

16. Ibid., pp. 258–268.

17. See Maurice Duverger, *Political Parties*, London: Methuen, 1954, pp. 20–21, 25–27.

18. See Joseph La Palombara, "Political Party Systems and Crisis Governments: French and Italian Contrasts," *Midwest Journal of Political Science*, 2 (May 1958), 131–135.

19. See Giuseppe Maranini, *Storia del potere in Italia: 1848–1967*, Firenze: Vallecchi, 1967, pp. 409–410.

20. See Giuseppe Reale, "I partiti del centro sinistra e la crisi di governo del giugno 1963," *Partiti e democrazia: Atti del III Convegno di San Pellegrino*, Roma: Edizioni Cinque Lune, 1964, p. 906.

21. See Otto Kirchheimer, "The Transformation of the Western European Party Systems," in Joseph La Palombara and Myron Weiner, eds., *Political Parties and Political Development*, Princeton, N.J.: Princeton University Press, 1966, pp. 182–183.

22. See P. A. Allum, *Italy—Republic Without Government?*, New York: W. W. Norton, 1973, pp. 70–71.

23. See Di Palma, op. cit., p. 261, and Gianfranco Pasquino, "Crisi della DC e evoluzione del sistema politico," *Rivista Italiana di Scienza Politica*, 5 (December 1975), 461.

24. See Gianfranco Pasquino, "The Italian Socialist Party: An Irreversible Decline?," in Howard R. Penniman, ed., *Italy at the Polls: The Italian Parliamentary Elections of 1976*, Washington, D.C.: American Enterprise Institute for Public Policy Research, 1977, p. 188.

25. See Di Palma, op. cit., p. 261, and Pasquino, "Crisi della DC," p. 461.

26. Ibid.

27. Galli, op. cit., pp. 154–157.

28. Ibid., pp. 157–162.

29. See Di Palma, op. cit., pp. 264–268. See also Giuseppe Di Palma, "Christian Democracy: The End of Hegemony?," in Penniman, ed., op. cit. pp. 127–131, and Sidney G. Tarrow, *Peasant Communism in Southern Italy*, New Haven, Conn.: Yale University Press, 1967, pp. 322–332.

30. See Mattei Dogan, "Political Cleavage and Social Stratification in France and Italy," in Seymour M. Lipset and Stein Rokkan, eds., *Party Systems and Voter Alignments*, New York: Free Press, 1967, p. 184.

31. See Dogan, op. cit., pp. 146–148. See also Giorgio Braga, *Sociologia elettorale della Toscana*, Roma: Edizioni Cinque Lune, 1963, pp. 12, 110.

32. See Joseph La Palombara, *Interest Groups in Italian Politics*, Princeton, N.J.: Princeton University Press, 1964, pp. 235–246.

33. See Giorgio Galli, ed., *Il comportamento elettorale in Italia*, Bologna: Il Mulino, 1968, pp. 205–211, 242–245, 274, 304–306. Co-authors include V. Capecchi, V. Cioni Polacchini, and G. Sivini.

34. See Galli, ed., *Il comportamento elettorale*, p. 243.

35. See Stephen Hellman, "The Longest Campaign: Communist Party Strategy and the Elections of 1976," in Penniman, ed., op. cit., pp. 176–178, and Arturo Parisi and Gianfranco Pasquino, "20 giugno: struttura politica e comportamenti elettorali," *Il Mulino*, 25 (May–June 1976), 356.

36. See Pasquino, "The Italian Socialist Party," in Penniman, ed., op. cit., pp. 213–215.

37. See Parisi and Pasquino, loc. cit., 344, 348–349, 363, 368–369, 382–383.

38. See Achille Ardigò, "Il volto elettorale di Bologna," in Alberto Spreafico and Joseph La Palombara, eds., *Elezioni e comportamento politico in Italia*, Milano, Comunità, 1963, pp. 825, 839–840.

39. See Barnes, op. cit., chap. 4.

40. See Parisi and Pasquino, pp. 362–363, 368–369, and Gianfranco Pasquino, "Before and After the Italian General Elections of 1976," *Government and Opposition*, 12 (Winter 1977), 64.

41. See Pasquino, "Before and After," p. 64. See also Angelo Panebianco, "Analisi di una sconfitta: il declino del PSI nel sistema politico italiano," *Il Mulino*, 25 (September–October 1976), 673–703, especially pp. 677–679, 687–688, and

Stefano Bartolini, "Per un' analisi dei rapporti tra partiti socialisti e comunisti in Italia e Francia," *Rivista Italiana di Scienza Politica*, 6 (December 1976), 439–481, esp. pp. 459–461.

42. See Sani, "Le elezioni," loc. cit., 266–274, and Giacomo Sani, "Ricambio elettorale e identificazioni partiche: verso una egemonia delle sinistre?," *Rivista Italiana di Scienza Politica*, 5 (December 1975), 517–526.

43. See Sani, "Secular Trends," op. cit., p. 7, and Parisi and Pasquino, loc. cit., p. 356.

44. See Sani, "Ricambio elettorale," loc. cit., p. 536.

45. See Parisi and Pasquino, loc. cit., pp. 356–360.

46. See Sani, "Ricambio elettorale," loc. cit., pp. 526–532, esp. p. 531.

47. See Parisi and Pasquino, loc. cit. pp. 373–375.

48. See Sani, "Secular Trends," pp. 1–2, and n. 3.

49. See Sani, "Le elezioni," loc. cit., pp. 272–273.

50. See Luigi Anderlini, "I partiti tutti contro tutti," *L'Astrolabio*, April 30, 1975, pp. 6–7.

51. On grass-roots collaboration and exchange among politicians of different parties, see Sidney Tarrow, *Between Center and Periphery: Grassroots Politicians in Italy and France*, New Haven, Conn.: Yale University Press, 1977, pp. 180–182. See also for a provocative analysis of various models of the Italian party system and for a discussion of vertical and horizontal political exchange in that system, Sidney Tarrow, "The Italian Party System Between Crisis and Transition," *American Journal of Political Science*, 21 (May 1977), 193–224.

PART TWO

The Smaller Democracies

INTRODUCTION TO
PART TWO

Peter H. Merkl

THE MAJORITY of Western European countries have populations of less than
10 million. With the possible exception of the Netherlands (14.6 million)
and the rather new democracies of Spain (36 million) and Portugal
(10.2 million), the game of politics in these countries is evidently determined
by settings rather different from the megasystems of 55–65 million
described in Part One. How do the party systems of these smaller countries
differ from their larger cousins? In the smaller democracies, at first
glance, there appears to be more consensus, more of a sense of community
and integration, than in the larger ones where the stakes of power are high and
the likelihood of domination of one region by another is greater.

The number of parties in each system alone appears to bear this out. The
large party systems by and large have not been able to maintain the luxury
of many small parties representing traditional social elements of various
descriptions, such as agrarian, regional, or religious minority parties. Even
France and Italy are now well on their way toward bipolar majoritarianism
despite the occasional resurgence of regionalisms such as the Occitan and
Breton splinter movements in France or their Scotch and Welsh equivalents
in Great Britain. The smaller democracies, by comparison, have the most
pluralistic party systems among them, especially Denmark, Finland,
Switzerland, Norway, the Netherlands, and Belgium (Table 1–3), and with
five or more parties are generally of the "extreme pluralistic" type according
to Sartori. The only exceptions or near-exceptions among them, curiously,
are the minisystems of Luxembourg and Iceland, the next smallest country,

155

Ireland, and Austria, a country whose party system still bears the marks of the polarization period of the 1920s[1] just as Ireland's bears that of the splitting of the independence movement in the 1930s over the treaty issue. The new democracies, Spain, Portugal, and Greece, have pronounced traditional and regional elements, much like Switzerland, Belgium, and others, which will continue to inhibit complete polarization for some time to come.

The other difference may be found in internal characteristics of the relationship of the party systems to their respective societies. Until a decade ago, a chief point of emphasis in essays on such countries as the Scandinavian and Benelux countries, Switzerland, and even Austria were various interpretations of consociational democracy.[2] *In essence, consociationalism is usually defined as a system of mutually exclusive, highly cohesive* familles spirituelles, Zuilen *(pillars), or* Lager *(battle camps), whose leaders have successfully kept down confrontation and competition among them by patterns of cooperation and coalition over long periods of time. In his seminal work on "segmented pluralism," Val Lorwin ascribed a high degree of it to Austria and the Benelux countries, a medium extent to France, Italy, Germany, Switzerland, and the United States, and a low degree to Ireland, Great Britain, and the Scandinavian countries.[3] He also traced its gradual decline of which some of the most recent developments are described in Galen Irwin's contribution on the Netherlands in this book. The concept has even been applied to such countries as Lebanon,[4] Colombia, Uruguay, and Canada until their recent breakdowns of consensus. Sometimes the pact of cooperation has been laid down in constitutions or formal agreements, other times it may be carried out through top-level councils or informal networks of group leaders. Unfortunately, we must refer the reader to other sources on such classic consociational cases as Belgium and Switzerland,[5] although we can present electoral statistics on them (Tables II–1 and II–2). The table relating to Belgium shows the relative stability of the partisan vote over time—the growth of the ethnic parties and the Liberals in the 1960s at the expense of the Christian Social party and the Socialists was the only change of consequence. The Swiss pattern is even more stable, owing among other things to the very low turnout. Both the Belgian and the Swiss systems show their ethnic and, in the Swiss case, also religious pluralism as the major barriers to polarization and party competition. It stands to reason that such extremes of segmented pluralism would hardly have survived politically in a larger, less protected setting.[6]*

The consociational patterns in the Scandinavian countries, by common consensus, have been far weaker even though, in their large numbers of parties and relative geographic protection, they seem to resemble those of the Benelux countries and Switzerland. Sten Sparre Nilson, in his chapter on Norway and Denmark and his note in Part Four, discusses conflicting

TABLE II-1. Belgian Chamber Elections, 1946–1974 (Percent)

	1946	1949	1950	1954	1958	1961	1965	1968	1971	1974
Christian Socials	43	44	48	41	46	41	34	32	32	32
Socialists	32	30	35	37	36	37	28	28	27	27
Liberals	9	15	11	12	11	12	22	21	15	15
Communists	13	7	5	4	2	3	5	3	3	4
Volksunie	—	2	—	2	2	4	7	10	11	10
Walloons	—	—	—	—	—	1	2	6	11	11
Others	3	2	1	4	3	2	2	—	1	1
	100	100	100	100	100	100	100	100	100	100

157

TABLE II–2.   Selected Elections to the Swiss National Council (Number of Seats)

	1919	1928	1939	1947	1959	1967	1975
Catholics	41	46	43	44	47	45	46
Radicals	63	58	51	52	51	49	45
Socialist	41	50	45	48	51	51	55
Farmers	25	31	22	21	23	21	21
Independents	—	—	9	9	10	16	11
Liberals	9	6	6	7	5	6	6
Communists	—	—	—	7	3	5	4
Others	10	7	11	6	6	6	10
	189	198	187	194	196	199	198

conceptions of "salient cleavages," fragmentation, aggregation, and polarization with regard to the recent developments in the Norwegian and Danish systems. The question of whether cross-cutting cleavages divide or unify a body politic is an old issue in political sociology.

Another feature likely to be prevalent in the less developed smaller countries though not entirely absent in larger ones like Italy or France are competing structures of political articulation and aggregation from the past. Constitutional monarchy still inhibits partisan competition in many of the smaller democracies including Spain and so does the powerful presidency of Finland. The armed forces, and, less often, the bureaucracy may play a similar role in countries like Spain and Greece. Patron-client relationships as the antecedents of parties or as mediating structures inside parties are another major factor holding back party competition in Ireland, in Mediterranean countries, and elsewhere as well.

Notes

1. See Alfred Diamant, *Austrian Catholics and the First Republic: Democracy, Capitalism, and the Social Orders*, Princeton, N.J.: Princeton University Press, 1960, pp. 73–80, and Peter C. J. Pulzer, "The Legitimizing Role of Political Parties: The Second Austrian Republic," *Government and Opposition*, 4 (1969), 324–344.

2. See esp. Arend Lijphart, "Consociational Democracy," *World Politics*, 21 (1969), pp. 207–225.

3. "Segmented Pluralism: Ideological Cleavages and Political Cohesion in the Smaller European Democracies," *Comparative Politics*, 3 (1971), 141–175. Religious dissension and particular socioeconomic issues played a major role in the formation of the pillars during the political development of these countries.

4. See, for example, Tawfic Farah, *Aspects of Consociationalism and Modernization: Lebanon as an Exploratory Test Case*, Lincoln, Neb.: Middle East

Research Group, 1975, and Alvin Rabushka and Kenneth A. Shepsle, *Politics in Plural Societies*, Columbus, Ohio: Merrill, 1972 for other examples.

5. See esp. Val Lorwin, "Belgium: Conflict and Compromise" in Kenneth D. McRae, ed., *Consociational Democracy: Political Accommodation in Segmented Societies*, Toronto: McClelland & Stewart, 1974, pp. 179–206; Roger Girod, "Geography of the Swiss Party System," in Erik Allardt and Yrjo Littunen, eds., *Cleavages, Ideologies, and Party Systems*, Helsinki: Academic Bookstore, 1964, pp. 132–161; and James A. Dunn, *Social Cleavage, Party Systems, and Political Integration: A Comparison of the Belgian and Swiss Experiences*, Unpublished Ph.D. dissertation, University of Pennsylvania, 1970. But see also the critical view expressed by Brian Barry, "Political Accommodation and Consociational Democracy," *British Journal of Political Science*, 5 (1975), 477–505 and in "The Consociational Model and Its Dangers," *European Journal of Political Research*, 3 (1975), 393–412.

6. Of course, there have also been breakdowns of consociationalism such as the language riots in Belgium and the Jura problem in Switzerland. On the other hand, the Canadian problems with Quebec demonstrate dramatically what may happen in a larger, less protected setting once the supraregional consensus breaks down. See esp. McRae, pp. 235–261 and the other contributions on Canada there. McRae suggests that, in the Canadian case, the majoritarian attitude of the English Canadians all along made the growth of consociationalism there doubtful and eventually engendered its equivalent among the French Canadians. Ibid., pp. 300–302.

CHAPTER 6

THE NETHERLANDS

Galen A. Irwin

TO THE FOREIGN OBSERVER, the Dutch party system has often seemed bewildering in its variety. The large number of parties that take part in the elections, the similarly large number that secure representation in the Parliament, and the number of small parties that seem to compete for the same small group of voters combine to require considerable devoted study before one can feel at ease in any political discussion. In recent years, for example, there have been two parties bearing the label Catholic, four (sometimes five) Protestant parties, three labeled socialist (including a somewhat right-of-center variety), plus radicals, communists, and progressive democrats. In addition, there has been a wide offering of other sorts, including in 1977 an Old Folks party, a Maoist-oriented Socialist party, a Taxpayers party, a Retailers party, and a League against Bureaucratic Capriciousness. Through the years the list has been wide and virtually endless.

Yet despite the bewilderment for the outsider, to the Dutchman, who knew exactly where he fit, it has been quite understandable. "Until recently politics in the Netherlands were of exemplary stability . . . ," wrote Ter Hoeven in 1970.[1] In a comparative study of the same year, Rose and Urwin classified the Dutch party system as static; the percentages for the parties displayed few cumulative trends and few fluctuations over time.[2] Despite the number of small parties that have added much color to Dutch politics, five parties have dominated the scene since even before the institution of universal suffrage. Between 1918 and 1963, these Big Five never received less than 83.9% of the votes cast and reached a high of 91.6% in 1959.[3] Moreover, the proportions of the vote received by each of the Big Five and the two more permanent smaller

161

parties (the small Calvinist Political Reformed party and the Communist party) was quite stable. In 1948, only 4 of the 100 seats changed hands at the election. After the expansion of the Parliament to 150 seats, the number of seats that changed hands at the elections of 1956, 1959, and 1963 was only 7, 8, and 9, respectively.[4]

In the mid-1960s the traditional party system began to show the signs of strain. In 1963 a Farmer's party, sometimes described as *Poujadist*, succeeded in gaining 2.13% of the vote and three seats in Parliament. This, and its subsequent rather dramatic successes in the following municipal elections, might easily have been dismissed, had not a series of events occurred in 1966 that definitely established that the system was under pressure. Government uncertainty and/or mishandling of such affairs as the marriage of Princess Beatrix, provo agitators and the demands of construction workers eroded faith in the governing elite. Citizens began to become less "passive" and more "politicized."[5] In the second edition of his book, Lijphart found it necessary to add a new concluding chapter on "the breakdown of the politics of accommodation," in which he wrote, "The system of accommodation reached its heyday in the 1950's but declined rapidly in the following decade. By the late 1960's, it had broken down completely. The Second Chamber elections of 1967 marked the turning point, and this year can therefore be regarded as the end of half a century of accommodation politics."[6]

The events of 1966 made themselves felt politically at the parliamentary elections of February 1967. Following the elections in 1963, a Liberal-Confessional cabinet had been formed, which fell in 1965 on a question concerning commercial television. The Socialists were then drawn back into government only to be dumped the following year. An interim cabinet was formed to carry on until new elections could be called. Yet frustration was high with a political system which could produce three cabinet combinations without resorting to elections. After first examining the "market" through careful research, a new party—Democrats '66—was formed with the express purpose of "exploding" the existing party system and bringing about other reforms of the political system. By Dutch standards the success of this new party was astounding, achieving seven seats in the first try for Parliament, and the impact was felt quickly. Soon thereafter, a young politician, who eventually became the Socialist party leader in Parliament during the period 1973–1977, wrote "Constitutional revision is 'in.' After the overwhelming electoral successes of D'66 there is no party that does not have 'an open eye' for the need for revision of our democratic institutions."[7] Within Van Thijn's own Socialist party, changes were also being pushed by a group calling themselves New Left. This group was committed to achieving, among other things, greater participatory democracy and demanded changes in the style, policy, and orientation of the party.

The British political scientist Kenneth Gladdish has summarized a number of complaints, which were (and still often are) leveled at the Dutch political system:[8]

1. "the recurrently inconclusive outcome of elections"—no party and, often, no single bloc gains a majority of the seats in Parliament;
2. "the unresponsiveness of cabinet formation to electoral fluctuation"— "in 1971 the five party coalition government which eventually took office included four parties which had lost seats at the election";
3. "delays in cabinet formation";
4. "the unaccountability of party strategy"—"the reluctance of party leaders to commit themselves before elections to any prescribed formula for post-election strategy" and the unaccountability which "occurs where coalitions are dismantled and new combinations formed without further reference to the electorate, as happened in 1958, 1965, and 1966";
5. "the invertebrate character of governing coalitions"—the "tendency for the style of multi-party government to be reconciliationist, rather than dynamic and incisive";
6. "the confusions of multiple choice and the absence of polarisation";
7. "the inertias and anachronisms of the party machines";
8. "the anonymity of the list system of voting and the absence of locality representation."

Although it is beyond the scope of the present discussion to deal with all of these criticisms here, several will become evident in the course of the discussion.

The Parties and Their Development

The political party system of the Netherlands clearly reflects two traditional cleavages in the society. The older cleavage derives from religious orientation and can be traced back to the Spanish occupation of the sixteenth century. Nationalism and Protestantism coincided in opposition to the Spanish Catholics. With the expulsion of the Spanish, Protestantism had established itself as the dominant religion in the northern provinces. Although the Catholic faith was never forbidden, as this was a matter of personal belief and conscience, Catholics (along with Jews and adherents to numerous dissident Protestant sects) were relegated to second-class citizenship. Catholics were not allowed to hold public religious services or to hold public office. Most lived in the conquered territory of Brabant and Limburg, the so-called "lands of generality," which were governed virtually as colonies; heavy taxes and other measures helped to keep them backward politically, economically, and culturally.

Within the dominant Dutch Reformed church, many shades of opinion were found. Although the theological arguments are complex, the basic questions generally centered around orthodoxy versus Latitudinarianism and a centralized church organization versus freedom for local churches. Orthodox groups favoring freedom for local churches broke away in 1834 (*Afscheiding*) and in 1886 (*Doleantie*). Eventually most of these groups unified in the *Gereformeerde* church and a Gereformeerde group within the Dutch Reformed church. Throughout the nineteenth century, orthodox Calvinists belonging to such groups were the object of various degrees of church, social, and judicial discrimination.[9]

Cutting across, although in some cases reinforcing, the religious cleavage was social class. The Industrial Revolution was relatively late in reaching the Netherlands, so that the rise of an industrial proletariat was similarly late in developing, but preindustrial classes were quite evident. By the sixteenth century certain merchant and commercial families had come to dominate the social and political life of the cities and towns. The lack of a powerful aristocracy had facilitated their rise of power, and the lack of a strong central government prior to 1795 left their authority untouched until the mid- to late nineteenth century. It was, of course, virtually inconceivable that a member of this "regents" class would be Catholic, but neither were they necessarily strongly orthodox Calvinist. Their source of influence was economic, and they neither needed nor utilized the support of the church.

Despite certain social and religious restrictions, the Netherlands was long known for its tolerant atmosphere, so that when liberalism finally arrived as a philosophy it did not take the form of an emancipation movement. By the mid-nineteenth century, middle- and upper-class liberals, aided by property qualifications for voting, were in firm command of the political scene.

Beneath this dominant structure, at least two important groups must be distinguished. One was the class of small shopkeepers, artisans, fishermen, inland shippers, independent farmers, and lower-level public employees whom Abraham Kuyper called the "little men." These were generally quite orthodox in their faith, and it was they whom Kuyper organized into the first national political party (see the discussion following Protestant Tradition).[10] The other group was composed of workers and paupers, often without any strong religious preferences, who formed the bottom of the social ladder.

This brief description of the social situation in the Netherlands of the nineteenth century provides us with four groups that are relevant to the emergence of the party system—the dominant liberal class, the Protestants, the Catholics, and the workers. Understanding these social origins and the factors that led to the establishment of the first political parties is perhaps more important than an examination of current party programs for understanding the Dutch political party system.

THE LIBERAL TRADITION

Prior to the establishment of modern political parties, groupings of like-minded representatives were found in Parliament. In the mid-nineteenth century Netherlands, the most important of these groupings were the Liberals. Despite the rather liberal attitudes of the ruling classes, liberalism as a philosophy was rather slow in taking hold. When it did arrive, the growing demands for freedom centered around two questions: (1) the role of the monarch versus the role of the ministers and Parliament and (2) the role of the church in political affairs. Although Liberals agreed on freedom of conscience for all in religious matters, even when they disagreed on other matters, they were generally united in their anticlericalism in matters of state.

The Liberals flourished most during the third quarter of the century under the leadership of Johan Rudolf Thorbecke. Thorbecke's political philosophy is well summed up in his definition of the state:[11]

> the mark of a liberal state and a liberal movement [is], that it encourages the development of self-sufficiency; self-sufficiency in province, municipality, organization, and individual. Encouragement, that means providing the general conditions, by which the development is made possible. . . . Does this mean that the state must attend to everything, to heal all the evils and shortcomings of society? On the contrary. The first demand is abstinence; abstinence from that which goes beyond her calling as legal union.

Difficulties in seeking a balance between the progressive principle of encouraging self-sufficiency and the more conservative principle of abstinence have continued to manifest themselves in the thinking and programs of the various Liberal parties to the present day. Thorbecke left his lasting imprint on the Dutch political system through a revision of the constitution and in a law organizing the government of municipalities. Through the constitutional revision, the principle of ministerial responsibility was introduced, Parliament was granted increased powers, and the Second Chamber of Parliament was thenceforth elected directly rather than by the provincial legislatures.

The period of Liberal dominance actually preceded the founding of the first Liberal party in 1885. This Liberal Union was a loosely organized party, strongly united only in its anticlericalism. Not too long after its establishment, a radical democratic group split off to form the Radical League (1892). A further split occurred when the Liberal minister, J. P. R. Tak van Poortvliet, introduced a law which would have substantially extended suffrage. The anti-Takkians, as they were called, eventually founded the League for Free Liberals.

With the rise of mass political parties, as described below, and the extension of suffrage, the influence of the Liberals began to decline. During the 1920s and 1930s only a small percentage of the vote was gained. After World War II, during which time the democratic parties were banned by the German occupiers, many Liberal leaders questioned the basis for reestablishing a separate Liberal party and cooperated with the prewar socialists in founding the Labor party (PvdA). This cooperation was short-lived, however, and in 1948 the People's Party for Democracy and Freedom (known almost exclusively by its abbreviation, VVD) was established. The new party quickly obtained the approximately 10% of the vote which the Liberals had held before the war.

Yet the image of the new party was still associated with the "regents" of times past, until in 1972 the party made a move to create a new, more modern image. The barely 30-year-old chairman of the parliamentary party, Hans Wiegel, was placed at the top of the party list of candidates. Glib, aggressive, and clever in his use of the mass media, Wiegel helped to give the party a more dynamic and youthful image. Rather than an intellectual liberal line, he talked in direct terms and in a manner designed to appeal to a wide range of supporters. While fighting against the bigness and pushiness of government, he stressed that the aged and those who worked need not fear that social benefits would be curtailed. Those who were genuinely needy would be helped, but freeloaders would be cut off.

In making such appeals, Wiegel attempted to break down the middle- and upper-class image of the party, and to an extent he has succeeded. The party virtually doubled its vote to 18% in 1977. His critics, however, protest that he has done so by deserting the liberal heritage of the party, turning it into an ideologically conservative party. Moreover, the strategy of polarization has made cooperation with the PvdA virtually impossible, thus removing an important alternative for the formation of a cabinet. At the moment, the criticism is stilled by the party's good fortune in gaining an opportunity to form a government with the Christian Democrats (CDA). Although the party will be forced to deal with the problems of government, this should also provide an opportunity to increase exposure for other prominent VVD leaders and allow time for the party to consider its future course.

THE CATHOLIC TRADITION

With the introduction of more liberal ideas, the political emancipation of the Catholics became possible. The constitutional revision of 1848 brought freedom of worship and organization, so that in 1853 the episcopal hierarchy could be reestablished. Although in the effort to secure equal rights, the Catholics had allied with the Liberals, this alliance was soon tested and eventually broken. Disagreement arose over Liberal support of anticlerical nationalists in Italy, a papal encyclical, *Quanta Cura*, warned of the improper influence of liberalism and in a *Syllabus Errorum* stressed the need for Catholic schools. This collided with the Liberal policy of neutral schools, and, when the Calvinists proved willing, a new Christian alliance was formed.

Although Catholics were elected to Parliament, it took considerable time before they could be unified into a parliamentary party, and even more years elapsed before a mass political party structure was erected. The movement attempted to encompass all Catholics, regardless of social class, in an effort to bring all out of their second-class status. On questions such as the school question, which directly affected their religion, Catholics were reasonably unified. On other issues, differing group interests proved difficult to balance. The question of extension of the franchise, for example, divided the Catholics as deeply as it did the Liberals.

It is difficult to say just when the first Catholic political party was established. Lipschits treats the General League of Roman Catholic Voter's Clubs (1904) as at least the forerunner of a Catholic party.[12] The Roman Catholic State party was founded in 1926, and remained the predominant Catholic party until World War II. Following the war, many Catholic political leaders questioned the necessity for reestablishing a separate Catholic party. Theological considerations had always played a lesser role in the justification of the party than for the Calvinists, and the need for a party of emancipation was less imminent. However, at least partially as a result of efforts by the church hierarchy, a new Catholic People's party (KVP) was established, picking up pretty much where its predecessor had left off. It has been no less susceptible to the internal difficulties that arose from attempts to pacify the many diverse interests within the party. Most recently, a conservative Roman Catholic party of the Netherlands (1972) appeared, based primarily on objections to the mother party's stand on abortion. In contrast to the Protestants, and even to the VVD and the PvdA, the dominant Catholic party has always managed to fend off such attacks and remain essentially unified. This is perhaps best accounted for by the historical traditions of common discrimination and the direct efforts of the church hierarchy in maintaining unity.

The success of the Roman Catholic State party and the KVP in gaining the support of Catholic voters was quite remarkable. Most research indicates that between 1917 and 1967, some 80–90% of all Catholics supported the party.[13] Relying upon this solid base of about 30% of the total voting population, the party was generally the largest party in Parliament. In the 1960s the Catholic church in the Netherlands underwent extreme changes, moving from serving as one of the Vatican's strongest supporters to becoming almost a renegade. Whether the influence on the voters was direct or indirect, from 1967 the percentage of the vote for the KVP began dropping dramatically, with important consequences not only for the party but for the entire political system.

In contrast to the Calvinist Antirevolutionary opposition to liberalism, Catholics have seemed more to fear socialism. As a movement for the emancipation of the working class, socialism was in direct competition for the votes, if not the souls of Catholic workers. Following the lead of Kuyper and the Protestants, separate organizations were created to protect Catholics from unwanted influences. Certainly not the least important was the organization of Catholic trade unions (NKV). As late as 1954, the bishops threatened to refuse the sacraments to any Catholic who joined a Socialist union or, for that matter, listened to radio broadcasts of the Socialist network. Although this mandate has never been officially retracted, it has long since ceased to have meaning. Nevertheless, despite various periods of cooperation between the KVP and the PvdA in forming a government, considerable mistrust has remained.

THE PROTESTANT TRADITION

Most appalled by the emergence of the new liberal philosophy, which they saw as rising out of the principles of the French Revolution, were the orthodox Calvinists (Gereformeerden). The idea that authority, and in particular political authority, might arise from the people and not from God was especially repulsive. "Against the Revolution, the Gospels," stated Groen van Prinsteren as the motto for the antirevolutionaries. Opposition to the liberal rational-humanistic philosophies led to a desire not only for a resurgence of Calvinist influence, but protection through insulation from these new influences.

Not only was the Calvinist movement a reaction against liberalism, it was an attempt to emancipate the "small man" who was discriminated against because of his social position and his faith. The means of this emancipation was mass organization, and in the clergyman Abraham Kuyper a great organizer was found. In the time span of a single generation, Kuyper organized a daily newspaper, an Anti-School Law League, a mass petition movement against the Liberal School law, the first national political party—the Anti-Revolutionary party (ARP)—the Free University in Amsterdam, and a separate church organization after the walkout in 1878.

Somewhat paralleling, but extending beyond American ideas of separation of church and state, Kuyper believed that God had organized the world in various spheres, such as family, factory, school, and nation. Separate authority was transmitted by God to these spheres, so that each was "sovereign in own sphere" and could not intrude on another. This philosophy clashed with the liberal principle of neutral schools, and the ensuing battle continued until the compromise of 1917 in which the principle of equal governmental financing of confessional schools was recognized.

Groen van Prinsterer had written that God reveals Himself in two ways, through revelation ("it is written") and through Christian history ("it happened"). The terms "antirevolutionary" and "christian-historical" were thus originally virtually synonymous.[14] However, when the ARP split into Takkian and anti-Takkian factions over the question of extension of franchise, the leader of the party in Parliament, A. F. de Savornin Lohman, broke with Kuyper and helped to form a new party. After a transformation and merger with some other parties, this new party became in 1908 the Christian-Historical Union (CHU). De Savornin Lohman had taken the more conservative position on franchise, and in general the party received more support from middle- to upper-class Protestants. Furthermore, it received more support from members of the Dutch Reformed church, many of whom felt that the influence of the Gereformeerden was too great in the Anti-Revolutionary party.

A break within the Gereformeerde church over the question of separation of church and state and the possibility of cooperation with Catholics led eventually to the formation in 1918 of a new party, the Political Reformed party (SGP). This ultraconservative, ultra-Calvinist party has been continuously represented in Parliament since 1922. After World War II, differences of theology again led to a group walking out of the Gereformeerde church and eventually establishing their own political party. This Reformed Political League (GPV) first gained a seat in the Second Chamber in 1963.

THE SOCIALIST TRADITION

Undoubtedly, the late arrival of the Industrial Revolution in the agricultural Netherlands goes a long way in accounting for the late introduction of socialism into the country, making an impact only some 25 years after it had become important in Germany, 40 years later than in France, and half a century later than in England.[15] Although there had been a Dutch branch of the First International since 1870, a Social Democratic party was first founded in 1881. In the absence of a strong industrial proletariat, the early successes for the socialist movement were in certain agrarian areas, often those hit hardest by depression and where strong social conflict reinforced religious conflicts.[16] It was in the rural district of Schoterland that the first Social-Democratic member of Parliament, F. Domela Nieuwenhuis, was elected in 1888.

Although initially influenced by Marxism, Domela Nieuwenhuis was deeply disappointed by his experiences in Parliament and soon turned more in the direction of anarchism. This produced the first major split within the Socialist movement and led in 1894 to the founding of the Social-Democratic Workers party (SDAP). The new party, led for 25 years by Pieter Jelles Troelstra, quickly dominated. The growth of the SDAP shifted the emphasis from the rural areas to the large cities. Yet this growth was stopped short of goals and expectations by the strong competition from the Calvinist and Catholic emancipation movements. Even after the introduction of universal manhood suffrage, the party usually received only between 20% and 24% of the vote. This competition not only retarded the growth of the SDAP, but helped to contribute to the mistrust which developed between the Socialists and the Confessionals.

The early programs of the Dutch Socialist movement were heavily influenced by those of their German counterparts. The program of the Social Democratic League leaned heavily on the Gotha Program and that of the SDAP on that of Erfurt. However, relying only on an examination of this program would lead one to conclude that the Dutch party was more Marxist than would an examination of what the party did in practice. A radical Marxist group split off from the party at the Deventer congress in 1909; this group reorganized and in 1918 became the Communist party of the Netherlands (CPN).

The foremost early political goal of the SDAP was the introduction of universal manhood suffrage. (Other important issues concerned the eight-hour working day and government pensions.) The extension of franchise had led to serious divisions within the other parties and was finally only resolved in the great compromise of 1917. By this compromise, all elementary schools, that is, including those run by religious groups, were to receive financial assistance from the state based on the size of their enrollments. Universal manhood suffrage was introduced (women were added in 1922), and the list system of proportional representation replaced the election of members of Parliament by district.[17]

The stimulus which the introduction of universal suffrage might have given to the Socialist movement was lost in the "revolution" of Troelstra of 1919. Following the November 1918 events in Germany, Troelstra announced in and out of Parliament that the revolution had come to Holland and that the worker class would seize power. Within a few days it became clear that this was a major misperception, which he himself was forced to admit. This misjudgment had long-lasting consequences, reinforcing the image among the other parties that the Socialists were not truly democratic and could not be trusted. In 1913 the Socialists had refused participation in a government, thinking that they should wait until a majority had been achieved. After 1919 they were not again given a chance to participate until 1939, a longer wait than in any other Western European country.

After the war and the occupation, the former Socialist leaders joined with Liberals and some radical Christians in forming a new Labor Party (PvdA). This was to be a "breakthrough" party, rejecting religion as the basis of political parties. However, with the revival of all of the religious parties and the departure of important Liberal leaders to form the VVD, the party may again be considered a Socialist party. Its slogan and program stress the need and demand for more equal distributions of income, power, and knowledge.

The postwar Socialist movement has not been spared from internal dissention. In 1957 the Pacifist-Socialist party was founded as a protest to the militarism of East and West in the Cold War. It is now considered to be left of the PvdA. In the 1960s a group of young radicals, calling themselves the New Left, gained considerable influence within the party.[18] At the party congress in 1967, 7 supporters of New Left were elected to the 21-man party executive. In 1969, at the instigation of New Left, the party adopted a resolution that it would refuse to cooperate with the KVP after the election in the formation of a cabinet. As a reaction to the success and influence of New Left, a group left the party in 1970 to form the Democratic-Socialists '70 (DS '70).

DS '70 was led to success (7 seats) at the election of 1971 by the son of the former Prime Minister W. Drees. Subsequently, the party joined with the religious parties and the Liberals in forming a cabinet, whose fall it forced only a little more than one year later. Its electoral appeal has since declined substantially. Despite its Socialist origins, the party is now considered by most observers to be somewhat to the right of center.

STABILITY AND THE BEGINNINGS OF CHANGE

Allowing for some renaming of parties after World War II, five political parties (ARP, CHU, KVP, PvdA, VVD) from these four traditions have dominated the political scene. From the constitutional revision of 1917 until 1967, these five parties never polled less than 83.9% of the vote and generally obtained close to 90.0%. Until 1971, no other parties were included in the governing coalitions, and during this half century one can definitely speak of a "frozen" party structure. Not only did these five parties dominate national politics, Dutch society was equally rigidly structured, with many organizations such as trade unions, employer's organizations, newspapers, radio (and later television) networks, schools, and sport clubs organized along the lines of the four traditions just outlined. The Netherlands was literally divided into "segments" or "pillars" (*zuilen*) along religious and class lines.[19]

During this period of great political stability, voters were legally obligated to appear at the polls, and in casting a vote one bore witness to his place in society. The percentages cast for the parties varied only slightly, and the number of seats changing hands in Parliament was minimal. (Of course, this did mean that minor changes took on major importance.) In the first three columns of Table 6-1, one sees evidence of this considerable stability. The variations for the Big Five are quite small. The Labor party did show a loss of 4.7% across the three elections, but 1956 had been an all-time high percentage for the party. For the religious parties, the greatest variation was only 1.2% for the ARP, whereas the others varied only in tenths of a percentage point. The VVD showed some ups and downs.

The dominance of the Big Five certainly did not mean that other parties did not compete in the elections and occasionally gain representation. The Netherlands has long been noted for its large number of political parties, and the 10% to 15% of the vote which the Big Five were not able to obtain was split among them. Early splits with the socialist movement led to the founding of the Communist party and within the Calvinist movement to the SGP. These two parties have been represented continually in Parliament since 1918 and 1922, respectively. The SGP has consistently received a bit more than 2% of the vote; the Communists reached a high point immediately after World War II and lost heavily after 1956 because of the party's stand on the Russian invasion of Hungary (see Table 6-1).

TABLE 6–1.   Results of Elections to the Second Chamber, 1956–1977 (Percent)

	1956	1959	1963	1967	1971	1972	1977
Major parties							
Labor	32.69	30.36	28.01	23.55	24.60	27.34	33.81
Catholic People's party	31.69	31.60	31.88	26.50	21.84	17.65	} CDA[a]
Anti-Revolutionary party	9.91	9.39	8.72	9.90	8.59	8.84	} 31.91
Christian-Historical Union	8.43	8.11	8.58	8.14	6.32	4.79	
Liberal party	8.77	12.21	10.29	10.73	10.34	14.45	17.95
Long-standing minor parties							
Communist party	4.75	2.41	2.77	3.61	3.90	4.47	1.73
Political Reformed party	2.26	2.16	2.30	2.01	2.35	2.21	2.13
Newer minor parties							
Reformed Political League	0.65	0.67	0.74	0.86	1.61	1.77	0.96
Pacifist-Socialist party	—	1.84	3.03	2.87	1.44	1.50	0.94
Farmers party	—	0.66	2.13	4.77	1.10	1.94	0.84
Democrats '66	—	—	—	4.48	6.78	4.15	5.43
Democratic-Socialists '70	—	—	—	—	5.33	4.12	0.72
Radical party	—	—	—	—	1.84	4.80	1.69
Retailers party	—	—	—	—	1.51	0.45	—
Roman Catholic party	—	—	—	—	—	0.92	0.40
Other	0.85	0.60	1.56	2.58	2.46	0.60	1.49
Total	100	100	100	100	100	100	100

[a]The Christian Democrats (CDA) are a merger of the Catholic People's (KVP), Anti-Revolutionary (ARP), and Christian Historical Union (CHU) parties.

In addition to these two smaller parties with continuing support, numerous parties have entered electoral contests, sometimes with (temporary) success. At the first election following the introduction of universal manhood suffrage (1918), no less than 32 party lists of candidates were presented, and 17 won seats. In 1922 the number of lists increased to 48; however, due in part to a hike from 0.5% to 0.75% in the percentage of the vote required to gain a seat, only 10 were successful. The number of parties competing reached a peak in 1922 when no less than 54 submitted lists, of which 14 won seats. Following that election, parties were required to make a deposit that was returned only if a specified percentage of votes was achieved. From then until 1967 the number of lists seldom exceeded 13, and the number acquiring seats never exceeded 10.[20]

Despite the large number of lists and the number of parties represented in Parliament in the 1917–1967 period, these smaller parties had little impact on the political system. The first signs of change in the party system began to appear in 1963. The number of lists submitted rose to 18, and the Farmer's party (BP) entered Parliament with 3 seats. Sometimes described as *poujadist*, this new party received support not only from farmers but many others who were alienated from the dominant politics. The party's successes in the municipal elections of 1966 indicated that this discontent was more widespread than first thought. In the parliamentary election of 1967, the Farmers reached a highpoint of 7 seats, and despite numerous internal conflicts continue to be represented in Parliament. The party takes a strongly anti-Socialist line, but also an antibig-party line. Although of some interest because of its role in bringing about change in the party system, the party has never had any real political influence.

Of those parties falling outside the four major political traditions, the most important has been Democrats '66 (D'66). Its founders were primarily young academics and journalists from Amsterdam, most of whom had only loose ties with any of the existing political parties. The party was founded only after market research had convinced them that there was an opportunity for a new party that would break through the old traditions. Under strong influence from the American political system and American political science, they sought to "explode" the existing Dutch party system. They complained that the old parties were based on cleavages that were no longer relevant to the political problems of the modern world and explicitly rejected religion as a basis for parties, pointing out the conflicting political opinions that were presumably based on the same Bible.[21] Instead, they sought to replace the extreme multiparty system with a two-party system, somewhat along American lines. The direct election of the prime minister was proposed as was the return to a district system for election of the national legislature. One means of achieving this would be to encourage or in some way force the parties to indicate before the election with which other parties they would be willing to join in a coalition after the election.

D'66 caught on quickly among the voters. After its foundation in the fall of 1966, it gained almost 4.5% of the vote only a few months later in the February 1967 election. Even more shocking to the politicians, perhaps, were public opinion polls from the fall of 1967 which showed that, if elections were held then, D'66 could expect to be the third largest party in Parliament.[22] Unfortunately for D'66, elections were not held then. In fact, to the party's misfortune, the De Jong cabinet was the only cabinet since World War II to complete a full four-year term in office, and by 1971 the steam was gone from the D'66 train. The party did join with the PvdA and the Radicals to produce a "shadow cabinet" that would rule in the (highly unlikely) event that the combination received a majority of the parliamentary seats. The increase of 2% and 4 seats in 1971 was far less than had been hoped for earlier. The very fact of achieving one of its goals, namely a preelection agreement, apparently had a negative effect on some voters, convincing them to turn to the senior member of the combination—Labor—rather than a junior member. The D'66 voter corps has always been relatively young and volatile, and in 1972 the young turned to the Radicals. D'66 dropped back to 6 seats, and by the provincial elections of 1974 the party could gain only 1% of the vote. In 1976 the party kept itself in the news mainly with discussions of whether it should disband or not.

Thus the party's recovery in 1977 is almost as striking as its original success. In the fall of 1976 the popular leader of the party, Jan Terlouw (also a physicist and writer of children's books), threatened not to return as the party's top candidate. In relenting he demanded that the party faithful obtain 66,000 signatures supporting the party and sign up 1,666 new members. With renewed enthusiasm these goals were achieved. Remaining true more to its pragmatic origins than to its founding principles, the party now refused to continue its preelection accord with PvdA and the Radicals, although it did indicate that it would not enter a cabinet with the Liberals. Instead, the party chose the election slogan "A Reasonable Alternative." Somehow it all worked and D'66 became the only new, small party to succeed in 1977, actually increasing its 1972 vote by more than 1%.

A CHRISTIAN DEMOCRATIC APPEAL

Between 1967 and 1977, several new parties emerged to achieve prominence previously unheard of in Dutch politics. The smaller parties began to gain larger and larger percentages of the vote. The DS'70, the D'66, and the Radicals took part in governing coalitions. Concomitantly, the traditional Big Five suffered. In 1967, their percentage of the vote dropped below 80%, falling even further four years later to less than 72%. Some of this loss is accounted for by losses for the PvdA (probably due to increased offerings on the left), but most was the result of severe losses by the Catholics and the CHU. Both were almost halved within the space of nine years, a stark contrast to previous periods of stability. Such enormous losses, especially for the Catholic party which had almost always been the largest party, could not help but have major consequences.

An easy explanation for what set this process of "deconfessionalization" in motion is not available, and a lengthy treatment is not possible here. Survey data do tell us something about what was happening, even if it tells less about why. Comparison of a 1966 survey with one from 1975 shows that the percentage of the population reporting identification with a church declined from 74% to 58%. Although this shrinking base was certainly of importance to the religious parties, the attitudes of those still reporting religious adherence was equally important. In 1966, just under 45% of the church identifiers felt that a political party should be based upon religious principles. This percentage was less than the percentage which felt that the broadcasting networks should be based on such principles,[23] but more than those who felt that labor unions should be so based. After a drop in the percentages for all three in 1970, the percentages for the broadcasting networks and labor unions showed a slight upturn in 1975. The percentage favoring political parties based on religious principles continued to decline, in all cases looking only at those stating a religious preference.[24] In terms of votes, although some previous religious party supporters did turn away, of perhaps greater importance was that very few younger voters followed their parents in voting along the traditional lines.

The decline in votes for the religious parties led to renewed interest in the possibilities of fusion into a single Christian-democratic party. Yet despite these pressures, the long-standing differences made this appear unlikely, and, as late as 1975, Wolinetz concluded[25]

> Recent polls indicate . . . increased support for a unified Christian Democratic party, should it materialize; but at the moment that seems unlikely. Although the plans announced in 1972 and approved in succeeding years call for the submission of a common Christian Democratic list in the next parliamentary elections, divisions between the Catholics and Anti-Revolutionaries appear to preclude this. . . . The difference is serious, and the Catholics are now developing "emergency" plans to contest the elections on their own.

Although few would have questioned this analysis when it was written, a common list did materialize. Two factors would seem to have been the catalysts which helped overcome the reservations of the ARP leaders. In his analysis, Wolinetz relied on interviews with higher- and middle-level party leaders. In the ARP these leaders were long hesitant about the Christian-Democratic alliance and in stalling for time used the argument that the alliance would be difficult to sell to their followers. Yet, in local meetings, party supporters began to indicate increasing support for the idea. For several years the parties had been collaborating at the local level, and this had generally gone smoothly. With this rug pulled from under them, the leaders could do little to forestall the merger.

The second important factor was agreement on a leader for the combined ticket at the 1977 election. It would have been very difficult to choose one of the three party leaders in Parliament as the number-one man for the party list. Moreover, since the Catholics were still by far the largest of the three, they had the best claim for supplying the new party's leader. A Catholic who nevertheless could inspire Calvinist voters emerged in the person of Minister of Justice Andries van Agt. Van Agt had gained considerable publicity in his efforts to close a particular abortion clinic and in his fight against a Socialist-Liberal proposed abortion law. He quickly broadened and solidified his image by speaking of a need for an "Ethical Revival." Although criticized by the Socialists for his handling of the case of a suspected (later convicted) war criminal, his popularity rose correspondingly in other circles. His zeal and Christian conviction appealed to the Calvinists, and large numbers of all religious groups turned out during the campaign. The Christian-Democratic Appeal (CDA) obtained one more seat in Parliament than the three parties had held prior to the 1977 election. Initial analysis indicates that Protestants supported the new party relatively more strongly than Catholics.[26]

The 1977 election has not ended the problems among the three religious partners. Difficulties arose within the new parliamentary party over the election of the leadership, and the long cabinet negotiations revealed considerable differences in preferences for coalition partners. After it became apparent that cooperation with the Socialists was not possible, a cabinet was formed with the Liberals.[27] However, this coalition is only "tolerated" by a portion of the Christian-Democratic MP's who refuse to be bound to support for the cabinet. Nevertheless, despite these internal differences, the three parties have announced that a complete merger will take place by 1980.

Cabinet Formation

For the average citizen, an election generally means the conclusion of a period of heightened political interest and activity. For the elected politician, however, it is only a beginning. This is particularly true in a parliamentary system, where on the basis of the election results a new cabinet must be formed. In the Netherlands, the formation of a cabinet has never been an easy matter. No party has ever come close to obtaining a majority of the votes, so cabinets are, of necessity, coalition cabinets. Agreeing on a coalition is generally a time-consuming process; before World War II postelection cabinet formation lasted an average of 46 days but since then has increased to almost 90 days. In 1977 a new record was set of 207 days of negotiations before the new cabinet could be installed.[28]

With so many parties and, often, with so few changes after an election, it has not always been obvious what the voters have "said" through the election. Therefore, the Queen has often felt it necessary to appoint an "informateur" to inform her as to the most realistic possibilities before deeming it appropriate to appoint a "formateur" who may attempt to form a government. The "informateur" may search the party platforms for points of common interest and inquire among the various party leaders as to their preferences. He can, in many ways, pave the way for the "formateur." Nevertheless, few "formateurs" are able to complete the process without setback, and, during a single cabinet formation, several "informateurs" and "formateurs" may be appointed.[29] In 1977, five "informateurs" and two "formateurs" were involved before a cabinet was finally formed.

Cabinets must have a base in Parliament, preferably the support of a majority of the members. The translation of election results into parliamentary seats is done by the d'Hondt method which favors the larger parties. The number of parliamentary seats corresponding to the election results in Table 6–1 are presented in Table 6–2.

The key to understanding Dutch cabinet formation is the role and position of the KVP. Until its recent decline, this party was generally the largest party in Parliament, with about one-third of the seats. As a party which saw its mission as representing all Catholics, regardless of socioeconomic position, it has always followed the center course necessary to keep potentially hostile

TABLE 6–2.   Number of Seats in Second Chamber Held by Various Parties, 1956–1977

	1956	1959	1963	1967	1971	1972	1977
Major parties							
Labor	50	48	43	37	39	43	53
Catholic People's	49	49	50	42	35	27 ⎫	CDA[a]
Anti-Revolutionary	15	14	13	15	13	14 ⎬	49
Christian-Historical Union	13	12	13	12	10	7 ⎭	
Liberal	13	19	16	17	16	22	28
Long-standing minor parties							
Communist	7	3	4	5	6	7	2
Political Reformed	3	3	3	3	3	3	3
Newer minor parties							
Reformed Political League	—	—	1	1	2	2	1
Pacifist-Socialist	—	2	4	4	2	2	1
Farmers		—	3	7	1	3	1
Democrats '66	—	—	—	7	11	6	8
Democratic-Socialists '70	—	—	—	—	8	6	1
Radical	—	—	—	—	2	7	3
Retailers	—	—	—	—	2	—	—
Roman Catholic	—	—	—	—	—	1	0
Total	150	150	150	150	150	150	150

[a]Christian Democratic Appeal is the merger of the three religious parties.

interests within the party from causing a split. Thus, in socioeconomic terms, this party formed a keystone with the other two religious parties grouped around it, the PvdA to the left and the VVD to the right. The size and position of the party meant that it was virtually impossible to form a cabinet without its participation, and the party has participated in all cabinets since World War II.

From this central position, the Catholics virtually dictated what form the cabinet would take. Generally, one or both of the Protestant parties were included in a cabinet along with either the PvdA or the VVD. One reason for the dominance of the Catholics was that, in most instances, they and the Protestants controlled a majority of the seats. Although the margin of this majority was quite small, usually no more than one or two seats, it meant that the religious parties potentially could form a government alone if they so chose. Certainly no majority could be formed without one or more of them. If either the PvdA or the VVD were to participate in a cabinet, it was necessarily to an extent by the grace of the religious parties.

Despite the possibility of ruling without one or other of the secular parties, the Catholics seldom chose to do so. With the exception of some short-term rump cabinets, they opted not for a "minimum winning coalition" with only the Protestants but included one of the secular parties. When one of the secular parties had been a clear winner at the election, the choice for cooperation was clear. Yet even such a winner needed the support of the KVP to turn its gains into a position in government. In his analysis of coalition behavior, De Swaan has described the actions of the KVP as follows:[30]

> The outspoken performance on the part of the Catholic People's Party for "broadly based" governments, even at the cost of losing some portfolios to additional parties . . . is explained by its desire to maintain its options; this, in turn, springs from the urgent necessity to keep internal factions of trade union, farming, and entrepreneurial interests at bay by avoiding a clear commitment to one political side or another. . . .[30]

Rather than favoring a policy that would most profitably divide the "spoils" of the election, the party preferred to look ahead to subsequent elections and the possibility of sharing the "blame." De Swaan has called these coalitions "supercoalitions," that is, a coalition of the Catholics with the Protestants and of the Catholics with the PvdA (or the VVD). The Catholics occupied "the key position of being a member in both minimal range, minimal winning coalitions." Moreover, concluded De Swaan, "It appears that they were able to extend this privileged position into the Cabinet coalition proper by including both alternatives in the super coalition, thus holding on to their options beyond the moment of formation."[31]

If a cabinet fell, there were always other parties with which a coalition could be formed, often without even resorting to new elections. For example, after the cabinet formed in 1963 of the religious parties and the VVD fell in 1965, a new cabinet was formed with the Socialists. Only a year later, the right wing of the KVP brought this cabinet down, and a rump cabinet of the KVP and ARP carried on until the election. The frustration among the PvdA was great. Not long thereafter, the party congress of the PvdA adopted a resolution vowing that the party should not cooperate in future cabinets with the KVP in its (then) current form. In 1972, this resolution had to be ignored as it was again necessary to have the support of the Catholics if the PvdA were to govern again.

Nevertheless, the frustration with a system that could produce quite different cabinets on the basis of a single election has brought changes. It is now felt that it is no longer possible to form a new government after the fall of a cabinet without calling new elections. It has also led to increased pressure on all parties to indicate in advance of the elections their preference for future coalition partners. Understandably, the religious parties have been quite reluctant to announce such preferences in advance, as this would severely inhibit their ability to maneuver.

The cabinet formation period in recent years has been longer, even by Dutch standards—163 days in 1972–1973 and 207 days in 1977. Andeweg, Dittrich, and Van der Tak have listed several structural factors that help to account for the greater length.[32] First, they indicate that the loosening of the bands with the traditional parties has brought larger numbers of party "switchers" into the electorate. Whereas once the elections were often merely a registration of allegiance for voters, now many other factors have become important. The parties, in their turn, must take greater account of the voters. Polarization and conflict have resulted, with each party attempting to create a clear identity. Yet after the election, some of this identity must be sacrificed if one is to join a coalition with other parties. Time is needed to make clear to the voters just where and why compromises must be made.

The situation is exacerbated by the greater openness of the cabinet formations. Whereas once cabinets were formed by the leaders behind closed doors in a style of "summit diplomacy,"[33] negotiations are now brought much more into the open. When a politician speaks to the voters through the medium of television, he also is speaking to his political opponent. Speaking openly, and often bluntly, to one's voters may do little to facilitate negotiations.

To these factors of polarization and openness, one might add the altered position of the KVP. Together, the religious parties have only as many seats as the KVP once had alone. These parties no longer have the majority needed to govern alone. They, too, now depend on either the PvdA or the VVD for securing a majority. This greatly strengthens the bargaining position of the secular parties, again aggravating and lengthening the formation process. In the past, the inability of the PvdA and the VVD to join in a cabinet has contributed to the keystone position occupied by the religious parties. Moreover, the two secular parties were too weak in numbers to provide an alternative majority. Although at present the discussions of cooperation seem rather remote, in 1977 for the first time these two parties achieved sufficient seats to make it theoretically possible to form a majority coalition, and leaders of the parties are beginning to admit that future cooperation must not be ruled out completely.

Social Bases of the Parties

In our discussion concerning the four traditions that produced the major Dutch political parties, the social base of each party has been quite evident. Developments since 1967, however, have weakened these bases considerably, and it is useful to examine the extent to which the electorate still divides along traditional lines.

The success of the KPV and the ARP in mobilizing their respective religious groups was quite extraordinary. The limited survey evidence which exists from the pre-1967 period indicates that close to 90% of all persons identifying themselves as Catholic voted for the KVP. The percentage of orthodox Calvinists (Gereformeerden) voting for the ARP was a bit lower, but this group also provided support for the SGP and some splinter Calvinist parties. The CHU was never as successful in obtaining a large portion of the Dutch Reformed vote. In 1954 only 27% of the Dutch Reformed indicated a preference for the CHU and another 13% supported the ARP.[34]

In 1977 the three major religious parties presented a single list, so it is impossible to examine the trends for the various parties individually. However, one can examine the percentage of the religious groups supporting the new Christian Democratic Appeal (CDA). Only slightly more than half of the Catholics are now found to support the CDA, whereas almost one-quarter now find it possible to vote for the PvdA without relinquishing their religious identification. Calvinists remain strong in support of Christian parties; more than three-fourths support the CDA, and a few percent more support the smaller Calvinist parties. Part of the stability in this vote is accounted for in part by the greater coherence of the orthodox Calvinists and in part by the fact that a break with the party would in many cases go hand in hand with a rejection of religious identification. Again, the Dutch Reformed is lowest in its support for the CDA. Less than one-third support this party, and small percentages of orthodox Calvinists within the Dutch Reformed church support the smaller Calvinist parties.

Part of the drop in religious voting is accounted for by the behavior of those voters with rather loose ties to a church. Thus, among those who attend church services weekly, more than three-fourths support religious parties, but for those who do not attend church services regularly, the percentages are considerably smaller (see Table 6-3). The weaker the identification with the religious group (as measured by the frequency of church attendance), the less the likelihood one has of voting for a religious party.

During the past few years, the importance of religion in social life has been decreasing in the Netherlands. This can be seen in the declining attendance at church services and in increasing numbers of persons professing no religious preference or affiliation, and is especially prevalent among younger groups. Moreover, even among those maintaining religious beliefs, these beliefs are increasingly seen as irrelevant for politics and political questions. The combination of these factors has contributed to the decline of the religious parties over the past decade. In 1977 the newly formed CDA was only able to obtain 8% of those with no religious identification. If it is not able to reverse these trends, it too faces the prospects of further losses in the future.

SOCIAL CLASS

The socialist PvdA has an obvious class orientation in its program; the VVD, despite attempts in recent years to broaden their support, remain somewhat middle and upper class. Neither, however, has ever mobilized their respective social groups with success comparable to the Catholics and orthodox Calvinists. Much of the reason for this is, of course, precisely because of the success of the religious parties. Even today, the PvdA does not gain half of the votes of manual workers and their families (this would exceed 50% if smaller left-wing parties were included). The VVD obtains even less (22%)

TABLE 6–3. Vote Choice by Religious Preference and Church Attendance (Percent)

	ATTEND CHURCH WEEKLY			ATTEND CHURCH LESS THAN WEEKLY			
PARTY	Catholic	Dutch Reformed	Orthodox Calvinists	Catholic	Dutch Reformed	Orthodox Calvinists	No Religious Preference
Christian-Democratic	75	64	78	40	21	50	8
Other religious parties	0	17	17	—	—	4	0
Labor	12	9	3	34	44	14	58
Liberal	8	9	1	15	24	25	16
Democrats '66	5	—	—	6	8	—	10
Other	—	1	1	6	4	7	9
Total	100	100	100	101	101	100	101
Number of seats	183	59	90	254	194	28	412

Source: 1977 Dutch National Election Study.

TABLE 6–4.   Voter Choice and Social Class

	MANUAL WORKERS	NONMANUAL WORKERS
Labor Party	48	28
Liberal Party	6	22
Christian-Democrats	34	36
Other religious parties	4	2
Democrats '66	3	8
Other	5	4
Total	100%	100%
Number of Seats	498	691

Source: 1977 Dutch National Election Study.

among nonmanual workers, and only does substantially better (42%) among the professionals, managers, and the like in the higher-status occupations of the middle class (see Table 6–4).

The importance of the religious parties in drawing support away from the more class-based parties is seen in the roughly equal percentages obtained from both the manual and nonmanual groups. Among working-class families with no more than weak ties to a religious group, approximately two-thirds support the Labor party. It is interesting to note that this percentage has changed rather little over the past years, but with the decline in the importance of religion this percentage now applies to a larger portion of the population and has resulted in added votes for the Labor party.[35]

Notes

1. P. J. A. Ter Hoeven, "Social Change and the Rise of Political Studies," *Sociologica Neerlandica*, 6 (1970), 108–120.

2. R. Rose and D. Urwin, "Persistence and Change in Western Party Systems since 1945," paper presented to the Conference on Comparative Social Science, University of Cologne, May 1969.

3. H. Daalder, "De kleine politieke partijen—een voorlopige poging tot inventarisatie," *Acta Politica*, 1 (1965–1966), 172–196.

4. "De mannen erachter," special supplement to *Vrij Nederland*, April 17, 1977.

5. H. Daalder, *Politisering en Lijdelijkheid in de Nederlandse politiek*, Assen: Van Gorcum, 1974.

6. A Lijphart, *The Politics of Accommodation*, 2nd ed., Berkeley, Calif.: University of California Press, 1975.

7. E. van Thijn, "Van partijen naar stembusaccoorden," in E. Jurgens et al., eds., *Partij Vernieuwing? Open Brief 2*, Amsterdam, 1967 (my translation).

8. K. Gladdish, "Two-Party versus Multi-Party: The Netherlands and Britain," *Acta Politica*, 7 (1972), 342–361.

9. I. Lipschits, *De Protestants-Christelijke Stroming tot 1940*, Deventer: Kluwer, 1977, pp. 19–23.

10. Ibid., p. 22.

11. Cited in W. Banning, *Hedendaagse Sociale Bewegingen*, Arnhem: Van Loghum Slaterus, 1964, p. 51 (my translation).

12. I. Lipschits, *Politieke Stromingen in Nederland*, Deventer: Kluwer, 1977, p. 29.

13. See, for example, *De Nederlandse Kiezer: Een onderzoek naar zijn gedragingen en opvattingen*, 's-Gravenhage: Staatsdrukkerij en Uitgeversbedrijf, 1956.

14. Lipschits, *De Protestants-Christelijke Stroming tot 1940*, p. 18.

15. Banning, loc. cit., p. 186. The discussion of the Socialist movement presented here relies heavily on the interpretation of Banning.

16. H. Daalder, "Nederland," in *Repertorium van de Sociale Wetenschappen*, Amsterdam: Elsevier, 1958.

17. Lijphart, loc. cit., pp. 110–111.

18. S. Wolinetz, "New Left and the Transformation of the Dutch Socialist Party," paper presented at Annual Meeting of the American Political Science Association, San Francisco, California, September, 1975.

19. The discussions of "verzuiling," in H. Daalder, "The Netherlands: Opposition in a Segmented Society," in R. A. Dahl, ed., *Political Oppositions in Western Democracies*, New Haven, Conn.: Yale University Press, 1966; J. Goudsblom, *Dutch Society*, New York: Random House, 1968; and Lijphart, loc. cit., will help the reader better to understand its social and political importance in The Netherlands.

20. Daalder, "De kleine partijen . . .".

21. D. J. Hoekstra, ed., *Partijvernieuwing in Politiek Nederland*, Alphen aan den Rijn: Uitgeverij Samsom, 1968.

22. Ibid., p. 213.

23. For a description of the Dutch television broadcasting system, see A. J. Heidenheimer, "Elite Responses to Ontzuiling: Reels within wheels in Dutch Broadcasting Politics," paper presented to the International Political Science Association, Eighth World Congress, Munich, 1970.

24. Sociaal en Cultureel Planbureau, *Sociaal en Cultureel Rapport 1976*, 's-Gravenhage: Staatsuitge-verij, 1976.

25. S. Wolinetz, "Dutch Politics in the 1970's: Re-alignment at a Stand Still?," *Current History*, 70 (April 1976), 163–167, 182.

26. Ph. C. Stouthard, "Godsdienst en Politiek," in G. A. Irwin, J. Verhoef, and C. J. Wiebrens, eds., *De Nederlandse Kiezer '77*, Voorschoten: Uitgeverij VAM, 1977.

27. The formation of a cabinet following the 1977 parliamentary elections has been described by R. B. Andeweg, K. Dittrich, Th. van der Tak, *Kabinetsformatie 1977*, Leiden, Brill, 1978.

28. For the lengths of the various cabinet formation periods, see ibid., p. 117.

29. For further information, see G. Ringalda, "De kabinetsformatie," in A. Hoogerwerf, ed., *Verkenningen in de Politiek*, vol. I, Alphen aan den Rijn: Uitgeverij Samsom, 1971.

30. A. De Swaan, *Coalition Theories and Cabinet Formation*, Amsterdam: Elsevier, 1973, p. 221.

31. Ibid., p. 226.

32. Andeweg, Dittrich, and Van der Tak, op. cit., pp. 118–120.

33. Lijphart, op. cit., pp. 26–27.

34. *De Nederlandse Kiezer*, loc. cit.

35. R. B. Andeweg, "Factoren die het stemgedrag mede bepalen," in Irwin, Verhoef, and Wiebrens, eds., op. cit., p. 163.

CHAPTER 7

SWEDEN

M. Donald Hancock

SWEDEN'S NATIONAL ELECTION in 1976 marked an apparent watershed in the continuing evolution of its multiparty system. The three nonsocialist parties—the Center, the Liberals, and the Moderates (Conservatives)—won a narrow majority of 50.8% of the popular vote, thereby forcing the Social Democrats (SD) into parliamentary opposition for the first time in 44 years. Conservative skeptics in Europe and North America immediately hailed the outcome as further confirmation of a universal voter backlash against the bureaucratization and high costs of advanced welfare systems, in Sweden as elsewhere. The Social Democrats were quick to rebut their external ideological critics; their defeat, they claimed, was attributable instead to the negative effect of immediate campaign issues, including a spirited debate on nuclear energy and a series of untimely political scandals involving leading cultural and labor figures. The truth, of course, is more complex than either of these facile explanations. First, the election results were the product of a historical process of increased bloc competitiveness between socialists and nonsocialists that had transformed a previously single-party dominant system into a functional bipolar system. And, second, the campaign provided an early preview of what is likely to become a major ideological issue during the coming decades in other advanced industrial societies as well—namely, conflicting partisan efforts to promote potentially contradictory goals of sustained productivity and economic democracy.

For both reasons, Sweden constitutes an important case study in the comparative assessment of the postindustrial prospect among the world's advanced democracies. The 1976 election itself will become increasingly

185

relegated to historical interest, as subsequent events (noted in later paragraphs) revealed that it is likely to prove only an interruption in the long-term pattern of Social Democratic predominance rather than the beginning of a new era of stable nonsocialist governance. But underlying changes in the structure of the Swedish party system and the ideological principles espoused by its constituent parts, which came to the fore during the 1976 campaign, pose analytical issues of more lasting concern. Will contrasting Social Democratic and nonsocialist policy priorities reenforce the postwar trend toward party bipolarity? Or will the simultaneous debate over nuclear policy and fundamental property rights lead to a realignment of the multiparty system? Answers to these questions will be sought through an examination of developmental trends in modern Sweden and recent programmatic innovations by party and other group leaders.

The Swedish Multiparty System: Historical Origins

In contrast to recurrent periods of party decomposition in Western Europe and the United States during much of the twentieth century,[1] Sweden's multiparty system exemplifies a striking record of structural continuity. The contemporary five-party system—which ranges on a conventional left-right continuum from the Left Party-Communists to the Social Democrats, the Center, the Liberals, and the Moderates—dates from the early 1920s. As in other advanced democracies, the parties are products of both industrialization and the diffusion of ideological consciousness among diverse social strata. A precipitous growth in industry from the 1880s onward led to the concomitant economic and social changes associated with modernization—including a basic transformation in the structure of the labor force (see Table 7–1), urbanization, social mobilization, and a proliferation of specialized interest groups and idealistic associations. Among the last segment were industrial

TABLE 7–1.   Transformation of the Swedish Labor Force, 1860–1930

		PERCENTAGE EMPLOYED IN		
YEAR	ABSOLUTE NUMBER OF WORKERS (IN MILLIONS)	AGRICULTURE	MINING AND MANUFACTURING	SERVICES
1860	1.037	64.0	16.8	15.1
1880	1,802	59.4	9.7	9.5
1900	2,072	53.8	19.9	8.9
1920	3.057	34.6	26.4	10.7
1930	3,327	31.3	27.8	11.8

Source: Calculated from absolute data in Brian R. Mitchell, ed., European Historical Statistics, 1750–1970, New York: Columbia University Press, 1975, p. 162.

trade unions which made their initial appearance during the 1880s and converged to form a national Swedish Federation of Trade Unions (LO) in 1898; a Swedish Employers Association (SAF) founded in 1902; and various temperance and free church associations. These changes prompted the gradual emergence of modern political parties representing the socioeconomic interests of, respectively, the industrial workers, middle-class groups, farmers, and an urban-based upper social class. The Social Democrats were the first of the contemporary parties to establish themselves as a formal political organization in 1889; they were followed by the Liberal party in 1900, the Conservatives (Right party) in 1917, the Agrarian party in 1921, and a miniscule breakaway Communist party in 1921.[2]

Sweden's socioeconomic development was accompanied by a sustained struggle among the Liberals, the Social Democrats, and traditional Conservatives over political democratization. Claiming a long tradition of constitutionalism and separation of powers which displays striking historical parallels with the evolution of rule by law in England,[3] Sweden nonetheless fell behind its Scandinavian neighbors in achieving suffrage reform and parliamentarianism. Denmark had introduced manhood suffrage as early as 1849, followed by Norway in 1898. And both countries had implemented parliamentary democracy by the turn of the century. Sweden, in contrast, remained governed throughout the nineteenth century by a ruling coalition composed of the hereditary monarch and a well-educated bureaucratic elite anchored socially and economically in affluent urban strata and the nobility.

The Liberals and the Social Democrats joined forces in opposing the prevailing pattern of conservative dominance. Efforts by the two parties of "radical reform" to promote Sweden's democratization were abetted by at least four factors of historical significance: (1) an evolutionary growth of parliamentary authority vis-à-vis the king and his royal advisers, which followed the introduction of a bicameral legislative system in 1865–1866; (2) the parallel emergence of organized Liberalism and Social Democracy during the 1890s, which facilitated their collaboration on behalf of shared reform objectives; (3) a sustained growth in the numerical strength of Liberal and Socialist supporters, which progressively eroded the social base of Conservative electoral strength; and (4) external events in the form of the Bolshevik revolution of 1917 and the collapse of the German monarchy a year later, which prompted conservative spokesmen in Sweden to accept constitutional-political change as inevitable.

The confluence of these sociopolitical trends and events resulted in Sweden's peaceful transition from a constitutional oligarchy to a parliamentary democracy. The major breakthrough occurred in 1907–1909, when the conservative ruling elite accepted the Liberal and Social Democratic demand for manhood suffrage in exchange for introducing proportional representation in national and local elections as a means to preserve its own relative share of political influence. This so-called "Great Compromise" among the Conservatives, the Liberals, and the Social Democrats constituted a decisive link between Sweden's past and present, for it embodied a new synthesis of political values among the nation's leading political actors. On the basis of their shared commitment to representative institutions and rational political choice, the principal political protagonists were subsequently able to concur on the introduction of parliamentarianism in 1917 and universal suffrage in 1919–1921.

Thus, by the beginning of the 1920s, the basic contours of both parliamentary democracy and Sweden's contemporary multiparty system were firmly established. Henceforth, executive leadership was vested in the prime minister and his cabinet colleagues, who were dependent for their tenure in office on the majority support—or at least the tolerance of a majority—of the members of the Riksdag (Parliament) rather than the personal confidence of the king. Simultaneously, the Social Democrats (along with their Leninist offshoot, the Communist Party of Sweden), the Liberals, the Agrarians, and the Conservatives had consolidated their claim to a monopoly of seats in the newly democratized Riksdag. Important changes ensued in party programs, the distribution of electoral support among them, and in some of their names— but the five-party structure has remained basically intact to the present day.

Social Democratic Ascendancy and the Rise of the Welfare State

An immediate consequence of Sweden's democratic breakthrough was the appearance of political instability. National elections from 1921 to 1928 revealed a fluctuating Social Democratic plurality (see Table 7–2), but no party or coalition could command a reliable parliamentary majority. The result, as in other parliamentary regimes throughout interwar Europe, was a

TABLE 7–2. Percentage of the Popular Vote in National Elections, 1914–1932

YEAR	COMMUNISTS	SOCIAL DEMOCRATS	AGRARIANS	LIBERALS	CONSERVATIVES
1914	—	36.4	0.2	26.9	36.5
1917	—	39.2	8.5	27.6	24.7
1920	—	36.1	14.2	21.8	27.9
1921	4.6	39.4	11.1	19.1	25.8
1924	5.1	41.1	10.8	16.9	26.1
1928	6.4	37.0	11.2	15.9	29.4
1932	8.3	41.7	14.1	11.7	23.5

Source: Allmänna valen, Sveriges Officiella statistik, Stockholm: Statistika Centralbyrau, for the years in question.

period of persistent executive discontinuity. Between March 1920 and September 1932, eight cabinets held office. Three were minority Social Democratic governments, two were Conservative, two were Liberal, and one was a nonpartisan caretaker ministry.

Swedish politics entered a new era of "majority parliamentarianism" in response to the global economic crisis of 1929. Rising unemployment and falling farm prices, which followed the near collapse of the European banking system and a precipitous decline in international trade, prompted a realignment of the Swedish electorate. Clearly the recipients of a groundswell of protest votes cast by industrial workers and farmers—the two social groups most adversely affected by the depression—the Social Democrats and the Agrarians advanced to 41.7% and 14.1% of the popular vote, respectively, in the 1932 parliamentary election. Leaders of the two parties subsequently reached an historic decision to form an informal coalition on behalf of an interventionist program of economic recovery. Consequently, the Social Democrats formed a "majority" government in September 1932 with indirect Agrarian parliamentary support whose proclaimed policy task was the restoration of Swedish productivity through a combination of public works and farm price supports—both to be financed by the then novel concept of deficit government spending.

The rise of the Social Democrats to executive power with majority backing marked the beginning of over four decades of single-party dominance in domestic affairs. From late 1932 through September 1976, the Social Democrats governed alone for 29 years, in formal coalition with the Agrarians for another 9, and as senior partner in a national wartime coalition for 6 years. Only once during this 44-year period did they relinquish cabinet office—and then only for a brief period to the Agrarians during the summer of 1936.[4]

Both product and cause of long-term Social Democratic leadership was the party's architectural role in establishing one of the world's most advanced welfare states. Under the able leadership of Per Albin Hansson, who served as prime minister from 1932 until his death in 1946, and his successor, Tage Erlander, who relinquished the premiership upon his retirement in 1969 to Olof Palme, the Social Democrats initiated successive measures to promote individual economic and social security through collective action. With the support of their Agrarian allies, they obtained parliamentary endorsement between 1934 and 1937 of national programs of unemployment insurance, comprehensive retirement benefits, home construction subsidies for large families, and maternity benefits. The advent of World War II temporarily suspended government efforts to extend welfare services, but with the cessation of hostilities in 1945 the Social Democrats resumed their reform momentum. In partial collaboration with both the Agrarians and the Liberals (who had abandoned their earlier opposition to activist economic and social policies with the adoption of a new program of social liberalism during the war), the Social Democrats introduced a compulsory national pension program in 1946 and the legal basis for a comprehensive national health system a year later.[5]

Accompanying the implementation of Sweden's welfare state were complementary processes of social harmonization and material growth. A major factor accounting for the former was a comprehensive agreement reached in 1938 between leaders of the LO and the SAF to promote labor peace. Known as the "Saltsjöbaden agreement" after the Baltic resort where it was negotiated, the labor-management pact outlawed unauthorized strikes and established national grievance procedures for resolving disputes over wage contracts. The resulting decline in conflict on the labor market facilitated a largely sustained period of continued industrialization and a corresponding increase in national and per capita wealth. Swedish industrial production rose from an index of 100 in 1929 to 166 by 1939, accompanied by a 16% increase in the country's exports and a 58% growth in imports.[6] The growth rate leveled off during World War II but subsequently accelerated to an average annual rate of 3.7% during the postwar decades from 1950 to 1971.[7] By the early 1970s Sweden had achieved a per capita income second only to that of the United States among industrial nations ($6,140 in 1973 compared with a U.S. per capita average of $6,170).

The parallel extension of welfare services and economic expansion rebounded to the political advantage of the governing Social Democrats. Their percentage of the popular vote rose steadily during the 1930s to an absolute majority of 53.8% in the parliamentary election of 1940. Aggregate nonsocialist strength declined accordingly, with both the Conservatives and the Liberals losing an appreciable share of their earlier support. Only the Agrarians retained a relatively stable following within the bourgeois camp during the first decade of Social Democratic rule; their share of the popular vote averaged 13.5% between 1932 and 1940.

The Social Democrats entered a period of electoral decline in the mid-1940s, due to a combination of public discontent over wartime economic controls and the Liberal party's ideological transformation under chairman Bertil Ohlin into a more progressive movement affirming both individualism and the welfare state. The Liberals' popular support nearly doubled in the 1948 parliamentary election, when it increased from 12.9% recorded four years previously to 22.8%, as Ohlin led the nonsocialist forces in a vigorous campaign against the Social Democrats' declared intention to implement a system of national economic planning and selective nationalization in the postwar era.[8]

Confronting an imminent loss in their parliamentary majority, the Social Democrats decided in 1951 to renew their earlier alliance with the Agrarians by inviting them to rejoin the cabinet in a formal coalition. Simultaneously, party leaders embarked on an ambitious new welfare initiative in an effort to extend their base of electoral support among middle-class voters. Emboldened by LO pressure to augment the existing retirement program with additional personalized benefits, the Social Democrats introduced legislation in 1958 over the united opposition of the three nonsocialist parties to create a new compulsory supplementary pension system. Their move was preceded by an inconclusive national referendum on alternative pension proposals and the Agrarians' angry resignation from the cabinet, and provoked modern Sweden's first vote of no-confidence and dissolution election. Thanks to a slight increase in Social Democratic popular support and the abstention by a Liberal deputy in the final parliamentary vote, the Social Democrats' version of the bill finally passed by a narrow majority in May 1959.[9]

The voters' response to the government's victory in the supplementary pension conflict vindicated Social Democratic hopes that their version of the measure would attract the endorsement of crucial middle-class strata. The Social Democrats restored their absolute majority of the popular vote in the communal election of 1962, and with the indirect backing of Communist deputies in parliament they succeeded in retaining control of the national executive through the mid-1970s.

Toward a Bipolar Party System

The Social Democrats' success in the supplementary pension controversy proved a major turning point in interparty relations. Whereas the electoral realignment of 1932 had resulted in the emergence of a "red-green" legislative alliance between the Social Democrats and the Agrarians, the parliamentary outcome of 1959 prompted a move toward bipolarity between the socialist and nonsocialist blocs. From the early 1960s onward, the three nonsocialist parties began moving closer together—both ideologically and strategically—to comprise a relatively cohesive countervailing force to the Social Democrats and the Communists on the left. Simultaneously, both the Social Democrats and their nonsocialist opponents embraced new programmatic principles in response to perceived shortcomings of the established industrial-welfare system.

A combination of social and political changes determined the move toward bipolarity. In the first instance, Sweden's ongoing process of economic development yielded not only a predictable decline in the agrarian sector of the economy but also a perceptible increase in the number of white-collar workers. As indicated in Table 7–3, the percentage of persons employed in farming, forestry, and fishing declined from 24.5% in 1945 to 13.8% in 1960. Simultaneously, the percentage of those engaged in public and private services—a key empirical indicator of emergent postindustrialism[10]—rose from 17.1% to 19.8% and continued to climb through the remainder of the decade into the 1970s. One result of the former trend was a continuous loss of electoral support by the Agrarian party. From a zenith of 14.3% of the popular vote recorded in 1936, Agrarian strength had gradually declined to a postwar

TABLE 7–3. Transformation of the Swedish Labor Force, 1945–1975

| | ABSOLUTE NUMBER OF WORKERS | PERCENTAGE EMPLOYED IN | | |
YEAR	(IN MILLIONS)	AGRICULTURE	MINING AND MANUFACTURING	SERVICES
1945	2,988	24.5	30.6	17.1
1950	3,105	20.4	32.9	17.0
1960	3,243	13.8	35.9	19.8
1975	3,548	6.4	29.9	28.4

Source: Percentages for 1945–1960 calculated from absolute data in *European Historical Statistics, 1750–1970*, p. 162; percentages for 1975 from *Yearbook of Nordic Statistics 1977*, p. 42.

nadir of 9.4% in 1956. Demographic trends suggested an inevitable demise of the movement unless party spokesmen undertook corrective measures which would attract new electoral clientele. Acting on this realization, Agrarian leaders changed the name of their organization to the Center party in 1957 and adopted a new program two years later that was designed to extend the party's appeal to small businessmen and civil servants. Among its principal features were tax reforms designed to enhance the status of the self-employed and families. In addition, the newly christened Center party declared its support for "a policy that promotes local self-government, a decentralized construction of homes and industry, and a rich provincial and local cultural life."[11]

In the second instance, various political trends encouraged the discovery of a community of values among the three nonsocialist parties. Historically fragmented because they represent distinct social strata and varying degrees of commitment first to democracy and later to the welfare state, the Center, Liberal, and Conservative parties no longer seemed as distant from one another on the center-right ideological scale by the beginning of the 1960s. On the contrary, their joint opposition to the Social Democratic concept of a compulsory system of supplementary pensions underscored the extent to which they had come to share common beliefs in economic, cultural, and political individualism. Accordingly, a new generation of party leaders— among them, Per Ahlmark and Ola Ullsten of the Liberals, Thorbjörn Fälldin of the Center, and Gösta Bohman of the Moderates—began groping toward the formation of a joint nonsocialist policy alternative to continued dominance by the Social Democrats. The key elements of such an alternative, as they evolved in the course of successive electoral campaigns and legislative initiatives during the 1960s and early 1970s, included tax reform, political decentralization, and policies designed to promote regional economic growth. As a distinctive theme of nonsocialist criticism of Social Democracy, the Center party embraced a populist "green wave" orientation that emphasized the conservation of natural resources and existing communities in preference to material growth at all costs.

The incipient move toward greater nonsocialist unity gradually transformed the character of Swedish elections. Traditionally, the nonsocialist parties had competed as much among themselves for popular support as they had against the Social Democratics—thereby indirectly contributing to much of the latter's electoral successes from the early 1930s through the early 1960s. But the proclamation of a moratorium (*Borgfreden*) on internecine political attacks within nonsocialist ranks prior to the 1966 communal election inaugurated a new phase of bloc competition between the bourgeois and socialist parties.[12] Increasingly, election results came to be measured in terms of the aggregate performance of the three nonsocialist parties in relation to the combined parliamentary strength of the Social Democrats and their Communist rivals—who, despite fundamental ideological cleavages between them, could be expected to vote together on crucial policy issues for the sake of continued Social Democratic executive leadership. Thus, the earlier pattern of single-party legislative dominance in the face of a fragmented political opposition gave way to the emerging contours of a functional bipolar party system.

The Social Democratic Response

The trend toward increased bloc competitiveness, which had become clearly evident by the mid-1960s, coincided with ideological renewal within the Social Democratic movement itself. For complex international and domestic reasons, Sweden's Social Democratic party unexpectedly confronted the necessity to redefine its long-range social and political objectives. Despite its electoral recovery during the early 1960s, the party's support fell marginally in the 1964 election and plummeted abruptly to 42.2% in the 1966 communal election—its lowest point in over three decades.

A principal cause for the Social Democrats' sudden electoral decline was the advent of Radical criticism directed toward their failure to transform property relations or to promote enhanced equality among individuals and social classes despite their long period of executive dominance. Such criticism came in part from outside the movement in the form of impassioned Radical Socialist attacks on government policy levied by a new generation of revisionist leaders who rose to power in the early 1960s in the Swedish Communist party.[13] But loyal Social Democrats and many rank-and-file members of the LO also began to mount a critical campaign from within, calling for a renewed commitment to comprehensive democratization of economic and social power relations.

Multiple causes of ideological renewal within the Social Democratic party (and the Swedish left generally) included such diverse trends as the radicalization of international public opinion in the wake of the Vietnamese conflict, the diffusion of new forms of critical theory among younger intellectuals, and the external example of efforts by Communist leaders in Italy and Czechoslovakia to achieve an effective synthesis between democracy and socialism. More specifically relevant to the Swedish case was the dawning realization among party and union stalwarts that domestic socialist and nonsocialist critics were empirically as well as morally justified in citing persistent deficiencies in the established industrial-welfare system. As a proliferation of partisan tracts as well as objective economic surveys during the 1960s and early 1970s revealed,[14] Sweden did in factc manifest multiple shortcomings: an uneven distribution of income and access to economic power among different individuals and social groups, social discrimination against women, and a growing sense of powerlessness among industrial workers.[15] An ominous expression of the last factor was an outbreak of spontaneous wildcat strikes at the end of the decade—including an illegal walkout of some 5,000 workers at the state-owned iron mines in the northern party of the country.

In response to the radical critique of persisting social inequities and employee restlessness within the trade union movement, both the party and the LO undertook a series of programmatic innovations aimed primarily at subjecting private economic power to greater social control. Establishment Social Democrats hoped thereby to promote enhanced socioeconomic equality while simultaneously lessening systemic causes of worker alienation. Their most important initiatives included the following measures:[16]

1. Parliamentary endorsement of cabinet proposals submitted in 1967 to establish a state-owned investment corporation and an investment bank, both of which were established to serve as alternative sources of investment capital to facilitate industrial expansion in areas in which private entrepreneurs are reluctant to invest.

2. The creation of a department of industry in 1968 to coordinate national economic planning and the activities of state-owned enterprises.

3. An LO endorsement of the West German principle of industrial codetermination between labor and capital at its congress in 1971, whereby unions would acquire the right to appoint two members to the boards of firms employing 100 and more workers to represent the interests of organized workers and gain "insight" into the internal financial transactions of the companies concerned. The Social Democratic leadership obtained parliamentary approval to implement the codetermination experiment on a trial basis in 1972; permanent legislation was subsequently enacted in 1976.

4. The culmination of an intense LO campaign during the early 1970s to limit the discretionary right of private employers to hire, assign, and dismiss labor in the Social Democrats' securing the Riksdag's endorsement of legislation in June 1976 that provides for the transformation of such decisions into a joint management-union endeavor.

5. The adoption of a new Social Democratic program in 1975 which outlines future steps toward the eventual attainment of economic democracy as the next stage in Sweden's development. As its political objective, the party proclaims, "the Swedish working class movement will continue its struggles to achieve a fundamental transformation of Swedish society, a struggle that now to an increasing degree is directed toward the democratization of economic life. . . ."[17]

The most sweeping reform proposal was advanced by the LO at its June 1976 congress. Determined to redress the imbalance of economic power between organized labor and private capital that is inherent in Sweden's system of free enterprise, an overwhelming majority of delegates affirmed a proposal formulated by the LO's chief economist, Rudolf Meidner, to introduce a new system of collective capital formation. The long-range objective of the so-called "Meidner report" would be to achieve a substantial modification of existing property relations by establishing a centralized "equalization fund" to be administered by elected union officials. According to Meidner's initial, admittedly highly tentative conception, the fund would be financed through annual payments of 20% of pretax profits contributed by companies employing 50 and more workers. Half the dividends earned by the transferred shares would be invested in the purchase of additional stocks in the individual companies; the remainder would be spent on educational purposes on behalf of the trade union movement. Over a 20- to 30-year period, the projected increase in the value of the equalization fund would enable the LO to purchase majority ownership of Sweden's leading industrial enterprises.[18]

The LO's blueprint for a long-range shift in the contemporary mix between public and private ownership in the Swedish economy was promptly tabled by Prime Minister Olof Palme, who referred the proposal to an extraparliamentary committee of experts which he appointed during the summer of 1976 to study alternative models of profit-sharing and investment formation. Palme's action was designed partly to blunt bourgeois criticism of the proposal and partly to allow party and union members more time to consider its potential merits and defects.[19] He succeeded in the latter objective but failed in the former—at least to the extent that the Meidner plan inevitably became a controversial campaign issue. As such, it helped bring about the Social Democratic defeat in the 1976 election.

The 1976 Election

The Social Democrats' loss in 1976 capped a spiraling decline in the party's share of popular support since the beginning of the decade. As indicated in Table 7–4, the percentage of Social Democratic electoral strength progres-

TABLE 7–4.   National Election Results in Sweden, 1960–1976 (Percent)

PARTY	1960	1964	1968	1970	1973	1976
Revolutionary Marxist Leninists	—	—	—	0.4	0.2	0.1
Communist Party of Sweden	—	—	—	—	0.4	0.3
Leftwing Communists	4.5	5.2	3.0	4.8	5.3	4.8
Social Democrats	47.8	47.3	50.1	45.3	43.6	42.7
Center party	13.6	13.4	16.2	19.9	25.1	24.1
People's party (Liberals)	17.5	17.1	15.0	16.2	9.4	11.1
Moderate Unity party (Conservatives)	16.5	13.7	13.9	11.5	14.3	15.6
Christian Democrats	—	—	—	1.9	1.8	1.4

SEATS IN RIKSDAG

	1960		1964		1968		1970		1973		1976	
Leftwing Communists	7	} 198	10	} 201	4	} 208	17	} 180	19	} 175	17	} 169
Social Democrats	191		191		204		163		156		152	
Center Party	54		54		79		71		90		86	
Liberals	73	} 185	69	} 182	60	} 196	58	} 170	34	} 175	39	} 180
Moderates	58		59		57		41		51		55	

sively declined from an absolute majority of 50.1% in 1968—which was garnered at the height of the Czechoslovak crisis of that year—to 43.6% in 1973. Concomitantly, total nonsocialist support (excluding votes cast for a small Christian Democratic Union) rose from 45.1% to 48.8%. Within the nonsocialist bloc, the Centrists displaced the Liberals as the largest party as early as 1968 and gradually increased their following to over a quarter of the electorate by 1973. Electoral outcomes were translated into a narrow majority of ten seats commanded by the Social Democrats and the Left Party-Communists between 1970 and 1973 and an ostensible legislative deadlock of 175–175 between the socialist and bourgeois blocs during the 1973–1976 session of the Riksdag.[20]

The Social Democratic decline was attributable to multiple factors—including the sudden advent of "stagflation" in 1973 which followed a general economic slowdown among the industrialized nations, voter disillusionment with Prime Minister Palme's leadership style, and public wariness in response to the labor movement's new set of reform initiatives. Conversely, the surge in Center party support revealed a substantial shift in the social base of the party's electorate. Since the adoption of its new name and program in the late 1950s, the Center has gradually extended its social base from farmers—who as late as 1960 still comprised 57% of the party's supporters—to include over a quarter of Sweden's lower-level salaried employees and a fifth of the industrial workers.[21] This trend was the result largely of the party's success in establishing itself as an ideological fulcrum between the collectivist tendencies associated with Social Democracy and the conservative economic principles identified with the Moderates and to a lesser extent the Liberals. In addition, Center chairman Fälldin emerged by the beginning of the 1970s as Sweden's most outspoken advocate of active environmentalism—a stance that earned him widespread support among the country's conservationists.

These factors converged in the 1976 electoral campaign. The economy had begun a minor recovery from the slump of 1974–1975, but the annual rate of inflation nonetheless had risen to 11%. Much more importantly, the Social Democrats and the nonsocialist parties confronted each other in an unprecedented ideological debate over Sweden's future. The Meidner report generated partisan conflict when Fälldin sharply criticized the LO proposal as containing the potential for an undemocratic concentration of economic power. Complicating the issue was that the Social Democratic party had failed to follow the LO's lead in explicitly affirming the report, thereby creating a public impression of party and union disunity over the new reform initiative.

In the midst of the summer campaign, yet another issue emerged that quickly overshadowed the Meidner controversy itself: the question of nuclear energy as a partial supplement for Sweden's reliance on hydroelectric power and imported oil and gas. Center Chairman Fälldin unexpectedly attacked the government's nuclear policy when he declared his party's opposition to a parliamentary agreement endorsed the preceding year by the Social Democrats, the Moderates, and with some reservations the Liberals providing for an increase in the number of Sweden's nuclear power plants from 5 to 13. Convinced that nuclear waste products posed a serious risk to the Swedish environment, Fälldin called for an alternative national energy policy based on the development of solar and eventually fusion technologies. Moreover, he demanded that no further nuclear plants be placed into operation and that existing installations be eventually closed down.

Voter ambivalence about the implications of the Meidner report and a last-minute swing among many younger voters to the Center party determined the election outcome. Social Democratic support fell still further to 42.7%, while both the Liberals and the Moderates marginally advanced. The Center declined one percentage point compared with the 1973 election—but their attainment of 24.1% was a marked improvement over the party's slump to 22.8% recorded in opinion polls conducted in May 1976.[22] Electoral analysts attributed most of the recovery to widespread public endorsement of Fälldin's stance against the proliferation of nuclear energy. Together, the three nonsocialist parties amassed 50.8% and 180 seats compared with 47.5% and 169 seats for the Social Democrats and the Communists. Accordingly, Palme relinquished his chair as prime minister. In his place, Fälldin formed a three-party nonsocialist coalition—the first such instance of executive bourgeois unity in Swedish political history.

The Aftermath

Electoral analysis of the 1976 campaign reveals a new phase of "voter uncertainty" in Sweden. As Olof Petersson and his colleagues have demonstrated, the number of persons who switched their party preference as compared with results in the preceding national election increased to 19%—a sizable jump from the average of 7% noted during the 1950s.[23] The reasons are enormously varied and include such diverse tendencies as increased social mobility, structural change in the composition of the labor force, and a decline in the traditional link between subjective class identity and partisan political preference. The cumulative effect of these socioeconomic and cultural trends is that political issues have become increasingly paramount in voter choice, as demonstrated by the dual salience of the Meidner proposal and nuclear energy during the 1976 campaign.

Both political blocs acted on this insight in the aftermath of the election. Responding to internal and campaign criticism that the original Meidner report failed to specify adequate democratic controls over the contemplated equalization fund, the Social Democratic party and the LO appointed a joint study group in 1977 to revise the labor movement's concept of a national system of employee funds. For his part, Center chairman Fälldin utilized his new status as prime minister to attempt to induce his Liberal and Moderate coalition partners to accept a moratorium on the further development of nuclear energy. These parallel efforts culminated in a series of dramatic domestic events in 1978 that underscored the lessons of 1976 for the continuing evolution of reform strategies and the multiparty system itself.

The Social Democratic-LO study group released its revised version of the Meidner proposal in February 1978. The newest document, entitled "Wage Earner Funds and Capital Formation," modifies the LO's original concept of employee funds by restricting the obligatory profit-sharing scheme to companies employing 500 and more workers. But, otherwise, the joint report retains Meidner's basic notion that the annual transfer of 20% of pretax profits into a national system of employee funds would eventually enable organized labor to become the majority owner of Sweden's largest industrial firms. A significant addition is that the revised proposal also calls for the establishment of two national and 24 regional development funds—to be financed by an annual payroll tax of 3%—whose purpose would be to provide additional "risk capital" for investment in industrial expansion. The funds would be administered by a combination of appointed union and "social" representatives; the latter would be designated by the elected members of Parliament and the various local assemblies. A third feature of the joint report is the contemplated introduction of a new "codetermination fund," which would be financed through a 1% payroll tax levied against those companies not participating in the employee fund system; its function would be to help finance trade union activities aimed at the further democratization of the economy.[24]

The publication of the joint report received a mixed reception among nonsocialist spokesmen. Fälldin endorsed the report's emphasis on the need to devise additional sources of investment capital as a necessary condition of future industrial expansion but asserted anew that his party "cannot accept a system that seeks centralized control or the socialist exercise of power."[25] In even more strident terms, the Moderates announced their opposition to all forms of collective profit sharing—as well as collective capital formation. In contrast, the principal white-collar union—the Central Organization of Salaried Employees (TCO), which traditionally has been loosely aligned with the Liberal party—issued a report of its own on employee funds in February 1978 that is strikingly similar to the Social Democratic-LO document.[26] Like the Social Democrats and the trade union leadership, the TCO advocates the creation of a national system of collective funds and capitalization. The TCO report differs from the revised Meidner plan largely in its greater emphasis on the parallel necessity for the government to increase incentives for individual savings. Largely in deference to the TCO's recommendations, the Liberals adopted a cautious recommendation at their party congress in late 1978 affirming the simultaneous need for increased capital formation through collective savings and further economic democratization.

The release of the joint report midway through the 1976–1979 legislative session initially indicated that the Social Democrats intended to elevate employee funds into a major campaign issue prior to the next scheduled election in September 1979. Unexpectedly, however, party and union officials announced at a press conference on June 30, 1978 that final consideration of the proposal will be postponed until the party's next congress in 1981. The declared purpose of the delay is to permit the committee of experts, whom Palme appointed in 1976 to consider the employee fund issue from an ostensibly nonpartisan perspective, sufficient time to release its own report. In the meantime, party and LO leaders will seek to extend codetermination by pressing for an expansion in the number of union representatives on the governing boards of Sweden's larger private firms.

Simultaneously, the nuclear issue reasserted itself toward the end of the summer when the three nonsocialist coalition partners opened deliberations on whether the government should proceed with the scheduled activation of two additional nuclear plants in accordance with the original Social Democratic decision of 1975. Center chairman Fälldin had risked his personal credibility in the nuclear issue upon assuming office as prime minister in October 1976 when he reluctantly agreed to Moderate and Liberal demands that one plant which had already been completed prior to the election should be placed in operation. By August 1978, however, his resistance to any further concessions had stiffened. Moderate leader Bohman and Ola Ullsten, who had been elected chairman of the Liberal party the preceding March to succeed Ahlmark,[27] tentatively concurred with Fälldin in late September on postponing a decision about the two new plants. But, when Swedish scientists announced a week later that they had located a safe location for the deposit of nuclear wastes, Bohman declared that the government should proceed with their activation.

The result was the prompt resignation by Fälldin and other Centrist members from the national cabinet. Ullsten, who had served as vice premier under the former Center prime minister, succeeded him as head of a caretaker government. On October 12 Parliament formally affirmed Ullsten's status as prime minister of a minority Liberal cabinet. Abstaining in the vote of investiture were the Riksdag's 152 Social Democrats and 86 Centrists; opposing Ullsten's ascension to office were its 17 Communist deputies and 55 Moderates. Thus, Sweden's first experiment with a three-party nonsocialist government came to an ignominious end.

Prospects for the Future: A New Realignment?

The events of 1978 confirmed Sweden's changing political agenda in response to continued economic and social transformation. The concept of a collective system of employee funds—which conceivably can lead to the emergence of a distinctive form of "labor socialism"[28]—and the more immediate controversy surrounding the nuclear energy issue galvanized Swedish politics to an extent that no one could have predicted even five years previously.[29] Not only does Sweden appear to be on the verge of another protracted ideological controversy comparable to the socialist-nonsocialist conflict over supplementary pensions 20 years earlier, but the unanticipated problematic of material growth itself, which prompted the Social Democrats to extend Sweden's nuclear capability in the first place, introduced an unforeseen source of divisiveness between the parties as well as among concerned citizens at large.

The confluence of these issues points toward a potential realignment of the established multiparty system. Nonsocialist unity is now shattered and will remain so until at least the nuclear energy issue is resolved to the satisfaction of Center leaders (and it may never be). Simultaneously, Social Democratic advocacy of a collective system of employee funds and capital formation indicates the probability of renewed ideological conflict between the left and the right. Yet the coming debate on the reciprocal rights of labor and capital in Sweden is not likely to involve a conventional division between the socialist and nonsocialist parties, as was the case in both the "planned economy" and supplementary pension disputes earlier in the postwar era. To be sure, the Moderates and employer interest groups can be expected to voice their strong opposition to any formula for collective savings and profit sharing; presumably they will be joined in their effort by the Center party. But the fact that the TCO has endorsed a compulsory system of employee funds reveals a lack of nonsocialist unity on the issue. Because of their strong social anchorage among salaried employees and industrial workers, the Liberals may well follow the TCO's lead in supporting the final Social Democratic version of enabling legislation when it is presented to the Riksdag in 1981.

Thus, to answer the questions posed at the outset of this chapter, the ideological and policy debates of the 1980s in Sweden are not likely to reenforce the postwar trend toward increased bloc competitiveness. On the contrary, the post-1960 pattern of socialist-nonsocialist bipolarity may already have given way to the incipient restoration of a Social Democratic-Liberal alignment reminiscent of their earlier alliance on behalf of political democratization at the turn of the century.

Notes

1. The concept of "party decomposition" is most closely associated with the writings of W. D. Burnham, who defines the phenomenon as a combination of party disaggregation and the loss of partisan support. As such, party decomposition is hardly a new phenomenon; witness the disintegration of the multiparty system in Weimar Germany and pre-fascist Italy. Burnham's most comprehensive work on the subject is his *Critical Elections and the Mainsprings of American Politics* (New York: Norton & Co., 1970). For an application of the concept to contemporary Scandinavian politics, see Gösta Esping-Andersen, "Social Democratic Party Decomposition in Denmark and Sweden," *Comparative Politics* (October 1978).

2. The actual origins of the major parties lie, of course, much further back than their formal founding dates. A liberal faction had emerged within parliament by the 1840s, while a Ruralist Party was established in 1867 which served as a partial forerunner to both the Agrarian and the Conservative parties of the twentieth century. The best English-language description of the origins of the modern party system in Sweden remains Dankwart A. Rustow's *The Politics of Compromise: A Study of Parties and Cabinet Government in Sweden* (Princeton, N.J.: Princeton University Press, 1955).

3. Useful accounts of Sweden's historical development include Douglas Verney, *Parliamentary Reform in Sweden, 1866–1921* (Oxford: Clarendon Press, 1957); Ingvar Andersson, *A History of Sweden* (London: Wiedenfeld and Nicolson, 1956); Franklin Scott, *Sweden: The Nation's History* (Minneapolis: University of Minnesota Press, 1977); and Steven Koblik (ed.), *Sweden's Development from Poverty to Affluence, 1750–1970* (Minneapolis: University of Minnesota Press, 1975).

4. Swedish cabinets from 1932 to September 1976 included the following:

   1932–1936:   Informal SD coalition with the Agrarian Party
   Summer 1936: Interim Agrarian minority ministry

1936–1939:　SD-Agrarian coalition
1939–1945:　Wartime "grand coalition" composed of the Social Democrats, Agrarians, Liberals, and Conservatives
1945–1951:　SD majority government
1951–1957:　SD-Agrarian coalition
1957–1960:　Minority SD government, with indirect Communist support
1960–1965:　Majority SD government
1965–1968:　Minority SD government, with indirect Communist support
1968–1970:　Majority SD government
1970–1976:　Minority SD government, with indirect Communist support

5. Standard sources on the evolution and scope of Sweden's social services include Karl Höjer, *Social Welfare in Sweden* (Stockholm: The Swedish Institute, 1949); Albert H. Rosenthal, *The Social Programs of Sweden: A Search for Security in a Free Society* (Minneapolis: University of Minnesota Press, 1967); Joseph Board, *Government and Politics of Sweden* (Boston: Houghton Mifflin and Company, 1970); Hugh Heclo, *Modern Social Politics in Britain and Sweden: From Relief to Income Maintenance* (New Haven: Yale University Press, 1974); and Leif Hulgersson and Stig Lundström, *The Evolution of Swedish Social Welfare* (Stockholm: The Swedish Institute, 1975).

6. Kurt Samuelsson, *From Great Power to Welfare State: 300 Years of Swedish Social Development* (London: George Allen and Unwin, Ltd., 1968), p. 239.

7. Assar Lindbeck, *Swedish Economic Policy* (Berkeley and Los Angeles: University of California Press, 1974), p. 2.

8. The best discussion of the "planned economy debate" in postwar Sweden is Leif Lewin's *Planhushållningsdebatten* (Stockholm: Almqvist & Wiksell, 1967).

9. A comprehensive account of the supplementary pension dispute can be found in Björn Molin, *Tjänstepensionsfrågen* (Göteborg: Akademieförlaget, 1965). I summarize the controversy and its outcome in M. Donald Hancock, *Sweden: The Politics of Postindustrial Change* (Hinsdale, Ill.: Dryden Press, 1972), pp. 214–222, as does Christopher Wheeler in *White-Collar Power: Changing Patterns of Interest Group Behavior in Sweden* (Urbana, Ill.: University of Illinois Press, 1975), pp. 66–91.

10. Admittedly ambiguous, the concept of "postindustrialism" is minimally defined in Western social science literature to mean a form of advanced industrial society in which the number of white collar workers gradually equals (and eventually exceeds) the number of industrial workers. A more complex attribute is Daniel Bell's notion of the increased centrality of theoretical knowledge as the central distinguishing feature of emergent postindustrial society. For early efforts to define the concept, see Bell, "Notes on the Post-Industrial Society," Parts I and II, *The Public Interest*, 6 and 7 (Winter and Spring 1967), pp. 24–35 and 102–118; "Toward the Year 2000: Work in Progress," *Daedalus*, 96 (Summer 1967); Herman Kahn and Anthony Wiener, *The Year 2000: A Framework for Speculation on the Next Thirty-Three Years* (New York: Macmillan, 1967); and Bell's comprehensive *The Coming of Post-Industrial Society* (New York: Basic Books, 1974).

11. Hans Wieslander (ed.), *De politiska partiernas program* (Stockholm: Bokförlaget Prisma, 1964), p. 39.

12. I discuss the shift toward nonsocialist unity and the 1966 communal election in Hancock, *Sweden*, pp. 132–145.

13. A leading proponent of the radical left revival in Sweden was C. H. Hermansson, who was elected chairman of the Communist Party in 1964. His best-known critique of Social Democratic policy and the alleged shortcomings of Swedish industrial-welfare society is *Vänsterns väg* (Stockholm: Rabén & Sjögren, 1965).

14. Among the critics of bureaucratic centralization and political "fossilization" in Sweden were a number of young Liberals and Centrists, who, under the editorship of Per Ahlmark, published several impassioned tracts calling for nonsocialist revitalization in the mid-1960s: Ahlmark, et al., *Mitt i 60-talet* (Stockholm: Bonniers, 1965), and Ahlmark (ed.), *Många liberaler* (Stockholm: Bonniers, 1966). In response to criticism of the welfare state from the left and the center, the government commissioned an empirical survey of income levels during the latter part of the decade; its findings are summarized in Sten Johansson, "The Level of Living Survey," *Acta Sociologica*, 16 (1973), pp. 211–219.

15. I discuss these features of contemporary Sweden in "The Swedish Welfare State: Prospects and Contradictions," *The Wilson Quarterly* (1977), pp. 111–126.

16. Succinct summaries of recent Social Democratic and LO reform efforts include Andrew Martin, "From Joint Consultations to Joint Decision-Making: The Redistribution of Workplace Power in Sweden," *Current Sweden*, April 1976; Martin, "In Sweden: A Union Proposal for Socialism," *Working Papers for a New Society*, Vol. 15 (1977), No. 2; Martin, "Workers' Participation: Contrasting Union Strategies," *Scandinavian Review*, II (1977), pp. 15–21; Sandra Albrecht, "The Nature of Participatory Democracy in Sweden," a paper delivered at the 1978 annual meeting of the Society for the Advancement of Scandinavian Studies; and my "Productivity, Welfare and Participation in Sweden and West Germany: A Comparison of Social Democratic Reform Prospects," *Comparative Politics* (October 1978).

17. Sweden, Socialdemokratiska arbetareparti, *Partiprogram och kommunalt principprogram* (Stockholm, 1975).

18. The original report was published as *Kollektiv kapitalbildning genom löntagarfönder: Rapport till LO-kongressen 1976* (Stockholm: Prisma, 1976) Meidner has subsequently published an English translation, *Employee Investment Funds* (London: George Allen and Unwin, 1978).

19. Employer groups issued a counter-proposal to the Meidner report in 1976 which envisions the creation of a voluntary system of capitalization and profit-sharing. See *Företagsvinster. Kapitalförsörjning. Löntagarfonder. Rapport fran en arbetsgrupp inom näringslivet* (Stockholm: Sveriges industriförbund, Svenska arbetsgivareföreningen, 1976).

20. Despite the parliamentary deadlock, the Social Democrats retained control of the cabinet because they remained the largest party in the Riksdag.

21. Bo Särlvik, "Recent Electoral Trends in Sweden," in Karl H. Cerny, *Scandinavia at the Polls* (Washington, D.C.: American Enterprise Institute for Public Policy Research, 1977), p. 91.

22. Ibid., p. 121.

23. Olof Petersson, "Väljarnas ökanda osäkerhet," paper presented to the Nordiska partiforskningsgruppen in Sandbjerg on January 26–29, 1978; "1976 års val,"

Samhällsdebatt, Nr. 2, 1976 (Stockholm: Forum för samhällsdebatt); Petersson and Bo Särlvik, "När de borgerliga vann," *Statsvetenskaplig tidskrift*, 1977:2, pp. 79–92; and Petersson.

24. *Löntagarfonder och kapitalbildning. Förslag från LO-SAPs Arbetsgrupp* (Stockholm: Tiden, 1978).

25. Quoted in *Sverige-Nytt*, April 11, 1978, p. 8.

26. *Löntagarfonder ur TCO-perspektiv—en debattskrift* (Stockholm: Tjänstemännens Centralorganisation, 1978).

27. Ahlmark resigned the party chairmanship in January 1978 for personal reasons.

28. Hancock, "Sweden's Emerging Labor Socialism," in Bernard E. Brown (ed.), *Eurocommunism and Eurosocialism: The Left Confronts Modernity* (New York: Cyrco Press, distributed by Bobbs-Merrill, 1978).

29. In a series of interviews with 60 leading Swedish public and private officials which I conducted during the winter of 1972–73, not a single respondent mentioned either employee funds or nuclear energy as a potential source of political conflict during the foreseeable future. Most persons interviewed did predict, however, that employees would acquire greater influence over their work environment in the years ahead. See Hancock, "Elite Images and System Change in Sweden," in Leon Lindberg (ed.), *Politics and the Future of Industrial Society* (New York: David McKay Company, 1976).

CHAPTER 8

NORWAY AND DENMARK

Sten Sparre Nilson

AFTER DECADES OF STABILITY, the party systems of Denmark and Norway in the last ten years have undergone striking changes. In 1970 the party system still strongly resembled that of the 1920s, when the large Social Democratic Labor parties were flanked by the smaller Socialist and Communist groupings and opposed by the Conservatives, the Agrarians, and the Liberals. By the 1950s, according to Dankwart Rustow, after several decades and through a World War and occupation, social and economic differences continued to provide the main stimulus for party division. The Conservatives, Agrarians, and Socialists represented the interests of employers, farmers, and workers, respectively, while those middle-class elements not readily identified with any of these groups provided the chief support for the Liberal parties.[1]

Much of this stability, notes Seymour Martin Lipset and Stein Rokkan, reflected the nearly complete mobilization of many of the European nations' citizens, the Scandinavians among them, for electoral participation during the 1920s. In this they saw the reason for party constellations remaining largely unchanged. The parties, they wrote, that were able to entrench themselves before the final drive toward complete mobilization were also the parties that survived. The narrowing of the "support market" brought about through the growth of mass parties during the final thrust toward full-suffrage democracy left very little opportunity for newcomers.[2]

At the beginning of the 1970s this condition still seemed to be generally true for both Denmark and Norway. The old parties constituted "the political establishment," dividing the parliamentary arena between them, though the differences that separated them had become notably smaller and the non-

205

socialist parties often formed coalition governments. These governments were opposed by Labor, but they pursued much the same domestic and foreign policies as the Social Democrats, maintaining the welfare state at home and adhering to the NATO alliance abroad. So the multiparty systems had become almost dualistic, separated into two "blocs." At the same time the decreasing differences between the blocs could not escape notice. Aggregation and stability had become the main characteristics of both. In Norway a Christian Democratic party had been launched, and in both countries new socialist parties had appeared to the left of the Social Democrats, but this did not seem to portend any major change.

Suddenly and almost simultaneously, the pattern of stability was destroyed, in Norway in the election of September 1973 and in Denmark in the election of December the same year, triggered in both countries, it appears, by the referendums on Common Market membership that had taken place a year earlier, in September and October 1972. But certain other factors had also eroded some of the established bases of party stability. In both countries the relation between political parties and the mass media underwent a change in the 1960s from the period between World Wars I and II, when the party systems were molded and the importance of the daily press was paramount.

Most leading Scandinavian newspapers had very close ties to one or the other political party. And the mobilization of voters at election time depended to a large extent on the efforts of the dailies. The advent of broadcasting during the early 1930s had no great effect on politics. But the introduction of television in the 1960s was important, especially as it coincided with a weakening of the party affiliation of the press. The pressure of competition in the newspaper industry brought about increasing concentration. As dailies became fewer and bigger, they were forced to appeal to a broader public, and the leading newspapers became less partisan than before. In addition, television is strictly nonpartisan. No longer do Danish and Norwegian parties each possess a kind of information monopoly over a particular segment of the electorate as they did during the first half century after World War I.[3]

This is a potential source of instability, but it does not fully explain the breakdown in 1973. So the extraordinary event of a nationwide referendum on entry into the European Community (EC) that was held in both countries should be considered. Although this too does not constitute the entire explanation, voters who disagree with "their" party's stand at a referendum or who find it split on the issue in question may be drawn to other parties. Such was the case both in Denmark and in Norway, not the least because the principal traditional foes—Labor and the Conservatives—suddenly appeared campaigning cordially together in favor of Common Market membership.

In Norway the consequences followed quickly and clearly. The Liberal party split in two, while the Left Socialists and Communists merged their forces and were joined by a sizable number of dissidents from the Social Democratic Norwegian Labor party. Together these groups formed a Socialist

Electoral Alliance with a view to the 1973 election, at which they won a number of seats as a result of their strong common opposition to EC membership. There was also a rebellion on the right, with an antitax party gaining four seats in 1973. Some would argue that the latter phenomenon was unrelated to the struggle over the Common Market. But, even if we assume that the 1972 EC referendum had an impact on all aspects of the 1973 election in Norway, it may not have been a permanent impact. The next election to the Norwegian Parliament, in 1977, largely restored the old balance of forces, at least for the time being.

In Denmark the 1972 referendum did not have as clear and immediate an impact. Nevertheless, the voter rebellion seems to have been of a more lasting kind in Denmark than in Norway.[4]

And there were other differences. In Denmark a majority of the electorate favored joining the EC in 1972; in Norway the majority was against. The relative economic positions of the two countries had a great deal to do with these choices. Denmark is an exporter of farm products. Her agriculture stood to gain by getting access to the Common Market. Norwegian agriculture, on the contrary, feared that once inside the EC it would be badly hurt by competition from other member countries. The referendum campaigns may have precipitated the recent changes in the party systems of both countries, but the two campaigns did not have the same character. In Denmark all established parties favored entry; in Norway the Agrarians opposed it. The fact indicates the existence of a separate dimension in Norwegian politics, a dimension that made itself felt not only in 1972 but also during the previous decade, although with greatly varying force.

In the Norwegian case it is necessary to follow the course of events over a considerable period to get into perspective the evolution of the last few years.

Norway: Two Dimensions

POLITICAL FLUCTUATIONS

From the beginning of the 1960s to the latter half of the 1970s, political life in Norway was influenced by two main sets of issues. There was a left-right conflict line between people in the lower and higher income brackets and an EC conflict line between periphery and center. Now the former, now the latter dimension, was the more prominent. A cyclical pattern ensued.

Up to the beginning of the 1960s, the left-right cleavage had dominated the political scene. But in 1961–1962 an EC dimension became salient; it cut across the left-right cleavage, producing a political climate of acute conflict and an incipient fragmentation of the party system. From 1963 on, the left-right axis reemerged and superseded the EC dimension. The aggregation of parties reasserted itself. Finally, in the 1970s the cycle was repeated once more. First came a resurgence of the EC dimension, with a concomitant splitting of parties and intensification of conflict. Then the left-right cleavage reasserted itself. There was renewed party aggregation and a dampening of conflict.

The Norwegian experience seems to show that cross-cutting cleavages do not always moderate conflict, in accordance with phenomena that have been reported from other countries. In *Politics in Plural Societies*, Alvin Rabushka and Kenneth A. Shepsle assert that there are examples from both European and Third World nations of politics that remained moderate as long as the left-right cleavage was forefront, but turned violent after an ethnic cleavage cut across it. Direct comparisons between countries of widely different social and economic background are not easy to make. But it seems of general interest to ask what makes one cleavage rather than another salient in any given case. The political entrepreneur can be said to activate political cleavages, but he does not have a free hand in so doing. He is constrained by "social arrangements, citizen preferences, and official political institutions," to quote Rabushka and Shepsle. They indicate the desirability of having "a theory of political entrepreneurship" worked out.[5] I shall sketch tentatively a few elements of such a theory and try to indicate its relation to the phenomenon of salience. The conditions of political competition are important. In politics as in economics, entrepreneurs are constrained not least by the investments which they themselves have made and by the actions of other entrepreneurs.

The course of events in Norway can be regarded from two perspectives—that of the pro- and that of antimarketeers. In such a situation note must be taken of the role played by different sets of entrepreneurs, the established ones as well as the leaders of protest groups and new parties. In Norway the former, many of them strongly in favor of joining the EC, regarded the leaders of the ad hoc "Popular Movement Against EC Membership" as manipulators. The antimarketeers themselves saw their role as that of helping to articulate a strong and deep-seated citizen preference. They accused the established leaders, and more particularly the Labor party leadership, of being the Machiavellians. But both groups would probably agree that the role played by political entre-preneurs was important. Their actions, from both sides, must have influenced citizens' choice of an alternative to a considerable degree.

At the end of 1971, when propaganda in favor of entry had not yet got under way and the antimarketeers were in full swing, nearly 75.0% of all who had taken a stand declared against membership, according to opinion polls. But the figure was reduced to 53.5% at the referendum in September 1972. When the issue had first been debated, in 1962, there also occurred a certain mobilization of opinion against entry, but it was not as strong as that in 1971, and mass propaganda from the pro-EC side scarcely got under way before De Gaulle enunciated his veto. It is quite possible to argue that a referendum held in 1963 would have had a different outcome from the one conducted in 1972. For example, according to the former Labor party chairman who was prime minister in 1962–1963, in 1963 there woula nave bccn a majority in favor of entry. The change in citizens' basic preferences which seemed to take place in the course of a decade can be explained with reference to the country's economic development.

THE ECONOMIC BACKGROUND

No fluctuations characterized the Norwegian economy. The general development was unidirectional. The period from the 1950s right through the 1960s and most of the 1970s was one of economic growth and prosperity in Norway, a prosperity shared by the whole population through an elaborate system of steeply progressive income taxation, extensive social services, and large subsidies for the primary branch of the economy.

With conditions improving for people at all levels, controversy between those in the lower and higher income groups was resolved with relative ease. Issues of taxation and social welfare were handled in a pragmatic way, and these remained the issues which occupied most of thc attcntion of politicians in the 1950s and 1960s. Thc rural-urban contrast was not as marked as before. To the extent that it did assume political importance, this kind of conflict also was solved pragmatically. Transfers of income from the industrial branch of the economy reconciled many people in the countryside to the expansion of manufacturing industry. The latter increasingly attracted rural labor, which led to a reduction of agricultural manpower and a decline in the number of farms. Up to a point, however, fewer farms in a given area could mean larger, more profitable units, and mechanization of agriculture could make up for the reduction in the labor force. People in the countryside accepted the increasing industrialization, urbanization, and centralization of Norwegian society as an inescapable fact. Many welcomed the changes, though others regretted them.

Leadership of the Agrarian party, concluding that the farmers' share of the electorate was bound to decline, decided to changc its namc to that of Center party in thc late 1950s, in the hope of attracting some urban voters. In the country's largest party—Labor—the fisherman-smallholder wing was still important, accounting for about 20% of the party's voting strength in the late 1950s. Within this group uneasiness even resulted in confrontations with the party leadership. When the Labor government refused to agree to an increase in farm prices in 1956 and a motion of censure was put forward by the Agrarian party in Parliament, for example, it was supported by legislators representing Labor's smallholder wing. But such an incident was exceptional and solutions were usually found at the level of the interest organizations, with the government acting as an intermediary. Economic growth made it possible to manage conflicts rather easily through accommodation. This applied to rural-urban conflict as well as to disputes between workers and management. Services and manufacturing industry could offer increasingly high remuneration to labor, and they attracted young people in the countryside, while small farms at the margin of production were gradually abandoned. Growth and social mobility made it possible to avoid a decisive confrontation for a long time and work out viable compromises.

However, at the beginning of the 1960s the level of economic growth itself began to raise rather serious problems. The drain of manpower to the cities and industrialized areas depopulated outlying districts to the extent that in 1961–1966 more elementary schools in rural districts had to be closed down than in the previous 15 years. At the same time the rapid process of centralization created strains in the urbanized areas. Rural-urban conflict, or rather a new form of center-periphery conflict, could become serious if the same kind of growth continued—especially if it were to be accelerated. And the prospect of acceleration was raised when Norwegian entry into the more strongly industrialized Common Market became a possibility in 1961–1962.

In the fall of 1961 Great Britain, Norway's most important trade partner, applied for entry. The leading Norwegian politicians, particularly those of the two largest opposing parties, Labor and the Conservatives, found that it was best for their country to follow suit. But this led to a heated public debate. Agrarian spokesmen feared the consequences for the primary branch of the economy, and there was opposition from defenders of the traditional values of the countryside, who deplored the trend toward urbanization and industrialization. Equally opposed to membership were urban radicals, who regarded the institutions of the Common Market as instruments of ruthless monopolistic capitalism. In other words, a new EC conflict dimension cut straight across the existing left-right cleavage. When the question of initiating negotiations with the EC was put to a vote in the Storting in April 1962, Agrarian representatives voted with the socialist Left against Social Democrats and Conservatives. And the cross-cutting produced the opposite of a moderation of conflict. The intense controversy revealed an antagonism between the opposing camps which was much sharper than usual in Norwegian politics. But the struggle was suddenly brought to an end when General De Gaulle vetoed British membership in January 1963. The whole issue was shelved in Norway.

In the period that followed, Norwegian economic development continued as before. There was prosperity and growth, but also increasing centralization in many fields, from business mergers and the construction of ever larger manufacturing plants, whether private or publicly owned, to administrative reorganization into units of increasing size. Small communes disappeared, to be superseded by large ones, a process facilitated by the increased technical efficiency of transport and communications. As a consequence, there was a transfer of authority to fewer decision-making centers. This strengthened the position of a few centrally placed cities, particularly the position of the national capital. In the course of this process, outlying districts stood to lose more and more control of their own conditions of life. Small elementary schools were closed, and the children transported by bus to and from larger schools in fewer, more centrally placed localities. The activity of small hospitals in outlying districts was curtailed to strengthen the staff and technical apparatus of a few larger units. Like the schools, the big hospitals were more efficiently equipped and offered more diversified services, but they were located far away from a great number of patients and their relatives.

Although in some respects material conditions were improving in the country as a whole, progress was more rapid in central than in peripheral areas, producing a feeling of relative regional deprivation in the latter. The impact was greatest in North Norway. Annual net migration from the three northernmost provinces reached more than 2,000 a year during 1961–1965, and the following four-year period was characterized by a further strong increase in the rate of migration. The number of persons moving southward from North Norway amounted to some 15,000 according to the official statistics:

1966	3,030
1967	2,782
1968	4,117
1969	5,140

Similar phenomena could be noted in other countries, such as neighboring Finland, where the Populist Protest party increased its electoral support tenfold between 1966 and 1970. Causes of its rapid upsurge included industrialization, centralization, and migration from rural areas to the towns.[6] New arrivals to the city were more susceptible to various mass movements than were people who had grown up in an urban environment. But in particular the new party appealed to the population of Finland's outlying districts, which was said to find itself in a state of general alienation, reinforced by factors such as the extension of the Finnish television network to cover the whole country. The information coming from television about the higher standard of living in central areas contributed toward alienation.

When television was introduced in the 1960s in Norway, the effect of migration was felt not only in farming families but throughout the countryside. The decline in population led to a reduction of services for the remaining inhabitants in many places. The profits of business declined as the population dwindled, and many small enterprises faced the threat of having to close. There was a feeling in the periphery that people were about to become the victims of sinister forces, which must somehow be resisted.

In Norway, the EC symbolized these forces. The prospect of having to join an emergent industrial superpower was fought with passionate strength, a passion no less than that exhibited earlier in class conflict. The whole development since 1945 seemed to many people to indicate that, while differences between those in higher and lower income brackets had diminished to a point where they had become small and tolerable, the difference between people in central and outlying districts was growing rapidly.

It seems plausible to attribute at least some of the intensity of the EC conflict to this kind of feeling. The sense of relative regional deprivation seemed to grow steadily in the 1960s. It produced a reaction against the Common Market idea in 1961–1962 and an even stronger one ten years later. One fact, however, is hard to fit into this line of reasoning. Serious preparations for entry into the EC were also made in Norway in 1966–1967, but then practically no protest was heard. At that time the left-right dimension was the salient one, obliterating the EC cleavage.

There is no doubt that economic development can have important political consequences. But the evolution of party constellations can also be a significant factor.

CROSS-CUTTING DIMENSIONS

Resistance to Norwegian membership in the EC was strong in 1962 and still stronger in 1972. But in 1967 it was almost unnoticeable, submerged by a cross-cutting dimension. The contrast between socialists and nonsocialists had become highly noticeable by 1966–1967, yet the contrast was not intense or sharp.

It was not possible to talk about a schism in the sense that incompatible courses of action were proposed or strong popular feeling aroused. On the contrary, the nonsocialist parties had come to accept the principle of the welfare state, and for a number of years their objections to the way in which it was administered by the Labor government had been rather weak. However, after a certain amount of mismanagement in public affairs was revealed in the summer and fall of 1963, the bourgeois parties staged an offensive. They succeeded in gaining a parliamentary majority at the election of 1965, whereupon they proceeded to form a coalition cabinet, and the Labor party became the opposition after having been in office practically without interruption for 30 years. Such was the situation when the British government renewed its application for entry into the Common Market in 1966.

When the EC issue arose for the first time, in the fall of 1961, there had been another political constellation in Norway. At that moment the left-right cleavage was not very obvious. The Labor party lost its parliamentary majority at the election in September 1961. A new Socialist People's party gained two seats, which meant that there was still a socialist majority in Parliament, but the Labor cabinet was not inclined to seek the newcomers' support. The latter took a neutral stand and opposed the NATO alliance. This dimension differed from the left-right cleavage but did not cut across it. In foreign and defense policy, the Labor government was assured of support from the bourgeois parties. There was also a possibility of entering into regular collaboration in domestic affairs with the Liberals, who were generally considered to stand somewhat to the left of the other nonsocialists. Such a constellation had long been characteristic of Danish politics. But the Norwegian Labor party, accustomed to many years of majority rule, hardly relished the idea of tying its hands in this or any other way. The situation remained undecided in the months that followed the 1961 election. The socialist-nonsocialist opposition still seemed to be the main dividing line, but it was not a sharp one.

Then, early in 1962, Norwegian politicians had to decide whether or not to initiate negotiations for Common Market membership. And here they proved to touch on a truly cross-cutting conflict line, which produced serious divisions among both socialists and nonsocialists. After the question was shelved in 1963 it came up again on more than one occasion, with the same results. Its force was varying over time, but in the end it led to party splits on both sides of the left and the right. Tables 8–1 and 8–2 give a rough impression of how the constellations shifted back and forth at the parliamentary level during the 1960s and 1970s.

The Norwegian Parliament, the Storting, is elected at regular intervals for four-year terms. The present term extends until 1981. There is no possibility of dissolution. Elections were held in the autumn months of 1961, 1965, 1969, 1973, and 1977. In the first and the two last terms, there was a slight socialist majority. In the 1965–1969 and 1969–1973 terms, there was a nonsocialist majority (see Table 8–1). As a result of the elections, a Labor government took office or remained in office in 1961, 1973, and 1977, while a coalition government of Conservatives, Agrarians, Christian Democrats, and Liberals took office in 1965 and remained in office in 1969. But the coalition cabinet stayed only until March 1971. The question of Common Market membership had not been an issue in any election in the 1960s, and when it became salient in 1970–1971 it produced a cleavage that cut across the socialist-bourgeois dimension of conflict. The question was to be resolved through a nationwide

TABLE 8–1. Distribution of Seats in the Norwegian Storting, 1961–1977

	RESULT OF ELECTION HELD IN THE AUTUMN OF				
PARTIES	*1961*	*1965*	*1969*	*1973*	*1977*
Labor	74	68	74	62	76
Left Socialist	2	2	0	16	2
Socialist total	76	70	74	78	78
Conservative	29	31	29	29	42
Agrarian	16	18	20	21	12
Christian Democrat	15	13	14	20	21
Liberal	14	18	13	2	2
New Liberal	—	—	—	1	0
Progress (Antitax)	—	—	—	4	0
Nonsocialist total	74	80	76	77	77
Total number of seats	150	150	150	155	155

TABLE 8–2.   Roll Calls on the EC in the Storting, 1962–1971

PARTIES	1962		1967		1970		1971	
	Yes	No	Yes	No	Yes	No	Yes	No
Labor	63	11	63	4	66	7	66	8
Left Socialist	0	2	0	2	—	—	—	—
Socialist total	63	13	63	6	66	7	66	8
Conservative	29	0	31	0	29	0	29	0
Agrarian	1	15	11	7	13	7	0	20
Christian Democrat	8	7	10	3	11	3	10	4
Liberal	12	2	18	0	13	0	8	5
Nonsocialist total	50	24	70	10	66	10	47	29
Grand total	113	37	133	16	132	17	113	37

referendum, and, when the time for this consultation approached, visible strains became apparent in Parliament. The same thing had happened in 1962, when negotiations for EC membership were first decided. At that time the issue was shelved before negotiations had started. In 1967 it was decided to resume them, but again the matter was postponed. Both times the reason was a French refusal to enlarge the EC. Finally, the issue emerged once more in 1970, this time in earnest. By March 1971 it had produced so great a strain within the bourgeois coalition that the government found it necessary to resign. It was replaced by a Labor government pledged to seek entry into the Common Market. But there was opposition to the idea within the socialist as well as the nonsocialist camp. A vote on the question of initiating negotiations was taken in Parliament four times, in April 1962, July 1967, June 1970, and June 1971 (see Table 8–2).

Tables 8–1 and 8–2 indicate the shifting importance of two different dimensions of conflict. It is true that Table 8–1 shows a multiparty system, but it could be argued that party differences were largely of historic rather than contemporary interest.[7] The bourgeois coalition acted in many ways like a single party.[8] Table 8–2 shows, however, that there were cases when another line would cut across the socialist-nonsocialist schism. These were important cases too, since the roll calls in question referred to negotiations for entry into the Common Market, a step which could be presumed to have far-reaching consequences. But the cross-cutting did not seem to be serious in 1967, when only small minorities on either side of the left and the right voted in opposition to the main line. It was more serious in 1962 and again in 1971, when the Agrarian party had become unanimously anti-Common Market, the Liberals were badly split, and signs of a steadily growing opposition had appeared within the Labor party. Nineteen seventy was a year of transition.

This cyclical pattern of resistance to the EC was even more clearly visible outside of Parliament. In 1962 the difference of opinion over the Common Market cut straight across the left-right cleavage in the Norwegian electorate. An analysis of Gallup poll data showed Conservative voters in favor, Agrarian and Left Socialist voters against, and Liberals and Christian Democrats divided into an urban and a rural wing; there was also a serious split within the Labor party, in which smallholders and fishermen were opposed to the EC. Among workers the opposition was most marked in the largest cities and in the most sparsely populated areas. Nor is there any doubt that many people felt strongly about the issue. Observers noted the unusually heated debate and the violent mass campaigns.[9]

The anti-EC movement of 1962 was certainly strong, but it is difficult to say how broad it was. At the height of the campaign a slight majority of those who had taken a stand seemed to be against negotiating for entry, according to a Gallup poll. But one-third of the voters had not made up their minds. Similarly, what little public opinion research was conducted in 1967 also showed voters largely undecided, which is not surprising, since at that time no mass campaigns got under way. Only in 1971–1972 was active campaigning resumed. A cleavage similar to the one in 1962 appeared again, and this time the whole electorate was clearly affected. Political entrepreneurs, marketeers as well as antimarketeers, succeeded in mobilizing their adherents through appeals which to a large extent broke up the usual party lines.

There is no doubt that the entrepreneurs made the EC cleavage salient in 1961–1962 and especially in 1971–1972. But they also had their part in keeping it submerged for a long time in between.

THE ROLE OF ENTREPRENEURS

Politicians, it has been said, can either activate or suppress conflict. But they cannot do so at will. In Norway some of the constraints on politicians were quite clear. They were not at liberty to activate the EC cleavage line; Great Britain had to take the lead. However, once the British made the issue salient by asking for entry into the EC, two possibilities were open to Norwegian political entrepreneurs. They could set the agenda as far as their country was concerned, by deciding that the issue was a controversial one or by declaring that there was nothing much to fight about. In 1967 they chose the latter alternative.

American authors have written about what they term "nondecision making" by politicians who "effectively prevent certain grievances from developing into fully-fledged issues."[10] In 1967 the Common Market question was effectively prevented from developing into a full-fledged issue in Norway. Five years earlier the antimarketeers had made the Labor party leadership accede to their demand that a referendum should be held before membership was decided upon. In the summer of 1967 the chairman of the party had hoped to avoid the national referendum. Unless strong reasons to the contrary can be adduced, he said, it will be better to save the trouble and expense of holding it. And it seemed as if he had little to fear. He made his statement in Parliament without meeting any opposition. As one of his collaborators wrote a few months later in November 1967, "The agitation in connection with the parliamentary debate on the EC this year was only a faint summer breeze compared to the storm that was created five years earlier," and, we can add, five years later.

The whole matter was treated in quite a special atmosphere in 1966–1967. When the British Labor government raised the question of entry toward the end of 1966, the Norwegian Labor party was quick to pressure the nonsocialist government for a Norwegian declaration of support. Similar pressure was applied inside the coalition. The marketeers felt that now was *their* time. The leading Conservative member of the cabinet, Foreign Minister John Lyng, relates in his memoirs how political activists, particularly within his own party, put forward their demands for a clear government stand in favor of Norwegian membership.[11] Several cabinet members, the Agrarian prime minister among them, had been opposed to this solution in 1962. But they were in the minority, and if they maintained their stand it would mean the breakup of the newly launched coalition, the fruit of their electoral victory. The political investment made would have been wasted, the patient work of the last few years would have been all in vain. Possibly there would be a return to decades of Labor predominance. The former antimarketeers in the cabinet felt that they had no choice. They agreed to the initiation of membership negotiations.

The necessity of making the coalition work, as well as the necessity of keeping a united socialist front *against* the coalition, carried most of the antimarketeers along on both sides. The EEC cleavage line was obliterated by the left-right line. In the year 1967 the latter dimension was so pronounced that opinion leaders did not want to be distracted by any other disputes. Yet this cannot be called an example of a dimension's becoming salient because of its intensity. No strong opposition between left and right was noticeable at the mass level. The main driving force behind the nonsocialist rally had been irritation among parliamentarians rather than widespread fear or hatred in groups of the population. The bourgeois government had some pet programs, like the building of a specified number of dwelling units in their four-year term of office, but they offered no alternative policy to that of the welfare state. Their declared aim was to administer the latter in a better way than the Labor party had done. Still the change was felt to be important by all who took an interest in politics. For the first time in a generation Labor had been forced out. Was this to be only the beginning of more thoroughgoing change? Nobody could tell.

When the question of an enlargement of the EC was raised anew in this situation, the government hesitated for a short while, then it declared the struggle over Norwegian negotiations to be a thing of the past as far as the coalition partners were concerned. And there was no more of a struggle on the socialist side. Things looked quite different from what they had been five years earlier. For once in modern Norwegian history, Socialists were on the defensive after the resounding electoral victory of their adversaries in 1965. It had been a shock to everyone on the left. "We must not be overwhelmed by pessimism," said the Labor party chairman at his party's National Congress in the spring of 1967. "Many of our opponents see before them the prospect of a lasting period of decline for the Labor movement," he added, "and there is only one way for us to get through this difficult time. We must stick together and work together despite all difficulties, he said, appealing to the rank-and-file to show patience and understanding in a time of adversity." Nor did he appeal in vain. The delegates at the National Congress showed remarkable willingness to support the leadership and put aside old hobbyhorses. Their restraint in the matter of the EC was not the least striking. There was only indirect opposition, mainly in the innocuous form of a proposal on the part of the Iron and Metal Workers' Union to make a study of the socialist policy that Norwegians ought to pursue once they had become members of the EC.

ISSUES AND DIMENSIONS

No doubt there were some, both among socialists and others, who would have liked to see a new anti-EC campaign launched in 1967. It would have been surprising if no signs of uneasiness had come to light. There was unrest in agricultural circles as urbanization and industrialization continued. In the period 1949–1959, on the average 2,023 farmsteads had been abandoned each year. The figure increased to 6,669 per year in 1964–1969. At first only smallholders had left for the town. They were the people who had always had to take some extra jobs outside agriculture, because they could not make a decent living out of farming alone on their small plots of land. But by the middle of the 1960s it had come so far that even medium-sized family farms were being abandoned. In 1962 only the Labor-affiliated Smallholders' Association had expressed apprehension at the prospect of entry into the Common Market. In 1967 it was joined by the Farmers' Association, closely related to the Agrarian party.

But leading politicians turned a deaf ear. Only a minority of parliamentarians from the Agrarian party maintained their opposition, and on the other side very few Labor members showed any willingness to join the anti-EC stand of the Left Socialists. However, this does not mean that the leading politicians were unaware of the problems which the process of centralization increasingly entailed. In retrospect it may seem as if a close and necessary connection existed between the issue of EEC membership and the territorial center-periphery conflict line. But that was not self-evident. If proper safeguards could be obtained from the EEC, entry into the Common Market might not upset Norwegian agriculture. The majority of Norwegian politicians regarded further centralization as undesirable, but the remedies they sought in the middle of the 1960s had little to do with the EEC issue. To many nonsocialists it seemed that the Labor party, with its policy of a planned national economy under central government control, must bear the main responsibility. The Agrarians in particular emphasized this theme in the 1965 parliamentary campaign. Labor politicians responded by pointing to the trend toward concentration in private business. In their view the remedy was to be sought not in a weakening but in a strengthening of government regulation. "Planned decentralization" was their watchword. In short, the territorial center-periphery dispute was incorporated into the left-right dimension of conflict. And there it remained as long as the Common Market issue was not on the agenda. By 1969 Labor politicians were in a position to argue that four years of nonsocialist coalition government had only aggravated the center-periphery problem. The undesirable consequences of centralization had become more clearly visible than ever. Obviously, according to Labor spokesmen, the *laissez-faire* policy of the bourgeois government was responsible for the accelerating depopulation of the outlying districts. Voters seemed to respond. In the 1969 election the Labor party made considerable gains in the periphery, particularly in North Norway, the area hardest hit by the tendency of the times.

But the center-periphery dispute did not stay for long within the confines of the socialist-nonsocialist dimension of conflict. In 1971–1972 the EC issue emerged once more. It was necessary to take a clear stand in the matter of Common Market membership. And the relations between parties had changed considerably since 1966–1967, a fact that led to a new development. The bourgeois coalition was no longer a new and exciting adventure. It had suffered a setback at the 1969 election, and for the Agrarians in particular the question arose as to whether their party really stood to gain by continuing in a government which was unable to stem the rising tide of centralization. Friction developed over other issues as well, but it was the EC question that made the coalition fall apart. It still apparently stuck together in June 1970, when a vote was taken in Parliament on whether or not to open the third round of EC negotiations. As will be seen from Table 8–2, there seemed to be as large a majority of "Yes" votes in the coalition parties as there had been in 1967. But this was only an outward appearance. In the 1970 debate a number of parliamentarians voted affirmatively but had reservations sufficiently strong to make it clear that they were actually against the idea of membership. While voting in favor of opening negotiations, one speaker after another let it be understood that he hoped they would fail or expected that they would lead to no acceptable result. The debate revealed that in the parliamentary group of the Agrarian party, there was now actually a majority against joining the EC.

On the socialist side, the 1970 vote showed growing opposition to the EC within the Labor party group as well. In the 1969 election the party had been successful at the polls. It had called for a rally behind the largest socialist party to defeat the bourgeois coalition, and the appeal seemed to work. The Socialist People's party lost its two seats, and the Labor party came very close to obtaining a parliamentary majority. But this in itself made the bourgeois coalition look less threatening than before. No longer did it constitute an unknown and disquieting menace to the working class. It could rather easily be beaten.

Soon socialist unity began to break up. When it became clear that the governing coalition was seriously divided over the EC issue in 1970, antimarketeers within the Labor movement could afford on their side to oppose the policy of the Labor leadership. Despite the tradition of strict discipline in Labor party parliamentary voting, the number of negative votes in roll calls increased. Other data, however, showed much more clearly the extent of internal opposition. At the district conferences of the party, held early in 1972, about one-third of the delegates were opposed to the leadership. The antimarketeers organized their own Workers' Information Committee within the party. They campaigned actively against the official party line in the 1972 EC referendum and at the 1973 parliamentary election many of them joined hands with the Socialist People's party and the Communist party to form a Socialist Electoral Alliance. It succeeded in having no less than 16 candidates elected, one a Communist, the others belonging to the Socialist People's party or the Workers' Information Committee. The Labor party's share of the total vote in the election was reduced by almost one-fourth, and its losses were particularly heavy in the outlying districts. In 1969 it had posed as defender of the periphery, but after it had come out strongly in support of EC membership in 1971–1972, the periphery turned against the party as well as against the EC. Seventy-three percent of the electorate voted "No" in communes of low centrality at the 1972 referendum, whereas 55% voted "Yes" in communes of high centrality.[12] And the "No" to EC was particularly marked in North Norway, as was the loss of the Labor party the following year. In the largest Northern province of Nordland, where the party had obtained 53% of the total vote in 1969, that figure was reduced to 36% in 1973.

A new political pattern emerged while the Common Market issue was salient. Before October, 1965, a socialist government had been faced by a nonsocialist opposition; then a nonsocialist government took over. But, when it fell apart in March 1971, the Labor party government which was formed had its *raison d'être* not as a socialist, but as a pro-EC cabinet. It was faced by an antimarketeer opposition till the autumn of 1972, when it resigned after losing the referendum. An anti-EC government took over and held office till after the 1973 election.

When the Labor party formed a government again in 1973, it had accepted the antimarketeers' Commercial Treaty with the EC. For a while it looked as if the Common Market issue would continue to play a role in Norwegian politics, and such might perhaps have been the case if the country's position outside the EC had proved difficult. It did not, however. The failure to enter had no noticeable consequences; on the contrary, the importance of the EC seemed to be on the wane after 1973. The leading Common Market countries disagreed on important items of monetary and economic policy. When for the first time in more than 30 years Norway was threatened by a serious recession in 1977, the EC controversy was no longer a live issue. The electoral campaign of 1977 was to a large extent dominated by the question whether voters had confidence in the full-employment policies of the Labor government. The socialist-non-socialist cleavage line was once more in the foreground. The left-right constellation of previous decades largely reasserted itself, with Labor and the Conservatives as the two main parties. The Agrarians, and still more the Left Socialists, who had profited most from the EC dispute four years earlier, now lost heavily.

To sum up, the territorial center-periphery contrast has played an intermittent, but important, role in the last two decades besides the economic left-right contrast. And it is a remarkable fact that whenever opposition between pro- and antimarketeers was the salient dimension, sharp conflict characterized Norwegian politics. The opposition between parties that called themselves socialist and nonsocialist, respectively, was much milder in nature.

I said, when describing the economic development, that differences between central and outlying districts caused anxiety, whereas many people thought the difference between high and low incomes had diminished to a point where it could be regarded as insignificant and tolerable. Consequently, stronger passion was fanned by the center-periphery conflict than by the right-left conflict. This is part of the story, but not the whole story. Not everyone felt alike; there were many who wanted a further reduction or a total abolition of both income differences and private property rights over the means of production. They thought that Norwegian entry into the EC would make such policies impossible; it would probably lead to an increase in income differences and the power of private capital. One reason for the sharpness of the Common Market controversy was that it served to infuse ideological fervor into the left-right cleavage. The struggle over EC membership was not solely a question of urban-rural or center-periphery opposition. The left-right dimension was also incorporated, and in a form different from the one it had assumed in recent decades, as a mild dispute over a little more or a little less welfare state regulation. Suddenly, irreconcilable socialist-capitalist principles again became politically relevant. Only in a limited sense did the EC cleavage cut across the left-right cleavage.

Similarly, it could be said that in the latter half of the 1960s the contrast between periphery and center was incorporated into the socialist-nonsocialist dimension. And it received a form which made for mildness of conflict. The issue of decentralization was treated in a pragmatic way, not as a question of great or dramatic steps involving the whole future of Norwegian society, but as a question of slightly different forms of practical regulation of the economy. The issue was defused.

Cautious and pragmatic leaders were in control in the second half of the 1960s and determined the climate of Norwegian politics. Today they are in control once more, but it is impossible to know for how long. The impact of political entrepreneurs is often dependent on constellations over which they themselves have only limited influence.

THE MORAL-RELIGIOUS DIMENSION

One additional dimension, the moral-religious line of conflict, must be mentioned separately. It has played a subordinate, but still noticeable, role in Norwegian politics. Studying Norwegian voters' perceptions of party distances in the second half of the 1960s, Philip E. Converse and Henry Valen found the left-right axis to be dominant, but the moral-religious cleavage came next in importance.[13] In the early 1970s there was added a third dimension, according to Valen: the Common Market dispute had a major impact on perceived configurations in the party system.[14] But the two dimensions from the late 1960s were still clearly recognizable.

At present the picture would seem to be again more similar to that of the later 1960s, with the left-right cleavage dominant and the moral-religious one second. The rather great salience of the latter is related to the fact that Norway alone in Scandinavia has a religious party of some significance—the Christian Democrats; these have recently improved their position to the point of becoming the country's third largest party at the 1977 election.

The party split off from the Liberals in the 1930s but gained national importance only in 1945. In the Nordic countries, with their established Lutheran churches and no significant religious minorities, parties of this type seemed out of place. However, various religious groups were activated politically during the Nazi occupation, when disputes arose between the established church and those who had taken over the apparatus of the state. The Christian Democratic party was launched on a national scale at the end of hostilities. It could benefit from the traditional political involvement of certain religious or semireligious organizations, not least those connected with the temperance movement. The latter once constituted a force of great importance in Norwegian politics. They were affiliated in the main with the Liberal party, which has now been largely superseded by the Christian Democrats. For a number of years between the two World Wars, alcohol prohibition was a dominant issue. The temperance question still remains salient to a number of voters, and the emergent problem of narcotics may have made this type of moral issue look increasingly important. A similar role has been played in recent years by the public debate on abortion and related topics. This too has helped make moral issues salient.

It can be noted that, unlike her neighboring Nordic states, Norway is a country facing the Atlantic and that transatlantic influences are stronger here in some respects. For a long time Norwegian temperance organizations were in close contact with their American counterparts. But another and more special factor, which played a role in the buildup of the Christian Democratic party, can also be mentioned. The prewar party was a small, strictly local phenomenon on the Western coast. It had a low-status, rather rural character, and only during the occupation was contact established with other religious circles. At the crucial moment of party organizing in 1945, members of a high-status urban revival movement—the so-called Oxford Group Movement, which had been brought to Norway in the 1930s by an American, Dr. Buchman—played an important role in providing an active element with more widespread national connections than what the original leadership possessed.

In Denmark as well as in Finland and Sweden, attempts have been made in recent years to launch Christian Democratic parties on the Norwegian model, but so far they have had no success.[15] It can scarcely be said that Norway is less secularized than the rest of Scandinavia. Yet the fact remains that it constitutes the one Nordic country where the moral-religious cleavage plays a political role which, though subordinate, is not without a certain significance.

PARTIES AND CLEAVAGES: AN ILLUSTRATION

Table 8–3 illustrates the relationship between parties and cleavages at a given point of time. Respondents were asked about their stand on three different issues: how they had voted at the EC referendum in 1972, what was their view of restrictive laws on abortion, and how they viewed proposals to increase public control over banks. They were also asked what party they had voted for at the 1973 election. For example, 32% of those who voted Labor in 1973 had voted "No" to EC at the 1972 referendum; 37% of Labor party voters were in favor of restrictive legislation on abortion (while their party was

TABLE 8–3. Parties and Cleavages in Norway

	VOTED IN 1973 FOR				
	Labor	Conservatives	Agrarians	Christians	Left Socialists
Voted on EEC 1972	32	12	4	20	10
Restrictions on abortion	37	48	25	11	26
More control with banks	26	10	39	28	10
Number	523	263	194	177	156

against, as was also the case with the Left Socialist party); and 26% of Labor party voters were against extending public influence over private banks, whereas their party (again like the Left Socialist party) favored such extension. Conservative voters agreed strongly with their party both on the question of free enterprise and on the EC. The opposite stand on the EC, taken by the Agrarian party, was supported by 96% of its voters. The Christian Democratic party got the strongest support from its voters in the matter of legal restrictions on abortion. The Conservative and Agrarian parties, who had similar planks in their platforms, were much less in agreement with their voters. But this may not have done them too much harm, if few of their adherents regarded the abortion issue as overly important. In the case of the Agrarian party, however, it seems that voter support was weakened as the EC issue receded into the background, while questions related to the left-right conflict line became more important. The outlook for the Left Socialists could be considered better in 1973, since 90% of those who voted for them agreed with their stand not only on the EC but also on the question of public influence versus private capital. But they lost support largely because of a number of disagreements among leaders over personal and organizational matters. The Socialist Electoral Alliance of 1973 became the Left Socialist party only after the majority of Communists had refused to continue cooperation with their partners in the alliance. More serious than the bolting of the Communists, perhaps, were later quarrels among leaders which made the new party lose a good deal of its credibility. This redounded to the advantage of the Labor party at the 1977 election. Finally, it can be noted from the table that in 1973 there seemed to be a good deal of party identification with Labor even on the part of voters who failed to agree with specific points on its program. Many voted for it apparently less because of particular issues than because they regarded it as "the party of common people." Even at this low point in its fortunes, it remained the linchpin of the Norwegian party system.

Denmark: A One-Dimensional System Under Stress[16]

There is general agreement that during the last half century the Danish party system has been characterized mainly by one single dimension.[17] Parties have been situated from left to right, according to the interests of groups with low income and middle or high income, respectively, the extent of public expenditures on welfare measures, and the distribution of burdens and benefits of taxation. What is still often called the Agrarian party used to be the party of the farming interest, but today it has an urban as well as a rural electorate, and for decades antagonism between city and country has been of decidedly subordinate importance. As in Sweden and Norway, the Social Democratic party is the largest party in Denmark, but unlike those in the neighboring countries it has never succeeded in obtaining a parliamentary majority, and the characteristic constellation of Danish politics used to be a minority government of Social Democrats supported in Parliament by the votes of the Liberal party, or a coalition government formed by these two parties.

In other words, the party system of Denmark as a whole could be placed somewhat to the right of those in Sweden and Norway. In 1966 there was a change in the small Socialist People's party, which had been launched in the late 1950s to the left of the Social Democrats, that increased its representation at the parliamentary election sufficient for the Social Democrats to establish a majority with left socialist support. Until then the Social Democrats had refused to have anything to do with the "splinter" party. But now cooperation between the two was initiated, and the system moved leftward. The Liberals, Agrarians, and Conservatives approached one another. At the 1968 election these three parties together obtained a majority of parliamentary seats, and they formed a coalition government. But the event could not be said to constitute a markedly rightward move. The prime minister was a Liberal, and the coalition chose what it considered a cautious line. It did not initiate any break with the past, but rather followed the general trend that had marked Danish policy during the preceding years. It might have been assumed that no great consequences would follow, but soon it became clear that the development was getting out of hand.

This is not the place to evaluate the impact of political parties on public policy, but the subject must be mentioned briefly. It has been said that, compared with parties in a country such as the United States, the parties of Western Europe and not least those in Scandinavia have been impressively effective in pushing through large-scale social reform in fields such as health care and housing policy.[18] But this is not to say that Scandinavian political parties have been uniformly successful and efficient instruments of reform. There are instances of control being lost, and voter rebellions against the established parties have resulted. The phenomenon has been particularly evident in Denmark. No attempt shall be made here to determine whether the chain of events was triggered mainly by an unforeseeable international economic development or by a lack of foresight on the part of established party leaders. In any case around 1970 the actual impact of reforms on the daily life of citizens had been badly miscalculated. As the relation between Danish exports and imports developed unfavorably and inflationary pressure mounted, control was lost. Taxes increased from 31% of the gross national product in 1965 to 34% in 1968 and to 44% in 1971. The 1969 Danish income tax law did assume increases in personal exemptions as prices rose, but like most national tax laws it did not provide for any automatic alteration in tax rates as inflation pushed money incomes up. Confronted with inflation, the need to implement newly adopted tax legislation, and the need to prepare for Denmark's entry into the Common Market, the tax authorities were not able to cope imaginatively with the many problems that arose in the course of a few years.

Voters grew increasingly restive. At the 1971 election the bourgeois government lost its majority. There was no dramatic change, however. The Social Democrats once more formed a government leaning on the Socialist People's party. But the main attention of voters and parties in 1971–1972 focused on the question of entry into the European Community. The restive mood of the electorate was reflected in opposition to entry, which was shown by opinion polls to be quite considerable. However, the leaders of the main established parties were agreed on the necessity of securing Danish membership. Social Democrats, Agrarians, and Conservatives fought side by side in what has been called "undoubtedly the most extensive political campaign ever undertaken in Denmark."[19] The leaders of the Danish establishment won the referendum. But perhaps they overplayed their hand. Sensing that the Danish population was dissatisfied with steadily deteriorating economic conditions, they stressed the advantages which they thought were to accrue from joining the EC. Their effort was intense, and the voters turned out with a record participation of 90.1%. But improved conditions did not follow immediately; on the contrary there was further deterioration. Frustration seemed to be the result.

A little more than a year after the EC referendum, at the parliamentary election of December 1973, the storm broke. Voters found instruments which they thought suitable for expressing their displeasure with the traditional parties. In particular, one of the most eye-catching protest votes ever seen in any country was generated by the lawyer Mogens Glistrup, a man who has recently been sentenced to the payment of a million-dollar fine because of tax evasion. Launching what he called the Progress party, he used an antitax platform to attract almost half a million voters away from the established parties, permitting him to emerge overnight as the leader of the second largest party in the Folketing, the Danish Parliament. Glistrup appeared on Danish television at a most opportune moment, when in 1973 he attacked the expansion of the public bureaucracy and the income tax increases which had been legislated by both bourgeois and Social Democratic governments. As inflation moved money incomes up, higher tax rates and reduced subsidies caused some middle-income groups to incur marginal income reductions of over 100%. A faultily designed income tax reduction scheme caused many voters to receive end-of-year notices of additional tax debt just before the December 1973 election. And Glistrup was not the only protester. Actually the election was triggered by a Social Democrat who broke with his party because of its proposal, supported by the left socialists, to increase taxes on homeowners. He launched his own party, the Center Democrats, which contributed to the transformation of the Danish party system, as did also the appearance of some smaller new parties. But Glistrup's success was the most sensational feature.

Table 8–4 shows the composition of the Danish Parliament after the last "normal" election of 1971, the first protest election of 1973, and the most recent election, held in 1977.

With all its fragmentation the Danish party system can still be termed unidimensional. It is true that there is some doubt about the position of Mogens Glistrup on certain issues. He once declared that the Progress party aimed at disbanding the Danish armed forces, replacing them with something much cheaper: a phonograph record which would send out the message "We surrender" (in Russian) at the approach of an invader. This would place him in a position near some extreme leftists in defense matters if he were to be taken seriously on this point, which seems doubtful. The traditional parties, while regarding him as rightist, have refused to take him seriously in any connection. But his continued great electoral strength remains a fact.

In any case it is clear that the same economic issues as before, mainly concerning welfare expenditure and the incidence of taxation, still dominate Danish politics. The efforts of the small Christian Democratic party to raise moral and religious questions have not been successful. But in a special sense it may be said that a second dimension has appeared in addition to the left-right conflict line in Denmark: there is also a cleavage between the political establishment and the recently launched parties of protest. Survey analysis has made it possible to gain some insight into the background of this old party-new party dimension. Jerold G. Rusk and Ole Borre, studying the elections of the 1970s, found that people who held views compatible with "socialist" and "bourgeois" ideologies, respectively, maintained their identification with the traditional parties.[20] But, although the highest attitude item on this dimension was *ideology*, the highest on the new party-old party dimension was *political distrust*. In other words, the left-right conflict line is the product of social class

TABLE 8–4. Number of Seats Obtained in the Folketing

	1971	1973	1977
Social Democrats	70	46	65
Conservatives	31	16	15
Agrarians	30	22	21
Liberals	27	20	6
Socialist People's party	17	11	7
Progress Party (anti-tax)	—	28	26
Center Democrats	—	14	11
Christian Democrats	—	7	6
Communists	—	6	7
Legal Justice party	—	5	6
Left Wing Socialist party	—	—	5
Total[a]	175	175	175

[a]In addition there are two members from the Faroe Islands and two from Greenland. In 1971 the majority of these supported the Social Democrats, enabling them to form a government.

identifications and issues which led in the past to the development of socialist and bourgeois ideologies. The other "dimension," if it can be called that, is caused by more immediate factors of political distrust and concern with current problems.

Rusk and Borre conclude that the new parties are not anchored in any new cleavage, whether ethnic, religious, or regional. Nor do they reflect any basic realignment of the existing lower class-middle class cleavage. They have succeeded in pitting some members of the middle class against one another, and some members of the lower class against one another. There are "cynics of the left" in Denmark as well as "cynics of the right," although the former are fewer than the latter. Rusk and Borre refer to a similar phenomenon in the United States, where it was found that, in the 1968 election, distrust was associated with sympathy for either George Wallace or Eugene McCarthy.[21] The Danish "cynical" or "distrustful" voters, whether they support one or the other new party, of the left or right, are pitted against those who still retain their belief that the traditional parties are best fitted to solve the pressing problems of the country. Rusk and Borre assume that, as the new parties are forced to reveal that they have no quick and easy solution to those problems, the left-right dimension will continue to shape Danish politics. "Some of the new parties will weaken and possibly disappear; others will regroup along the left-right dimension."[22] There are few signs that this is about to happen. But perhaps it is the most likely outcome.

A Note on Fragmentation, Aggregation, and Polarization

When a society is divided politically into two main groups, the opposition can be either mild or sharp. A number of different terms have been used to describe this condition: mild or sharp polarization, weak or strong dualism, muted opposition, implacable cleavage, and still other expressions. Often the term *aggregation* is employed to denote the formation of two parties or coalitions advocating only slightly divergent policies, whereas *polarization* is taken to mean that the two are irreconcilably opposed. I shall follow that usage here.

A condition of more than two main opponents is customarily called *fragmentation*. Now political fragmentation can be either an enduring or a transitory state of affairs. The undesirable aspects of durable fragmentation have been pointed out by many authors. No decisive political action is taken, a lack of direction and purpose prevails. One example of fragmentation is the Third Republic in France, with its timid political leadership drawn from the ranks of the so-called Radical party, a party having no policy or discipline and no consistency in its choice of allies. "Its deputies joined every majority and its ministers sat in every cabinet, bewildering and disgusting the voter by ensuring that he was never presented with clear alternatives."[23] Yet the politicians of the fragmented Third Republic contrived to keep the contending groups of French society in a balanced state of mild dissatisfaction, which most of them after all found "preferable to any serious alternative."[24] Possibly the choice of an alternative would have been not only serious, but tragic. After seeing three years of civil war in the neighboring country across the Pyrenees, a hostile critic of the French Radicals conceded reluctantly: "Perhaps it was a Radical party that Spain lacked in 1936."[25] Subsequent to a period of fragmentation in the early 1930s, the Spanish political system went through a process of polarization, in the course of which their Radical, that is, Centrist, politicians were rapidly eliminated.[26] Some years earlier, in the German Weimar republic, fragmentation was replaced (at least partly) by polarization, when the Nazi and Communist parties seemed about to divide an increasingly great share of the electorate between them. Civil war was avoided, but it was done by giving one set of extremists, the Nazis, the opportunity to suppress all opposition.

In France's Third Republic fragmentation was maintained for a surprisingly long time. Usually it represents, in its strong form at least, only a short transitional phase, as in Germany and Spain, or in the United States in the last century. In the latter half of the 1850s, "everyone was, to some degree, suspicious of everyone else."[27] In the American election of 1860 four major parties sought the presidency. No candidate came close to winning a majority of popular votes. Lincoln got 40%, Douglas 30%, Breckenridge 18%, and Bell 12% of the total vote. Both geographical sections were split, but all four parties were wholly or mainly sectional:[29]

Percentage of votes won by regions

	NORTH AND WEST	SOUTH	TOTAL
Republicans (Lincoln)	99%	1%	100%
Democrats (Douglas)	88	12	100
Constitutional Democrats (Breckenridge)	33	67	100
Constitutional Union (Bell)	13	87	100

This fragmentation quickly gave way to polarization, and civil war between the sections ensued.

But polarization is not the necessary outcome of transitional fragmentation. The result can also be aggregation. The United States went through a stage of fragmentation in the late 1840s, when both the slavery question and other issues, such as the fight over internal improvement of rivers and harbors, threatened to split the two main party organizations. However, after a compromise on slavery had been reached in 1850, a reaggregation of the mildly opposed Whig and Democratic parties ensued.[29] The fragmentation created on the American scene by the Vietnam war and other events of the 1960s was followed by aggregation in the 1970s. Robert A. Dahl remarks that, contrary to expectation, the highly fragmented pattern was followed by a return to the "old politics" in the first half of the new decade.[30] The result of the 1976 election seems to show that this meant a return to aggregation. Not only did the candidates of the two major parties get practically all the votes, but policy differences between them were also very mild. Some would use the word insipid, and certainly many voters seemed to think that only a choice between Tweedledum and Tweedledee was offered them. Turnout was very low. But, although very few are satisfied, it can at least be said that the present American system is neither polarized nor strongly fragmented.

The aggregation achieved after the compromise of 1850 did not prove durable. For how long the present state of aggregation or weak dualism will last remains to be seen. Experience shows that political change can be rapid, in the United States as elsewhere. And the relation between aggregation, fragmentation, and polarization is a complex one.

The experience of two small countries like Denmark and Norway can provide only a limited contribution to the study of a vast subject. But perhaps they can be said to illustrate certain tendencies of contemporary democracy. Denmark is at present a somewhat fragmented polity. If the trend that was inaugurated in 1973 should continue, and the basis of the established parties be further eroded from right and left, the Danish situation might come to resemble in certain respects that of the Weimar republic. But this is a very unlikely prospect. After all, the elements of aggregation or muted dualism still seem much stronger in Denmark than the elements of fragmentation.

The shifting constellations in Norway raise the question of what exactly we mean by fragmentation. It seems to be in effect another word for cross-cutting cleavages, which tends to be used when the author regards the cross cutting as undesirable. Robert A. Dahl remarks that American opinions about Vietnam cut across other cleavages, fragmenting the two political parties, a phenomenon he seems to regard as regrettable.[31] As used by Lawrence C. Mayer in the present volume, fragmentation has a still more clearly negative connotation. I shall use it in the following without either laudatory or pejorative connotations, simply as a synonym for the more cumbrous "state of affairs characterized by cross-cutting cleavages."

Schematically, the Norwegian political system can be said to have gone through six different phases since the early 1960s:

1. fragmentation, 1961–1963
2. aggregation, 1963–1970
3. fragmentation, 1970–1971
4. polarization, 1971–1973
5. fragmentation, 1973–1977
6. aggregation, 1977–

The three phases of fragmentation differed somewhat in character. It could be said that in 1970–1971 there was simple fragmentation, whereas the periods 1961–1963 and 1973–1977 were characterized by compound fragmentation.

The fragmentation period of 1961–1963 was characterized by a double splitting up. There was antagonism between those who were for and against membership in the Common Market, but in addition the antimarketeers were disunited among themselves. While the Left Socialists would have no form of affiliation with the EC, the Agrarians favored a Treaty of Association (as did some Christian Democrats and Liberals). Different antimarketeer organizations were launched, working separately for their different aims. Only at the beginning of 1963 did they try to come together, but by then the whole issue was about to be taken off the agenda. In other words, while there was a breakup of the political spectrum, only weak tendencies toward a regrouping or new alignment were visible.

In 1970–1971 the various antimarket groups did come together. A common organization, the People's Movement Against Membership in the EC, was formally launched. A prominent conservative agrarian was made its chairman, with a prominent left socialist its vice chairman. There was agreement not only on the negative goal of "no membership," but also on the solution to be sought: a simple Commercial Treaty with the EC. More important still, a common ideology was now taking shape. No doubt there were still separate strands of anticapitalist propaganda from the left, antiindustrialist and anti-Catholic propaganda from the right, but a common theme of resistance to centralization was slowly emerging, although not without some difficulty.

In Norway 1970 and part of 1971 was a period of fragmentation in the sense that the left-right cleavage was still strong enough to keep the government together, but at the same time the force of internal opposition was growing and made the continuation of negotiations with the EC increasingly difficult. The bourgeois coalition was falling apart, and the opposition joined hands with the left wing of the equally disunited socialists in a way which foreshadowed the emergence of the next stage, with its polarization along a pro- and anti-Common Market axis.

Several factors contributed to this implacable opposition. Besides those mentioned already, it should be added that the issue was perceived by most active participants not as a question of practical adjustments, but of taking a decisive and irrevocable step.[32] In the eyes of many, acceding to the Treaty of Rome was tantamount to giving up Norwegian sovereignty forever. It became a vote for or against independence, for or against a separate national existence, perhaps not least in the opinion of many young people. There was a strong mobilization of youth during the EC struggle. And, as Max Weber once remarked, the young tend to prefer an absolutist ethic to a pragmatic one.

The movement against entry derived great strength from its ideology of decentralization, which united, on the one hand, left and right, farmers and peripheral small business impatient with government regulation, and, on the other, radical labor dissatisfied with the restraining influence of the strong Central Federation of Labor in wage negotiations.[33] The common ideology was fragile, and once the struggle against entry had been won there was little to hold the two wings of the movement together. A swift disintegration was to set in during the fragmentation period from 1973 on. But, while the EC appeared as a threatening enemy, the anticentralization ideology provided a strong cohesive force. It contributed to the creation of an intense cleavage, cutting across the less intense one which divided the parties labeled "socialist" from the ones labeled "bourgeois."

I shall not try to provide arguments for deciding whether or not the period of polarization was preferable to the preceding or the ensuing period of aggregation. Some might even regard the intermediate periods of fragmentation as better than either alternative. These are probably a minority. But the fragmentation periods at least hold interest for academics who wish to study certain aspects of political entrepreneurship. The newly launched Anders Lange's Party for Sharp Reduction in Taxes and Public Restrictions got 100,000 votes in 1973, which, although only one-third of the share obtained by Mogens Glistrup's antitax Progress party in Denmark, was quite impressive for Norway. But when Anders Lange died not long afterward, the whole movement collapsed in a very short time, as his successors quarrelled among themselves. The equally striking decline in support for the socialist left, which had obtained nearly a quarter of a million votes at the 1973 Norwegian election, could also be attributed largely to problems of leadership. Public disagreement between prominent members of the Left Socialist party, many of them academics, made it appear at times more like a debating society than a party. Its leaders were no doubt gifted people, but voters seemed to prefer the diffident Labor party style of leadership with its emphasis on working in a team. Similarly, on the bourgeois side, the split within the Liberal party proved catastrophic, and the sharp decline in support for the Agrarians—Norway's Center party was also connected with leadership problems. The chairman resigned at the beginning of the election year 1977, and there followed a long struggle over the issue of succession. By way of contrast, a similar succession problem was solved much more quickly and harmoniously by the Christian Democrats. Entrepreneurship certainly has a good deal to do with changing party fortunes. Over and over again it has been confirmed that disunity is damaging at the polls.

Those who are involved in entrepreneurship on various levels must always give some thought to the preservation of unity. But it is a consideration which weighs more or less heavily with different groups of political entrepreneurs at different times. Thus it appears that in 1962 many leaders of the Norwegian Iron and Metal Workers' Union were more interested in keeping their country out of the Common Market than in sticking to the Labor party line. In 1967 the aim of strengthening the party was held to be much more important; and though many middle-level entrepreneurs probably still regarded its program and its leadership with mixed feelings, they nevertheless supported it energetically.

One is reminded of the ambivalence expressed by certain American politicians after the slavery question had been shelved in 1850. They had tried hard to make it the one salient issue, to split both major parties down the middle and bring about a realignment of South and North. But, when their aim was frustrated, they rallied once more to the support of Whigs and Democrats, respectively. The "cursed bonds of party," wrote James Seddon of Virginia in 1852, "paralyzed our strength and energy when they might have been successfully exerted, and now as some partial compension must sustain and uphold us from dispersion and prostration."[34] There were political actors in Norway who seemed to feel likewise in 1967 for a time, particularly in 1966–1967.

Thus it appears that the fragmentation of a party system or its opposite—be it aggregation or polarization—is determined to considerable extent by political entrepreneurs, but these again are largely influenced in their actions by what they perceive as constraints imposed upon them through the party constellation itself.

Notes

1. Dankward A. Rustow, "Working Multiparty Systems, in Sigmund Neumann, ed., *Modern Political Parties*, Chicago: Chicago University Press, 1956, p. 176.

2. S. M. Lipset and Stein Rokkan, eds., *Party Systems and Voter Alignments*, New York: Free Press, 1967, Introduction and p. 51.

3. Steen Sauerberg and Niels Thomsen, "The Political Role of Mass Communication in Scandinavia," in Karl H. Cerny, ed., *Scandinavia at the Polls*, Washington, D.C.: American Enterprise Institute, 1977, pp. 181–216.

4. On the 1972 referendums, see articles in *Scandinavian Political Studies*, 8 (1973), 214 ff. On the subsequent elections, ibid., 9 (1974), 197 ff.

5. Alvin Rabushka and Kenneth A. Shepsle, *Politics in Plural Societies: A Theory of Democratic Instability*, Columbus, Ohio: Merrill, 1972, p. 61.

6. Risto Sänkiaho, "A Model of the Rise of Populism and Support for the Finnish Rural Party," *Scandinavian Political Studies*, 6 (1971), 27–47.

7. Philip E. Converse and Henry Valen, "Dimensions of Cleavage and Perceived Party Distances in Norwegian Voting," *Scandinavian Political Studies*, 6 (1971), 107–152. They find in the data of the 1960s an "almost geologic" record of the past.

8. In about 95% of all cases, parliamentary members of the disciplined Labor party opposition voted together, but so did the members of the four coalition parties in just as high a proportion of all cases.

9. Stein Rokkan and Henry Valen, "Regional Contrasts in Norwegian Politics," in E. Allarde and Y. Littunen, eds., *Cleavages, Ideologies and Party Systems*, vol. 10, Helsinki: Transactions of the Westermarck Society, 1964, p. 199.

10. Peter Bachrach and Morton S. Baratz, "Decisions and Nondecisions: An Analytical Framework," *American Political Science Review*, 57 (1963), 641.

11. John Lyng, *Mellom öst og vest*, Oslo: Cappelen, 1976, p. 213.

12. As defined in the official statistics. See *Yearbook of Nordic Statistics*, 11 (1972), 231 n.

13. Converse and Valen, loc. cit.

14. Henry Valen, "National Conflict Structure and Foreign Politics: The Impact of the EEC Issue on Perceived Cleavages in Norwegian Politics," *European Journal of Political Research*, 4 (1976), 63.

15. John T. S. Madeley, "Scandinavian Christian Democracy: Throwback or Portent?," *European Journal of Political Research*, 5 (1977), 267–286.

16. As a national of Norway, not of Denmark, the author can claim no intimate knowledge of the Danish party system. For more details, the reader is referred to the numerous articles on Danish politics to be found in the yearbook *Scandinavian Political Studies*, 1 (1966) and subsequent volumes.

17. See, for example, Erik Damgaard, "Stability and Change in the Danish Party System over Half a Century," *Scandinavian Political Studies*, 9 (1974), 104.

18. Arnold J. Heidenheimer et al., *Comparative Public Policy: The Politics of Social Choice in Europe and America*, New York: St. Martin's Press, 1975, pp. 272–275.

19. Nikolaj Petersen and Jörgen Elklit, "Denmark Enters the European Communities," *Scandinavian Political Studies*, 8 (1972), 206.

20. Jerrold G. Rusk and Ole Borre, "The Changing Party Space in Danish Voter Perceptions, 1971–1973," *European Journal of Political Research*, 2 (1974), 329–361.

21. Ibid., p. 357.

22. Ibid.

23. Philip M. Williams, *Crisis and Compromise*, Hamden, Conn.: Archon Books, 1964, p. 131.

24. Ibid., p. 11.

25. François Goguel, *Esprit* (May 1939), quoted in Williams, p. 31.

26. In part this was due to the introduction of an electoral system modeled on that of Great Britain. Under conditions different from those of Britain, it did not help to produce aggregation but, rather, polarization. The Weimar system of proportional representation, with all its shortcomings, presented greater obstacles to a near complete polarization of politics. See the author's review, "The Consequences of Electoral Laws," *European Journal of Political Research*, 2 (1974), 287.

27. Joel H. Silbey, *The Transformation of American Politics, 1840–1960*, Englewood Cliffs, N.J.: Prentice-Hall, 1967, p. 29.

28. Computed by Robert A. Dahl from data in Walter Dean Burnham, *Presidential Ballots, 1836–1892*, Baltimore: Johns Hopkins Press, 1955, p. 78. Also, see Dahl, *Democracy in the United States: Promise and Performance*, Chicago: Rand McNally, 1976, p. 430.

29. Joel H. Silbey, *The Shrine of Party*, Pittsburgh: Pittsburgh University Press, 1967, pp. 83 ff.

30. Dahl, ibid., p. 415.

31. Ibid., p. 408.

32. The author, for one, disagreed and did not believe that the EEC would become a strong supranational organization. Another factor that made for antagonism in the EEC dispute should be mentioned: for a number of people it could be said that the urban-rural and center-periphery dimensions "worked in a parallel direction, reinforcing one another" (Valen, op. cit., p. 71). For example, fishermen in the outlying districts who felt that there was too much interference in their local affairs from the central government in faraway Oslo were against transferring authority to Brussels, which was still farther away. In addition, they thought that their branch of the economy was being sacrificed in the interest of manufacturing industry, when it was proposed to give vessels from Common Market countries access to Norwegian fishing grounds in return for advantageous conditions offered to Norway's export industries. The fishing population had a double reason for being against entry and therefore opposed it with particular force, a fact that supports one of Edward A. Ross's propositions: ". . . when . . . lines of cleavage coincide . . . they reinforce one another." (*Principles of Sociology*, New York: The Century Co., 1920, p. 164)

33. It has been argued that the concepts of "periphery" and "low social position" can be taken as synonymous, but this is doubtful. See the author's article, "In What Sense Is a High Social Position also a Central Position?," *Journal of Peace Research*, 13 (1976), 67–71.

34. Letter to R. M. T. Hunter quoted in Silbey, *The Shrine of Party*, op. cit., p. 275.

CHAPTER 9

FINLAND

Pertti Suhonen

The Historical Development of the Party System

THE FINNISH PARTY INSTITUTION is relatively young. The first political parties in the proper sense of the word were not founded until after the middle of the nineteenth century. At that time Finland was an autonomous part of the old Russian Empire with its own parliament, the traditional Diet of the Four Estates. The formation of parties was first based on the language issue. The Finnish party, founded in 1860, demanded increased educational and other rights for the Finnish-speaking majority. It strove for the substitution of Swedish by Finnish as the official language. The Swedish-speaking minority had had a leading position both in culture and economy in the six centuries that Finland had been a part of Sweden. The Finnish party soon gained a majority in two estates in the Diet: the clergy and the peasants. In the 1870s the Swedish party was established as a counterforce. It dominated the estates of the nobility and the burgesses in the Diet.

At the end of the century a new cleavage emerged in political life: the question of Finland's relations with Russia. A group broke off from the Finnish party and formed the Young Finnish party. The Young Finns did not agree with their party's tolerance of the unconstitutional Russification program of the czar.

New social problems at the end of the 1890s, linked with the rising capitalistic industry, led to the rise of the Finnish labor movement. The Finnish Labor party was founded in 1899 and four years later the name of the party was

235

changed to the Social Democratic Party of Finland. The party adopted a pure Marxian program, which was based on the so-called Erfurtian program and the program of the Social Democratic Party of Austria. The new Labor party soon became a conspicuous political force in Finnish society and it had a leading part in the campaign for Diet reform. In the first election after the reform in 1907, equal and universal suffrage having been adopted, the Social Democratic party won 37% of the votes and eighty of the 200 seats in Parliament. In connection with the first election of the unicameral Parliament a new party, the Agrarian Union, was born. It was founded to advocate the interest of the farming population and to foster the ideological inheritance of the country-side.

Finland's independence was declared by the Finnish Diet in December 1917, soon after the Bolshevik revolution in Russia. Political upheavals in the first year of independence led to a party realignment. In the winter of 1918 the radical wing of the Social Democrats and the Red Guards under its direction declared a revolution. They had no success and the Civil War, which followed, ended in the victory of the Whites. The Red leaders, who had fled to Russia, founded the Finnish Communist party. The moderate part of the labor movement retained the name of the Social Democratic Party. The left-wing opposition of the party took part in the elections in the 1920s, together with the Communists, under different names, e.g. the Socialist Workers' Party. The Communist party and its organizations were outlawed in the period of 1930–1944.

Also, the right wing underwent political reorganization. Both the old Finns and the Young Finns fell into two parts as a consequence of the issue of monarchism: the monarchists founded a new party, the National Coalition party, and the republicans formed the National Progressive party. The Parliament elected in 1919 passed a republican Constitution. Before World War II, the only other change in the Finnish party system worth mentioning was the appearance of the Patriotic People's Movement in the 1930s. It was an antidemocratic, fascist organization. Its maximum electoral vote was 8.3%. The movement was outlawed after World War II.

The end of World War II caused changes also on the left side of the party system. The Communist party became legal again and started its activity in October 1944. A left-wing opposition group separated from the Social Democratic Party during the war. This group and some other socialist groups, together with the Communist party, founded a new political organization for cooperation, the Finnish People's Democratic League (PDL). It soon changed into a political party and functioned as the electoral organization for Communists and left-wing socialists. The Communist party has not taken part in the postwar elections under its own name. Its candidates have always been put forward under the label of the PDL. In every Parliament a great majority of the PDL representatives have been communists.

In the light of the election returns in 1945, the Finnish party system turned out to be the same in its basic structure as in the first years of independence. The biggest parties were Social Democrats, the Communists, the Conservative Coalition party and the Agrarian Union, as had already been the case in 1922. As we can see in Table 9–1, the same basic structure has remained for more than 30 years after the wars. The four biggest parties can be distinguished as their own groups, with their votes making up a total of 75–85%. Even though the basic structure of the party system has been very stable, some variation has been caused by the rise, growth and fall of some small parties in the elections of the last decades.

The Progressive party, having declined gradually, was dissolved in 1951. In the same year the Finnish People's party was founded to represent the liberalism of the Finnish middle class. In 1965 it changed its name to the Liberal People's party in connection with a merger with the small Liberal League. Since then the party has been declining gradually.

As a result of disagreements within the Social Democratic party, once again, the left-wing opposition split off from the party and a new party with the name of the Social Democratic League of Workers and Smallholders (SDL) was formed at the end of the 1950s. Its largest vote was 4.4% in 1962. Since then its support has declined gradually. A change in the political course followed by the Social Democrats brought back a part of the former members and voters, while some of them moved to the PDL. The SDL was suspended by the majority of the party convention in 1973. The minority, which opposed the suspension, founded the Socialist Workers' Party in the same year.

The Agrarian Union gave heed to the rapid urbanization process and the declining agrarian population. It followed the Swedish and Norwegian examples and changed its name to the Center party in 1965. The following year the Smallholders' Party adopted the name of the Finnish Rural Party (FRP). The party was founded in 1959 by Veikko Vennamo, a former minister and member of Parliament of the Agrarian Union. The populistic program of the Rural party and the charisma of the party leader had an effect on the alienated voters of the "old parties," particularly on those of the Center party and the PDL. The FRP gained a surprising victory with 18 seats in Parliament and 10.5% of the votes in the general election of 1970 (versus 1 seat and 1% in the previous election). It was the biggest change in party support since World War II. (Sänkiaho 1971; Suhonen 1972, pp. 52–57). The Rural party succeeded in only two general elections. There were disagreements within the party and, at the beginning of 1973, FRP members of Parliament defected from the Rural party and formed the Finnish People's Unity Party. In the parliamentary elections of 1975, the new party obtained 1.7% and the Rural party 3.6% of the votes.

In the 1970s a new dimension appeared in the Finnish party system. The Christian League increased its number of seats in Parliament from one in 1970 to nine in 1975. This party was founded as early as 1958 as a protest of the fundamentalist Christian circles against the seemingly indifferent attitude of

TABLE 9–1. Results of the Parliamentary Elections in Finland, 1945–1972 (Percent)[a]

	1945	1948	1951	1954	1958	1962	1966	1970	1972	1975
Socialist parties										
People's Democratic League	23.5 (49)	20.0 (38)	21.6 (43)	21.6 (43)	23.2 (50)	22.0 (47)	21.2 (41)	16.6 (36)	17.0 (37)	18.9 (40)
Social Democratic League	—	—	—	—	1.7 (3)	4.4 (2)	2.6 (7)	1.4 (—)	1.0 (—)	0.3 (—)
Social Democrats	25.1 (50)	26.3 (54)	26.3 (53)	26.2 (54)	23.2 (48)	19.5 (38)	27.2 (55)	23.4 (52)	25.8 (55)	24.9 (54)
Total	48.6 (99)	46.3 (92)	47.9 (96)	47.8 (97)	48.1 (101)	45.9 (87)	51.0 (103)	41.8 (88)	43.8 (92)	44.1 (94)
Centrist parties										
Finnish Rural Party	—	—	—	—	—	2.2 (—)	1.0 (1)	10.5 (18)	9.2 (18)	3.6 (2)
People's Unity Party	—	—	—	—	—	—	—	—	—	1.7 (1)
Center Party	21.3 (49)	24.2 (56)	23.2 (51)	24.1 (53)	23.1 (48)	23.0 (53)	21.2 (49)	17.1 (36)	16.3 (35)	17.6 (39)
Progressives/Liberals	5.2 (9)	3.9 (5)	6.0 (10)	8.2 (13)	6.2 (8)	6.4 (14)	6.5 (9)	5.9 (8)	5.2 (7)	4.3 (9)
Swedish People Party	7.9 (14)	7.7 (14)	7.6 (15)	7.0 (13)	6.7 (14)	6.4 (14)	6.0 (12)	5.7 (12)	5.4 (10)	5.0 (10)
Total	34.4 (72)	35.8 (75)	36.8 (76)	39.3 (79)	36.0 (70)	38.0 (81)	34.7 (71)	39.2 (74)	36.1 (70)	32.2 (61)
Right-wing parties										
Christian League	—	—	—	—	0.2 (—)	—	0.5 (—)	1.1 (1)	2.5 (4)	3.3 (9)
National Coalition	15.0 (28)	17.1 (33)	14.6 (28)	12.8 (24)	15.3 (29)	15.0 (32)	13.8 (26)	18.0 (37)	17.6 (34)	18.4 (35)
Constitutional People's Party	—	—	—	—	—	—	—	—	—	1.6 (1)
Total	15.0 (28)	17.1 (33)	14.6 (28)	12.8 (24)	15.5 (29)	15.0 (32)	14.3 (26)	19.1 (38)	20.1 (38)	23.3 (44)

[a]Seats in parentheses.

existing parties toward Christian values and morale. The Christian League took its model from the other Christian parties in Scandinavia.

Of the other small parties we might briefly mention the Constitutional People's party, which was founded by the right-wing members of the National Coalition and the Swedish People's party in 1973. It obtained one seat in Parliament and 1.6% of the votes in 1975.

Perhaps the clearest trend in the development of the Finnish party system, even though it is one of no great significance, is the slow, regular decline in the votes of the Swedish People's party. The decline is connected with the decreasing Swedish-speaking minority in Finland. At the beginning of the independence the party's support was more than 12% and in 1975 5%.

Aims and Programs

Even though the basic structure of the party system has remained fairly stable for the whole period of the Finnish independence, there has been quite a lot of development in the goals of the party programs. In the following pages we shall deal with the programs and policies of six different political parties. In addition to the four big parties, also the LPP and the SPP will be discussed even though there has been a decline in the support of these parties. Both of them have until quite recently had a much more significant role in the political life of Finland than their small size would presuppose.

THE SOCIAL DEMOCRATIC PARTY

Although the first, clearly Marxian program of the Social Democratic party was in force until the 1950s, the party had, in fact, given up these principles much earlier. It was not until 1952 that the party renewed its program of principles, basing it on the principles of western social democracy. It is the ideas of Keynes rather than those of Marx that serve as the economic-theoretical starting point for the present program. In the long run, the SDP aims at "democratic socialism"; in the shorter run, it aims at developing a "welfare state."

When talking about democratic socialism, the SDP tries to draw a line between itself and the Communists, and especially the left-wing socialists of the PDL. Democratic socialism refers to a model of society in which the production media and the central components of the economy are democratically controlled by the citizens. This control operates in the form of the present multiparty Parliament with representatives of the people and at the lower levels in the form of industrial democracy. Another aspect of the idea of democratic socialism is that all social changes are to be carried out through parliamentary measures. As a central, practical goal for realizing this type of democratic socialism, the SDP has emphasized the importance of constitutional reform in such a way that majority rule, whenever it constitutes a barrier to economic democracy, should be abolished. Three central goals have been set for the development of a welfare state: maintaining full employment, securing economic growth, and creating a social security system. Farm policy has been seen as the biggest obstacle to economic growth, since this policy maintains inefficient and population-binding agriculture at the expense of the productivity of the manufacturing industries. The SDP has actively participated in the implementation of comprehensive sociopolitical reforms in the 1960s and 1970s.

However, there has been some variation in the emphasis given to these goals and in their implementation, depending on who the leaders of the party have been. Within the party there continues to be disagreement concerning the line of operation. An active reform period started in the mid-1960s, when Rafael Paasio, representing the ideological center of the SDP, became chairman of the party. Before that the party had been under the direction of fairly right-wing leaders. The leader of the party had been Väinö Tanner, the "grand old man" of the Social Democrats, who had had a leading position in the party ever since its formation after the Civil War. Tanner's relations with the Soviet Union were quite poor, and this meant that as far as foreign policy was concerned the SDP had difficulties.

Rafael Paasio proposed that the party change its direction "a few points toward the left." In addition to activating internal reform policy, this also meant the beginning of a new cooperation with the PDL as well as revaluation of the foreign policy line and improved relations with the Soviet Union. This new line did not, however, prevent the SDP from supporting Finland's free trade agreement with the European Community. The present chairman of the party, Kalevi Sorsa, has continued along the lines of his predecessor. Sorsa has been a member of the cabinet several times, both as the foreign minister and the prime minister, which post he is holding at the moment.

A line of economic and social policy which is more right wing than the basic party line has lately been advocated by the social democratic governor of the Bank of Finland, Mauno Koivisto. He has also been a cabinet minister in the past. For example, he was the minister of finance and prime minister at the end of the 1960s.

THE FINNISH COMMUNIST PARTY AND THE FINNISH PEOPLE'S DEMOCRATIC LEAGUE

The FCP is a Marxist-Leninist labor party which aims at realizing socialism by means of a social revolution. In addition, the party supports all those reforms which increase the standard of living of the citizens and improve their social status. The party aims to function as the vanguard of the working class in the realization of socialism. As compared with the previous programs, the party program adopted in 1969 presents a more moderate definition of the ways and means through which the socialist revolution will be carried out.

While the program of the FCP deals with the theoretical and long-range questions of the struggle of the working class, the program of the PDL is of a more practical nature and is more clearly linked with its activity in Parliament and other political arenas. Since the PDL started developing in the direction of a party (originally it was a cooperation organization) also, some general principles were included in its new program which was adopted in 1967. For example, it is demanded in the program that there should be a gradual move toward a socialist society with the help of socialist reforms which give more power to the people. "Since the aim is to build a more democratic society than the present one, it is clear that all the changes must happen democratically."

The demands for reforms in social policy are not very different from the corresponding Social Democratic goals. Consequently, during the last decade extensive cooperation has been possible between the two labor parties with regard to these questions. In the field of cultural policy, however, the PDL is clearly more radical than the Social Democrats. The PDL is aware that the slowness of social reforms is partly due to the ideological domination by the right wing, and therefore it aims at restricting the right wing's power in the schools, the church, the mass media, the sciences, the arts, and so on.

In their foreign policy both the FCP and the PDL have emphasized the great significance of the good relations between Finland and the Soviet Union with regard to not only the security but also the economy of Finland. They have opposed Finland's joining the Western economic groupings, and particularly the free trade agreement with the EC.

The liberalization of the party program and some practical political solutions in the 1960s, for example, the PDL's participating in the work of the cabinet, led to an aggravation of ideological disagreements within the FCP. The minority group, whose leader has been the vice chairman of the party, Taisto Sinisalo, has accused the majority of the party of reformism and of participation in solutions which are not in the interests of the working class. The chairman of the party, Aarne Saarinen, on the other hand, has repeatedly emphasized the fact that the improvement of the position of the workers specifically requires participation in the work of the cabinet in cooperation with the SDP and the parties of the center. When locating the goals of the PDL program on the political party map, the party seems to fall somewhere between the ideology of the majority group of the Communists and that of the Social Democrats. The party goals are most clearly supported by the PDL socialists, that is, the members who do not belong to the Communist party. One of these left-wing socialists is Dr. Ele Alenius, who has for quite a long time now acted as the chairman of the PDL.

CENTER PARTY

The central aim of the program of the Center party (the former Agrarian Union) has been to attend to the interests of the farming population and to foster peasant culture. Due to rapid urbanization, the farming population kept declining. This made it necessary for the party to alter its program in the direction of such social aims as would suit large masses of people even in an advanced society. Because of the center position of the party, there were certain prerequisites for such a change. In its new program of 1962 the party began to emphasize its own center qualities, on the one hand, by criticizing the socialist parties for their socialistic aims and, on the other hand, by pointing out the problems caused by capitalism.

An original feature in its program is the idea of decentralization. This idea is directed against the centralization of power, be it economic or political. According to this idea providing people with better opportunities of using power directly is a necessary condition for democracy. This could be achieved, for example, by realizing provincial self-government, by referring important social issues to the electorate for advisory decision by means of a referendum, and by changing the system of the presidential elections so that the president would be elected directly by a general vote of the people. Another aim in the program which results from the idea of decentralization is the tendency to equalize the regional differences in the development of society, including cultural as well as material differences. No obligations, however, should be imposed on the economic and industrial sector; instead, the regional guidance of economy and industry must be carried out by creating, with the help of government measures in the developing regions, conditions favorable to private enterprise.

The Center party/Agrarian Union has been a significant reformer of social conditions, together with the labor parties. However, perhaps the most important achievement of the party has been its cooperation with other parties, particularly with the PDL, in the field of foreign policy. It has played an important role in the formation of Finland's postwar foreign policy. This has been partly influenced by the fact that Urho Kekkonen, president of Finland since 1956, originally came from this party. Another outstanding expert in foreign policy, coming from the Center party, is Dr. Ahti Karjalainen. He has been a member of the cabinet several times as the prime minister and foreign minister. Even today agricultural policy represents an important sector in the activity of the Center party. Dr. Johannes Virolainen, a long-time chairman of the party, is the minister of agriculture in the present cabinet and thus in charge of farm policy.

THE NATIONAL COALITION

Traditional conservatism in the Finnish political system has been represented by the National Coalition Party. The party, however, reformed its program first in 1957 and then again at the beginning of the 1970s, with the result that the program is now more liberal. "Traditional values," so typical of conservatism, are no longer so strongly emphasized as before, and similarly, the Communists are not opposed so much as in the past; instead, a new idea of a pluralistic society has emerged. In its program of 1957 the party still characterized its political line as "dynamic conservatism," whereas in the most recent program the whole concept of conservatism has been abandoned. The new line means that the party is taking a more active stand to the development of society. Previously the Coalition party had always resisted sociopolitical reforms, particularly if they involved transfers of income from the taxpayers. The present party program contains a great number of items for sociopolitical development. On the other hand, it also mentions that the growth of the expenditure of the public sector must be adapted to the average growth of the national income.

The Coalition party regards private ownership and a free market economy as the cornerstones of economic development. The best results from the point of view of both individuals and society are achieved by free competition. The participation in enterprising activity by the public authority is acceptable in exceptional cases only. The economic system which the party aims at is described as "socially selective economy." It means that in solving economic problems the effects of the solutions on the individual and the environment must be taken into account.

The new program of the Coalition party repeatedly emphasizes the role of the individual and his right to make his own choice, but on the other hand, it also stresses the individual's responsibility for his solutions and for his own well-being.

The Coalition party has found it difficult to establish a credible line in foreign policy. After World War II the party's negative attitude toward the Soviet Union continued for a long time, and the party kept criticizing the way Finnish foreign policy was managed. Among other things, this attitude led to a cold relationship between the Coalition party and its natural cooperation partner, the Center party. Harri Holkeri, the present chairman of the party, and a group of reformers supporting him tried to develop the party's foreign policy line in the direction followed by the other parties. In its new program the Coalition party declares that it supports the Finnish foreign policy known by the name of Paasikivi-Kekkonen line.

The leaders of the party have had some difficulties with a group in the extreme right within the party. This group has conspicuously criticized Finnish foreign policy and the fact that the Coalition party supports this policy. In other respects as well, the new program of abandonment of some of the old conservative principles has aroused dissatisfaction in the extreme right of the party, at the same time making ideological room for a new extreme right-wing party, that is, the Constitutional People's party. Similarly, the political rise of the Christian League has assumed new strength as the Coalition party in its new program has abandoned its earlier commitment to Christian values and, instead, has proceeded to defend pluralism of values like the other parties.

THE LIBERAL PEOPLE'S PARTY

The Liberal People's party, which represents the ideology of the Western European liberal parties, was founded in 1965. As far as its program and activity are concerned, the party regards itself as dating from the Young Finnish Party at the turn of the century. On the basis of its central sociopolitical aims the party can be located somewhere between the Coalition party and the SDP. It stresses the inviolability of private ownership and the significance of free enterprise as the basis of the economy. However, the party also realizes that the favorable development of society presupposes planning and long-range social policy. Thus it emphasizes the importance of the freedom of individual, but at the same time it stresses the responsibility of society for its members. This line of policy is characterized by the party as "social liberalism."

A special feature of the program and activity of the LPP is the dominant part which education and culture, have in it. The party was quite active in the Finnish school reform; the comprehensive school system is now operating in the whole of Finland. Perhaps the most outstanding figure in this sector has been Jaakko Itälä, the present minister of education, who was recently elected the chairman of the party. The versatile cultural connections of the party are also illustrated by the fact that a former party chairman, chancellor of the University of Helsinki and president of the Lutheran World Federation, Mikko Juva, was elected the archbishop of the Finnish Lutheran Church in 1978.

THE SWEDISH PEOPLE'S PARTY

The force holding this party together is primarily nationalistic ideology and national interest. With regard to its general sociopolitical line the party is clearly one of the nonsocialist parties. However, it has no strong, uniform stand in the central questions of economy, culture and social policy. Within the party there are several competing interest groups, because of the heterogeneous nature of the party. After all, it is at the same time the party of the Swedish-speaking upper class and intelligentsia, the Swedish-speaking farmers and partly also the Swedish-speaking workers. On the basis of the general program adopted in 1964 and the policy practiced by the present leaders, the SPP can be included in the parties of the political center.

In addition to the party programs of political principles and short-range aims in different fields, the special party-affiliated organizations have prepared their own programs. Particularly the programs of the youth organizations of the parties adopted during the last ten years are worth mentioning. The youth organizations and student organizations, ranging from the SDP to the Coalition party, have in their programs adopted a line clearly different from their own party line. Their ideas are more leftish and more radical, and their attitudes toward society are more critical. The active and fruitful work of the youth organizations has contributed to many of the reforms in the aims of the mother parties.

The Party Organization[1]

At the beginning of independence there were considerable dissimilarities in the organization of different parties. At the time the Social Democratic party was the only mass party which made an effort to obtain as large a membership as possible. Only the SDP carried on systematic political education. On the other hand, the National Coalition, the Progressive party and the Swedish People's party were typical cadre parties in the sense of Duverger's conception (Duverger 1969). Their membership was numerically small and inactive. Organized activity and fieldwork characteristic of modern parties was not started by the National Coalition until after the war. As for now, on the basis of their activity and organization, all the major parties may be regarded clearly as mass parties.

The lowest level of the party organization is formed by the membership. According to the information given out by the parties the number of members in each party in 1972 was as follows:

	MEMBERS	PERCENT OF VOTES IN 1972
People's Democratic League	170,000	39
Social Democrats	80,000	12
Center Party	276,000	61
Liberals	18,000	14
Swedish People's Party	47,000	36
National Coalition	87,000	18

The Center party was the most successful in getting its voters to participate in the party work. The membership of the biggest party, the SDP, is relatively small.

The local organizations are formed by the rank-and-file. They are usually formed on a regional basis; the small parties aim to found a local organization for at least each commune, and the large ones at least one for each voting district or population centre. In addition to this the labor parties have occupational and workplace associations. The Communist party has the most of them, and the People's Democratic League and the SDP have some too. Both the FCP and the PDL have their own organizations and, to a great extent, their own separate memberships.

Each party requires that a candidate applying for memebership approve the principles and aims of the party and that he not be a member of any other party. The membership applications are normally handled on the local level. The Communist party is an exception in this respect because in it new members are approved.only at the city or district level. To become a member of a party is most easily done with the Coalition party and the two liberal parties, the LPP and the SPP. In addition to obtaining and approving new members, it is the task of the local organizations to provide political education for the members as well as to practice political propaganda in housing areas and places of work. Special activity is required in connection with elections, for example in fund raising, in the nomination of candidates and in the practical organization of election posters and advertisements.

In most parties the next level above the local organizations is the communal organization, that is, in communes with several local organizations. Their task is to facilitate participation in communal policy.

The district organization of the political parties is based on the country's division into 16 constituencies. In each constituency a party in most cases has one or two district organizations. In the district organization, the highest authority in decision making is the district convention to which the local and communal organizations send their representatives. A district committee appointed by this convention functions as an executive organ. The task of the district organizations is to join together the local organizations in the district and to act as a connecting link between the local organizations and the central leadership of the party. They control the activity of the local organizations and attend to educational and publishing activity. An important task of the district organizations is to manage the preparations for a general election in the district.

Above the districts there are the central party organs, the highest of which is the party convention. The party convention of the Swedish People's party meets every year and those of the Center party, the Liberal People's party, and the National Coalition every two years. The party conventions of the socialist parties, the Social Democratic party, the Communist party, and the PDL, meet only every three years. The representatives for these conventions are elected on the district or local level. In the socialist parties the representatives are elected by a general vote of the members and in the other parties by the meetings of the organizations.

The task of the party convention is to make decisions on important questions of principles. The convention evaluates the state of society and the party and decides on the necessary measures to be taken. It adopts the rules and the programs of the party and elects the members of the representative body, which exercises decisive power in the intervals between party conventions.

Even though the hierarchical organizations of the Finnish parties may seem fairly similar, there are differences in the principles of their functioning. A central principle concerns the relations between the different levels of the party organization. The socialist parties typically have a more rigid organization in which administration is centralized but decision making is based on the activity of the members and an extensive organizational democracy. For example, all the questions concerning the program are thoroughly discussed on the local level. It is also quite common that important questions are referred to the members for decision by a general vote.

From the point of view of practical operation, centralized decision making means that the lower levels of the organization are bound to follow the instructions coming from the upper levels. This model of organization is the farthest developed in the FCP, which, following the traditions of the socialist labor movement, aims to realize the principle of "democratic centralism." This principle means, briefly, that the preparation of issues is carried out democratically on all the levels of the party, but after that all the levels are bound by the decisions that have been made. No opposition is allowed concerning the democratic decision by the organization. The functioning principles of the organizations of the Coalition party and the liberal parties are in many respects different. Due to the passivity of the members, activity at the local and district levels is concentrated in the leadership of these levels. The local and district organizations are also fairly independent of the central leadership of the parties, even in ideological questions.

These differences between the socialist and nonsocialist parties have diminished in the last few years. In fact, the nonsocialist parties have been trying to improve party discipline and to produce a more uniform party line at the lower levels. Organizational democracy is also increasing. In the nomination of candidates for election, for example, the right-wing parties have started using the same method as the left wing, that is, arranging a general vote by the members for nominating the candidates. On the other hand, the principle of democratic centralism in the Communist party has not been fully realized because of internal disagreements. The minority group of the party may accuse the party leadership of breaking jointly adopted principles, interpret the majority decisions in its own way, and act according to its own interpretations. It may form an organized opposition within the party, and control a part of the district organizations. Such an opposition can have its own leadership, organization, and even its own newspaper, which may regularly criticize the party leadership.

Most parties have a special election organization in addition to the organization described above. The task of the election organization is to carry out the preparation work in the field, to distribute propaganda material, and to bring the party's supporters to the polls on election day.

A special problem in the Finnish political system is created by the relationship between a party's organization and its parliamentary group. According to the Constitution, the authority of the members of Parliament is based only on the mandate received from their electors. But in actual practice the members of Parliament represent their party rather than the electorate. Each party's deputies form parliamentary groups in which the members work and vote quite coherently. There are no great differences in group cohesion from one party to the next. Group cohesion has been the strongest in the socialist parties and the Center party, and somewhat weaker in the other parties. The same kind of difference has also prevailed in the relationship between the party leadership and the parliamentary group. The group's dependence on the party organization is weakest on the right wing of the party system and greater toward the left. However, no parliamentary group of any party has more power than the party organization. Whether the party should participate in the government, however, is a question in which the parliamentary group has its say in most Finnish parties.

The varied activities of mass parties, which are based on a wide organization and a great number of salaried party officials as well as costly election campaigns, requires lots of financial resources. The parties give out little information on the financing of their activity, and therefore this question has been a difficult one to study. Today, all the parties charge membership fees, which has been an important source of income, particularly for the socialist parties. Contributions made by enterprises, associations, and private citizens have formed a substantial part of the financing, particularly during election campaigns. Especially the right-wing parties, but also the SDP to a certain extent, have received financial support from commercial and industrial circles in connection with elections. Since 1967, the state has granted substantial annual subsidies to all the parties that are represented in Parliament. Moreover, the state also grants financial support to various auxiliary organizations of the parties, such as educational, youth, sports, and cultural organizations. These may be only very loosely connected with the actual party organizations, but are to a considerable degree responsible for political education.

Voting Behavior

When studying the Finns' voting behavior it has often been noted that social class and occupation very strongly influence the choice of the party. International comparisons show that this link is stronger in Finland than perhaps anywhere else in the world (Allardt 1964, p. 102; Uusitalo 1975, Rose 1974). As can be seen in Table 9–2, the majority of the voters have chosen their party in such a way that it corresponds to their occupational status. Two-thirds of the farming population supported the agrarian parties, the Center party or the Rural party. Seventy-one percent of the workers supported either one of the two labor parties. Forty-seven percent of the middle class and 67% of the

TABLE 9–2.   Party Preference by Occupation in Finland in 1972
(Percent)[a]

	FARMER	WORKER	MIDDLE CLASS	EXECUTIVE
Communists				.
(PDL)	6	30	8	5
Social Democrats	8	41	26	14
Rural Party	11	4	3	—
Center Party	54	8	8	5
Liberals	—	3	14	10
Swedish Party	6	4	6	9
Christian League	1	3	2	—
Nationalists	14	7	33	57
Total	100	100	100	100
Number of Respondents	277	451	258	84

[a]Results are based on national survey data. Respondents without party preference omitted.
Occupational grouping by head of household.
Source: Suhonen 1976, p. 29.

executives supported the National Coalition of the Liberal People's Party.

The starting point for this situation can be found as far back as the beginning of this century. At that time, when the country's party system was first shaped, it came to correspond to the conflicting interests of the workers and the burgesses, on the one hand, and the agricultural producers and consumers, on the other. The citizens' status in the occupational and industrial structure of society directs their political choices in two ways. First, their status determines what kind of experiences they have from earning their living and working, and, second, their status links them to an environment which has its own special ideology.

The differences between the farming population and the workers, as far as political preferences are concerned, are not due to differences in the level of income. In Finland the average income of the farmers is somewhat lower than that of the workers. At the same time, the differences in the level of income are greater among the farming population than among the other population groups (Suhonen 1976, pp. 32–33). But the level of income is not a decisive factor in the very uniform political choices of the farming population; instead, the basic reason is that the income is earned mainly in the same way—by supplying agricultural products for trade and consumption and timber for the wood-processing industry.

A political choice which can be regarded as unexpected on the basis of the occupational status is of special interest. Here we shall deal with some of the factors that work in the direction opposite to the basic tendency observed. First, it has to be noted that the occupational development has led to a situation in which it is difficult to draw a clear line between the working class and the middle class—neither the level of income nor the type of work can be used as the basis for making the distinction.

The age of the voters proved an essential intervening factor. It was the youngest and the oldest age groups that deviated the most from the voting behavior presupposed by their occupation (Suhonen 1976, pp. 38–40). Age as a biological variable does not directly affect party preferences, but it links people in quite different ways to their occupations, the historical stages of society and the different cultures of different age groups. This all certainly affects party preferences.

A concrete example of this is the change in party preference that occurs among people with a higher academic education. Traditionally, people with academic degrees have been fairly conservative. The majority of them have voted for the National coalition and the rest, with very few exceptions, for the two People's parties. In the 1970s this type of voting behavior has begun to change, and there are now increasingly more exceptions to the rule, particularly among the younger voters. According to the 1972 study by this writer, of the voters with an academic degree and over 35 years of age, 6% supported one of the socialist parties, 1% the Center party, and 65% the Coalition party. The corresponding figures for those under 35 years of age were socialist parties 21%, the Center party 6%, and the Coalition 39%. A similar difference can be observed with those who have completed secondary education (Suhonen 1976, pp. 35–36). This deviation in the younger age groups not only has something to do with youth but is as such a passing phenomenon, as the corresponding deviation has not been observed in the previous academic generations. A permanent change in the political division of the people with a higher academic education can be expected on the basis of the strong and permanent leftward movement among the university students at the end of the 1960s (Suhonen 1975).

In many European countries religion has a great effect on the party preferences of the citizens. This is also the case in Finland, even though this question has not been much studied. Finland is a 90% Lutheran country, so the differences between the various denominations have no significance. Instead, the people's personal relation to religion often influences their choice of party (see Table 9–3).

Religion is clearly a factor which alienates a part of the workers from the socialist parties. Alternatively, adopting the materialistic ideology of socialism results in a negative attitude toward religion. Religiousness among the agrarian population strengthens the support of the Center party, whereas in the middle class it strengthens the support of the other nonsocialist parties.

The stable support of the four major parties described here is rather surprising considering the development that has taken place in the structure of industries and population (see Table 9–4). In the period after World War II the relative proportion of the farming population has decreased by about 50%. Correspondingly, there has been an increase in the proportions of the workers

TABLE 9–3. Party Preference by Religious Involvement and Occupation in 1972 (Percent)

	RELIGIOUS INVOLVEMENT		
	+	0	−
Workers voting for the socialist parties	58 (233)	72 (362)	82 (77)
Agrarian population voting for the Center party	64 (211)	59 (190)	46 (28)
Middle class and executives voting for the right-wing parties	75 (159)	54 (160)	36 (25)

+ – Believers and religious persons.
0 – Persons with favorable attitude toward religion.
− – Persons with indifferent or negative attitude toward religion.
Source: National survey data. Suhonen 1976, p. 41.

TABLE 9–4. Main Groups of Voters of Four Big Parties, 1948, 1966, and 1974 (Percent)

	1948	*1966*	*1974*
Workers among Communists	80	82	78
Workers among Socialists	75	74	67
Farmers among Center Party	90	72	63
Middle Class and Managers among National Coalition	48	68	69

in the manufacturing industry as well as (particularly recently) in the service industry and also in the proportion of the clerical workers. One could have expected structural changes of this kind to weaken the position of the Center party and to strengthen the support of, above all, the Coalition. Why this did not happen can be explained by the different developmental features which affected the structure of the groups of people voting for the various parties.

The CP has been able to keep up its support because it now has a great number of voters outside the farming population. The proportion of the farming population of the voters of the Center party decreased from 90% by nearly a third by the middle of the 1970s. The new voters came from the expanded working class as well as from the middle classes. The party has made an effort to expand into towns and cities by changing its name and program. Even though its support among urban population has not grown much, its proportion of urban voters has grown at the same rate as the proportion of the urban population in the total population of the country.

Another factor which helped the Center party to resist a decline in its support, even though the farming population was declining, was the fact that more farmers than ever before concentrated their votes on their own party. As a consequence, the National Coalition lost some of its farmer voters. To replace them, the Coalition obtained new voters from the expanding middle class. As a result, the structure of the supporters of the party became strongly one-sided. While at the end of the 1940s less than 50% of the voters of the Coalition were clerical workers or executives, by the beginning of the 1970s their proportion had risen to nearly 70%. Thus the development of the structure of the supporters of the National Coalition was quite contrary to the development in the other major parties. Mainly due to the growing number of the middle classes, the voting support of the labor parties is also gradually getting more varied.

The Role of Parties in the Finnish Political System

The position and tasks of the political parties were radically changed in connection with the Diet reform of 1960. In fact, it was only then that the central forum for the activities of modern parties was created. Even though the new Diet act contained no mention of the political parties, the parties have from the very beginning attended to many tasks, which have been essential from the point of view of the work of Parliament: political education and activation of voters, candidate nomination for elections, and organization of parliamentary work. Ever since the first unicameral Diet, the members of Parliament have formed their own groups, by parties, in which a considerable part of the preparation of the questions to be discussed takes place. In all the parties the parliamentary group also acts as an organ which controls the activity of the party's individual members of Parliament, thus strengthening the role of parties at the supreme national level of decision making. The position of political parties has also been reinforced by legislation. In the Election Act of 1969, the priority of the parties to enforce nomination of candidates in parliamentary elections was confirmed. Also, legislation is being prepared concerning official recognition of the work done in the parliamentary groups.

The proportions of the parties in Parliament mainly follow the distribution of votes in the election (see Table 9–1). The d'Hondt rule for allocation of seats and small constituencies makes the electoral system unfavorable to small parties. The big parties get more seats in Parliament than their share of votes would presuppose. This forces the small parties into electoral alliances, either among themselves or with the big parties. The number of small parties in the Finnish party system is fairly large, because, without a minimum vote barrier, the proportional representation and the opportunity of electoral alliance make it possible for them to win a seat in Parliament even with a fairly low number of votes. As the constitutional reform is in preparation, all the big parties, except for the People's Democratic League and the Communist party, have proposed adopting a voting minimum in order to eliminate the small parties.

Even though the Constitution of Finland grants the president of the Republic a substantial amount of power, it can be said that Finland has a parliamentary system of government. The basic rule of parliamentarism means that the ministers—the members of the cabinet—must enjoy the confidence of Parliament and are responsible to Parliament for their actions. Since the beginning of independence, when the new Constitution was passed, this has implied that the political parties had an important role in the forming of governments. To ensure that the government maintained the confidence of a majority of Parliament, the cabinet had to be composed of the politicians of those parties which were in the majority in Parliament. Consequently, the ministers were generally committed to some parties, or directly chosen by parties.

Participation in the work of the cabinet in Finland is not divided according to the proportions of seats in Parliament. The fragmentation of the party system means that a government which enjoys the confidence of the majority of Parliament must necessarily consist of at least two parties. Since World War II, Parliament has in most cases been composed in such a way that not even two parties would have sufficed (see Table 9–5). Of decisive importance in the composition of government is the question of which parties can agree on a joint government policy and selection of ministers.

Due to the cleavage structure of the Finnish party system and particularly the parties' position in the left-right dimension, it has not been possible to form many different kinds of majority coalitions. The position of the two big parties—the PDL and the National Coalition—at the extremes of the basic dimension of the party system means that they cannot work in the same cabinet. Therefore, no majority government can be formed without the participation of either the Social Democratic party or the Center party. When these two parties have not been able to agree on the policy of the government and the composition of the cabinet, half-way solutions have had to be adopted, such as caretaker or minority governments. The position of the Liberal People's party and the Swedish People's party in the center of the party system has made them quite well suited for participation in governments, and both of them have frequently served in different types of government.

The parties also have an important role in the presidential elections. In all the presidential elections since World War II that have been arranged in the normal procedure, the candidates have been nominated by political parties. Similarly, the candidate nomination for the 300 electors, who elect the president, as well as the campaigns for the presidential elections have been attended to by the parties. The two postwar presidents, J. K. Paasikivi and Urho Kekkonen both were outstanding and experienced politicians who as presidents placed themselves above the parties, without feeling committed to their elector parties.

Advanced communal self-government is another essential part of the Finnish political system. On the communal level the authority of decision is with the municipal councils, which are elected every four years in a general election. In the last decades the municipal elections have changed in such a way as to reinforce the position of political parties. Candidate nomination and other election work is almost totally in the hands of the parties. The voters

TABLE 9–5. Parties in the Cabinets (without Caretaker Cabinets), 1944–1978

	People's Democratic League	Social Democratic League	Social Democratic Party	Agrarian Union	Center Party	Progressive Party	Finnish People's Party	Liberal People's Party	Swedish People's Party	National Coalition
1944–1945	✓		✓	✓		✓			✓	
1945–1946	✓		✓	✓		✓				
1946–1948	✓		✓	✓						
1948–1950			✓						✓	
1950–1951				✓		✓			✓	
1951–1953			✓	✓		✓			✓	
1953			✓	✓					✓	
1953–1954							✓		✓	✓
1954			✓	✓					✓	
1954–1956			✓	✓			✓		✓	
1956–1957			✓	✓			✓		✓	
1957				✓			✓			
1957		✓		✓			✓			
1957				✓			✓			
1958–1959			✓	✓			✓		✓	✓
1959–1961				✓			✓			
1961–1962				✓						
1962–1963				✓			✓		✓	✓
1964–1966				✓			✓		✓	✓
1966–1968	✓	✓	✓		✓					
1968–1970	✓	✓	✓		✓				✓	
1970–1971	✓		✓		✓				✓	
1972			✓							
1972–1975			✓		✓			✓	✓	
1975–1976	✓		✓		✓			✓	✓	
1976–1977					✓			✓	✓	
1977–1978	✓		✓		✓			✓	✓	

choose their candidates primarily on the basis of the party and not so much on the basis of some special local problems, which often happened in the past (Suhonen 1976, pp. 20–22).

In addition to the decision-making forums of the state and the communes, the parties are reinforcing their position also in many other places where social decision making and influencing takes place. A struggle for power is going on between the different parties in the central interest groups and organizations of society. In the trade union organizations of the workers this struggle is between the Social Democrats and the Communists, in the organizations of the clerical workers and officials between the Social Democrats and the nonsocialist parties, and in the agricultural organizations between the Center party and the National Coalition. In the various civic organizations, for example, in the field of culture and sports, decisions and choices are made on the basis of political criteria. Students of the universities and other educational institutions today elect their own governing bodies from among candidates nominated by party groups. The parties even nominate candidates of their own in the elections of parish councils of the Lutheran church.

Activity in several fields has become more visibly dependent on and committed to political parties. However, it is quite hard to answer the question of whether or not the power of the parties has grown. Some people believe that the power of the parties has grown in excess, whereas others point out that essential decision making is being moved outside the parliamentary machinery. In the last few years government and Parliament have frequently had no choice but to confirm, by means of legislation, decisions which had already been made in the mutual negotiations between the representatives of employers and industry, workers, and agricultural producers. The growing significance of the interest groups can also be seen in their more and more extensive participation in the work of committees and planning and preparatory organs of the state and communes. Whether it is the parties or the pressure groups which represent the interests of the different groups of population, there still remains the essential question from the point of view of democracy: What voice do the various group interests get in the decision-making process?

Note

1. The main source for this chapter was Nousiainen, 1971.

References

ALLARDT, ERIK. "Patterns of Class Conflict and Working Class Consciousness in Finnish Politics," in Erik Allardt and Yrjö Littunen, eds., *Cleavages, Ideologies and Party Systems*. Turku: Transactions of the Westermarck Society, vol. X, 1964.

DUVERGER, MAURICE. *Political Parties*. London: Methuen & Co., 1969.

NOUSIAINEN, JAAKKO. *The Finnish Political System*. Cambridge: Harvard University Press, 1971.

PESONEN, PERTTI. "Finland: Party Support in a Fragmented System," in Richard Rose, ed., *Electoral Behavior. A Comparative Handbook*. New York: Free Press, 1974.

ROSE, RICHARD. "Comparability in Electoral Studies," in Richard Rose, ed., *Electoral Behavior. A Comparative Handbook*. New York: Free Press, 1974.

SUHONEN, PERTTI. *Liikkuva äänestäjä Suomen monipuoluejärjestelmässä* (Floating Voter in Finnish Multiparty System). University of Tampere: Institute of Political Science, Research Report no. 26, 1972.

SUHONEN, PERTTI. *Korkeakouluopiskelijoiden poliittinen muutos Suomessa* (Political Change of University Students in Finland). University of Tampere: Institute of Political Science, Research Report no. 41, 1976.

SUHONEN, PERTTI. *Äänestäjien valinnat ja puoluejärjestelmän etäisyysrakenne* (Voters' Choice and Distances in Finnish Party Structure). University of Tampere: Department of Sociology and Social Psychology, Research Report no. 14, 1976.

SÄNKIAHO, RISTO. "A Model of the Rise of Populism and Support for The Finnish Rural Party," *Scandinavian Political Studies*, New York: Columbia University Press, 1971.

TÖRNUDD, KLAUS. *The Electoral System of Finland*. London: Hugh Evelyn, 1968.

UUSITALO, HANNU. *Class Structure and Party Choice: A Scandinavian Comparison*. University of Helsinki: Research Group for Comparative Sociology, Research Report no. 10, 1975.

CHAPTER 10

IRELAND

Michael J. Carey

Parties and the Irish Political System

IRISH POLITICAL PARTIES, like those in other Western European parliamentary democracies, are critical to the political system. The difference between these systems is in the key role that parties play in Irish politics. Due partially to a cabinet system of executive government and partially to a lack of other strong political actors such as interest groups, the political arena in Ireland is left unusually open to those most organized groups, the political parties. As centers of national power, the principal governmental institutions such as the Oireachtas (Parliament), the Taoiseach (prime minister), and the cabinet are understandable mainly as reflections of party politics. Party competition and a pattern of "ins and outs" (or styles of opposition)[1] largely determine the nature of these centers of national power. A remarkable lack of organized interests marks this modern European polity. Whereas the bureaucracy may be susceptible to "colonization" or clientelism in some cases, for example, the Irish Farmers Association and the Department of Agriculture and Fisheries or the Confederation of Irish Industries and the Department of Industry and Commerce, generally interest groups are so weak that they cannot forge tight links at administrative levels and, also, usually avoid identification with any of the parties. Groups thus freed may approach governments of either party. The closest link of organized interests and party is labor unions and the Irish labor party, although, as discussed in the following paragraphs, even this link is weak (as is this party). The church constitutes a powerful interest in one sense, but its

257

pervasiveness is more a determinant of the political culture. It should be more properly considered elsewhere under that rubric.

Other significant political actors include the presidency, bureaucracy, military, police and courts. The president is elected in partisan campaigns and is only a figure head. A recent presidential resignation over a dispute with a minister resulted in a nationwide election for a new president rather than the fall of a government. The bureaucracy, which is highly professionalized, avoids partisan identification[2] but plays a role in the dominant political culture as a bogy which a local party man can slay.

The military is not identified with parties today, although this has not always been the case due to Ireland's recent revolutionary past. The civil war and first transfer of power between the major parties provides an example of military involvement. The transfer of power from the "winners" of the civil war after independence to De Valera's "losers" when the latter won the 1932 election could have been but was not prevented by the army. This same army fought against De Valera's forces and had as a consequence some motivation to prevent the transfer of power to the "radicals." Among a number of intervening factors which inhibited the military was a willingness on the part of the government in power to submit to electoral defeat.[3] That event, if not others, signaled the ascendancy of political parties to the primary position among political organizations in Ireland.

The police and courts, as is typically the case in Northern Europe, remain nonpartisan, but, under governments of the leading party, admission to the bench may depend on partisanship.

Although other structures of the political system remain very "British," the parties have not. Indeed the parties' significance to the system itself is different. Ireland's revolutionary past shaped the party system and contributes to the parties' significance. At least the two dominant parties are the constitutional and institutionalized cadres of the revolutionaries. In its rather complete break with the past, the revolution spawned the new party system. The ensuing civil war divided the cadre of revolutionaries. Today nearly all of them have passed from the scene and certainly from positions of power. The point remains, however, that these organizations—the principal parties—were made up of followers led by the two sets of revolutionary leaders. Given this background even in a "British" style parliamentary democracy, it is not unusual that parties such as these play key roles in the political system.

The case of Ireland, then, is somewhat similar to that of Austria; postwar party politics provide the key to understanding that political system. On the other hand, the Irish party system has been compared with those in the Third World.[4] Here the argument centers upon parties, again, as organizations embodying the revolutionary leadership, cadres, militia, and so on, which became the source of mobilization during and after the revolution of independence. Of course, despite the ensuing civil war, the Irish system is more European than any other twentieth century example of independence movements; the Irish revolution provided a stable parliamentary democracy unlike other such movements outside of Europe.

Parliamentary democracies reflect the trend among industrialized nations toward centralization of power in the executive. In this respect, Ireland is no different. It may be argued, then, that the executive institution, the Taoiseach and his cabinet, becomes the most significant political organization in Ireland. A complete analysis of the political system indicates, however, that in several ways such a conclusion is inaccurate. The executive is the head of a party and attains the elected position via a responsible party electoral process (examined subsequently). Indeed, a defeated Taoiseach may lose his post as party head if it appears that he cannot lead his party back to electoral success; this was demonstrated after the 1977 elections. Taoiseach and party, as well as opposition and party in the Dail (lower house), constitute parts of a party system.

In addition, from the electorates' point of view as well, the party system not only provides the method for transfer of power in their political system, but equally or even perhaps more importantly provides for a type of a brokerage. This brokerage system of "representation" is identified both with personalities and parties. So, on at least two levels, one which is common and on another which is rare in Western Europe, the Irish party system is remarkable for its role in the overall political system. Further, a brokerage role in the party system displaces interest groups from fulfilling that role. Interest groups in many Western European systems act as brokers articulating and, perhaps, aggregating demands and even interceding with governmental institutions such as the civil service or local authorities to fulfill the needs and demands of interest group members. "Cozy triangles"[5] in the United States or clientelism in Italy provide examples of this form of interest group activities. In Ireland, however, brokerage takes place via individuals (local personalities) within the party framework, hence displacing interest groups.[6]

In short, the role of the party system in Irish politics is either paramount to explaining the system on the one hand or primary to explaining the operation of other components of the system on the other. One analyst, in describing the vast differences in scope and powers of Irish parties compared with those in Britain, concluded that the local bias of parties and politics lent an "amateurish" and underdeveloped look to Irish parties.[7] On the contrary, Irish parties are more comprehensive (while even more simplified) than are parties in Britain. Perhaps a more salient comparison should be made to continental (and more comprehensive) parties.

Political Party Development

The Irish party system, only in operation a short time compared with other Western European systems, lacks the antecedents which are common to independent countries. Groupings or factions within parliaments in Europe preceded or assisted party development, for example, in Scandinavia or the United Kingdom. In striking contrast to this lack of longevity, the Irish system has been uninterrupted for 55 years, with no hiatus such as France, Germany, Austria, or Italy which were occupied during World War II. The Irish system was not reconstructed after World War II with Allied influence as in West Germany, Austria, or Italy.

Parties existed before the Irish revolution, for example, the parliamentary home rule party of Parnell. Parnell's party represented Ireland in Westminster, instead of in Dublin or Belfast even though elected in Ireland. The Unionist party, which represented the Protestant Irish, existed simultaneously but ended up as a Northern Ireland party within the United Kingdom. Serious discontinuities existed between the earlier parties and Sinn Fein—the independence movement. It replaced the Parnellite party and in fact broke the links with the past constitutional parties in Ireland.

The development of the Irish party system over the past 30 years has been toward a stable bipolar (or perhaps two and a half) party system.[8] Bipolarity best describes this system, as one of the three permanent parties, the Irish Labor party (LP), remains too small to alternate in power outside of a coalition with the other "usual" out party. On the surface, the Irish system is similar to that of West Germany or the United Kingdom at least in terms of numbers and possibilities for "ins and outs." Bipolarity is an apt term in other respects as well, because the original split of the revolutionary independence party, Sinn Fein, into two armed camps (one in power) was caused by a political disagreement, not the usual class or religious cleavages which are so common to European party development.

Although essentially bipolar numerically, the main parties have been catchall parties since their inception. That is even more the case today. The two principal parties, Fianna Fail (F/F) and Fine Gael (F/G), attracted electoral support across the electorate, though "tendencies" for particular segments to be attracted to one or other of the main parties exist. Labor's peculiar development is reflected in its virtual exclusion from urban eastern politics until recently. Its support was found instead among the rural agricultural "proletariat" in specific regions. Labor remains unlike labor elsewhere in Europe even after its shift in support; it may be described as a nonsocialist labor party. Although the same may be said of the German SPD since the Bad Godesberg program and of the moderate wing of the British Labor party, these parties once articulated socialistic ideologies[9] whereas the LP did not. The two main parties, F/F and F/G, have been catchall in terms of electoral support. The lessening of political bipolarity as memories of the civil war fade contributes as well to the increasingly catchall nature of these parties. Examination of shifts in electoral support and "tendencies" of overrepresentation of one group or another also demonstrates the catchall nature of the parties.

Ideology is not a pronounced source of differences among the two main rightist, antisecular, and nationalistic parties, but at one time it appeared to provide a point of comparison. That largely illusionary difference centered on the radical nationalism of F/F; even this radicalism faded quickly. Because there was so little ideological content to party differences, it is overstating the case of Irish parties to call the shift part of the decline of ideology. The increased similarity in rhetoric and policy of the two main parties (indeed, even Labor) contributes to the growth of a catchall party system. On the other hand, the Irish party system may face a novel infusion of ideology from an unexpected source if the young turks of the most right-wing party (F/G) succeed in injecting a leftist social-democratic program into F/G as an attempt to rejuvenate and resurrect the party after its 1977 defeat. The new party leader is one of these "radicals."

A unique characteristic of party development in Ireland is the system's origin in a revolution of independence which severed ties to the imperial United Kingdom. A significant consequence is that pro-unionists left either for the United Kingdom or the Northern six counties of Ireland which remain part of the United Kingdom. Thus, a potential electoral group left the country. Since these partisans were mainly Protestant, it eliminated a key potential cleavage from Irish politics. Protestants in the border counties participate within the Irish party system but are so few in number that they create only a tiny minority. It has been suggested that most Protestants remaining in the Free State after independence found the predecessor to F/G the most satisfactory party because it was less radically nationalistic than F/F.[10] The abstentionist policy of F/F in the early years no doubt contributed to the electoral support pattern of minority Protestants.

Since the North remained attached to the United Kingdom, the revolution appeared to be incomplete. Another significant consequence of independence was that the revolution created a homogeneous population in the Free State. The outcome in the Free State was that the leaders and cadres of the revolutionaries quite simply took over the machinery of government and fell to quarreling amongst themselves.

A political dispute occurred over the treaty with the United Kingdom which recognized Ireland's independence or self-rule and described the country as part of the Commonwealth. Though the emphasis of this study is on post-1945 Irish parties, this dispute within the ranks of the revolutionaries should be briefly described. It led to the primary cleavage in the party system. The revolutionaries split over whether or not the treaty adequately recognized Ireland's independence and removed the symbols of British rule. The "solution" of the Northern issue was unsatisfactory to nearly all in the Free State, but one group accepted it, if only temporarily. Pro-treaty and anti-treaty sentiments split Sinn Fein. One group had control of government and the army. The other group of more radical nationalists had an irregular militia. The political conflict degenerated into political violence marked by atrocities and deep hatreds on both sides. The pro-treaty party in power was the forerunner of F/G, and it underwent a metamorphosis in the 1930s. The radicals followed abstentionist tactics after the civil war while contesting elections. The charismatic leader, De Valera, led his "new" party, F/F, into the Dail to become the opposition after abstentionism failed. F/F came to power in 1932 and has been the dominant party since that time.

The Irish party system was transformed into a European-style party system, when, after the civil war, parties fell into recognizable roles which were "normal" to political parties in Western Europe. These were participation in the Dail, striving for electoral support to become governing parties, and rejection of abstentionism, among others. While the development of F/F into the dominant political force in the system has been called "the decisive event in the political history of the new state,"[11] the transformation of the Irish party system into a functioning bipolar system with the potential for democratic alteration in power was of greater consequence. As a result of party development, national independence had been gained, political violence between the nationalists foregone, and party politics initiated. An overview of the governing parties is found in Table 10–1.

Little attention is paid here to the minor parties which flourished at times in Ireland. Given their short lives (usually) and often low impact on national politics, these parties are better understood as regional phenomena or as an expected outcome of a proportional representation system which may help them flourish.[12]

In summary, the Irish party system has become more "simplified" in the postwar era as the number of parties declined and political differences disappeared. In terms of parties in power and in opposition, Ireland's system is

TABLE 10–1.   Governing Parties in Ireland

Governing Party(ies)	*Date*
Pro-treaty	1922
Cumann na nGaedheal[a]	1923–1932
Fianna Fáil	1933–1948
Coalition of Fine Gael, Labor, and Clann na Talmhan, with support of Clann na Ploblachta)[b]	1948–1951
Fianna Fáil	1951–1954
Coalition (same parties)	1954–1957
Fianna Fáil	1957–1973
Coalition (Fine Gael, Labor)	1973–1977
Fianna Fáil	1977–

[a]Predecessor to F/G.
[b]Clann na Talmhan is the Farmers party.
 Clann na Ploblachta are "left" nationalists supporting but not participating in coalition government.

bipolar, with parties becoming ever-more catchall in nature.[13] The alternations in government over the past 25 years appear to indicate a stable pattern with one dominant party (F/F) and one large (F/G) and one minor party (LP) forming a coalition to alternate in government.

Party Structure

In theory Irish party structures are centralized and bureaucratized but in practice powerful decentralizing tendencies inhibit a tight, top-down party structure of the type ordinarily found in Western Europe. Although the parties are organized on a branch style locally (rather than by caucus or cell), they try to operate at the national level like responsible parties in the European tradition. They are characterized by discipline, centralized decision making, hierarchy, authority, localism, personalism, and a brokerage system. The last three elements are such pervasive factors of the Irish political culture that they work against "centralism" at the local level. In fact not only at the local level do party practices inhibit centralism, as in a kind of periphery versus center or "have-nots" versus elites conflict, but in practice national parties use brokerage, personalism, and localism to win elections. If the analyst merely examines the party system from a subsystemic level, only then the system itself takes on an excessively parochial outlook.[14] The analyst should, of course, analyze both levels, local and national, to produce a comprehensive description.

As is the case with catchall party systems, the ultimate criterion of success is electoral victory. That goal affects party structure. Organizational goals, for example, hierarchy and responsibility, may be displaced by electoral goals. National parties develop catchall strategies, which to a great extent tap into local political culture. On the other hand, catchall parties are not solely election machines but also political organizations with habits, traditions, identities, and, obviously, structure. Catchall parties are neither mere reflections of present political interests, nor attempts to attract ephemeral floating voters. Partisans have to be satisfied as well and kept within the fold. Hence, some value, issue, or other difference from the other parties will be expressed (or exaggerated) for their benefit even by a catchall party. Since habit is so strong in political action, partisans will be ignored only at the expense of losing them. Drawing in the floaters and giving them an identity may make them habit-following partisans as well. So electoral strategies reflect both local practices in Ireland that work against centralism and a party organization of politics that tends to reinforce structures.

For the catchall party, structures are critical to electoral success as well as for the party in government. Structure in this sense means the apparatus to organize, finance, direct, and change party processes that promote participation via voting. Structures would be of little consequence if parties were not the main instruments of participation in Ireland.

Descriptions of national party structures of the three main parties share the following points. All are structurally similar; parties are cadre-dominated by parliamentary (or governmental) party leaders. Local clubs or branches (cumann in F/F) are organized on a ward or parish basis. Constituency organizations link these local branches together. Nationally, an annual convention of delegates (Ard Fheis) and central office (national executive) tie the system together.[15] Salaried organizers are limited in number but are often key figures in internal party politics.[16] Youth organizations have become increasingly significant to F/F and F/G in the past five years; these did not previously exist.[17] The consequences of young voters are significant as this group makes up such a large portion of the population. This group will make Irish politics different from other European politics in the next general election.

The Ard Fheis is the dominant national decision-maker in theory but in reality it is largely symbolic. Decision-making is actually centered in the parliamentary party elites, not unlike the process in the United Kingdom. Of course, if the party is in power, the Taoiseach is the nominal and often real center of the party hierarchy. Chubb points out that this elite has a virtual monopoly in formulating policy.[18] This elite is the apex of the structure, a fact that is underscored by the lack of branch influence at that level. Even ordinary members of the parliamentary party act as followers, as its party members are not strictly organized along party lines and its members play rather limited roles at the national party level. The Oireachtas is, as a consequence, "one of the worst organized, equipped and informed parliaments in the democratic world."[19] The bureaucracies of the parties—the central offices—are very small and their functions severely limited.[20] Small staffs provide few services to members, and even at election time resources for public relations and information services are limited. A change appears to be taking place in the two major parties' bureaucracies. F/F expanded the roles of the central office and its available resources after its 1973 defeat. F/G has been in the same process in the wake of its 1977 defeat.[21] Because finances and expenditures are not well publicized, the degree of change, at least as indicated by expenditures by party bureaucracies, cannot be accurately determined. Overall, it appears that neither party is in "danger" of becoming overly bureaucratized, as personalities of leaders continue to play such key roles—even in reorganization— whereas the local factors discussed below further inhibit bureaucratization.

The final point at the national party level concerns the question of party discipline and responsibility. Recent evidence indicates that the F/F operates as a responsible party with the discipline to expel members over national policy issues. The case in point is the expulsion of party leaders from the cabinet in 1970 when these ministers were accused of collaboration in gunrunning to the North. Later, they were exonerated in the courts. Nevertheless, this rather spectacular incident demonstrates responsibility by the party. On the other hand, because so many local politicians are either elected to the Dail on the basis of service to the constituency in local government or reelected on the basis of past service in the Dail, rather than on the basis of a party platform, one condition of party responsibility seems to be undercut. Also, the lack of national party assistance to campaigns may undercut party responsibility. Both factors work against a responsible party system because elections are more determined by localism and brokerage than by national party identity and party policies.

Powerful decentralizing tendencies work against national party structures in Ireland. Such tendencies, due to branch practices, localism-personalism, and brokerage, create a party system more similar to the chaotic, "irresponsible" American party system than the disciplined, responsible European party system. Although national structures appear to be centripetal forces in Ireland, local structures defeat this with their own centrifugal pressures.

At the bottom of the party structure are the clubs based on either parishes or wards. Labor claims a few hundred clubs whereas F/F claims to have about 2,000, with F/G in between with about 1,700.[22] Clubs average about 10 to 30 members with, of course, a hard core of gladiators. Club tasks are recruitment of party members, nomination, and campaigning. The campaigning activity is paramount. Bax found that clubs do not act as communication channels "between the people and the center";[23] rather, a parallel structure of personal networks of politicians and local notables act as communication channels. Another study found F/F local organization to be more pervasive, that is, numbers of organizations within a constituency that was described as being specifically geared to cover territory with an even network.[24]

The bottom-level organizations profoundly influence nominations. A local nominee is put forward on the premise that the local person will pursue garnering benefits and going to bat for the area. "In spite of the party leaders presiding over the national and local conventions for the selection of candidates, the center by no means controls nominations."[25] Localism, personalism, and brokerage reinforce one another and work against the center, at least in regard to nominations and getting elected. In the latter it is most clear that brokerage is a key factor. (Brokerage is the use of an intermediary seen as necessary to any relationship between the citizen and the state—especially with the bureaucracy.) Most often, when a citizen seeks a service or even only information from "government" in Ireland, rather than make direct contact, a go-between is used. Most often that is a local official (of local government) or the representative in the Dail (a T.D.). Further, a T.D. is evaluated in terms of the service provided to the constituency, be it road repairs or council housing, via the state and by the T.D.'s actions as an intermediary on behalf of constituents. The literature on brokerage in Ireland[26] emphasizes that this political relationship is different from the unequal patron-client relationship in less modern polities. Political and cultural characteristics such as an emphasis on the local area, trusting a "neighbor" from the area, the importance of face-to-face contacts, kinship linkages, and other left-overs from a peasant society are part and parcel of Irish brokerage politics. Recent survey research confirms this description of Irish party politics.[27] Such a system goes far beyond the notion of pork-barrel politics, because brokerage becomes the main function of most T.D.s.

The key influence of brokerage on party structure and politics is in this reemphasis of the local and personal over the national and central. Faced with persistent demands for this type of service which is obviously time-consuming for the T.D., the T.D. has little time for other considerations. The voter with such a clear-cut method of evaluating candidates continues to demand services. The system of proportional representation with a single transferable vote allows the voter to discriminate (unlike in a pure list system) even between candidates of the same party within his district (constituencies are multi-member). Hence the pressure is on party politicians to perform as expected; such a local emphasis is a powerful centrifugal force on the party's national structures.

Party Elites and Party Processes

Party elites are composed of locals, parliamentary party members, and top elites centered around the Taoiseach or opposition leader and his cohorts. One of the last two sets of the elite are already well enough analyzed to describe in general, that is, the top elite (Taoiseach). Data is available for comparison of recent parliamentary party elites, for example, biographical data on the 1973 T.D.'s and, to a lesser extent, those elected in 1977 (see Tables 10–2, 10–3, 10–4, and 10–5).[28] General conclusions can be drawn from this data for 1973; at the parliamentary party level the population is nearly all male, nearly all local, that is, from in or near the constituency represented (86.8%), and serve on local authority (local government) concurrently (72.2%), middle aged, with a "decent" representation of youthful T.D.'s (22.7%) largely from middle-class and professional occupations across a fairly broad range (publicans to professors). Roughly one-quarter of the T.D.'s had politicians for parents or for husbands. Three of the four women in the 1973 Dail are widows; inclusion of widows in the calculation increases the figure to 26.4%. There is good reason to include them since kinship and personalism in Irish party politics are demonstrated by both of these groups of T.D.'s.

Not included in the tables are the following points. Nearly all the T.D.s are Catholic, many are relatives (nieces, nephews, etc.) of famous politicians in addition to the sons, daughters, and widows mentioned above, some made a name in athletics before politics, and many cite sports organizations among their important memberships. Taken together with the variables concerned with locale and parents, these are significant indications of the importance of

TABLE 10–2.   Membership of the Dail, 1973 and 1974

	1973		1977	
PARTY	Percent of Total	Seats	Percent of Total	Seats
Party				
Fianna Fáil	46.5	67	56.7	84
Fine Gael	38.9	56	29.1	43
Labor	13.2	19	11.5	17
Independent	1.4	2	.027	4
Age				
Under 41	22.7	32	29.1	34[a]
41–56	54.6	77	53.8	63
Over 56	22.7	32	17.1	20
Occupation				
Politician	15.3	22	20.1	29[b]
Business	35.4	51	34.0	49
Teacher	8.3	12	9.0	13
Farmer	18.1	26	17.4	25
Trade union official	4.9	7	3.5	5
Legal (barrister, solicitor)	9.0	13	7.6	11
Labor	2.8	4	2.1	3
Labor	2.8	4	2.1	3
Medical (doctor, etc.)	3.5	5	4.2	6
University professor	2.8	4	2.1	3

[a]31 missing.
[b]4 missing.

TABLE 10–3.   Localism, Personalism, and Party, 1973 Dail (Percent)

	FIANNA FAIL	FINE GAEL	LABOR	INDEPENDENTS
Local[a]	89.6%	85.7%	78.9%	100.0%
Nonlocal	10.4	14.3	21.1	0.0
Parents in politics[b]	26.9	21.4	21.1	50.0
No parents in politics	71.6	76.8	73.7	50.0
Widow	1.5	1.8	5.3	0.0

[a]Birthplace in or near (e.g., within the county) the constituency represented.
[b]Immediate parent having been an important political figure in Ireland. Nephews, nieces, other "indirect" relationships are not included. Most women in the Dail are widows of politicians.

localism, personalism, and kinship. Hence, personalistic and brokerage politics are major characteristics of Irish political parties.

Party elites in 1973 and 1977 show a shift in the two main parties towards younger T.D.s, the biggest increase is found in F/G. F/G also "lost" middle aged and elder T.D.s. Compared with 1973 F/F is now more similar to F/G in

TABLE 10–4. Age and Party Affiliation, 1973 and 1977 Dail

	FIANNA FAIL		FINE GAEL		LABOR		INDEPENDENTS	
	Percent of Total	Seats	Percent of Total	Seats	Percent of Total	Seats	Percent of Total	Seats
1973 Dail								
Under 41	25.8	17	18.5	10	26.3	5	0.0	0
41–56	47.0	31	63.0	34	52.6	10	100.0	2
Over 56	27.3	18	18.5	10	21.1	4	0.0	0
1977 Dail								
Under 41	30.0	18	34.1	14	14.3	2	0.0	0
41–56	53.3	31	51.2	21	64.3	9	50.0	1
Over 56	16.7	10	14.6	3	21.4	3	50.0	1

TABLE 10–5. Occupation and Party Affiliation, 1973 and 1977 Dail

	FIANNA FAIL		FINE GAEL		LABOR		INDEPENDENTS	
	Percent of Total	Seats	Percent of Total	Seats	Percent of Total	Seats	Percent of Total	Seats
1973 Dail								
Politician	17.9	12	8.9	5	21.1	4	50.0	1
Businessperson	41.8	28	35.7	20	15.8	3	0.0	0
Teacher	11.9	8	7.1	4	0.0	0	0.0	0
Farmer	16.4	11	25.0	14	0.0	0	50.0	1
Trade union official	0.0	0	0.0	0	36.8	7	0.0	0
Legal (barrister, solicitor)	6.0	4	16.1	9	0.0	0	0.0	0
Laborer	1.5	1	3.6	2	5.3	1	0.0	0
Medical (doctor)	4.5	3	1.8	1	5.3	1	0.0	0
University professor	0.0	0	1.8	1	15.8	3	0.0	0
1977 Dail								
Politician	6.2	5	34.9	15	47.1	8	33.3	1
Businessperson	48.1	39	18.6	8	11.8	2	0.0	0
Teacher	11.1	9	9.3	4	0.0	0	0.0	0
Farmer	18.5	15	0.0	0	5.9	1	33.3	1
Trade union official	0.0	0	18.6	8	29.4	5	0.0	0
Legal (barrister, solicitor)	8.6	7	9.3	4	0.0	0	0.0	0
Laborer	2.5	2	2.3	1	0.0	0	0.0	0
Medical (doctor)	3.7	3	2.3	1	5.9	1	33.3	1
University professor	1.2	1	4.7	2	0.0	0	0.0	0

terms of numbers of elders. Labor lost some of its youthful orientation in the 1977 general election and now have a substantial underrepresentation of young T.D.s. Clearly middle-class professions are predominant, a trend that becomes even more apparent in 1977. This trend has been at Labor's expense.

The composition of top party elites centered around the Taoiseach or leaders of the opposition has changed in at least two very significant ways in the past several general elections. The revolutionary elite has passed from positions of power, and localism connected with the first change has been reinforced. For example, four of the nine men forming the F/F cabinet under De Valera in 1932 were still in office when he resigned in 1959 (with a couple of periods in opposition), and, when F/G formed the government in 1948, three former cabinet members returned.[29] The revolutionary generation finally passed, as "no member of the new Government ('73) was a participant in the revolutionary era."[30] Once the aura of revolutionary service passed the voters turned to more pragmatic reasons to elect T.D.s and, indirectly, the government. The brokerage and localism rationale became paramount. In terms of career patterns of the government formed in 1977, unlike the revolutionary era elite, F/F has mostly ministers with professional backgrounds, for example, intelligentsia, barrister, solicitor, company director, and so on.[31] There were, however, no women in the last three governments; hence they cannot make up part of the key party elites.

There are no primaries in Ireland. Candidates are selected for the voter by activists at conventions made up of the branches in a constituency. A T.D. will try to guarantee his office by using his influence at a convention to keep the competition weak.[32] In multimember constituencies with the single transferable vote, the T.D.s, or for that matter, any candidates' need to ensure enough votes to get elected and prevent a fellow party member from intruding on this voting "turf."

A candidate is not required by law to live in the constituency in which he stands, but nearly all do so. A deposit of £100 is required along with various applications to election officials.[33] The most significant factors in the nomination process are the informal ones. As mentioned, branches nominate local candidates. As a result nearly all candidates are locals, and Chubb points out the important consequences of this: locals largely fight their own campaigns because they can expect little help from the center.[34] Here again, centrifugal forces are in effect.

Two studies investigated the nomination process and underscored the effect of the decentralizing factors. In a study of a Northwestern constituency by Sacks, politicians and party notables in F/F and F/G nominated candidates on local considerations. Local issues included religion, the border, and the formation of bailiwicks within the constituency based on intraconstituency locales where a "neighbor" stood for election and organized a miniature political machine.[35] Final choices were determined by strength of machines, personal appeal, religious division, and past performance of candidates. Very little if any of this had to do with national parties or their policies.

A second study in another section of Ireland described the nomination battle which took place at the local level before the convention itself. The battle was waged by several potential contenders trying to gather support for the nomination. Four years later the convention too was largely determined by preconvention negotiation (and sabotage) by potentials.[36] An important function of these nominations and prenomination haggling is the division of territory within the constituency and, in extreme cases, the creation of bailiwicks. Multimember constituencies must be divided for effective canvassing and to tap into those narrowly local strengths of various candidates. In short, nominations reflect localism, personalism, and brokerage.

National party elites intrude on the local nomination process occasionally at their own peril. For the 1977 general election, F/F demonstrated its superior organizational capabilities as nominating conferences were held in some cases before dissolution of the government. F/G and the LP, which were in power, were either late in organizing conventions or in the case of the LP were rent by factionalism. The central office of F/F intruded into nominations to add nominees in some areas, for example, women, with such intrusions resented locally.[37]

As mentioned, Irish parties alternate in power rather than form complex coalitions or consociational systems of parties in power, as in some other small Northern European democracies. The lack of class, religious, and secular divisions undercuts the social bases for consociational politics, although the period of civil war marks a cleavage which is similar in some respects to the background of consociational polities.

Neither F/G nor Labor could hope to play a role in government without a coalition, but the LP must play the minor role due to its low average electoral support. Ministerial posts are divided with the lion's share going to F/G. The lack of ideological distance between these coalition partners made the marriage of convenience an easy one. Compared with Austria and its coalition government during 1945–1966, there exist no deep-seated differences between the parties. On unsettling issues such as Northern Ireland, Labor and F/G both are moderate in marked contrast to F/F. Differences within the cabinet over an "emergency powers" bill revealed some differences but the policies pursued proved the coalition a like-minded group.

F/F has usually had the strength, as it does now, to rule as a dominant party with a majority and without dependence on "understandings" within the Dail. At times, however, the party was dependent on coalitions composed of independent T.D.s or the tacit support of small parties in the Dail. In its early years in power F/F was supported by Labor.

Thus, in terms of roles in government and in opposition, the norm in Ireland has become one dominant party (F/F) and a coalition (F/G and Labor) which can occasionally displace it and alternate in power.

Cleavages: Voters and Members?

Although Ireland's bipolar, two-and-a-half party system resembles British and continental systems with its alternations in power and similar structures, in many respects the Irish system remains a deviant case. Previously mentioned were various local centrifugal forces and the lack of ideological differences. Another significant difference is apparent when contrasting the British and Irish systems. Mass parties were alien to Irish politics when such parties developed in the United Kingdom. Industrialization, urbanization, and class politics came much later to Ireland, if at all. Indeed, class politics never really developed, nor was secularization a source of political divisions. As mentioned, a vertical cleavage over a political issue (the treaty) was the original division between the two main parties. Irish party politics are referred to as "politics without social bases."[38] Analysts have described the lack of cleavages under various labels, often finding tendencies within regions or social groups to support a particular party. The rural versus urban split assumes the role of a cleavage as well and is discussed below. The point is that, when religion-secularism, class, race, language, or clear-cut regional differences exist, these social factors are often reflected in the party systems. Ireland with its homogeneous population and relative underdevelopment lacks those bases for parties. At most, tendencies may be found among groups, and over time even those change, especially as parties become more catchall.

Generally, these tendencies are described in regards to the first main party, Cumann na nGaedheal (forerunner to F/G), as the conservative middle-class party with support of the business community, church hierarchy, and well-to-do farmers. F/F attracted western small farmers (generally poor), urban and rural working classes, and republican middle class and clergy.[39] By the end of World War II, F/F was respectable enough for major business support to shift to it. Labor counted on agricultural workers in the south and east until fairly recently. Other parties tapped narrower sentiments like extreme republicanism, or special farmers' interests; none lasted for long.

As the main parties became more catchall, the tendencies of various groups to support one or other party grew even less distinct. This was accentuated by the shift to an emphasis on economic development in the late 1950s and more outward orientation of the parties marked by promotion of industrialization, international trade, and the Europeanization of Irish foreign policy.[40] The main parties supported state intervention in the economy, development, and an active role by promotional agencies and state participation in enterprises. Policy goals became ever more similar as memories of the civil war faded. Especially for the main parties, support could be found throughout society; for example, a survey in 1969 found that 45% of the middle class supported F/F, 28% F/G, and 14% Labor, whereas 42% of the working class supported F/F, 16% F/G, and 28% Labor. Forty-two percent of the farmers supported F/F, 40% F/G ,and 3% Labor.[41] Party support by all classes was 43% F/F,

25% F/G, and 18% Labor (14% other). A more detailed analysis of classes revealed important levels of support for the two main parties except among unskilled laborers, where F/G garnered 14% of this group's support.

General support for the parties revealed an important shift in the 1977 general election landslide for F/F, when the dominant party captured 84 seats in the Dail to 43 for F/G, 17 for Labor, and 4 others (total 148 seats). Comparing the 1973 and 1977 general elections, the first preference votes by party were F/F 46.24% and 50.63%, F/G 35.09% and 30.49%, and Labor 13.67% and 11.63%, respectively.[42] The coalition in 1973 gained 48.76% total first preference votes, dropping to 42.12% in 1977. F/F in 1977 received more than half the first preference votes in 22 of the 42 constituencies, "ranging from 33% in a Dublin constituency to an unprecedented 69% in Clare" (the rural west).[43] Large well-to-do farmers gave up on F/G in Munster and Leinster according to one analysis; normally that group supported F/G.

Studies that looked for cleavages and found only tendencies among electoral supporters of particular parties indicate a peculiar volatility among Irish voters. Class bases for support were found to be generally less distinct than those supporting parties in most Western European democracies.[44]

One clear-cut group particularly supportive of F/F are the Irish speakers; F/F is notably the party of Irish language restoration. F/F strength with farmers shifted over time, especially during World War II and immediately after. Voters in the wealthiest and most industrialized areas also shifted support away from F/F during the 1950s. In the 1969 and 1973 general elections, F/F was strongest in the most agricultural regions and weakest in the least agricultural areas.

In the same periods, F/G's support was highest "in constituencies with a high proportion of employers and managers and where the rateable value of land was high."[45] Where the labor force in agriculture and emigration rate was high, F/G support was low in 1954. Overall up to 1961 these relationships between F/G support and ecological variables were generally low. This "pattern" was totally reversed in the 1965 election, which was marked, among other changes, by a F/G election manifesto that gave the impression that F/G had shifted to the left as a social democratic party.

Labor's electoral support, in class terms, can be described as agricultural laborers, and this is borne out by ecological analysis. Areas with farmers but few or no farm laborers did not support labor. In 1969 and 1973, Labor finally broke its urban barrier and increased its support in Dublin. Yet its overall weakness indicates that "likely" supporters are turning elsewhere. Attempts to find class cleavage rationales for the Irish party system find, at most, tendencies which more accurately depict an unstable electorate!

Other possible cleavage sources in Ireland are based on the notion of center versus periphery or urban versus rural regions. Within rural regions one analysis identifies agrarian classes as well-to-do farmers, poor farmers, and landless laborers.[46] The rural region (with its own internal conflicts) separated from the cosmopolitan urban areas in economic and social functions. The image is that of cities surrounded by a sea of peasants and farmers who dominated politics until the World War II era. Since then, emigration to the cities extended the tentacles of the rural party style into the city with F/F's organizational forms. Basically, the conclusion that can be drawn from this attempt at describing cleavages is that F/F got its start in the western, poor rural periphery and spread from there to the cities. F/G in these early years simply had no one regional or class center of gravity as did F/F. In that sense F/G was more catchall to start with. Labor is described no differently in this context than in the ecological analysis of support. Overall then, the periphery-urban analysis may be more useful in describing party *membership* cleavages than party *support* cleavages.

Age was thought to be significant to F/F's 1977 win, but one survey suggested there was no major swing to F/F by the 25-and-under age group. Those voting for F/F were probably only slightly above their proportion in the electorate.[47]

Electoral support for particular Irish parties as indicated in the 1969 survey is fairly broadly based and not explained by social or regional cleavages. One is tempted to acknowledge that Ireland is indeed an example of "politics without social bases."

Perhaps, then, a clearer picture of cleavages can be gained from party membership analysis. Chubb suggests that in the late 1960s party membership amounted to not more than 60,000 (total population of the Republic was about 2.9 million). Leaving aside mere membership where statistics are difficult to obtain, the activists, for example, those who enter into local government, demonstrate that Irish party politics is like politics elsewhere in the West, dominated by notables.[48] One membership study examined a single urban constituency in Dublin, in which 2% of the adult population were "paid up members of one or another of the three main parties."[49] F/F activists (defined here as regular participants in party activities) came from a more varied set of socioeconomic backgrounds. Among the activists interviewed, many were originally from rural areas. Dublin's population is about 33% rural born; the activists were 51% "rural" in F/F, 36% in F/G, and 33% in Labor. These activists were also generally well-educated and belonged to secondary associations as well.[50]

Turning to a more general comparison in the age and occupation party tables for 1973–1977, some slight differences are found. These party members are, of course, the second most select group of members. Here, F/F and Labor both have slight overrepresentations of young Dail members. F/G has a definite overrepresentation of the middle age group; by 1977, F/F and F/G both shifted toward younger T.D.s. It is also apparent in general that younger members are no more nonlocal than are their elders. In terms of occupation, F/F attracts those in business and teaching and many full-time politicians. Farmers are slightly underrepresented in F/F, but that percentage increased in

1977. F/G is a magnet for farmers and those in legal fields. Labor naturally attracted trade union officials and laborers in 1973 and strongly attracted those in medical fields and professors in 1973. The two main parties draw business support (F/F especially). The sharpest occupational cleavage in membership appears between Labor and the other two parties. However, the overall preponderance of middle-class occupational backgrounds appears to be the most important characteristic and that is even more apparent in 1977. In this membership sense, the parties are not catchall.

Like parties in many Western European nations, Irish political parties are significant political institutions. On the other hand, they are unique among Western European parties in terms of lack of cleavages in voter identification, party membership, structure, roles, and processes. Too, they are significantly affected by localism and personalism. Yet, in another sense, they are quite similar to other Western European catchall political parties in that they are motivated by a desire to mute ideologies, to expand their electoral base, and to win elections.

Notes

1. For a general discussion, see Robert Dahl, ed., *Political Oppositions in Western Democracies*, New Haven, Conn.: Yale University Press, 1966, pp. xiii–xxi.
2. See Basil Chubb, *The Government and Politics of Ireland*, London: Oxford University Press, 1974, pp. 218–245 for a description of the civil service.
3. David E. Schmitt, *The Irony of Irish Democracy*, Lexington, Mass.: Lexington Books, 1973, p. 34.
4. Tom Garvin, "National Elites, Irish Voters and Irish Political Development," *Economic and Social Review* (ESR), 8 (April 1977), 161–186. Despite this comparison, the Irish party system resembles European styles much more than those in the Third World, the similarity in independence movements may be overdrawn.
5. See, for example, Garth Youngberg, "U.S. Agriculture in the 1970's," in James E. Anderson, ed., *Economic Regulatory Policies*, Lexington, Mass.: Lexington Books, 1976, and Roger Davidson, "Policy-making in the Policy Making Subgovernment," in Michael P. Smith, ed., *Politics in America: Studies in Policy Analysis*, New York: Random House, 1974.
6. See discussion of personalism, localism, and brokerage.
7. Basil Chubb, "The Republic of Ireland," in Stanley Henig and John Pinder, eds., *European Political Parties*, London: PEP, 1969, p. 456. One dilemma of colonialism in this case is the tendency to only compare Irish political phenomena to those in the United Kingdom.
8. This section on party development benefited from the comprehensive studies of Irish political parties found in Chubb (1974), Chubb (1969); Maurice Manning, *Irish Political Parties*, Dublin: Gill and Macmillan, 1972; J. F. S. Ross, *The Irish*

Election System, London: Pall Mall, 1959; Garvin (1977); Tom Garvin, "Political Cleavages, Party Politics and Urbanization in Ireland: The Case of the Periphery-Dominated Center," *European Journal of Political Research* (EJPR), 2 (1974), 307–327; and R. K. Carty, "Social Cleavages & Party Systems: A Reconsideration of the Irish Case," *EJPR*, 4 (1976), 195–203. More generally, see Gordon Smith, *Politics in Western Europe*, New York: Holmes & Meier, 1972, Chap. 4; Roy Macridis, ed., *Political Parties*, New York: Harper & Row, 1967, passim; Leon Epstein, *Political Parties in Western Democracies*, New York: Praeger, 1967, passim.

9. The Irish Labor party lost its radicalism when Connolly and Larkin left the scene, see Chubb (1969), p. 450.

10. See Manning (1969), p. 30.

11. Garvin (1977), p. 175.

12. See Manning (1969) for a discussion of the development and significance of minor parties. For proportional representation and the electoral systems, see A. S. Cohan, R. P. McKinlay and A. Mughan, "The Used Vote and Electoral Outcomes: The Irish General Election of 1973," *British Journal of Political Science*, 5 (June 1975), 363–383; C. Robson and B. Walsh, "The Importance of Positional Voting Bias in the Irish General Election of 1973," *Political Studies*, 22 (June 1974), 191–203; M. Gallagher, "Disproportionality in a PR System: The Irish Experience," *Political Studies*, 23 (December 1975), 501–513; P. Mair and M. Laver, "Proportionality, P.R., and S.T.V. in Ireland," *Political Studies*, 23 (December 1975), 491–500.

13. See Frank Wilson, *The French Democratic Left, 1963–1969*, Stanford, Calif.: Stanford University Press, 1971, pp. 1–20 for a cogent discussion of catchall party development in post-World War II Western Europe.

14. Mart Bax, *Harp Strings and Confessions*, Assen: Van Gorcum, 1976 concentrates on a local analysis and concludes, naturally, that Irish politics are marked by parochialism, p. 42. Such a microscopic analysis needs to be set against the background of national politics (e.g., parties) to make sense of Irish parochialism.

15. See, for example, Chubb in Henig (1969); Garvin, *EJPR* (1974); and Bax (1976), pp. 34–36.

16. Garvin (1974), p. 317.

17. See, for example, *The Irish Times*, January 14, 1978, p. 5, and February 6, 1978, p. 5; Chubb, in Henig (1969).

18. Chubb, in Henig (1969), p. 458.

19. Ibid.

20. Ibid.

21. See, for example on F/F, *Irish Press*, May 20, 1977, p. 3, June 22, 1977, p. 3, and June 23, 1977, p. 10; *The Irish Times*, June 30, 1977, p. 10 and November 5, 1977, p. 14. On F/G, see *The Irish Times*, June 21, 1977, p. 1 and February 6, 1978, p. 5.

22. See Bax (1976), p. 35; Chubb, op. cit., 456.

23. Bax, Ibid.

24. Garvin, *EJPR* (1974), p. 318.

25. Bax, op. cit.

26. See Schmitt (1973), Chap. 5; Paul M. Sacks, *The Donegal Mafia*, New Haven, Conn.: Yale University Press, 1976; and Bax, op. cit. Also, see Peter Gibbon and M. D. Higgens, "Patronage, Tradition, and Modernization: The Case of the Irish 'Gombeenan,' " *ESR*, 6 (October 1974), 27–44; Basil Chubb, "Going About Persecuting Civil Servants: The Role of the Irish Parliamentary Representation," *Political Studies*, 11 (1963), 272–286.

27. John Raven and C. T. Whalen, "Irish Adults Perceptions of their Civic Institutions and their Own Role in Relation to Them," in Raven et al., eds., *Political Culture in Ireland—The Views of Two Generations*, Raven et al., eds., Dublin: 1976, pp. 52–54.

28. These frequency distributions for party members were computed by this writer from biographical data for each 1973 T.D. found in Ted Nealon, *Ireland: A Parliamentary Directory, 1973–1974*, Dublin: Institute of Public Administration, 1974, and from a list published after the 1977 general election in *The Irish Times*, June 20, 1977, p. 8; Al Cohan, *The Irish Political Elite*, Dublin: Gill and Macmillan, 1972; Basil Chubb, *Cabinet Government in Ireland*, Dublin: Institute of Public Administration, 1974; Brian Farrell, "Dail Deputies: The 1969 Generation," *ESR*, 23 (April 1971), pp. 309–313.

29. Brian Farrell, "The Irish Prime Minister," *Parliamentary Affairs*, 25 (Winter 1971), 77.

30. A. S. Cohan, "Continuity and Change in the Irish Political Elite, A Comment on the 1973 Election," *BJPS*, 4 (April 1974), 250. See also A. S. Cohan, "Career Patterns in The Irish Political Elite," *BJPS*, 2 (April 1973), 213–228.

31. See the list of elected T.D.s, *The Irish Times*, June 20, 1977, p. 8.

32. James Knight and Nicolas Baxtor-Moore, *Republic of Ireland, The General Election of 1969 and 1973*, London: Arthur McDougal Fund, 1973, p. 7.

33. Ibid., pp. 32–33.

34. Chubb in Henig, op. cit., p. 457.

35. Paul M. Sacks, "Bailiwicks, Locality, and Religion: Three Elements in an Irish Dail Constituency Election," *ESR*, 1 (July 1970), 537–539. See also Sacks, *The Donegal Mafia*, op. cit.

36. See, for example, Bax, op. cit., p. 118.

37. Brian Farrell, "The Irish General Election, 1977," *Parliamentary Affairs*, 31 (Winter 1978), 26.

38. J. H. Whyte, "Ireland: Politics without Social Bases," in Richard Rose, ed., *Electoral Behavior*, New York: Free Press, 1974.

39. Nicolas Baxter-Moore, op. cit., p. 27.

40. See Michael J. Carey, *The Europeanization of Irish Foreign Policy, 1958–1975*, Santa Barbara, Calif.: University of California at Santa Barbara, unpublished dissertation, 1977.

41. Gallup Survey of April 1969, in Manning, op. cit., Appendix A, p. 114. These "classes" constitute 31%, 48%, 21% of the total population, respectively.

42. These figures are from a table in Farrell, op. cit., p. 36.

43. Ibid., p. 29.

44. Michael Gallagher, *Electoral Support for Irish Political Parties, 1927–1973*, Beverly Hills, Calif.: Sage, 1976, p. 69. The discussion of class is largely informed by this study.

45. Ibid., p. 36. On Labor, see M. A. Busteed and Hugh Mason, "Irish Labor in the 1969 Election," *Political Studies*, 18 (September 1970), 372–379. On stability, see Tom Garvin and Anthony Parker, "Party Loyalty and Irish Voters: The EEC Referendum as a Case Study," *ESR*, 4 (October 1972), 35–39; C. Gillman, "Party Loyalty and Irish Voters: The EEC Referendum as a Case Study—A Comment," *ESR*, 4 (January 1973), 269–271; Garvin and Parker, "A Reply," *ESR*, 4 (January 1973), 273–275; C. McCarthy and T. Ryan, "Party Loyalty at Referenda and General Electives: Evidence from Recent Irish Contests," *ESR*, 7 (April 1976), 279–288. More generally on stability, see J. F. S. Ross, "Ireland," in S. Rokkan and J. Meyriat, eds., *International Guide to Electoral Statistics*, The Hague: Mauton, 1969; Tom Garvin, "Continuity and Change in Irish Electoral Politics, 1923–1969," *ESR*, 3 (April 1972), 359–372; Enid Lakeman, "The Irish Voter—1968 Pattern," *Parliamentary Affairs*, 22 (Spring 1969), 170–174.

46. Garvin, *ESR* (1977), p. 172. The discussion of center-periphery cleavages is largely informed by this study and Garvin, *EJPR* (1974) and Carty, op. cit.

47. See *The Irish Times*, June 30, 1977, p. 10 and June 20, p. 1.

48. Chubb (1974), pp. 94–95.

49. Garvin, *EJPR*, p. 317.

50. Ibid., p. 321.

CHAPTER 11

AUSTRIA

Margareta Mommsen-Reindl

Preliminary Remarks

THE POLITICAL LANDSCAPE of contemporary Austria is usually characterized as a "lame" three-party system or a "two-and-a-half" party system.[1] The
two major parties are the Socialist Party of Austria (SPO) and the Austrian
People's party (OVP). The Liberal Party of Austria (FPO) is considered the
"lame" element. The fourth party, the Communist Party of Austria (KPO), is
numerically so weak that it is not necessary to consider it in this connection.

The relative strength of the Austrian parties has scarcely changed since the
resurrection of the Austrian Republic in 1945.[2] In the First Republic, which
lasted from 1918 to 1945, the numerical relationship between the parties was
also virtually the same as it is today. But, whereas during the First Republic a
bourgeois bloc of the right predominated, in the Second Republic a Great
Coalition between the two major parties ruled for over 20 years. The longevity
of joint rule led some political scientists to conclude that the structure of the
Austrian party system made coalition government unavoidable.[3] But the
collapse of the coalition in 1966 refuted this analysis, and now the Anglo-
Saxon model of weak one-party rule with a strong opposition seems to best
characterize Austrian political life.

Although the advent of one-party rule in 1966 seems to have been a turning
point in the political system of Austria, this development scarcely altered the
usual forms of interaction between the major parties; "consociational democracy" and "proportional democracy"—concepts developed during the Great
Coalition period to explain Austrian politics—are thus still held valid by many

278

political scientists today.[4] These two concepts encompass a number of interrelated phenomena: the patterns of interaction between the political parties, the ideological belief systems of the parties, the attitudes of party members toward the solution of political conflict, the internal structure of the mass parties and the relationship of the mass parties to other factors in the system such as the church and the ministerial bureaucracy, and, finally, the relationship of the voters to the political parties and their different subcultures.

The contemporary relationship of the Austrian political parties to one another can best be understood by examining briefly the historical development of the Austrian political system. This background will also illuminate the unique profile of each party and thus enable us to answer specific questions about party organization and voting behavior in contemporary Austria.

The Parties' Development Within the Political System

Although political parties emerged with the parliamentarization of the Hapsburg Empire in the 1860s, many obstacles hindered the development of modern forms of political life: multinational fragmentation, restricted and indirect suffrage (*curiae*), and the limited range of parliamentary rights.[5] Nonetheless, a political right and left formed during the first years of parliamentary life. The left saw itself as the constitutional party; that is, its major task was to defend the newly acquired political rights. The right, on the other hand, considered itself the protector of the historic rights of the individual crown lands, not only against possible usurpations by the monarchy but also against the political left. The organization of these two blocks was at first quite rudimentary. A number of loosely bound parliamentary clubs rather than sharply defined political parties characterized the system. The early political polarization within the Imperial Parliament (*Reichsrat*) was not the outcome of parliamentary rules but, rather, resulted from a crisis of legitimacy. It was precisely the question of whether the new Reichsrat was a legitimate political institution which divided the two blocs.[6]

The franchise reform of 1882 extended political rights to the petty bourgeoisie and the peasantry of all the monarchy's nationalities. Not surprisingly, this electoral reform did not assuage parliamentary antagonism as was hoped but, rather, brought new socially hostile groups into the Reichsrat. Moreover, thanks to the homogeneous curiae and constituencies, not only did other social groups form new parties, but the non-German nationalities were politicized. And, in addition to these new political centrifugal forces represented in the Reichsrat, there arose extraparliamentary groups, the first being Georg von Schoenerer's Pan German League, followed later by the Christian

Social Union, created by the Catholic Social reformers. In 1889, the Social Democratic party reemerged as the Marxist spokesman of the growing working class.

Universal manhood suffrage introduced in 1907 brought large contingents from these hitherto extraparliamentary parties into the Reichsrat. Of the 516 Reichsrat deputies elected in 1907, 96 were Christian Socials and 86 Social Democrats, making these two parties undisputably the strongest among the parliamentary factions. A comparison of the parliamentary clubs in the Reichsrat in 1887 with the party constellation of 1907 shows that a basic change had taken place in the structure of the Austrian party system.[7]

The older "intraparliamentary parties" that arose on the basis of specific political demands and later functioned as political platforms for the various nationalities of the monarchy gradually dissolved, their members drifting to the new mass parties. Thus many conservatives found a new home in the Christian Social party, whereas former Liberals joined forces with the German National Association (*Deutscher Nationalverband*).

The new political structure and culture born in 1907 inherited some of the characteristics of the old political order. Corresponding to the sharpening of the nationality conflict and social strife in the years before universal manhood suffrage was the increasingly ideological character of the parties after 1907. Each party now sought to embody the opposition to the Imperial government, and this further strengthened the trend toward political fragmentation and sectionalization. The increasing encapsulation of the parties in ideological shells served a double function. On the one hand, it was a shield against the Imperial executive, on the other, a weapon against other social groups. The growth of party subcultures further hardened the traditional divisions along class and ideological lines. Trade unions and peasant associations increasingly rallied to the ideological banners of the parties.

This emergence of blocks organized along coherent ideological and societal axes has been characterized by the military term *Lager* (encampment).[8] This concept indicates not only the militancy of the political parties and their subcultures, but also their mutual intransigence. Even after the collapse of the monarchy in 1918 freed the parliamentary system from the incumbencies of Imperial prerogative and the predominance of the ministerial bureaucracy, it proved difficult to regulate political conflict, for the parties remained the shock troops of a society divided into hostile political encampments.

But for a short time hostilities were temporarily suspended. Military defeat in 1918 discredited Old Austria and created a revolutionary situation. Politicians from all three Lager found themselves summoned to constitute German-Austria as a new state. The Social Democratic theoretician Otto Bauer described the founding of the new Austrian Republic in these words: "The German-Austrian state had emerged from a *contrat social*, a state-founding treaty between the political parties representing the classes of the

German-Austrian people."[9] Thus the common task of creating a new state had led to a temporary consensus among the class enemies. In this atmosphere of cooperation in the face of a common crisis arose the first great coalition of the Christian Socials and the Social Democrats.

Otto Bauer ascribed this development to an "equilibrium of class forces."[10] In a similar cooperative spirit the major parties wrote the Constitution of 1920, a document which seemed to provide the basis for the full development of parliamentary life. Moreover, the election results of 1919 seemed to promise a viable parliamentary system: The Social Democrats obtained 41% of the vote, the Christian Social party 36%, and the liberal national groups 18%. The last group included the Pan German People's party and the Agrarians (*Landbund*).

In all subsequent elections the major parties always captured at least 75% of the vote, whereas the Liberal Nationals could never rally more than 12% of the electorate. The consistency of voting patterns from the last election in the monarchy in 1911 into the Second Republic conforms to the aforementioned model of the "two-and-a-half" or "lame" three-party system. But this model, which attempts to explain the stability of a political system by referring to the relative strength of the competing parties, fails to explain subsequent Austrian developments. Indeed, the fate of the First Republic shows that a willingness to cooperate with political opponents and mutual tolerance are of much greater importance to political stability than mere numerical considerations. Closer examination of Austrian conditions finally led one critical observer to the conclusion that the First Austrian Republic reflected a *bipolar* party structure with very strong centrifugal tendencies. The resultant conclusion was that "the Austrian system could survive only on convergent drives" but that between 1919 and 1933 these drives were divergent."[11]

The political culture of a "divided society" that characterized the last decades of the monarchy increasingly took on the form of a bipolar antagonism during the crisis years of the First Republic, bringing the parties to the verge of civil war. Unschooled in parliamentarianism and imprinted by a militant "Lager mentality," the signatories of the contrat social of 1918 squandered all chances for internal stability within the republic. The general crisis of legitimacy of the political system was intensified by external threats. The sharpening of the internal political crisis therefore went along with the growing ideologization and politization of the Lager. A milestone on the path to the final deadlock was the militarization of politics in the form of paramilitary forces. On the right were the Defense Leagues (*Heimwehren*), split into two camps, one chiefly Christian Socials, the other of Nationals; on the left stood the republican Protective Association (*Schutzbund*). The Schutzbund and Heimwehren were originally self-defense organizations against internal and external threats. As such, they were no danger to the republic. Only with the sharpening of political conflict and the advent of the so-called "crisis of parliamentarism" did these private armies become a grave obstacle to the creation of political consensus. In addition to these paramilitary forces, the rise of national socialism and the depression further undermined the fragile basis of Austrian democracy.

The programmatic war of party ideologies began at the latest in 1926, when the Social Democrats announced their Linz Program. To counter a possible dismantling of democracy by the right, the Linz Program called for a "dictatorship of the working class." In a similar fashion, the Christian Socials glorified in their party programs clerical and corporatist ideals.[12]

It was commonly feared that the party that won the majority would change the state according to its own ideology. The coup of 1934 justified this apprehension. The death of parliamentary life was followed by the bloody defeat of the Social Democrats in February 1934 and the erection of an authoritarian corporatist state. All traces of pluralistic party life disappeared for years to come.

This so-called "*Dollfuss-Schuschnigg* era" was followed in 1938 by the incorporation of Austria into the Third Reich. But 11 years of authoritarian and Nazi rule did not destroy all Austrian democratic traditions or forces. On the contrary, the bitter experience of national socialist oppression led to a certain rapprochement between the Austrian right and the left, pushing these groups to the conclusion that mutual respect and a willingness to compromise had to replace a "Lager mentality" and the self-fulfilling prophecies of secular religions.

In Nazi concentration camps and in the Resistance movement, the leading moderates of the Christian Socials and the Socialists were brought together. They began to prepare for a liberated Austria. The reconstitution of the Austrian Republic thus took place under the aegis of an epochal consensus between the two great parties, the bitter enemies of yesterday.

On April 27, 1945 the "executives of the political parties of Austria" proclaimed the restoration of the republic. Representatives of all of the so-called "democratic parties" formed a provisional government.[13] Due to the Soviet presence, the Communists, who had been a miniscule force in the First Republic, attained parity with the two major parties in the provisional government. This lasted, however, only until the first parliamentary elections in November 1945. Then the successor party to the Christian Socials, the OVP polled 50%, the SPO 45%, and the Communists 5% of the vote. 480,000 Austrian citizens were prohibited from voting in the election because of their "Nazi past." Similarly, the Allied military authorities refused to allow members of the earlier "national" Lager to stand for election.

The election results gave the OVP the possibility of forming a single-party government. It was considered essential, however, to continue cooperating with the SPO. It was not only easier for a coalition government based on a broad majority to represent Austrian interests via-à-vis the four occupation powers, but, above all, such common political responsibility would facilitate the internal "restoration" of Austria. Indeed, during the election the OVP advocated creating the conditions necessary for a "democracy of equality" (*Demokratie der Gleichberechtigung*).[14] The legitimacy of the Austrian political system depended on mastering this task.

The great coalition at the beginning of the First Republic had been, to a large extent, merely an "armistice in the class war." Consequently, it had soon collapsed. By way of contrast, the coalition in the Second Republic was intended to be a permanent feature of political life. The class struggle would no longer be fought out on the streets but, rather, negotiated in the government's conference chambers. After much reflection both parties had concluded that it was prudent to negotiate political conflict. As their new People's party name Volkspartei indicated, the successors to the Christian Socials sought to secularize their party. Seeing itself as the new "party of the middle," the OVP professed "democratic ideals," "solidarity," and "the knightly form of settling conflict between political opponents."[15] The party's program as well as innumerable writings appearing with the party's imprimatur proclaimed that this new faith was not merely lip service to democratic ideals.

In the socialist camp, it was the moderate leaders Renner, Helmer, and Schärf, who now set the party's course. After the November elections of 1945, Schärf rejected Otto Bauer's view that the SPO was destined by nature to play the role of an opposition.[16] Schärf insisted that only within the government could the SPO be certain of influencing the democratic development of the country. Despite protests from the former revolutionary socialists against what they saw as a fatal willingness to compromise the interests of the working class, the moderates refused to change course. The SPO's "action program" of 1947 insisted that "the free play of political parties is the necessary basis of democracy."[17] Implicitly, the Linz Program of 1926 which had contained the threat of a dictatorship of the proletariat was now obsolete.

In fact, cooperation between the major parties became the basic feature of Austrian political life for the next two decades. After each election to the Nationalrat in 1949, 1953, 1956, 1959, and 1962, the coalition pact was renewed. The theory of an "equilibrium of the classes" advanced in 1918 was replaced by a new theory of equilibrium which ascribed to a quasi-fatalistic perpetuation of the coalition. Empirically, this theory was based on the results of the parliamentary elections and the elections of the federal president.[18] The political pendulum swung regularly from right to left, if only slightly.

Each parliamentary election "corrected" the results of the last; the election results led perforce to new coalition negotiations. Curiously, the loser in the election was usually the winner of the coalition negotiations; that is, despite election losses the losing party could preserve its position. Finally, although there was always a "black" (OVP) federal chancellor, the SPO found compensation in the repeated election of one of their own to the office of federal president. All these developments seemed to augur well for the continuation of the Great Coalition.[19]

In addition to this electoral geometry, there were yet other factors which were of decisive importance for this extended cooperation. Above all, both political parties persisted in the wish to avoid anything which could again lead to the *itio in partes* or polarization of the First Republic. Characteristic of this political psychology of voluntarism was the generally recognized necessity of continuing cooperation, even after the state treaty of 1955 ended the four-power occupation that resulted in a fundamental increase in freedom of maneuver in domestic politics. Even if, especially at the beginning of the Second Republic, the exertions to political cooperation had been forged by the difficult task of asserting Austrian interest against the "four elephants in the Austrian rowboat,"[20] there is no reason to overestimate the impact of the stabilization introduced from the outside by the occupying powers. Rather, the most important reason for the persistence of the coalition appears to have been an internal one. The new system of conflict resolution had indeed become the indispensable determinant of politics.

The decision-making process of this coalition system has been characterized by the terms "concordance," *Proporz* (proportionality), or "consociational" democracy.[21] Basic to the functioning of the coalition system are two factors, the aforementioned psychological factor of goodwill and the specific organizational structures of the parties, such as their interrelationships with various interest groups.

In relation to the second factor, we will discuss the importance of the interpenetration of the parties and the interest groups. Suffice it here to say that the three organizational and ideological camps persisted into the Second Republic. Albeit that these camps now fought with blunted ideological weapons, they were still distinguished by a dense organizational structure which included innumerable ties to various pressure groups. Within each Lager, the articulation of political interests occurred in the parties and the great interest groups. These interests were then aggregated and negotiated through common political institutions vis-à-vis the coalition partner.

The coalition pact which was bargained out at the beginning of each legislative period established common responsibility between the two major parties, specifically excluding all other parties.[22] A rigid coalition contract carved out political preserves for each party. The election results and the outcome of the coalition negotiations served as the key to the distribution of power. This was what was meant by "proportionality"—the right of appointments within the allocated preserve. This patronage of office led to a thoroughgoing politicization of many branches of the administration.

The heart of the system beat in the coalition executive where both parties were equally represented. The decisions reached here were binding for the parliamentary deputies of each party which, to be sure, also meant a certain denaturation of the classical functions of Parliament. Nevertheless, there was also a place for control and opposition in this proportional democracy. It took the forms of the so-called "departmental" opposition and the "built-in" opposition.[23] Departmental opposition permitted each coalition partner to criticize the activities of the other partner within his preserve. State secretaries usually served this monitoring function, for it had become common practice to appoint, for example, an SPO state secretary in a ministry controlled by the OVP.

It was in the coalition committee and in the cabinet that the principle of built-in opposition came into play, and this decisively shaped the decision-making process. In short, compromise was unavoidable. Years of cooperation made the governing partners increasingly innovative in the art of political bargaining. In Austrian slang the word *Packeln* (horse trading) was used to characterize the new political culture. In the parlance of political science, it was called "concordance strategy" or "consociational behavior."

The specific structure of the decision-making process, to which belonged the organizations and subcultures peculiar to each party, became an independent factor in the maintenance of the system. But, by the end of the 1950s, the first cracks in the political regime appeared: The psychological necessity to cooperate faded as the older generation of politicians committed to cooperation died out. Consequently, crises became increasingly frequent. The taboo against coalitions with the "third camp" disappeared; during the "Hapsburg crisis" of 1963, parliament even temporarily regained its original sovereignty as the battleground of political conflict. In the last years of the coalition, signs increased that the supporters of the coalition system were striving to emancipate themselves from each other, while the proportional system emancipated itself from its original supporters.[24]

When the elections of 1966 gave a majority to the OVP, coalition government collapsed. To be sure, the OVP shied away from assuming sole governmental responsibility. But, after the usual coalition negotiations got nowhere, the step to an alternating two-party system had to be taken. Although the momentary solution of 1966 appeared to many to be a temporary solution, it has in fact lasted until the present, although this new model of one-party government has been under the SPO's flag since 1970.

That a smooth transition from the system of the Great Coalition to the Anglo-Saxon form of party government took place probably had two major causes. The common endeavors of both political parties led to a closing of the confidence gap which had killed the First Republic. In the Second Republic both parties had proved their legitimizing role and thus made possible an alternating one-party government. Each could allow the other to rule without fearing for its own existence. Naturally, one-party rule today does not exclude possible coalition governments in the future. Another important reason for the smooth Anglicization of Austria is to be seen in the fact that despite one-party rule many structures of the old proportional democracy, and with them the typical Austrian attitude toward compromising, have remained. "The coalition may be dead, the *Proporz* mentality is not,"[25] wrote Peter Pulzer.

This attitude toward democracy is grounded in the structure of the political parties, their subcultures, and the institutional limitations imposed on both the ruling and opposition parties. Thus, to evaluate the viability of democracy in contemporary Austria, we now turn to the structure of these parties and the development of Austrian voting behavior patterns.

The Structure of the Electorate

Two basic factors characterize voting behavior in Austria: a high degree of voter participation and, as already mentioned, the fundamental loyalty of the voter to one of the two political Lager (see Table 11–1).

The high level of voter participation is primarily due to the electorate's strong loyalty to the traditional Lager. The Lager mentality inculcates in each member the duty to vote for his party. This same sociopsychological motive helps explain the consistency of voter preference.

As is indicated in Table 11–2, a threefold division of votes has increasingly given way to a bipolar system. This concentration upon the two major parties could lead one to the conclusion that Austria is finally developing into a classical two-party system. Before making this conclusion, however, one must take into account the possible effects of the most recent electoral reform. In contrast to the ideal model of the two-party system, this reform reasserted the principle of distributing Nationalrat seats according to the proportion of votes received by all parties. Furthermore, fond memories of coalition government are still alive, and such a government, as opposed to one-party rule, still remains a possibility.

It is interesting to note that the percentage of uncommitted voters has climbed from 5% to 10% since the Great Coalition. There also have been noteworthy changes in the occupational structure of the electorate (see Table 11–3).

There are unquestionably definite social blocks primarily adhering to each party and largely corresponding to the occupational groups. However, as is shown by the occupational composition of the OVP and FPO vote, these blocks are by no means monolithic. Furthermore, some occupational groups, such as the white-collar workers and civil servants, are less inclined to vote the party line than are other groups, say, peasants and blue-collar workers. Moreover, even within these last two groups, which have traditionally been strongly identified with specific Lager, there is a perceptible shift in voter loyalties.

The SPO itself has spoken of its "epochal" successes in the peasant villages,[26] whereas the OVP has been able to attract an increasing number of blue-collar workers. To be sure, these shifts are less important than changes in voter behavior caused by the general change of social structure. In any case, on the basis of both developments one can predict a continual blurring between the traditional Austrian Lager.

TABLE 11-1. Elections to the Nationalrat 1919–1975 (Percent)

	1919	1920	1923	1927	1930	1945	(1945)	1949	1953	1956	1959	1962	1966	1970	1971	1975
CSP/ÖVP	35.9	41.8	45.0	41.4	41.9	49.8	(42.9)	44.0	41.3	46.0	44.2	45.4	48.4	44.9	43.1	43.0
SDP/SPÖ	40.8	36.0	39.6	42.3	41.1	44.6	(38.4)	38.7	42.1	43.0	44.8	44.0	42.6	48.4	50.0	50.4
"3. Lager"	18.4	17.3	12.8	13.1	15.0	0	(13.9)	11.7	10.9	6.5	7.7	7.1	5.3	5.5	5.5	5.4
KPÖ	0	1.0	0.7	0.4	0.6	5.4	(4.7)	5.1	5.3	4.4	3.3	3.0	0.4	0.9	1.4	1.2
Others	4.9	4.0	2.0	2.8	0.6	0.2	(0.1)	0.5	0.4	0.1	0.1	0.5	3.3	0.3	—	—
Voter participation	84	80	87	89	90	94	97	97	96	96	94	94	94	92	—	—

287

TABLE 11–2. Major Party Voting Trend

ELECTIONS TO THE NR	TWO GREAT PARTIES	OTHERS
1920	77.8	22.2
1930	76.8	23.2
1949	82.7	17.3
1959	89.0	11.0
1970	93.1	6.9
1971	93.1	6.9

1920 and 1930: Social Democrats and Christian Socials; then SPÖ and ÖVP.

TABLE 11–3. Occupational Structure of the Electorate (Percent)

	SPÖ		ÖVP		FPÖ	
	1969	1973	1969	1973	1969	1973
Professionals, self-employed	2	5	13	16	11	11
White collar workers, civil servants	25	30	29	34	40	55
Blue collar workers	68	62	23	25	26	29
Farmers	5	3	35	25	23	5
	100	100	100	100	100	100

HOW MANY OF THESE ELECTORS ARE PARTY MEMBERS?

In comparison with various parties in other democracies, both major Austrian parties are characterized by an above average organizational density. They are indeed typical membership parties which have bound a high percentage of their voters organizationally to the party (see Table 11–4).

The key to understanding this fact is again to be found in the ever-present traditions of the Lager. The precursors of the great parties, understanding themselves parties of social integration, always sought to extend the organizational framework of their parties so as to make every voter a party member. This organizational principle still determines the profile of both political parties and explains the party's strong tendencies toward bureaucratic

TABLE 11–4. Organizational Density: Voters and Party Members (in thousands)

	VOTERS	MEMBERS	ORGANIZATIONAL DENSITY
SPÖ	2.280	698	30.6
ÖVP	1.965	838	42.5
FPÖ	248	30	12.1

organization and internal discipline. The Lager mentality—the complete identification with a specific political party—chiefly explains why so many Austrians carry a party book.

Of the many motives for party membership those of tradition and protection are of particular importance to the Austrians, not a specific participatory engagement. A party member in Austria expresses his loyalty to the party chiefly by paying membership dues and, of course, by voting. To this extent the membership of the large parties in contemporary Austria has been largely reduced to the role of regularly voting the party line.

PARTY ORGANIZATION AND INTERNAL DEMOCRACY

The party organization of the OVP is characterized by so-called *bündische* or professional structures as well as by federal components. The party rests on the following five pillars: the Austrian League of Workers and Employees (*Österreichischer Arbeiter-und Angestelltenbund*, OAAB), the Austrian Peasant's League (*Österreichischer Bauernbund*, OBB), the Austrian Business League (*Österreichischer Wirtschaftsbund*, OWB), the Austrian Women's Movement (*Österreichische Frauenbewegung*), and the Austrian Youth Movement (*Österreichische Jugendbewegung*). The three leagues (*Bünde*) clearly reflect the corporate traditions of the Christian Social Lager. On the basis of members brought into the party, the power relationship between the three leagues is as follows: OAAB 45.6%, OBB 38.4%, and OWB 16.1%.[27]

The internal structure of the party can be seen in the threefold division of power among the leagues. In view of the relatively few party members mobilized, the OWB appears to be overrepresented. The principle of parity between the leagues also applies to the division of government offices and in the composition of the OVP fraction in the Nationalrat. At the state (Land) level, however, the threefold parity principle is most strongly enforced. At the Land level, the leagues enjoy a high degree of autonomy. As the traditional heartland of the OVP, Lower Austria was regularly overrepresented within the leadership of the leagues in comparison with the other Länder. Most of the top politicians since 1945 such as Leopold Figl (chancellor from 1945 to 1953) and Julius Raab (chancellor from 1953 to 1961) have come from Lower Austria.

The leagues are financially autonomous: membership subscription is fixed by each provincial league. Ten percent of membership dues are turned over to the federal party executive. The leagues may adopt their own programs and statutes. Whereas the OBB resembles an umbrella organization for the Peasant Leagues of each Land, the OWB acts more as an economic interest organization. Only the OAAB has its own program, understanding itself as "a political movement for christian social theory in all aspects of society."[28]

Moreover, the OAAB is distinguished by a hierarchical organization. Thanks to its continual membership increase, the OAAB appears to be the most dynamic of the three federations. This gradual shift in power between the leagues is undoubtedly in large part due to the general change in the social structure.

Unlike the SPO, which has a dense network of organizations affiliated with the party, the OVP has only a few unimportant auxiliary organizations. Whereas in the SPO the coming generation rises through the party's affiliates, for the OVP a number of Roman Catholic organizations which are only loosely bound to the party serve as the ladders to political prominence. The most important recruiting ground for party leaders is undoubtedly the Catholic Student League (*Cartellverband der Katholischen Studentenverbindungen*, CV). It surprised no one that the federal chancellors, the party's presidents, and its general secretaries, at least until 1970, came from this organization.

In contrast to the loose structure of the OVP, the SPO is strongly centralized, has a large number of affiliated organizations, and binds its membership directly to the party. In keeping with tradition, the Land organization of "Red Vienna" recruits the greatest number of party members and provides most of the party's leaders. Although the influence of the party's Land organizations has increased since 1945, this has by no means led to a federalization of the party. Nonetheless, a more equitable geographic distribution of seats in the various party organizations has occurred, above all, in the unitary party executive, which was created in 1967.[29]

In addition to a high degree of organizational density, the functionary density of the SPO, the number of party members holding the office of trustee (*Vertrauensmann*), is particularly striking. Trustees constitute nearly 10% of the party's membership. This army of minor officeholders exercises functions corresponding to the model of engaged party activists. To be sure, one of the most important functions of the trustee is the rather prosaic task of collecting party dues.

The extensive internal differentiation of the socialist Lager becomes clear when one examines the number and variety of party affiliates—to name only a few, the parents' organization *Kinderfreunde*, the Central Association of Amateur Gardeners, Settlers and Small Animal Breeders, the sports league Askö, and the League of Socialist Academics, Intellectuals, and Artists. The last organization serves as the recruiting ground for the party elite and thus functions for the SPO as the Cartellverband does for the OVP.

The procedures involved in the nomination of candidates within the two major parties sheds some light on how each party practices internal party democracy. Both parties naturally advocate the principle of party democracy. The party statutes, however, reveal the trend toward oligarchy, which in practice is far stronger than even these statutes indicate.[30] In the OVP the democratic principle is undermined even in the selection of chiefs (*Obmänner*) for the leagues. They are "elected" by only a small circle of party functionaries and delegates. For example, the Obmann of the OBB is named by its federal executive (*Bundesvorstand*) from among the members of the OBB's executive committee; these members are themselves ex officio members of the federal executive. Nor are the executive committee or the federal executive democratically elected. To be sure, members are recruited from OBB, government, and members of parliament on the one hand and delegates from the *Land* Peasant Leagues, the Presidential Conference of the Chambers of Agriculture, and the agricultural cooperatives on the other hand. But, instead of democratic elections from top to bottom, reciprocal delegations of the leading groups within the party pass back and forth in an almost impenetrable confusion. Without a doubt, the OVP has to struggle with integration problems because of its league structure. This is reflected in the latent tension between the federal party leadership and the various leagues. Finally, as is characteristic of a stable party oligarchy, the party leaders and general secretaries of the OVP, once elected, hold their offices for a long time.

Until 1967 it was the rule within the SPO that, while the party convention (*Parteitag*) elected the 50-member party executive composed of the executive (*Parteivorstand*) and the central commission (*Parteikontrolle*), the rank-and-file was excluded from all further nominations. Instead, the executive, once elected, filled the other party offices such as the president, the vice president, the treasurer, the general secretary, and so forth. The 1967 Convention, however, changed the statutes so that subsequent appointments by the party chairman (*Parteivorsitzender*) and his vice chairman required the approval of the convention; this confirmation is decided by secret ballot.

The conventions rarely serve as forums for political disputes. Occasionally, however—and this also applies to the conventions of the OVP   the question of the successor of the party chairman can lead to open conflict.

The selection of candidates within the major parties corresponds only faintly to the ideal type of internal party democracy.[31] The behavior of the party leaders is in fact usually oriented toward those sections of the electorate it hopes to woo in the next election, not to the wishes of party members. This attitude is particularly pronounced in the OVP; undoubtedly the loose affiliation of members to this party exaggerates the tendency towards the extraparty orientation of its leaders. In selecting candidates for the Nationalrat, the seniority principle holds sway in both parties. That is, the "safe" places on the party list are assigned to those party members who, like civil servants, have made a career chiefly by time serving. Within the OVP the seniority principle operates within the leagues, where, to be sure, it is supplemented by the aforementioned inner-league proportionality principle. To democratize candidate selection, the OVP experimented with the American form of primary elections in 1969 and 1970. This had only a limited success, however, since there was no open campaigning and the election results were only partially published.

In the SPO, the seniority principle chiefly functions within the framework of the party's Land organizations. In selecting candidates for the Nationalrat, the federal party executive acted in accordance with the competent Land executives. This meant that as a rule the federal party executive approved the suggestions given to it "from below" and thereby revealed the relatively strong position of the middle-level organizations within the party. In the interest of "central party necessity," the SPO organizational statutes were changed in 1968; henceforth, to prevent the self-perpetuation of the "apparatus," there would be a freer selection of candidates.[32] Recently, the seniority principle has increasingly been supplemented by the technocratic career model. In both parties the increasing applicability of this new model is reflected in the candidacy of party members for the Nationalrat or higher party offices who have been either "independent" or have not yet completely fulfilled their "time serving" within the party organization.

PARTY FINANCING

The financing of the Austrian mass parties is through three channels: membership dues and party taxes (*Parteisteuern*), individual and collective donations, and state financing.[33] The first source is usually not sufficient to cover a party's budget, especially in the case of the OVP as its leagues claim the lion's share of the membership dues. Party taxes are levied on party functionaries as a type of "remuneration" for the positions they hold. Similarly, party business undertakings such as newspapers and publishing houses contribute to the general party treasury.

For the OVP, donations from private industry are of particular importance. Collective donations are usually funneled into the parties' coffers through their affiliated organizations; whereas the Union of Austrian Industrialists supports the OVP, the SPO's budget profits from payments made by the Austrian Trade Union Federation.

Due to the ever precarious state of party finances, the call for state financing has become increasingly louder. Although there is still no general regulation providing for this type of support, there are already such agreements at the Land level.

THE INTERPENETRATION BETWEEN PARTIES
AND INTEREST GROUPS

Austria can be viewed as the prototype of the interest group state. The country is covered by a thick network of economic interest groups, many having their origins in the nineteenth century. These groups exercise such decisive influence in the political process that the question has been raised as to whether or not it would be more appropriate to designate Austria an interest group rather than a party state. But, considering the interpenetration of the parties and the interest groups, it is probably best not to even try to answer such a question. Rather, let us examine the extent of this interpenetration.

The four big interest groupings that rule the political scene are: the Trade Union Federation (OGB), the Chambers of Commerce, the Chambers of Agriculture, and the Chambers of Labor. Whereas the chambers are self-governing bodies in which membership is automatically granted, the unions are fundamentally voluntary organizations; two-thirds of all workers, however, are union members. Even if the OGB and the chambers are officially "above parties," party influence is clearly evident in these organizations. Thus the OGB is itself divided into party factions, whereas within the chambers officers are elected as representatives of the political parties.

In 1970 the distribution of party mandates within the highest organs of the large interest groups was as given in Table 11–5. Usually the SPO dominates the Chambers of Labor, whereas the OVP enjoys a comfortable majority in the Chambers of Commerce and Agriculture. Nonetheless, during the last decades certain structural changes can be perceived. For example, the OVP has continually been able to expand its influence in the chambers of workers and employees.

The interpenetration between the parties and interest groups is guaranteed by the strong presence of interest group members in the parties, in the Nationalrat, and in the government administration. The pivot between the SPO and the socialist-dominated associations is the "socialist fraction" within the OGB, a large partisan union that fills the key positions both within the OGB and as well as in the Chambers of Labor. For the OVP the leagues are the transmission belt between the party and the chambers; the OBB and the OWB have the majority in their respective chambers and thus influence these bodies according to the wishes of the party. Personal union is a further important factor in the coordination of the politics of the parties and interest groups. For instance, Julius Raab was federal president of both the Chamber of Commerce and the OWB on becoming chancellor in 1953; in the 1970s Anton Benya combines the presidency of the OGB with the vice presidency of the Nationalrat.

TABLE 11–5. Parties within the Interest Groups (Percent)

	SPÖ	*ÖVP*	*FPÖ*	*KPÖ*	*OTHERS*	*TOTAL*
Chambers of Commerce	10	85	—	—	5	100
Chambers of Agriculture	10	84	2	—	4	100
Chambers of Labor	69	24	5	1	1	100
Austrian Federation of Trade Unions	75	17	—	7	1	100

This interest group aggregation became a constituent part of the political system with the advent of the so-called "social partnership."[34] The institutional expression of this partnership is the Joint Commission on Prices and Wages (*Paritätische Kommission für Lohn- und Preisfragen*) in which the four major groups not only resolve specific wage and price questions but also address more general economic problems. Commentators on Austrian politics unanimously agree that the personal and institutional interpenetration between the parties and the interest groups represents the most important bridge between the two segments of Austrian society, thus guaranteeing both the dynamism and the stability of the political system.

Conclusions

Undoubtedly, Austria's political parties underwent many a change on the way from the monarchy to the republican 1970s. From class and ideological parties, they have turned into people's and platform parties which are obviously hard-pressed to rise to their own occasional challenges to bring about a "spiritual rebirth" in their programs. Already in the 1950s, Kurt L. Shell said of the SPO that "no other Socialist party has travelled a longer road faster from Left to Right."[35] This government party of today, in fact, regards itself as a middle-of-the-road party. It is portentous for the partnership among Austrian parties to read in the new SPO program of 1978 that the road to social democracy calls not for solitary effort but for "cooperation with the progressive-minded people in this country." The SPO is an "open party" and appreciates progressive forces even outside the Socialist movement, in "Catholicism and . . . Liberalism,"[36] two stand-in words for the other parties.

The OVP in its discussions of principles of recent years committed itself to coping better with modernity, a better quality of life, more self-government, and pluralism. Only the FPO has not yet managed (despite its quest to borrow images from the West German FDP) to discard its traditional exaggerated nationalism, an obsolete ideology.[37]

We may not be mistaken in concluding that the trends toward deideologization in both great parties, the rising percentage of the floating vote of recent elections, and the realignments going on among the voters, all point toward the image of more pragmatic and hence interchangeable party programs. Despite the heightened mobility shown by the voters, however, landslides in future Nationalrat elections are hardly to be expected. The all-too-solid Lager alignments of the past have retarded any quick and radical development in the prevailing voting patterns regardless of the manifest trends toward "opening up" of the campaigning parties.[38] Thus Austria's political profile will continue yet for a long time to be structured by high, if latent, party membership figures and the intensive "integration" of the citizen into Austrian society by means of party-affiliated mass organizations.

The political elites have not lost their touch for political horse-trading as long as the monopolistic paracoalitions between parties and interest groups can flourish even under one-party dominance. Such kinds of direct contacts and top-level bargaining seem to be as beneficial to the stability of the system as is the relative isolation of the average party member behind the protective shield of his Lager. We can learn from Austria that competitive politics and "concordance democracy" need not be mutually exclusive. In the course of a painful historical learning process, the political system developed this curious mixture of patterns. In the last analysis, however, the preference for political togetherness instead of destructive competition may be implicit in the rationale of a small state.

Notes

1. See Jean Blondel, *An Introduction to Comparative Government*, London: Weidenfeld & Nicolson, 1969, p. 153 ff, advocating the term "two-and-a-half" party system; on the other hand, Wolfgang Mantl, in *Der österreichische Parteienstaat*, Retzhof Leibnitz: Volksbildungsheim, 1969, p. 26 speaks of a "lame" (*hinkendes*) three-party system.

2. See Table 11–1.

3. See, for instance, Gustav E. Kafka, *Die Einheit Österreichs*, Grazer Universitäts-reden, no. 2, Graz: Kienreich, 1966, p. 13; René Marcic, *Die Koalitions-demokratie*, Karlsruhe: Müller Verlag, 1966, p. 12.

4. See Gerhard Lehmbruch, "Politisches System und politische Kultur in der Schweiz und in Österreich," in *Recht und Staat in Geschichte und Gegenwart*, Tübingen: J. C. B. Mohr, 1967, pp. 225 ff; Arend Lijphart, *The Politics of Accommodation*, Berkeley-Los Angeles: University of California Press, 1968; Lijphart, "Typologies of Democratic Systems," *Comparative Political Studies*, 1 (1968), 3–44; Lijphart, "Consociational Democracy," *World Politics*, 21 (1968–1969), 207–225.

5. See Gustav Kolmer, *Parlament und Verfassung in Österreich*, vols. 1–8, Vienna: Carl Fromme, 1902–1914. See also Brita Skottsberg, *Der österreichische Parlamentarismus*, Göteborg: Elanders Boktryckeri, 1940, chap. 3, pp. 53 ff.

6. See Peter Pulzer, "The Legitimizing Role of Political Parties: The Second Austrian Republic," *Government and Opposition*, 4 (1969), 324–344. Pulzer's analysis of the parties in the monarchy focuses on its specific crisis of legitimacy.

7. See G. Kolmer, op. cit.

8. See Adam Wandruszka, "Österreichs politische Struktur," in H. Benedikt, ed., *Geschichte der Republik Österreich*, München: R. Oldenbourg, 1954, pp. 289–485; Alfred Diamant, "The Group Basis of Austrian Politics," *Journal of Central European Affairs*, 18 (1958), 134–155; Rudolf Steininger, *Polarisierung und Integration, Eine vergleichende Untersuchung der strukturellen Versäulung der Gesellschaft in den Niederlanden und in Österreich*, Meisenheim am Glan: Verlag Anton Hain, 1975.

9. Otto Bauer, *Die österreichische Revolution*, Vienna: Vorwärts, 1923, p. 96.

10. Ibid., pp. 126 ff.

11. Peter Pulzer, op. cit., p. 334.

12. See Klaus Berchtold, *Österreichische Parteiprogramme, 1868–1966*, München: R. Oldenbourg, 1967, pp. 34 ff., 59 ff.

13. See Karl Renner, *Denkschrift über die Geschichte der Unabhängigkeitserklärung Österreichs und Bericht über drei Monate Aufbauarbeit*, Österreichische Staatsdruckerei, Vienna, 1946, p. 19.

14. This was an election slogan of the ÖVP in the elections to the Nationalrat in November 1945; see the ÖVP journal *Österreichische Monatschefte*, 1 (November 1945).

15. See Leopold Figl in "Zum Geleit," in *Österreichische Monatshefte*, 3 (1947), 1.

16. *Parteitagsprotokoll SPO*, Vienna, 1945, pp. 85 ff.

17. *Parteitagsprotokoll SPO*, Vienna, 1947, p. 140.

18. See Table 11–1.

19. See Margareta Mommsen-Reindl, "Widersprüche in der Proporzdemokratie," *Politische Vierteljahresschrift* 15 (1974), 175–212 and, by the same author, *Die Österreichische Proporzdemokratie und der Fall Habsburg*, Vienna-Cologne-Graz: Hermann Böhlaus Nachf., 1976.

20. Lois Weinberger attributes these words to Karl Renner; see Lois Weinberger, *Tatsachen, Begegnungen und Gespräche*, Vienna: Österreicheischer Verlag, 1948, p. 281.

21. See note 4.

22. See Kurt Schneider, "Die Koalitionsvereinbarungen der österreichischen Regierungsparteien," in Rodney Stiefbold et al., eds., *Wahlen und Parteien in Österreich*, Vienna: Österreichischer Bundesverlag, 1966, pp. 779 ff.

23. See Frederick C. Engelmann, "Austria: The Pooling of Opposition," in Robert A. Dahl, ed., *Political Opposition in Western Democracies*, New Haven, Conn.: Yale University Press, 1966, pp. 270–273. Otto Kirchheimer, "Vom Wandel der politischen Oppositionen," *Archiv für Rechts- und Sozialphilosophie*, 43 (1957), 59–86.

24. See Margareta Mommsen-Reindl, *Die Österreichische Proporzdemokratie und der Fall Habsburg*, pp. 96 ff.

25. Peter Pulzer, "Austria," in Stanley Henig and John Pinder, eds., *European Political Parties*, London: G. Allen & Unwin, 1969, p. 314.

26. So did Chancellor Bruno Kreisky in an interview on Austrian television after the elections of 1971.

27. Anton Pelinka and Manfred Welan, *Demokratie und Verfassung in Österreich*, Vienna-Frankfürt-Zürich: Europa Verlag 1971, p. 287.

28. Kurt Steiner, *Politics in Austria, A Country Study*, Boston: Little, Brown, 1972, p. 143.

29. See Pelinka-Welan, op. cit., p. 304.

30. See Reinhold Knoll and Anton Mayer, *Österreichische Konsensdemokratie in Theorie und Praxis, Staat, Interessenverbände, Parteien und die politische Wirklichkeit*, Vienna-Cologne-Graz: Hermann Böhlaus Nachf., 1976, pp. 34 ff.

31. See Heinz Fischer, "Die parlamentarischen Fraktionen," in *Das politische System Österreichs*, op. cit., pp. 120 ff.

32. Ibid., p. 123.

33. For an evaluation on party financing, see Peter Gerlich, "Parteien zwischen Tradition und Reform," *Die Republik*, 2 (1973), 26:

	SPO	*OVP*	*FPO*
Membership dues and party taxes	64%	20%	19%
State financing	32	42	48
Donations	4	38	33
Total	100%	100%	100%

34. See Egon Matzner, "Funktionen der Sozialpartnerschaft," in *Heinz Fischer*, ed., *Das politische System Österreichs*, op. cit., pp. 429 ff. See also Knoll and Mayer, op. cit., pp. 105 ff.

35. Kurt L. Shell, *The Transformation of Austrian Socialism*, New York: State University of New York, 1962, p. 4.

36. See the special issue of the *Österreichische Zeitschrift für Politikwissenschaft*, 7 (1978), entitled "Ideologiedebatte in den Parteien." See especially Norbert Leser, "Die SPO gibt sich ein Programm. Analyse des Gestaltwandels von Programmvorbereitungen," pp. 141–154, Egon Matzner, "Zu den wissenschaftlichen Grundlagen des Entwurfs des neuen Parteiprogramms der SPO," pp. 157–171, and Peter Diem, "Zu den Grundsätzen des neuen SPO-Programms und seiner Genese," ibid., pp. 187–198.

37. Ibid., pp. 173 ff. and pp. 209 ff.

38. See Klaus Liepelt, "Esquisse d'une typologie des électeurs allemands et autrichiens," *Revue française de Sociologie*, 9 (Janaury–March 1968), 13–32.

CHAPTER 12

SPAIN AND PORTUGAL

Howard J. Wiarda

SPAIN AND PORTUGAL have long been considered a part of Europe, and yet apart from it. This is true not only in a geographic sense (Lisbon is still a solid four days' driving time from Paris, Madrid three) but in a social, political, economic, psychological, even moral sense as well. A recent American secretary of state was not the first European to let slip that he didn't really understand very well those nations that lay over the Pyrenees (and in his case, a certain unspecified nation that lay over the Alps as well).[1]

At least from the time of Charlemagne and Roland,[2] there has existed a certain European prejudice toward Iberia, and a certain vague hostility. This historic prejudice undoubtedly has complex racial, social, cultural, religious, and political roots. At the same time the sense of both distance and rejection which the nations of Iberia feel has bred in them a sense of separateness, a certain national inferiority complex and, frequently, a desire to "go it alone" regardless of the wishes of Northern Europe, to strike off in their own directions and thumb their noses at a Europe that refuses to treat them as equals and cannot appreciate distinctively Iberian ways and institutions.

During the long Franco and Salazar eras this sense of isolation, distance, and rejection continued—of course at least as much for the nature of these regimes as for any historic prejudices. Spain and Portugal remained outcasts of the European community, a position that often strengthened their own resolve to maintain the distance and distinctiveness of their sociopolitical structures. But the long-standing authoritarian regimes of these two nations have by now been relegated to the past, either by revolution (in the case of Portugal since 1974) or a very rapid evolution (in the case of Spain since 1975). In their place

298

has come the new institutional structures of "democracy," including democracy's various accoutrements: a gamut of political parties, a full-fledged party system, elections, and "party" government. This transition has been accompanied by a new opening toward Europe on the part of the Iberian nations, a sense that they are no longer outcasts but part of the Western democratic community, as well as a new acceptability and legitimacy for Spain and Portugal in European liberal and social-democratic circles.[3]

In this chapter we shall be assessing the role and functions of political parties and the party systems of Spain and Portugal, focusing specifically on the transition from the authoritarian politics of the Franco and Salazar eras to the more open and democratic period of the present. The questions we will be focusing on are these: What was the nature of "party" politics under the Franco and Salazar regimes? To what degree was this "distinctive"? How well have the newer parties of the post-Franco and post-Salazar eras been institutionalized? What are the role and functions of elections in these systems? To what degree have party government, democracy, and representative rule now been established? Ultimately the question to which we shall return is the one with which we began, namely, to what extent does Europe still stop at the Pyrenees, how accurate is the assessment that Spain and Portugal are now part of the Western democratic community, and to what degree do parties, party government, and systemic politics in Iberia still diverge from, or correspond to, the broader European model, as described in this book?

Parties and the Party System: Their Multifaceted Dimensions

The Spanish and Portuguese party systems, like the party systems of other nations, can be approached from a variety of perspectives. One can, for example, focus on the ideological spectrum and policy goals presented by the parties. One can concentrate on their organizational structure and the classic distinctions between cadre and mass parties. Their electoral bases may be studied in order to formulate certain theses about voting behavior. Or one may deal with the parliamentary party, as well as its extraparliamentary organization, in the making and unmaking of governments, the passing of legislation, parliamentary debates, and the like.[4]

All these approaches may be constructively utilized in the examination of the Spanish and Portuguese parties and party systems. But the suspicion remains that these may not necessarily be the only, or the most useful, approaches to studying Iberian parties and politics. The question is still open, in fact, as to whether parties and elections in Iberia stand for or mean the same thing as elsewhere in Europe, whether the "party phenomena" really describe adequately where political power lies and how it is manipulated, whether there are not other more important political arenas and centers of power and decision making to which the parties remain peripheral.[5]

In Spain and Portugal the fact the parties which have recently burst forth still operate frequently at the periphery rather than the center of national politics may in part be explained by the very short history of the parties, their submergence under protracted authoritarian rule, the long-time restrictions on their activities and the downright repression they often felt, the absence of trained cadres, leaders, and the like. These factors help explain the lack of institutionalization, the relative weakness and fragility of the parties—and of democracy itself—in both Spain and Portugal.

But there are other explanations as well, which provide us with a number of provocative approaches, in addition to those already mentioned, for understanding parties and the party systems of Iberia. These have to do with the relations of the parties to a state structure which has historically been far stronger and more important than the parties themselves; the nature of broad, nationwide systems of patron-client relations which frequently render the parties of secondary importance; the tentative nature of elections in both Spain and Portugal and the fact that other legitimized routes to power (such as the skillfully executed coup d'état, the heroic guerrilla struggle, direct action in streets and factories) also remain open; the existence of other "parties," such as the church, the army, or the financial oligarchy, which may have more importance in domestic politics than do the parties themselves; and the pervasive presence of corporatist and functionalist influences and modes of representation based on a structure of group, regional, or sectoral privileges and *fueros*, hierarchical and inegalitarian assumptions and, hence, the denial of some of the fundamental assumptions of democratic rule, such as the principle of one man, one vote.[6] These areas merit our serious attention as much as do the more conventional approaches to parties and party systems.

Intraparty Politics, Factions, and the Emergence of a Party System

The origins of the Spanish and Portuguese parties and party systems go back to the nineteenth century. Some would trace their origins even earlier, to the eighteenth century, and the emergence of the "two Spains" or the "two Portugals" phenomena. The one was Catholic, traditionalist, and inward looking; the other more secular, rationalist, "enlightened," and European looking. Although, as we shall see, this fundamental schism in the Spanish (and Portuguese) soul still importantly shapes Iberian politics, parties per se did not emerge until later. When they did, furthermore, they tended to be based on only incompletely digested conceptions of British parliamentarism. Right from the beginning the Spanish and Portuguese parties were fundamentally different from their Northern European counterparts.[7]

The nineteenth century Spanish and Portuguese parties were almost exclusively cadre or elitist parties, and they remained so. The suffrage was extended to newer social groups exceedingly slowly and reluctantly. A bow was made to liberalism and republicanism, then in fashion, in terms of the organization of "parties," but the functions performed were quite different. The parties remained the personal mechanisms of rival elite groups, families, and local notables and were almost totally devoid of ideological or programmatic pretensions. They served as the means by which the elites mobilized client support to gain power and to distribute patronage and spoils to the deserving once power was achieved. The "parties" also served as the mechanism for rival *caciques*, or political "bosses," similarly to secure a clientelistic following and to achieve power.[8] The crown served as the "moderating power," balancing, checking, sometimes leading the contending factions.

With social and economic change in Spain and Portugal, principally the gradual development of sizable middle class and trade union groups, toward the end of the nineteenth and the beginning of the twentieth centuries, new political associations began to emerge. These included, in Portugal, not just the liberal, democratic, and republican factions that helped usher in the ill-fated Republic of 1910–1926, but a variety of Catholic, Monarchist, Integralist, Corporatist, Nationalist, Fascist, and Socialist groups as well. In Spain many of the same or similar parties were present, along with the Falange, the Communists, the Anarcho-syndicalists, and various regional groups.

Although we cannot review here the entire history of parties and party politics in Spain and Portugal during this period, carrying us through the establishment of a republic in Spain as well as in Portugal, several features merit particular attention. First, the new parties were among the principal means to power for the emerging Spanish and Portuguese middle sectors and reflected the gradual transition, itself reflective of broad-scale socioeconomic changes, from aristocratic to middle-sector dominance of the two nations' major institutions: army, government, universities, bureaucracy, and so forth. Even the Socialist, Communist, and Anarcho-syndicalist groups, while obviously reflecting rising working-class consciousness, tended to be dominated in their executive committees by aspiring middle-sector politicians and intellectuals.[9]

Second, while reflecting a growing middle-class society, that middle class in both Spain and Portugal was severely divided internally. It had no consciousness as a class, tended to ape upper-class ways, while also using an informal alliance with the rising worker elements to wrest control from the old oligarchic groups. Third, reflecting these deep divisions within the middle class, no one party could command a majority, and the distances were so great between these contending factions that lasting coalitions were all but impossible as well. The party spectrum ranged from Communists, Anarcho-syndicalists, and Socialists on the left to Fascists, Monarchists, Falangists, and Integralists on the right—and all of them dominated by emerging, aspiring, ambitious, rival middle-sector groups. With a weak or nonexistent center, equally divided, the situation was one of fragmentation and gradual polarization, leading to a condition in both countries of incipient civil war, complicated by rising class consciousness and aspirations (especially in Spain) for regional autonomy.[10]

The result, fourth, was a republican form in which parties and parliament seemed incapable of governing. For its frequent coups, cabinet shuffles, corruption, bombs, and sheer instability and seeming incompetence from 1910–1926, Portugal's Republic became the butt of the cruelest and national character-based European jokes.[11] The Spanish Republic, 1931–1936, seemed almost equally incapable of concerted, effective government policy making and implementation. And, as the pendulum there swung ever more violently from left to right and back to a left popular front in 1936, with each party faction recruiting large private militias, the Civil War seemed to loom inevitably.

It is certainly true that one of the primary characteristics of both the Salazar and Franco regimes involved their efforts to harness and control this emerging pluralism, and particularly to control and suppress if necessary the perceived looming threat (to the middle sectors now uncertainly established in power) of organized labor. However, this posture must be placed in perspective. For based on their experiences under both the elite-dominated systems of the nineteenth century as well as the chaotic republicanism of the twentieth, Franco and Salazar were not just hostile to the working-class parties but to *all* parties. Like George Washington and De Gaulle, they saw "party" as diminishing the unity, integrity, and grandeur of the nation. They dissolved, absorbed, or stripped of power both the Socialist and Communist factions *and* the Integralist, Fascist, and Monarchist ones. In keeping with an older Spanish and Portuguese conception going back at least as far as the "Golden era" of the sixteenth century, they sought to rule in an authoritative and technocratic fashion, *devoid of all party politics*. The model was that of an organic and corporate state system in which divisive, political parties were to have no or little role. Rather than the one-party regimes, with which we are familiar from the literature and which leads sometimes to mistaken labels being applied, the Spanish and Portuguese systems were essentially no-party states dominated by a technocratic-bureaucratic structure, supported by a number of corporate elites (church, army, and landed and industrial wealth) and held together at the top by an overpowering and immensely politically skilled *caudillo* (Franco and Salazar), who functioned in ways comparable to the monarchy in the nineteenth century, as the "moderating" or "directing" power.[12]

Of course both these regimes did have official appendages which they called "parties," thus contributing further to our difficulties in categorizing them. But these "parties" did not carry out the functions usually thought of as appropriate for political parties. Only incidentally and almost as an afterthought did they present candidates for elections, devise party programs, or exercise parliamentary functions. The chief purposes of these "parties" were otherwise. For one thing they served, in the historic fashion, as giant patronage agencies, helping to put both friends and enemies of the regime, as well as virtually the entire emerging middle class, on the public payroll. They served as agencies of charity and benefices, doling out bicycles and toys to children, rocking chairs and sometimes sewing machines to old women, and jobs to aspiring politicians and university graduates as well as compliant labor officials. The party machinery served as a convenient place to test out and bring along rising and politically ambitious persons, as well as to "pension off" older or out-of-favor ones.

The "party" was also a fund-raising mechanism and an agency for securing loyalty and service, as all government bureaucrats had to join and pay to it a portion of their salaries. The party hence served as an accommodator of various views as well as an agency to suppress some others. It was the eyes and ears of the regime in the countryside, designed both to tap public opinion (though not necessarily by means of elections) and to help publicize and administer government policies. The party served both to lock out some groups and to absorb others through its monopolization of political activity. It was thus more a giant bureaucratic apparatus of the regime than a party per se. It liked to be called a "movement," a "union," or a "civic action association" rather than a "party." Hence, whereas on one level the Franco and Salazar regimes were one-party states, on another they were not. Even the official "parties" themselves were in fact antiparty.[13]

Because they absorbed a number of groups and parties that had existed under earlier regimes, the official "parties" of Franco and Salazar were never quite the monolithic organizations they are often pictured. Rather, the various factions, largely party-based, existent within the "party" always had to be kept in balance. Moreover, as socioeconomic development continued inexorably in the postwar period and as Spain and Portugal became more complex nations and socially differentiated, the number of factions that had to be juggled and balanced in this way also grew. There emerged left Falangists, whose ideology was hardly distinct from that of the Socialists or Anarcho-syndicalists, as well as rightist ones; Christian Democrats, Monarchists, and Social Democrats also found something of a home within the official apparatus.

These factions became, by the 1950s and 1960s, critically important in determining the direction of the regime. By studying the makeup of new cabinets, government appointments, and rotations within the top leadership of the "party" itself, astute observers could determine which faction was rising or falling in power and hence what could be expected in public policies.[14] The Franco and Salazar regimes, in turn, used the "party" mechanism to raise, check, and balance off these contending factions. The official "parties," never really monolithic, became the agencies to express and reflect, within limits, the growing societal and political pluralism of these two regimes. Moreover, within the official "party" differences had to be worked out between the rival factions in ways that were not entirely undemocratic. The situation was increasingly analogous to the old one-party American South, where distinct political factions fought it out in the primaries and within the single Democratic party apparatus and where the subsequent general elections served chiefly to ratify the choices already made.[15]

The emerging pluralism of the Franco and Salazar regimes, however, remained a limited pluralism.[16] Not all groups could be accommodated in the traditional cooptive way, particularly the more militant Socialists and Communists. In some instances these groups continued to be persecuted. But in others they too were allowed to function, in a certain grudging recognition of new realities. In Portugal the Socialist opposition was allowed to participate in a series of elections, although its campaign and organizational activities remained severely hamstrung. Socialist leader Mario Soares was allowed into the country on an on-again, off-again basis, most notably for the 1969 parliamentary elections which were among the freest Portugal had ever had. During the period of Salazar's successor, Marcello Caetano, successive national "congresses of the democratic opposition" were also held, and even though opposition "parties" remained largely proscribed, opposition "study groups" that were in fact the nuclei of the later parties met regularly.[17]

The Communists also remained illegal but in both countries they had built up a considerable underground apparatus, most notably in the workers' commissions organized parallel to the official *sindicatos*. As the workers' commissions grew in strength, furthermore, the two governments, especially Spain in Franco's last years and Portugal under Caetano, became increasingly inclined to deal with them realistically. Though they remained illegal and, hence, though the government could not admit its dealings with them publicly, it became increasingly inclined to negotiate with the workers' commissions instead of its own official syndicates as the true representatives of labor. Of course labor relations, like the situation with the opposition parties, went through various vicissitudes and ups and downs. But this is still a considerable distance from the image we frequently have of a monolithic fascist structure.[18]

By the 1960s, therefore, the bases for a future, more competitive network of parties and a broader party spectrum had already been laid. These included (1) the official "party" with its several major and many minor internal factions; (2) the bureaucratic state apparatus with its divisions and contending elements; (3) the Socialist, Communist, and social-democratic opposition, now operating both below and in some areas above ground; and (4) the various exile groups, centered in Paris, London, or, in the case of Portuguese Communist party leader Alvaro Cunhal, Prague. The exile groups tended to be small, personalistic, and highly factionalized, but they would also serve as the nuclei for an even broader party spectrum once Franco and the Salazar-Caetano regime had gone.

Toward the end of the period of authoritarian rule, the dynamics of politics in both Spain and Portugal, and a wrenching internal decision particularly for the opposition groups, revolved increasingly around whether to work within or outside "the system." Both the Franco and Caetano regimes were now sufficiently open that it was possible for the opposition, on some levels, to function. Agreeing to this, however, involved considerable costs, for by its willingness to participate the opposition not only received certain advantages but also gave added legitimacy to a regime in power the opposition had long fought. But continuing to work outside the system was also problematic. It enabled the opposition to maintain the purity of its doctrines, but the costs here meant being cut off from the new opportunities, in the new climate, for organization and proselytizing. Without going into the details here, it can be said that most opposition groups opted for varying degrees of both. That is, they chose to try at one level to work within the system and gain certain advantages from it, while at another they sought to maintain their separate existences as "out" and "persecuted" groups. Generally, it can be said that prior to 1974 in Portugal and to a somewhat lesser degree in Spain before 1975, the more moderate democratic opposition tended to be increasingly incorporated and hence coopted by the existing regimes while the more radical opposition, principally the Communists, maintained their image of martyrdom. The Socialists, especially in Portugal, were a mixed case, popular at some levels for their heroic opposition but coopted and compromised at others.[19]

Party Organization

The political parties and the "party systems" that have recently emerged in Spain and Portugal are fragile and only weakly institutionalized.[20] While many commentators have taken in the past few years to referring to the emerging Spanish and Portuguese "democracies," to a considerable degree, especially as it is based on the presence of parties and a party system, that evaluation represents more wishful thinking than an accurate description of reality. Indeed some other commentators would go so far as to say a "party system" as such, as the dominant means by which political power is mobilized and transferred, does not yet exist in either country.

The weakness, fragility, and lack of institutionalization of the parties and party systems have to do primarily with their short histories and the conditions under which, up till recently, they have been obliged to operate. During the 30-odd years of the Salazar and Franco dictatorships, the parties were illegalized, exiled, forced underground, or so hamstrung in their activities that a free and independent existence was impossible. Alternatively, they and their leaders were coopted by the regimes in power, which provided about the only opportunities for employment and/or survival. The parties were never able to build an effective national organization or to develop grass-roots cadres. These organizational weaknesses continue to plague the parties today and make their very continued existence precarious. We shall be considering these organizational problems under four major categories: the relations of the parties to the state, the parties and their parliamentary groups, the parties and their relations with extraparliamentary groups and clientela, and internal party organization.

Historically, in Iberia it has been difficult for any party to survive, let alone prosper, without state support and assistance. Indeed it is precisely because of the critical importance of official access and favors given the "party" that dominate the state machinery that the competition for those positions has been so intense. Membership dues are usually insufficient to keep an "out" party alive, jobs and patronage flow usually only from control of the state machinery, and elections are at best tentative and irregular and thus there is no automatic rotation of the parties into office. Without access to the great public watering trough, the parties tend to atrophy and disappear.[21]

In Portugal the official apparatus of the Salazar-Caetano regime has been disbanded and most of its leading members ousted from official positions, and/or exiled. The period of military rule that came with the Revolution of 1974 meant for a time that no party, except the military "party," had access to the usual spoils and patronage. The formation of a Socialist government in 1976 provided that party with some, limited special privileges and jobs, but there has not been a wholesale reshuffling of the bureaucracy under the Socialists, and they did not use their position in the government to reorganize as a new official party. The precarious nature of the Socialists' mandate was one cause of this, the fact the Socialists shared power with the armed forces another. And none of the other parties have gained access to official favors either. The relation of the parties to the state is hence still weak and uncertain with none of them able to enjoy the wholesale advantages that control of or special access to the state machinery usually implies.[22]

The situation in Spain is different. That is so both because the transition from the Franco regime was not so abrupt and revolutionary as in Portugal and because the military has not so far stepped overtly into power. Prime Minister Adolfo Suárez inherited most of the governmental machinery, including the largely moribund "party" machinery, from the old dictatorship. Though himself more a technocrat in the "apolitical" tradition, in the 1977 election Suárez moved to coopt the center of the Spanish political spectrum by affiliating his name with, and in a sense taking over, the so-called Union of the Democratic Center (UDC), a hastily formed alliance of 15 other centrist, moderately Catholic, and bureaucratic groups. In keeping with an older tradition, the Union is not really a party but a "movement," "alliance," or "rally," and thus far it has remained of secondary importance in the power structure of the evolving new regime. It will be interesting to see, however, if Suárez begins to reconstruct the Union as the new official "party" appendage and patronage mechanism of the government, not altogether different from the old regime system but perhaps updated with greater responsibilities and a more broadly based sectoral representation as in the Mexican Revolutionary Institutional party. It seems likely that the felt need for greater discipline and organization now that the euphoria of the immediate post-Franco celebration is giving way to more sober appraisals, plus the economic controls and austerity the government is forced to impose, may compel Suárez in that direction. The effects of the creation of such a new official appendage on the opposition parties will likely also be serious, and most probably damaging; however it may in any case be that the opposition is too strong and Suárez's UDC mandate so weak that he would not be able to bring off the creation of such a new official, umbrella-like organization.[23]

The parties' relations with their parliamentary blocs are also weak and uncertain. That is so, especially in Spain, because the Parliament has yet to emerge as a major center of political authority within the broader system. Spain's is simply not a parliamentary government, and, even though it is uncertain where exactly power does lie in Spain—king, prime minister, armed forces, economic elites—it is certainly not in the Cortes. In Portugal too, the Parliament must share power with the armed forces under a pact still in effect that allowed elections to be held but reserved for the military a special position as the ultimate arbiters of national affairs. The internal politics of the military and the several armed forces factions are thus at least as important as the rivalries of the parliamentary blocs; additionally, the president, a military man, has the power to dismiss the prime minister. Within the parliamentary groups, moreover, especially the Socialists and the Popular Democrats, party discipline and organization have been weak, loyalties have frequently been fleeting, and there have been numerous instances of party splits, lack of discipline, and disaffection.

The relations of the parties with their extraparliamentary and clientelist groups are complex. Probably the strongest links have been forged, in both countries, between the Communist parties and the trade unions. This is a long-standing alliance going back a considerable period, even during the era of the dictatorships. In both countries the Socialists have moved recently and with some success to wrest control of the union structure, or at least some unions and some workers, from the Communists. It is likely, though we lack many monographic studies, that the same kinds of linkages have been fashioned, or at least various attempts made, by other parties with distinct clientelist groups. However, each party has sought also to establish a tie with like-thinking groups within the military. No doubt Suárez's UDC has begun to develop a network within the governmental bureaucracy; indeed that is where much of its electoral support in 1977 came from. And in Portugal, the rightist Social Democratic Center (CDS) began to build its support among the conservative, Catholic peasantry in the northern provinces of the country. But the overall impression that one has is that all these links are still weak and tenuous, that the parties have been in existence too briefly for any strong or permanent ties to have been forged, and that the parties' relations with extraparliamentary and clientelist groups are still uncertain, shifting, uninstitutionalized, further retarding the strength and growth of the parties themselves.[24]

The internal structure of the parties presents a similar picture. It is generally conceded that in both countries, because of long, arduous, underground struggles against the dictatorships, the two Communist parties are tough, strong, disciplined and well-organized. In Portugal some of that strength has been sapped because of the Communists' failures in 1975 and 1976, but in both countries the nuclear organization remains powerful. The rightist parties have been weak and fragmented, both because they represent the presently discredited old regime and because in the past their other, more informal connections were such they had little need for a strong party organization or a mass following. They can be expected to begin formulating plans for a political comeback; in both Spain and Portugal, indeed, there are numerous signs that the Right is reorganizing.

The two main parties in Portugal are the Socialists (PS) and the Social Democrats (PSD—formerly known as the Popular Democrats, or PPD). Neither is particularly well organized. Both are led by upper-middle-class elements often more at home in the ideological debates and the social-democratic salons of Western Europe than in the harder, "dirtier" nuts-and-bolts activities of party organization.[25] Both are deeply divided internally at the top, and neither has as yet developed the cadres and grass-roots organizations to weld a strong national organization—although, when the Socialists were in power in Portugal, there were some efforts to use the advantage of control of the state machinery to fashion a stronger organization and to lure the workers and peasants away from the Communists.

In Spain Felipe González's Socialist Workers party (PSOE) presents a formidable opposition to the government. The party has been successful in wresting trade union support away from the Communists [as far as one can tell, the Socialist General Labor Union (UGT) has outdistanced the Workers Commissions (CCOO); unlike Portugal, Socialist labor in Spain is number one] and, with 29% of the vote, it has a sizable mass following. But its organization remains weak; as the principal opposition it may lose some support by trying to be all things to all men; it has to some degree more a regional than a genuinely national base; and there are many who question whether without its attractive leader the party would enjoy the same level of popularity.

Prime Minister Suárez's UDC is not really a party at all but a loose collection of local or regional notables, establishmentarians, regime officials, bureaucrats, and others, from a variety of loosely knit centrist, Catholic, and moderately rightist groups, who tend to support the government no matter which government happens to be in power. It is really a coalition movement or, as its name implies, a "union" of diverse interests and of the Spanish "people," largely devoid of ideology, program, or strong organization. Indeed it was only after the apolitical prime minister determined to affiliate his name with the UDC and pull it together that it began to flourish and showed signs of becoming the largest "party." That step, as the Madrid newspapers prominently played it, also marked the end of the UDC as an independent entity and led to considerable initial resentment on the part of some early UDC leaders.[26] But their resentments were lessened by the benefits immediately showered upon the "party" as the chosen agent of the popular prime minister. Although the UDC organization remains weak and though after the election it was consigned to the oblivion that often befalls official machines once their immediate usefulness has expired, there is a potential though now rusting organizational framework "out there" that could form the nucleus of a stronger governmental apparatus. It will be interesting to see if the prime minister decides to avail himself of that possibility or whether he will allow the UDC to continue rusting while the government retains its more personalistic orientation.

Parties and Their Programs

The emergence of a broad, modern, European-style party spectrum, with a range of left, center, and right parties, is of relatively recent origins in Spain and Portugal. The very newness of the parties and party spectrum contributes to the frequent ambiguity, lack of clarity, and shifting nature of the party ideologies and programs. So does the historic lack of importance afforded parties in the Iberian tradition, as well as the special relationships the parties must maintain vis-à-vis the armed forces or the state machinery. Nevertheless a party spectrum has emerged, and the party phenomenon has gained increasing importance.

The party spectrum in Portugal ranges from the right to far left, with no single party able to command a majority, with opinion deeply divided, and with few discernible trends toward a stable, center, middle of-the-road politics. These features of the new Portuguese party system were particularly evident in the governmental crisis of late 1977 when the ruling (but minority) Socialists suffered a vote of no confidence and the government fell, and hence the unhappy situation developed of a new Socialist-dominated coalition even weaker and more likely to be immobilized and stalemated than the one before. In the summer of 1978 these divisions and the stalemate became such that the government fell again, and this time Socialist Prime Minister Mario Soares was not asked to try to form a new government.

On the left the most prominent party is the Communist party (PCP) led by Alvaro Cunhal and a hard core of able, long-time leaders whose heroic exploits against the old dictatorship are frequently heralded in party propaganda by the combined years (over 300) that these leaders have spent in jail. The PCP is an old-time Moscow-oriented Communist party which was the only one in

Western Europe to applaud the Soviet Union's brutal stifling of liberalism in Czechoslovakia in 1968. The party has so far remained immune to the influences of more liberal Eurocommunism, although in the wake of its debacle in 1975 when the party failed to elbow its way into power and then in 1976 when it did badly at the polls (16%), there is now some evidence that Cunhal may have begun to moderate his position.[27]

The PCP has problems on both its right and its left flanks. The Portuguese Socialists have chipped away at its once solid trade union structure. And on the left there are a variety of Maoist, Trotskyite, Fidelista, and Anarcho-syndicalist groups, strong particularly among young people, who argue that the party is old, tired, closed to new influences, bureaucratized, Stalinist, and so illiberal as to be unacceptable. A more accurate reading of the situation, however, is that, while the PCP has some problems, it has retained its strength and vigor particularly among the working classes and, in the current situation of spiraling societal chaos and economic collapse in Portugal, may well be strengthening its position. Despite the sniping of his numerous critics, whose analysis of the situation is often based on wishful thinking as regards the development of Eurocommunism in the PCP, it may be that Cunhal's harder-line position will prevail and remain the correct one for his party.[28]

Because of the special problems Portugal faces, the Socialist party has not been able to function as a real socialist party, nor is there much prospect that it will. The Socialists came to power during a period when economic restraints, wage stabilization, and general belt-tightening had to be imposed, but these policies also had the effect of largely eroding its socialist stance and program. Moreover because it governed only at the suffrance of the army in Portugal and during a period of widespread popular desire for a return to order, the Socialists were cast in a peculiar position. Their socialist and reformist legitimacy was undermined by the conservative policies that they were forced to follow. For example, it was a Socialist government that began to roll back the agrarian reform, strip the trade unions of their independent bargaining power, return some nationalized properties to private hands, impose police controls on the universities, knuckle under to IMF and U.S. Embassy advice, and so on.[29] Moreover there is much doubt as to just how socialist Mario Soares and his fellow well-coiffed and manicured Socialists are. In the nineteenth century Portuguese liberals were often known as "cafe liberals" or *liberais do chá* because they much preferred the comforts of intellectual discussion in Lisbon's elegant coffee houses to the difficulties of governing. The suspicion lingers that the Soares party consists of "cafe socialists."

The PSD is similarly somewhat less than meets the eye. Led by parliamentary deputy Francisco Sá Carneiro and *Expresso* editor Francisco Pinto Balsemão, the Social Democrats are not really a social-democratic party but perhaps more the Portuguese equivalents of the liberal wing of the American Republican party (if such a dubious comparison can be made at all). That is, they are classic but conventional and rather bourgeois liberals who favor some reform but not too much. Similarly well-coiffed and manicured, the PSD want above all else to get to power. They represent a portion of the bourgeoisie who had been excluded from enjoying the benefits and perquisites of governmental position during the Salazar-Caetano era and who desire to make up for these missed opportunities. It may be that, with the increasingly conservative Portuguese electorate, their wish may come true.

The more conservative CDS is, in effect, the Christian Democratic party of Portugal. It is Catholic (though nonconfessional) and oriented toward the protection of the family, order, stability—although it represents a fairly moderate and mainstream position on these issues, not the extremes. Like some others, it does not consider itself a party but a "league" or an "alliance." Led by Diego Freitas do Amaral, the CDS has been gaining in strength and for a brief time shared power in a coalition with the Socialists. It has recently attracted many government bureaucrats, officials, and others associated with the former regime. Whereas in the immediate postrevolutionary period many of the old *Salazaristas* and *Caetanistas* called themselves "Socialists" because that was politically the thing to do, now they have begun abandoning the Socialists and joining the CDS, seeing perhaps a brighter future there.

There is still a Monarchist faction alive but not necessarily well in Portugal, and a certain hard core of real Fascists (as distinct from those associated with the old regime who were not Fascists but have been discredited by the use of that label). In addition, there are a number of prominent individuals who someday might attempt a political comeback basing their support on charisma, their name and stature, and a "following" rather than a "party." These include General Antonio de Spinola, the monocled man on horseback whose book helped destroy the old regime and who still harbors ambitions to be the Portuguese De Gaulle; Marcello Caetano who in exile in Brazil maintains a certain bitterness at the unfair pilloring his well-meaning regime received following the Revolution and may still have some hopes for vindication; General Kaula de Arriaga, once Spinola's rival and still with strong ambitions; Franco Nogueira, Caetano's rival, tough and ambitious; Adriano Moreira, a former Caetano protege with ambitions of his own; and perhaps even General Ramalho Eanes, the current president, who may become tired of the present party bickering, abolish them all, rule directly, and perhaps launch a "movement" of his own.

In Spain the Communist party (PCE), in contrast to its Portuguese cousin, is most famous for its moderation, its Eurocommunism,[30] and its curious, sometimes mutually supportive relationship with the center-right government of Adolfo Suárez (if Santiago Carrillo can bow and kiss the hands of the King," say Spanish wags, "perhaps the Pope will be next"). The party's program is temperate and progressive, calling for the defense of democracy, Spain's entry into the Common Market, and some (unspecified) nationalizations. Because it largely owes its above-ground existence and legality to a political decision made by the king and the prime minister, it has concentrated its attacks on the far right and not the government. The PCE also has a history of long exile and underground activity directed against the Franco regime as well as a strong position within the trade unions. But, under the wily and genial Carillo, its position has been moderate indeed. In part at least this has to do with the tactical strategy of the party, for unlike the situation in revolutionary Portugal the Spanish Communists never had a chance to come to power "by fiat," and thus they sought to put their most reasonable and democratic face forward. Then too, the Spanish Communists made a poor electoral showing in 1977 (9% of the vote), in contrast with the strong 29% polled by the PSOE. And to outflank the Socialists and blur their image as the dominant party on the left, the PCE has tried to corral the Socialists into a broad popular opposition front (in which the PCE would presumably have a stronger voice than its electoral strength showed it merited), while also working in alliance with the government on crucial parliamentary votes. To this end, Carillo has taken a curiously familiar "above politics" stance and called for a "government of concentration." This has all given the PCE an acceptability it lacked before, but many Spaniards are either aghast or bewildered at the party's position and some, who recall its hard-line past, not a little bemused.

With nearly a third of the popular vote, Felipe González's PSOE has emerged as the principal opposition group in Spain, to the surprise of the government and even the Socialists themselves. For the 1977 elections the PSOE fashioned a moderate program that was hardly distinguishable from that of the government: a mixed economy, nationalization of "key" but unnamed industries, free unions, entry into the Common Market. It accused the government of working with the right and the Francoists to defeat the left, and it has been the beneficiary of a widespread desire in Spain for change and a sense of discontent with the existing regime. Since it is the principal opposition, the U.S. Embassy and, to a lesser degree, the Common Market social democrats have moved quickly to try to coopt and capture the Spanish Socialists, as they had the Socialists of Portugal. That may not be so easy since the PSOE's basic program, as enunciated in its December 1976 Congress, is potentially quite radical and the party is probably more militant than the Portuguese Socialists and with a stronger basis in the trade union movement. Nevertheless support for the PSOE may not be all that firm. Its base is often regional and having to do with the autonomy issue more than national and having to do with socialist issues; Felipe González has proved a charismatic vote getter who garners considerable support from his personal attractiveness independent of the issues he stands for; and the PSOE, and to some degree the PCE, benefited from a fairly widespread protest vote against the remnants of Francoism and that may prove to be only temporary. Having registered these reservations, however, the point remains that the PSOE garnered nearly 30% in the 1977 balloting and will be a major, perhaps *the* major, force to reckon with in any future political consideration.[31]

So far as can be determined the UDC, the prime minister's adopted apparatus, has no clear-cut program of its own. It has sought to capture the broad center and moderate right of the Spanish political spectrum, and with 166 seats in the Cortes (to the PSOE's 118) has largely succeeded in doing so. Its ideology, however, is largely the prime minister's ideology, and that means almost no ideology at all. It is pragmatic, vaguely Catholic, technocratic, centrist. As an alliance of some 15 vaguely liberal, middle-of-the-road, and moderately conservative groups, it is an amalgam of largely middle-class bureaucrats and Social and Christian Democrats. It favors the drafting of a new and somewhat more democratic constitution, economic reform (un-defined), a streamlined bureaucracy, free unions, expanded social security, limited regional autonomy, closer relations with Europe. Seeking to avoid the historic polarizations, it advocates a "safe road to democracy." It favors Spain's gradual entry into NATO and the Common Market, but would not be entirely averse to Spain's going it alone. It favors a gradual dismantling of the outdated control mechanisms of the old regime, but without that implying a breakdown of law and order. It recognizes the need to deal with Spain's pressing economic problems, but would do so through a mixture of private and state capitalist structures, not socialism. In short, what there is of a "party" here supports the government and its program and is inseparable from them.

The right in Spain is, for now, discredited and without a popular base. The Popular Alliance (again an "alliance" rather than a "party") of Manuel Fraga Iribarne (considered a "liberal" when he was in the Franco cabinet) polled only 8% of the popular vote (16 seats in the Cortes); other rightist groups hardly even bothered to campaign. The Alliance advocated retaining "the best of Franco"; called for limited reforms, law and order, and the outlawing of the Communist party; and drew support from Spain's traditional corporate elements—big business, Opus Dei, old-time Francoists, Roman Catholic lay groups, and some sectors of the armed forces. But its poor showing in the 1977 elections should not be taken as the final measure of the right's influence. First, it recognizes that numbers of ballots are not the only measure of political influence in Spain, nor are elections the only route to power. Second, the right feels the early post-Franco euphoria will pass and that as the country settles down again the need for order and discipline will once more become apparent. Third, the right is betting that Suárez's UDC will eventually split up and that it will receive the support of many conservatives, moderates, and Catholics who presently support the prime minister. Fourth, as indicated, the right remains strong within the army, the church, the economic oligarchy, and some key areas of the state machinery—all of whose strength is considerably greater than the individual votes of its members. The right feels that if the need arises or a crisis situation develops, it can call on the support of any of these key elite groups who can act above and beyond the electoral arena. Though one might wish otherwise, the right in Spain, particularly an updated, refashioned non-Francoist right, is by no means dead yet.[32]

In addition to these national organizations, Spain also has a number of regional "parties" with some representation in the parliament. The chief of these are the Catalan Democratic Pact (11 seats) and the Basque Nationalist party (8 seats). The regional autonomy issue is of course a volatile one in Spain; contrary to what Karl Deutsch and others have said, national integration, in Spain and elsewhere, is not a necessary and inevitable consequence of modernization.[33] Sentiment in favor of regional autonomy remains very much alive, and especially in Catalonia and the Basque country it is intertwined with complex class and economic issues.[34]

Party Membership and Leadership

There have been few, if any, studies as yet of either Portuguese or Spanish party membership, and probably it is premature for such studies to be done. Although there was remarkable continuity in voting patterns between the 1975 and 1976 elections in Portugal, party membership in both countries nevertheless remains highly unstable and shifting. The tendency to shift party allegiance is still strong, and most Portuguese and Spaniards are not yet inclined to join definitively any party. This helps explain why party membership for all the parties in both countries remains small, although the voting turnout was remarkably heavy. Prudently, most Portuguese and Spanish voters are still waiting to see which way the political winds blow before committing themselves. One is inclined to accept Converse's hypothesis that perhaps several generations of competitive elections and party development are required before fixed party allegiances emerge—whatever the social bases of the cleavages that do eventually develop.[35]

But, if the membership remains shifting and the claims of the parties themselves suspect, so much so in both cases that the figures are all but totally worthless, it is nevertheless possible to distinguish between "hard" and "soft" voting patterns. The few opinion surveys and election analyses that have been done in the two countries show the vote for the Communist party to be the "hardest," firmest, and probably most permanent of all the major parties. In Portugal the vote for the PS and in Spain for the PSOE was considerably "softer," although in both cases there was an identifiable "hard core" of party loyalists. These studies and surveys seem to indicate the vote for the Socialist position may be less firm than that for the Communists and hence more fluid, shifting, and susceptible to major changes. The vote for the conservative and Catholic parties seems to occupy an intermediary position between these other two, while the vote for the center parties (Prime Minister Suárez's UDC and Portugal's PSD) seems to be the "softest" of all.[36] Whether this implies the possibilities for instability in the middle and the potential for major shifts on the part of the electorate cannot at this time be finally ascertained. This plus other evidence to be set forth in the following paragraphs, however, provides little optimism for the growth of a stable, happy, bourgeois, middle-of-the-road polity in either Spain or Portugal.

The information on party leadership is much more complete than is that on party membership. Although some few bows have been made by the left parties to the principle of direct worker representation in their executive committees, in fact *all* the party leaderships are dominated by middle-class or middle-sector representatives. Not only are few workers represented but the old oligarchic elites have been largely bypassed as well, even in the conservative parties. This marks a significant class shift in both Spain and Portugal from the aristocratic era preceding the 1930s and is a major indicator of the social changes that occurred inexorably under Franco and Salazar-Caetano regardless of the generally conservative and authoritarian nature of these two regimes. From this point on politics in Spain and Portugal, at least as defined by the social makeup of the various parties' executive committees (and probably also as defined in other important institutions such as the military officer corps and the public service) is essentially middle-sector politics. The dynamics of political struggle involve no longer elite versus bourgeoisie but rival factions within the middle sectors themselves, obviously taking quite disparate ideological positions and looking differentially toward the lower classes for electoral mass support.[37]

Voting Strength and Bases of Cleavage

If the data on party membership are often incomplete and misleading, a useful means for determining the class bases of the polity and the sources of other societal cleavages is provided by the voting itself. The data are incomplete, but they nonetheless indicate certain important electoral phenomena characteristic of both countries (see Table 12–1). Among the most important of these are (1) the high turnouts and levels of participation, (2) the strongly class and regional basis of the balloting, (3) the weakness and isolation of the extreme left and the extreme right, and (4) the relative strength of the center in these early electoral contests, seemingly reflecting a desire on the part of the Spanish and Portuguese electorates to avoid the polarization that had previously torn their countries apart.

In both countries the electoral turnout was over 80% (90% in Portugal in 1975). Although some of the high turnout undoubtedly had to do with the practice of compulsory voting begun under the old dictatorships, the chief factor was simply the desire of the people, after so many years of silence, to express themselves and their opinions at the polls. Election day was a major "national holiday," and the campaign itself a long festival of joy, high hopes, and celebration culminating in the vote. For Portugal it was the "first free election in 50 years" (actually the first free election ever),[38] whereas for Spain it was the first free election in 40 years. Both countries experienced a sudden and rapid escalation in participation, what Huntington calls a "burst of

TABLE 12–1.   Spain and Portugal: Voting Percentages

Spain: 1977	
Union of the Democratic Center	34
Socialist Workers Party	28
Communists	9
Popular Alliance	8
Others (Christian Democrats, regional parties, independent socialists, etc.)	20
Portugal: 1975 Constituent Assembly Elections	
Socialists	38
Social Democrats	26
Communists	12
Center Social Democrats	8
Others (chiefly extreme Left or null and blank ballots)	16
Portugal: 1976 Elections for the National Assembly[a]	
Socialists	35
Social Democrats	24
Center Social Democrats	16
Communists	16
Others	9

[a]The most striking changes from 1975 to 1976 are that the Socialists and Social Democrats lost somewhat, the Communists gained (in large part because other extreme left parties chose not to participate), the number of blank ballots and votes for "others" declined significantly, and the CDS doubled in strength (reflecting both a growing conservatism in Portugal and the influx of many embittered "returnees" from Angola and Mozambique).

explosive energy" when civil freedoms are restored after a long period of repression. The longer-range implications of such a sudden burst of popular participation and high expectations provide some interesting hypotheses for comparative study. Huntington speculates that such sudden expansion typically leads to a conservative reaction and renewed efforts by rightist groups to again reduce political participation and restore a more narrowly based political order.[39] It generally leads also to widespread disillusionment when the hopes generated produce few measurable benefits.

The strongly class and regional basis of the voting is apparent in both countries (see Table 12–2). Both demonstrated a comparatively high articula-

TABLE 12–2.   Distribution of Votes by Region and Size of Place: Portugal 1975 (Percent)

	SOCIALISTS	SOCIAL DEMOCRATS	COMMUNISTS	CENTER DEMOCRATS
Rural North	29.9	38.6	3.8	1.2
Urban North	41.7	27.4	7.1	9.5
Rural South	41.8	8.5	28.2	2.3
Urban South	45.1	12.4	22.7	4.3

Source: John L. Hammond, "Das Urnas as Ruas: Electoral Behavior and Noninstitutional Militancy: Portugal, 1975." Paper presented at the conference on "Crisis in Portugal," Toronto, April 15–17, 1976.

tion of class interest, and in both countries the class and regional bases of the parties overlapped. In Portugal the PCP won strongly among rural wage earners in the large estate-dominated provinces of the Alentejo (the southern so-called "red belt") and in the industrial concentrations of the center region, Lisbon, Setúbal, and so on. The more conservative parties—the PSD and CDS—were more attractive to rural smallholders of the northern regions, to Catholics, and to the urban bourgeoisie, both north and south. The PS attracted the votes of workers outside the dominant mode of regional production—that is, industrial workers in the predominantly agricultural north and rural smallholders in the south—and also of workers in the tertiary sector. The PS also attracted the urban bourgeoisie and intellectuals of Lisbon, and many of those associated with the old regime seeking to establish their "socialist" legitimacy. But note John Hammond's carefully researched and important conclusion that a Socialist vote appeared often to have been a vote against the party of the most numerous class, in favor of the alternative nearest on the spectrum in the direction that the affected constituency's interests led it (i.e., to the left for nonproprietors in the north and to the right for agricultural or industrial workers in the south). Thus it would appear that the actual vote supports our earlier conclusion regarding the "softness" of Socialist support. Or, as Hammond put it, "the PS's campaign and the electorate's response appear to have led it to victory by turning it into a residual category."[40]

In Spain in 1977 the patterns were not altogether unlike those in Portugal. First there was a definite regional split, although not so clear-cut as in Portugal, between the more conservative, rural, and agricultural provinces of the south and west and the more urban and industrial concentrations of the north and northwest. The UDC, Prime Minister Suárez's electoral alliance, did well in the more rural, conservative, and Catholic regions and among the urban bourgeoisie and government workers (often synonymous). The left did well in the urban, industrial, and more cosmopolitan centers, sweeping such cities as Barcelona, Valencia, Madrid, Sevilla, and the Basque provinces. A significant correlate of the last was the relative decline of the Basque nationalist party and a sharp move toward the left in these provinces. One conclusion that might be drawn from the vote here is that, while the Basque region seems to be becoming more radicalized by the growing industrialization of its work force, it may be becoming somewhat less inclined toward Basque separatism.[41]

The votes show, additionally, the weaknesses of the extreme left and right in both countries, and the corresponding—and new—strength of the center. Of course, it depends on how one counts. In both countries the combined vote for the left (including Socialist, Communist, and some small independent and fringe groups) was over 50%. But looked at another way, and given the relative conservativeness and "acceptability" of the Socialists in both countries, as well as the sharp differences between them and the Communists, another and perhaps more valid interpretation is possible. The Communists in Spain polled only 9% of the vote and won 20 seats in the Cortes; in Portugal they won only

12–16%, and recent indications are that their support has since slipped even further. Indeed in Portugal the Communists actively campaigned to force a cancellation of the election, not wishing to have their weak electoral strength clearly demonstrated by the votes.

The Portuguese right was discredited and prohibited from participating in the election, whereas in Spain Fraga's Popular Alliance polled only 8% of the vote and garnered only seventeen seats in the Cortes. Thus in Spain, if we are correct in assuming that the PSOE is not outside the mainstream and is in fact rather moderate, then the combined moderate or center vote (PSOE and UDC, plus some small parties) runs upward of 80% of the electorate. And in Portugal, if the Socialists, liberal-democratic PSD, and Catholic-moderate CDS may similarly be considered all middle-of-the-road and moderate, then the center vote there also surpasses 80%. Although the case must not be overstated and one should not underplay the divisions between these parties, as well as the obvious class differences that continue to exist, it could easily be that the lack of support for either extreme and the seeming strength of the center has to do with the increasing "embourgeoisement" of both Spain and Portugal, their increased prosperity, literacy, and overall modernization, and the growth in both of a strong middle class since the 1920s and 1930s, when extremes of wealth and the absence of a strong middle class tore both countries apart.[42]

The Electoral System and the Other "Parties"

Although Spain and Portugal have both witnessed the emergence of new political parties and had democratic elections that can and should be celebrated, we should not forget that there are other "parties" in the system and that elections are not viewed as the only means to power. Indeed the case could be made that the parties and elections are really peripheral to the main centers of power and influence in these two systems. The elections thus served as useful opinion polls to gauge the relative strength of the various factions, but real power continued to lie elsewhere, little changed as a result of the elections, and the main arenas of politics had little to do with the votes and parties per se. Let us see what these other arenas, power centers, and "parties" are.

THE ELECTORAL SYSTEM AND THE EFFORTS TO CIRCUMVENT, REGULATE, AND CONTROL THE ELECTION RESULTS

The Spanish electoral system was fashioned in, and was an integral part of, the struggles involving the post-Franco decompression.[43] The principal actors included the king, Juan Carlos; the army; the new generation "liberals" who supported the king; and the old Franco state apparatus, headed by the Generalissimo's hand-picked prime minister, Carlos Arías Navarro.

Arías Navarro was willing to hold parliamentary elections but he insisted the entire process be tightly controlled and regulated to preserve the continuity of the Franco regime. He proposed a bicameral legislature with the lower house popularly elected by universal suffrage, but the PCE would be excluded from participating and regime loyalists would be the chief candidates. The upper house was to be appointed from among the traditional corporate interests: the army, the church, central and provisional government authorities, government labor unions, and business associations. Additionally, the upper house could veto any action by the lower house, and all legislation would require approval by the prime minister's cabinet.

But moderates and the left claimed the election and a Cortes would be meaningless if they were not democratically based and open to all political groups including the PCE. The king and his supporters concurred, and, in a series of intricate and politically deft steps that followed in 1976, he moved to legalize the PCE, get rid of Arías, diminish the strength of the Francoists (the so-called "bunker"), increase his own standing and popularity, retain control and the support of the army, appoint his own prime minister (Suárez), and promulgate a new electoral law. The Juan Carlos-Suárez Political Reform Act called for a two-house Cortes consisting of a Chamber of Deputies of 350 members elected by universal suffrage, with its membership proportionate to the population of Spain's various provinces and with each province guaranteed a minimum number of seats. The Senate would have 244 members, 204 popularly elected, 40 appointed by the king, and with each province having equal representation. The Senate could still veto legislation of the lower house, and the king was to select the prime minister. Juan Carlos and Suárez then moved to gain the approval of the old Cortes for their plan, which would give it democratic legitimacy but require Cortes members to vote for a proposal that put their own positions at severe risk. Passage was assured both by subtle threats and by the promise of at least 150 sinecures to those who voted for the measure and then subsequently might themselves be ousted in the balloting. The PCE was also legalized.

Election day brought some surprises, chiefly in terms of the low level of support for the government coalition, the UDC, especially considering *all* (from its own point of view) it had done for "democracy" in Spain. Even though the Political Reform Act ensured a moderate outcome by favoring rural and conservative provinces at the expense of populous and heavily industrial ones (the 15 smallest provinces with 3.4 million population had 53 seats in the Cortes, while the largest province, Catalonia, with 4.5 million population, had only 33 seats), the UDC still did not gain its expected parliamentary majority. It won only 34% of the popular vote but, because of the electoral system, garnered 47% of the parliamentary seats: 166 of 370 in the Chamber and 107 of 204 in the Senate. The results were apparently so disappointing to Juan

Carlos-Suárez that they have been despondent and largely immobilized ever since, slowing considerably the process of Spanish liberalization and reform policy implementation. As another indicator of how the election results have been read, the American Embassy began putting some distance between itself and the government while establishing new links with, and thus giving added legitimacy to, Felipe González and the PSOE.

In Portugal of course the situation was different. There was no king or prime minister to provide continuity. Rather, the Salazar-Caetano regime had been destroyed by military coup d'état, the so-called "revolution of flowers." The Revolution had been led by the Armed Forces Movement (MFA), and, though elections had been promised by the revolution's leaders, evidence mounted in late 1974 and early 1975 that the MFA enjoyed its leading and heroic position and wished to perpetuate its supervisory role. By this time it had built an elaborate set of military cum political agencies parallel to and often bypassing the civilian ones and had also become the nation's strongest "political party," more coordinated, better organized, and, at least in its own eyes, more popular and with a stronger sense of the national will than the perpetually squabbling civilian parties. Its leading officers had come to believe that further institution-alization of the MFA was necessary and that it should continue to play a directing role even after the scheduled elections for a Constituent Assembly.[44]

To this end the MFA began to downgrade the importance of the elections and make efforts to control their results. Although it could not cancel them altogether and thus run the risk of sacrificing its democratic legitimacy, it did postpone them as long as possible (to April 25, 1975, the first anniversary of the Revolution). It also hinted that it intended to continue playing a primary role in the drafting of a new constitution. It established an institutional structure giving an especially privileged place to the armed forces and enabling them to continue serving as "guarantors" of the Revolution. Among other things, the MFA insisted on a system of representation in the Constituent Assembly that would guarantee a dominant voice for the military itself. It demanded the "right" (like the traditional military foro) to reserve to itself the selection of the defense and economic ministers and the right to approve beforehand (and presumably reject) any presidential candidate. The Council of State, which the MFA officers already controlled, was to be converted into a "superior" upper chamber which, as in Spain, would hold veto power and also enable the army to stay in power indefinitely and ensure that its program would be carried out. Some MFA officers flirted with the idea of forming a party of their own which would surely sweep the elections, and leftist Premier Vasco Gonçalves vowed in a nationwide TV speech that the military in control of the government might ignore or discount any election vote which "did not express the will of the people"—presumably as defined by the MFA.

These notions were formalized in an accord that the civilian parties were forced to sign only two weeks before the election and that gave the military the power to choose the president, to veto unacceptable legislation, and to continue to rule for at least three to five years. This accord considerably diminished the importance of the election by tying the hands of the Constituent Assembly even before its members had been chosen and eliminating the possibility for an effective opposition or alternative to the MFA. However the civilian parties had no choice but to sign it or risk their own legality and continued ability to function, as well as the possibility the election would be cancelled.

Even after the elections were held (with the PS getting 38%, the PSD 26%, the CDS 8%, and the PCP 12.5%), the MFA, particularly Gonçalves and the PCP, continued to disparage their importance. The Constituent Assembly met under a cloud and continuously faced the threat it would be disbanded. The streets remained at least as important a political arena as the ballot box. Only after the turnaround of November, 1975, when Gonçalves was forced out and the PCP deprived of some of its special access, did the civilian parties and electioneering (new elections for the parliament were scheduled for 1976) begin to emerge as preeminent. But even with the establishment of a civilian, parliamentary system and the eventual formation of a Socialist government, the president remained a military man and the armed forces continued as the ultimate arbiters of national affairs.

OTHER "PARTIES" WITHIN THE SYSTEM

In both countries, thus, the party arena, on this and other issues, was not the primary focus and there were clearly other and often more important "parties" operating in the system.[45] In Spain this meant the king, the armed forces, the bureaucracy, the church, the Francoist element, the economic elites, and the prime minister (who is appointed by the king and whose position does not derive necessarily from his electoral strength). In Portugal the principal nonparty "party" was the MFA, but there are other groups and individuals, as we have seen, that must be taken into account.

In Spain also the principal political arenas were not necessarily party-related: the king and his efforts to build his own popularity, the king's relations with the armed forces, the internal politics of the military institution, the trade union struggle, the changeover in the prime minister's offices, the relations of the government to the Cortes, and so on. In Portugal the principal arenas were also the internal politics of the armed forces and the MFA, the relations of the premier to the Communist party, the struggle for control in streets, factories, and government agencies. All these arenas either took precedence over, or were just as important as, the party arena.

Similarly as regards elections. They are significant to be sure, but one should not read too many implications into them. They are tentative rather than definitive.[46] The elections in Portugal were, in effect, a referendum on the Revolution and the MFA; in Spain on the king, the prime minister, and their performance. They were an indication of the current balance of political forces.

In Portugal they did not offer a full range of choices (the right groups were excluded, as were prominent personalities like Spínola) and their importance had previously been downgraded by the military. The elections in Spain provided a set of signals, like an opinion poll, which did not convey definitive legitimacy to any groups or party. At best they provided a tentative mandate. Hence the elections in both countries may be seen as part of an ongoing political process which afforded new opportunities for some groups and a new defensiveness for others. Other routes to power remain open and are presently being actively explored by a variety of forces, which again implies that arenas other than the party one must also command our attention.

The Role of Parties within the Spanish and Portuguese Systems

Political parties, a party system, and party government are comparatively new phenomena for Spain and Portugal. Indeed with the exception of the chaotic and short-lived republics of two generations ago, neither country has ever had a functioning party system. In fact, some would go so far as to say that the parties and party systems in Spain and Portugal have been—and remain— mere concessions to foreign fads, or else that they are the contrived and rather synthetic creations for satisfying the a priori conditions for U.S aid and entry into NATO and the Common Market. They serve, expediently, some argue, to show the Iberian nations are as "modern" and as "democratic" as the rest of Europe, when in fact a little scratching of the surface reveals the parties to be ephemeral and not central to the functioning of the political system. As the novelist and reporter José Yglesias has written, "In Spain there has been a tendency to think of politics much more as aesthetics than as an attempt at the practical manipulation of reality in a positive determined sense. There has been no effort to fit political formulations to the exigencies of reality in its rambling process of change, but to adapt that reality to an a priori scheme of ideas totally conceived outside its conditions."[47]

The findings in this paper lend support to these contentions, *in part*. With the exception of the Communists and possibly the far right, the parties and party systems in both countries are exceedingly weak. To some extent they do seem to represent rather artificial creations, derived from a priori, often foreign criteria. They are not well organized, their leadership is terribly thin, funds are scarce, membership is small, party identification is "soft," loyalties are fleeting, the parties are splintered and fragmented, and party government has not as yet been strongly or irrevocably established. At the same time, the real foci of power in both countries lie oftentimes outside the party arena, with the army, the bureaucracy, the state machinery, the king (in Spain) or a prime minister independent from the parties, the president (in Portugal) who is also an army general, powerful economic groups, and other corporate and institutional interests. Elections, similarly, provide one route to power, but other means are also available.

And yet parties and a party system have emerged and a system of "party government" is evolving. One cannot discount the impressive turnouts at the polls, the "explosion of participation" (to use Huntington's phrase), the new climate of liberty and freedom, and the obvious, often spontaneous joy and outpouring in favor of democratic rule. The parties have been established, and party government and respect for the results of the ballot box have gained new-found legitimacy. That legitimacy is now sufficiently strong and democracy sufficiently well established that no military or civil-military faction, employing some other route to power, could afford to ignore entirely or ride roughshod over these newer expressions of democratic legitimacy.

The result, in both Spain and Portugal, is a dual system of political power and authority. On the one hand, there are the parties and the institutional paraphernalia that go with them: Cortes, elections, campaigns, public opinion, parliamentary maneuvering, and so on. On the other, there is the army, the state structure, and a variety of powerful vested and corporate interests. The political system rests on a complex set of relationships and often an uneasy balance between these two sets of institutional pillars. Hence the old question of the "two Spains" or the "two Portugals," the one largely urban, rationalist, parliamentary-democratic, and European-looking, the other rural, Catholic, traditionalist and more inward-looking, a fissure in the Spanish and Portuguese soul and society that dates at least back to the eighteenth century, is still very much alive. What is interesting is to study not only the internal dynamics of each of these clusters of interests but also the involved interactions and potential for conflict between them.[48] Still open to much further analysis is the issue of whether Spain's and Portugal's new affluence, their younger generations, and their rising "embourgeoisement" may have transcended these historic differences. Or, alternatively, will the economic crunch and political crises that both countries are experiencing (Portugal far more so than Spain) bring on a new fragmentation and polarization producing stalemate, conflict, breakdown, and the renewed and familiar turning toward an authoritarian solution?

The signals are mixed, but they provide little cause for optimism. The social gaps and problems in both countries remain large and seemingly intractable. The Spanish economy is in trouble and the Portuguese a shambles. Politically, Portugal has gone through an inconclusive revolution which has bred increasing governmental paralysis, immobilism, collapse, and, eventually, a return to more authoritarian methods and a form of military-civilian, "non-partisan," technocratic rule. The "revolution of flowers" has wilted, living standards are declining, the national mood is foul, and there is much weariness of politics. In Spain there is also widespread disillusion that "democracy" has not brought brighter prospects, violence is increasing, and the nation seems adrift. In both countries it has proved far easier to dismantle the structures of the old regimes than to build viable democratic ones to replace them. In both countries there is much malaise and sense of misplaced hopes, if not despair. The political parties in both countries report a sharp drop in enthusiasm, and in both the parties themselves have been increasingly shunted aside in favor of more traditional, "statist" methods of rule. The party/electoral arena seems no longer as important as other arenas, but whether that is the result of a certain disinterest in parties and platforms in the interregnum between elections or of a deeper and longer-term process of party atrophy it is impossible at this time to say.

The question therefore remains whether Iberia, with its new elections, parties, and party systems, is now a part of Europe or still apart from it. The answer remains: both. There is much survey and other data that point to the conclusion that Spain and Portugal may in some areas be even more authoritarian, conservative, inward-looking, and oriented toward the preservation of historic, traditionalist values and institutions than were their own authoritarian-conservative governments: Franco and Salazar. There are also many indicators of change, movement, even revolutionary upheaval. Or, as Prime Minister Suárez once noted optimistically, "Spain will surprise you." Which way the balance will tip is still an open question, and the complex currents, blends, and overlaps that provide possibilities for both clash and reconciliation between them also furnish numerous opportunities for further research on a whole series of important and interesting issues raised here but only incompletely explored.

Notes

1. As reported on a "not for direct attribution" basis during the course of one of the secretary's shuttles about Europe.

2. In the legend of Roland, it is only the Moorish armies of Iberia that are able to defeat the forces of Christendom led by Charlemagne, and Roland himself was killed in Spain, apparently in the Basque country by the "Saracens."

3. Portugal, however, continues to flirt with Third World ideologies, and Spain is not entirely certain it really wants to join NATO. At the same time a number of the European nations have yet to be convinced that they want Spain and Portugal in the Common Market. Although the thrust has been mainly toward integration with Europe and the Western democratic community, the old prejudices are still often strong and the Iberian nations stand ready, yet and again, to "go it alone" if necessary, to reject Europe and "the West" to some degree, perhaps even to jettison their newly evolved democratic forms in favor of a more traditional Iberian model.

4. The approach here, as well as the major chapter headings, derive from Raphael Zariski, *Italy: The Politics of Uneven Development*, Hinsdale, Ill.: Dryden Press, 1972, chap. 5. Also Peter H. Merkl, *Modern Comparative Politics*, Hinsdale, Ill.:

Dryden Press, 1977, chap. 4; and Joseph La Palombara and Myron Weiner, eds., *Political Parties and Political Development*, Princeton, N.J.: Princeton University Press, 1966.

5. On the role of political parties in the Iberic-Latin culture area, see Douglas A. Chalmers, "Parties and Society in Latin America," *Studies in Comparative International Development*, 7 (Summer 1972), 102–128; Robert H. Dix, "Latin America: Opposition and Development," in Robert A. Dahl, ed., *Regimes and Opposition*, New Haven, Conn.: Yale University Press, 1973; and Margaret McLaughlin, "Political Parties in Latin America." Unpublished manuscript, Amherst: University of Massachusetts, Department of Political Science, 1977.

6. See Glen C. Dealy, *The Public Man: An Interpretation of Latin American and Other Catholic Countries*, Amherst: University of Massachusetts Press, 1977; Howard J. Wiarda, "Toward a Framework for the Study of Political Change in the Iberic-Latin Tradition: The Corporative Model," *World Politics*, 25 (January 1973), 206–235; Wiarda, ed., *Politics and Social Change in Latin America*, Amherst: University of Massachusetts Press, 1974; and James M. Malloy, ed., *Authoritarianism and Corporatism in Latin America*, Pittsburgh, Penn.: University of Pittsburgh Press, 1977.

7. The best historical survey is Stanley G. Payne, *A History of Spain and Portugal*, 2 vols., Madison: University of Wisconsin Press, 1973.

8. Especially Raymond Carr, *Spain 1808–1939*, Oxford: Clarendon Press, 1966; Miguel M. Cuadrado, *Elecciones y partidos politicos de España, 1868–1931*, Madrid: 1931; Juan Linz, "The Party System of Spain: Past and Future," in S. Lipset and S. Rokkan, eds., *Party Systems and Voter Alignments*, New York: Free Press, 1967, pp. 197–282; Robert Kern, ed., *The Caciques: Oligarchic Politics and the System of Caciquismo in the Luso-Hispanic World*, Albuquerque: University of New Mexico Press, 1973; Marcello Caetano, *Constituçoes portuguesas*, Coimbra: Coimbra Editora, 1958; A. H. de Oliveira Martins, *History of Portugal*, Vol. II, New York: Columbia University Press, 1972; and Douglas L. Wheeler, *Republican Portugal: A Political History, 1910–1926*, Madison: University of Wisconsin Press, 1978.

9. Gerald Brennan's *The Spanish Labyrinth: An Account of the Social and Political Background of the Spanish Civil War*, Cambridge: Cambridge University Press, 1971, is the best book on this period and one of the best ever written about Spain. On the parties, see especially Linz, "The Party System" and Wheeler, *Republican Portugal*. It should be said that some of the Spanish working-class parties, the PSOE-UGT and FAI-CNT were remarkably free of middle-class intellectual domination.

10. See José Ortega y Gasset, *Invertebrate Spain*, New York: Norton, 1937.

11. Douglas L. Wheeler, *Republican Portugal: A Political History, 1910–1926*, Madison: University of Wisconsin Press, 1978.

12. Kenneth N. Medhurst, *Government in Spain*, Oxford: Pergamon Press, 1973; and Lawrence S. Graham, *Portugal: The Decline and Collapse of an Authoritarian Order*, Beverly Hills, Calif.: Sage, 1975.

13. The Spanish Falange became the "Movimiento"; see Juan Linz "From Falange to Movimiento-Organización: The Spanish Single Party and the Franco Regime, 1936–1968," in Samuel P. Huntington and Clement H. Moore, eds., *Authori-*

tarian Politics in Modern Society, New York: Basic Books, 1970, pp. 128–203. In Portugal it was the União Nacional under Salazar, remodeled and rebaptized as the Aliança Nacional Popular by Caetano; see Howard J. Wiarda, *Corporatism and Development: The Portuguese Experience*, Amherst: University of Massachusetts Press, 1978, chaps. IV, IX, X.

14. See especially Graham, op. cit.

15. V. O. Key, *Southern Politics in State and Nation*, New York: Knopf, 1949. Specifically, see Charles W. Anderson, *The Political Economy of Modern Spain: Policy-Making in an Authoritarian System*, Madison: University of Wisconsin Press, 1970; and Wiarda, *Corporatism and Development*. An important qualifier should be introduced for Spain. While the description given above holds for the earlier period, it is not a correct description of the Francoist state party mechanism after the late 1950s. By then the Movimiento had become so restricted and limited that the functions described were carried out generally through direct bureaucratic manipulation without normally bothering with the state party as such.

16. Juan Linz, "An Authoritarian Regime: Spain," in E. Allardt and Y. Littunen, eds., *Cleavages, Ideologies and Party Systems*, Helsinki: Westermarck Society, 1964, pp. 291–342 for a discussion of systems of "limited pluralism."

17. For the nature and "givens" of these elections, see Steven Ussach, "The Portuguese Presidential Election of 1958." Unpublished manuscript, Amherst: University of Massachusetts, Department of Political Science, 1974. During a period of extensive research in Portugal in 1972–1973, the author attended several meetings of the socialist and social-democratic opposition; a major congress of all the "democratic opposition" was more or less freely held at Aveiro.

18. Jon Amsden, *Collective Bargaining and Class Conflict in Spain*, London: Weidenfeld and Nicolson, 1972; and Wiarda, *Corporatism and Development*, chap. IX.

19. For some general comments on the cooptation versus repression strategies, see Howard J. Wiarda and Harvey F. Kline, *Latin American Politics and Development*, Boston: Houghton Mifflin, 1979, part I.

20. The materials in this section are based on field work in Portugal and Spain in 1972–1973, 1974, 1975, 1977.

21. An interesting case study, with broader implications, though not specifically focused on Iberia, is Michael J. Kryzanek, *Political Party Opposition in Latin America: The PRD, Joaquin Balaguer, and Politics in the Dominican Republic, 1966–1973*. Unpublished Ph.D. dissertation, Amherst: University of Massachusetts, Department of Political Science, 1975.

22. On the importance and role of the state, see Wiarda and Kline, *Latin American Politics*, chap. V.

23. The author was in Spain in the spring of 1977 when there was much public discussion of the possibility of "the Mexican model."

24. For Portugal these events may be best followed in *Expresso* and *Jornal Novo*; for Spain, see *Cuadernos para el Diálogo* and *Cambio*.

25. In office Mario Soares proved an abler and tougher politician than most observers anticipated; nevertheless the criticism holds.

26. See the coverage in the daily press for April–May 1977.

27. The most devastating portrayal of Cunhal was his celebrated interview with Oriana Fallaci, *New York Times Magazine*, July 13, 1975; in more recent statements Cunhal has begun to shed some of his "Stalinist" image.

28. Author's assessment, based on field research in Portugal in 1977.

29. These events may be followed in *Expresso* and *Jornal Novo*. During the period preceding the cabinet crisis of December, 1977, there was much talk in the Portuguese press about the vacuum of political leadership, the ineffectiveness of the government, and the widespread desire for a "government that really governs." On these and related themes, see Howard J. Wiarda, "The Transition to Democracy in Portugal: Real or Wishful?" Paper presented to the Joint Seminar on Political Development, Center for International Affairs, Harvard University, Cambridge, Mass. and Center for International Studies, Massachusetts Institute of Technology, Cambridge, Mass., December 8, 1976; excerpts and discussion published in the minutes of that JOSPOD meeting.

30. See Santiago Carillo's recently published book with this title.

31. Based on interviews with U.S. Embassy and SPOE officials.

32. Based on the field work in 1977 and interviews with elite group representatives.

33. Deutsch, *Nationalism and Social Communication*, Cambridge: MIT, 1966; but see Milton DaSilva, *The Basque Nationalist Movement: A Case Study in Modernization and Ethnic Conflict*. Unpublished Ph.D. dissertation, Amherst: University of Massachusetts, Department of Political Science, 1972; and Juan Linz and Amando de Miguel, "Within Nation Differences and Comparisons: The Eight Spains," in R. L. Merritt and S. Rokkan, eds., *Comparing Nations*, New Haven, Conn.: Yale University Press, 1966, pp. 267–319.

34. The upheavals and general strike in the Basque country in May 1977 struck many observers as based on class conflict rather than regional aspirations.

35. Philip Converse, "Of Time and Partisan Stability," *Comparative Political Studies*, 2 (July 1969), 141–142.

36. For Spain, see the Fundación FOESSA surveys and the data and studies done for them by DATA S.A. under the direction of Amando de Miguel, as well as the Gallup surveys; for Portugal, see especially John L. Hammond, "Das Urnas as Ruas: Electoral Behavior and Noninstitutional Political Militancy: Portugal, 1975." Paper presented at the conference on "Crisis in Portugal," Toronto, April 15–17, 1976.

37. On these changes, see Herminio Martins, "Portugal," and Salvador Giner, "Spain," in Margaret Archer and Giner, eds., *Contemporary Europe: Class, Status, and Power*, London: Weidenfeld and Nicolson, 1971; also João B. N. Pereira Neto, "Social Evolution in Portugal Since 1945," in R. S. Sayers, ed., *Portugal and Brazil in Transition*, Minneapolis: University of Minnesota Press, 1968; and Amando de Miguel, "Changes in the Spanish Social Structure Under Francoism." Unpublished manuscript, New Haven, Conn.: Yale University, Department of Sociology, 1977.

38. Douglas Wheeler, "Portuguese Elections and History." Unpublished manuscript, Durham: University of New Hampshire, Department of History, 1975.

39. Samuel P. Huntington, *Political Order in Changing Societies*, New Haven, Conn.: Yale University Press, 1968, p. 407.

40. Ibid., p. 8. See also *Eleicão para a Assembleia Constituinte 1975*, Lisbon: Instituto Nacional de Estatística, 1975.

41. Based on the field research in the spring of 1977, the electoral results as provided by Spanish Embassy in Washington and an anonymous paper entitled "Some Thoughts on the Meaning of Basque Voting Patterns in the 1977 Spanish Elections."

42. William T. Salisbury and Jonathan Story, "The Economic Positions of Spain and Portugal in 1980: The Official View." Paper presented at the conference on "Spain and Portugal: The Politics of Economics and Defense," Institute for the Study of Conflict, London, May 29–31, 1975; and Juan Linz, "Spain and Portugal: Critical Choices." Paper presented at the "Mini-Conference on Contemporary Portugal," Yale University, New Haven, Conn., March 28–29, 1975.

43. Two accounts by Stanley Meisler, in the *Atlantic Monthly*, May 1977, and *Foreign Affairs*, October 1977, offer useful overviews of this chronology.

44. See the analysis in Howard J. Wiarda, *Transcending Corporatism? The Portuguese Corporative System and the Revolution of 1974*, Columbia: Institute of International Studies, University of South Carolina, 1976.

45. For a general discussion of this phenomenon, see Wiarda and Kline, *Latin American Politics*, chap. V.

46. On the role of elections in the political process of Iberia and Latin America, see Charles W. Anderson, "Toward a Theory of Latin American Politics," Occasional Paper no. 2, Graduate Center for Latin American Studies, Vanderbilt University, Nashville, Tenn., February 1964.

47. *The Franco Years*, Indianapolis: Bobbs-Merrill, 1977.

48. On these more general and theoretical issues, see James M. Malloy, ed., *Authoritarianism and Corporatism*; Frederick Pike and Thomas Stritch, eds., *The New Corporatism: Social and Political Structures in the Iberian World*, Notre Dame, Ind.: University of Notre Dame Press, 1974; and Wiarda, ed., *Politics and Social Change*.

Comparative Research Topics

INTRODUCTION TO
PART THREE

Peter H. Merkl

W E HAVE ALREADY ENCOUNTERED *comparative macrotheories in the introductions to this book and to Part Two, as well as in some country articles such as that of Sten Sparre Nilson on cross-cutting cleavages in Norway and Denmark. In this part, the five authors all raise comparative perspectives that go beyond the country-by-country approach to Western European party systems, although they differ considerably in how theoretical or how empirical they are.*

Lawrence C. Mayer addresses himself to the central problem of all party systems: ". . . governments must govern," "stable government requires a stable majority," "Parties are the only available institution capable of exercising such discipline over individual legislators." Two-party systems or what goes by this label in Europe are more easily associated with the governing and opposition functions. However, even some multiparty systems are capable of acting according to the British adversary model provided that they aggregate their multiple group interests in such a way as to create at least one bloc of parties capable of governing. Unlike other theories that undertook to measure the "fractionalization" of party systems, Mayer focuses on how majority coalitions may be built of dominant and junior parties and juxtaposes an index of aggregation to one of political instability for most of the European countries we have considered and several democratic nations outside of Europe.

John C. Thomas tackles the "decline of ideology" thesis, interpreting it as a decline of ideological issue differences and a failure of the parties to develop new ideological issues for the politics of postindustrial societies.

331

His comparison is limited to the four major European democracies, Austria, and the United States and looks mainly at the larger parties and especially at the two political poles of each party system. We would expect to find major differences in the trend toward the decline of issue differences over the last 60 years between such often-cited examples of ideological decline as Austria and the Federal Republic and, on the other hand, Italy and France. Thomas examines both traditional and so-called postindustrial issues including many of the new issues of the late 1960s and the 1970s. Yet he finds that the proverbial Italian and French examples of ideological fragmentation have not been exceptions to the trend of convergency which led the late Otto Kirchheimer to speak of the "waning of opposition" and many others of the decline of ideology. The reduction of issue differences, moreover, has involved more of a leftward movement of the right wing than it has moved the left toward the right.

C. Neal Tate examines the centrality of party in voting choice, an undertaking that aims at yet another aspect of the decline of ideology, namely the alleged decline of parties in the cognitive political maps of the voters. Comparing election studies in Great Britain, the Netherlands, West Germany, the United States, and Canada between the mid-1960s and the 1970s, he reduces the voting choices to left-right dichotomies. His key variables are party identification and party affect and he finds that, according to the data at hand, the former has indeed declined whereas the latter has increased. We are thus left with the conclusion that a demonstration of the "decline of parties" thesis strictly depends on how such a decline is defined, by party identification or by party affect. As with the decline of ideology, the decline of parties is an ambiguous slogan lacking in empirical specificity. It can be confirmed or disconfirmed depending on what we mean by it, and it is a useless concept unless it is explained further.

The study of ideological and basic attitudes among Italian and West German Socialists and Christian Democrats by Peter H. Merkl is an attempt to move the examination of partisan ideologies from their diffuse and elusive presence in mass publics to the more solid ground of the beliefs of party members. These beliefs and the complex relationships among several levels of beliefs are compared for the two nations as well as for the two sets of partisan subcultures. The replacement of traditional ideological syndromes, such as Socialist anticlericalism, class solidarity, and anticapitalism (or Christian Democratic clericalism, solidarism, and conservatism) with new sets of political beliefs is also related to such attributes as social distrust, socioeconomic status, age, and involvement in party activity. In the end, attitude profiles for each of the four major parties emerge and can be compared.

Part Three ends with a critical essay by Sten Sparre Nilson about the familiar spatial models of party competition. The models and curves of several authors are examined and tested against concrete problems of politico-economic bargains and trade-offs. The Third Republic of France, in which a middle bloc "equally opposed to clerical reaction and to socialist experiment" in effect prevented all real change, is the test case which reveals the limits of such competition modeling of party systems. Nilson shows in a more pragmatic way what David Robertson called the four ways in which competition modeling has failed to capture the essence of how party systems function: "For Downs there is never any reason why a party might not want, might not be able, might not suffer from failing, or might [not] expect it to be rewarding ... to adopt the vote maximising point on the spectrum."[1] Like other insightful models, mapping competition makes its point by leaving out all but one dynamic element of a complex mechanism and suffers the consequences of such deliberate omission.

Note

1. David Robertson, *A Theory of Party Competition*, New York: Wiley, 1976, p. 31. The four simplifications are said to be the number of parties, the constitutional structure of states, actor motivation, and standards of voter rationality.

CHAPTER 13

PARTY SYSTEMS AND CABINET STABILITY

Lawrence C. Mayer

THE COLLAPSE OF PARLIAMENTARY DEMOCRACIES in Europe prior to World War II generated a search for the internal weaknesses of such systems. Out of this search came the suggestion from several quarters that multiparty parliamentary democracies were more prone to cabinet instability than were two-party systems.[1] Parliamentary democracies, beset with such cabinet instability, cannot govern effectively. Therefore, it was suggested, such unstable systems were readily replaced by more authoritarian political regimes that appeared better able to provide for the efficient functioning of the system.

At first glance, the logic behind such a proposition appears unassailable. Governments must govern; that is, they must possess a measure of discretion in choosing among alternatives of public policy and possess the capacity to impose such choices on society. Governments in parliamentary systems by and large govern only at the sufferance of a majority of the lower house of the legislature.[2] Therefore, stable government requires a stable majority in that house. It is highly unlikely that a majority of several hundred autonomous individual legislators would spontaneously arrive at agreements over a wide range of issues. An institution or structure must exist to command support for the government from individual legislators who may disagree with the government's position on one or more issues. Parties are the only available institution capable of exercising such discipline over individual legislators.

A strict two-party system will produce a majority of one party capable of being disciplined in support of the government. In a three- or more party system (usually called multiparty), such a majority is less likely to result from an election. In such systems, governments normally must be formed from

335

coalitions of two or more autonomous parties. Although parties may discipline their own members, they do not have the same power over coalition partners.

This suggested relationship between multiparty systems and cabinet stability seemed to its early proponents to explain the instability of the Third and Fourth French Republics, Weimar Germany, prewar Austria, and Italy, in contrast with the manifest success of parliamentary democracy in Great Britain. However, as political scientists began to devote increasing attention to the smaller parliamentary democracies, the realization grew that there were numerous stable parliamentary democracies with three or more parties in the legislature. The Low Country and Scandinavian democracies constitute obvious examples of such "deviant cases."

Part of the confusion lies in the manner in which the variables of party systems and cabinet stability have been conceptualized. Therefore, the primary task of this paper is to more adequately conceptualize both cabinet stability and one of the variables that putatively influence such stability.

A secondary purpose of this paper is to utilize these indices in a test of the relationship between party system aggregation and cabinet instability. It is suggested that these variables are negatively correlated and that party aggregation, as herein conceptualized, will more fully account for the variation in cabinet stability than other conceptualizations of party system variables that have previously appeared in the literature including the number of parties (Hermens, 1951; Milnor, 1959; Duverger, 1963) or Rae's index of fractionalization, discussed below (Rae, 1968).

The Number of Parties

The concepts of two-party and multiparty systems do not group specific party systems in such a way that the similarities within a category and differences between categories emerge as significant.

As an illustration of the conceptual difficulties in the conventional treatments of party systems, we might take note of Leslie Lipson's widely accepted definition of a two-party system:

1. Not more than two parties at any given time have a genuine chance to gain power.
2. One of these is able to win the requisite majority to stay in office without help from a third party.
3. Over a number of decades, two parties alternate in power. (Lipson, 1953:338)

By this formula, Australia would not qualify as having a two-party system. During much of the post-World War II era, Australia had been governed by an apparently indissoluble coalition of the Liberal and Country parties with the

Labour party, holding a plurality, in opposition. It is unclear whether Lipson's phrase "gain power" encompasses participation in a governing coalition; nevertheless, Australia clearly did not meet his second criterion. Yet it is manifestly clear that the Australian party system operates with greater similarity to the two-party model of Great Britain than to the multiparty models of the Third and Fourth French Republics. The same could be said of Canada's party system, although Maurice Duverger classifies it as a four-party system (1963:223). A government is essentially controlled by one of two parties, although minority governments in Canada have not been all that rare.

Thus, one must go through intellectual contortions to construct a definition of a two-party system that will include those systems that essentially behave like the classic two-party model—that is, where two stable and relatively cohesive forces alternate in and out of power. In the Australian example, a Country-Labour coalition is inconceivable given the intensity of antipathy between them, hence, the former cannot play a balance of power role.

Moreover, the variation of system types within the category of multiparty (three or more) is so great as to render that category virtually meaningless. Clearly, a three-party system such as Belgium's generates a different set of expectations with regard to cabinet stability than a twelve-party system as found in the Netherlands or in the Weimar Republic. The probability of the loss of a government's majority is certainly greater when the majority depends on the continued cooperation of four or five parties than when the majority depends on the continued cooperation of two parties. It may make more sense to think of party systems as a continuous variable than as a dichotomous typology.

Party Dominance

Although the number of parties is an important consideration, the size of the largest party also affects the impact of the party system on cabinet stability. Thus, Sweden's party system features five parties; however, the largest party, the Social Democrats, has maintained either a majority of seats in the Riksdag or close to it for 43 years. It has been able to govern unfettered by coalition partners or with the alliance of a small Communist party, a party that lacked any other options. Clearly, there is no reason for a system such as this to produce any more instability than the classic two-party model. Indeed, one might expect less turnover at more or less regular elections than in the two-party model due to the fragmentation of the opposition in the Swedish system. Clearly, one would expect greater cabinet stability in Sweden than in a system of five parties of approximately equal strength.

Arian and Barnes have suggested that a dominant party system, a system in which one party retains essentially hegemonic control of the government over a long period of time despite more or less regular elections, is *sui generis*, essentially distinct from either the two-party or multiparty system. They have suggested that such a system is capable of extreme stability (Arian and Barnes, 1974:600).

Arian and Barnes use Italy and Israel as examples. In these systems, no party is close to majority status; apparently, majority status is not necessary to be labeled a dominant party. What is needed is a clear explication of why a party that is significantly stronger than its rivals although far short of majority status should be stable.

In such systems, it is virtually impossible to form a government that excludes the dominant party. Although governments are by coalition, all but one member of that coalition become junior coalition partners. Because the strongest party is indispensable, the junior coalition partners are unable to bargain effectively with the dominant party even though that party is not a majority party. The dominant party may be able to choose from among several junior partners, whereas the junior partners have nowhere else to go but out of power. Smaller parties are thus under considerable pressure to reach accommodation with the dominant coalition partner. To the extent that one can assume that any party is better off as part of the governing coalition than in opposition, it is against the interest of such smaller coalition partners to bring down the government.

Dominance may be usefully conceptualized as an overwhelming plurality of seats in the lower house of the legislature. Thus conceptualized, dominance is clearly a matter of degree. The Italian Christian Democrats are dominant according to Arian and Barnes with about a third of the seats in a typical Italian legislative session, yet they are less dominant than the Swedish Social Democrats with a little more or a little less than half of the seats in the Riksdag since 1932. The unanswered question is whether or not cabinet stability is to a significant extent a function of degree of dominance.

Toward a New Conceptualization of System Types

Rather than speak of a simplistic typology of a two- or multiparty system, it is being suggested that it is preferable to speak of a continuous variable with the continuum running from fragmented to aggregated.

It is further suggested that *two dimensions* must be included in the measurement of this variable: the number of parties and the relative strength of the largest party. The latter variable is indicated by the average percentage of seats that party has in the lower house of the legislature for the time period in question. An aggregation score may be calculated as the average percentage of the largest party divided by the average number of parties having seats in that legislative assembly: $A = (S/L)/P$, where A is the aggregation index, S is the mean number of seats that the largest party in any given legislative session has for the period in question, L is the mean number of seats in the lower house of the legislature for the period, and P is the mean number of parties holding seats in that house averaged for the period in question. The higher the score, the more aggregated the system and the less instability one would expect from that system. Accordingly, the aggregation index should correlate negatively with the instability score.

This measure differs from and, I believe, has an advantage over Douglas Rae's index of "party fractionalization" in terms of potentially explaining cabinet instability (1968). Rae's index, like the one offered here, is a continuous variable that avoids the oversimplified artificiality of the two- and multiparty categorization. However, Rae's index is based on the number of parties and the number of seats held by each party. Therefore, Rae's index makes no distinction between the aggregation of the government and that of the opposition. For example, according to Rae's index, Israel is one of the most highly fractionalized of systems and Sweden is somewhere in the middle. Yet, with their respective dominant parties, both systems are characterized by considerable cabinet stability. Taylor and Herman also utilize Rae's fractionalization index in their attempt to explain cabinet stability.

Thus being sensitive to the size of the largest party in the government coalition, the principal advantage in the measure offered here in the attempt to explain cabinet stability over the Rae index as utilized by Taylor and Herman (1971) is that the index offered here makes a distinction between the aggregation of the government coalition and of the opposition. It is not surprising that Taylor and Herman (1971:32) find virtually no negative correlation between the fragmentation of the opposition and cabinet stability. One could almost expect the opposite result. The more fragmented the opposition, the less viable an alternative government will appear, a supposition in which Taylor and Herman concur. The logic of the party dominance thesis applies to only the government, and the aggregation index offered here takes account of the logic.

Usually, but not always, the largest party in the legislature is part of the government. As discussed earlier, this is due to the bargaining power of that party. If its plurality is not overwhelming, however, the next strongest party may coalesce with a smaller party to exclude the largest party in the legislature from the government. In such cases, the largest party in the government rather than the largest party in the legislature is used in the aggregation index. (In Australia, for example, the Labour party has occasionally been placed in opposition by a Liberal-Country coalition. The permanence of that coalition may cause some to question as to whether or not they ought to be viewed as autonomous parties.)

Conceptually, aggregation connotes the extent to which parties bring together (aggregate) a number of diverse demands and interests under one party label. The aggregation index measures the extent to which the government is dominated by one power center rather than having to bargain and compromise among several *autonomous* power centers in order to hold the government together. The autonomy of these other power centers is thought to be a function of the two dimensions in the aggregation index. Thus, it is suggested that the index combining the two dimensions possesses face validity; if it explains a significantly large portion of the variation in cabinet instability than previously explained, it would possess construct validity. The term avoids the necessity of having to rationalize systems such as those in Australia, Austria, Canada, and West Germany under the two-party label because they behave more like the British system than, say, that of the Fourth French Republic.

Fragmented refers to those party systems in which governments are formed by a process of negotiation, bargaining, and compromising after the elections. Thus, the composition of the government in such systems and its policy outputs are not determined to a great extent by the outcome of the election. In aggregative systems, the composition of the government is determined to a great extent by the outcome of the election; consequently, policy alternatives are affected by such elections as well. Those who prefer fragmented systems as more democratic are therefore conceptualizing democracy in terms of representation, the input side of politics, rather than in terms of responsive policy dimensions, the output side of politics. In such fragmented systems, the homogeneity of each party's clientele is preserved by the absence of bargaining and compromise within each party's structure.

Cabinet Stability

The dependent variable, cabinet stability, is also in need of reconceptualization. The basic concern with regard to unstable government is the lack of coherence and continuity in policy making, the inability of a government to produce a coherent, relatively predictable policy output over time and over a range of specific issues. Leon Hurwitz (1971) perceptively points out that the Taylor and Herman conceptualization of cabinet stability, a conceptualization that equates stability with duration, fails to weight the different types of events. It is suggested here that different kinds of events have different impacts on the aforementioned capacity to govern coherently. There are four types of events that should have a negative impact on that capacity. The probable strength of this impact varies with these types of events; hence, these events should be weighted accordingly.

The heaviest weighting is given to unscheduled resignations of the government due to a loss of confidence in the legislature and the reformation of the government under a prime minister or premier of a different party label.

Next in weighting is an unscheduled election not compelled by a loss of legislative support which results in a change in which party controls the head of government role. Such a personnel change is reasoned to have a greater impact on probable policy output and therefore to have a greater disruptive effect than when the government is reformed under the control of the same party. A loss of confidence in the legislature is an indicator that the tenure of any given government is tenuous and that the placing of the control of the government on the line is forced upon the government.

Third in weighting are unscheduled resignations of the government due to a loss of support in the legislature (i.e., no confidence) and the reformation of the government under the same party label. Italy would manifest this condition most clearly with 36 governments since World War II, but almost invariably under Christian Democratic leadership.

An unscheduled election in which the same party retains control of the head of government role is the fourth in weighting. Such elections may or may not be called to avoid a possible loss of confidence. These types of events are scored from four to one in the order in which they are mentioned.

A cabinet resignation forced by the legislature on a confidence vote clearly is an indication of more instability than one that is voluntary to call new elections. Moreover, when a cabinet cannot be reconstituted without elections, this may suggest a highly unstable situation. Therefore, when a forced resignation is followed by new elections, both events are scored unless, as in Britain and the older Commonwealth, elections must follow such a resignation. In those systems, the constitution (in the extralegal British sense of the term) dictates the dissolution of Parliament; hence, the following elections cannot be taken as an indication of an inability to form a government. Finally, the duration of cabinet crises must be included in the analysis, a variable omitted from previous analyses of cabinet stability.

Clearly, whatever the nature of the events, a cabinet crisis lasting a great length of time is at least as destabilizing or more so as several of the same types of events of short duration. Furthermore, the longer each cabinet crisis lasts, the fewer crises that nation can have given the same disposition toward stability or its antithesis.

Recall that we are interested in stability not for its own sake as are Taylor and Herman (1971) but in terms of its logically supposed impact on the capacity to govern coherently over time. Accordingly, cabinet crises that last from one to three months are scored as one point, from three to six months two points, in addition to the score of the event itself. This should reflect the situation of nations like the Netherlands where a highly fragmented party system might be expected to produce destabilizing events, even a weighted enumeration. Inclusion of the duration variable will make the Netherlands a less deviant case. It is thus possible to construct a quantitative score for cabinet stability that, albeit based on some judgmental decisions, is somewhat more complex than unidimensional conceptualizations and does permit the dependent variable to be used in quantitative analysis.

Party Aggregation and Cabinet Stability

The data presented in Tables 13–1 and 13–2 include the universe of industrial parliamentary democracies. Other nations in the Afro-Asian-Latin areas may have the political forms of parliamentary democracies; however, these nations often lack a genuinely competitive political system, a fact which would seriously distort any study of cabinet stability. It is not unreasonable to suggest that industrial democracies, because of cultural and social characteristics distinctive to them, operate differently from newly independent and less industrialized parliamentary systems. Hence, the geographical universe of this paper is industrial parliamentary democracies.

A 15-year data base was selected, from 1960 through 1974. The Fourth French Republic was included due to the relative scarcity of fragmented systems since its demise. Obviously, a different time period was required in the case of France since the Fourth Republic was supplanted by the Fifth Republic in 1958, so the years 1948 through 1957 were used. Because this paper is not

TABLE 13–1.   Aggregation Factors and Indices for Seventeen Nations

	MEAN NUMBER OF PARTIES IN LEGISLATURE	MEAN PERCENTAGE SEATS OF LEADING PARTY	AGGREGATE INDEX
Australia	3.0	40.0	15.20
Austria	3.0	50.4	16.80
Belgium	5.0	36.9	7.38
Canada	4.0	48.0	12.00
Denmark	6.7	35.6	5.27
Finland	8.0	27.0	3.37
France (Fourth Republic)	12.0	21.0	1.70
Germany (Bonn)	3.0	47.6	15.80
Great Britain	3.5	54.0	18.00
Iceland	4.5	37.9	8.44
Ireland	4.0	50.0	12.50
Israel	11.7	38.3	3.28
Italy	9.5	41.9	4.40
Japan	6.0	58.5	9.75
Luxembourg	5.0	33.9	6.78
Netherlands	10.2	29.0	2.84
New Zealand	2.3	54.0	23.40
Sweden	5.5	46.0	8.36

TABLE 13–2. Factors and Index of Government Instability

	Unscheduled Elections, Same Party	Unscheduled Cabinet Resignations, Same Party	Unscheduled Elections, Party Change	Unscheduled Cabinet Resignations, Party Change	Duration of Crises (2 mo = 1 pt)	Istability Index	Aggregate Index
Australia	3	3	0	1	2 mo = 1	11	13.20
Austria	1	1	0	0	2 mo = 1	3	16.80
Belgium	2	3	0	2	3 mo = 1	16	7.38
Canada	1	2	1	1		12	12.00
Denmark	2	0	1	2		13	5.27
Finland	1	1	0	6	9 mo = 3	30	3.37
France (Fourth Republic)	1	0	0	15		61	1.70
Germany (Bonn)	2	2	0	0	0	6	15.80
Great Britain	2	0	2	0		8	18.00
Iceland	0	1	1	1		9	8.44
Ireland	1	1	1	0		6	12.50
Israel	2	4	0	0	8 mo = 1	11	3.28
Italy	2	13	0	0		28	44.00
Japan	4	6	0	0		16	9.75
Luxembourg	1	1	0	0	10 mo = 4 }	3	6.78
Netherlands	2	1	0	2	2 mo = 1 }	15	2.84
New Zealand	0	1	1	0		4	23.40
Sweden	0	0	0	0		0	8.36

Pearson's r = −.57   sig. = .007
Spearman's ρ = −.62   sig. = .003
Kendall's τ = −.48   sig = .003

343

concerned with changes in these political systems, it did not seem legitimate to claim an expansion of data points by using several points in time.

Correlations were calculated between the two indices offered in this note using Spearman's rho (ρ), Pearson's r, and Kendall's τ. Since we are dealing with continuous, interval data, the product moment coefficient seemed a natural choice. However, the Pearson coefficient is particularly sensitive to extreme outlying cases (such as the data on Fourth Republic France). The Spearman's, being a rank order correlation, is not sensitive to such outlyers; therefore, it was included to counterbalance that particular distortion. Kendall's is also reported, as it is not sensitive to ties as is Spearman's.

Whereas the Pearson product moment coefficient should be inflated by the outliers, it should be depressed by the somewhat curvilinear shape of the regression line (see the scattergram in Figure 13–1). Pearson's r assumes linearity. Thus, by the logic Spearman's should be higher than Pearson's,

Figure 13-1.   Scattergram and Linear Regression Line

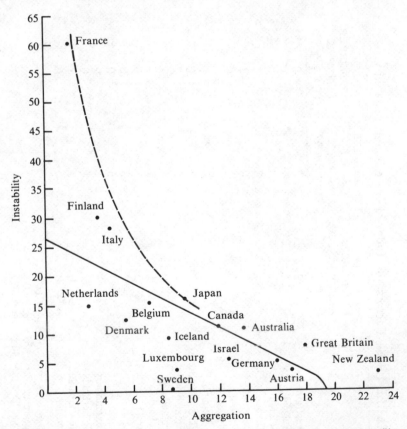

NOTE: If France were included, the line of best fit (dashed line in figure) would be curvilinear.

because Spearman's is not distorted by the assumption of linearity. The same logic should also apply to Kendall's rank order coefficient; however, τ, unaffected by ties, should be lower than ρ with 3 ties in 18 cases. Negative correlations should be obtained on all measures. That is, the higher a nation's aggregation index, the lower its instability score and vice versa. All measures are in the expected direction and are indicative of a moderate to strong relationship. The hypothesis of a negative relationship between my indices of aggregation and cabinet instability are thus clearly supported by Pearson's r of $-.57$ and a Spearman's ρ of $-.62$, and a Kendall's τ of $-.48$. These figures also confirm the expectations derived from the logic of the measures as discussed above with Spearman's ρ being higher than r and both being higher than τ. The data are drawn from the universe of industrial parliamentary democracies. If, however, one tends to regard diachronic expansion of the data as adding distinct data points rendering the reported time frame a "sample" of such democracies or if one wishes to regard these 18 nations as a sample of all nations having the forms of parliamentary democracies (a universe including such places as Mexico, Botswana, and Rhodesia), then the .007 significance level of the Pearson's correlation, the .003 level of Spearman's, and the .003 level of τ become relevant.

Obviously, cabinet stability or, more specifically, the events that comprise the stability score, are a product of numerous factors of which the party system is only one. It would therefore be unreasonable to expect an extremely high correlation between a measure of party aggregation and the instability index. What has been suggested is that the party aggregation factor can, despite the debunking of the vulnerable Herman thesis, explain some significant portion of the variation in cabinet stability if both variables are properly conceptualized and measured. The data are not inconsistent with this proposition. The coefficient of determination, r^2, suggests 32.3%—almost one-third—of the variation in cabinet stability is accounted for by this conceptualization of party system aggregation.

Conclusion

The utility of any measure of a variable lies in its ability to account some significant portion of another variable that we wish to explain. Cabinet instability in those parliamentary democracies characterized by genuine political competition has been a phenomenon that political scientists have long endeavored to explain. It has been intuitively plausible that certain characteristics of party systems contribute significantly to such instability; yet, early efforts of scholars like Herman (1951) to specify the nature of such a relationship left many glaring deviant cases. Later, more sophisticated efforts such as that by Taylor and Herman constituted a major improvement in explaining "government stability." Yet, even here, the correlations, while quite strong (running around .3 to .4), can be improved upon with more adequate conceptualization of the variables.

The data presented here support the contention that there is a relatively strong relationship between party systems and cabinet stability. A Pearsonian correlation of −.57 is considerably stronger than any result reported by Taylor and Herman supporting my contention that a more adequate conceptualization of the variables will account for a greater percentage of the variation in the explicandum. Not only is the coefficient strong; the slope in the scattergram indicates that the independent variable has considerable impact on the dependent variable. The major outlier, the Fourth Republic of France, is characterizable less as a deviant case than as an extreme example of the negative relationship herein asserted. Omitting France changes the r very little from −.57 to −.56.

By incorporating additional dimensions into our conceptualization of cabinet stability (such as kinds of events and duration of cabinet crises) and in our conceptualization of party system aggregation (such as the distinction between government aggregation and the opposition), our ability to explain the variability in the capacity of parliamentary democracies to govern coherently can be enhanced significantly. In a heuristic sense, perhaps F. A. Hermens has made a contribution after all.

Notes

1. Such studies rendered themselves especially vulnerable to criticism by suggesting that the fragmentation of the party system was predominantly a function of the election system.
2. The Netherlands does not specifically require a government to resign upon the loss of parliamentary support on a given issue. However, repeated losses of parliamentary votes by the government, especially in the Tweede Kamer (the lower house) results in the resignation of the government.

References

ARIAN, ALAN and BARNES, SAMUEL. 1974. "The Dominant Party System: A Neglected Model of Political Stability," *Journal of Politics*, 36 (August), 592–614.

DUVERGER, MAURICE. 1963. *Political Parties*, trans. Barbara and Robert North. New York: Wiley.

HERMENS, F. A. 1951. *Europe Under Democracy or Anarchy*. Notre Dame, Ind.: University of Notre Dame Press.

HURWITZ, LEON. 1971. "Communications to the Editor," *American Political Science Review*, 65 (December), 1148–1149.

LIPSON, LESLIE. 1953. "The Two Party System in Great Britain," *The American Political Science Review* 57 (June), 337–358.

MILNOR, ANDREW. 1964. *Elections and Political Stability*. Boston: Little Brown.

RAE, DOUGLAS. 1968. "A Note on the Fractionalism of Some European Party Systems," *Comparative Political Studies*, 1 (October), 413–418.

TAYLOR, MICHAEL and HERMAN, V. M. 1971. "Party Systems and Government Stability," *American Political Science Review*, 65 (March), 28–37.

CHAPTER 14

IDEOLOGICAL TRENDS IN WESTERN POLITICAL PARTIES

John Clayton Thomas

TRADITIONALLY, political parties in Western democracies have been viewed as offering distinct choices on what government should do and how it should operate. Those choices were based on party ideologies and were expressed in clearly differing stands on major public issues. The choices have been viewed as the primary basis for partisanship, that is, for people voting for parties in elections and, for parties aiding in governmental policy-making.

Recently, however, some observers have questioned whether the distinct issue differences between Western parties may be declining or disappearing, thus reducing the basis for choice between parties. If so, partisanship itself might be placed in doubt. What happens to partisan competition if the parties are no longer distinguishable from each other?

The possible changes in partisan issue differences have usually been discussed in terms of party ideologies, with two principal assertions being offered. One assertion holds that there has been a decline in the influence of traditional ideologies (e.g., socialism, liberalism, conservatism) on party policy positions.[1] As those ideologies have lost influence, parties have supposedly drifted closer together on traditional partisan issues. The second assertion holds that parties have failed to develop new ideologies to deal with the rapidly changing conditions of the so-called "postindustrial" era.[2] The absence of new ideologies supposedly means no partisan differences arising on new issues.

This research examines the validity of these two assertions for domestic policy questions in six Western party systems. (The area of foreign policy

348

questions was deemed beyond the scope of this research.) The research will examine first how party positions on traditional domestic policy questions have changed in recent decades. It will then examine how, if at all, parties are dealing with new domestic issues. A concluding segment will then speculate on what the changes might mean for the future of partisanship.

Method

This research examines the party systems of Austria, France, Great Britain, Italy, the United States, and West Germany. These six were selected, from among the many possible, because they offer useful contrasts. Austria and West Germany, for example, have been frequently described as countries in which partisan policy differences have declined sharply, whereas Italy and France, by contrast, are viewed as party systems where radical partisan policy differences still flourish.[3] Great Britain has usually been viewed as somewhere between those two extremes. The U.S example presents a final contrast as a party system where ideology and large partisan differences have been said never to have flourished.[4]

The research was designed to examine all significant parties within these party systems. A party was considered significant, and so selected for study, if it averaged during the period of study either (1) 5% of the seats in the lower house (e.g., the House of Representatives in the United States) or (2) 5% of the total votes for seats in the lower house.

The parties were studied on two types of domestic issues, the "traditional" and the "postindustrial." The traditional issues, adapted from earlier research,[5] are ten ordinal dimensions of policy questions on which major divisions between Western political parties have been based. Some have to do with social and economic matters, others with matters of the structures and procedures of government. This research will focus primarily on the former because the latter have had little relevance in recent years.

The issues were operationalized as scales usually covering a ten-point range. They were defined in left-right terms, the terms in which parties have usually viewed them. The scales are presented in Figures 14–1 through 14–10 in abbreviated form, including the issue name (with, parenthetically, its abbreviation for use in later tables), the extreme positions, and the range of the scale.

These scales were used as the basis for scoring party stands on traditional issues in several time periods. The 1971–1976 period was used for contemporary years, with historical periods of 1957–1962, 1950–1956, and 1911–1915.

Parties were scored through content analysis of contemporary and historical literature on parties and societies. Excerpts were selected by the author based on an exhaustive search of library materials, including political histories, essays on politics, and the like. Two coders were then provided with the excerpts, one party system at a time, and instructed to code the parties on each policy dimension in each period. Consideration was to be given in the coding both to what parties said they wanted and to what they actually sought. In other words, party scores were to be based on a compromise between platform and practice.

After the coders completed their coding independently, they were to record their codes and then meet to resolve any differences. These records produced intercoder reliabilities ranging from .709 on one party system to .920 on another. In addition, the pre-1970 data correlated well—from .779 to .863— with similar data produced independently by Lawrence C. Dodd.[6]

The new, or "postindustrial," issues were dealt with more subjectively. Drawing from the literature excerpts for the 1971–1976 period, the research attempted, first, to identify any major new issues in these countries, second, to compare the issues to postindustrial themes, and, third, to discern whether the issues were prompting new partisan differences.

Figure 14-1. Nationalization and Control of Means of Production (Industries)

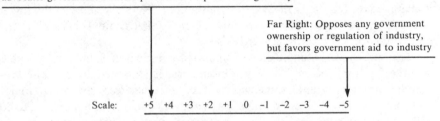

Far Left: Strongly favors government ownership;
advocates government ownership of all basic industries;
advocates government ownership of means of production generally

Far Right: Opposes any government ownership or regulation of industry, but favors government aid to industry

Scale: +5   +4   +3   +2   +1   0   −1   −2   −3   −4   −5

Figure 14-2. Government Role in Economic Planning (Planning)

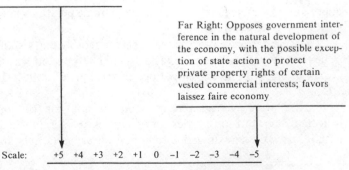

Far Left: Advocates government prescription of the level and nature of resource allocation, commodity production and distribution; often represented by the promulgation of "five-year plans" and the like

Far Right: Opposes government interference in the natural development of the economy, with the possible exception of state action to protect private property rights of certain vested commercial interests; favors laissez faire economy

Scale: +5   +4   +3   +2   +1   0   −1   −2   −3   −4   −5

Figure 14-3.   Distribution of Wealth (Taxes)

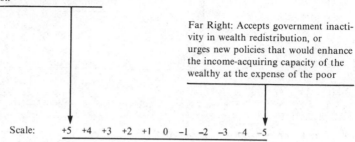

Far Left: Advocates extreme vertical redistribution from rich to poor to achieve the goal of almost total equalization of income and wealth; favors land nationalization and redistribution (or state ownership) of land plus confiscatory income taxation, to achieve income and wealth redistribution

Far Right: Accepts government inactivity in wealth redistribution, or urges new policies that would enhance the income-acquiring capacity of the wealthy at the expense of the poor

Scale: +5   +4   +3   +2   +1   0   –1   –2   –3   –4   –5

Figure 14-4.   Providing for Social Welfare (Welfare)

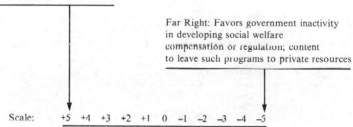

Far Left: Favors universally available, "cradle-to-grave," social welfare through a program of public assistance (including aid to the poor, aged, young, and including health care and medical benefits) with at least subsistence-level benefits

Far Right: Favors government inactivity in developing social welfare compensation or regulation; content to leave such programs to private resources

Scale: +5   +4   +3   +2   +1   0   –1   –2   –3   –4   –5

Figure 14-5.   Secularization of Society (Religion)

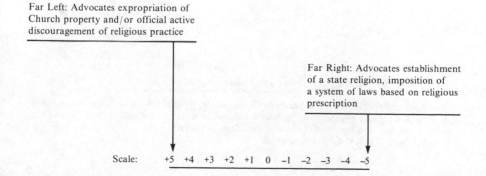

Far Left: Advocates expropriation of Church property and/or official active discouragement of religious practice

Far Right: Advocates establishment of a state religion, imposition of a system of laws based on religious prescription

Scale: +5   +4   +3   +2   +1   0   –1   –2   –3   –4   –5

Figure 14-6.   Extension of the Franchise (Franchise)

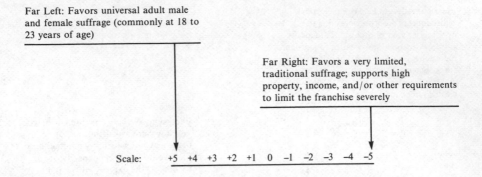

Far Left: Favors universal adult male
and female suffrage (commonly at 18 to
23 years of age)

Far Right: Favors a very limited,
traditional suffrage; supports high
property, income, and/or other requirements
to limit the franchise severely

Scale: +5 +4 +3 +2 +1   0 −1 −2 −3 −4 −5

Figure 14-7.   Electoral System (Electoral)

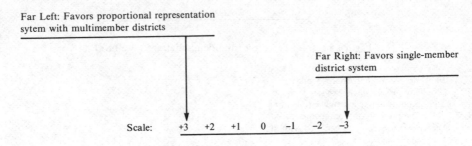

Far Left: Favors proportional representation
sytem with multimember districts

Far Right: Favors single-member
district system

Scale: +3   +2   +1   0   −1   −2   −3

Figure 14-8.   Party Government*

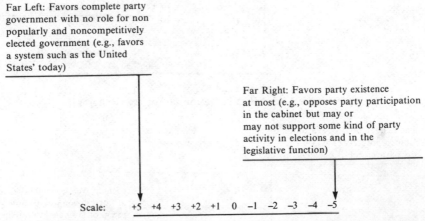

Far Left: Favors complete party
government with no role for non
popularly and noncompetitively
elected government (e.g., favors
a system such as the United
States' today)

Far Right: Favors party existence
at most (e.g., opposes party participation
in the cabinet but may or
may not support some kind of party
activity in elections and in the
legislative function)

Scale: +5 +4 +3 +2 +1   0 −1 −2 −3 −4 −5

*"Party government" is a common historical shorthand for the question of how much control of the
legislative and executive branches of government should be based on the outcomes of popular (e.g.,
open to mass participation), competitive elections. Operationally, the question has usually concerned
hwo much control should be given to parties.

Figure 14-9.   Governmental Centralization (Federalism)*

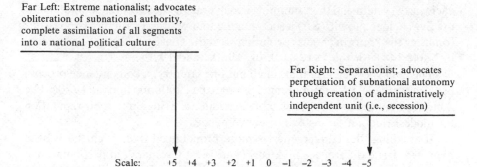

Far Left: Extreme nationalist; advocates
obliteration of subnational authority,
complete assimilation of all segments
into a national political culture

Far Right: Separationist; advocates
perpetuation of subnational autonomy
through creation of administratively
independent unit (i.e., secession)

Scale: +5 +4 +3 +2 +1   0 −1 −2 −3 −4 −5

*The fit of left-right terminology is not as good here as on the other issues. The terminology is retained, nonetheless, for consistency with the other issues.

Figure 14-10.   Reform vs. Revolution

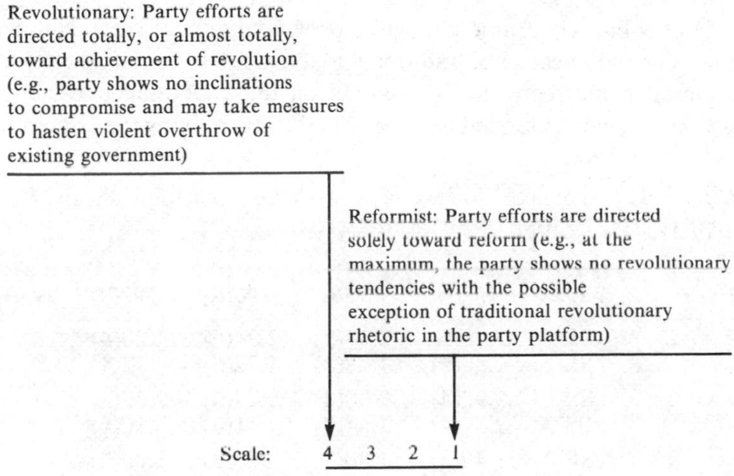

Revolutionary: Party efforts are
directed totally, or almost totally,
toward achievement of revolution
(e.g., party shows no inclinations
to compromise and may take measures
to hasten violent overthrow of
existing government)

Reformist: Party efforts are directed
solely toward reform (e.g., at the
maximum, the party shows no revolutionary
tendencies with the possible
exception of traditional revolutionary
rhetoric in the party platform)

Scale: 4   3   2   1

Traditional Issues I:
Convergence Within Party Systems

What has happened to traditional partisan differences in Western party systems? To answer that question, a measure of average issue differences was developed. The purpose of the measure is to indicate the average distance between parties in a party system at a given time. It is computed by first averaging the differences on each issue for all possible pairs of parties within each party system and then summing and averaging those scores separately for the five socioeconomic (SE) issues and the four political structure (PS) issues (omitting the "reform versus revolution" issue). These averages are presented in Table 14–1 for the 1910s, 1950s, 1960s, and 1970s.

The data show clearly that, in all but one country, a convergence process began after the 1910s and continued through the 1960s and into the 1970s. The American parties are the predictable exceptions, living up to their reputation for modest fluctuation instead of convergence.

If anything, the convergence is more pronounced than might have been expected. Issue differences in Austria and West Germany, in particular, had declined markedly. Indeed, by the 1970s the Austrian and West German parties differed less than did the supposedly indistinguishable American parties.

The convergence process appeared almost completed in Austria. There the Socialist party and the People's party no longer differed in the 1970s on such traditional sources of controversy as how much control government should have over industry, what government should do about the distribution of wealth, and what government should provide by way of social welfare programs. The only vestige of traditional ideological divisions was a slim one-point difference between the two parties on the economic planning issue.

The convergence extended to France and Italy, belying the contentions of

TABLE 14–1.   Average Differences of Issue Positions within Party Systems, 1910s, 1950s, 1960s, and 1970s

COUNTRY	ISSUE TYPE	1910s	1950s	1960s	1970s	SIGNS[a] 1960–1970
France	SE	3.48(5)[b]	2.44(5)	2.34(5)	1.20(4)	+
	PS	1.30(5)	1.28(5)	1.72(5)	.73(4)	+
Italy	SE	3.90(4)	3.00(4)	2.27(4)	2.23(4)	+
	PS	2.67(4)	1.44(4)	1.11(4)	.50(4)	+
Austria	SE	3.40(3)	1.40(3)	.67(3)	.20(2)	+
	PS	.50(3)	0(3)	0(3)	0(2)	0
West Germany	SE	3.08(5)	2.13(3)	1.73(3)	.44(3)	+
	PS	3.51(5)	.33(3)	.33(3)	0(3)	+
Great Britain	SE	2.47(4)	1.47(3)	1.10(3)	.53(3)	+
	PS	2.60(4)	1.00(3)	1.00(3)	1.00(3)	0
United States	SE	.80(2)	1.40(2)	1.20(2)	1.40(2)	−
	PS	.75(2)	.25(2)	.25(2)	.25(2)	0

[a]In this table and in Table 14–2, signs in the right-hand columns indicate whether there was no change between the designated periods (0) or, if change occurred, whether it was in the predicted direction (+) or not (−).
[b]In this table and in Table 14–2, the figures in parentheses represent the number of parties on which the average deviation is based.

some that ideological differences have persisted undiminished there. Those contentions have been directed particularly at France; yet, it is France which shows as much convergence as any of the six countries from the 1960s to the 1970s. Partisan differences may still be large in France—for who is to say what is "large" in ideological terms?—but they are obviously smaller than in prior decades and no longer much greater than the American party differences.

The Italian data are difficult to interpret because they are distorted by the inclusion of one minor extremist party, the Neo-Fascist party (or Neo-Fascist-Monarchist party in the 1970s), in the computations. If that minor party were excluded from the 1970s computations, the figures for Italy would drop to 1.07 for the socioeconomic issues and zero for the political structure issues.

That problem suggests a flaw in the statistic: It treats all parties equally regardless of size, thus giving weight to extremist minor parties probably far out of proportion to their actual importance in party systems. That flaw is especially disturbing in an era when many Western multiparty systems, including France and Italy, are viewed as moving toward two-party, or at least bipolar, party systems. This problem suggests the utility of another comparison of party systems, one focusing only on the two major parties or party blocs in each party system. This comparison is presented in Table 14–2 for each of these bipolar competitions: (1) Socialists-Communists versus Gaullists (UDR) in France; (2) Socialists-Communists versus Christian Democrats in Italy in the 1950s, Communists versus Christian Democrats in 1970s; (3) Socialists versus People's in Austria; (4) Social Democrats versus Christian Democrats in Germany; (5) Labour versus Conservatives in Great Britain: (6) Democrats versus Republicans in the United States (identical to Table 14–1).

TABLE 14–2.   Average Differences of Issue Positions for Bipolar Party Systems, 1950s, 1960s, and 1970s

COUNTRY	ISSUE TYPE	1950s	1960s	1970s	SIGNS 1960–1970
France	SE	2.90	2.50	1.60	+
	PS	1.33	1.83	1.00	+
Italy	SE	3.10	1.70	1.40	+
	PS	.90	.50	0	+
Austria	SE	1.60	1.00	.20	+
	PS	0	0	0	0
West Germany	SE	2.00	1.00	.80	+
	PS	.40	.40	0	+
Great Britain	SE	2.40	1.40	.60	+
	PS	0	0	0	0
United States	SE	1.40	1.20	1.40	−
	PS	.25	.25	.25	0

The different statistic changes the numbers, but not the basic finding of convergence, either for Italy or any other party system. Traditional partisan issue differences in the five Western European countries have declined uniformly between the 1960s and the 1970s, regardless of whether the comparison is restricted to the two major party blocs or extended to all parties with a 5% share of the vote.

These findings dispute the argument of some party theorists that multiparty systems will tend toward extremism, resisting convergence.[7] According to these theorists, a party in a multiparty system must maintain an extreme ideological position to distinguish itself from other parties in the market for voters. It may be true that multiparty systems tend toward extremism more than do two- or two-and-a-half party systems; such is the case for France and Italy as compared with Austria and West Germany. However, the findings on France and Italy show that Western multiparty systems are not impervious to convergence.

The impression of nonconvergence in the French and Italian party systems may have been fostered by a confusion between policy distance and partisan hostility. Although policy distances between parties have narrowed in these countries, partisan hostility may have persisted, especially in France. That hostility may have been misinterpreted as meaning that the real policy distances between parties remain as large as ever. They do not.

Traditional Issues II:
Convergence between Left and Right

Another way to view the data is by seeing how types of parties have changed. In particular, we can examine how the parties of the left and of the right have changed to create convergence within party systems. This can tell us something about who the winners and losers have been in the compromising of traditional partisan issue differences.

Earlier research showed that the parties of the left, the parties of labor, had fared better in the compromising at least to the early 1960s.[8] They had moved toward the right less than other parties had moved toward the left. That pattern could have changed in recent years. Western politics are widely viewed as becoming more conservative, in part because Western government may have taken on more responsibilities than they can handle.[9]

To determine the actual pattern, the parties in this research were dichotomized into labor and nonlabor types. The labor parties include all parties with some historical socialist or communist ideological allegiance, whereas the nonlabor include all other parties (e.g., conservative, liberal, Catholic). Means, presented in Table 14–3 below, were computed for the two types for the five socioeconomic issues in the 1957–1962 and 1971–1976

**TABLE 14–3.   Comparison of Changes in Mean Policy Positions of
Labor and Nonlabor Party Types between 1957–1962 and 1971–1976**

NAME OF ISSUE	LABOR MEANS					NONLABOR MEANS	
	1960s	*1970s*	*Diff.*[a]	*Diff.*[a]		*1960s*	*1970s*
Industries	3.14	3.29	.15	−1.10		.90	2.00
Planning	3.14	2.86	− .28	− .46		1.10	1.56
Taxes	2.71	2.14	− .57	− .40		.60	1.00
Welfare	3.00	4.29	1.29	−1.61		1.50	3.11
Religion	.43	− .57	−1.00	.71		−1.40	−2.11
Number of parties	7	7				10	9

[a]To facilitate the comparison, movement in the expected direction by a party type between the 1960s and 1970s is given a negative sign, with movement in the direction opposite to that expected being given a positive sign. Thus, rightward movement by labor parties between the 1960s and 1970s is recorded with a negative sign, but rightward movement by nonlabor parties would be recorded with a positive sign.

periods. (Means were not computed for political structure issues because there were few changes on those issues in this period. The only significant changes are described in the text.)

The table indicates that the pattern may have changed. The two party types moved roughly the same distances toward the political center from the 1960s to the 1970s, thus varying from the historical pattern of more nonlabor party movement leftward. The nonlabor parties did move slightly more leftward than the labor parties moved rightward during this period, but the difference was modest.

This pattern of roughly equivalent compromises is most pronounced on the first three economic issues. On the economic planning and taxation issues, in particular, each party type appeared to be giving ground gradually in the direction of the other.

Changes on the remaining two issues represent important exceptions to the general pattern. On the social welfare issue both party types had moved consistently and sizably leftward since the early 1960s. In fact, all parties changing their positions on this issue since the early 1960s—five labor and nine nonlabor parties—moved toward the left. This exception supports the frequently heard contention that Western parties have increasingly tended to bid for votes against each other by escalating their promises of welfare benefits. There are, in other words, few if any opponents of the welfare state among European parties.

On the secularization issue, by contrast, both party types have tended rightward, continuing a long-standing pattern of increasing support for the traditional privileges of organized religion. This may reflect a tendency of both party types to bid for the support of Catholic voters by promising more governmental assistance for private schools.

Changes on these last two issues may, taken together, show each party type learning when the other has a successful issue. Thus, nonlabor parties may have abandoned their opposition to welfare programs after observing the electoral popularity of those programs, and labor parties may have abandoned their opposition to state support for private schools when they recognized how many voters have children in those schools.

On the political structure issues labor parties made the only notable changes, and they suggest a continued muting of the once-revolutionary rhetoric of labor parties. In the first place, the two Communist parties in the sample moved from either opposition to or ambivalence on parliamentary democracy (the "party government" issue) in the early 1960s to support for it in the 1970s. In the second place, those two parties and two other labor parties in the sample became more reformist in orientation on the "reform versus revolution" tactical question. Thus, labor parties were becoming more accepting of the procedural norms of Western democracy.

Do these findings mean that Western politics have taken a conservative turn? The answer to that question depends on how one defines "conservative turn." If it is defined as rightward movement, the answer is "no." On the other hand, if it is defined to include centrist movement at variance from the historical leftward trend, then there has been a conservative turn. In any event, there has been a significant change, whatever one wishes to call it.

The Prospects for New Partisan Issues

As Western parties move toward consensus on traditional partisan issues, the question arises as to whether or not new issues are developing to supplant the old as the basis for partisan conflict. The research for this section suggests a number of possible candidates for new partisan issues. They are discussed as follows in two major segments, one on economic issues and the other on all other issues.

NEW ECONOMIC ISSUES

If there was one preeminent economic issue to emerge during the 1960s, it was that of economic growth and stability. Parties in many Western countries were increasingly arguing over which of them were best able to maintain that growth and stability. The German Social Democratic party, for example, began to campaign for "stable economic growth."[10] Its Austrian counterpart, the Socialist party, actually repudiated traditional issues of income and wealth distribution, declaring economic growth the top priority.[11]

However, this is not an issue with definable opposing sides, no party being opposed to economic growth. It is instead a question of leadership. Which party has the more competent leadership, not the better programs, to maintain economic growth? Thus, the 1966 Austrian electoral campaign could be fought in part on the issue of which party had the better technical economic experts.[12]

Seen in this light, the growth issue becomes more evidence of declining partisan issue differences and not a possible new partisan issue. Parties have gone from arguing about which principles to embody in economic policies to arguing about which party is more capable of assuring achievement of the consensually accepted principles of economic growth and stability.

The unemployment-inflation dilemma may hold more promise as a potential new partisan issue. This dilemma finds Western nations recognizing the trade-off between unemployment and inflation and debating as to whether or not to tolerate more of the one or of the other. It may be a good example of the complex unsolvable issues which some have suggested will dominate post-industrial politics.[13] The partisan promise of the issue lies in the tendency for labor parties to be more willing to tolerate inflation, with nonlabor parties more willing to tolerate unemployment. At the same time, partisan differences on this issue have thus far been modest, being a matter of emphasis on inflation versus unemployment and not a sole concern with one or the other. That fact suggests that, if this does persist as a partisan issue, differences on it are unlikely to be greater than the modest contemporary differences on traditional economic issues.

The unemployment-inflation dilemma has been less central to partisan politics in France and Italy, in part because traditional ideological issues (e.g., nationalization of industries, distribution of wealth) persist there, but it began to make inroads when the unemployment-inflation dilemma was transformed to "stagflation" (i.e., inflation combined with economic stagnation instead of growth) in the 1970s. In France this turnaround led the Socialists to suggest a reworking of their Common Program with the Communists:[14]

> The Socialists, to state it plainly, hope that a growing economy will placate the rich and powerful during the period of radical changes, just as non-socialist govern-ments during the postwar period have taken advantage of economic expansion to postpone egalitarian reforms. Thus, the Socialists are now of necessity interested in a general rethinking of the Common Program. . . .

In Italy this dilemma has been cited as giving the Communist party reason to be happy it has yet to move into the ruling role, where the dilemma would have challenged the party's traditional ideological tenets.[15]

Another emerging issue is that of "industrial democracy" or "economic democracy," the question of whether workers and consumers should have more control over the operation of industries. This represents an intriguing possibility for a new partisan issue because it fits nicely with a theme prominent in the literature on postindustrial politics. That theme is the argument that popular values are changing to give more emphasis to individuals being able to participate in any decisions affecting their lives.[16] Because they are better educated and more affluent, people are supposedly less willing than they have been historically to have decisions imposed on them. In particular, they may be less willing to have decisions on their jobs made without their involvement in the decision-making.

Despite this theoretical promise, the issue has achieved only limited partisan salience. In Austria the differences between the two major parties on this issue have been more rhetorical than actual.[17] In Great Britain the partisan differences are real, but not great.[18] Little different can be said for the other party systems in this research. Thus, as with the unemployment–inflation issue, the economic democracy issue may be a new partisan issue, but not one prompting pronounced interparty differences.

Finally, new partisan economic issues might develop from the evolving problems of scarce resources (e.g., oil) in the West. Such issues are suggested by observation of evolving Western problems, including the "no-growth" problem discussed earlier. If Western economies do not resume their growth, persisting economic inequalities could become intolerable for those at the bottom of the income and wealth distribution, thus prompting a revived interest in distribution of wealth issues.

However, this study provides no evidence of a partisan revival of the distribution of wealth issue. Quite to the contrary, earlier findings documented the continuing decline of partisan differences on this issue, a decline culminating in Austria in the Socialist abandonment of the issue.

Several tentative conclusions emerge from this survey of possible new economic issues. First, there are several candidates for new partisan economic issues. Second, those candidates may be less "new" issues than extensions of traditional economic issues. The unemployment-inflation and economic democracy issues, in particular, have usually been interpreted along traditional ideological lines. Finally, if these issues do become new partisan issues, the range of disagreement on them will be limited, probably comparable to the modest persisting differences on the traditional economic issues.

OTHER NEW ISSUES

The late 1960s and early 1970s found a number of new essentially noneconomic issues achieving prominence in the West. Of these the most popular candidate for a new partisan issue may be that battery of problems concerning the costs of industrialization, principally problems of environmental conservation and pollution. These problems have been expected to achieve prominence as part of a postindustrial turn toward quality of life concerns. Their salience has, in fact, grown rapidly in many industrialized nations.

However, salience does not necessarily mean partisan salience; an issue may be prominent, yet not be a basis for interparty differences. Such may be the case here. Parties do not appear to be taking opposing stands on this issue. The inclination seems to be more toward, as in West Germany, "all-party agreement on the desirability of protecting and improving the environment."[19]

The issue may have failed to become partisan because it divides voters along other than traditional partisan group lines. As Tsurutani explains,[20]

... the costs of advanced industrialism in the form of increasingly apparent negative externalities tend to be egalitarian, catholic, indiscriminate, hence cross-stratal in impact. In Japan, the rich and poor alike suffocate in the polluted air, at least when they are outdoors; are sickened or disgusted by contaminated water when they go to rivers, lakes, and ocean beaches; and suffer from urban congestion whether they travel by private cars or by public transportation.

That being the case, an established party might be reluctant to take a side on this issue for fear of risking part of its traditional constituency without any assurance of gaining an equivalent or greater new constituency. Parties may prefer to stick to low-risk traditional appeals.

Partisan salience appears likely for this issue only if new parties develop and are able to inject the issue into partisan debates. New parties, having no traditional constituencies to protect, might be interested in appealing across traditional class lines for votes. This has already happened in some Western countries, Australia and New Zealand being two examples. However, the Australia party and the New Zealand Values party, after faring well in their initial electoral efforts, have faded recently, suggesting that the environmental issue may have a limited potential for partisan salience under any conditions.[21]

A second possibility for a partisan noneconomic issue is the issue of sexual and personal freedoms, including questions of abortion, divorce, homosexuality, and birth control. These appear natural issues for a postindustrial politics expected to give more emphasis to personal and social values over traditional economic values. In fact, the issue has been raised in some form in at least five of the six countries during the 1970s.

This issue could have partisan potential since divisions on its frequently parallel traditional interparty religious divisions. In Italy, for example, the divorce issue was described as having "re-opened the thorny old nineteenth century issues about Church-State relations and the place of the Vatican in Italian life...."[22]

However, Western parties have generally downplayed these issues and their potential partisan implications. Thus, in West Germany where the Christian Democrat-Social Democrat competition traditionally had some religious basis, the issues of sexual and personal freedoms "tend not to be party-political issues...."[23] Avoidance of partisanship on these issues may be based on the fact that established parties long ago moved away from narrow religious appeals and toward broader, so-called "catchall" appeals for votes. Returning to narrow religious appeals, especially on emotional issues like abortion and divorce, could jeopardize part of a party's broad base, and without much promise of adding to that base in any significant way. As parties may be afraid of making new appeals on the environmental issue, so they may fear reviving old appeals on the issues of sexual and personal freedoms.

The same generalization may apply to the evolving issue of cultural pluralism, which has touched Western countries in many different ways. The United States has its racial problem. Great Britain recently has developed a similar problem, but the British have also had problems with regional cultural minorities, first in Northern Ireland and then in Scotland. Other Western countries have faced demands from their own cultural minorities. Yet, for the most part established parties have not drawn partisan lines on questions of cultural pluralism. The presumption, as with the earlier noneconomic issues, is that parties see risks in any radical departures from their traditional appeals for voters and so will not attempt to win new voters on this issue.

Here, however, the development of new parties may be a realistic means for cultural pluralism to become a partisan issue. This may already have happened in Britain as regional cultural parties, especially the Scottish Nationalist party, have grown greatly in parliamentary strength in recent years. It could conceivably happen in other countries, particularly if their cultural minorities are so geographically concentrated that they can convert their numbers into parliamentary power.

Finally, in the area of political structure issues there has been a modest push in some of these countries for increasing public participation in governmental decision-making, analogous to the push described earlier for more participation in industrial decision-making. This kind of push is interesting given its fit to the postindustrial issue of pressures for more participation in decision-making. However, the issue has barely surfaced in these countries, and it certainly has not become a major partisan issue.

Overall, there is little evidence that any noneconomic issue is becoming a major basis for partisan divisions among the established parties. Those parties appear, in fact, to be trying to prevent any such change occurring. On the other hand, there is some prospect for new partisan divisions developing, especially on cultural pluralism issues, between established parties and new parties, *if* the new parties form and *if* they remain viable.

Conclusions: Parties and Issues in the Future

The findings show that, as predicted, Western political parties have become less differentiated on major public issues over the past 20 years. Earlier research indicated that this trend actually began before World War II or, in some countries, even before World War I.[24] Since that time partisan differences on traditional issues have declined, in some cases almost disappearing, without being replaced by partisan differences on new issues.

Most of the evidence points toward the trend continuing on both traditional and new issues. On the traditional issues the only limiting point appears to be a state of no significant issue differences. Parties may then argue, as has already happened in Austria, over which has the better leaders, not the better programs. It has sometimes been suggested that the limiting point might be differences comparable to the usual modest policy differences between the American Democratic and Republican parties, but current research has shown that policy differences in the Austrian and West German party systems have already fallen well below that magnitude.

Some prospect can be held out for a modest revival of interparty differences on traditional economic issues. This research indicates that a revival is possible based on new economic issues (e.g., unemployment–inflation, economic democracy, distribution of wealth) to which traditional ideological principles can be applied. Any revival, however, is likely to be modest. History tells us that in most of these party systems even the Depression did not produce an increase in partisan policy differences. The trend has instead been toward decline, almost regardless of other factors. Thus, a revival might produce interparty issue differences no larger than the modest differences characterizing most of these party systems in the 1950s.

New noneconomic issues appear unlikely to revive partisan conflict, at least among established Western parties. Those parties have thus far tended either to sidestep new noneconomic issues or to agree with each other on how government should deal with the issues, and they appear to have good reasons for continuing that tendency. For one thing, taking sides on these new issues could place some of a party's traditional constituency in jeopardy since the new issues cross-cut traditional party constituencies. Parties may be unwilling to take that risk because, in increasingly bipolar party systems, most parties have a good chance of attaining or maintaining ruling status without taking the risk. As well, the issues have yet to prove so salient that a change in party policies could be viewed as likely to attract a large new constituency.

These noneconomic issues could achieve partisan salience based on the development of new parties. New parties in Great Britain may already have made cultural pluralism a partisan issue. On the other hand, new parties in Australia and New Zealand apparently have failed to make other postindustrial issues a basis for partisan conflict. In addition, the long-term success rate of new parties in most Western countries is so poor that one has to be very skeptical of their likely future success. New parties may be more likely to be absorbed and moderated by one of the major forces in each bipolar system, as has happened cyclically in American politics, than to become institutionalized as independent forces.

The future, then, probably will not bring any major revival of partisan issue differences. Western parties appear headed instead toward emulation of one of two existing models of partisan differences. A modest revival of those differences might mean that Western parties, with issue differences now comparable to those between the major American parties, had begun to emulate the American pattern of fluctuating modest partisan issue differences. If there is no revival, these parties could be headed toward the kind of partisan consensus which now characterizes Austrian politics.

This choice of possible futures raises questions about the future of partisanship. In particular, what will happen to partisanship in elections and in governance if parties do not offer distinct choices on what government should do?

The answer to half of that question may already be clear. Partisanship in governance—that is, the role for parties in policy making—almost certainly has decreased significantly and will likely continue to decrease. Responsibility for policy making seems to have moved away from parties toward other institutions as parties have approached consensus on major public issues. The popular sentiment is that policy decisions have moved from "politics to administration," as Peters explains in describing the current stage of Western political development:[25]

> The third and final stage of the development is characterized by a pattern of nondecision making by the political system. . . . That is, once the government decides upon the response which it desires to make to certain environmental changes, it leaves the decisions on day-to-day responses to relatively low-level officials.

Partisanship in elections stands a better chance for survival. For one reason, the differences on traditional issues, although smaller and on fewer issues, remain consistent with traditional left-right distinctions, thus giving voters a semblance of their traditional basis for distinguishing between parties on issues. For another, even if the issue differences disappear, there often are other bases for continuing to vote for party labels. Engelmann and Schwartz have made this argument for group ties as the continuing basis for partisanship in Austria, where the current research found party differences all but nonexistent:[26]

> . . . it is the group ties themselves, without any necessary or obvious connection with parties, that are currently operative. That is, loyalty to a group and identification with its members propel individuals in a partisan direction, even when it is not completely evident, at a particular point in time, what the party does for the group.

Thus, the reduction in differences between Western parties on major public issues probably has eviscerated the policy-making role of parties, but has left intact the role of parties in providing cues to voters in elections. Parties have not yet become simply vestigial traces of an earlier era of politics, although the scope of their influence has diminished significantly.

Notes

1. See, for example, M. Rejai, ed., *Decline of Ideology*, Chicago: Aldine Atherton, 1971.

2. S. D. Berger, G. D. Feldman, G. Hernes, J. LaPalombara, P. C. Schmitter, A. A. Silver, "New Perspectives for the Study of Western Europe," *Social Science Research Council Items*, 29 (September 1975), 34–37, p. 35.

3. On West Germany, see J. D. Dowell, "The Politics of Accommodation: German Social Democracy and the Catholic Church," *Journal of Church and State*, 7 (1965), 78–90; on Austria, see O. Kirchheimer, "The Waning of Opposition in Parliamentary Regimes," *Social Research*, 24 (Summer 1957), 127–156.

4. C. I. Waxman, *The End of Ideology Debate*, New York: Simon & Schuster, 1968, p. 5.

5. K. Janda, "Measuring Issue Orientations of Parties Across Nations," Paper prepared for delivery at the Midwest Conference of Political Scientists, Chicago, Illinois, May 1970; J. C. Thomas, "The Decline of Ideology in Western Political Parties: A Study of Changing Policy Orientations," *Sage Professional Papers in Contemporary Political Sociology*, 1 (1975), 1–68.

6. L. C. Dodd, "Party Coalitions in Multiparty Parliaments: A Game-Theoretic Analysis," *American Political Science Review*, 68 (September 1974), 1093–1117.

7. A. Downs, *An Economic Theory of Democracy* (New York: Harper & Row, 1957), p. 115; G. Sartori, "European Political Parties: The Case of Polarized Pluralism," in J. LaPalombara and M. Weiner, eds., *Political Parties and Political Development*, Princeton, N.J.: Princeton University Press, 1966, pp. 137–176, pp. 139–141.

8. Thomas, p. 41.

9. On the conservative turn, see M. Ledeen, "Left, Right, Right: Europe's New Conservatism," *The New Republic*, 175 (November 13, 1976), 15–18, on the responsibilities of government, see A. King, "Overload: Problems of Governing in the 1970s," *Political Studies*, 23 (June–September 1975), 284–296.

10. L. J. Edinger, "Political Change in Germany: The Federal Republic after the 1969 Election," *Comparative Politics*, 2 (July 1970), 549–578, p. 557.

11. W. T. Bluhm, *Building an Austrian Nation: The Political Integration of a Western State*, New Haven, Conn., and London: Yale University Press, 1973, p. 122.

12. Ibid., pp. 121–123.

13. T. LaPorte and C. J. Abrams, "Alternative Patterns of Post-industria: The California Experience," in L. N. Lindberg, ed., *Politics and the Future of Industrial Society*, New York: David McKay, 1976, 19–56, p. 42.

14. R. Tiersky, "French Communism in 1976," *Problems of Communism*, 25 (January–February 1976), 20–47, p. 37.

15. S. Tarrow, "The Italian Party System Between Crisis and Transition," *American Journal of Political Science*, 21 (May 1977), 193–224, p. 219.

16. R. Inglehart, "The Nature of Value Change in Postindustrial Societies," in L. N. Lindberg, ed., *Politics and the Future of Industrial Society*, New York: David McKay, 1976, pp. 57–99.

17. E. Barker, *Austria 1918–1972*, Coral Gables, Fla.: University of Miami Press, 1973, p. 271.

18. J. Eaton and A. Fletcher, "Workers' Participation in Management: A Survey of Post-War Organized Opinion," *Parliamentary Affairs*, 29 (Winter 1976), 82–92.

19. G. K. Roberts, *West German Politics*, London: The Macmillan Press, 1972, p. 167.

20. T. Tsurutani, "Japan as a Postindustrial Society," in L. N. Lindberg, ed., *Politics and the Future of Industrial Society*, New York: David McKay, 1976, pp. 100–125, p. 105.

21. On Australia, see D. Kemp, "Social Change and the Future of Political Parties: The Australian Case," in L. Maisel and P. M. Sacks, eds., *The Future of Political Parties*, Beverly Hills, Calif., and London: Sage Publications, 1975, pp. 124–164, p. 154; on New Zealand, see N. S. Roberts, "The New Zealand General Election of 1975," *Australian Quarterly*, 48 (March 1976), 97–114, p. 103.

22. M. Clark and R. E. M. Irving, "The Italian Political Crisis and the General Election of May 1972," *Parliamentary Affairs*, 25 (Summer 1972), 198–222, p. 200.

23. G. K. Roberts, p. 168.

24. Thomas, pp. 14–15.

25. B. G. Peters, "The Development of Social Policy in France, Sweden, and the United Kingdom: 1850–65," in M. O. Heisler, ed., *Politics in Europe: Structures and Processes in Some Postindustrial Democracies*, New York: David McKay, 1974, pp. 257–292, p. 292.

26. F. C. Engelmann and M. A. Schwartz, "Partisan Stability and the Continuity of a Segmented Society: The Austrian Case," *American Journal of Sociology*, 79 (January 1974), 948–966, p. 964.

CHAPTER 15

THE CENTRALITY OF PARTY
IN VOTING CHOICE

C. Neal Tate

THE APPARENT DECLINE of political parties has been a much-noted phenomenon in the recent politics of industrialized democracies. The Joint Committee on Western Europe of the Social Science Research Council and American Council of Learned Societies identified the decline in the effectiveness of political parties (and their narrow-minded cousins, interest groups) as one of the deep and "long-term shifts in the structure of Western Industrial societies" that underlie the traumatic events which shook European society and politics in the late 1960s and early 1970s (Joint Committee on Western Europe, 1975: 35). Leon Epstein closed his *Handbook of Political Science* essay on political parties by noting that most democratic parties are "subject to a new skepticism concerning their efficacy and relative importance" (Epstein, 1975:266). And certainly one of the principal objectives of Otto Kircheimer's critique of the "transformation of the Western European party systems" was to highlight this perceived decline in the effectiveness of the parties of industrialized democracies (Kircheimer, 1966; esp. p. 200).

If the decline of political parties in industrialized democracies is real, and if the consequences of the decline may be as significant as they are alleged to be (Kircheimer, 1966:200), then surely it represents a political change worthy of the serious research attention of political scientists. It is the purpose of this paper to give it some of that attention by examining the extent to which parties may be determined to have declined in significance in recent years as agencies helping to structure the voting choice of individual electors. As such, the focus here is on the "centrality" of party-related variables in causal models of voting choice for different points in time for a number of industrialized democracies.

367

The Centrality of Party:
Definitions and Analytical Strategy

The basic hypothesis which will be examined in this paper—that there has been a decline in the recent past in the centrality of party as an agency structuring the voting choice of electors in industrialized democracies—is easily stated. But, once stated, it gives rise to a large number of thorny questions regarding definitions and strategies for analysis.

TIME PERIOD AND NATIONS CONSIDERED

It is clear that those who discuss the decline of parties have in mind a phenomenon that is relatively recent. Just how recent is rarely discussed very clearly. Usually the 1950s and 1960s seem to be the relevant decades. Unfortunately, problems of availability of usable data will make it impossible to carry the analysis very effectively back into the 1950s for most of the industrialized democracies.

What nations constitute the "industrialized democracies?" Like the question of the extent of the recent past, this question is rarely answered very specifically. Ideally, an analysis of the centrality of party in voting choice should be based on data from about 20 nations. Practically, the number of nations which can be included in the analysis is much smaller, due to the lack of data appropriate to the testing of the decline of parties hypothesis.

Because the hypothesis of concern here deals with the behavior of individual electors, it is best examined through the use of national survey data. Because it posits a *decline* in the centrality of party in voting choice, it requires that comparable national surveys be available for at least two preferably widely separated points in time. The national surveys to be used must be fairly elaborate and definitely election-focused. Otherwise, they will be too deficient in measurements of the variables which are crucial to the analysis to be of use. Finally, they must involve a postelection interview, as the dependent variable to be analyzed is voting choice, an uncertainty until after an election. The effect of these requirements is to limit the present analysis to Great Britain, the Netherlands, West Germany, the United States and Canada. For none of the other industrialized democracies was sufficiently rich national survey data available for at least two sufficiently widely separated points in time.

The number of usable surveys available for the five nations ranged from 3 to 12. The specific surveys utilized are summarized as follows:

United States: SRC/CPS national election studies from 1952 through 1976. The studies include seven surveys conducted during presidential election years and five conducted for the "off-year" or congressional elections since 1958.

Canada: The 1965, 1968, and 1974 national election studies.

Great Britain: The 1964, 1966, 1970, February 1974, and October 1974 national election studies.

West Germany: The 1961 and 1965 postelection studies, the 1969 pre- and postelection study, and the 1972 three-wave election study.

The Netherlands: The 1970 electorate sample and the 1971 and 1972 panels from the parliamentary election panel study of 1970–1973. The 1970 respondents are analyzed with respect to their votes in the 1967 Second Chamber elections, thus making the effective time span for the Netherlands five years, 1967–1972.

VOTING CHOICE

For those citizens who choose to vote, voting choice involves the selection of a candidate and/or party from among those presented to them in a given election. Making the choice may be difficult or easy for the citizen. Deciding how to categorize and analyze the citizens' choices is almost always very difficult for the scholar engaged in comparative research. For convenient analysis, the decisions made should reflect dichotomous choice situations. In fact, they often do not.

The analytical needs of this paper require a dichotomous voting choice. Consequently, voting choice has been dichotomized so that respondents' votes are classified as being "for" or "not for" the largest left party in the party system. These parties are the American Democrats, the Canadian Liberals, the British Labour party, the German Social Democrats, and the Dutch Labor party. This dichotomization is most satisfactory for the United States, since only in 1968 did any third party receive a substantial number of votes. It is least satisfactory for The Netherlands, where the Labor party has been only one of several parties of the left and where it did not receive even a third of the votes for any of the elections considered.

Parallel dichotomizations of voting choice could have been made for other major parties. But the one used here can be defended on two grounds which make it most suitable for use in this analysis. First, the parties used for this dichotomization have been for all five nations in most of the elections considered the parties which have been the objects of the party identification of a plurality of the voters. Any decline in the centrality of *these* parties in voting choice must consequently be one which is highly significant for the party system. Second, this dichotomization is in conformity with much existing research utilizing causal models. Irvine's models of Canadian voting choice in 1965 (Irvine, 1976) and Thomassen's models of Dutch voting choice (Thomassen, 1976) used identical classifications.

THE CENTRALITY OF PARTY

The centrality of party will be assessed with respect to the position and significance of party-related variables in causal models of voting choice. The *significance* of the party-related variables will be indicated by their (direct and indirect) impacts on voting choice as measured by the path coefficients linking the party variables to voting choice. The greater the magnitude of the sum of the direct and indirect path coefficients linking the party variables to voting choice, the greater the significance of the party variables and the more central an influence on voting choice is party. The *position* of the party variables in the causal models will be described in terms of their linkages to other, nonparty-related variables included in the model as direct or indirect causes of voting choice. The more numerous and strong the path coefficients linking these other variables to the party-related variables, the more central the position of party in the causal model.

The specific party-related variables to be utilized are *party identification* and *party affect*. Party identification is an index combining respondents' answers to questions asking them, first, to name a party with which they "generally" identify and, second, to indicate how strongly they feel about their identification. One extreme of the party identification index includes those who strongly identify with the particular left party being analyzed, whereas the other extreme includes those who strongly identify with other parties. Voters who are independent, neutral, or apolitical are placed at the midpoint of the index.

The party affect measures are intended to measure the balance of the respondents' feelings about the left party being analyzed in comparison with its principal opposition. A respondent who liked many things and disliked nothing about a particular party and disliked many things and liked nothing about its principal opposition would end up at one or the other extremes of the party affect index, depending on which party he or she liked. Respondents whose feelings were neutral for both parties or equally positive or equally negative for both parties would end up at the midpoint of the party affect index.[1]

In summary, "party" in this context means party identification and party affect. The "centrality" of party is examined by assessing the position and significance of party in causal models of voting choice. These models will include, in addition to the party-related variables, other variables assumed to be relevant in structuring the voting choice of citizens in industrialized democracies.

PARTY AND OTHER CAUSES OF
VOTING CHOICE: THE MODELS

Party is only one of several psychological and sociological phenomena which may structure voting choice. To examine the centrality of party in structuring voting choice, it is necessary to specify what other phenomena may be expected consistently to have a direct or indirect impact on voting choice in the five nations considered here. What is needed is a model of voting choice which specifies the factors that may be expected to structure it and the interrelations of those factors.

Clearly the most highly developed and well-tested model of voting choice is the one that emerges from *The American Voter* (Campbell et al., 1960). Somewhat inchoate as originally stated, the model has been clarified and formalized through the causal modeling efforts of Goldberg (1966), Knoke (1974), and Schulman and Pomper (1975). In generic form, it has been comprehensively stated in a recent essay by Budge, Crewe, and Farlie (1976a). After a perusal of these statements of the "Michigan model" of American voting choice, a model was developed to guide the construction of the causal models of voting choice in the 12 American elections studied here. That model is presented in Figure 15–1. It is identical to that used by Knoke except for its inclusion of a specific measure of party affect and a more comprehensive set of exogenous characteristics of the respondents and their social settings.[2]

The model summarized in Figure 15–1 presents party identification as an intermediate cause of voting choice which is strongly linked both to the set of exogenous variables characterizing the respondents and their social settings and the set of attitudinal variables (including party affect) intervening between it and voting. The arrows depicting causal paths are meant to show the nature of the causal linkages to be expected in such a model. A complete set of path coefficients for this model was calculated for each of the 12 American data sets. Only when a variable was not measured in and could not be constructed from the existing data was it excluded from the model for any election. The results of those calculations are presented in the path diagrams constituting Figures 15–2 through 15–13. These results are discussed in the following paragraphs.

The model in Figure 15–1 seems most appropriate to depict the structuring of voting choice of Americans. There is much evidence to suggest that it is not completely appropriate for the residents of Western European democracies. The research of Kaase (1976:99–101), Schleth and Weede (1971:88), Thomassen (1976:77) and Butler and Stokes (1976:22–28) supports the proposition that, at least in the European nations considered here, party identification is a very immediate cause of vote (and possibly an *effect* of prior vote), if not, in fact, merely another, slightly imperfect expression of voting preference. Party identification in these settings does not appear to occupy the central and independent position which it does in the American models.

The position of party identification in Canada is more ambiguous. Irvine's models of the 1965 election assigned it the position it occupied in the American models (Irvine, 1976:357–358), despite the weakness of the paths between vote and the issue measures which intervened between party identification and voting choice. Recent research by this author (Tate, 1977) tentatively suggests that in Canada, too, party identification may best be viewed as an immediate, rather than intermediate, cause of voting choice. It will be so viewed here.

Figure 15–14 depicts a model in which party identification appears as an immediate cause of voting choice. It is otherwise identical to Figure 15–1. It was used to guide the calculation of the path coefficients for the causal diagrams for the Canadian and European data sets. Every variable listed in Figure 15–14 was included in each of the 15 causal models presented in Figures 15–15 through 15–29, unless it proved impossible to measure from the existing data. The results presented in Figures 15–15 through 15–29 are discussed in the following paragraphs.

Figure 15-1.   Party I.D. as Intermediate Cause of Vote

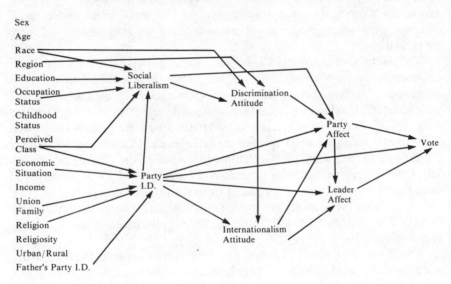

Figure 15-2.   Effect of Economic Situation on U.S. Presidential Voting Choice, 1952

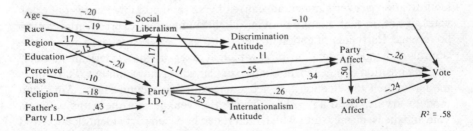

Figure 15-3.   Effect of Father's Party I.D. on U.S. Presidential Voting Choice, 1956

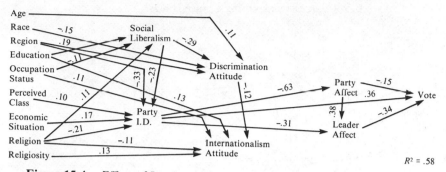

$R^2 = .58$

Figure 15-4.   Effect of Leader on U.S. Congressional Voting Choice, 1958

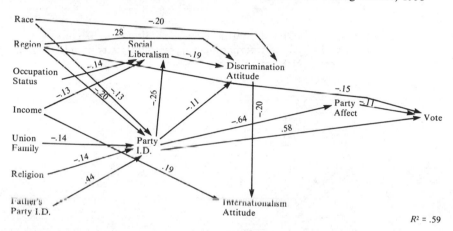

$R^2 = .59$

Figure 15-5.   Effect of Father's Party I.D. on U.S. Presidential Voting Choice, 1960

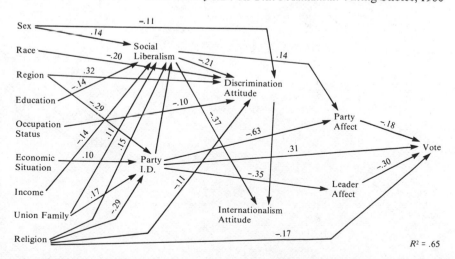

$R^2 = .65$

Figure 15-6.   Effect of Childhood Status, Economic Situation, Union Family, Father's Party I.D., Internationalism Attitude, Party, and Leader on U.S. Congressional Voting Choice, 1962

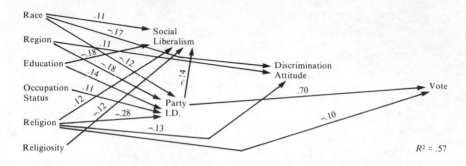

Figure 15-7.   Effect of Childhood Status, Economic Situation, Union Family, Father's Party I.D., Internationalism Attitude, Party, and Leader on U.S. Presidential Voting Choice, 1964

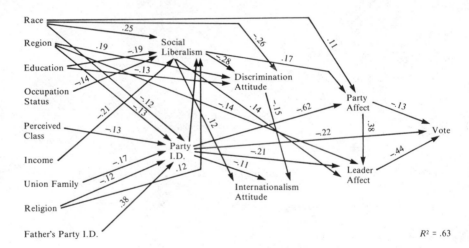

Figure 15-8.   Effect of Father's Party I.D., Social Liberalism, and Leader on U.S. Congressional Voting Choice, 1966

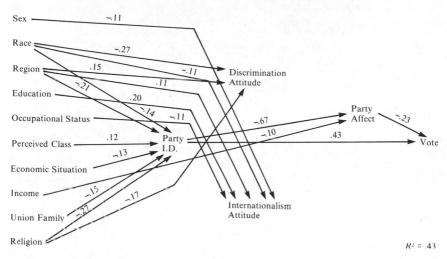

Figure 15-9.   Effect of Father's Party I.D., Social Liberalism, and Leader on U.S. Presidential Voting Choice, 1968

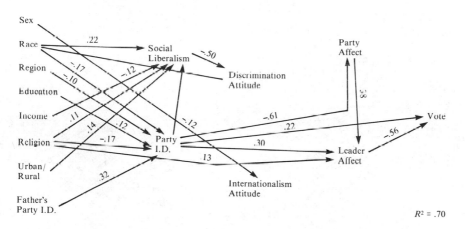

Figure 15-10.   Effect of Father's Party I.D., Social Liberalism, and Leader on U.S. Congressional Voting Choice, 1970

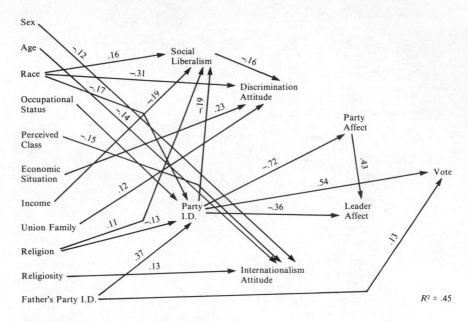

Figure 15-11.   Effect of Discrimination Attitude on U.S. Presidential Voting Choice, 1972

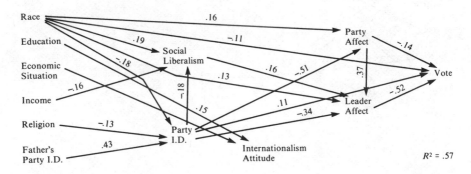

Figure 15-12. Effect of Internationalism Attitude on U.S. Congressional Voting Choice, 1974

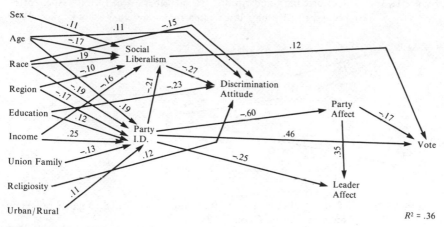

$R^2 = .36$

Figure 15-13. Effect of Childhood Status on U.S. Presidential Voting Choice, 1976

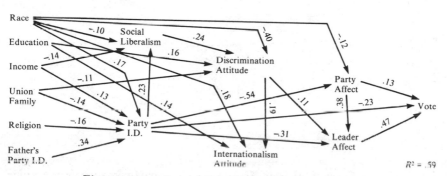

$R^2 = .59$

Figure 15-14. Party I.D. as Immediate Cause of Vote

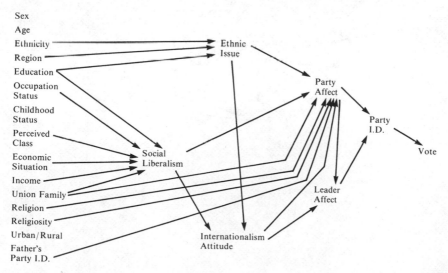

Figure 15-15.   Effect of Childhood Status, Social Liberalism, Ethnic Issue, Internationalism Attitude, and Leader on Canadian Voting Choice, 1965

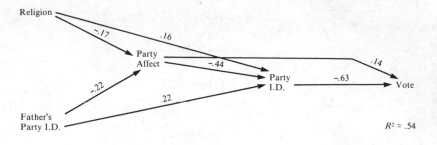

Figure 15-16.   Effect of Union Family, Father's Party I.D., and Social Liberalism on Canadian Voting Choice, 1968

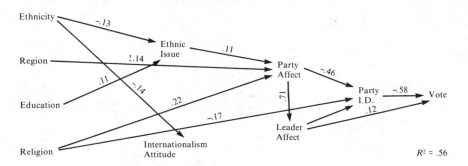

Figure 15-17.   Effect of Ethnicity, Social Liberalism, and Internationalism Attitude on Canadian Voting Choice, 1974

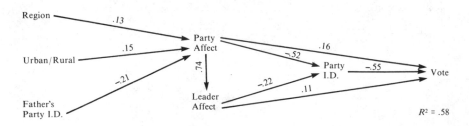

Figure 15-18. Effect of Urban/Rural, Ethnicity, and Ethnic Issue on British Voting Choice, 1964

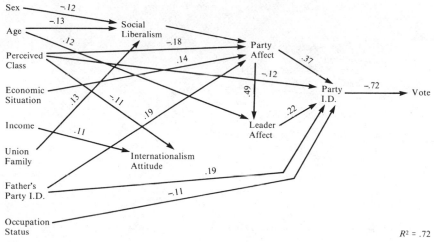

Figure 15-19. Effect of Urban/Rural, Ethnicity, and Ethnic Issue on British Voting Choice, 1966

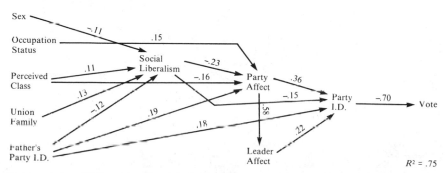

Figure 15-20. Effect of Urban/Rural, Ethnicity, and Ethnic Issue on British Voting Choice, 1970

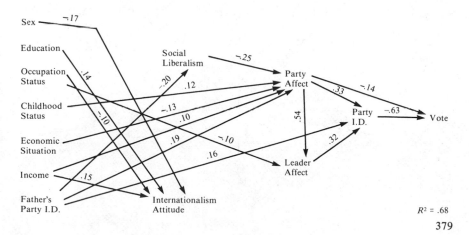

379

Figure 15-21.   Effect of Ethnicity, Religion, Religiosity, Urban/Rural, and Ethnic
Issue on British Voting Choice, February 1974

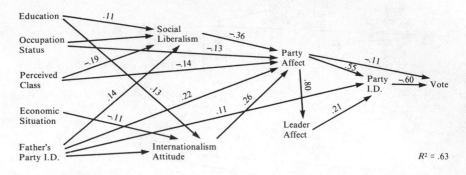

$R^2 = .63$

Figure 15-22.   Effect of Ethnicity, Urban/Rural, and Ethnic Issue on British Voting
Choice, October 1974

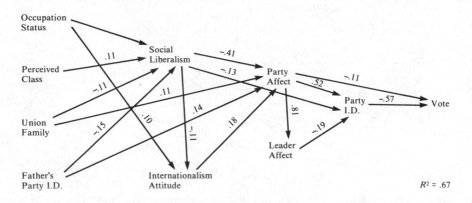

$R^2 = .67$

Figure 15-23.   Effect of Ethnicity, Childhood Status, Perceived Class, Union
Family, Religiosity, Father's Party I.D., Social Liberalism, Internationalism Attitude, and Ethnic Issue on German Voting Choice,
1961

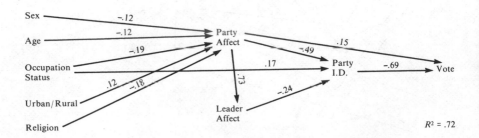

$R^2 = .72$

Figure 15-24.   Effect of Ethnicity, Childhood Status, Perceived Class, Father's Party I.D., Social Liberalism, Internationalism Attitude, Ethnic Issue, and Party I.D. on German Voting Choice, 1965

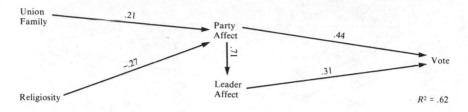

Figure 15-25.   Effect of Ethnicity, Perceived Class, Social Liberalism, Party I.D., and Ethnic Issue on German Voting Choice, 1969

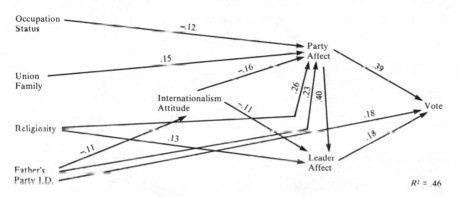

Figure 15-26.   Effect of Ethnicity, Perceived Class, and Ethnic Issue on German Voting Choice, 1972

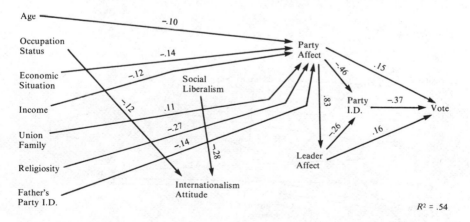

Figure 15-27. Effect of Ethnicity, Ethnic Issue, and Leader on Dutch Voting Choice, 1967

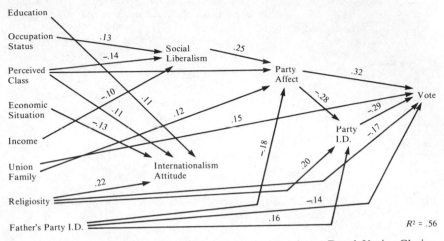

Figure 15-28. Effect of Ethnicity, Ethnic Issue, and Leader on Dutch Voting Choice, 1971

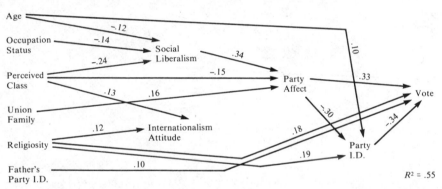

Figure 15-29. Effect of Ethnicity, Ethnic Issue, and Leader on Dutch Voting Choice, 1972

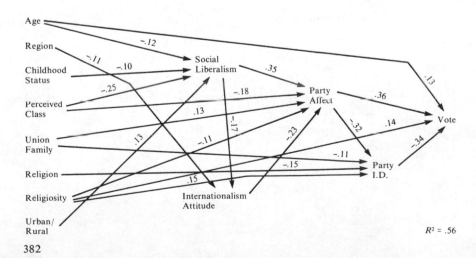

OPERATIONALIZATION OF THE MODELS

All the empirically estimated models were operationalized as straightforwardly as possible. For two reasons, the temptation to recode and introduce complications was indulged only when necessary. First, the large amount of data analysis required to produce 27 causal models including up to 22 variables each necessitated simple operationalizations. Second, simplicity of measurement increased the interpretability of the numerous models. Table 15–1 summarizes in general terms the operationalization of the variables in the models. It is self-explanatory and should be consulted whenever the meaning of any variable is not transparent in any of the models.

TABLE 15–1. Operationalization of Models

VARIABLE	*OPERATIONALIZATION*
Voting choice	Recalled vote dichotomized as either "for" or "not for" largest "left" party. Direction of dichotomy varies across nations.
Party identification	Seven- or five-point index ranging from "strong left party identifier" through "independent" or "neutral" to "strong other party identifier."
Party affect	Indexes of feelings toward political parties. Indexes have varying ranges and are computed by subtracting from left party effect for its principal opposition party. Effect for the left party and its opposition is measured either by feeling thermometer ratings or by subtracting party "dislikes" from party "likes."
Leader affect	Indexes of feelings toward principal leaders of political parties. Computed in same manner as party affect indexes.
Internationalism attitude	Indexes of desires to see the nation play an inactive/active role in international politics. Computed by summing answers to questions relevant to this issue dimension. Higher scores indicate internationalist attitudes.
Discrimination attitude	Indexes of desires to maintain discriminationist practices against blacks in the United States. Computed by summing answers to questions relevant to this issue dimension. Higher scores indicate discriminationist attitudes.
Ethnic issue	Indexes of sympathy for French Canadian autonomy/separatism. Computed by summing answers to questions relevant to this issue dimension. Higher scores are pro-French Canadian.
Social liberalism	Indexes of support for government sponsored social programs and significant economic role for government. Computed by summing answers to questions relevant to this issue dimension. Higher scores indicate "liberal," pro-government attitudes.
Father's party I.D.	A three-point index ranging from "left party supporter" through "supported no party" or "none recalled" to "other party supporter."
Urban/rural	Indexes with varying ranges indicating the degree of urbanization or size of community of residence. Higher scores are more urban.

	Religiosity
Religiosity	Four- or five-point indexes indicating frequency of church attendance. Higher scores indicate more frequent attendance.
Religion	A dichotomy: Protestant/not Protestant.
Union family	A dichotomy: Nonunion member/union member in family.
Income	Ordinal scales of income categories. Number of categories varies. Higher scores indicate higher incomes.
Economic situation	A trichotomy: things are worse/ same as/ better than a year ago. (Slight variation in questions across countries.)
Perceived class	Indexes of perceived social class membership with from two to seven categories. Higher scores indicate higher status.
Childhood status	Questions tapping perceived well-being of R's family when R was a child. Usually a dichotomy with higher score indicating higher status.
Occupation status	Indexes of socioeconomic status of family head's occupation. Number of categories varies. Higher scores indicate higher status.
Education	Number of years of formal education.
Region	A dichotomy: doesn't/does live in most culturally distinct region.
Race	A dichotomy: nonblack/black.
Ethnicity	A dichotomy: not French Canadian/French Canadian.
Age	In years.
Sex	Higher score indicates females.

Findings

It will not be possible to discuss the causal models presented in Figures 15–2 through 15–13 and 15–15 through 15–29 in any detail. Rather, the discussion will necessarily focus on the position and significance of the party-related variables in the models. It will seek to identify changes in their position and significance which document any trends in their centrality in the models. However, before proceeding to a discussion of the models for particular countries, it will be helpful to describe the assumptions and conventions under which the models were constructed.

All the models are recursive; they do not allow for reciprocal causation or feedback loops. As noted, two slightly different generic models were fitted to the data for the five countries. The model summarized in Figure 15–1 was used for the American elections, whereas that in Figure 15–14 was employed for the elections from the other nations. Within the limitations imposed by data availability, *all* the variables depicted in the generic model for a particular nation were included in each empirically estimated model for that nation. However, for simplicity of presentation, those variables not linked by "significant" path coefficients to other variables in the empirically estimated models are not graphically portrayed in Figures 15–2 through 15–29. Thus in Figure 15–2, for example, sex, occupation status, and religiosity are not listed because they have no significant links to subsequent variables. If a variable could not be measured in the model for a particular election, it is listed as "not available" (NA) in the figure for that election. For example father's party I.D. is so listed in Figure 15–3 because it was not available in the 1956 American election study data.

The numbers accompanying the arrows in the models are path coefficients, standardized regression coefficients (beta weights) for the regression of the variable at the head of an arrow on the variable at its tail, controlling for the effects of all other variables prior to the variable at the head.[3] For an arrow to appear in the model, the path coefficient appropriate to it was required to have a magnitude of at least .100. For simple random samples as large as the ones used here, this value is considerably larger than that required for statistical significance even at the .01 level. However, given the complicated sample designs used for these surveys and the complexity of the models, it seemed undesirable to adhere to a concept of statistical significance which was probably not appropriate and which would lead to "cluttering up" the models with arrows that expressed relationships which were of little if any substantive significance. The arbitrary .100 cutoff point was selected to ensure at least a modicum of substantive significance for the causal linkages to be depicted in the models.

Each model is accompanied by an R^2 figure. This R^2 expresses the proportion of the variance in voting choice which is accounted for by *all* the variables in the model, including those which may not have significant direct or indirect links to voting choice. It is thus a measure of the total potency of the variables in the model and can be used to compare the explainability of voting choice across elections and nations, given the models employed and the limitations of the data.

UNITED STATES

Figures 15–2 through 15–13 present the empirically estimated models of voting choice based on the American surveys. There is considerable continuity of measurement of the variables in the generic model (Figure 15–1), with one major exception—1962. The 1962 election study is much less comprehensive than any of the others. Nevertheless, a model based on it has been included for the sake of continuity. Despite its limitations, the 1962 model should prove useful in the search for trends in the centrality of party.

The only other major source of discontinuity in the American models is father's party I.D. Although it stands as a consistently important cause of respondent's party identification, father's party I.D. was not measured in five of the studies (1956, 1960, 1962, 1966, and 1974).

The upper panel of Table 15–2 presents the effects[4] of the party-related variables—party identification and party affect—on voting choice in the American elections. It may be used to assess the significance of these variables as causes of voting choice. The direct, indirect, and total effects of each variable are separately presented for each election. In addition, the right-most column presents the combined effects of the two party-related variables. An examination of the direct effects of party identification revealed that these effects have quite different magnitudes for presidential and congressional elections. Because the former are dominated by highly visible presidential candidates whose personalities may be emphasized far more than their party ties, this is what one should expect. Consequently, Table 15–2 presents the effects for presidential and congressional elections separately.

Looking first at the direct effects of party identification for the presidential election years, one can discern a declining trend through 1972. From a high point around .35 in the 1950s, the direct effect of party identification declines to a low of .11 in 1972. However in 1976, this effect increases to the level characteristic of 1964 and 1968.

The direct effects of party identification for the congressional election years are all larger than are the largest direct effects for a presidential year. But a pattern for these larger effects is not clear. The largest direct effect shows up in 1962. However, if one examines the model for 1962 (Figure 15–6), one can see that all but one of the variables which in other models intervene between party identification and voting choice are missing in 1962. One should therefore expect party identification to have a larger direct effect in 1962 than in other years. A reasonable estimate of its direct effect *had these intervening variables been present* would place its magnitude about .53.[5]

If one uses .53 as an estimate of the direct effect of party identification in 1962, the downward trend which was evident for the presidential election years appears for the congressional election years 1958, 1962, and 1966. It does not continue, however. The direct effect for 1970 is of the same magnitude as the effects for 1958 and 1962, whereas the effect for 1974 is about the same as that for 1966. The average of the effects for the two earlier elections is larger than that for the later three. But a two-election moving average of these effects shows a shallow U shape, not a downward trend. Consequently, one can hardly conclude that there has been a steady decline in the direct effects of party identification on voting choice in American congressional elections.

The indirect effects of party identification on voting choice have been broken down into those which occur through the other party-related variable, party affect, and those which occur through other intervening variables, principally leader affect. The indirect effects of party identification are higher on the average for presidential than for congressional election years. The indirect effects through party affect vary only from .13 to .22 and show no trend.

For congressional elections the indirect impacts of party identification through party affect are rather small and also show no trend. Its indirect effects through other variables are even smaller. In all congressional election years they are listed as "not significant," indicating the absence of the path or paths necessary for the indirect impact to occur. Again this is what one should expect to find, given that the principal intervening variable through which these indirct effects would act is leader affect, a variable which is unlikely to play a serious role in congressional elections.

For presidential elections the indirect impacts of party identification through variables other than party affect show a pattern which largely supports the hypothesis of a decline in significance for party identification taken alone. They show a rough upward trend, indicating that, in the late 1960s and 1970s at least, a substantial portion of the impact retained by party identification in presidential elections became indirect, working through attitudes toward the party leaders, the presidential candidates.

The total effects of party identification on voting choice, analyzed separately for presidential and congressional elections, show an irregular decline in the significance of party identification. The trend for the presidential election years shows a slight reversal in 1968 and a more substantial one in 1976, but it is downward. The two-election moving average for the presidential elections declines until 1972–1976, when it experiences a small upturn.

For congressional elections the total effects of party identification also show a somewhat unsteady but downward trend. The two-election moving average for these elections declines steadily.

The effects of party affect on voting choice can be dealt with much more summarily. For congressional elections, its indirect effects cannot be measured in four cases and are not significant in the fifth. Consequently, its total effects are the same as its direct effects—and these show no real pattern. To be sure the average for the 1970s is lower than it is for the two earlier elections (1958 and 1966), but this is solely due to the 1966 effect. The 1958 effect is identical to the mean of the 1970s effects.

The effects of party affect in presidential election years are somewhat more interesting. Although there is no firm trend for the direct effects, the average for the 1964–1976 period is distinctly below that for the 1952–1960 era. Conversely, the indirect effects of party affect show a higher average for 1964 than for 1952–1960. Similar patterns of effects were found for party identification.

The net results of the patterns just discussed can be traced in the combined effects displayed in the right-most column of Table 15–2. With the exception of a single reversal in 1964, these effects clearly decline from 1952 through 1970. However they then steadily increase from 1970 through 1976. The combined

TABLE 15-2. Effects of Party-Related Variables on Voting Choice

U.S. MODELS

	PARTY IDENTIFICATION EFFECTS: INDIRECT THROUGH				PARTY AFFECT EFFECTS			COMBINED
						Party		
ELECTION ELECTION TYPE/YEAR	Direct	Party Affect	Others	Total	Direct	Indirect	Total	COMBINED EFFECTS[a]
Pres 1952	.34	.22	.06	.62	.26	.12	.38	.78
Pres 1956	.36	.17	.11	.64	.15	.13	.28	.75
Pres 1960	.31	.19	.11	.61	.18	.12	.30	.72
Pres 1964	.22	.18	.09	.49	.13	.17	.30	.61
Pres 1968	.22	.13	.17	.52	NS	.21	.21	.60
Pres 1972	.11	.17	.18	.46	.14	.19	.33	.62
Pres 1976	.23	.17	.15	.55	.13	.18	.31	.69
Cong 1958	.58	.10	NS	.68	.15	NP	.15	.73
Cong 1962	.70	NP	NS	.70	NP	NP	NP	.70
Cong 1966	.43	.15	NS	.58	.23	NP	.23	.66
Cong 1970	.54	NS	NS	.54	NS	NP	NS	.54
Cong 1974	.46	.10	NS	.56	.17	NS	.17	.63

OTHER NATIONS' MODELS

NATION AND ELECTION YEAR	PARTY IDENTIFICATION EFFECTS: TOTAL (DIRECT)	PARTY AFFECT EFFECTS: INDIRECT THROUGH				COMBINED EFFECTS
		Direct	Party I.D.	Others	Total	
CAN 1965	.63	.14	.27	NP	.41	.77
CAN 1968	.58	NS	.38	.09	.47	.67
CAN 1974	.55	.16	.38	.08	.62	.79
GB 1964	.72	NS	.35	NS	.35	.72
GB 1966	.70	NS	.34	NS	.34	.70
GB 1970	.63	.14	.32	NS	.46	.77
GB Feb 1974	.60	.11	.43	NS	.54	.71
GB Oct 1974	.57	.11	.38	NS	.49	.68
GER 1961	.69	.15	.46	NS	.61	.84
GER 1965	NP	.44	NP	NS	.66	.66
GER 1969	NP	.39	NP	.22	.46	.66
GER 1972	.37	.15	.25	.07	.38	.65
NETH 1967	.29	.32	.08	.13	.40	.61
NETH 1971	.34	.33	.10	NP	.43	.67
NETH 1972	.34	.36	.11	NP	.47	.70

[a]Direct effects plus indirect effects through others, that is, direct effects plus indirect effects not through party-related variables.

NP = not possible due to absence of necessary variable.

NS = "Not significant," that is, one or more necessary paths is less than the .1 cutoff value.

effects of the party-related variables at the end of this increasing trend are of the same magnitude as the effect for 1962—still below the level of the 1950s effects, but well above that of the 1964–1970 period.

The declining trend from 1952 through 1970 will hardly startle those familiar with the literature on American voting, since it is one of the principal findings documented by other means in such work as that of Nie, Verba, and Petrocik (1976, esp. Chap. 4). But the increasing trend for the 1970s may be more of a surprise. It seems to suggest a "bottoming out" of the decline in the centrality of party in shaping voting choice, if not yet a return to the status quo ante *The American Voter*. A brief look at the position of the party-related variables in the causal models will provide another perspective on these conclusions regarding the centrality of party.

Assessing the position of the party variables involves more qualitative judgment than documenting their significance, because it cannot be based solely on numerical coefficients. It will involve examining the causal links from prior variables to the party variables and from the party variables to subsequent variables in the causal network.

Looking first at the linkage from party identification to subsequent variables in the 1952 model (Figure 15–2), one sees that party identification is a cause of social liberalism, internationalism attitude, and leader affect. Turning to the 1956 model (Figure 15–3), one sees that the link to internationalism no longer exists but that there are no other changes in the causal paths linking party identification to subsequent variables. Furthermore, this pattern prevails for all later elections in which social liberalism, party affect, and leader affect are measured. The only changes which occur involve the addition of a single link to an issue variable—discrimination attitude in 1958 (Figure 15–4) and internationalism attitude in 1964 (Figure 15–7). Otherwise party identification occupies a very stable position with respect to subsequent variables in the models.

The causal arrows linking the individual's social characteristics to party identification demonstrate the manner in which party identification is linked to social structure. The 1952 model shows party identification to be linked directly to four prior variables: father's party I.D., religion, perceived class, and region. If one regards perceived class as one of a number of potentially substitutable indicators of socioeconomic status, these four relationships tie party identification firmly to the family, the religious system, the socio-economic system, and to history (via region). It thus appears to be well grounded in the social structure.

The 1952 pattern described in the preceding paragraph continues with only minor change—such as the inclusion of an additional socioeconomic status indicator—for several elections. The appearance and disappearance of father's party I.D. as it is or is not measured seems to have little impact on the other relationships. In 1956, 1958, and 1960 party identification is consistently caused by religion, two socioeconomic indicators, and region. Significantly, race enters as an additional cause in 1958 but drops out again in 1960. The first continuing change in the pattern occurs in 1962, when race enters the list of causes of party identification, this time to stay.

Except for the addition of the link between race and party identification, the models for 1962 through 1968 continue to resemble the earlier models with respect to the position of party identification. A subtle change does occur between 1966 and 1968, when the number of socioeconomic indicators with causal links to party identification drops from three, its high point, back to one. One such indicator remains in the 1970 model, but party identification loses its link to history, as region drops out. In 1972 the remaining link to the socioeconomic system disappears.

In the late 1960s and early 1970s party identification becomes less dependent on social structure. The 1974 and 1976 elections, however, reveal a reversal of this trend. In the model for 1974 party identification has more links to social structure than it does in any previous year, in that for 1976 it has more links to social structure than it does in the models for 1968, 1970, and 1972.

There is little point in any extended discussion of the position of party affect in the American models. It is always linked strongly to leader affect, the only variable which intervenes between it and voting choice. Its principal cause is always party identification, though it is also related to social liberalism on four occasions. Its links to social structural variables are usually indirect, passing through party identification, social liberalism, or both. Thus its position in the models is principally dependent on that of party identification.

In summary of the evidence from the American models, one could conclude that party did indeed decline from the 1950s to 1970 in its centrality in American voting choice. It declined as an influence on the votes of individual electors and in the degree to which it is determined by social structure. However the decline of party was more consistent and noteworthy in presidential than in congressional elections. Furthermore the evidence suggests that the decline has been reversed in the 1970s.

CANADA

The data needed to assess the significance of the party-related variables in the models for Canada and the other non-American nations are contained in the lower panel of Table 15–2. Because these models posit party identification as the immediate cause of voting choice, it is not possible for party identification to have indirect effects on vote. This simplifies to some extent the task of describing the impact of the party-related variables.

Looking first at the direct (or total) effects of party identification in Canada, one discerns a slight but fairly downward trend: its direct effect declines from .63 in 1965 to .55 in 1974. However the total effects of party affect show exactly the opposite: these increase from .41 to .62 across the same time period. Substantial proportions of the total effects of party affect are transmitted through party identification. If these proportions are removed from the total effects of party affect, they no longer yield an upward trend. But the impact of party affect is still greater in 1974 than in either previous election.

The net result of the patterns of effects discussed above can be seen in the combined effects of party identification and party affect in Canada. The trio of combined effects yields a V-shaped pattern: high in 1965, somewhat lower in 1968, equally high in 1974. If there was a decline in the significance of party in structuring Canadian voting choice, it occurred through the late 1960s and early 1970s, but it had apparently been reversed by 1974. Unfortunately usable survey data for the 1972 election, which would help document any such decline, are lacking.

In discussing the position of the party-related variables in the Canadian models, one should focus first on party affect, as it is the more remote from voting choice. In all three elections it is firmly linked to party identification and leader affect, the two variables which succeed it in the models. In 1965 it is caused only by religion and father's party I.D. In 1968 (with father's partisanship unmeasured) it is directly caused only by religion and region, but it is also indirectly linked to ethnicity and education through their impact on ethnic issue attitudes. Then in 1974 it is caused by region, urbanism, and, again, father's partisanship.

The most striking thing about the position of party affect in the Canadian models is its nearly complete lack of ties with the major indicators of social status, such as perceived class, union membership, or occupational status. Religion and region provide such grounding in Canadian social structure as party affect has, and that is not much. The R^2 values for the regression equations predicting party affect from all prior variables are quite small: .12 for 1965, .11 for 1968, and .15 for 1974.

What is true for the position of party affect in the Canadian models is also true for party identification: it is no more strongly linked to social structure than party affect. In 1965 it is directly caused by party affect and father's party I.D., as one would expect, and by religion. In 1968 religion is again the only social structural variable which has any direct impact on party identification, but in 1974 no variable other than party affect and leader affect has any direct link with party identification. In all three elections the only indirect impacts of social structural variables are passed through party affect. As noted, these are few in number.

It is difficult to maintain that there has been any change in the position of the party-related variables in the Canadian models. Only the disappearance of religion as a cause of either party variable in 1974 might suggest some cutting loose of the few traditional ties of party to social structure. But the replacement of religion by the urban/rural indicator may simply indicate a slight shift in the manner and not the amount of the determination of the party variables by social structure.

Students of Canadian politics will not be surprised at the results presented here. They recognize the weakness of the links between support for the major Canadian parties and the socioeconomic structure of Canadian society. But the implications of these results for the focus of this paper may not be already well understood. Only the pattern of direct effects of party identification on voting choice suggests that there has been a decline in the centrality of party in structuring Canadian voting choice. The other data concerning the significance and position of the party variables in the Canadian models do not support the decline of party hypothesis.

GREAT BRITAIN

The pattern of direct effects for party identification in the five British elections shows a slow but steady decline from 1964 through October, 1974. This trend parallels those for the equivalent Canadian and U.S. 1952–1972 presidential election effects. The total effects of party affect for Great Britain roughly show the increasing trend of the equivalent Canadian effects, though with a mild reversal in October 1974. The direct effects of party affect do not detract from this ascending pattern. They are not significant for the 1960s elections, but are just above .10 for the three 1970s elections. The indirect effects of party affect are all transmitted through party identification. No significant paths link leader affect to voting choice; hence party affect can have no significant indirect effects through that "other" variable. The indirect effects of party affect through party identification are quite stable in magnitude through the 1970 election, but they show an increase for the 1974 elections which may be more due to changes in the operationalizations underlying the party and leader affect measures than to changes in the respondents' political behavior.

The net result of the two contrary trends described here is a rather stable pattern of combined effects for the party variables in the British elections. Four of the five effects are around .70, whereas the fifth is slightly higher at .77. The overall significance of party in structuring voting choice appears not to have changed. But the manner in which party achieves that significance has changed. Voters now appear to vote slightly more in accord with their feelings toward the major parties and slightly less in accord with whatever established loyalties may be represented in party identification.

The positions of the party variables in the 1964 British model suggest a substantial determination of party affect and identification by the structure of British society. Party affect is, to be sure, directly caused only by father's partisanship and the respondent's perception of the economic situation. But through the intervening variable social liberalism it is indirectly linked to union membership, sex, and age. Furthermore 1964 party identification also has direct links with three exogenous variables—occupation status, perceived class, and father's party I.D.—and an indirect link through leader affect with age. Given the mutual link between the party variables and their links to leader affect, the 1964 British model shows the party variables to be highly central. They are strongly interconnected and also firmly related to social structure.

The 1966 British model bears a strong family resemblance to its 1964 cousin. Party affect is caused directly by occupation status, perceived class, and father's party I.D. and indirectly through social liberalism by perceived class and father's partisanship again and by union membership. Party identification is caused directly only by father's party I.D. among the exogenous variables. But through social liberalism it is indirectly linked to sex, perceived class, union membership, and (yet again) father's party I.D. Again the party variables are firmly related, meaning that party identification is indirectly linked to all the social structural variables which appeared as causes of party affect. The linkage between the party variables is both direct and indirect through leader affect.

The 1970 model shows party affect to be caused directly by father's partisanship and by three socioeconomic measures: childhood status, perceived economic situation, and income. It exhibits fewer indirect links than the earlier models, however. Only father's party I.D. is linked to party affect through social liberalism. Party identification occupies a somewhat different position. It is directly linked to only one of the exogenous variables, father's partisanship. It is indirectly linked only to occupation status, and this path passes through leader affect, rather than social liberalism as in the previous models. The result is that the party-related variables seem in 1970 to be a bit less central to the model of voting choice than in 1964 or 1966.

In the February 1974 model party affect returns to a position which is firmly linked to the exogenous social and economic characteristics. It is directly linked to father's party I.D., occupation status, and perceived class. Through social liberalism it is caused again by father's partisanship, perceived class, and occupational status, as well as by education. Finally, father's party I.D. also affects it indirectly through internationalism attitudes.

Unlike party affect, party identification in February 1974 is not independently well linked to the social structural variables. Its only link—other than the indirect ones through party affect, of course—is the direct one with father's party I.D. February 1974 thus continues the trend begun in 1970 in which party identification is more removed from the influence of social structure.

Party affect is directly linked only to union family and father's party I.D. among the exogenous variables in October 1974. Through social liberalism it is linked to the same two variables plus perceived class, whereas through internationalism attitude it is linked to occupation status. Party affect is thus less firmly linked to exogenous social and economic characteristics than it is in any earlier election.

Party identification is more removed from the influence of social structure in October 1974 than in any previous election. It is directly linked to no exogenous variable, not even father's party I.D. It is indirectly linked to perceived class, union family, and father's party I.D. through its direct link with social liberalism, as well as through the exogenous variables' links with party affect.

Overall the positions of the party-related variables in the British models do not appear to support the hypothesis of a decline in the centrality of party in the structuring of individual voting choice. Party affect occupies a fairly central position throughout the period studied. The R^2 values for the regression equations predicting party affect from all prior variables are .24, .26, .24, .47, and .44 for 1964 through October 1974, respectively. These certainly do not suggest that party affect became less connected to social structure during this time. And, although it is clear that party identification did become more remote from the social structural variables in 1970 and February 1974, what this appears to mean is that the impact of these variables became more concentrated through party affect. In support of this conclusion is the fact that the R^2's for party identification predicted from prior variables (.61, .65, .64, .75, .72) also show no decline during this period.

The conclusions for the British analysis are in many ways like those for the Canadian. Except for the decline in the direct impact of party identification on voting choice, there is little evidence to support the hypothesis of a decline in the centrality of party in structuring British voting choice. As noted, it may be that in Britain (and possibly in Canada as well) voters have come to rely more directly on their feelings about the parties and less on their party loyalties. If this were the case, party would remain a central force in the determination of British voting choice, but for different reasons.

WEST GERMANY

The biggest problem in dealing with the Germany models is the absence of an appropriate measure of party identification in the 1965 and 1969 election studies. This is especially unfortunate because of the sharp difference in the total (direct) effects of party identification for the two widely separated elections for which it is measured, 1961 and 1972. It is tantalizing to speculate as to whether or not 1965 and 1969 might have exhibited values for the direct effects of party identification which would have fitted the steep downward trend line defined by the 1961 and 1972 values.

In the absence of party identification for 1965 and 1969, most attention should be focused on the total effects for party affect, which is measured consistently across all four elections. These four values define a downward trend line, with a small reversal in 1965. From 1965 to 1972 the slope of the line is steeper than for any previously encountered trend. All things considered, then, a fearless conclusion would be that the significance of party variables in structuring voting choice did indeed decline in West Germany from 1961 to 1972.

The position of party affect in the German models does not necessarily suggest the conclusion of a decline in the centrality of party. It is directly caused by sex, age, occupation status, urbanism, and religion in 1961. In 1965 it is directly linked only to union membership and religiosity, but in 1969 it is again linked to several variables: directly to union membership, religiosity, occupational status, and father's partisanship and indirectly to father's party I.D. through internationalism. Finally in 1972 it is causally linked to still more social structural variables: age, economic situation, income, union membership, religiosity, and father's partisanship. The position of party identification when it is measured adds little of significance to this picture. It is caused by party and leader affect and, in 1961, by occupational status.

The position of party affect appears to have become more central in the German models from 1961 to 1972. This conclusion is supported by the R^2 values for the regression equations predicting party affect from prior variables. These increase from .13 in 1961 to .20 in 1965 to .26 and .25 in 1969 and 1972.

The overall conclusion for the German case is relatively clear. The significance of party as an influence on voting choice appears definitely to have declined from 1961 to 1972. At the same time party appears no less—perhaps even more—firmly grounded in German social structure in 1972 than in 1961.

THE NETHERLANDS

The coefficients for the effects of the party variables in the three Dutch models stand out from those for the other non-American nations. In every column of Table 15–2 the Dutch coefficients exhibit an increasing (or at least monotonic) trend. The difference between the first and third values in these trends are not large, but neither is the time period covered by the Dutch data. The conclusion to be drawn here is brief and unambiguous: party increased in significance in structuring Dutch voting choice from 1967 to 1972.

The positions of the party-related variables in the Dutch models also paint a rather unambiguous picture. In 1967 party affect was directly caused by perceived class, union membership, and father's party I.D. Indirectly it was linked to income, perceived class, and occupational status. The R^2 for the regression equations predicting it from prior variables was .32. In 1971 it remained well linked to social structural variables: directly to perceived class and union membership and indirectly to perceived class, age, and occupational status through social liberalism. Its 1971 R^2 was a larger .39. Finally in 1972 party affect was directly linked to perceived class, union membership, and religiosity and indirectly caused by age, childhood status, perceived class, and urbanism through social liberalism and by region through internationalism. Its 1972 R^2 was a still larger .47.

The position of party identification was more stable throughout the period. Most of the influence of social structural variables reached it through party affect, and its R^2 values (.28, .30, .30) were stable. In all three elections it did have an independent link with religiosity. In 1967 it was also caused directly by father's partisanship, in 1971 by age, and in 1972 by religion and union membership. Certainly these patterns of relationships do not suggest that party identification declined in centrality in Dutch elections from 1967 to 1972.

All the Dutch evidence points not to a decline, but to an increase in the centrality of party in Dutch voting choice. This sets the Netherlands apart from the other four nations considered. Why is the Dutch case so different? At least three answers to this query can be suggested.

First, it is possible that the Dutch findings are an artifact of the data utilized. After all, the three Dutch surveys, unlike all the others used here, were not taken for independently selected samples, but for a continuing and unsupplemented panel. It is possible that panel attrition would leave unrepresentative samples of Dutch voters for whom party is indeed a very central concept.

Second, it is possible that the time period covered was simply too short. By using the recalled 1967 vote that period was stretched to five years, barely half as long as the minimum period used for any other nation. In actuality, of course, the time between the first and third surveys was less than three years. Perhaps the trends discussed here would appear insignificant across a longer time span.

Finally, it is possible that the Dutch trend is an accurate reflection of what happened in Dutch politics from 1967 to 1972. The 1967 election is often cited as one which broke down the traditional accommodationist pattern of Dutch politics. The years following 1967 are also cited as a period of realignment in the Dutch party system.[6] During such a period one should expect that citizens might be forming new loyalties to parties or, perhaps, reaffirming their shaken ones to their old parties. Such a process would produce a pattern of findings like the one reported here.

Conclusion

Technical precautions and tentative substantive conclusions have been noted for each analyzed nation in the body of the paper. There is no point in repeating them here. It will be more helpful to return to the general hypothesis with which the paper began—that there has been a decline in the recent past in the centrality of party as an agency structuring the voting choice of electors in industrialized democracies. How may this hypothesis be evaluated in light of the findings presented here?

As is usual, it is difficult to give a concise overall evaluation of a hypothesis as broad as the one stated here. If "party" is defined as "party identification," the evidence is relatively clear: in four of the five nations party identification generally declined in its impact on voting choice. If party is defined as "party affect," the preponderance of evidence might support the opposite conclusion. If party is defined as some combination of these, as it has been here, the preponderance of evidence again supports a decline in the causal impact of party on voting choice. When one takes an alternative view of the centrality of party and regards it as a variable which, if central, ought to be well imbedded in a network of social structural and relevant attitudinal measures, the preponderance of evidence suggests a decline in the centrality of party.

It is necessary to speak in terms of the "preponderance of evidence" because, as is again usual, the trends depicted by the causal models are not uniform across nations. The findings from the two Continental European nations rather clearly support opposite conclusions concerning the decline in the centrality of party. The two British Commonwealth nations yield similar but mixed findings: whether party has declined depends on how one chooses to define it. The findings from the United States are generally supportive of the decline hypothesis. But the enthusiasm with which one can support the hypothesis must be less intense for U.S. congressional than for presidential elections and for the 1970s than the 1960s.

Ironically, much of the support found here for the decline of party hypothesis—which has been often and vigorously stated by scholars concerned with Western European politics—comes from the United States, perhaps the least "European" of the industrialized nations considered. Why do the European nations provide less than totally clear support for the hypothesis? The answer appears that the role of party in structuring voting choice in some European nations has perhaps not declined so much as it has simply changed. In Great Britain and the Netherlands in particular there has been an apparent waning in the power and centrality of the traditional major parties, but not necessarily a decline in the relevance of party in general to *the choices made by those who do vote*. Other parties have been the beneficiaries of the major parties' losses in this area. The result is less support for the decline of party hypothesis in these European nations than might have been supposed.

Notes

1. The party affect index has its origins in the American election study open-ended questions asking respondents to name their "likes" and "dislikes" about the major political parties. In the later American studies and in most of the non-American studies used here, these questions were replaced or supplemented by "feeling thermometer" type questions which asked respondents to indicate how "warmly" they felt toward a particular party by placing that party at a particular point on an ordered scale referred to as a "thermometer" or (in the German case) "skalometer." Where the latter were available, they were used to construct the party affect index on the grounds that they came closer to tapping pure affect toward the parties than the former. Otherwise the index was constructed from the likes/dislikes questions.

When thermometer ratings were used, party affect was equal to the left party rating minus the opposition party rating. When the likes/dislikes questions were used, party affect was computed by the following simple formula: party affect = (left party likes − left party dislikes) − (opposition party likes − opposition party dislikes).

2. It is also very similar to that given by Budge, Crewe, and Farlie (1976a:6). The principal difference between the two is that Figure 15–1 omits the "campaign issues" and "campaign candidates" included in the latter and places the respondents' economic perceptions (of the goodness/badness of the times) as an exogenous variable. The campaign-related variables are omitted because they do not represent concepts which can be measured consistently across time. Economic perceptions seemed to be closely related to the respondents' social situations. Hence it was treated as an exogenous variable.

   Figure 15–1 is also in the spirit of the Goldberg (1966) and Schulman and Pomper (1975) models. It looks rather different because it does not include the complicated summary indexes of respondents' and respondents' fathers' political and socioeconomic predispositions which were included in these earlier models. Instead, it includes the list of basic socioeconomic and political characteristics on which these summary indexes were based.

3. For some purposes—specifically the comparison of the impact of particular variables across time and/or nations—it might have been preferable to have used unstandardized regression coefficients. (See Asher, 1976:47–48; Wright, 1960; Blalock, 1967.) However, this would have required that the variables be measured on "determinate" scales across time and nations for the comparison to be meaningful. This condition could not be achieved with these data. So the familiar beta weights have been used.

4. The signs have been omitted from the effects in Table 15–2 for the sake of clarity of presentation. Because the signs of the path coefficients used to calculate these effects are usually determined only by the arbitrary and reversible assignments of direction to the variables, they are not very significant, especially for the purposes that Table 15–2 is intended to serve. Furthermore there are no instances in which one of the party-related variables has exhibited a positive direct effect and a negative indirect effect (or vice versa). Hence the signs are truly arbitrary and can be ignored with no fear of error resulting.

5. This estimate is derived by subtracting from the 1962 direct effect given in Table 15–2 (.70) the median total effect (.17) of the most important intervening variable, party affect, in the three congressional elections in which it had a significant total effect. Other estimates within a range of ±.05 would have no effect on the conclusions drawn in the text.

6. On these points see, for example, Lijphart, 1975; Thomassen, 1976; Miller and Stouthard, 1975.

References

ASHER, HERBERT B. (1976). "Causal Modeling." Sage University Papers series on Quantitative Applications in the Social Sciences, 07-001. Beverly Hills, Calif. London: Sage.

BLALOCK, H. M., JR. (1967). "Causal Inferences, Closed Populations, and Measures of Association," *The American Political Science Review* 61 (March), 130–136.

BUDGE, IAN, IVOR CREWE, and DENNIS FARLIE (1976a). "Introduction: Party Identification and Beyond," in Budge, Crewe, and Farlie (1976b), pp. 3–20.

———— (1976b). *Party Identification and Beyond.* London and New York: Wiley.

BUTLER, DAVID, and DONALD E. STOKES (1976). *Political Change in Britain*, 2nd coll. ed. New York: St. Martin's Press.

CAMPBELL, ANGUS, PHILIP E. CONVERSE, WARREN E. MILLER, and DONALD E. STOKES (1960). *The American Voter.* New York: Wiley.

EPSTEIN, LEON D. (1975). "Political Parties," in Fred I. Greenstein and Nelson W. Polsby, eds., *Handbook of Political Science*, Reading, Mass.: Addison-Wesley, Vol. 4: *Nongovernmental Politics*, pp. 229–278.

GOLDBERG, ARTHUR S. (1966). "Discerning a Causal Pattern among Data on Voting Behavior," *The American Political Science Review* 60 (Sept.), 913–922.

IRVINE, WILLIAM P. (1976). "Testing Models of Voting Choice in Canada," in Budge, Crewe, and Farlie (1976b), pp. 353–364.

IRWIN, GALEN A., and JACQUES THOMASSEN (1975). "Issue Consensus in a Multi-Party System: Voters and Leaders in the Netherlands," *Acta Politica* 10 (Oct.), 389–420.

JENNINGS, M. KENT (1972). "Partisan Commitment and Electoral Behavior in the Netherlands," *Acta Politica* 7 (Oct.), 445–470.

JOINT COMMITTEE ON WESTERN EUROPE of the Social Science Research Council and the American Council of Learned Societies (1975). "New Perspectives for the Study of Western Europe," *Items* 29 (Sept.), 34–37.

KAASE, MAX (1976). "Party Identification and Voting Behavior in the West German Election of 1969," in Budge, Crewe, and Farlie (1976b), pp. 81–102.

KING, ANTHONY (1969). "Political Parties in Western Democracies," *Polity* 2 (Jan.), 112–141. As reprinted in Louis J. Cantori, ed., *Comparative Political Systems.* Boston: Holbrook Press, 1974.

KIRCHHEIMER, OTTO (1966). "The Transformation of the Western European Party Systems," in Joseph LaPalombara and Myron Weiner, eds., *Political Parties and Political Development.* Princeton, N.J.: Princeton University Press.

KNOKE, DAVID (1974). "A Causal Synthesis of Sociological and Psychological Models of American Voting Behavior," *Social Forces* 53 (Sept.), 92–101.

MAYER, LAWRENCE, with JOHN H. BURNETT (1977). *Politics in Industrial Societies: A Comparative Perspective.* New York: Wiley.

MILLER, WARREN E., and PHILIP STOUTHARD (1975). "Confessional Attachment and Electoral Behavior in the Netherlands," *European Journal of Political Research*, 3 (Sept.), 219–258.

NIE, NORMAN H., SIDNEY VERBA, and JOHN R. PETROCIK (1976). *The Changing American Voter.* Cambridge, Mass. and London: Harvard University Press.

SCHLETH, UWE, and WEEDE, ERICH (1971). "Causal Models on West German Voting Behavior," in Rudolph Wildenmann et al., eds., *Sozialwissenschaftliches Jahrbuch für Politik*, Band 2. Munchen: Olzog Verlag.

SCHULMAN, MARK A., and GERALD M. POMPER (1975). "Variability in Electoral Behavior: Longitudinal Perspectives from Causal Modeling," *American Journal of Political Science*, 19 (Feb.), 1–18.

TATE, C. NEAL (1977). "Causal Models of Voting Choice: An Eight Nation Analysis." Paper presented to the Annual Meeting of the Midwest Political Science Association, Chicago.

THOMASSEN, JACQUES (1976). "Party Identification as a Cross-Cultural Concept: Its Meaning in the Netherlands," in Budge, Crewe, and Farlie (1976b), pp. 63–79.

WRIGHT, SEWALL (1906). "Path Coefficients and Path Regressions: Alternative or Complementary Concepts?," *Biometrics*, 16 (June), 189–202.

CHAPTER 16

ATTITUDES, IDEOLOGY, AND POLITICS OF PARTY MEMBERS

Peter H. Merkl

THE PARTY SYSTEMS that evolved in much of Western Europe with the onset of mass politics in the twentieth century, according to Seymour M. Lipset and Stein Rokkan,[1] were largely the products of the social structures prevailing then and throughout the first half of the century. The members of these parties, too, to a considerable extent never entirely shared the attitudes and belonged to the particular social classes and groups they represented.[2] Since the 1950s and especially since the 1960s, however, social change has begun to alter the original group basis of party politics, leaving the party members increasingly detached from what used to be their relatively transparent backgrounds. Although we seem to know less about them, the parties are as powerful as ever—all the more reason to take a close look at the attitudes and motives of party members of major parties. Partisan ideologies once used to be intimately related to their social group background in ways that were easy to fathom. Today, we may have to probe a member's underlying psychological attitudes and try to contrast their influence on his (or her) ideology with that of his occupational status. Ideology has become so unpredictable a guide to actual policy preference, in fact, that we also have to ask the question whether there is not a perceptible tendency for the basic attitudes to relate directly to day-to-day policy preferences, shortcutting the importance of partisan ideology. Behind these interrelated questions we are examining, finally, there is the variable of political change as it may be mirrored in the ages of the respondents and in the times when they chose to join their respective parties.

For several reasons, this attempt to cope with the questions raised above will have to deviate somewhat from the deceptive tidiness and finished look of most quantitative studies. It will do so not only because it is part of a larger study of the ideological attitudes and other characteristics of 415 West German and Italian Socialists and Christian Democrats, much of which has appeared elsewhere,[3] but also from a sense of uneasiness about burying the richness and significance of these data in a quantitative summation. Readers who are impatient for the bottom line are directed to the factor analysis of the data in *Comparative Social Research* (II)[4] to which we will occasionally refer. But the message of this essay is really that getting there was far more interesting than the final goal of the research journey.

The Sample

The original plans called for a sample of 100 members each of the West German SPD and CDU and the Italian PSU (a temporary merger of the PSI and PSDI) and DC to be gathered in 1968 and 1969 by Doxa of Milan and Infas of Bad Godesberg. The timing had to do with the Italian and German election campaigns of those years and also with the presence of controversial grand coalition governments in both countries. Those were also the days of the Vietnam agony, although its reception in Italy and West Germany was quite different and more ideological than in the United States itself.[5] The ensuing upheaval, particularly among German and Italian university youth, at first seemed to make this timing seem unfortunate as there are evidently no obvious young rebels in the sample.[6] With the benefit of hindsight, however, the timing now appears to enhance the historical perspective on that point in party history which preceded the era of *Ostpolitik* in West Germany and the dramatic surge of the Italian Communists (PCI) to the gates of power.

It was not possible to draw samples from membership files in either country. The Italian sample of 215 was drawn in a geographically representative manner in August of 1968 from a list of known party members previously interviewed by DOXA, as follows. From the three provinces of the industrial Northwest, 30 DC and 32 PSU; from the agrarian Northeast, 9 DC and 8 PSU; from Central Italy, 21 DC and 36 PSU; from the South, 25 DC and 24 PSU; and from the islands, Sicily and Sardinia, 17 DC and 13 PSU—altogether 102 DC and 113 PSU respondents. The most obvious weakness of the sample drawn is that it is considerably higher in the level of education than both parties are thought to be. The German sample of 200 was based on a random sample drawn from a large party member study conducted by Nils Diederich in Hesse, North Rhine Westphalia, and Lower Saxony:[7] 53 CDU and 34 SPD from Lower Saxony, 17 CDU and 21 SPD from North Rhine Westphalia, and 30 CDU and 45 SPD from Hesse. Although this appears to be a well-balanced cross-section, the lack of geographical coverage should be noted.

To describe some of the basic dimensions of the two samples, we have set them side by side by size of commune, Table 16–1(a), by occupation, Table 16–1(b), and by age, Table 16–1(c).

Ideological Attitudes

The study focused on the political socialization and views of the respondents. Among many other questions, they were asked ten dichotomous attitude questions which attempted to fathom their ideological attitudes at several levels:

1. Dedication to Party: Private orientation

   Underlying Attitudes

2. Social Trust: Distrust
3. Democracy: Authoritarianism
4. Probureaucracy: Bureaucratophobia

   Ideological Issues

5. Class Barriers (Class Order): Free Social Mobility
6. Capitalistic Development: Interventionism (Revolution)
7. Clericalism (Tolerance): Anticlericalism (Secularism)

   Topical Issues

8. Grand Coalition (Centro-Sinistra): Anticoalition
9. European Integration: Gaullism
10. United States in Vietnam: Anti-Vietnam

These questions were presented in dichotomous pairs to maintain their dialectical nature and to facilitate processing of the data.[8] A few extra parameters were added for the German respondents which obviously had no Italian equivalent and are included here only as a tangential perspective. They were also of a topical nature:

11. Outlawing the NPD: Toleration
12. Recognizing the DDR: Nonrecognition

We expected that the questions of suppressing either the neo-Nazi NPD or the New Left, and of course the recognition of the East German Republic, would divide the SPD and CDU and relate in interesting ways to the other dichotomies. The cross-tabulations carried out among them indeed showed

TABLE 16–1. Basic Dimensions of the Sample

	ITALIANS			GERMANS		
	DC	PSU	Average	CDU	SPD	Average
a: Party Members by Size of Commune (Percent)						
Below 2,000	5.9	5.3	5.6	17	34	25.5
2,000–5,000	19.6	15.0	17.2	14	15	14.5
5,000–10,000	5.9	5.3	5.6	23	6	14.5
10,000–20,000	15.7	13.3	14.4	8	4	6.0
20,000–100,000	29.4	25.7	27.4	28	13	20.5
Italy 100,000–200,000 (Germany 100,000–250,000)	2.9	15.9	9.8	1	5	3.0
Italy 200,000 and over (Germany: 250,000 and over)	20.6	19.5	20.0	9	23	16.0
Total	100 (n = 102)	100 (n = 113)	100 (n = 215)	100 (n = 100)	100 (n = 100)	100 (n = 200)
b: Party Members by Occupation (Percent)						
Independents and family helpers	10.8	12.4	11.6	27	3	15.0
Professions	4.9	5.3	6.1	2	—	1.0
GGE, students	12.7	15.9	14.4	—	—	—
Managers, high civil servants, teachers	20.6	21.3	20.9	14	3	8.5
Public service	19.6	11.5	15.4	9	8	8.5
White collar, private	13.7	12.4	13.0	22	26	24.0
Blue collar	11.8	17.7	14.9	10	34	22.0
Retired, on pension	—	—	—	15	25	20.0
Farmers	5.9	3.5	4.7	—	—	—
Not available	—	—	—	1	1	1.0
Total	100 (n = 102)	100 (n = 113)	100 (n = 215)	100 (n = 110)	100 (n = 100)	100 (n = 200)

TABLE 16–1 (continued)

	16–24	25–34	35–44	45–54	OVER 54	TOTAL
c: Party Members by Age (Percent)						
Italians						
DC	9.8	29.5	25.5	17.6	17.6	100 (n = 102)
PSU	9.9	27.9	26.2	18.9	17.1	100 (n = 111)
Average	9.9	23.6	25.8	18.3	17.4	100 (n = 213)
West Germans						
CDU	6	17	38	24	15	100 (n = 100)
SPD	—	17	34	26	23	100 (n = 100)
Average	3	17	36	25	19	100 (n = 200)

some surprising linkages. In both parties, for example, members exhibiting social trust were significantly more tolerant toward the NPD but also more inclined not to want to recognize the West German DDR than were the distrustful ones. Those who showed less dedication to their party and those who were more democratically inclined, and exhibited probureaucratic attitudes (especially in the CDU), also were more often tolerant toward the NPD but not the DDR than their opposites. The upshot appeared to be a kind of establishment consensus on the NPD and on nonrecognition of the DDR, among the *bien-pensants* of both parties and especially in the CDU which was still in power then. The more traditional attitudes among the more distrustful Social and Christian Democrats tilted more toward banning the NPD and recognizing the DDR.[9]

The ten questions were grouped on three levels to test hypotheses deriving the topical positions from broad ideological attitudes and the latter from deeper dimensions of social adjustment and personal integration. Our choice of underlying issues turned out to be quite revealing, especially the social trust-distrust and the authoritarian-democratic dimensions. Hatred of bureaucracy appears to be too unevenly distributed today to facilitate comparisons although it appeared in many pivotal relationships. Dedication to party was unexpectedly ambiguous, although the pronounced difference between the organization-happy Germans and the private-oriented Italians alone was a feature worth noting (Table 16–2). The breakdown by individual party, by country, and by party label across the boundaries shows the only major differences to be between the countries. About one-fourth more West Germans than Italians are dedicated to their party. This measurement can be deepened by reference to participation in party activities and other indicators. Asked how frequently they participate in party meetings, for example, 76% of the very or rather dedicated CDU respondents reply "always" and another 21% "almost always," whereas the private-oriented have fewer "always" (50%) and "almost always" (27%) responses. The SPD respondents, on the other hand, turn out to participate generally less in meetings: 40% say "always" and 24% "almost always." The "dedicated" Social Democrats, in fact, participate somewhat less often than the less dedicated and private-oriented respondents. Their lower rate of participation is borne out also by the responses to another question about the time of the last meeting attended. The dedicated CDU respondents included 52% (SPD, 23%) who attended a meeting during the last four weeks, 26% (SPD, 20%) who had done so a month ago and 9% (SPD, 20%) who had attended one a quarter of a year ago. Among the Italians, where the private orientation is very pronounced in both parties, the highest participation also occurs not among the very dedicated of either party, but among the rather dedicated, the less dedicated and those in the middle.[10] There is a paradox here between self-styled dedication and actual attendance which goes begging for an explanation for the time being.[11]

TABLE 16–2. Dedication to Own Party (Percent)

	SPD	CDU	WEST GERMANY	ITALY	PSU	DC	ALL SOCIALISTS	ALL CHRISTIAN DEMOCRATS
Very dedicated	20	24	22.0	5.1	6.2	3.9	12.7	13.9
Rather dedicated	11	9	10.0	2.8	3.5	2.0	7.0	5.4
In the middle	17	12	14.5	5.1	5.3	4.9	10.8	8.4
Rather private-oriented	16	21	18.5	17.2	15.0	19.6	15.5	20.3
Very private-oriented	33	31	32.0	67.9	66.4	69.6	50.7	50.5
Don't know, neither	3	3	3.0	1.9	3.6	—	3.3	1.5
Total	100	100	100	100	100	100	100	100
Number	100	100	200	215	113	102	213	202

Underlying Attitudes

At the next level we have three measurements of underlying attitudes that are not usually spelled out in overt ideological statements although they may influence the latter to a considerable degree. The first involves social trust and distrust in the personalized form of "people taking advantage of me."[12] Behind an identification with Meier-Rossi who complains about being taken advantage of is a stress on childlike dependency needs and a kind of social masochism. Whether anyone ever took advantage of him or not, the respondent likes to think of himself as exposed to exploitation and would like for someone to come and protect or nurture him as his parents might do.

Table 16–3 shows these dependency needs and social distrust to be far higher among the Italians than among the Germans, and nearly as much higher among socialists in both countries than among the Christian Democrats. The general population sample of the Almond-Verba study had brought out a German percentage of 81% (Italy, 73%) who agreed that "people will take advantage of you" and of 72% (Italy, 61%) who felt that "no one is going to care much what happens to you."[13] Evidently Socialist party members are generally more dependency-oriented and the Italian Socialists nearly outstrip even the general population in this. We may conjecture that strong feelings of this sort may well be related to a concern for the underdog and that Italian society generally lacks many of the self-help opportunities and perhaps also the training for self-reliance which West German society possesses. If this reasoning about socialism holds true, it would follow for the Christian Democrats that the social distrust-trust dichotomy among them describes the division between the more socialistically inclined and those whose dependency needs are met by the existing society or by their faith in God.

How do the distrustful Italians differ from the trusting? The supplementary remarks of many respondents throw some light on how they interpreted the question. The more distrustful Christian Democrats tended to relate personal experiences of people taking advantage of them or to refer to pushy people or crooks. The more trusting tended to address themselves critically to the distrust of many people in the altruism of their fellow man or spoke of getting to know and understand people or of "making people respect you." Distrustful Socialists also stressed personal experiences and facts of life, pushy people, crooks, and exploiters. But they also spoke disapprovingly of rampant distrust in society "because the state does not step in" and of the callous selfishness of the collectivity. Trusting Socialists stressed faith in the altruism of their fellow man and of getting to know and understand people.

Social Trust

The respondents were also asked to rank five categories of people they would trust with problems regarding their personal future. The results were

TABLE 16-3. People Take Advantage of You (Social Distrust) (Percent)

	SPD	CDU	WEST GERMANY	ITALY	PSU	DC	ALL SOCIALISTS	ALL CHRISTIAN DEMOCRATS
They sure do	11	8	9.5	28.6	35.4	21.6	23.9	14.9
They rather do	15	13	14.0	24.1	26.5	21.6	21.1	17.3
In the middle	18	18	18.0	16.3	13.3	19.6	15.5	18.8
Not really	31	32	31.5	14.4	8.0	21.6	18.8	26.7
Definitely not	21	23	22.0	12.1	11.5	12.7	16.0	17.8
Don't know, neither	4	6	5.0	4.5	5.3	2.9	4.7	4.5
Total	100	100	100	100	100	100	100	100
Number	100	100	200	215	113	102	213	202

rather striking in view of often-stressed characteristics of Italian political culture such as Banfield's "amoral familism," the role of the church, and the prestige of education. Regarding relatives and family members, the more trusting DC members tended to place them in first or second place, whereas the distrustful often rated them third or fourth. If you cannot even trust your family, they seemed to say, you have a right to be distrustful. The distrustful Socialists did the opposite, placing the family first, second, or third, whereas the trusting placed them third or fourth. Here evidently the distrustful are more familistic and the trusting socially integrated in the wider society. In both parties, the family gets the highest trust scores. Priests, the second most popular confidants among the DC members, did best among the distrustful but almost as well among the trusting. Among the Socialists, where they enjoy the least respect, they did somewhat better among the trusting than among the distrustful, of whom more than half went out of their way to give them the lowest place on their list.

Having thus disposed of Don Camillo, Socialists gave Peppone his due by placing fellow party members second on their list of trust. Ironically, however, it is chiefly the distrustful Socialists who place their trust first and second in their party comrades, leading one to speculate on the presumable connection between distrusting people in general and trusting fellow Socialists. The PSU evidently still considers itself still very much as an underdog party in which the exploited band together against their oppressors, a view which leaves little room for the parties on their left.

The Christian Democrats were less trusting of their fellow party members, placing them after relatives, priests, and teachers. The more trusting among them rate party members higher as confidants, but many of them also place them at the bottom of their list. Teachers, as persons of trust, were given a very strong second place rating by both parties. The distrustful Christian Democrats appreciate teachers more than do the trusting, which reinforces the impression that distrustful DC members felt neglected by their families. Among the Socialists, it is the trusting who give their teachers a high rating and who, it will be recalled, are also less familistic. Finally, there are the fellow trade union members who grace the bottom of the Christian Democratic lists of trust and, if it were not for the priests, would do no better with the PSU. The distrustful DC members still treat them more kindly than the more trusting, and the same is true of the PSU.

Because some of these differences in ranking may well leave a confusing picture in the mind of the reader, let us sketch profiles of the trusting and distrustful of each party. Considered in this fashion, the distrustful Christian Democrats in Italy trust family members the most, followed closely by priests, and at some distance by teachers, fellow party members, and fellow trade unionists. The trusting DC member trusts people in the same order, but at equal intervals and more clearly. The distrustful Socialist also trusts his relatives most, but after them come fellow party members, teachers, fellow trade unionists, and, finally, priests. The trusting PSU members, after their family members, directly place their trust in teachers, and then in fellow party members, trade unionists and priests. It is with all four groups a choice of political significance, hardly an accidental tally of personal idiosyncrasies. Indeed, one can read a modernization differential into the shifting patterns of social trust from family to the priests and teachers or, alternatively, to fellow party members or trade unionists. Furthermore, because the family-oriented of the DC are more trusting whereas those of the PSU are most distrustful, this line of argument tends to juxtapose different paths of emancipation from the bonds of familism for the clientele of the two parties, from the traditional DC family to trust in priests or teachers, and with the already transitional PSU family, where social distrust seems to be the political atmosphere, to the equally distrustful party.

How do the German respondents compare with this? The German interviews did not use any ranking, but merely asked the respondents to pick out one of the five categories as the most trustworthy. They also accepted additional categories. This change had the unexpected result of reducing the numbers for the five categories and of bringing in a new preferred category, namely, "friends." Nearly half of the more trusting CDU members chose "friends" as their most trusted category. The rest split more or less between "teachers and clergymen" (combined for lack of numbers) and relatives. Distrustful Christian Democrats named these last two, relatives and clergymen, most often. Relatives were also the preferred category of the distrustful SPD members. The trusting Social Democrats, by comparison, tended to name fellow party members and trade unionists.

The contrast between the Italian and the West German social trust responses could hardly be greater. Apart from the equally dominant role of relatives, the Italian combination of social distrust with socialism and trust in fellow party members has no parallel in Germany. There on the contrary it is the trusting Socialists who trust their fellow party members and trade unionists. Social distrust, in other words, does not seem to be of the same political significance as with the PSU, whereas social trust relates to the comradely atmosphere of party and labor movement. The CDU members were noticeably less beholden to clergymen than were the Italian DC. Major differences in the meaning of social trust are, of course, to be expected since the popular understanding of the two cultures ascribes more of an atmosphere of social cooperation to the Germans than to the Italians. And it will be remembered that the German party members were far less distrustful than the Italians, especially the PSU, to begin with.

What other differences are there between the trusting and the distrustful of both countries and parties? In Italy, for one thing, there is a noticeable regional differential. Italian party members in the South, the islands, and in Central Italy are more distrustful than are those living in the North. More specifically, the distrustful PSU members tend to live in the Northeast and in the South and the island areas where the DC happens to dominate partisan politics, whereas the trusting Socialists live more often in the Northwest or in the Central "red belt" where the left-wing parties are dominant. The Christian Democrats, conversely, are distrustful in the Northwest and Center and more trusting in the Northeast and the South. Apart from the not unexpected difference between North and South, the sense of social trust is evidently related to whether or not the respondent's party or ideological subculture (such as Communism-Socialism) is dominant in the area. We can go a step further and suggest that perhaps a person's social distrust has partisan overtones and expresses a deeper existential and ideological anxiety which motivates the person to join a party to ward off the threat. If this is what distrust denotes in a party member, an expression of social trust would mean the absence of this anxiety as a motive for becoming active in politics.

What about other indices of location and occupation? The more trusting Italians tend to live in communities under 10,000,[14] are farmers or laborers, and have grown up without moving from the place of their birth. Distrustful Christian Democrats tend to be born where they now reside, while distrustful Socialists often pulled up stakes when they were teenagers. The most distrustful occupations are professionals, business and handicraft,[15] and university students, whereas teachers, civil servants, and public employees are the least distrustful. This is true of both parties, although the Socialists also include distrustful farmers and blue- and white-collar workers. The size of the company or economic unit where the respondents work also distinguishes the level of trust. Socialists are more distrustful in companies of less than ten employees, and Christian Democrats are more trusting there than in larger units. Socialists are also more likely to be distrustful the shorter the time they have been with a given company. Only after 15 years with the same outfit do they tend to give a trusting response. This relationship applies to the DC as well but not as clearly. It is understandable that long-time employees should feel more secure, even though dependent labor in both parties appears to be more trusting than the independents and family helpers are. It hardly will surprise anyone that in both parties distrust and trust closely relate to dissatisfaction and satisfaction with the respondent's income and the nature of his work.

Is social trust related to education? Christian Democrats, who never went beyond the middle-school level and those who attended the university tend to be more distrustful, whereas those who went to upper-middle schools are notably more trusting. With the Socialists, it is precisely the upper-middle school graduates who are the most distrustful and hence in line with the distrustfulness of their party. Does attendance at a church school allay anxiety? On the contrary, the religious school graduates are more distrustful than those who never attended such a school. One wonders what they learn in these schools. Respondents who have attended adult education or training programs also are more distrustful, perhaps because they are upwardly mobile, than those who did not.

We also asked respondents whether they had many friends left from their school days in an effort to find out whether they had been loners at school. The more school friends after graduation, the more trusting is the respondent on our scale, especially among the Christian Democrats. The Socialists conform less clearly to this pattern. Specifically, there are many distrustful respondents who report having many old school chums still around. One gets the impression that, in a Socialist milieu, even the chummiest can feel and express social distrust because it is the thing to feel. It may be a catch phrase or a common verbal means to establish rapport in this case rather than a sign of individual alienation.

With the German parties, their regional differential is less clear. To be sure, distrustful Christian Democrats tended to live in Hesse, the "reddest" of the three states, whereas the more trusting lived more often in Lower Saxony and North Rhine Westphalia. But the SPD members also are more distrustful in Hesse and more trusting in North Rhine Westphalia. The size of the community gives us no clue either. The more trusting of both parties tend to be in communes under 2,000 as well as in metropolitan areas. The more trusting, especially in the CDU, also tend to be long-time residents or to have been born where they now reside, whereas the distrustful are from somewhere else in Germany, from Berlin, or even from the DDR or the East.

Regarding their occupations, the distrustful Christian Democrats tend to be independents, professionals, or workers, whereas the trusting are more likely pensionists or white collar. The pensionists in the SPD also tend to be trusting, but white and blue collar are distrustful. Thus there are some similarities to the Italian pattern, although one would expect workers to be more convinced that "people take advantage" of them in any case. As among the Italians, also, the Socialists are more likely to be distrustful if they work in companies with under ten employees, whereas Christian Democrats in the same size of economic unit are more trusting. Generally, far fewer Socialists (12.0%) than Christian Democrats (31.8%) work in enterprises that small. Socialists in economic units with 100 and more employees again are slightly more likely to be distrustful rather than trusting, whereas the CDU members present the opposite picture. The level of distrust among CDU members also tends to be higher in agriculture, mining, commerce, and transportation, whereas the public service and handicraft and construction are more trusting industries. The exact obverse of this obtains among the SPD. With the Christian Democrats, also, as with the Italians, people are less distrustful after they have been with the same company for 15 years or more. The SPD members, on the other hand, are more distrustful after five years on the job. Both CDU and SPD members, just like the two Italian parties, are the more distrustful the more dissatisfied they are with their income and work.

The level of their education again brings out significant differences. The less educated (elementary school plus vocational training) Christian Democrats and the better educated Social Democrats are the most distrustful. The

SPD member of little education, and probably working-class status, the "regular labor movement man," once again tends to be trusting. Attendance at denominational primary schools among the CDU members (one-third of whom attended such a school) seems to make for more trusting responses, whereas nonattenders are slightly more distrustful. Among the SPD members, however, attendance at these religiously influenced schools clearly makes for social distrust and nonattendance for trust. We may conjecture that it is not so much the nature of the school as of the local community which may produce distrust. These denominational schools were a matter of local option in most parts and having opted for one is likely to characterize a community as fairly religious and probably CDU-oriented. The Italian respondents of both parties also showed more distrust if they had attended religious schools, though obviously for different reasons. The German responses to the question about school friends remaining after graduation produced opposite partisan reactions.

Of those who replied that they still remained in touch with *many* old school chums, the CDU members tended to be distrustful and the SPD members trusting. Those who responded that they had "some" showed exactly the opposite reaction. Distrustful CDU members and trusting SPD members again made up the bulk of those who had "only one or two" school friends left. And the opposite combination was typical of those without school friends. It hardly added up to a pattern, except that there were many more Socialists (25%) than CDU members (16%) without any school friends.

To pursue this matter a little further, let us look at the responses to another question, "Do you have many good friends, apart from relatives?," which explores the trust patterns outside of the family. The question was answered seven to one in the affirmative by both parties, but the distrustful CDU and SPD members were noticeably more friendless, especially in the SPD, than the trusting. The Italian DC shows the same reaction but the PSU does not; the special significance of social distrust for Italian Socialists obscures the natural relationship between trust and friendship and produces more expressions of social trust among the friendless.

Generally, group memberships denote social integration and trust, but running trust against trade union membership indicates the complexity of the relationship. Among both the CDU and the SPD members, the union members tend to be more distrustful than the nonmembers which leads one to suspect that a fear of being taken advantage of is typical of workers and may lead to union membership. The distrustful union members of both parties also participate more in union meetings than the trusting. The patterns of other organizational memberships show significant variations. Among the CDU members, the trusting are proportionally more involved in nearly all groups, sports, church groups, welfare and cooperative or interest groups, and trade unions, except for social or cultural groups in which the distrustful stand out. In the SPD, it is likewise the social and cultural groups, but also the welfare and cooperative associations and the trade unions, in which the distrustful stand out. Only 10–15% in both parties, and among the trusting as often as the distrustful, are without other organizational memberships. Why are there more distrustful respondents in social, cultural, and, with the SPD, in welfare, cooperative groups, and trade unions? These groups may be of special significance to the ideological commitment of party militants on both sides.

Union membership among the Italians does not seem to denote the same as in West Germany. Hence in both parties, the nonunionists tend to be more distrustful than the union members. Only among the holders of union offices and those who participate frequently in union meetings do the distrustful stand out. As for the other organizational memberships, of which the Italian party members have far fewer,[16] the more ideological (ACLI, ENAL, Catholic associations) enroll more of the distrustful, at least in the DC, than is the case with the various sports, cultural and assistance groups in either party.

Relating Distrust to Other Attitudes

How do the attitudes of the social trust-distrust question fit in with the other underlying attitudes? We have cross-tabulated these parameters with social distrust and arranged them in series of two-by-two tables (Tables 16–4 and 16–5) which contain only the pro and con responses in absolute numbers, leaving off the undecided and the don't knows. Each two-by-two table indicates to what extent social distrust or trust in each party are related to the dichotomies of the other issues. For example, the very first juxtaposition is of social trust and dedication to party: it shows 12 of the 100 SPD respondents to be both dedicated and distrustful, 10 private-oriented and distrustful, 16 dedicated and trusting, and 26 private-oriented and trusting. Private orientation and social trust are obviously the most highly related for the SPD, whereas for the PSU it is private orientation and social distrust. Christian Democrats of both countries mirror the same tendencies as the Socialists, but much more weakly. This is one way of looking at these tables. Another way is by going down vertically and seeing, for instance, how distrust relates to each of the other issues. Let us take a look at the distrustful and trusting of each party issue by issue.[17]

Distrustful German Socialists tend to profess some dedication to their party, authoritarianism, and sympathy for the bureaucrats. We will encounter this DDA (distrust-dedication-authoritarianism) syndrome again soon. The trusting SPD members, by way of contrast, are private-oriented with regard to the party, distinctly democratic, and friendly to the civil service in their underlying attitudes. On the same basis, we can also say that dedicated SPD members as well as the private-oriented tend to be trusting and that authoritarian Socialists are about evenly divided between trust and distrust, whereas the democratically inclined are trusting. Private orientation, trust, and democratic attitudes also form a syndrome, PTD, which will come up again. The antibureaucratic SPD members are more distrustful, whereas those sympathetic to the civil servants tend to be trusting. Antibureaucratism as a part of the DDA syndrome, as will soon become evident, is very prominent among the Italian Socialists who do not share the positive feelings of the Germans toward the bureaucracy.

On the basic ideological issues, the SPD distrustful believe that there are no class barriers to social mobility, that capitalistic development can break the shackles of poverty, and that church influence should not be tolerated. The trusting SPD members agree regarding the effect of capitalistic development and feel even more strongly that there are no class barriers in West Germany, but they are very tolerant toward church influence. Reading horizontally, Social Democrats who believe that there are still class barriers are evenly split on social trust, whereas those who reject this notion heavily turn out to be trusting. Those who expect capitalistic development to solve the problems of the underdog tend to be trusting, though no more so than the advocates of decisive political changes. Anticlerical SPD members, finally, tend toward social distrust, whereas their more tolerant comrades are far more likely to trust their fellowman. The influence of the underlying attitudes, and particularly of the DDA syndrome, seems to make for a noticeably harder or softer ideological line. The DDA syndrome appears to relate strongly to anticlericalism and, less so, to class consciousness. The PTD syndrome, on the other hand, relates more strongly to religious tolerance and to deemphasis on class, but also, if to a weaker extent, to demands for drastic political change.

As for the day-to-day issues, distrustful German Socialists are for the Grand Coalition, for the American involvement in Vietnam, and strongly in favor of a true European federation, but not quite as strongly as the trusting, especially with respect to the Grand Coalition, a subject of great controversiality in the SPD. They also favor tolerating the NPD and the recognition of the East German Republic (DDR). Trusting SPD members are heavily in favor of the Grand Coalition, European federation, and Vietnam. They are less heavily in favor of tolerating the NPD and are against recognition of Pankow. Horizontally read, the enemies of the Grand Coalition are split evenly between the trusting and the distrustful, whereas its friends tend to be trusting. The supporters and opponents of the American presence in Vietnam both tend to be trusting folks, especially the latter. So are the good Europeans as well as the Gaullists, the sworn enemies of the NPD as well as those who are prepared to tolerate it, and the advocates of DDR recognition as well as its supporters, but especially the latter. Distrust seems to make Social Democrats noticeably more intolerant of the NPD, but also to encourage an identification with the DDR. We can either interpret this to signify an underlying, left-wing ideological dimension of social distrust in the SPD, or as a psychological projection mechanism which leads opposition within the party and the state to

TABLE 16-4. Various Ideological Parameters and Social Distrust (in absolute numbers)

	SPD		CDU		PSU		DC	
	Distrust	Trust	Distrust	Trust	Distrust	Trust	Distrust	Trust
Dedication to party	$Q = .322$		$Q = .048$		$Q = .181$		$Q = .257$	
Dedicated	12	16	8	20	7	3	2	1
Private oriented	10	26	11	25	59	19	39	33
	$X^2 = 1.621$		$X^2 = .020$					
Authoritarianism	$Q = .571^{**}$		$Q = .450$		$Q = .584^{**}$		$Q = .400$	
Authoritarian	16	17	14	22	16	2	14	6
Democratic	9	35	7	29	42	20	28	28
	$S^2 = 6.793^{***}$		$X^2 = 3.292^{*}$		$X^2 = 3.494^{*}$		$X^2 = 2.308$	
Hatred of bureaucracy	$Q = .805^{**}$		$Q = .729^{**}$		$Q = .737^{**}$		$Q = .698^{**}$	
Antibureaucratic	7	2	4	2	37	4	10	2
Probureaucratic	17	45	15	48	21	15	24	27
	$X^2 = 9.525^{***}$		$X^2 = 3.078^{*}$		$X^2 = 10.861^{***}$		$X^2 = 5.486^{**}$	
Class barriers	$Q = .464^{**}$		$Q = .236$		$Q = .624$		$Q = .451$	
Classes present (or desirable)	8	8	5	9	27	4	11	4
No barriers	15	41	12	35	25	16	26	25
	$X^2 = 3.109$				$X^2 = 6.468$		$X^2 = 3.009$	
Capitalistic development	$Q = .031$		$Q = .316$		$Q = .197$		$Q = .701^{**}$	
Procapitalistic	14	25	14	23	21	13	11	2
Revolutionary (intervention-istic)	10	19	6	19	41	17	27	28
							$X^2 = 5.679$	

418

Church influence
Tolerant (proclerical) | Anticlerical

$Q = .607**$	$Q = -.029$	$Q = .837**$	$Q = .215$
11 | 39	10 | 24	31 | 20	7 | 4
15 | 13	11 | 28	35 | 2	35 | 31
$X^2 = 8.150***$		$X^2 = 13.482***$	

Grand Coalition
In favor | Against

$Q = -.471**$	$Q = -.884**$	$Q = -.345$	$Q = -.145$
14 | 39	9 | 44	42 | 16	29 | 25
8 | 8	10 | 3	27 | 5	14 | 9
$X^2 = 3.149*$	$X^2 = 18.990***$		

United States in Vietnam
In favor | Against

$Q = -.361$	$Q = -.442$	$Q = -.255$	$Q = -.068$
13 | 37	17 | 44	22 | 9	31 | 27
3 | 4	2 | 2	33 | 8	5 | 5

Europeanism versus Gaullism
Europeanist | Gaullist

$Q = -.041$	$Q = .135$	$Q = -.415$	$Q = .008$
21 | 38	21 | 48	23 | 13	29 | 19
3 | 5	— | 3	30 | 7	9 | 6

Toleration of NPD
Get rid of it | Tolerate it

$Q = .164$	$Q = .084$
$Q = .164$	$Q = .084$
10 | 16	9 | 19
13 | 29	10 | 25

Recognition of DDR
In favor | Against

$Q = .454*$	$Q = -.600**$
12 | 15	8 | 6
9 | 30	12 | 36
$X^2 = 3.338*$	$X^2 = 5.177**$

419

TABLE 16–5. Various Ideological Parameters and Dedication to Party (in absolute numbers)

	SPD Dedicated	SPD Private Oriented	CDU Dedicated	CDU Private Oriented	PSU Dedicated	PSU Private Oriented	DC Dedicated	DC Private Oriented
Social distrust	$Q = .322$		$Q = -.048$		$Q = -.181$		$Q = .257$	
Distrust	12	10	8	11	7	59	2	39
Trust	16	26	20	25	3	19	1	33
Authoritarianism	$Q = .159$		$Q = .181$		$Q = -.354$		$Q = -.655^{**}$	
Authoritarian	12	23	18	24	1	21	4	25
Democratic	18	25	13	25	6	60	2	60
							$X^2 = 2.209$	
Hatred of bureaucracy	$Q = .333$		$Q = .420$		$Q = -.380$		$Q = .388$	
Antibureaucratic	4	3	4	3	3	39	2	13
Probureaucratic	26	39	25	46	6	35	4	59
Class barriers	$Q = -.504^{**}$		$Q = .245$		$Q = .291$		$Q = .127$	
Classes present (or desirable)	8	6	4	9	4	30	1	15
No barriers	18	41	22	30	3	41	5	58
	$X^2 = 3.343^*$							
Capitalistic development	$Q = -.272$		$Q = .024$		$Q = -.567^{**}$		$Q = .441$	
Procapitalistic	16	28	17	25	2	38	2	12
Revolutionary/interventionistic	12	12	11	17	8	42	4	62
					$X^2 = 3.138^*$			
Church influence	$Q = -.224$		$Q = .107$		$Q = .318$		$Q = .071$	
Tolerant (proclerical)	19	35	16	22	8	51	1	13
Anticlerical (secular)	12	14	17	29	3	37	5	75

Grand Coalition

	In favor	Against	Q
	21	37	$Q = -.213$
	7	8	
	22	36	$Q = -.177$
	7	8	
	6	60	$Q = -.250$
	5	30	
	2	66	$Q = -.714**$
	4	22	$X^2 = 2.958*$

United States in Vietnam

	In favor	Against	Q
	16	39	$Q = -.529**$
	4	3	$X^2 = 1.172$
	26	44	$Q = -.083$
	2	4	
	4	31	$Q = -.075$
	6	40	
	5	61	$Q = -.031$
	1	13	

Europeanism versus Gaullism

	Europeanist	Gaullist	Q
	24	39	$Q = .573**$
	12	6	$X^2 = 2.055$
	33	44	$Q = -.636**$
	2	6	$X^2 = 4.416**$
	5	35	$Q = .000$
	5	35	
	1	55	$Q = -.746**$
	2	16	$X^2 = 1.320$

Toleration of NPD

	Get rid of it	Tolerate it	Q
	12	15	$Q = .333$
	12	30	
	21	13	$Q = .675**$
	10	32	$X^2 = 11.104***$

Recognition of DDR

	In favor	Against	Q
	13	20	$Q = .148$
	13	27	
	9	8	$Q = .372$
	18	35	

identify with the most hated, external antagonist. Other than this, the trust-distrust dimension seems to have little impact on the topical orientations in the SPD.

What about social distrust in the German CDU, the other major political subculture in the Federal Republic? We have to assume that an attitude of distrust may mean something entirely different from what it meant in the SPD. Distrustful German Christian Democrats tend to be private-oriented toward their party, authoritarian, and sympathetic to the bureaucracy. Trusting CDU members also tend to be private-oriented but democratic and heavily in favor of the civil service. By the same token, we can say that dedicated CDU members tend to be as trusting as the private-oriented. Authoritarians also tend to be trusting, though not as heavily as democrats. Antibureaucrats are more often distrustful, whereas the friends of the civil service tend toward trusting their fellowman. At first glance, it appears, social distrust in the CDU is highly related to authoritarianism, but only slightly to private orientation, and not much more to antibureaucratism. Trust by the same token goes with democratic and probureaucratic attitudes.

On the basic ideological issues, distrustful Christian Democrats believe that there are no barriers to social mobility and, strongly, that West German economic development shows indeed the superfluous role of economic intervention. Nearly as many distrustful CDU members give proclerical responses as express a preference for political autonomy from church influences. Trusting CDU members strongly agree that there are no class barriers and, by smaller margins, agree also that no state intervention in the economy is needed and that politics should be autonomous from church influence. Reading across, both the CDU members who believe social classes are natural and those who think there are no more class barriers today tend to be trusting, as do both capitalistic development groups and both church influence groups. Distrust seems to make the Christian Democrats more procapitalistic and more attached to the traditional role of social classes and of the church. Social trust makes for secularism, faith in social mobility, and relatively more concern about the underdogs of society.

As for the topical issues, distrustful Christian Democrats are against the Grand Coalition, but heavily in favor of the American presence in Vietnam and of a European federation. They also favor tolerating the NPD but oppose recognition of the DDR. Trusting CDU members heavily support the Grand Coalition, Vietnam, and a European federation. In almost identical numbers they support these typical policies of the establishment within the party, whereas the distrustful have noticeable misgivings about the alliance with the SPD. The trusting are also prepared to tolerate the NPD and, by a big margin, oppose recognition, whereas the distrustful are obviously less favorable to the NPD but somewhat more willing to recognize the DDR. On these issues, the CDU rather resembles the SPD.

Comparing the two German parties (Table 16–6), there is an amazing number of similarities in their responses, especially on the underlying and basic ideological issues. One glaring difference, to begin with is, of course, the fact that dedicated Socialists tend to be socially distrusting, whereas in the CDU dedicated members are as trusting as the private-oriented. There are also the distrustful SPD authoritarians and trusting SPD democrats, whereas the CDU authoritarians tend to be trusting. But from there on, the parallels predominate. The distrustful antibureaucrats and the trusting friends of the civil service, the trusting believers in *freie Bahn dem Tuechtigen* (no barriers to the upwardly mobile), and the trusting procapitalists. On church influence, always a fundamental issue between the two parties, there are differences again: the distrustful, anticlerical Socialist and the trusting, tolerant, one and the narrow edge of the secular-minded Christian Democrats, whether trusting or distrustful, over the proclerical, religious conservatives of the CDU. On the Grand Coalition, the only surprise is that distrustful CDU members oppose it, whereas distrustful SPD members don't. The reason for the SPD reaction may well lie in the weak representation of the younger cohorts in our German sample. The Vietnam issue for the same reason failed to produce more negative reactions in the SPD. The European, NPD, and DDR responses hold little surprise, though the last two are worth a closer look. In both cases, social distrust appears to reinforce attitudes not in conformity with West German majority opinion. On the NPD, the distrustful of both parties were noticeably more extrapunitive, as indeed they were on the bureaucrats and on the clergy. On recognition of the DDR, they tended to be more radical and alienated from their own society, as indeed they were also on dedication to party, authoritarianism, the presence of classes, radical political change, and on the Grand Coalition.

As for the Italians, there are profound differences from the West German responses in many respects. The distrustful Socialists heavily tend to be private oriented, rather democratic, and antibureaucratic. The trusting PSU members disagree only in being more heavily democratic and decidedly sympathetic to the civil service. Looking horizontally at the two-by-two tables, we note that dedicated socialists tend to be socially distrustful but that the private-oriented are so even more. Authoritarians heavily tend toward distrust far more than the democrats. And the antibureaucrats also heavily tend toward social distrust, far more than the friends of civil servants who are often civil servants themselves. In other words, here is the PDDA syndrome (private-distrustful-democratic-antibureaucratic) counterpointed only weakly by PTDP (private-

TABLE 16–6. **Trust–Distrust Patterns of Underlying Issues**

	SPD	*CDU*	*PSU*	*DC*
First tendency	PTDP	PTDP	PDDA	PDDP
Second tendency	DDAP	PDAP	PTDP	PTDP
Third tendency	DDAA	PDAA	DDAA	PDAA

NOTE: Each pattern follows the sequence Dedication-Private orientation, Trust-Distrust, Authority-Democracy, Pro-Antibureaucratism.

trusting-democratic-probureaucratic), the dominant tendency among both German parties. But there is also a significant undercurrent linking distrust with authoritarianism, dedication to party, and prejudice against the bureaucracy (Table 16–6).

On the ideological issues, the distrustful PSU member just barely prefers to believe that underdogs have no chance in the class society present and, more strongly, insists on drastic political changes and on an anticlerical position. Trusting Socialists, conversely, strongly believe that there are no class barriers and are tolerant toward church influence. They mildly agree with the necessity for radical political change in Italy. Reading across, we note that Socialists who believe in the presence of class barriers tend far more heavily to be distrustful than are those who believe that anyone can rise by ability and hard work alone. The advocates of revolutionary changes also are noticeably more likely to be distrustful than are those who trust capitalistic development to free the poor. The anticlerical, finally, are infinitely more distrustful than those who are tolerant of clerical influence. Distrust thus makes for a hard ideological line of revolutionary change, anticlericalism, and class consciousness, whereas social trust seems to go with religious tolerance, faith in social mobility, and a weaker commitment to drastic political change. The impact of the underlying attitude on ideology is obviously profound.

Regarding the topical issues, distrustful PSU members are mildly in favor of Socialist participation in the *apertura a sinistra*, mildly against the American presence in Vietnam, and mildly sympathetic to the Gaullist stress on national sovereignty. Trusting Socialists, on the other hand, are strongly in favor of the Grand Coalition of Socialists and Christian Democrats and of a European federation and almost evenly split on Vietnam. Read across, the opponents of the *apertura* are far more distrustful than its supporters. And the anti-Vietnam respondents and Gaullists are also noticeably more distrustful than the Socialists on the other side of these issues. Social distrust on most issues is practically synonymous with the radical undercurrent in the PSU, it seems, and very important as a determinant of the party member's stand on the topical issues.

Distrustful DC members heavily tend to be private-oriented, and decidedly democratic and probureaucratic (PDDP). Trusting Christian Democrats, by the same token, are overwhelmingly private-oriented, democratic, and probureaucratic (PTDP). Both the dedicated and the private-oriented, in any case, tend to be socially distrustful. Authoritarians are mostly distrustful, whereas the democrats are evenly split between trust and distrust. Antibureaucrats in the DC tend heavily toward distrust, whereas the friends of civil servants are more often the trusting type. Distrust, antibureaucratism, and authoritarianism appear to supply together a subtle undercurrent in contrast to the more obvious tendencies.

On the ideological parameters, the distrustful DC member strongly believes that there are no class barriers but that the economy requires intervention whenever Christian charity calls for it. He heavily prefers the secular autonomy of the party to the direct influence of the church. Trusting DC members agree on all three issues, each time more heavily than the distrustful. Reading across, we note that respondents who believe social classes to be the natural order of society tend to be distrustful, whereas those who believe that anyone can rise by his work alone are almost evenly split between trust and distrust. On capitalistic development, likewise, the interventionists are about evenly split, whereas the antiinterventionists heavily tend toward social distrust. The proclerical Christian Democrats are more often distrustful than are those who prefer a secular politics. Thus distrust seems to go with clericalism and with social and economic conservatism, although the trend is not very strong.

Regarding the topical issues, finally, distrustful DC members rather favor the *apertura* and even more the American role in Vietnam and a European federation. The trusting agree more strongly on the Grand Coalition and, less strongly, on Vietnam and a United Europe. Horizontally, the DC opponents of the *apertura* are more distrustful than its supporters. The supporters of the American presence in Vietnam are also more often distrustful, whereas its opponents are evenly split between trust and distrust. The good Europeans and the Gaullists, finally, incline toward social distrust in the same ratio.

Comparing the two Italian parties, with a sidewise glance to the Germans, it is astonishing to see how differently the party members from the two countries responded to more or less the same questions, even if we grant a stronger measure of distrust to the Italians. Among themselves, the Italian responses are rather similar. The distrustful, private-oriented party member, the antiauthoritarian bias, the strength of anticapitalistic revolutionary or interventionistic sentiment, and the anticlerical or secular undercurrent are distinctive features of Italian political culture without a German parallel (Table 16–6). But there are other issues that seem to constitute partisan divisions, such as the antibureaucratic bias of distrustful Socialists or, more understandably, the Socialist stress on the class barriers that hold down the underdog. The partisan views on Vietnam and on a United Europe also deviate strongly, especially among the distrustful of both parties. The only issue on which German and Italian views seem comparable is the attitude toward the Grand Coalition. Even the parallels between Socialists or Christian Democrats of both countries seem to account for little apart from the relationship between social distrust and either conservatism or alienation and radicalism. Among the Italian Socialists, as among their German comrades, the distrustful hold more radical, alienated views than the trusting on many issues, such as authoritarianism, antibureaucratism, anticlericalism, or on class barriers and revolutionary change. The Christian Democrats who feel distrust similarly tend to have more extreme conservative views on the same subjects. With these exceptions, it appears, the role of social trust and distrust differs considerably in the two political cultures.

TABLE 16-7. Are Authority, Leadership Needed for Democracy (Authoritarianism)? (Percent)

	SPD	CDU	WEST GERMANY	ITALY	PSU	DC	ALL SOCIALISTS	ALL CHRISTIAN DEMOCRATS
Indeed they are	9	17	13.0	7.9	5.3	10.8	7.0	13.9
They rather are	17	16	16.5	8.4	4.4	12.7	10.3	14.4
In the middle	20	17	18.5	8.8	9.7	7.8	14.6	12.4
You need cooperation more than authority	28	25	26.5	22.8	23.0	22.5	25.4	23.8
Definitely no strong man needed	22	19	20.5	41.4	42.5	40.2	32.9	29.6
Don't know, neither	4	6	5.0	10.7	15.1	5.9	9.9	5.9
Total	100	100	100	100	100	100	100	100
Number	100	100	200	215	113	102	213	202

Authoritarianism and Democracy

The third dichotomy involves authoritarianism versus a faith in democratic cooperation, or at least an absence of fear of the anarchic interplay of grass-roots democracy.[18] At first glance, Table 16–7 appears to reveal only modest differences between Socialists and Christian Democrats. Closer examination, however, shows that the SPD respondents on the authoritarian side (not to mention the CDU) outnumber not only their Italian colleagues but even the Italian Christian Democrats. The edge of the SPD is further enlarged when we consider that the "agrees with both" group in the middle and even the "cooperation-more-than-authority" response still flirts with the idols of authority. Only 20.5% of the German party members (despite the strong-man image in their question) saw their way clear to the definitely nonauthoritarian answer chosen by over 40.0% of both Italian groups. Does this mean that German politicians still deeply believe in authority, whereas their Italian colleagues are a bunch of starry-eyed libertarians? What else?

Our question on authority and democracy was deliberately phrased in such a way as to make the authoritarian answer at least as reasonable as the democratic one. Still, one wonders how it was interpreted by the respondents and how broadly we can generalize from the responses. The Italian data include clarifying comments by both the democrats and the authoritarians (including "agree with both"). Nearly half the democrats of both parties motivated their response with references to the personal freedom of the individual. Other popular responses among them were in praise of opposition to an authoritarian government or stated that it is not possible to "guide" or "guard" another person's freedom without diminishing it. The authoritarians, by way of contrast, liked to refer to the "lack of maturity and self-discipline" and to the egotism and uncooperative attitudes of people which presumably make authority and leadership necessary. Some PSU members in particular felt that one could and should guide the exercise of individual liberty.

What sort of people are the Italian authoritarians and the democrats? Among the Christian Democrats, those from the South and the islands and, secondly, the industrial northwest are more authority-conscious than, for example, central Italy which, on the other hand, happens to be the home of many PSU authoritarians. Perhaps the political traditions of these regions in either party encourage authoritarianism. As to the size of their commune of residence, DC authoritarians predominate in cities over 10,000, whereas smaller communes are more democratic in their response. In the PSU, the authoritarians are concentrated in towns from 10,000–50,000, whereas the democrats are more often found in smaller or larger communities than that. In both parties, the authoritarians tend to be farmers or blue- and white-collar workers, whereas the democrats are more often business and professional people or university students. Among the DC members, moreover, the authoritarians tend to be in dependent positions, whereas the independents tend to be democrats. In the PSU, the opposite is the case. It is not clear whether this amounts to a juxtaposition of "working-class authoritarianism" and middle-class liberalism. The level of education of the DC authoritarians also is distinctly lower (up to junior high school only) than that of the democrats except for the somewhat more authoritarian university-educated respondents. One is reminded of the British working-class Tory. The PSU again has the opposite record, although the relationships are less clear. There is also a noticeable generational difference on this issue in both parties. Respondents under 35 are considerably more democratic than those between 35 and 54, the generation which grew up under Mussolini. Respondents over 55, again, for some reason, came out more democratic in both parties. Perhaps the life cycle brings greater tolerance and adaptability at this age.

How do the German authoritarians compare with the Italians? The authoritarians of SPD and CDU both seem to come more from Lower Saxony and North Rhine Westphalia, whereas Hesse has more democrats. As for the size of the commune, both parties seem to have more democrats in communities of less than 2,000 and more authoritarians in towns from 2,000–10,000. SPD members in towns from 10,000–100,000 also tend to be authoritarian. CDU respondents, on the other hand, are more often democratic in cities over 10,000 including metropolitan areas, in which the SPD respondents also tend more toward democracy. In notable contrast to Italy, however, the business and professional respondents and white collar (the only category similar to the Italian responses) tend to be authoritarian, and so are pensionists, presumably because of their age, which reaches back into earlier German eras. Civil servants are more democratic and so are workingmen, at least in the DC. In the PSU the workers are slightly more likely to be authoritarian. The German authoritarians also tend to be dissatisfied with their income and the nature of their job (not true in Italy).

The level of education has a strong bearing on authoritarianism, especially in the SPD which (like the DC) has the authoritarians concentrated at the lower level (elementary education and apprenticeship), whereas the upper levels are more democratic. In the CDU, on the other hand, the lowest and the highest levels (Abitur or better) are democratic, whereas the middle school or vocational level is the most authoritarian. Is authoritarianism, then, as in Italy a matter of social class? In the SPD, working-class respondents are clearly more authoritarian than middle-class respondents. One cannot help thinking of Robert Michel's thesis. In the CDU, however, which spans more strata, it is the middle- and upper-class respondent who tends to be authoritarian, whereas the upper-middle and working-class respondent is more likely to be democratic. However, we also have to consider the political overtones of authoritarianism. No one but a democrat would join the SPD from among the middle classes. And for middle-class authoritarians, of course, the CDU is a logical choice.

It is also worth noting that Protestants tend to be more authoritarian than Catholics and churchgoers more than those who never go to church. The factor of age, finally, is just as important as with the Italian parties. CDU respondents over 50, the generation that grew up 1915–1940, are notably more authoritarian than those below that age. In the SPD, the authoritarian age already begins with 35, but the older cohorts get more democratic again, as in the Italian sample.

Table 16–8 shows how the authoritarians and democrats of all four parties reacted to the other issues. The SPD authoritarians tend to be private-oriented, trusting, and heavily sympathetic to the bureaucrats. The democrats agree, except that they are even more heavily trusting and probureaucratic. Read across, the dedicated Socialists tend to be more democratic than the private-oriented ones. The distrustful tend toward authority, while the trusting are more often democratic. The antibureaucratic are mostly authoritarians and the friends of the civil service democratic, and so forth. The role of distrust and of the phobia about bureaucracy in SPD authoritarianism deserves special emphasis. We shall come back to these clusters when we discuss the ideological issues.

The Italian parties are also strongly influenced by this dichotomy. Authoritarian PSU members, for example, tend heavily toward private orientation, social distrust, and hatred for the bureaucracy. Democratic PSU members agree on the first two issues but tend to be sympathetic to civil servants. Horizontally, they all tend toward the democratic side although not to the same degree. The PDDA syndrome here appears to be split into democrats (PDDA) and authoritarians (PDAA).

The authoritarian DC members heavily favor private orientation, are more distrustful, and are sympathetic to the bureaucrats. The democrats in the *Domoorazia Cristiana* are even more inclined to be private-oriented and to favor the bureaucrats, but they are evenly split between trust and distrust. Dedicated Christian Democrats tend to be authoritarian, whereas the private-oriented are more often democrats. The trusting are more democratic than the distrustful, and so are the probureaucratic as compared to the bureaucrat haters. The PDDP syndrome we noted earlier still applies.

Hatred toward Bureaucracy

The next underlying dichotomy is the attitude toward bureaucracy. Rarely spelled out in programs or ideological statements, this attitude appears to be the Achilles heel of many a modern school of social reform. Especially to the Socialists, the bureaucrats have been simultaneously the indispensable and yet frustratingly imperfect tool of any state intervention or regulation, and also the authoritarian antidote to all libertarian or anarchistic undercurrents of socialism. In the form of a disdain for all experts and technocrats, antibureaucratic feeling has also played an important role among Italian Communists.[19]

TABLE 16–8. Various Ideological Parameters and Authoritarianism (in Absolute Numbers)

	SPD		CDU		PSU		DC	
	Authoritarian	Democratic	Authoritarian	Democratic	Authoritarian	Democratic	Authoritarian	Democratic
Dedication to party	$Q = .159$		$Q = .181$		$Q = -.354$		$Q = .655$**	
Dedicated	12	18	18	13	1	6	4	2
Private oriented	23	25	24	25	21	60	25	60
							$X^2 = 2.209$	
Social distrust	$Q = .571$**		$Q = .450$*		$Q = .584$**		$Q = .400$	
Distrust	16	9	14	7	16	42	14	28
Trust	17	35	22	29	2	20	6	28
	$X^2 = 6.793$***		$X^2 = 3.292$*		$X^2 = 3.494$*		$X^2 = 2.308$	
Hatred of bureaucracy	$Q = .800$**		$Q = -.173$		$Q = .385$		$Q = .595$**	
Antibureaucratic	9	1	4	5	11	26	9	7
Probureaucratic	29	46	42	37	6	32	15	46
	$X^2 = 9.500$***						$X^2 = 5.876$**	
Class barriers	$Q = .121$		$Q = -.341$		$Q = -.179$		$Q = .295$	
Classes present (or desirable)	8	7	6	11	7	26	8	11
No barriers	34	38	30	27	12	31	17	43

430

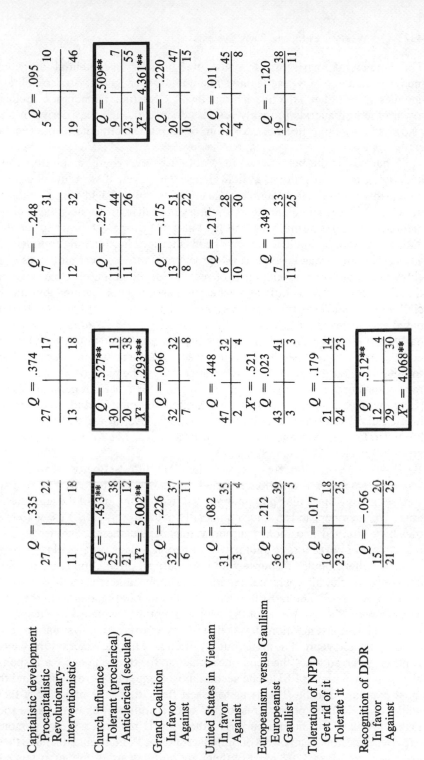

Capitalistic development
Procapitalistic / Revolutionary-interventionistic

- $Q = .335$: 27 | 22 ; 11 | 18
- $Q = .374$: 27 | 17 ; 13 | 18
- $Q = -.248$: 7 | 31 ; 12 | 32
- $Q = .095$: 5 | 10 ; 19 | 46

Church influence
Tolerant (proclerical) / Anticlerical (secular)

- $Q = -.453**$: 25 | 38 ; 21 | 12 ; $X^2 = 5.002**$
- $Q = .527**$: 30 | 13 ; 20 | 38 ; $X^2 = 7.293***$
- $Q = -.257$: 11 | 44 ; 11 | 26
- $Q = .509**$: 9 | 7 ; 23 | 55 ; $X^2 = 4.361**$

Grand Coalition
In favor / Against

- $Q = .226$: 32 | 37 ; 6 | 11
- $Q = .066$: 32 | 32 ; 7 | 8
- $Q = -.175$: 13 | 51 ; 8 | 22
- $Q = -.220$: 20 | 47 ; 10 | 15

United States in Vietnam
In favor / Against

- $Q = .082$: 31 | 35 ; 3 | 4
- $Q = .448$: 47 | 32 ; 2 | 4 ; $X^2 = .521$
- $Q = .217$: 6 | 28 ; 10 | 30
- $Q = .011$: 22 | 45 ; 4 | 8

Europeanism versus Gaullism
Europeanist / Gaullist

- $Q = .212$: 36 | 39 ; 3 | 5
- $Q = .023$: 43 | 41 ; 3 | 3
- $Q = .349$: 7 | 33 ; 11 | 25
- $Q = -.120$: 19 | 38 ; 7 | 11

Toleration of NPD
Get rid of it / Tolerate it

- $Q = .017$: 16 | 18 ; 23 | 25
- $Q = .179$: 21 | 14 ; 24 | 23

Recognition of DDR
In favor / Against

- $Q = -.056$: 15 | 20 ; 21 | 25
- $Q = .512**$: 12 | 4 ; 29 | 30 ; $X^2 = 4.068**$

The bureaucrats have further constituted masses of potential or actual members and voters whose feelings one could never ignore, or also political enemies at a rather effective irritant level. Christian Democratic feelings toward the bureaucrats probably run less deep, although they derive in part also from economic liberalism or from religious resentments of the secular state.

A hatred for the bureaucrats may not strike everybody as an important underlying political attitude at first glance. However, if we remember how crucial this phobia is, for example, to an understanding of right-wing thinking in the United States and in nineteenth century liberalism or to the antiestablishmentarian feelings of the New Left here and in Europe, we begin to see that antibureaucratism should never have been ignored. The clinching argument, in any case, is the antagonistic role of bureaucrats and political parties as rival elites in the political development of recent European nation-states such as Germany and Italy. As little as a generation ago, typical German and Italian civil servants and even many professors of constitutional or administrative law hated and despised parties as illegitimate interlopers in government, whereas party men could hardly help reciprocating these bitter feelings. In Italy, the conflict may have been less pronounced, but there as in Germany the totalitarian interlude signifies, among other things, the more or less successful rape of the bureaucracy by the totalitarian party. Because our populations are party members, then, measuring their antibureaucratic attitudes is to probe historically rooted residues of earlier conflicts, overgrown with changes in bureaucratic function and attitudes on both sides, not to mention the new attitudes of New Left and New Right.

How did the respondents interpret the dichotomy set before them?[20] The frank statement of the antibureaucratic prejudice elicited some strong responses among the Italian party members. Nearly one-third of the antibureaucratic DC members and an equal number of Socialists replied, "Yes, as soon as they have attained a position of authority, they neglect their assignments." The resentment of bureaucratic authority over people's lives is particularly salient here. Another popular response with both parties, often coming from public employees or claiming personal experience, simply called the public service "a bunch of loafers." The most frequent antibureaucratic response on the PSU side blamed "the system," not the people. Another frequent PSU response, next to the two just mentioned, was that it was an irremediable situation going on for years and years. The numerous DC friends of the bureaucracy, by way of contrast, averred that "the good ones make up for the bad ones," a response also popular with the PSU. The second most frequent DC response, and the most popular with the PSU, was to assert flatly that "the majority of them works hard." Other popular responses among both parties were "sure they make mistakes, but not on purpose—their job is not so easy," or personal experiences, frank disavowals of prejudice such as "one should not have these preconceived ideas," or "most of them are quite aware of the importance of doing their jobs." The interpretive responses, both pro and con, vary little in their distribution between the two parties, although antibureaucratism is far stronger in the PSU.

Table 16–9 should surprise some readers with the strong prejudice shown by the German party members in favor of civil servants (many of whom belong to the SPD and CDU). The German faith in authority evidently includes bureaucrats, and among the Christian Democrats even more than in the SPD. On the Italian side, by contrast, the PSU is split rather evenly by the issue, whereas the DC is decidedly probureaucratic. It is worth noting that among the Italians in both parties, blue- and white-collar employees and state employees are the most antibureaucratic, whereas business, the professions, and students tend to take a kinder view. Among the German CDU respondents, it is the civil servants who are most likely to defend the bureaucrats, and in the SPD it is blue collar. The most critical group in both countries is of white-collar occupations. Occupation, it appears, is highly related to attitudes toward bureaucracy.

A second question was designed to focus more squarely on the rivalry between bureaucrats and party politicians: "Who do you think is more honest and competent, the politicians or the civil servants?" The results among the Italian DC respondents were rather inconclusive and had more responses of "both," "neither," or other replies than actual choices made between the two. Of the small number (18%) who did make a choice, moreover, the antibureaucrats gave the edge to "civil servants," whereas the probureaucratic respondents opted for the politicians. The PSU respondents gave a higher pro or con response (26%), but likewise in the direction opposite to our hypothesis. A possible explanation for this result might be that the respondents draw a distinction between the "petty bureaucrats" whom they despise and the high-level administrators in whom they have more confidence. It is worth noting also that in both parties, especially in the DC, many of the probureaucratic respondents (29.2% in the DC, 21.4% in the PSU) replied that "both were equally honest and competent," just as if they were hastening to ward off the nasty prejudices that our questionnaire attempted to put in their mouths. There is no way of telling from our data whether such a response would indicate the absence or presence of antibureaucratic prejudice. A cautious attitude toward these data would seem to be in order.

The German respondents also gave an inconclusive answer to this question[21] as four out of five probureaucratic respondents preferred to answer "both" instead of taking sides. Of the few that did take sides, the CDU members tended to choose the civil servants, whereas the SPD members preferred their politicians regardless of pro or antibureaucratic sentiments.

Are there other differences in the backgrounds of anti- or probureaucratic respondents? Regarding regional differences, antibureaucratic CDU and SPD members are more often from Hesse, whereas the friends of the civil service in the CDU are more likely from North Rhine Westphalia and in the SPD from Lower Saxony. In the CDU, moreover, antibureaucratism grows in proportion

TABLE 16–9. Bureaucrats Are Petty, Lazy (Percent)

	SPD	CDU	WEST GERMANY	ITALY	PSU	DC	ALL SOCIALISTS	ALL CHRISTIAN DEMOCRATS
They sure are	4	4	4.0	15.0	20.8	8.8	12.8	6.4
They rather are	6	5	5.5	13.6	19.8	6.9	13.3	5.9
In the middle	10	3	6.5	15.5	15.3	15.7	12.8	9.4
They are really not	23	24	23.5	19.3	14.4	24.5	18.5	24.3
Definitely not	53	60	56.5	31.0	23.4	39.2	37.4	49.5
Don't know, neither	4	4	4.0	5.6	6.3	4.0	5.2	4.5
Total	100	100	100	100	100	100	100	100
Number	100	100	200	213	111	102	211	202

with the size of the commune of residence, whereas in the SPD it declines with growing community size. It is not clear why this should be so, although we can surmise that the German rural or small-town Christian Democrats are probably more often farmers, artisans, or businessmen which may account for their kinder attitude toward civil servants, whereas Socialists in this setting are more likely to be workers or teachers or in other service occupations which may explain their resentful attitudes. The antibureaucratic Socialist tends to be white or blue collar, the antibureaucratic CDU member also white collar. In the CDU, probureaucratic sentiment is concentrated among business and professional people and, of course, civil servants. In the SPD, the same groups and a fair number of workers are sympathetic to the civil service. White-collar resentment of civil servants is probably a matter of personal envy, especially among the public employees below civil service rank. It is worth noting also that antibureaucratic Socialists tend to work in smaller enterprises and antibureaucratic CDU members in the larger ones.

In Italy, antibureaucratic attitudes are generally higher in the South and the islands as compared with those in the Northwest which is the kindest to civil servants. This differential may well mirror the lag in development of the South. Within the parties, however, the distributions are more complex. In the PSU, for example, antibureaucratism is more pronounced in the Northeast and the South, whereas the Northwest and the "red belt" tend to be probureaucratic. This is almost like saying, "We only like the officialdom in the areas where the left wing is dominant," except that the DC is also more antibureaucratic in the South and probureaucratic in the Northwest. In both parties, antibureaucratic sentiment grows with the size of the community. In both parties also, the antibureaucrats tend to be white and blue collar, teachers, and farmers. The more sympathetic are business and professional people, students and the civil servants themselves. With the size of the economic unit, Italians are the opposite of the Germans. Antibureaucratic Socialists tend to work in larger enterprises, whereas antibureaucratic Christian Democrats are more often found in enterprises of less than ten employees. Table 16–10 shows how antibureaucratism and sympathy for the civil service relate to all the other pairs of issues.

Class Barriers

We are entering now the realm of the ideological issues properly so-called, philosophical issues which tie together the social predicament in which individuals find themselves with programmatic attempts to overcome the problems posed. The first of these issues concerns the survival of class barriers which keep down the underdogs of society. It is of course a highly subjective question in any society whether a person of humble origin could make his way

TABLE 16-10. Various Ideological Parameters and Hatred of Bureaucracy (in absolute numbers)

	SPD		CDU		PSU		DC	
	Anti-bureaucratic	Pro-bureaucratic	Anti-bureaucratic	Pro-bureaucratic	Anti-bureaucratic	Pro-bureaucratic	Anti-bureaucratic	Pro-bureaucratic
Dedication to party	$Q = .333$		$Q = .420$		$Q = -.380$		$Q = .388$	
Dedicated	4	26	4	25	3	6	2	4
Private oriented	3	39	3	46	39	35	13	59
Social distrust	$Q = .805^{**}$		$Q = .729^{**}$		$Q = .737^{**}$		$Q = .698^{**}$	
Distrust	7	17	4	15	37	21	10	24
Trust	2	45	2	48	4	15	2	27
	$X^2 = 9.525^{***}$		$X^2 = 3.078^{*}$		$X^2 = 10.861^{***}$		$X^2 = 5.486^{**}$	
Authoritarianism	$Q = .800^{**}$		$Q = -.173$		$Q = .385$		$Q = .595^{**}$	
Authoritarian	9	29	4	42	11	6	9	15
Democratic	1	46	5	37	26	32	7	46
	$X^2 = 9.500^{***}$						$X^2 = 5.876^{**}$	
Class barriers	$Q = .927^{**}$		$Q = .836^{**}$		$Q = .672^{**}$		$Q = .542^{**}$	
Classes present (or desirable)	7	8	5	12	20	7	6	10
No barriers	2	61	2	54	14	25	8	45
	$X^2 = 23.295^{***}$		$X^2 = 7.791^{***}$		$X^2 = 9.335^{***}$		$X^2 = 3.972^{**}$	
Capitalistic development	$Q = .070$		$Q = .344$		$Q = -.660^{**}$		$Q = -.058$	
Procapitalistic	6	38	6	39	9	22	2	11
Revolutionary-interventionistic	4	22	2	26	32	16	9	44
					$X^2 = 10.720^{***}$			

Church influence				
Tolerant (proclerical) / Anticlerical (secular)	$Q = -.718**$ 3 | 55 7 | 21 $X^2 = 7.496***$	$Q = .552**$ 6 | 38 2 | 44 $X^2 = 2.968*$	$Q = .774**$ 18 | 34 25 | 6 $X^2 = 16.334***$	$Q = .428$ 4 | 8 11 | 55
Grand Coalition				
In favor / Against	$Q = -.255$ 5 | 59 2 | 14	$Q = -.846**$ 3 | 60 6 | 10 $X^2 = 14.259***$	$Q = -.223$ 27 | 30 17 | 12	$Q = .311$ 12 | 42 3 | 20
United States in Vietnam				
In favor / Against	$Q = -.500**$ 3 | 54 1 | 6	$Q = .387$ 6 | 68 1 | 5	$Q = .021$ 14 | 15 17 | 19	$Q = .555**$ 14 | 44 — | 11 $X^2 = 3.377*$
Europeanism versus Gaullism				
Europeanist / Gaullist	$Q = -.034$ 8 | 60 — | 7	$Q = -.237$ 9 | 73 — | 5	$Q = -.190$ 16 | 20 20 | 17	$Q = .380$ 12 | 35 2 | 13
Toleration of NPD				
Get rid of it / Tolerate it	$Q = .169$ 4 | 27 4 | 38	$Q = -.222$ 4 | 28 4 | 44		
Recognition of DDR				
In favor / Against	$Q = -.038$ 3 | 30 4 | 37	$Q = .666**$ 4 | 11 4 | 55 $X^2 = 3.358*$		

by talent and hard work alone. Given many cases of failure and very few of success under these circumstances, it is largely up to the observer to decide whether to blame the person or such circumstances as "the class system." For the Christian Democrats, it is no less subjective to insist that "classes are the natural order of society" or to conclude that there are no class barriers to social mobility. Socialists who insist that class barriers exist and Christian Democrats who find class barriers a part of the natural order agree, of course, on their presence, although the former are more radical and the latter more conservative than respondents of either party who do not believe in the presence of class barriers. Hence, the Socialists had a choice between complaining about the class barriers and denying their existence altogether. The Christian Democrats chose between calling class barriers part of a well-ordered society and likewise denying their existence. As concerns Table 16–11, this means that the Socialist scales from top to bottom run the gamut from radical to liberal, while the Christian Democrats begin with conservatism at the top and go down to a liberal position. Comparing the two Socialist parties, in any case, we note that the Italians are almost evenly balanced between the radical and liberal positions, whereas the German Social Democrats rather incline toward liberalism, in this sense. It is worth noting that the Italian Socialists who deny the existence of class barriers tend to have been Social Democrats (PSDI) before they found themselves in the PSU, the union of PSDI and Nenni-Socialists. As for the two Christian Democratic parties, they split in similar ways between a small minority of conservatives and a majority of liberals. As the table shows, the Italians are more class-conscious than the Germans and the Socialists more so than the Christian Democrats.

Let us take a look at how the class-conscious of both parties differ from those of a more optimistic view. First, how were the alternatives interpreted by the various Italian groups?[22] DC members who believed in the "natural order of classes" nearly all replied that this was a dog-eat-dog world or that social equality simply won't work. Nearly one-third of the PSU members who felt that underdogs don't have a chance blamed the injustice of the government, whereas another one-fifth to one-fourth each either attacked the solid rock of social inequality or the egotism of the rich. The rest philosophized about the difficulties of improving oneself or about the causes of poverty. The more sanguine response that those who work hard can succeed was motivated with references to will power, ability, and faith in the quality of one's work by a good third of the respondents of both parties. Nearly as many DC members and quite a few Socialists pointed out that Italian society did allow some social mobility. About a sixth of the more sanguine DC members also spoke out against preconceived notions of social equality. The PSU members more often related the problem to the evolution of state and society or to a sense of courage and initiative, responses which also appealed to some DC members.

Do respondents of different social class backgrounds respond differently to the alternatives posed? In the German CDU, middle- and upper-middle-class

TABLE 16–11. Our Society Still Has Class Barriers (Percent)

	SPD	CDU	WEST GERMANY	ITALY	PSU	DC	ALL SOCIALISTS	ALL CHRISTIAN DEMOCRATS
It sure does (should)	7	9	8.0	15.8	20.4	10.8	14.1	9.9
It rather does	11	9	10.0	11.2	14.2	7.8	12.7	8.4
In the middle	10	18	14.0	15.8	16.8	14.7	13.6	16.3
It hardly does	27	19	23.0	19.1	15.0	23.5	20.7	21.3
Definitely not	45	41	43.0	32.1	25.7	39.2	34.7	40.1
Don't know, neither	—	4	2.0	6.0	8.0	4.0	4.2	4.0
Total	100	100	100	100	100	100	100	100
Number	100	100	200	215	113	102	213	202

respondents were considerably more sanguine about social mobility in Germany than were the few CDU working-class respondents of the sample. In the SPD, however, it is the other way around. Working-class respondents were more optimistic than were the middle-class respondents. It is not clear whether the latter were excessively concerned about the fate of the former or whether they were dubious of their own chances of rising beyond their present station. If we compare family income per month, Socialists earning below 1,000 marks were also more sanguine than those above that level. Among the CDU members, who generally make more money, the same would be true below and above the 1,000-mark level. As soon as we raise the level to 1,400 marks, however, Christian Democrats below that tend to consider the class order "natural," whereas those above it more often believe in upward mobility, especially their own. Their faith was shared by the dozen well-to-do SPD members.

In the DC and the PSU, the material circumstances of both sides to the class barrier show only minor variations. Class-conscious Christian Democrats were slightly less affluent and class-conscious Socialists slightly more so than the rest of the Italian sample. More revealing seems to be a breakdown by age. In both parties, and especially in the DC, the age cohorts under 45 tended to reject the notion of class barriers to social mobility, whereas those 45 or older either railed at them or pronounced them "natural." There are also other noteworthy differences. In both parties, respondents from the industrial Northwest and from Central Italy were more sanguine about social mobility than the respondents from the South, the islands, or from the agrarian Northeast, a differential which may well reflect real differences in opportunity. However, DC respondents from communes under 10,000 and PSU members from communes under 50,000 also tended to reject the notion of class barriers. We get the most persistent class consciousness from the most urban areas and from respondents living somewhere other than where they were born rather than from isolated villages and their native inhabitants.

By occupation, furthermore, Italian blue- and white-collar workers as well as the farmers in both parties tended to be optimistic about social mobility in contrast to teachers and other persons in the public employ. Business and professional people, on the other hand, decried the class barriers if they were Socialists and regarded them as "natural" if they were in the DC. By the same token, respondents in dependent positions in both parties tended to be more class-conscious than the independents and their family help. Finally, and not unexpectedly, respondents satisfied with their income and the nature of their work in both parties tended to think that a man can rise by work and talent. The PSU members who were dissatisfied with their jobs tended to blame the class barriers.

How do the German parties compare with these profiles? Regarding age, both the CDU and the SPD tended to be more class conscious among the younger age cohorts under 35 (CDU) or under 50 (SPD). We can explain this paradox only by contrasting the socially restorative postwar era with the turmoil of the war and the Nazi periods. There is little regional variation. Respondents from communities below 10,000 were more optimistic about social mobility if they were in the CDU and more pessimistic if they were in the SPD. Professional and business people in both parties were more sanguine about social mobility, and white collar and labor more class-conscious. Civil servants, however, were pessimistic in the CDU and optimistic in the SPD. Exactly like the Italians, furthermore, both parties tended to be dissatisfied with their income if they stressed class barriers and satisfied if they did not.

How do the class feelings of the respondents relate to their responses to the other issues? Let us take each party through the two-by-two tables on Table 16–12. SPD members who resent class barriers tended to be dedicated, as often distrustful as trusting, authoritarian, and less sympathetic to the bureaucracy (DDAP). Those who think there are no barriers to social mobility were heavily private-oriented, trusting, probureaucratic, and just barely on the democatic side (PTDP). Read horizontally, all but the antibureaucratic tended to see no class barriers in the way, but the private-oriented were less class-conscious than the dedicated, the distrustful less than the trusting, and the democrats less than the authoritarians. The antibureaucrats were very class-conscious, whereas the sympathizers with the civil service even more heavily trusted in untrammeled mobility.

On the other ideological issues, class-conscious Social Democrats just barely inclined toward satisfaction with capitalistic development and were as often anticlerical as tolerant, whereas the believers in upward mobility heavily favored capitalism and religious toleration. Read across, all groups tended to reject the idea of social barriers, but the procapitalists and the tolerant did so more heavily than their opposite numbers. So far it is rather obvious that preoccupation with class barriers made the SPD respondents tend toward dedication, distrust (authoritarianism), antibureaucratism (radical political change), and anticlericalism (see Table 16–13). How then did it affect their attitude on the topical issues? It evidently predisposed them to be more against the Grand Coalition and Vietnam, but for a United Europe, although the numbers in some of the last tables are too small to be significant. More surprisingly, it also seemed to incline them toward tolerating the NPD and rejecting the recognition of the DDR. Read across, the supporters of the Grand Coalition and of the American presence in Vietnam more heavily tended to deny the existence of class barriers. So did the Gaullists, the sworn enemies of the NPD, and the advocates of recognition, as compared with their opposite numbers.

How does the belief in a "natural class order" affect the responses of the CDU? It seemed to make them more private-oriented, but also relatively more distrustful and antibureaucratic (as compared with the less class-conscious) and more democratic. Perhaps we should rather focus on those who believe in rising by ability and hard work. They tended, in both parties, to be private-

TABLE 16-12. Various Ideological Parameters and Class Barriers (in absolute numbers)

	SPD		CDU		PSU		DC	
	Classes	No Barriers	Classes	No Barriers	Classes	No Barriers	Classes	No Barriers
Dedication to party	$Q = .504**$		$Q = -.245$		$Q = .291$		$Q = -.127$	
Dedicated	8	18	4	22	4	3	1	5
Private oriented	6	41	9	30	30	41	15	58
	$X^2 = 3.464*$							
Social distrust	$Q = .464*$		$Q = .236$		$Q = .624**$		$Q = .451*$	
Distrust	8	15	5	12	27	25	11	26
Trust	8	41	9	35	4	16	4	25
	$X^2 = 3.109*$		$X^2 =$		$X^2 = 6.468**$		$X^2 = 3.009*$	
Authoritarianism	$Q = .121$		$Q = -.341$		$Q = -.179$		$Q = .295$	
Authoritarian	8	34	6	30	7	12	8	17
Democratic	7	38	11	27	26	31	11	43
Hatred of bureaucracy	$Q = .927**$		$Q = .836**$		$Q = .672**$		$Q = .542**$	
Antibureaucratic	7	2	5	2	20	14	6	8
Probureaucratic	8	61	12	54	7	25	10	45
	$X^2 = 23.295***$		$X^2 = 7.791***$		$X^2 = 9.335***$		$X^2 = 3.972**$	
Capitalistic development	$Q = -.291$		$Q = .212$		$Q = -.759**$		$Q = .280$	
Procapitalistic	9	39	12	26	6	27	3	9
Revolutionary-Interventionistic	8	19	6	20	26	16	9	48
					$X^2 = 14.511***$			

The table below presents association coefficients (Q), fourfold contingency tables, and chi-square values (X²) for several political/attitudinal items. Each data cell shows the Q coefficient, a 2 × 2 contingency table, and (where given) the X² statistic. Boxed cells are indicated with [boxed].

	Column 1	Column 2	Column 3	Column 4
Church influence — Tolerant (proclerical) / Anticlerical (secular)	Q = −.416 9 | 51 9 | 21 X² = 2.812*	Q = .060 8 | 26 9 | 33	[boxed] Q = −.692** 14 | 35 22 | 10 X² = 12.727***	[boxed] Q = .787** 9 | 6 10 | 56 X² = 13.822***
Grand Coalition — In favor / Against	[boxed] Q = .718** 7 | 55 7 | 9 X² = 8.923***	Q = .043 13 | 39 4 | 11	[boxed] Q = −.590** 17 | 33 22 | 11 X² = 8.530***	Q = .030 13 | 44 5 | 18
United States in Vietnam — In favor / Against	Q = −.636** 6 | 54 2 | 4	Q = .176 14 | 49 1 | 5	Q = −.338 11 | 18 21 | 17	Q = .302 14 | 45 1 | 6
Europeanism versus Gaullism — Europeanist / Gaullist	Q = .238 13 | 56 1 | 7	Q = .181 15 | 52 1 | 5	Q = .151 14 | 19 15 | 16	Q = .685** 14 | 34 1 | 13 X² = 3.258*
Toleration of NPD — Get rid of it / Tolerate it	Q = −.103 5 | 26 9 | 38	Q = −.024 6 | 21 9 | 30		
Recognition of DDR — In favor / Against	Q = −.242 4 | 27 9 | 37	Q = .418 4 | 8 8 | 39		

TABLE 16–13.   Attitude Clusters of German Party Members Relating to Class Barriers

	SPD I	
Dedication	*Class Barriers*	Against Grand Coalition
Distrust	Radical Change	Less Pro-Vietnam policy
(Authoritarian)	Anticlerical	More tolerance for NPD
Antibureaucratic		More against DDR recognition
	SPD II	
Private-oriented	*Mobility-Minded*	Pro-Grand Coalition
Trusting	Procapitalistic	Pro-Vietnam policy
(Democratic)	Religious toleration	Less tolerance for NPD
Probureaucratic		Less against DDR recognition
	CDU I	
Private-oriented	*Classes Natural*	Pro-Grand Coalition
Trusting	Procapitalistic	Pro-Vietnam policy
Democratic	Less secular	Pro-European unification
Antibureaucratic		Pro-NPD toleration
		Less against DDR recognition
	CDU II	
Dedication	*Mobility Possible*	Less Pro-Grand Coalition
Distrust	Interventionism	Less Pro-Vietnam policy
Authoritarian	Secular-minded	Less Pro-European
Probureaucratic		Slightly Less for NPD toleration
		Heavily against DDR recognition

oriented, trusting, and probureaucratic. Only on authoritarianism, the CDU respondents tended to be authoritarian, whereas the SPD members were democrats. The mental image of the upward-mobility-oriented Christian Democrat is that of the nice guy who is deferential to authority but minds his own business. Nevertheless, read horizontally, dedicated CDU members tend more heavily to be sanguine about social mobility than the private-oriented.

On the other ideological issues, the belief in "natural classes" seems to make CDU members more inclined toward *laissez-faire* and slightly less intent on secularism than the other side. Those who believe that people can rise by ability and hard work alone are relatively less for *laissez-faire* and more for the secular autonomy of the party. Read across, the economic interventionists are more mobility-minded than the advocates of *laissez-faire*, and the secular minded more than the proclerical. So far, class consciousness in the CDU shows some relation to economic liberalism, but the trend is not very strong.

The Attitude Clusters

By now, the clusters of attitudes are clearly emerging. We have mapped two patterns each for the two German parties, SPD I and II, and CDU I and II. They cluster dichotomously around the perception of class barriers by the members of either party and relate these in particular to dedication and social distrust among the underlying attitudes and the Grand Coalition among the issues of day-to-day policy (Table 16–13).

How do the two German parties compare in their responses related to class views? There are a good many similarities in their patterns, as for example on antibureaucratism, capitalistic development, and most of the topical issues. There are also a few differences. Class-conscious Socialists tend to be dedicated to their party, whereas class-conscious CDU members tend to be of private orientation. On the issue of authoritarianism, there is a mirror image with the class-conscious as well as the sanguine of both parties tending in opposite directions. That class-conscious Socialists would be more authoritarian and the "natural class order" Christian Democrats more democratic is a paradox which may hide a generational difference in the SPD and a rural/urban one in the CDU. That those who believe that hard work and ability succeed tend to be more democratic in the SPD and more authoritarian in the CDU seems less puzzling in that it probably contrasts the collective (or trade union) way toward social advancement with the rugged individualism of the business and professional people in the CDU. On another issue—church influence—SPD members who are sanguine about social mobility tend to be religiously tolerant, whereas the CDU members of this description tend to be secular-minded, a difference which on a different dimension would have been nonexistent anyway. Finally, there are no less than three issues—social distrust, church influence, and the Grand Coalition—on which the class-conscious Socialists were evenly split between pro and con.

In the Italian PSU, the issue of class barriers produced lively reactions. Socialists who agreed that the underdog had no chance heavily tended to be distrustful, democratic, antibureaucratic, and private-oriented (PDDA). Those who saw no class barriers agree on all of these, though with lesser majorities except for the even heavier inclination to be private-oriented. Read horizontally, the dedicated tended to be class-conscious, whereas the private-oriented were mobility minded, and the same difference occurred with the distrustful and the antibureaucratic. The authoritarians tended more toward a belief in untrammeled social mobility than the democrats.

On the other ideological parameters, class-conscious Socialists heavily tended toward belief in radical political change, whereas their opposite numbers inclined toward accepting the blessings of capitalistic development. They also tended to be anticlerical, whereas the mobility minded took a tolerant view of church influence. Thus distrust, antibureaucratism, radical change, and anticlericalism together with democratic and private orientations, appear to constitute the cluster of attitudes relating to a preoccupation with class barriers (Table 16–14). On the topical issues, class consciousness seemed to make Socialists more opposed to the *apertura*, to Vietnam, and even to a European federation, whereas mobility mindedness seemed to push them strongly into the opposite direction. Read across, supporters of the Grand Coalition tended to see no barriers, whereas its opponents heavily did. The supporters of America in Vietnam also saw no barriers, whereas the dissenters did. And on a European federation, again the supporters tended to ignore class barriers, whereas the Gaullists were evenly split.

The "natural class order" responses in the DC also tended heavily toward private orientation and distrust and were more often democratic and pro-bureaucratic than the opposite. DC members who thought a person could rise by ability and hard work alone agreed on all these issues, but with smaller margins except for their even heavier support for the bureaucracy. Read horizontally, the dedicated Christian Democrats were more heavily for the sanguine view of social mobility in Italy, and so were the trusting, the democratic, and the probureaucratic, as compared with their opposites. On the other ideological issues, class-conscious DC members just barely endorsed economic intervention and secularism. Consequently, the economic interventionists tended more heavily toward the belief in unfettered opportunities, and so did the secular-minded DC members in comparison to their opposite numbers.

How did the impact of class consciousness, which seems to relate so highly to distrust, private orientation, authoritarianism, phobia of bureaucrats, and proclerical attitudes affect the DC responses to the topical issues? It increased the support for the Grand Coalition, the Vietnam action, and a United Europe, as compared with the more modest ratios of approval among the believers in rising by ability and hard work. Read across, however, the opponents of the Grand Coalition, the American presence in Vietnam, and a European federation tend more heavily not to perceive any class barriers than do their opposites.

The clusters of attitudes in the DC thus bring out a pattern of clerical conservatism on the one hand (DC I) and the modern, secular DC (DC II), complete with its public enterprises and its ambiguities on the topical issues. The attitude toward the class issue evidently separated the two into an "old" and a "new" DC, just as it had separated the orthodox PSU I from the accommodationist new PSU II (Table 16–14).

Capitalistic Development

The issue of capitalistic development, like that of class barriers, touches on the bedrock of the ideological faith of the two parties, at least in their historical

TABLE 16–14.   Attitude Clusters among Italian Party Members Regarding Class Barriers

PSU I

Less private	*Class Barriers*	Anti-center-left coalition
Distrustful	Revolutionary change	Anti-Vietnam policy
Democratic	Anticlerical	Anti-European
Antibureaucratic		unification

PSU II

Private	*Mobility-Minded*	Pro-center-left coalition
Less distrustful	Procapitalistic	Pro-Vietnam policy
Less democratic	Religiously tolerant	Pro-European
Probureaucratic		

DC I

Private	*Natural Class Order*	Procoalition
Distrustful	Less interventionist	Pro-Vietnam policy
Less democratic	Proclerical	Pro-European
Less probureaucratic		

DC II

Less private	*Mobility Possible*	Less procoalition
More trusting	Interventionistic	Less Pro-Vietnam
Democratic	Secular	Less Pro-European
Probureaucratic		

development. A generation or two ago there would have been no doubt about the Socialist answer to the choice between capitalistic development and radical political changes. Economic development was viewed not as a source of spreading prosperity for the masses, but as compounding the problems of capitalism and, hence, a signal for revolutionary change. Today, after decades of intermittent economic booms, many of the PSU and SPD respndents are quite willing to rely on the blessings of capitalism. The Christian Democrats, on the other hand, are at least as deeply split between *laissez-faire* and the strong social concerns of the Christian Democratic left. Table 16–15 shows the extent to which especially the Socialists have persuaded themselves that rising prosperity will set the underdog free. It is worth noting that the PSU respondents who think so tend to come from the PSDI, whereas the other PSU respondents tend to be from Nenni's PSI. The percentages of Socialists who believe only in basic political changes are worth comparing between Germany and Italy. Among the Christian Democrats, by comparison, the Italians appear far more progressive than the German CDU, where those who are still beating the dead horse of state intervention outweigh by far the socially concerned element. The German respondents generally show more faith in capitalistic development.

Let us see how the Italian respondents interpreted the alternatives before them.[23] The DC members who favored laissez-faire mostly tended to say that "free enterprise creates a better life for all," and some even cited democracy

TABLE 16-15. Does Capitalistic Development Free the People? (Percent)

	SPD	CDU	WEST GERMANY	ITALY	PSU	DC	ALL SOCIALISTS	ALL CHRISTIAN DEMOCRATS
It sure does	22	35	28.5	10.8	16.1	4.9	18.9	19.9
It rather does	29	14	21.5	16.9	23.2	9.8	25.9	11.9
In the middle	17	13	15.0	9.4	8.0	10.8	12.3	11.9
Drastic political change (intervention) is rather needed	16	15	15.5	12.1	11.6	33.3	13.7	24.4
Definitely needs drastic change (intervention)	14	16	15.0	36.6	37.5	35.3	26.4	25.9
Don't know, neither	2	7	4.5	4.2	3.6	4.9	2.8	6.0
Total	100	100	100	100	100	100	100	100
Number	100	100	200	213	112	101	212	201

which "lets people do what they want." Most of the many interventionists in the DC, however, strongly insisted that state intervention is necessary (61.4%). Others (15.7%) added that Italian society is too poor and too full of wants for the free play of enterprise, and some (5.7%) pointed to the need for political reforms. The Socialists who accepted the blessings of capitalist development felt that it allowed for a better life without exploitation (29.2%), simply stressed their faith in economic development (22.9%), or agreed that all had made some progress, even the peasants (18.8%). Some (12.5%) also shared the belief that "free enterprise creates a better life." Of the PSU members clamoring for radical change, the bulk called for political reforms (28.3%), pointed out that "some kinds of oppression still remained" (18.3%), or simply insisted on the need for state intervention (15%). Some also considered the division between rich and poor irremediable or philosophized that human nature would never really allow prosperity to spread (18.3%).

It is worth noting that in both Italian parties, respondents who accept capitalistic development were noticeably more satisfied with their party's record, whereas those calling for drastic change or state intervention tended to be dissatisfied. This suggests a look at the particular reasons cited for satisfaction or dissatisfaction in search of economic concerns. When asked what changes they had noticed in their party over the years, for example, many Socialists mention specifically a turning away from "class politics" to a more open approach. Comparable numbers of DC members similarly stress a turn toward working-class and other social problems in their party.

Laissez-faire Christian Democrats who were satisfied with their party cite in particular that it brought prosperity or simply "liberty" (a DC slogan), or mentioned its economic development programs, including agrarian development. The interventionists praised the party especially for its welfare legislation and its school and hospital construction and public works. Dissatisfied laissez-faire DC members objected to nationalization and public works projects, whereas the interventionists criticized their party for failing to bring prosperity and to provide for more welfare and the development of agriculture. Even the occasional charge of "do-nothings" was probably mainly economic in nature. Procapitalistic Socialists who were satisfied with their party also liked to cite prosperity, welfare legislation, development programs and public works, and unspecified social reforms. Dissatisfied but procapitalistic PSU members criticized their party particularly for its failures in the areas of welfare legislation and nationalization. PSU members who demanded radical changes were less intent on economic concerns and instead stressed such things as the need for administrative reform or their objections to the center-left coalition.

The respondents were also asked to name at least three main goals of their party. Paradoxically, DC members who believed in laissez-faire and PSU members in favor of radical change stressed such goals as a better distribution of income, better welfare and social security, reduction of unemployment, better pensions, low-cost housing, and agricultural betterment more than the

DC interventionists or the PSU procapitalists. The latter two groups emphasized administrative, fiscal, hospital, and educational reforms. The German CDU members who were for laissez-faire, by way of contrast, showed far less interest in the economic issues such as "economic stability" and social security than did the CDU interventionists. The SPD respondents in favor of radical political change also stressed the economic issues as chief party goals more than did those who relied on the spread of prosperity. We must conclude that in Italy even the laissez-faire Christian Democrats were rather interventionistic and that procapitalistic Socialists in both countries were amazingly indifferent about economic justice and equity.

Laissez-faire CDU members also tended to be more satisfied with their party's record than were the interventionists, whereas among the SPD members, paradoxically, it was those calling for radical change who were the most satisfied. In the CDU, economic policies were a main reason for the satisfaction of laissez-faire respondents, whereas the interventionists often cited social security and otherwise stressed domestic affairs as a reason for their dissatisfaction. The SPD members intent on capitalistic development prominently mentioned economic policy as one of the things they liked best about their party, whereas the radicals cited social welfare and other domestic affairs as a cause for dissatisfaction with their party.

Were there other notable differences between the procapitalists and the interventionists of the different parties and countries? In the CDU, laissez-faire respondents seemed to be concentrated in Lower Saxony and in cities over 10,000, whereas the Christian interventionists tended to live in North Rhine Westphalia and in smaller communes. It should occasion little surprise, moreover, that the advocates of laissez-faire were mainly professional and business people or white collar, whereas civil servants and blue collar (especially in enterprises smaller than 500 employees) tended to be on the side of state intervention. The length of employment also dramatically increased the love of free enterprise independent of job satisfaction and even of trade union membership. The SPD members, conversely, were most procapitalistic in North Rhine Westphalia and in smaller towns, and more interventionistic in Lower Saxony and Hesse, and in cities over 10,000. By occupation, the procapitalists in the SPD tended to be white collar or civil servants, whereas blue collar and the pensionists called for radical change, especially in enterprises of 500 employees or more. Here greater length of service with a large company seems to make for more radicalism.

The Italian parties presented a good deal of regional contrast on this issue. The DC respondents were more laissez-faire in the South and the Northeast, where they had less left-wing competition, and more interventionistic in the Northwest and in the central "red belt." The PSU, on the other hand, was most intent on radical change in the South where the left had just begun to mobilize against the conservative establishment. Elsewhere, the PSU tended to be satisfied with capitalistic development. Both parties were more interventionistic in communities below 10,000 and over 50,000, whereas the small towns between these limits preferred free enterprise.

By occupation, laissez-faire DC members tended to be in business and the professions or, to a lesser extent, civil servants or teachers rather than white or blue collar or farmers who all tended to be interventionists. In the PSU, too, business and the professions tended to be procapitalistic, whereas the farmers and blue and white collar wanted radical change. But the public employees also inclined toward revolutionary changes. In the DC and PSU, as in the German CDU, long-time service with the same company seemed to increase the zeal for free enterprise. This may also be a matter of age, as in both parties the respondents under 35 were notably more interventionistic than those over 35.[24] The German parties showed no such age differential.

The clustering of attitudes pro and con capitalistic development tends to resemble that on the role of class barriers (Table 16–16), so that we need not go into great detail. The fortuitous timing of the survey just before the great upheaval and the disintegration of center-left cooperation in both countries seems to show the two-party systems hovering on the brink of new departures, halfway into the future and half still in the past of traditional cleavage lines.

Clericalism, Secularism, and Anticlericalism

The third fundamental issue of ideology deals with clericalism in the form of influence of the clergy on secular issues. Because this is again one of the principal issues dividing the two parties, different dichotomies were used with each. For the Socialists, it was a choice between religious tolerance and freedom, on the one hand, and the traditional anticlericalism, on the other. Strong majorities, especially in the SPD, opted for tolerating clerical influences over a minority of *mangiapreti* (priest haters). For the Christian Democrats, the choice was between old-fashioned religious conservatism and the secular autonomy of the party, of politics, and even of culture from church influence. Surprisingly, the CDU members turned out to be far more church oriented than the DC members, although both parties have clear secular majorities. From looking at the table, one gets the impression that pro- and anticlericalism were dwindling in importance by 1968–1969 (Table 16–17).

The issues of church influence in politics and of the political reactions to it is such an ancient one in both Italy and Germany that we need not go into much elaboration. How were the alternatives interpreted by the respondents?[25] The proclerical Christian Democrats mostly limited themselves to calling church interference with civil affairs "inopportune." The secular-minded, on the other hand, liked to point to the division of church and state (39.8%) or would grant the church a right to guide society, but not the state (26.5%). Others would tell the church to stick to religious matters (10.8%). Some flatly denied that there

TABLE 16-16. Various Ideological Parameters and Capitalistic Development (in absolute numbers)

	SPD		CDU		PSU		DC	
	Pro-capitalistic	Revolutionary	Pro-capitalistic	Inter-ventionistic	Pro-capitalistic	Revolutionary	Pro-capitalistic	Inter-ventionistic
Dedication to party	$Q = .272$		$Q = .024$		$Q = -.567**$		$Q = .441$	
Dedicated	16	12	17	11	2	8	2	4
Private oriented	28	12	25	17	38	42	12	62
					$X^2 = 3.138*$			
Social distrust	$Q = .031$		$Q = .316$		$Q = .197$		$Q = .701**$	
Distrust	14	10	14	6	21	41	11	27
Trust	25	19	23	19	13	17	2	28
							$X^2 = 5.679**$	
Authoritarianism	$Q = .335$		$Q = .374$		$Q = .248$		$Q = .095$	
Authoritarian	27	11	27	13	7	12	5	19
Democratic	22	18	17	18	31	32	10	46
Hatred of bureaucracy	$Q = .070$		$Q = .344$		$Q = -.660**$		$Q = -.058$	
Antibureaucratic	6	4	6	2	9	32	2	9
Probureaucratic	38	22	39	26	22	16	11	44
					$X^2 = 10.720***$			
Class barriers	$Q = -.291$		$Q = .212$		$Q = -.759***$		$Q = .280$	
Classes present (or desirable)	9	8	12	6	6	26	3	9
No barriers	39	19	26	20	27	16	9	48
					$X^2 = 14.511***$			

452

	Column 1	Column 2	Column 3	Column 4
Church influence	$Q = .012$	$Q = .013$	$Q = .263$	$Q = .453*$
Tolerant (proclerical)	32 | 19	22 | 14	27 | 27	3 | 7
Anticlerical (secular)	19 | 11	26 | 17	14 | 24	10 | 62
				$X^2 = 1.993$
Grand Coalition	$Q = .475*$	$Q = -.335$	$Q = .702**$	$Q = -.674**$
In favor	38 | 18	32 | 26	37 | 28	6 | 54
Against	6 | 8	11 | 3	6 | 26	8 | 14
	$X^2 = 2.995*$		$X^2 = 12.405***$	$X^2 = 7.694***$
United States in Vietnam	$Q = -.476$	$Q = .322$	$Q = -.057$	$Q = .025$
In favor	34 | 16	40 | 26	14 | 19	11 | 47
Against	6 | 1	3 | 1	19 | 23	2 | 9
	$X^2 = 1.532$	$X^2 = 1.532$		
Europeanism versus Gaullism	$Q = .397$	$Q = .504$	$Q = .525**$	$Q = .562**$
Europeanist	40 | 23	44 | 29	22 | 19	11 | 40
Gaullist	3 | 4	1 | 2	9 | 25	1 | 13
			$X^2 = 5.769**$	$X^2 = 2.022$
Toleration of NPD	$Q = -.272$	$Q = -.206$		
Get rid of it	16 | 14	17 | 14		
Tolerate it	28 | 14	24 | 13		
Recognition of DDR	$Q = .048$	$Q = .171$		
In favor	19 | 12	11 | 5		
Against	23 | 16	28 | 18		

TABLE 16–17. Church Influence Should Be Tolerated (Percent)

	SPD	CDU	WEST GERMANY	ITALY	PSU	DC	ALL SOCIALISTS	ALL CHRISTIAN DEMOCRATS
It should indeed	42	24	33.0	23.7	39.8	5.9	40.9	14.9
It rather should	22	9	15.5	8.4	14.2	2.8	17.8	5.4
In the middle	13	12	12.5	13.5	18.6	7.8	16.0	9.0
Rather not	6	13	9.5	14.0	9.7	18.6	8.0	15.8
Definitely not	16	39	27.5	35.3	10.6	62.7	13.1	51.0
Don't know, neither	1	3	2.0	5.1	7.1	2.9	4.2	3.0
Total	100	100	100	100	100	100	100	100
Number	100	100	200	215	113	102	213	202

was any church interference (4.8%), and not a few opined that the parties ought to have "ideological autonomy" (12.1%). Anticlerical PSU members also declared church interference "inopportune" (19.2%) or called the church "too conservative" (30.8%). Some frankly stated their distrust of priests (15.3%), expressed their distaste for clericalism (11.5%), or admonished the church to stick to religion. Most of the tolerant PSU members motivated their choice with respect for the religious feelings of others and their freedom of religion (58.5%). Others pointed to the division of church and state (23.1%), granted the church a duty to guide society (6.2%), or praised its merits in the field of education, morals, and welfare (6.2%).

The German data lack an equivalent of this interpretative record, but there are other questions worth examining. When asked what they liked best about their party, for example, disproportionate numbers of proclerical CDU members replied "its Christian principles" as compared with the secular-minded who preferred to talk about the welfare achievements and the democratic attitude of their party. Proclerical CDU members also attended denominational schools more often than did the secular Christian Democrats who were generally better educated than the proclericals. The SPD anti-clericals also went more often to a denominational school and were less well-educated than were the tolerant Socialists (Table 16–18). Evidently, religious schooling will aggravate the conflict and make anticlericals out of Socialists, while a mixed or secular school encourages tolerance. In a Christian Democrat, on the other hand, the effect may indeed increase secular-mindedness, although we have to remember that these German denominational primary schools were often a matter of local option and hence a mixed school may only reflect the presence of a religiously mixed or secular-minded community. In Italy, the same relationships obtain between PSU anticlerical-ism or tolerance and religious education, and with DC proclericalism or secularism. Proclerical DC members also turned out to be less well educated than the secular-minded. PSU anticlericalists, however, is particularly strong among respondents with at least an upper-middle school education.

Let us take a look also at regional and location differences. Proclerical DC members were found most likely in the South, the islands, and in the Northeast

TABLE 16–18.   Religious Education and Anticlericalism (Secularism)

	SPD			*CDU*	
	Religious School	*Mixed or Secular School*		*Religious School*	*Mixed or Secular School*
Anticlerical	7	28	Proclerical	16	27
Tolerant	4	55	Secular	16	33
	PSU			*DC*	
Anticlerical	6	35	*Proclerical*	5	11
Tolerant	7	43	*Secular*	23	60

and in towns between 10 and 50,000, which may well be church centers. The secular abounded in central Italy and in larger cities or communes under 10,000. Anticlerical Socialists were strong precisely where proclerical DC members are strong, namely, in the South, the islands, and the Northeast and in the towns of 10,000–50,000. Tolerant Socialists were more often where the DC was secular, as in the "red belt" (actually an area of strong anticlerical traditions), or where the proclerical and secular elements were in balance, as in the Northwest. They were also strong in cities over 50,000 and communes under 10,000. Whether a respondent no longer lives in the place where he was born did not seem to make him less pro- or anticlerical. On the contrary, the secular DC member and the tolerant Socialist tended to be living elsewhere. However, the proclerical Christian Democrat tended to have moved away before he was 12 years old, whereas the secular-minded tended not to move until he was fully grown. It could be that early uprooting makes a person more dependent on the moral support of the church.

Anticlerical SPD members were somewhat more often from North Rhine Westphalia or Hesse and from towns between 2,000 and 100,000, whereas the tolerant were more often from Lower Saxony and either from rural or metropolitan areas. The anticlericals tended to be living where they were born or to have come from Eastern Germany or the Sudetenland, whereas the tolerant more often came from elsewhere in West Germany. The proclerical CDU members were most often from Lower Saxony and from communities under 10,000. They were born where they were now living or also came from the DDR or eastern areas, which gave them, as well as the SPD anticlericals, a traditional tinge. The secular-minded CDU members were frequently from Hesse and from cities over 10,000 and tended to have come in the last five years from elsewhere in the Federal Republic. By occupation, proclerical CDU members tended to be blue or white collar or pensionists, whereas business and professions as well as the civil service were predominantly secular in orientation. The anticlerical SPD members also tended to be blue or white collar, or even civil servants, whereas the tolerant were pensionists or professional persons. Among the two Italian parties, by contrast, business and the professions were pro- or anticlerical and blue and white collar and the farmers secular minded or tolerant. Only among the teachers and public employees do the DC members tend to be secular and the PSU members anticlerical. A greater contrast between the two countries is hard to imagine.

How do these views on church influence relate to the other issues (Table 16–19)? Again, the attitude clusters for each party are almost identical to those on the perception of class barriers. We have mapped them for easy comparison (Tables 16–20 and 16–21). They confirm our hypothesis that the underlying and the ideological issues are related in a fairly stable way. Even the topical issue patterns are largely in conformity with these patterns.

How do the two Italian parties compare with each other and with the Germans? There are more partisan differences in Italy than in Germany on this issue. The distrustful, for example, are anticlerical in the PSU and preoccupied with social classes. On Vietnam, supporters of the American action tended in opposite directions, and, vertically too the reactions in both parties were diametrically opposed, which confirms the impression that this was indeed a highly partisan issue. There are further differences on authoritarianism, capitalistic development, and Europeanism. At the same time, it should be noted that there seem to be more similarities on this issue between the German and Italian parties than on most others. Some patterns are quite parallel, such as dedication to party or Europeanism; others are nearly so, as for instance authoritarianism or class barriers.

The Topical Issues

Now that we have concluded the ideological core section, we can afford to dispose of the rest of the issues in a more summary fashion. Let us start out with the tables this time and then follow it up with other information about the background of each opinion grouping. If we set the three tables side by side, the similarity of the distributions for each party on all three topical tables becomes immediately obvious (Tables 16–22, 16–23, 16–24). Between 45% and 70% of the SPD, CDU, and DC appear to have supported all three of the policies. Only the PSU, which has less lopsided majorities on these issues than the others, shows significant variations. On all three issues, also, supporters tend more toward the private-trusting-democratic-probureaucratic (PTDP) combination than opponents, but, if read horizontally, each of the three presents a different pattern. On the Grand Coalition both tend toward support, and on Vietnam both tend toward opposition. But on a European federation, again, the dedicated-distrustful-authoritarian-antibureaucratic (DDAA) combination tends to be Gaullist, whereas PTDP is more likely on the side of a United Europe. With the earlier introduction of PTDP and DDAA, also, we indicated directions for the clusters of opinion. As the reader may have noticed, we now rearranged the ideological issues according to the findings of the last section to maintain among them the direction of the underlying issues. One direction there is CIC (class conscious-interventionist-clerical), and the other MCS (mobility-minded-capitalist-secular) for either party.

On the three day-to-day political issues, a person's position is presumably derived from his ideological and underlying attitudinal posture. Such an issue was, for example, the center-left coalition which was still a hotly debated question in both countries at the time of the survey (Table 16–25). The question had to be put in such a way as to account for the Italian multiparty system which seemingly gives the principals a choice between a Grand Coalition and other alternatives.[26] The PSU could have remained outside of the government and joined the extreme left in opposition to the DC. The SPD,

TABLE 16–19. Various Ideological Parameters and Church Influence (in absolute numbers)

	SPD		CDU		PSU		DC	
	Anticlerical	Tolerant	Anticlerical	Tolerant	Anticlerical	Tolerant	Anticlerical	Tolerant
Dedication to party	$Q = -.224$		$Q = .107$		$Q = .318$		$Q = .071$	
Dedicated	12	19	16	17	3	8	1	5
Private oriented	14	35	22	29	37	51	13	75
Social distrust	$Q = .607**$		$Q = .029$		$Q = .837**$		$Q = .215$	
Distrust	15	11	10	11	35	31	7	35
Trust	13	39	24	28	2	20	4	31
	$X^2 = 8.150***$				$X^2 = 13.482***$			
Authoritarianism	$Q = -.453*$		$Q = .527**$		$Q = -.257$		$Q = .509**$	
Authoritarian	21	25	30	20	11	11	9	23
Democratic	12	38	13	28	26	44	7	55
	$X^2 = 5.002*$		$X^2 = 7.293***$				$X^2 = 4.361**$	
Hatred of bureaucracy	$Q = -.718**$		$Q = .552**$		$Q = -.774**$		$Q = .428$	
Antibureaucratic	7	3	6	2	25	18	4	11
Probureaucratic	21	55	38	44	6	34	8	55
	$X^2 = 7.496***$		$X^2 = 2.968*$		$X^2 = 16.334***$			
Class barriers	$Q = -.416$		$Q = .060$		$Q = -.692***$		$Q = .787**$	
Classes present (or desirable)	9	9	8	9	22	14	9	10
No barriers	21	51	26	33	10	35	16	56
	$X^2 = 2.812*$				$X^2 = 12.727***$		$X^2 = 13.882$	

458

Capitalistic development				
Procapitalistic	$Q = .012$	$Q = .013$	$Q = .263$	$Q = .453$*
Revolutionary-Interventionistic	19, 32 / 11, 19	22, 26 / 14, 17	14, 27 / 24, 27	3, 10 / 7, 67 — $X^2 = 1.993$
Grand Coalition				
In favor	$Q = -.699$**	$Q = -.423$	$Q = -.178$	$Q = .234$
Against	15, 54 / 11, 7 — $X^2 = 10.464$***	27, 40 / 10, 5	27, 41 / 17, 18	12, 57 / 3, 23
United States in Vietnam				
In favor	$Q = -.756$*	$Q = -.737$**	$Q = .034$	$Q = -.142$
Against	17, 49 / 5, 2 — $X^2 = 6.783$***	34, 45 / 5, 1 — $X^2 = 2.181$	15, 21 / 18, 27	9, 60 / 2, 10
Europeanism versus Gaullism				
Europeanist	$Q = .647$*	$Q = -.082$	$Q = -.079$	$Q = .352$
Gaullist	28, 48 / 1, 8 — $X^2 = 2.830$*	39, 46 / 3, 3	16, 25 / 18, 24	12, 46 / 2, 16
Toleration of NPD				
Get rid of it	$Q = .120$	$Q = .447$		
Tolerate it	12, 22 / 15, 35	22, 14 / 18, 30		
Recognition of DDR				
In favor	$Q = .350$	$Q = .423$		
Against	15, 20 / 13, 36	11, 6 / 26, 35		

459

TABLE 16–20.   Attitude Clusters Among German Party Members Regarding Church Influence

	SPD I	
Less private	*Anticlerical*	Less Pro-Grand
Distrustful	Less mobility	coalition
Authoritarian	Less capitalistic	Less Pro-Vietnam policy
Less probureaucratic		Pro-European
		Less tolerant of NPD
		For DDR recognition

	SPD II	
More private	*Religiously Tolerant*	Pro-Grand Coalition
Trusting	Mobility-minded	Pro-Vietnam policy
Democratic	Procapitalistic	Less Pro-European
Probureaucratic		Tolerant of NPD
		Against DDR
		recognition

	CDU I	
Less private	*Proclerical*	Less Procoalition
More trusting	Less mobility	Less Pro-Vietnam policy
Authoritarian	Procapitalistic	Less Pro-European
Less probureaucratic		Against toleration of
		NPD
		Less against DDR
		recognition

	CDU II	
Private	*Secular-Minded*	Pro-Grand Coalition
Distrustful	Mobility-minded	Pro-Vietnam policy
Democratic	Interventionistic	Pro-European
Probureaucratic		Tolerant of NPD
		Against DDR
		recognition

by comparison, had no PCI to fall back on but only the FDP, which is hardly a left-wing party when viewed from the vantage point of the SPD. In any case, it is remarkable that so few of the German party members, even of the SPD, came out against the Grand Coalition, which had received a good deal more negative attention in the media. In Italy, the relative popularity of the Grand Coalition among the Socialists was equally surprising when we consider that the PSU directly after the 1968 elections for half a year refused to return to its coalition with the DC which showed no such reluctance to continue the *apertura a sinistra*.[27]

Because the PSU has less lopsided majorities than the SPD, let us take a look at how the PSU supporters and opponents of the coalition differ. PSU respondents who endorsed the center-left coalition most often motivated their preference by calling collaboration between the DC and the PSU more useful than opposition. Just as many respondents replied that the Communists (PCI)

TABLE 16–21. Attitude Clusters Among Italian Party Members Regarding Church Influence

	PSU I	
Private	*Anticlerical*	Less Pro-Center-Left
Distrustful	Class barriers	coalition
Less democratic	Revolutionary change	Less Anti-Vietnam
Antibureaucratic		policy
		Anti-European
		unification

	PSU II	
Less private	*Religiously Tolerant*	Pro-Center-Left
Less distrustful	Mobility minded	coalition
Democratic	Procapitalistic	Anti-Vietnam policy
Probureaucratic		Pro-European

	DC I	
Less private	*Proclerical*	Pro-Center-Left
Distrustful	Natural class order	coalition
Authoritarian	Less interventionist	Less Pro-Vietnam policy
Less probureaucratic		Pro-European

	DC II	
Private	*Secular-Minded*	Less Procoalition
More trusting	Mobility-minded	Pro-Vietnam policy
Democratic	Interventionistic	Less Pro-European
Probureaucratic		

were under the control of a foreign power or that their program was basically different from that of the PSU. The opponents of the coalition stressed that a policy of collaboration with the DC was out of step with the times or that working with the PCI was more in line with the times. If we check with which PSU leaders the opponents of the coalition identify, the names mentioned by 57% of them are Lombardi, Giolitti, and De Martino, whereas 53% of the supporters name Nenni, Pertini, Mancini, and Tanassi. This is almost exactly the factional split of the *disimpegno* (withdrawal from the coalition) of 1968. A check on previous party membership also shows relatively more of the opponents of the coalition to have come from the old PSI or even the PCI, whereas the supporters tend to have been in the PSDI before finding themselves in the PSU.

There are some questions on the SPD attitudes, but the answers do not shed much light. One of them asked the respondents whether they would ever vote for either the CDU or the FDP (one choice only). Those opposing the Grand Coalition actually showed relatively more sympathy for the CDU than did its supporters. The latter came out more strongly for the FDP, the party with which the SPD actually formed a new coalition a month after the survey. Opponents of the coalition were less satisfied with their party's record than the

TABLE 16–22. Various Ideological Parameters and the Grand Coalition (in absolute numbers)

	SPD		CDU		PSU		DC	
	Pro	Anti	Pro	Anti	Pro	Anti	Pro	Anti
Dedication to party	$Q = -.213$		$Q = -.177$		$Q = -.250$		$Q = -.714^{**}$	
Dedicated	21	7	22	7	6	5	2	4
Private oriented	37	8	36	8	60	30	66	22
							$X^2 = 2.958^*$	
Social distrust	$Q = -.471^*$		$Q = -.884^{**}$		$Q = -.345$		$Q = -.145$	
Distrust	14	8	9	10	42	27	29	14
Trust	39	8	44	3	16	5	25	9
	$X^2 = 3.149^*$		$X^2 = 18.990^{***}$					
Authoritarianism	$Q = .226$		$Q = .066$		$Q = -.175$		$Q = -.220$	
Authoritarian	32	6	32	7	13	8	20	10
Democratic	37	11	32	8	51	22	47	15
Hatred of bureaucracy	$Q = -.225$		$Q = -.846^{**}$		$Q = -.223$		$Q = .311$	
Antibureaucratic	5	2	3	6	27	17	12	3
Probureaucratic	59	14	60	10	30	12	42	20
			$X^2 = 14.259^{***}$					
Class barriers	$Q = .718^{**}$		$Q = .043$		$Q = -.590^{**}$		$Q = .030$	
Classes present (desirable)	7	7	13	4	17	22	13	5
No barriers	55	9	39	11	33	11	44	18
	$X^2 = 8.923^{***}$				$X^2 = 8.530^{***}$			

462

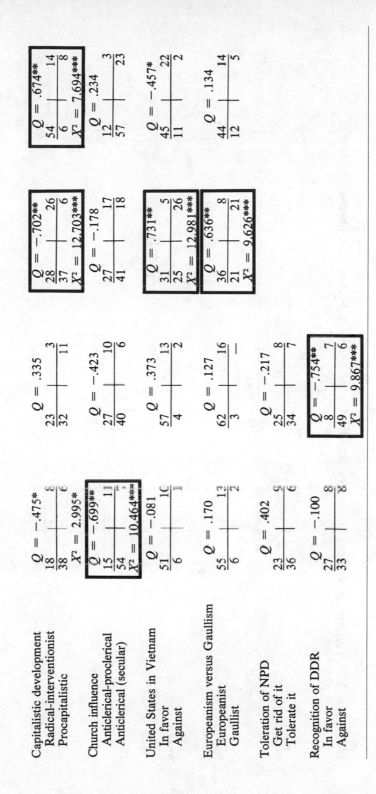

TABLE 16–23. Various Ideological Parameters and the United States in Vietnam (in absolute numbers)

	SPD		CDU		PSU		DC	
	Pro	Anti	Pro	Anti	Pro	Anti	Pro	Anti
Dedication to party	$Q = -.529*$		$Q = .083$		$Q = -.075$		$Q = .031$	
Dedicated	16	4	26	2	4	6	5	1
Private oriented	39	3	44	4	31	40	61	13
	$X^2 = 1.172$							
Social distrust	$Q = -.361$		$Q = -.442$		$Q = -.255$		$Q = .068$	
Distrust	13	3	17	2	22	33	31	5
Trust	37	4	44	2	9	8	27	5
Authoritarianism	$Q = .082$		$Q = .448$		$Q = .217$		$Q = .011$	
Authoritarian	31	3	42	2	6	10	22	4
Democratic	35	4	32	4	28	30	45	8
Hatred of bureaucracy	$Q = -.500*$		$Q = -.387$		$Q = .021$		$Q = .555**$	
Antibureaucratic	3	1	6	1	14	17	14	—
Probureaucratic	54	6	68	5	15	19	44	11
							$X^2 = 3.377*$	
Class barriers	$Q = -.636**$		$Q = .176$		$Q = -.338$		$Q = .302$	
Classes present (desirable)	6	2	14	1	11	21	14	1
No barriers	54	4	49	5	18	17	45	6

Capitalist development
Radical-interventionist
Procapitalistic

$Q = .476*$ $\dfrac{16}{34}\;\Big|\;\dfrac{1}{6}$ $X^2 = 1.532$

$Q = .322$ $\dfrac{26}{40}\;\Big|\;\dfrac{1}{3}$

$Q = .057$ $\dfrac{19}{14}\;\Big|\;\dfrac{23}{19}$

$Q = -.025$ $\dfrac{47}{11}\;\Big|\;\dfrac{9}{2}$

Church influence
Anticlerical-proclerical
Tolerant-secular

$Q = -.756**$ $\dfrac{17}{49}\;\Big|\;\dfrac{4}{2}$ $X^2 = 6.783***$

$Q = -.737**$ $\dfrac{34}{45}\;\Big|\;\dfrac{5}{1}$ $X^2 = 2.181$

$Q = .034$ $\dfrac{15}{21}\;\Big|\;\dfrac{18}{27}$

$Q = -.142$ $\dfrac{9}{60}\;\Big|\;\dfrac{2}{10}$

Grand Coalition
In favor
Against

$Q = -.081$ $\dfrac{51}{10}\;\Big|\;\dfrac{6}{1}$ $X^2 =$

$Q = .373$ $\dfrac{57}{13}\;\Big|\;\dfrac{4}{2}$

$Q = .731**$ $\dfrac{31}{5}\;\Big|\;\dfrac{25}{26}$ $X^2 = 12.981***$

$Q = -.457*$ $\dfrac{45}{22}\;\Big|\;\dfrac{11}{2}$

Europeanism versus Gaullism
Europeanist
Gaullist

$Q = .571**$ $\dfrac{55}{5}\;\Big|\;\dfrac{6}{2}$

$Q = .411$ $\dfrac{72}{5}\;\Big|\;\dfrac{6}{-}$

$Q = .346$ $\dfrac{20}{12}\;\Big|\;\dfrac{17}{21}$

$Q = .210$ $\dfrac{45}{11}\;\Big|\;\dfrac{8}{3}$

Toleration of NPD
Get rid of it
Tolerate it

$Q = .142$ $\dfrac{24}{34}\;\Big|\;\dfrac{2}{4}$

$Q = -.138$ $\dfrac{31}{41}\;\Big|\;\dfrac{2}{2}$

Recognition of DDR
In favor
Against

$Q = -.815**$ $\dfrac{22}{36}\;\Big|\;\dfrac{6}{-}$ $X^2 = 8.728***$

$Q = -.440$ $\dfrac{14}{54}\;\Big|\;\dfrac{2}{3}$

TABLE 16-24. Various Ideological Parameters and Europeanism (in absolute numbers)

	Europeanism	Gaullist	Europeanism	Gaullist	Europeanism	Gaullist	Europeanism	Gaullist
Dedication to party	$Q = .573$		$Q = .636**$		$Q = .000$		$Q = -.746**$	
Dedicated	24	1	33	—	5	5	1	2
Private oriented	39	6	44	6	35	35	55	16
			$X^2 = 4.416**$					
Social distrust	$Q = -.041$		$Q = .135$		$Q = -.415$		$Q = .008$	
Distrust	21	3	21	—	23	30	29	9
Trust	38	5	48	3	13	7	19	6
Authoritarianism	$Q = .212$		$Q = .023$		$Q = -.349$		$Q = -.120$	
Authoritarian	36	3	43	3	7	11	19	7
Democratic	39	5	41	3	33	25	38	11
Hatred of bureaucracy	$Q = -.034$		$Q = -.237$		$Q = -.190$		$Q = .380$	
Antibureaucratic	8	—	9	—	16	20	12	2
Probureaucratic	60	7	73	5	20	17	35	13

466

	Col 1	Col 2	Col 3	Col 4
Class barriers	$Q = .238$	$Q = .181$	$Q = .151$	$Q = .685^{**}$
Classes present (desirable)	13 / 56	15 / 52	14 / 19	14 / 34
No barriers	1 / 7	1 / 5	16 / 16	1 / 13
				$X^2 = 3.258^{*}$
Capitalistic development	$Q = -.397$	$Q = -.504^{**}$	$Q = -.525^{**}$	$Q = -.502^{**}$
Radical intervention	23 / 40	29 / 44	19 / 22	40 / 11
Procapitalistic	4 / 3	2 / 1	25 / 9	13 / 1
			$X^2 = 5.546^{**}$	
Church influence	$Q = .647^{**}$	$Q = -.082$	$Q = -.079$	$Q = .352$
Anticlerical-proclerical	28 / 48	39 / 46	16 / 25	12 / 46
Tolerant-secular	1 / 8	3 / 3	18 / 24	2 / 16
	$X^2 = 2.830^{*}$			
Grand Coalition	$Q = .170$	$Q = .127$	$Q = .636^{**}$	$Q = .134$
In favor	55 / 13	62 / 16	36 / 8	44 / 14
Against	6 / 2	3 / –	21 / 21	12 / 5
			$X^2 = 9.626^{***}$	
United States in Vietnam	$Q = .571$	$Q = .411$	$Q = .346$	$Q = .210$
In favor	55 / 6	72 / 6	20 / 17	45 / 8
Against	5 / 2	5 / –	12 / 21	11 / 3
Toleration of NPD	$Q = .040$	$Q = .409$		
Get rid of it	26 / 40	35 / 44		
Tolerate it	3 / 5	1 / 3		
Recognition of DDR	$Q = .136$	$Q = -.046$		
In favor	30 / 38	17 / 56		
Against	3 / 5	– / 3		

467

TABLE 16–25. Was Entering the Grand (Center-Left) Coalition an Unwise Step? (Percent)

	SPD	CDU	WEST GERMANY	ITALY	PSU	DC	ALL SOCIALISTS	ALL CHRISTIAN DEMOCRATS
It sure was	10	7	8.5	11.6	14.2	8.8	12.2	7.9
It rather was	8	9	8.5	3.7	1.8	5.9	4.7	7.4
In the middle	11	11	11.0	11.7	11.5	9.8	11.3	10.4
Not really	19	27	23.0	18.6	17.6	19.6	18.3	23.3
Definitely was not	50	42	46.0	48.0	46.0	50.0	47.9	46.0
Don't know, neither	2	4	3.0	7.4	8.9	5.9	5.6	5.0
Total	100	100	100	100	100	100	100	100
Number	100	100	200	215	113	102	213	202

supporters, of whom nearly one-fourth proudly cited the Grand Coalition as the thing which they liked the most. Members who only joined the SPD since 1955 were considerably less happy with the Grand Coalition than were their older comrades.

The Italian Socialists were also asked which parties they trusted more. Predictably, the supporters of the coalition came out heavily (1 to 9) for the DC, whereas its opponents opted almost as heavily (1 to 5) for the PCI or PSIUP. The opponents also showed a great deal more dissatisfaction with their party than the supporters, of whom many (32.9%) cited the center-left coalition as a special achievement of the PSU, whereas 12% of the opponents named it as the reason for their dissatisfaction. In contrast to the SPD, in the PSU it was the old Socialists, who joined before 1955, who were now less happy with the center-left coalition than their younger comrades. A check on age confirms this thesis.

On the issue of the American presence in Vietnam,[28] PSU supporters mostly (42.1%) referred to the need to contain the Communist policy of force with counterforce. Others spoke of preventing a Communist takeover in South Vietnam (15.8%) or cited Hungary or Czechoslovakia as examples of Soviet aggressiveness (10.5%). Opponents of the Vietnam policy motivated their preference mainly with the statement that a people ought to be free to make its choice without foreign intervention (25%). Another 12.5% insisted that one should fight Communism with ideas, not with arms. Others again suggested that the Vietnam action has failed to stop Communist expansion (5.2%) or that "the Soviet Union has," in fact, "respected the liberty of the peoples under its protection." From the Italian point of view, the role of the Soviet Union evidently loomed rather large in the South East Asian picture.

How much did anti-Vietnam Socialists identify with the PCI and PSIUP who were strongly committed on this, and how much with the DC which headed a government giving moral support (little else) to the U.S. position? A comparison between the relative trust set in either the DC or the PCI-PSIUP reveals that all three are highly partisan issues (Table 16–26). However,

TABLE 16–26. Trust in Parties and PSU Position on Topical Issues (Percent)

Trust in	VIETNAM POLICY		LEFT-CENTER COALITION		EUROPEANISM	
	DC	PCI-PSIUP	DC	PCI-PSIUP	DC	PCI-PSIUP
Pro	50.0	19.2	94.4	26.9	55.6	19.2
Anti	33.3	73.1	5.6	73.1	16.7	57.7
Both, neither, don't know	16.7	6.7	included in anti		28.7	23.1
Totals	100	100	100	100	100	100
Numbers	18	26	18	26	18	26

TABLE 16–27.   Italian Voters' Views on Vietnam Policy, 1968 (Percent)

WHO IS RIGHT?	ALL	PCI/PSIUP ADHERENTS	PSU/PRI	DC	RIGHT WING
U.S./South Vietnam	21.2	5.6	19.7	29.1	37.5
Viet Cong/North Vietnam	18.8	44.8	18.2	7.0	1.5
Both sides more or less	53.3	44.8	53.2	57.7	47.0

Vietnam did not stand out as the most partisan issue of the three, except in the sense that pro-Communist Socialists most heavily tended to be anti-Vietnam. As for identification with the DC, however, the center-left coalition and a United Europe clearly outdid the Vietnam issue. One possible reason for this might have been the cautious way in which the Italian government had expressed its endorsement and the presence of some anti-Vietnam sentiment in the DC.

In Italy, during the 1968 campaign, for example, Doxa ran a national poll with a representative adult sample on who was right in Vietnam, South Vietnam and the United States, North Vietnam and the Viet Cong, or both.[29] The results are broken down by party identification in Table 16–27. If these are the opinions of the population at large, our Italian party members are not far from the popular norm. The West Germans and the DC exhibited the strongest support for South Vietnam and the United States, although it is worth noting that even the DC, while giving very strong backing to the United States, had more Viet Cong supporters (12.7%) than did the SPD (Table 16–28). The PSU, on the other hand, had a substantial plurality for the Viet Cong and a suspiciously large number of responses which "agree with both," "agree with neither position," or claim not to know. The SPD also had 26% of such responses. It is most unlikely for Socialists in either country not to have been exposed to this issue considering the propaganda barrage of the PCI and the dissident Socialists (PSIUP) in Italy and of left-wing agitation in Germany on this issue. Thus it may be more correct in both cases to speak of a pattern of evasion due to a conflict of loyalties. As Table 16–28 indicates, Socialists in general and Italians in particular are far more anti-Vietnam than the Christian Democrats and the Germans.

The third issue of this set concerns the attraction of Gaullism versus the standard European commitment of both parties in Italy and West Germany.[30] The Gaullist stress on national sovereignty and European exclusiveness, as Table 16–29 shows, is considerably more popular among Socialists than Christian Democrats, and far more so in Italy than in West Germany. Christian Democrats historically took the initiative in the European direction, whereas the Socialists only came around at a later date to support European collaboration. But with the European tide still running so strongly, it is surprising to see the PSU almost evenly pro and con.

TABLE 16–28. Support for the United States in Vietnam (Percent)

	SPD	CDU	WEST GERMANY	ITALY	PSU	DC	ALL SOCIALISTS	ALL CHRISTIAN DEMOCRATS
Strongly supports United States	29	43	36.0	34.0	19.5	50.0	23.9	46.6
Rather supports United States	37	37	37.0	15.8	13.3	18.6	24.5	27.7
In the middle	16	4	10.0	7.4	8.0	6.9	11.7	5.4
Rather supports Viet Cong	4	3	3.5	8.4	12.4	3.9	8.5	3.5
Strongly supports Viet Cong	4	3	3.5	21.4	32.7	8.8	19.2	5.9
Don't know, neither	10	10	10.0	13.0	14.1	11.8	12.2	10.9
Total	100	100	100	100	100	100	100	100
Number	100	100	200	215	113	202	213	202

TABLE 16–29. A European Federation or a Europe of Fatherlands? (Percent)

	SPD	CDU	WEST GERMANY	ITALY	PSU	DC	ALL SOCIALISTS	ALL CHRISTIAN DEMOCRATS
Definitely for European federation	56	60	58.0	33.0	27.4	39.2	40.8	49.5
Rather European	20	28	24.0	16.3	12.4	20.6	16.0	24.3
In the middle	8	3	5.5	11.2	8.0	14.7	8.0	8.9
Rather Gaullist	5	3	4.0	8.8	12.4	4.9	8.9	4.0
Strongly Gaullist	5	3	4.0	19.1	24.8	12.7	15.5	7.9
Don't know, neither	6	3	4.5	11.6	15.0	7.8	10.8	5.4
Total	100	100	100	100	100	100	100	100
Number	100	100	200	215	113	102	213	202

What was it that would still make the European issue a partisan matter in the PSU, after 20 years of European initiatives and a decade of the Common Market? There was, of course, the strong PCI and PSIUP critique of the Atlantic Pact (NATO) from which these parties wanted to extricate the country. In their eyes, a European federation would create a politically pro-Western bloc, an international political alliance to go with the "international supercartel" of which they had been complaining. There was also the allure of what we have called Gaullism, the stress on national sovereignty and European independence from both the United States and the Soviet Union. Their anti-Americanism can be taken for granted, and Communist independence from Soviet influence had vociferously been proclaimed since the days of Togliatti's *Via Italiana al Socialismo*.

How did the PSU "Gaullists" interpret the question? Of the total, 54.8% stressed the desire to "keep out the U.S. and the USSR" and another 19.0% wanted to "avoid interference by any other country," presumably in Italian affairs. Another 11.9% expressed the necessity of maintaining intact the national sovereignty of Italy. The good Europeans, by contrast, emphasized the advantages accruing from such a union (33.3%) and the merits of an economic union (24.4%). More ideologically oriented responses stressed the "liberation to be gained by getting rid of frontiers," the ideal of a political union (11.1% each), or just collaboration among nations (6.7%).

The Unified Christian Democrats

What about the Christian Democratic responses to all the issues? The German CDU offers a good deal of consistency in its patterns of response on the underlying and ideological issues, but only on the Grand Coalition are its negative responses large enough to be worth further analysis. The DC, on the other hand, fluctuates more on the underlying and ideological issues, but has enough negative responses to encourage comparison.

Regarding the CDU, suffice it to say that opponents of the Grand Coalition tended to be from Hesse, and so were its SPD opponents. In the CDU, they also tended to be union members (not in the SPD), and they appeared to have no more prejudice against the SPD than those who endorsed the coalition. The CDU opponents of the coalition also showed relatively more support for a two-party system than did coalition supporters who more often express support for a system of three or four parties. The Grand Coalition was widely held to be antithetical to a working two-party system. Perhaps they rejected the easy way out by manipulating the electoral law to eliminate small parties, whereas those who welcomed the Grand Coalition also accepted a change of electoral law. In the SPD, the enemies of the Grand Coalition preferred a three- or four-party system, whereas its supporters strongly favored a two-party system. Nevertheless, the latter also toyed with changing the electoral law, whereas the opponents did not. It would appear that preference for a two-party system is not clearly related to support or opposition to the Grand Coalition, except in the CDU. In the SPD, the reasoning was more complex. Supporters of the coalition may well have felt with Wehner that the Grand Coalition was a temporary device to help the SPD become more competitive with the CDU, whereas its opponents may be part of the left wing of the party which worried about what a discriminatory electoral law might do to parties of left-wing dissent rather than to the NPD. Thus the division may also have involved the widespread fear that the ideal of a two-party system in the Federal Republic was really a design for the monopoly of a bipartisan power elite. In any case, the SPD coalition supporters inclined in about the same proportion (2 to 1) toward tolerating the NPD as its opponents preferred to get rid of it.[31] The latter also were less inclined to deny recognition to the DDR than were the coalition supporters, both divisions being rather similar to those in the CDU.

The DC members who supported the center-left coalition were at first glance considerably less MCS on the ideological issues than they were PTDP on the underlying issues, a relative loss of ideological direction which was also present in the CDU. The same differential appears among the Vietnam supporters and good Europeans of the DC, though less clearly than with the CDU. The DC opponents on the three issues showed more consistency between the underlying and the ideological issues. As for the topical issues on Tables 16–22, 16–23, and 16–24, the DC position seemed to be skewed similarly on all three between heavy pluralities on the pro-pro combinations and a negligible number of anti-anti combinations. With the CDU, the disparity was even greater. Let us take a closer look at the differences between the DC opinion groups.

The coalition supporters of the DC were more likely from the North, whereas the Central and Southern Italians tended to be more against the coalition. Its PSU opponents also came more often from the South, whereas its Socialist friends were from the Northwest and the Center. These regional patterns are rather reminiscent of the unity of both German parties in their reaction to the grand coalition in "red Hesse." Wherever partisan conflict is more acute, it seems that the idea of coalition has to overcome some resistance. By occupation, the Christian Democratic coalition supporters tend to be business and professional people (as in the PSU) and blue and white collar. The public employees in both parties oppose the coalition.

How did the DC members interpret the three topical questions posed? On the center-left coalition, some supporters tended to say that their earlier, right-wing coalition partners were not representatives of all the classes, whereas a DC-PSU coalition would be good for all classes (33.8%). The majority (50.7%) simply called the center-left coalition "modern," or "opportune," and their earlier coalitions "out of step with the times." Opponents of the coalition pointed out how the DC program differed from that of earlier partners such as the PLI, or that the PLI would never make a comeback.

On the Vietnam issue, DC dissenters tended to be from the "red belt" and the Northeast areas in which they may well have been more exposed to the Communists daily *L'Unità* and left-wing Socialist or PCI propaganda. Vietnam supporters in the DC most often came from the Northwest and tended to be blue or white collar or farmers. They often motivated their preference by saying that "Communist force has to be met with counterforce" (42.7%) or pointing out the necessity of preventing a Communist takeover in South Vietnam (18.3%). Other supportive reasons cited included "the U.S. has the task of defending liberty and self-government" (8.5%) or reminders of Soviet aggression in Hungary and Czechoslovakia. DC members opposed to the Vietnam action tended to express most often their belief in the freedom of a people from foreign intervention and, second, that Communism has to be fought with ideas, not with force. Comparing the trust expressed either in the PSU or in the right-wing parties by DC opponents of the Vietnam action with the opponents of the center-left coalition, we notice at once that right-wing influence plays a different role in both cases. On Vietnam, the right wingers in the DC were even more willing to support the American presence than were those who expressed trust in the PSU. On the center-left coalition, the right wingers tended to come out more against the coalition than those who trusted the PSU, which is hardly surprising (Table 16–30).

As for the European issue, the good Europeans in both parties of Italy tended to be from the Northwest, whereas Central Italy leaned more toward Gaullism and the Southerners had many undecided respondents. The farther one moves away from the other countries of Little Europe, it seems, the less interest there is in European federation. By occupation, the Gaullists in the DC tended to be blue and white collar or farmers and to have had a rather limited education (lower-middle school or less). The good Europeans, on the other hand, were more often business and professional (as in the PSU) or public employees including teachers (not among PSU) and generally better educated.

TABLE 16–30. Trust in Parties and DC Positions on Topical Issues (Percent)

TRUST IN	CENTER-LEFT COALITION		VIETNAM		EUROPEANISM	
	PSU	Right-Wing	PSU	Right-Wing	PSU	Right-Wing
Pro	89.7	50	65.5	75.0	65.5	75.0
Anti	3.4	50	13.8	12.5	10.3	12.5
Both, neither, don't know	6.9	—	20.7	12.5	23.2	12.5
Totals	100	100	100	100	100	100
Numbers	29	8	29	8	29	8

In the CDU, also, the Gaullists tended to be white collar or pensionists and to have had less formal education than the good Europeans. In comparing the partisan implications of this issue in the DC with the other two, there was a striking similarity between the patterns of responses on Europeanism and on Vietnam. Only on the center-left coalition was there more of a partisan tendency to associate trust in the PSU with support for the coalition.

The good Europeans in the DC tended to motivate their preference mostly with references to a "political union" (25.0%) or a more prosaic economic union (21.9%). Many stressed the advantages to be derived from a European federation (18.8%), spoke of collaboration among the nations (15.6%), or of the sense of liberation that would come with the abolition of frontiers (9.4%). The Gaullists truculently put "keeping out the U.S. and the USSR" (44.4%) first, followed by "keeping out the other powers" (33.3%), presumably the European partners. Some just stressed the need to maintain intact the national sovereignty of the country. It is difficult to escape the conclusion that Gaullism in the DC represented mostly the xenophobia and narrowness of some rather unenlightened people. And there was no reason to expect anything better from the handful of Gaullists in the CDU who were significantly lower in daily newspaper readership, weekly periodical consumption, and even in watching television news and news features or documentary programs than were the good Europeans.

Additional West German Issues

There were several more issues which were only used in Germany to counter the objection that this study might present a distorted picture by ignoring some of the most salient issues there. One was the recognition of the East German Republic (DDR)[32] which has meanwhile become even more intriguing as a result of Willy Brandt's Ostpolitik. In 1969, as Table 16–31 shows, not only the CDU but nearly a majority of our SPD respondents were not in favor of extending recognition to the East German regime. The second

TABLE 16–31. Recognition of DDR (Percent)

	SPD	CDU	TOTAL
Definitely in favor of recognition	21	9	15.0
Rather in favor	14	8	11.0
In the middle, neither	13	19	16.0
Rather against recognition	19	15	17.0
Definitely against recognition	30	47	38.5
DK	3	2	2.5
	100	100	100.0
			(200)

issue concerned the NPD which was still a worrisome menace to both parties at the time of the survey.[33] Its successes in various state elections since 1966 had endangered the survival of the FDP and frequently taken away SPD or CDU votes.[34] This issue should be viewed from the preoccupation of German politics with political monopoly and the democratic rights of the underdog however repulsive he may be. Both the CDU and the SPD, in fact, were evenly split on this issue with minor differences (Table 16–32).

There was a third such topical question asked in Germany, though not in the same dichotomous forms, which should be mentioned at this point. It concerned the treatment of the extraparliamentary opposition (APO) and offered a scale of six positions ranging from "more understanding for its demands" to arresting its ringleaders and deporting them to the DDR. The result was a strong partisan split which also indicates the potential of this issue for breaking up the SPD. SPD right wingers such as Helmut Schmidt had spoken out most forcefully against the APO even though there was obviously a good deal of sympathy for it in the party.[35] The CDU motives for tolerating the APO were not entirely pure, of course, as they counted on it to harrass and embarrass the SPD. In any case, a sizable majority of Social Democrats and a third of the Christian Democrats were quite willing to consider APO demands on their merits. On the other hand, there were nearly as many Social Democrats as CDU members ready to use extreme countermeasures (Table 16–33).

Toleration or nontoleration of the NPD involved complex sets of attitudes for our party members which require some interpretations before we begin to look into their actual behavior. In the SPD, for example, the tolerant might be those more committed to an open, democratic society, but also the young who had lost the well-rooted national fear of a resurgence of national socialism. The desire for suppressing the NPD could stem from an older generation, which remembered all too well the spell cast by the swastika in its own time, or it could come from the combative, sectarian left which is ever ready to see a fascist menace. Finally, there was a pattern of tolerance born of earlier involvement with the German military or the Nazis which, in both West German parties, simply produced a pragmatic attitude toward the NPD and the stability of

TABLE 16–32. Toleration of the NPD (Percent)

	SPD	CDU	TOTAL
Should be tolerated	25	35	30.0
It rather should	25	14	19.5
In the middle	13	10	11.5
Rather against toleration	7	9	8.0
Definitely against toleration	27	27	27.0
DK, either	3	5	4.0
	100	100	100.0 (200)

West German politics. Unlike the sense of panic in some minds, in other words, these citizens might have opted for toleration because they knew and did not overestimate the NPD phenomenon. Common CDU attitudes replicated the SPD patterns, including even the sectarian one, and may differ only in that there was a conservative wing that shared some of the NPD views on subjects such as law and order, the foreign workers, or anticommunism. In addition to this background, there were also regional variations which made CDU members in rural areas and especially in Lower Saxony opt for toleration while SPD members would not. In metropolitan areas and in highly urban/industrial North Rhine Westphalia, the situation was reversed. Here the SPD was for toleration and the CDU favored suppression of the NPD.

The sectarian element in both parties came out for suppression. Union members, workers, church group members, those very satisfied with their own party's record, and SPD members who some day "might vote for a party to the left of the SPD" all were leaning toward outlawing the NPD. In the CDU, the same was true of Catholics and children of CDU or Center party parents, as well as those over 50 and those who joined the party before 1955. By way of contrast, the professional, independent, well-educated, and white-collar members of both parties, members under 35, and recent joiners opted for toleration of the NPD. In the SPD, moreover, so did respondents who were past members of the Nazi youth and those who named German reunification as "the most important political problem today." As for CDU conservatives, toleration was advocated by members who were also prepared to use force on the left-wing APO and those who regularly watched the somewhat leftish television documentary series "Panorama." SPD fans of "Panorama," on the other hand, seemed to be left-wing Socialists, ready to suppress the NPD, whereas the tolerant were ready to tolerate APO as well.

We can also contrast the tolerant and the intolerant on the basis of the crosstabulations with all the other ideological attitudes (Table 16–34). Tolerant SPD members were noticeably more private-oriented, trusting, and probureaucratic; they made light of class barriers, favored capitalistic develop-

TABLE 16–33.   Policy Toward the APO

	SPD	CDU	TOTAL
More understanding	25	8	16.5
Yield to demands, if constitutional	32	26	29.0
Use courts and laws against APO threats	13	21	17.0
Use "authority and dignity"	14	16	15.0
Use police force, don't negotiate	5	10	7.5
Deport ringleaders	6	6	6.0
Other responses	—	3	1.5
Don't know, no answer	5	10	7.5
Totals	100	100	100
Numbers	100	100	200

ment, and were tolerant also of church influence. Finally, they favored the Grand Coalition more but Vietnam and European policy slightly less than did Social Democrats who wanted to suppress the NPD. All this seems to boil down to a modern democratic faith not unlike the main factor found for this party in the factor analysis, even though tolerance toward the NPD did not correlate any more with democratic than with authoritarian attitudes. Tolerant CDU members were likewise more private-oriented, trusting, and probureaucratic; they were also more procapitalistic and secular than the intolerant, and liked the Grand Coalition and American Vietnam policy better. And yet there was a noticeable conservative hue about them which was underscored by the presence of three of the four Gaullist respondents among them. Intolerant CDU members, moreover, clearly showed their sectarian color by being more dedicated, distrustful, authoritarian, pro-European, interventionistic, and pronouncedly proclerical. Here we clearly encounter both the DDAP and PTDP patterns mentioned earlier, as well as two of the factors that the factor analysis had turned up for the CDU.

On the question of the pre-Ostpolitik recognition of the DDR, likewise, SPD members ready before the 1969 elections to extend it were noticeably more trusting, less private-oriented, more democratic, ready to believe in social mobility and capitalistic development, but less tolerant of religion than were those who represented the conventional refusal to grant recognition. In the middle of an election campaign in which the SPD was accused of being the "party of recognition" by its erstwhile coalition partners and present antagonists in the CDU, it should not surprise us to find a willingness to recognize the DDR to go with less enthusiasm for the Grand Coalition and for Vietnam policy than among SPD standpatters who in other ways too still represented the traditional loyalties of the antirecognition stand of the SPD in the *Deutschland-Plan* of 1968. Those against recognition in the SPD typically came from rural communities and professional and independent members, but also from among the young (under 35) and leftish elements, especially in Hesse. Those in favor of recognition, on the other hand, tended to be better educated, older members, especially from Lower Saxony, interested in foreign policy and reunification and quite satisfied with their party's record. Recognition thus appears to be an issue cutting across the other alignments in the SPD, a harbinger perhaps of the shifting consensus in the party on the eve of its ascension to power in 1969.

The CDU members included a surprising number of advocates of recognition considering the adamant nonrecognition stance of the party. Who were these soft-liners in a traditionally hard-line party? They tended to be the less educated, low-income, working-class respondents who regularly watched "Panorama" on television. Their sectarian character came out clearly in their tendencies to be more dedicated, distrustful, authoritarian, even less probureaucratic, less mobility-minded, but more procapitalistic and proclerical. This line-up largely coincides with the *Christian conservatism* factor of the

TABLE 16-34. Various Ideological Parameters, Toleration of the NPD, and Recognition of the DDR (in absolute figures)

	SPD Outlaw	SPD Tolerate	CDU Outlaw	CDU Tolerate	SPD Outlaw	SPD Tolerate	CDU Outlaw	CDU Deny
Dedication to party	$Q = .333$		$Q = .675$**		$Q = .148$		$Q = .372$	
Dedicated	12	12	21	10	13	13	9	18
Private oriented	15	30	10	32	20	27	8	35
			$X^2 = 11.104$***					
Social distrust	$Q = .164$		$Q = .084$		$Q = .454°$		$Q = .600°°$	
Distrust	10	13	9	10	12	9	8	12
Trust	16	29	10	25	15	30	6	36
					$X^2 = 3.338$*		$X^2 = 5.177$**	
Authoritarianism	$Q = .017$		$Q = .179$		$Q = -.056$		$Q = .512$**	
Authoritarian	16	23	21	24	15	21	12	29
Democratic	18	25	14	23	20	25	4	30
							$X^2 = 4.068$**	
Hatred of bureaucracy	$Q = .169$		$Q = -.222$		$Q = -.038$		$Q = .666$**	
Antibureaucratic	4	4	4	4	3	4	4	4
Probureaucratic	27	38	28	44	30	37	11	55
							$X^2 = 3.358$*	

Class barriers	Q = -.103	Q = -.024	Q = -.242	Q = .418
Classes present	5[a], 9	6, 9	4, 9	4, 8
No barriers	26, 38	21, 30	27, 37	8, 39
Capitalistic development	Q = -.272	Q = -.206	Q = .048	Q = .171
Procapitalistic	16, 28	17, 24	19, 23	11, 28
Revolutionary-interventionistic	14, 14	14, 13	12, 16	5, 18
Church influence	Q = .120	Q = .447	Q = .350	Q = .423
Anticlerical-secular	12, 15	14, 30	15, 13	6, 35
Tolerant-proclerical	22, 35	22, 18	20, 36	11, 26
Grand Coalition	Q = .402	Q = -.217	Q = -.100	Q = -.754**
In favor	23, 36	25, 34	27, 33	8, 49
Against	9, 6	8, 7	8, 8	7, 6
United States in Vietnam	Q = .442	Q = -.138	Q = -.815**	X^2 = 9.867**; Q = -.440
In favor	24, 34	31, 41	22, 36	14, 54
Against	2, 4	2, 2	6, —	2, 3
Europeanism	Q = .040	Q = .409	Q = .136	Q = -.046
Pro-European	26, 40	35, 44	30, 38	17, 56
Gaullist	3, 5	1, 3	3, 5	—, 3

factor analysis which is evidently related to the traditions of the Christian trade unions rather than to the upper middle class Christian Democrats who represented the orthodox position on recognition.

The third additional issue for the Germans, how to deal with the APO, the left-wing street demonstrators of 1967–1968, was not couched in the same dichotomous form as the others and, for that reason, cannot be dealt with in quite the same fashion. It is a scale and has at least three significant positions, understanding/yielding, courts/authority, and force/deportation. The last of these, "deporting the ringleaders," even suggested that the latter belonged among or were put up to their actions by the Communists in the East. For the SPD, this was a painful issue separating the tougher, hard-lining elements from those feeling a kinship with APO concerns about the emergency laws and other left-wing issues buried by the Grand Coalition. SPD members who advocated understanding and even yielding to APO demands as long as they were not in violation of the constitutional order typically came from Hesse and from metropolitan areas and tended to be from the middle classes, including white collar. Many of them also held party offices, were children of ex-Nazis, were Protestant, and showed a lively social concern. The tough-minded Social Democrats, on the other hand, tended to be union members, especially active ones, workers in large enterprises, refugees, civil servants, farmers, Catholics, but also regular newspaper readers. They also expressed the feeling—shades of George Wallace—that "politics and government are simple matters to decide" and that "the government does care about what happens to its citizens," two items of belief not shared by the APO sympathizers.

In their underlying attitudes (Table 16–35), the tough-minded Social Democrats were heavily private oriented and rather more authoritarian and distrustful than the soft-liners. They also were less class conscious, more inclined toward radical change, and less tolerant of church influence in politics. On the topical issues, finally, they were not quite as much in favor of the Grand Coalition and European unification but, as we would expect, heavily in favor of the American role in Vietnam and against DDR recognition, two other anti-Communist issues. Outlawing the NPD, finally, was far more acceptable to the hard-liners than to the tolerant among whom two-thirds inclined toward tolerating the NPD as well as APO. Tolerant SPD members were trusting, more democratic and relatively more dedicated to their party, tolerant of religion, and even somewhat more inclined toward DDR recognition. Their ideological and topical attitudes otherwise resemble their tough-minded party friends. The APO clearly brought out the two wings of the SPD.

The CDU obviously could look at the APO with less of a sense of involvement and seemed to prefer using the courts and a show of "authority and dignity" against the street challenge. Here the sympathizers tended to be Catholics from North Rhine Westphalia, members of trade unions or of church-related organizations, and party officeholders or activists. The tough-minded Christian Democrats, by way of contrast, tended to be from low-income, less educated worker groups, especially in communes under 10,000.

TABLE 16–35. Various Ideological Parameters and the Extra-Parliamentary Opposition (APO) (in absolute numbers)

	SPD		CDU	
	Understanding/ Yielding	Force/ Authority	Understanding/ Yielding	Force/ Authority
Dedication to party				
Dedicated	21	9	12	17
Private oriented	27	19	17	30
Social distrust				
Distrust	12	14	8	9
Trust	33	16	17	29
Authoritarianism				
Authoritarian	24	18	16	25
Democratic	31	18	17	23
Hatred of bureaucracy				
Antibureaucratic	5	5	3	5
Probureaucratic	45	27	27	46
Class barriers				
Classes present (desirable)	11	6	7	10
No barriers	41	28	7	12
Capitalistic development				
Radical intervention	30	19	13	29
Procapitalistic	18	11	14	14
Church influence				
Anticlerical-proclerical	16	16	15	27
Tolerant-secular	40	22	17	26
Grand Coalition				
In favor	43	24	24	36
Against	8	8	6	9
U.S. in Vietnam				
In favor	35	27	23	46
Against	5	3	4	2
European unification				
Pro-European	42	31	29	47
Gaullist	5	5	3	3
Toleration of NPD				
Get rid of it	16	16	13	20
Tolerate it	33	17	15	29
Recognition of DDR				
In favor	23	11	7	9
Against	25	22	18	34

They tended to express feelings of powerlessness and conservative sentiments. In their underlying attitudes and ideological views, moreover, they heavily leaned toward private orientation, authoritarianism, and social trust (PTDP), as well as toward economic intervention, social mobility and clericalism. On the topical issues, too, the tough-minded CDU members were notably more in favor of the Vietnam and European policies and against DDR recognition, as well as tolerant toward the NPD. This orthodox line, admittedly, leaves little in the way of a different profile for Christian Democrats prepared to meet the APO with understanding and to yield to its demands as long as they were not in violation of the constitution. Aside from being slightly more democratic, they differed only on the ideological level by being more accepting of classes, more procapitalistic, and more secular.

Concluding Remarks

We have come to the end of this journey through the political cultures of four important European parties. Nearly half of our attention was lavished on the underlying attitudes alone to show their political relevance and the extent to which they differ between Italy and Germany. Social distrust in general, and in particular among Italian Socialists, appears to be the key to understanding wide-ranging patterns of political attitudes, whereas dedication to one's party, democratic attitudes, and hatred for bureaucracy vary in their significance from party to party. As compared with these basic psychological attitudes, the more specifically ideological views on class barriers, capitalist development, and church influence demonstrate both the current state of partisan ideology and the modifying impact of political change which has clearly set off the more contemporary positions from the traditional ideological orthodoxies of Socialists and Christian Democrats in either country.

In place of a summary,[36] we worked out the clusters of attitudes grouped around the party members' views of class barriers (Tables 16–13 and 16–14) and of church influence (Tables 16–20 and 16–21). These clusters link the underlying attitudes to ideological views and to topical positions and are remarkably similar to each other, a manifestation of the basic unity of the subject they are mapping out. The dichotomous design of the attitudinal questions appears to have been rather effective both in catching the range of opinions[37] and in bringing out the traditional-contemporary ideological divisions.

With the two lower levels well explored, however, there still remains a remarkable degree of freedom on the topical issues. To be sure, the party members' positions on them bear some relationship to their underlying and ideological views. The overwhelming majorities pro or contra the various topical issues, including the additional ones for the West Germans, however, suggest a conscious choice of politically active persons when they are faced with the need to make policy decisions. Rather than depicting political choices as mere reflections of social class or of the psychological compulsions of basic attitudes or the socialization process in given ideological subcultures, this study clearly shows the juncture at which the choice is rather free. Far from a deterministic world of human bondage, the politics of these European party members is still essentially a realm of free choice.

Notes

1. "Cleavage Structures, Party Systems, and Voter Alignments: An Introduction," in Seymour M. Lipset and Stein Rokkan, eds., *Party Systems and Voter Alignments: Crossnational Perspectives*, New York: Free Press, 1967, pp. 4–5, 30–33, and 50–56.

2. On the class and status of party members, see also my concluding chapter in this text. There is an increasing literature on party activists beginning with such works as Francesco Alberoni et al., *L'attivista di partito*, Bologna: Il Mulino, 1967; Samuel H. Barnes, *Party Democracy: Politics in an Italian Socialist Federation*, New Haven, Conn.: Yale University Press, 1967; and Giorgio Galli and Alfonso Prandi, *Patterns of Political Participation in Italy*, New Haven, Conn.: Yale University Press, 1970 as well as Galli, *Il bipartitismo imperfetto*, Bologna: Il Mulino, 1968. See, also, Stein Rokkan, *Citizens, Elections, Parties*, New York: McKay, 1970, pp. 367–368 and Kay Lawson, *The Comparative Study of Political Parties*, New York: St. Martin's Press, 1976, pp. 92–111. On West German party members, see esp. Juergen Dittberner and Rolf Ebbighausen, *Parteiensystem in der Legitimationskrise*, Opladen: Westdeutscher Verlag, 1973.

3. Peter H. Merkl, "Party Members and Society in West Germany and Italy," in Rudolf Wildenmann, ed., *Form und Erfahrung, ein Leben fuer die Demokratie, Festschrift fuer F. A. Hermens*, Berlin: Duncker & Humblot, 1976, pp. 153–172 and "Partecipazione ai sindicati e ai partiti in Germania Occidentale e in Italia," *Rivista Italiana di Scienza Politica*, 1 (1971), 326–329.

4. See Merkl, "Ideological Profiles of West German and Italian Socialists and Christian Democrats: A Factor Analysis," in Richard F. Tomasson, ed., *Comparative Social Research*, vol. 2, Greenwich, Conn.: JAI Press, 1979.

5. See the polls in Doxa, *Opinioni politiche degli Italiani alla vigilia delle elezioni*, May 1968, mimeographed, pp. 22–29.

6. Evidently the young Italian rebels never joined the PSU or its successors, whereas their German counterparts joined the SPD and became its *Jusos* only after the survey.

7. See Diederich, "Zur Mitgliederstruktur von CDU und SPD," in Dittberner and Ebbighausen, *Parteiensystem*, pp. 35–55. Diederich's sample was based on respondents who had indicated membership in either of these parties during previous Infas polls as well as further party members suggested by these respondents, for a total of 1,046. A pretest of the questionnaire was conducted in Baden-Wuerttemberg.

8. On the first question, dedication to party, for example, the question asked the respondent to identify either with a Mr. Meier (Rossi) who says, "My party is very

important to me. I wish all the members would get involved as much as I am so our cause can succeed," or with a Mr. Mueller (Bianchi) who says, "Sure I am a member and ready to do my share when I am needed. But a person has to have a private life, too." The responses were coded on a seven-point scale ranging from "strongly agrees with Meier-Rossi," "rather agrees with M-R," over "agrees with both," and "rather agrees with Mueller-Bianchi" to "strongly agrees with M-B." The last two categories were "agrees with neither" and "DK, NA." In the cross-tabulations, the Meier-Rossi responses and the Mueller-Bianchi responses form one group each, whereas "agrees with both" is sometimes combined with Meier-Rossi, Mueller-Bianchi, or "agrees with neither," depending on the substance of the juxtaposition. With this question as with most, "agrees with both" was cross-tabulated separately. For Tables 16–8 and 16–19, it was combined with the responses for Meier-Rossi.

9. The relationship between the ideological questions proper and these extra questions was not particularly revealing except for the religiously more tolerant SPD and the more secular CDU members who both favored tolerating the NPD and not recognizing the DDR. Among the topical issue groups, the opponents of the Grand Coalition (presumably the extremes in both parties) were for suppressing the NPD and DDR recognition. See Table 16–34. The cross-tabulation tables on all the ideological parameters are available on request as soon as the data are no longer being utilized.

10. Among the few very dedicated, in fact, a majority either admits they never attend or responds with "don't know."

11. The PCI members, by way of contrast, have a high sense of dedication to their party and its work. See esp. Robert D. Putnam, "The Italian Communist Politician," in Donald L. M. Blackmer and Sidney Tarrow, eds., *Communism in Italy and France*, Princeton, N.J.: Princeton University Press, 1973, pp. 177–178. Only about 10–15% of PCI members are activists.

12. The dichotomy was between "In this society everybody only thinks of himself—if you are not on your toes, people take advantage of you and step all over you" and "Not true—most people you meet are basically good and can be trusted." See, also, the formulations of Gabriel Almond and Sidney Verba in *The Civic Culture*, Princeton, N.J.: Princeton University Press, 1963, pp. 266–273 and the work of Morris Rosenberg in "Misanthropy and Political Ideology," *American Sociological Review*, 21 (Dec. 1956), 690–695 and "Misanthropy and Attitudes Toward International Affairs," *Journal of Conflict Resolution*, 1 (1957), 340–345.

13. Almond and Verba, *The Civic Culture*, pp. 265–269.

14. However, these small communities are also the place where many distrustful Socialists tend to live.

15. The high anxiety level of independent businessmen or artisans has often been commented on in the social science literature, often together with "aggressiveness." Social distrust would seem to fit in well with these characteristics.

16. Forty-one of the 102 DC respondents and 58 of the 113 PSU respondents have no other memberships save the party and for some (DC, 61; PSU, 68) the trade unions. See also this writer's "Party Members and Society in West Germany and Italy," pp. 153–173, and Diederich, pp. 44–45.

17. Table 16–4 also contains chi square (X^2) and Kendall's Q indices of the strength and significance of the relationships of each two-by-two table. Q values above $\pm.450$ and X^2 of 2.706 and more are emphasized to indicate strong nonrandom relationships. The number of asterisks marks degrees of strength.

18. Here the dichotomy was between "People here are so egotistical that they will not cooperate voluntarily in politics. Hence you need a man with sufficient authority to make them cooperate and toe the line" and "In a modern society you have to let people do as they please as long as they do not harm each other. (In Germany only: A strong man has no place here.) The difference in the German version was suggested by Infas with a view to the contemporary discussions about leaders such as Adenauer and Strauss or Herbert Wehner and Helmut Schmidt. The results showed this writer's fear of "overloading the dice" to be groundless.

19. See Putnam, pp. 180–182.

20. The dichotomy was between "Whenever I think of the state and what it could do for us, I visualize all these petty little bureaucrats at their little desks full of paper while they are thinking only of when they can go home, or of their next vacations" and "Of course there are petty and lazy bureaucrats, but the majority are men of competence and the goodwill to help the people." The German version of the first alternative is less picturesque and speaks of the "many petty civil servants who are supposed to be overworked and really do so little." Thus it does not focus only on desk jobs but includes the other kinds of civil servants who often belong to the SPD or at least to the trade unions (OeTV).

21. A subtle change in meaning occurred when the German polling institute changed the Italian "onesto e capace" to "men of integrity" and slipped in "politicians of your own party" in place of "politicians."

22. The dichotomy was, on the one hand, between "The social system of the Federal Republic is still full of injustice and a person can break through only under exceptional circumstances" (only for SPD) and "Life in Italy is unjust to those born in poverty and the well-to-do always squash any chance of poor people to get ahead" (only for PSU), and for all respondents, "Things are different now. If a person is able and willing to work hard, he can get ahead regardless of his origins." The Christian Democrats of both countries were given as their first alternative "A well-ordered society also includes social classes of which each makes its own contribution to the common good. Making everybody equal is contrary to human nature." This bifurcation in the question was designed to catch the Catholic conservative stance.

23. The dichotomy for the Socialists was between "In the last decade (Germany: Since the currency reform) there has taken place here an enormous economic development. The time may be near when rising prosperity will permit even the last citizen a dignified life without exploitation" and "It is true that there has been much development; but only the capitalists have profited from it. Only drastic political changes can free our lives of oppression." For the Christian Democrats it was between "Our economic development since the end of the war clearly shows that one can spread prosperity without socialistic state interventions into the economy" and "As Christians and democrats, it is far more important to us to contribute to the solution of social problems than to protect the economy from state intervention." The purpose of the bifurcation in this question was to catch the rather different lines of issues within the two parties.

24. In the PSU, the cohorts under 25 by themselves still incline to the pessimistic view of social mobility which may well reflect their youthful frustration with unemployment and Italian gerontocracy.

25. For the Socialists the dichotomy was between "In this country the churches still have too much influence. The clergy opposes so many political, social and cultural reforms" and "I don't approve of clericalism either, but we in the party must be careful not to offend people's religious feelings or infringe upon their religious freedoms." For the Christian Democrats it was "Modern society has abandoned the faith of our fathers. In these difficult times, we should pay more attention to the moral counsel of the church" and "Christian Democrats in the party and in the government can follow their Christian principles without giving the church direct influence on politics or culture." The issue obviously calls for formulations that will show up the divisions within each party.

26. The alternative for SPD and CDU was between "It was madness for our party to enter a grand coalition with the SPD (or CDU). Our alliance with the SPD (or CDU), which has completely different goals, may cost us our political profile" and "The Grand Coalition has its advantages for our party. Now we can finally tackle important legislative tasks and reforms for which the voters will give us credit." For PSU and DC, it was between "We must not break off our collaboration with the PCI (DC: Liberals) for the dubious cooperation of the DC (or PSU). The social problems of Italy can not be solved with compromises with the conservative parties (DC: Those who want revolution) but must be confronted by the parties of the left (DC: Of center and right wing) together" and "The PSU (or DC) did well not to collaborate with the PCI (DC, PLI) and to form a government with the DC (or PSU). Now the moderate forces in Italy can achieve advances in social reforms and progress. Socialist participation in the government makes more sense than staying in the opposition for so many years."

27. This strong support for the coalition among the PSU cannot be explained away with the socioeconomic bias of the sample. PSU respondents of manual occupations tend to support the coalition with the DC, whereas those of nonmanual occupations would rather have remained in league with the PCI.

28. The choice of all respondents was between "The American intervention in Vietnam is an unjust war by which American colonialism tries to prevent the self-determination of the people of Vietnam" and "I don't agree with the bombing of North Vietnam either, but we must remember that, if we let the Communists take over South Vietnam, they will go on to take over most countries of Asia, Africa, and Latin America (in Germany only: Vietnam is the general rehearsal for the seizure of power in all developing areas)."

29. The results appeared in *Oggi* in May 1968 and can be found in greater detail in Doxa, *Alla Vigilia delle Elezioni 1968*, mimeographed.

30. The alternatives were "I am still hoping that the Common Market will turn into a European federation (Germany) which can later on be enlarged with the inclusion of Great Britain (Italy. Such a federation would be of great benefit to Italy)" and "Whether we keep our national sovereignty in tact or collaborate with the European countries, the main thing is to keep out the interference of non-European powers such as the United States or the Soviet Union." This juxtaposition avoids tackling the issues head on and instead stresses a difference in emphasis.

31. From the cross-tabulations with the other issues, the sworn enemies of the NPD are slightly more DDAA, on the ideological issues more mobility minded but radical and anticlerical, and on the topical issues somewhat more anticoalition and anti-Vietnam (though pro-European) than those who would tolerate the NPD. This record clearly adds up to a slightly more radical position.

32. The choice was between "If we don't recognize the DDR, we are closing our eyes to reality. It has been there now for 20 years. Besides, recognition might make it possible to improve the relationship between the two states in many ways" and "Recognition would mean that we bury all hopes for reunification once and for all. And how do we know we could achieve anything with negotiations after recognition?"

33. The choice was between "The NPD must disappear under all circumstances. If the Federal Constitutional Court does not outlaw it, we must change the electoral law accordingly" and "As long as the NPD does not act contrary to the Constitution, every citizen has the democratic right to identify with the aims of this party."

34. See Chapter 1, pp. 50.

35. On the APO, see esp. Kurt L. Shell, "Extra-Parliamentary Opposition in Postwar Germany," *Comparative Politics*, 2 (1970), 653–680. Like other extreme left movements, the APO tended to attack SPD officeholders far more ferociously than the CDU or the far right.

36. See, also, the factor analysis of these data (but not of those on the NPD, DDR, and APO) in Merkl, "Ideological Profiles of West German and Italian Socialists and Christian Democrats: A Factor Analysis."

37. Only regarding the APO, a triple division into those who would treat the rebels with understanding, those insisting on law and authority, and the violent responses would clearly have been more revealing.

CHAPTER 17

MAPPING PARTY COMPETITION

Sten Sparre Nilson

Downsian Spatial Models

ANTHONY DOWNS, in his seminal *Economic Theory of Democracy*, speaks about different forms of two-party competition. An election, he says, is "a judgment passed upon the record of the incumbent party."[1] When the opposition's platform differs from that of the incumbent party, this judgment "expresses the voters' choice between the future projections of these two policy sets." But it is no longer so if nothing differentiates one party from the other. In this case, the judgment of citizens "expresses whether they rate the incumbents' record as good or bad according to some abstract standard."[2] Downs does not indicate clearly the nature of this standard, but perhaps certain inferences are permissible.

He presents his readers with a spatial model. The positions of voters and parties are denoted by points along a line—citizens vote for the party nearest to their own position. Downs mentions as an example the positions taken with regard to the question, How much government intervention in the economy should there be?[3] In the introduction to his book, he has made the general assumption that the citizen is a rational "political man," who approaches every situation with one eye on the gains to be had, the other eye on costs, and a delicate ability to balance them.[4] This would seem to imply, with regard to government intervention in the economy, that voters want the benefits of intervention to outweigh the costs, and preferably to outweigh them as much as possible. It is conceivable, moreover, that the magnitude of such costs and benefits could be measured empirically in some cases. If so, a spatial representation based on empirical data could be given of a situation in which voters compared the positions of two parties and also of a situation in which they simply reacted to the government's record.

Suppose that two such situations converge, that is, that after formerly taking different positions the parties start approaching one another. Downs illustrates such a case with the aid of a spatial model in which citizens are distributed unimodally along the political spectrum.[5] Both parties aim at maximizing the number of votes. Under certain conditions (of single-peaked preferences, etc.) they will be forced through competition to end by advocating the median voter's favourite policy, which is also found satisfactory by a majority of the electorate. When this has come about, the political system has reached a stable state of equilibrium.

In his model Downs indicates the equilibrium position with the aid of the figure 50, placed at a point exactly in the middle of the political scale. The figure does not denote an empirical magnitude; it has been chosen in order to express in symbolic form the idea of the median voter finding himself midway between the two extremes of the spectrum, which are marked 0 and 100, respectively, while the quartiles are marked 25 and 75.

While copying this Downsian model in my Figure 17–1, I have changed the notation to suggest that it might be possible to relate the model to empirically ascertainable magnitudes. These are meant to represent the costs and benefits of government intervention. It is assumed that the intervention takes the form of measures designed to reduce unemployment, the cost of which is an increased rate of inflation. If the number of unemployed is brought down to 175,000, the result is a 7.0% annual rise in the level of prices. If, on the other hand, the annual rate of inflation is brought down to 3.5%, unemployment rises to 325,000 (first and third quartiles, respectively). An unemployment level of 225,000 corresponds to a 5.0% annual rate of increase in prices (central

Figure 17-1.

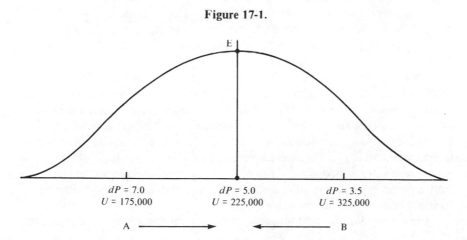

position E). In a unimodal two-party situation, both parties will pursue a policy of keeping the rate of inflation and unemployment at this level, and political equilibrium will obtain.

Political Indifference Maps

The figures just given correspond roughly with British data from the 1960s, which are presented in an article on "Political Economy" published in 1970 by C. A. E. Goodhart and R. J. Bhansali.[6] Starting from the theory of Anthony Downs, they go on to draw an indifference map (copied here in Figure 17–2) as an alternative to the Downsian type of graphic figure. They refer to the map when they describe one rather special political situation. It seems to me, however, that this kind of graphic model is suitable for illustrating a number of phenomena connected with party competition.

Goodhart and Bhansali posit that there exists, within the economy of a given country, a stable functional relationship of the kind known among economists as a Phillips curve, a relationship such that $dP = f(U)$, that is, that the rate of inflation is a function of the level of unemployment within the economy. The diagonal straight lines on the map, the public indifference lines, are supposed to indicate the reactions of the electorate by showing those combinations of inflation and unemployment levels that will result in the same lead for the government or the opposition. If the curve $dP = f(U)$ does not touch the zero lead indifference line, then no government can be viable in the long run, because it would be impossible structurally for the government of the day to establish that combination of high employment and stable prices which would induce the electorate to reelect it. The indifference lines marked +20%, +10%, +5%, 0, −5%, and so on indicate various combinations of policy measures, the implementation of which will result either in a lead for the governing party at the subsequent election (for instance, a 5% lead is represented by the line marked +5%), or a tie, that is, an equality in the number of votes cast for government and opposition (line marked zero), or a lead for the opposition, entailing a change of government (a 5% lead: line marked −5%).

It will be seen in Figure 17–2 that the Phillips curve and the zero lead indifference line intersect twice. On the map there is a hatched area within these two lines. According to Goodhart and Bhansali, any point in the hatched area denotes a situation in which the government can "organize the economy of the country so as to maintain power"; therefore, they speak about it as an "area of political viability."[7] But the situation referred to seems to be a rather special one. Apparently, Goodhart and Bhansali assume that the opposition is without influence on voters, and such a state of affairs will scarcely last very long, except under special circumstances.

Suppose that the incumbent party chooses to implement a policy entailing a

Figure 17-2.

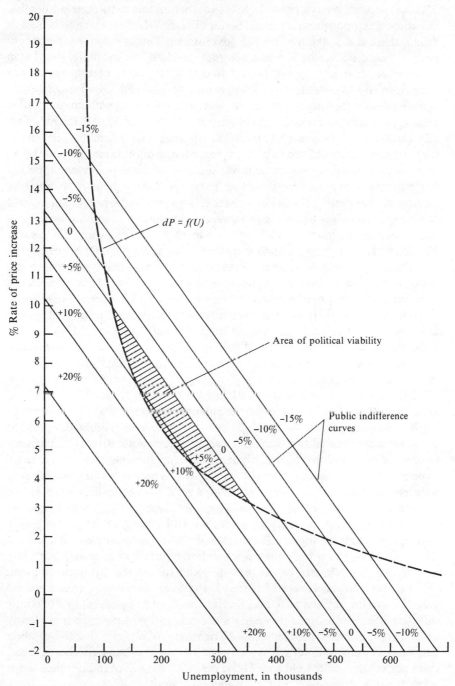

Reprinted with permission from *Political Studies,* vol. 18 (1970), p. 84.

yearly rise in prices of no more than about 3.5%, which means that some 350,000 persons are out of work. Most voters find this to be quite a tolerable situation. The opposition offers no better choice. When an election is held at time t_0 there is a 3–4% lead for the government. Voters judge the incumbent party's record according to some abstract standard, for example, the slogan "You never had it so good." They find that the costs of this policy are outweighed by its benefits. But the opposition party—call it A—is not likely to remain passive for long. At the next election it comes up with an alternative policy, promising to reduce unemployment to a level of some 175,000. This will entail an inflation rate of about 7% per year, but, as can be seen in the diagram, the benefits of such a policy is regarded as outweighing its costs by an even larger majority of voters than was the case with the policy combination implemented previously by the other party, B. Consequently, A wins the election held at time t_1. B still has a chance, however. In the next election, held at time t_2, it promises to cut the inflation rate to about 5% without increasing unemployment by more than 50,000, to a level of 225,000. Party B wins this election and proceeds to the implementation of its new policy. Only now does it succeed in organizing the economy of the country so as to maintain power—the opposition is unable to offer a better alternative. The point of equilibrium has been reached. This is illustrated in Figure 17–3, which corresponds to the Downsian Figure 17–1. The various phases through which the political system has passed are indicated in a manner somewhat more precise in Figure 17–3 than was the case in Figure 17–1. The diagram shows what economists term a "cobweb" of arrows, which forms a narrowing spiral and finally comes to a halt at the equilibrium point. In other respects Figure 17–3 is identical with Figure 17–2 (except that there is no hatched "area of political viability"; instead, the zero lead line has been dotted for the sake of clarity).

By introducing some further slight changes, we can use similar diagrams to illustrate other possibilities, such as a general rise in voter demands. The very process of party competition easily leads to a heightening of the electorate's expectations. In terms of the indifference map this means that the whole set of indifference lines moves downward, in a southwesterly direction.[8] If the movement goes no further than indicated in Figure 17–4, there is still an equilibrium point. A majority of voters are still willing—though just barely willing now—to settle for an inflation rate of 5% and an unemployment level of 225,000 in case this is the policy combination offered by the parties. Anthony Downs indicated in his figure that it would be offered by both of them.

We could ask, however, if Figure 17–1 does not represent a rather special case. Downs himself seems to take this into account as a possibility. He points out that often parties in a two-party system do present more or less clearly divergent programs to the electorate.[9] The reason is, among other things, their fear that extremist splinter parties may otherwise come into existence. Downs does not enlarge on the subject. However, with the aid of indifference maps some possible consequences can be demonstrated.

Figure 17-3.

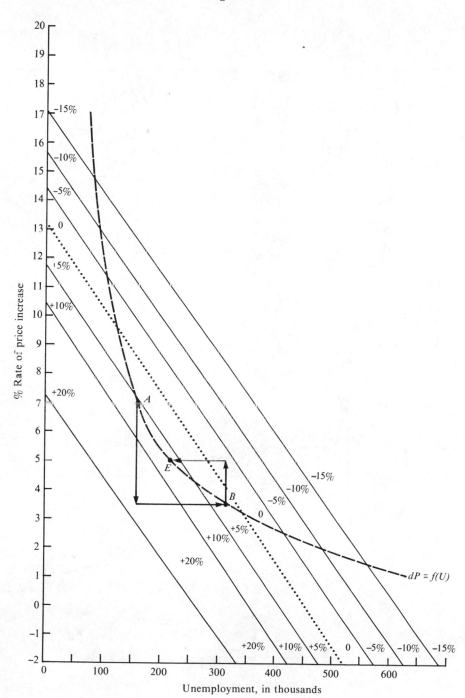

Figure 17-4.

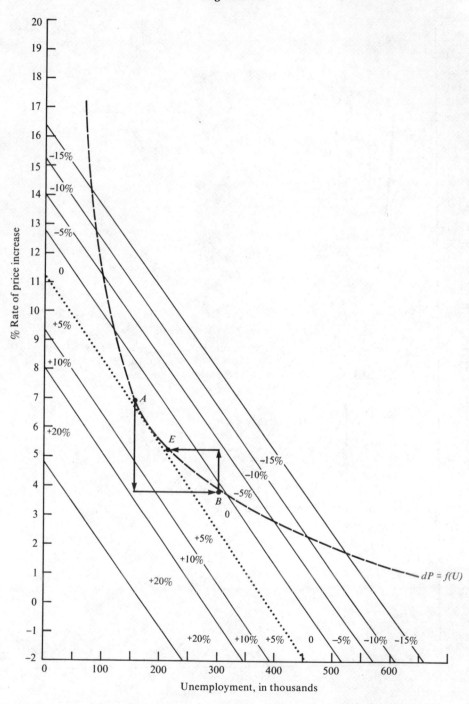

% Rate of price increase

Unemployment, in thousands

Suppose that voters' preferences are as indicated by the indifference lines in Figure 17–4. There is the possibility of an equilibrium. Both parties, however, insist on maintaining distinct positions on either side of the equilibrium point: A's program calls for the reduction of unemployment to a level of 175,000, which will entail a 7% inflation rate, whereas B's aims at half that rate, which means a level of unemployment of 325,000. (Goodhart and Bhansali remark at one point that the avoidance of inflation and the maintenance of a high level of employment can be regarded as conflicting interests of the bourgeoisie and the working class, respectively. If so, if seems not unreasonable to assume that two parties such as Labour and the Conservatives in Britain will favor different policy combinations, and some facts which point in that direction are cited by Goodhart and Bhansali.)[10]

In a case such as this, voters in the middle do not find their preferred position being taken either by party A or by party B. On the contrary, neither party is especially appealing to the undecided voters who are equally averse to inflation and unemployment. These crucial voters remain unsatisfied. Although a choice is offered to them, it is only a choice between two evils. The probable consequence is an increased instability in the political system, but not necessarily a breakdown.

Voters in the middle will give their support to whichever of the two alternatives appears to them as the lesser evil. But their views in this respect are hardly immutable. Full employment can be obtained only through a sharp rise in the general price level, and, while the left is in favor of combating unemployment at almost *any* cost, the right is committed to maintaining as far as possible a *stable* level of prices. Voters in the middle will let their choice be determined at any time by what their experience was during the period preceding an election. This means that the preferences of the electorate will shift periodically. After a period of rapidly rising prices, independent voters' dislike of inflation will be stronger than their dislike of unemployment, so they will turn from the inflationist to the deflationist party. But, when unemployment has increased for a while, during a period of rightist rule and price stabilization, the evils of deflation will loom large. The floating vote will shift to the left once more, returning the inflationist party to power. And so on. The system never comes to rest, it continues moving back and forth, but its movement is being kept within certain limits. In a sense it can be called a homeostatic system.[11] And its mode of functioning can be illustrated with the aid of indifference maps. The arrows in Figure 17–5 indicate roughly the movements of the system; but Figures 17–6 and 17–7 serve to illustrate more precisely what happens.

Both parties, under pressure from zealots, stick to their positions on either side of the median voter. When party A is the incumbent, it pursues an expansionist policy which leads to severe inflation. As a consequence A will lose in popularity. Party B sticks to a deflationary program which caused it to

Figure 17-5.

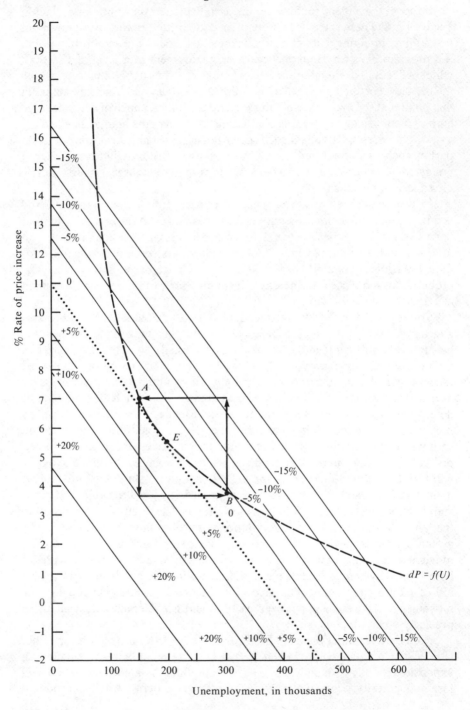

Unemployment, in thousands

Figure 17-6.

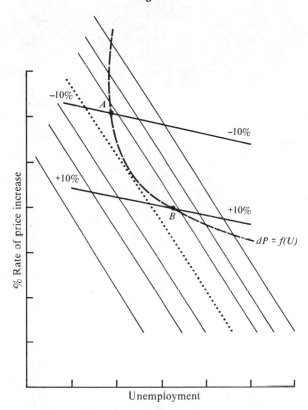

lose the preceding election. But after experiencing an inflationary process many voters come to think of deflation as the lesser evil. They are now willing to accept a significantly greater risk of unemployment than before, in return for a low rate of price increase. In other words, there is a *change in the slope* of the indifference lines. The new lines are less steeply inclined than the original ones. (For the sake of simplicity, only the new −10% and +10% lead lines have been drawn on the map in Figure 17–6.) As a consequence of the change in voters' tastes, party *B* wins the election on its deflationary program.[12] However, after a time voters develop a strong distaste for restrictionist monetary measures. Another shift in the slope of the indifference lines takes place, this time in the opposite direction (Figure 17–7). Now they become steeper than they were originally, so steep indeed that the inflationist party *A* is returned with a comfortable majority. And so the cycle starts over again. There is a pendulum movement, the political system being kept in a process of continuous, regular swings, yet staying all the while within definite limits as a result of voters' turning now to an inflationist, now to a deflationist party.

Figure 17-7.

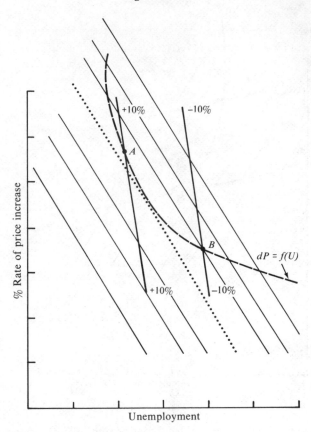

A Note on Assumptions

A movement such as the one just described can go on indefinitely, provided that the assumptions made continue to hold good. But there is no guarantee that they will. Economic relations may change, affecting the form of the Phillips curve, or displacing it. Or else there may be a change in the indifference lines, that is, in the reaction pattern of the electorate. A change in party reactions is also possible.

If one party chooses to take its position at the equilibrium point, the situation described in Figures 17–5, 17–6, and 17–7 will change into that indicated in Figure 17–4 (and in the Downsian Figure 17–1). The political system finds itself in equilibrium—but only for as long as economic conditions remain unchanged. If, for example, the Phillips curve is displaced upward, in a northeasterly direction, the political equilibrium will be destroyed. It will not be possible to obtain a lasting majority in support of any feasible policy combination. Voters become more or less ungovernable. Perhaps in the end the two-party system is replaced by a multiparty pattern, unless, on the other hand, the set of indifference lines shifts upward along with the Phillips curve, which means that voters are willing to settle for a higher rate of inflation and/or a greater amount of unemployment than before. A mood of resignation then permeates the electorate. Many different outcomes are conceivable, depending on the specific assumptions that we choose to make.

There is also the question of a more basic kind of assumption. Anthony Downs indicates what he regards as two main types of party competition.[13] The opposition party can try to defeat the government by creating a coalition of minorities through a combination of positions in different policy areas (agricultural prices, civil rights for blacks, etc.). Or it can try to win by taking a stand on some issue of importance to a majority of voters. In actual politics both kinds of strategy are found, often at one and the same time. For example, it has been said of the Democratic candidate in the 1976 American presidential election that not only did he appeal to different minorities on certain special issues, but he also had to attend to another problem—voters who were "terrified of unemployment" had to be reconciled with other voters who were "alarmed at inflation."[14]

This raises two questions. First, it appears that indifference maps can be used to illustrate only a rather restricted class of problems, the ones that have to do with party competition along a single dimension of conflict. And, second, it is a question of whether or not voters in such a case of unidimensional competition really do perform the kind of balancing of costs and benefits which Anthony Downs assumes. Some would argue that the electorate does not behave that way, at least not in the case of an issue such as the one we have considered. It has been contended that voters want to eat their cake and still have it, they desire full employment as well as stable prices, refusing to see that there can be a trade-off involved.[15] The argument is probably somewhat exaggerated. On the other hand, Goodhart and Bhansali declared the trade-off between inflation and unemployment to be the main theme of British politics. This was claiming too much for the analysis which they presented along with their indifference map.[16]

The map was designed for a rather special one-dimensional two-party situation. It can scarcely be employed as a general model of party competition. But perhaps it can be used to illustrate certain specific situations in which more than one dimension of conflict and more than two parties are involved.

A Two-Dimensional Model?

In conclusion just a tentative sketch can be drawn of the possible use of an indifference map in a multiparty situation. Consider the case of the Third

French Republic. Its many parties and their adherents could be divided roughly into three groups, rightist, centrist, and leftist, the right being capitalistic and clerical, the center capitalistic but anticlerical, and the left socialist and anticlerical. No policy combination was feasible which would produce a lasting majority. In successive periods, centrists governed the country in alliance now with one and now with the other extreme. A center-left coalition could be formed to carry out an anticlerical policy, but, to enlist the support of the left, it was necessary to concede certain economic measures. When the consequences of the latter became manifested after a time, there was a revulsion of feeling among centrist supporters which prepared the ground for a center-right coalition. In the following period, said coalition would implement a decidedly antisocialist economic policy, but, after a while, certain clerical measures were also carried out, representing the price demanded by the right in return for its support of the government. This led to a movement of protest in the center and a new shift to the left. And so on.

The available empirical data from the period must be characterized as scanty, but in principle a model could be constructed by a procedure similar to the one indicated in Figures 17–5, 17–6, and 17–7. In the French case it would be necessary to have indices measuring variations in clerical cultural policy on the one hand and leftist economic policy on the other. Figure 17–8 is a sketch of such a two-dimensional map, drawn as a counterpart to Figure 17–5. In Figure 17–8 the curve corresponding to the Phillips curve represents the combinations of economic and noneconomic measures which politicians were willing to consider (as indicated, say, by proposals put forward in the Chamber of Deputies). Points A and B indicate those particular combinations which were implemented at one time or another, A representing a leftist package adopted with the support of deputies from the center, B a rightist package adopted with similar support (after a reaction had set in against the former kind of policy among adherents of the center outside the chamber). The repeated movement back and forth between A and B is indicated by arrows. However, the process would have been more properly represented with the aid of two maps, as in Figures 17–6 and 17–7. These would have illustrated one and the other main phase of the process, in the course of which the slope of the public indifference lines became alternately more or less steeply inclined than is the case in Figure 17–8. As drawn in Figure 17–8, the lines can only be said to represent an average (over time) of the shifting actual attitudes of the French public toward its government.

Figure 17–8 has been drawn purely for expository purposes. There is no reason to insert any numerical values along its axes, the available data from the period being far too sketchy. It is possible to refer to certain roll calls and election results, but we have to rest content with a rather impressionistic picture. Its main lines seem clear, however. While a political breakdown was successfully avoided for many decades, there were continuous oscillations during most of the period of the Third Republic. The system never came to rest.

Figure 17-8.

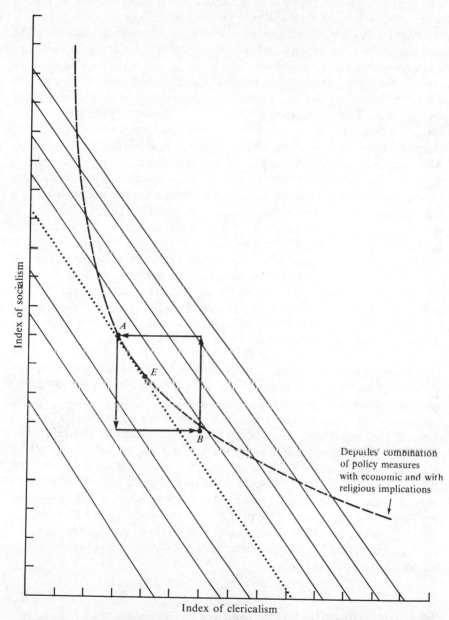

Index of socialism

Deputies' combination of policy measures with economic and with religious implications

Index of clericalism

Compromises which deputies agreed upon became unworkable after a few years, and then efforts to construct new ones must be laboriously undertaken. No such compromise proved to be lasting. But, while the ministerial instability of the Third Republic became proverbial, what was perhaps more important was the fact that fluctuations took place only within strict limits. There were incessant struggles over issues of no major importance. As has been said, governments changed often and policies very little.

It may seem questionable to argue that a one-dimensional model can be compared with a two-dimensional one in the way that I am doing. The idea of a trade-off between inflation and unemployment is perhaps more easily accepted than the suggestion that concessions in the religious and the economic sphere were "traded off" against one another. Yet such seems to have been actually the case in the Third French Republic. If we consider the two things which were feared by the center—socialist encroachment in the economic sphere and clericalist encroachment in the religious sphere—it is true that these are things which represent two different aspects of human existence. But in France there was a pronounced willingness among politicians to trade economic advantages for spiritual gains, and vice versa. This is perhaps not so surprising if we take into consideration the fact that political measures, whether classified as religious or economic, were largely of a symbolic nature. It was considered a not unimportant question for a center politician to decide if he should support or oppose a proposal that Good Friday be celebrated by the navy or that guards of honor should be supplied by the army for civil as well as religious funerals. The left insisted that, because the legislature was not to sit on Ascencion Day, it must not sit on Labor Day (May 1) either. Honoring Labor Day was one of the items which would have to be taken into account in the construction of an index to measure the extent of Socialist influence.

No such index has been constructed, but an author such as André Siegfried has referred to certain roll calls and other data. He speaks about strikingly nomothetic political fluctuations: "un cycle, toujours le même, que depuis cinquante ans nous avons vu se reproduire périodiquement, avec une régularité parfaite."[17] Siegfried's contention is somewhat exaggerated, but it does indicate a characteristic aspect of what went on during the Third Republic. Although political displacements one way or the other were often so small that it is hard to evaluate their significance, such was not always the case. From time to time the Republic did seem to be on the move toward some serious change of policy. Very soon the movement was stopped and reversed, however. As Philip Williams says, the aim of the middle bloc, "equally opposed to clerical reaction and to socialist experiment," was to prevent real change.[18] And it succeeded. Though there were incessant fluctuations, they stayed after all within rather strict limits.

Postscript: Political Dimensions

While referring to the type of situation presented in the first and third sections as one dimensional and the type described in the fourth section as two-dimensional, I made no attempt to define the concept of a political dimension.

It refers to the idea of ranging positions taken on political issues (by voters, legislators, or parties) along a continuum. When the relative positions of the actors are the same on two or more issues, these are often said to belong to the same dimension. For instance, in an article on the Danish party system, Erik Damgaard states that the four main parties—Social Democrats, Radical Liberals, Agrarian Liberals, and Conservatives—were ranged in that order between the two world wars on the left-right dimension.[19] As policy issues belonging to this dimension he mentions social welfare legislation and defense policy. For example, in 1922 a defense committee reported on the reorganization of the Danish defense system; each of the parties presented a proposal. The costs of implementing the four proposals were (in millions of Danish kroner):

Social Democrats	Radical Liberals	Agrarian Liberals	Conservatives
7.5	22.0	40.0	49.0

(Agrarian Liberals and Conservatives had a majority in Parliament between them, and they agreed on a compromise: 44 million.) In the same period there was also another dimension of some importance in Danish politics, however. The Agrarian Liberals and Radical Liberals were strongly in favor of free international trade, to the advantage of agriculture, whereas both the Social Democrats and the Conservatives were more inclined toward protectionist policies, to the benefit of manufacturing industry.

Certainly the latter was a separate dimension, with its own configuration of parties. But it might be argued that social welfare and military defense are such clearly distinct policy areas that we ought to speak of two different dimensions in this case as well. At least there is room for doubt, though it could be said that in such a situation one dimension has been for all practical purposes "fitted into" the other.[20]

Sören Holmberg, who studied the party system of Sweden in the late 1960s, found that the parties represented in the Diet were located as follows on five different issues:[21]

ISSUE	COMMUNISTS	SOCIAL DEMOCRATS	AGRARIANS	LIBERALS	CONSERVATIVES
1. Banks	1.00	1.18	2.44	3.77	4.30
2. Defense	1.00	2.47	3.10	3.75	4.89
3. Farming	1.66	2.76	4.89	3.65	4.33
4. Religion	1.00	1.19	4.10	2.75	3.80
5. Metropolitan areas	1.00	1.75	1.21	1.62	1.66

The issues in question were (1) To what extent should the government control private banks? (2) Should Swedish defense expenditure be increased, maintained at the existing level, or reduced? (3) Should subsidies for agriculture be increased, maintained, or reduced? (4) What should be the character of religious instruction in schools? (5) Should the government try to counteract the tendency toward increasing concentration of population in a few metropolitan areas?

The issue of banking belongs to the classic left-right (or socialist-nonsocialist, socialist-capitalist, socialist-bourgeois) domain. The defense issue could also be classified as left-right because the parties were located in the same relative positions along this line of conflict. But an objection can be raised, just as in the Danish case—defense and banking are two different policy areas.

The issue of farming differed from both of the preceding ones in that the Agrarian party took an extreme position; however, the other two nonsocialist parties were closer to the Agrarians on this issue than were the two socialist parties. Thus it can be said that the basic left-right pattern is still preserved. The farm issue belongs to the left-right dimension, or at least it fits partly into it and does not constitute an entirely separate dimension. The same can be said about the religious issue. It might be argued, however, that the two formed a separate (or semiseparate) rural/urban axis of conflict.

In any case the metropolitan issue belongs undoubtedly to a different dimension altogether. Here we find that Communists and Agrarians stood close to one another and were confronted by Social Democrats, Conservatives, and Liberals.

How about the situations discussed in the first and fourth sections? In the case of the Third French Republic, it might be argued that the economic and the religious dimensions fitted into one another to such an extent as to constitute in practice one single cleavage. But then objections could be raised both with reference to the different nature of the two sets of issues and with reference to the fact that they tended to be salient not at one and the same time but in different periods.

As to inflation and unemployment, it seems reasonable to say that they are only two aspects or components of one dimension. But it could be argued that, because the employment issue tends to be salient in one period and the issue of inflation in another, this case too partakes to some extent of the nature of a two-dimensional political configuration. After all, here, as in the case of the Third French Republic, the alternating changes in salience had as a result periodic changes in the relative distances between the actors.

To conclude, the concept of a dimension in politics is a complex one. It seems advisable that we indicate in any given instance the specific sense in which we use the term (or one of its synonyms, such as cleavage, conflict line, or conflict axis).[22]

Notes

1. Anthony Downs, *An Economic Theory of Democracy*, New York: Harper & Row, 1957, p. 41.

2. Ibid., p. 42.

3. Ibid., p. 116.

4. Ibid., pp. 7–8.

5. Ibid., p. 118.

6. C. A. E. Goodhart and R. J. Bhansali, "Political Economy," *Political Studies*, 18 (1970), 43–106, esp. diagram on p. 84.

7. It might be said that taking up a position *within* the "area of political viability" violates the assumption about the Phillips curve. The latter is said to represent the possible combinations of inflation and unemployment in the society. The answer, however, could be that it represents the *best* possible combination, if the majority of voters are willing to support even a government that does not give them any of the best possible combinations—so much the better for the inefficient government in question (and so much the worse for the inefficient opposition).

8. I have followed Goodhart and Bhansali in drawing straight indifference lines, although indifference curves might seem more realistic. Also, shorter lines, as indicated in Figures 17–6 and 17–7, might seem more realistic than the ones drawn by Goodhart and Bhansali.

9. Downs, op. cit., p. 131, esp. p. 117.

10. Goodhart and Bhansali, op. cit., p. 79.

11. On the notion of a homeostatic system, see Brian Barry, *Sociologists, Economists, and Democracy*, London: Collier-Macmillan, 1970, p. 170.

12. Anthony Downs assumed that voters' tastes were fixed, an assumption that gives a certain static quality to his theory. See Downs, op. cit., p. 140.

13. Downs, op. cit., pp. 55ff., esp. pp. 64ff.

14. Philip Williams and Graham Wilson, "The 1976 Election and the American Political System," *Political Studies*, 25 (1977), 198.

15. David Butler and Donald E. Stokes, *Political Change in Britain*, New York: St. Martin's Press, 1969, pp. 390ff. The authors regard the question of inflation versus unemployment as a pure "valence" issue, but they concede that "little is known about the reality of such dimensions to most voters" (p. 391).

16. Goodhart and Bhansali, op. cit. They refer to opinion polls showing the support given to the two major British parties in the 1950s and 1960s. Also, they claim that voters' ratings of the parties was determined mainly by the development of prices and unemployment. But the latter claim is supported only by reference to a few rather leading Gallup poll questions (pp. 45–46, note 3).

17. André Siegfried, *Tableau des partis en France*, Paris: Colin, 1930, p. 126.

18. Philip M. Williams, *Crisis and Compromise*, Hamden, Conn.: Archon Books, 1964, p. 10.

19. Erik Damgaard, "Stability and Change in the Danish Party System over Half a Century," *Scandinavian Political Studies*, 9 (1974), 104, 124.

20. See Ian Budge and Dennis Farlie, *Voting and Party Competition*, London: Wiley, 1977, p. 501. ". . . new cues are fitted into old and seemingly unrelated cleavages (e.g., the extent to which membership of NATO falls in The Netherlands and Norway into old Left-Right, working class-middle class divisions."

21. The method used to measure distances is described by Sören Holmberg in *Riksdagen representerar svenska folket* (*The Diet Represents the Swedish People*), Lund: Studentlitteratur, 1974, with English summary, pp. 377–392.

22. Paul Mosley has presented empirical data to show the alternating changes in saliency of the "price dimension" in Great Britain during recent decades. He also refers to other contributions on the use of political maps. See Mosley, "Images of the 'Floating Voter': Or 'The Political Business Cycle' Revisited," *Political Studies*, 26 (September 1978), 375–394.

PART FOUR

Research Trends and Perspectives

INTRODUCTION TO PART FOUR

Peter H. Merkl

THE ESSAYS IN PART FOUR *differ from those of the preceding part not so much by their subject as by their theoretical import and significance for the study of Western European party systems. Taken together, the seven theoretical essays and research notes open up new research perspectives by changing the ways in which conventional party theory has dealt with party systems.*

In the first essay, Lawrence C. Mayer deals with Otto Kirchheimer's thesis concerning the tendency of some party systems toward aggregation, "one of those impressionistic claims impossible to falsify in any definitive sense." He examines how aggregation has gone down, and fragmentation up, in 17 democratic party systems (including a few outside Europe) between 1965 and 1973. New ethnic parties and issues about the style or quality of life, in particular, contributed to this proliferation of parties where there was supposed to be greater aggregation. Only structural constraints, such as a plurality electoral law, Mayer concludes, could stem the increasing trend toward greater pluralism in the representative process in Europe.

In the second essay, Sten Sparre Nilson comes back to the effect of cross-cutting cleavages on a system, a question raised earlier in connection with his description of the Norwegian and Danish party systems. He weighs the evidence of whether cross-cutting cleavages increase or attenuate conflict in a given system and introduces the dimensions of intensity *and* salience *to distinguish the effects of various cleavages. If a sharply polarized cleavage is the more salient line of division, cross-cutting evidently is likely to increase conflict rather than to modify it. A great deal also depends on the*

511

management of conflict by political leaders who can do their share to make it worse or better.

Frank Wilson addresses himself to the question how whole party systems such as that of the Fifth Republic of France and the parties in it undergo major changes. His essay presents a model of party system transformation and tests the role of various causes in bringing about this change. The transformation of the years 1962–1977, still not completed today, was brought on rather suddenly after 17 years during which the French party system had remained more or less in the pre-World War II mold. What were the most important causes of this transformation, socioeconomic changes, institutional change, or changes in political socialization and culture? Wilson concludes that it was the new competitive situation arising from the challenge of the Gaullist presidency under the conditions introduced by the institutional changes of the early 1960s, especially 1962, far more than socioeconomic and politico-cultural trends. Again, the role of political leadership and of conscious efforts at party reform loom large in this explanatory model.

This essay is followed by an exploration, by Zelime Amen Ward, of one of the major contemporary challenges to the party systems of nine of our Western European countries and potentially to others as well. The direct elections to the European Parliament have been variously assessed along a spectrum ranging from a nonevent to the beginning of a revolution in the nature of the nine national party systems. At the first glance, the formation of transnational Christian Democratic, Socialist, and Liberal parties indeed seems to have the makings of a major process of political integration throughout the European community, counterpointed by the announcement of a number of very prominent politicians as candidates for the European parliament. The discomfiture of the Communist parties which cannot seem to get their act together despite decades of "proletarian internationalism" highlights the processes at work. Ward also indicates the support of the political leadership in general for strengthening the transnational ties among kindred parties. On the other hand, she also leaves no doubt about the weakness of these party organizations and the risk of giving up the double mandate which at least has given the European parliamentarians some real leverage with their national governments, parliaments, and parties. One hears of British Labour M.P.s who have hitherto been less than candid with their own constituents about their service in Brussels for fear that the constituents might not approve. When British party candidates now stand for the European parliament only, what will these constituents say? Will it bring out their isolationism or kindle a more realistic appreciation for the consequences and opportunities of membership in that foreign organization across the Channel? Dr. Ward has shown that the eagerness for European integration is substantially lower among the three most recent members of the European community. Even in the older members we are left once more with the vague "permissive consensus" on European integration which hides a great deal of popular ignorance about its particulars, at least until a controversial issue or an election campaign might bring them out.

The next two contributions show another major challenge to European parties from within their systems, in this case to the parties of the Federal Republic of Germany. Jutta Helm describes one aspect of the participational revolution outside the parties there, the "citizen initiatives" or citizen lobbies. Spontaneous, if rather middle-class, grass-roots movements, the citizen lobbies represent a massive uprising of the hitherto rather quiet German citizenry against local governments and especially against an unresponsive bureaucracy. Werner Kaltefleiter places similar phenomena into the context of the second crisis of legitimacy (the first was 1966–1969) of the Bonn Republic. So-called "green lists" of environmentalists are threatening the survival of the third party, the FDP, and thereby the linchpin of the whole party system. If the FDP fails to remain above 5% of the popular vote, the coalition government of SPD and FDP will fall and the opposition parties— the CDU and CSU—will return to power. Worse yet, there have been manifestations of a widespread disillusionment with political parties, a Parteiverdrossenheit, which extends even to the opposition and denies it the customary function of gathering in the bulk of the discontented electorate. There are also polls showing the large potential of a tax-payers revolt à la Denmark in Germany which could unhinge the consensus on the welfare state that hitherto characterized all the major parties of the Federal Republic.

The final essay of this part is a thoughtful note by Stephen L. Fisher on the bias against small parties which pervades most thinking about the alleged decline of parties. All indices of fragmentation, aggregation, or political instability, including the ones used in this volume, have an obvious slant in favor of the large parties even where the latter may be bent on confrontation and polarization. To speak of a "decline of parties" thus is really meant to bewail only the decline of one or more major parties while minor parties of the same system are very likely flourishing more than ever.

The last essay of this book, by the editor, is not a part of Part Four, but also is not exactly a conclusion in the customary sense. It was added mainly to bring together and compare party materials that have not received sufficient attention so far from students of parties and party systems. Information on the social composition of the membership of major European parties and whole party systems is becoming more available now and promises to shed more light on what still remains, to this day, a key element of the representative process in all democracies.

CHAPTER 18

A NOTE ON THE AGGREGATION OF PARTY SYSTEMS

Lawrence Mayer

THE END OF IDEOLOGY THESIS (Lipset, 1963; Bell, 1960) has become a well-established tradition among social scientists despite some notable dissenting views (LaPalombara, 1966). This thesis posits the decline in the great, comprehensive thought systems because of the diminishing relevance of such thought sytems to the issues of the coming postindustrial world.

Concomitant with the end of ideology thesis is Otto Kirchheimer's thesis concerning the aggregation of western party systems (Kirchheimer, 1966). Kirchheimer's oft-cited essay has now virtually reached the status of conventional wisdom in comparative politics. Essentially, his thesis is that parties have abandoned the traditional ideologies that have heretofore served as their programmatic base. They have become ideologically diffuse in seeking an ever wider and necessarily more variegated base of electoral support. The development of such parties of mass integration, labeled "catchall parties" by Kirchheimer, entails a significant change in party *systems* (the pattern of competition and interaction among parties) as implied by the title of his essay, "The Transformation of Western European Party Systems." This transformation essentially involves an aggregation of such party systems—fewer parties and major parties having a larger share of the seats in the legislature (Kirchheimer, 1966). It is, after all, doctrinal specificity that restricts the potential clientele of parties with a narrow electoral base. Ideological diffuseness seems to be a necessary if not sufficient precondition of aggregation. Therefore, the converse process, the fragmentation of the party system

515

may be grounds for suspicion that the relevance of rigid and narrow principle for party politics has not declined as much as the end of ideologists assert.

The Kirchheimer thesis, that the deideologized, expediential parties have a broader electoral base resulting in an aggregated party system, applies logically to those democracies in which structural arrangements permit the fragmentation of the party system. Specifically, in Anglo-American democracies, a single-member district plurality electoral system constitutes a structural impediment to the formal expression in the party system of political and social fragmentation. Clearly, the proportional electoral systems only permit party system fragmentation; they do not cause it. Nevertheless, aggregation becomes a meaningful concept only when its converse, fragmentation, is a possible alternative.

Accordingly, this paper examines the aggregation thesis in those relatively westernized democracies with some form of electoral system that *permits* the proliferation of parties. The data consist of the number of parties in each country holding at least one seat in the lower houses of their respective legislatures and the number of seats held by each of these parties at two points in time, September 1965 and September 1973. A complete listing of the relative strengths of the parties of the world may be found in the *Encyclopaedia Britannica Book of the Year* for these years.

It should be noted that Kirchheimer does not assert a statistically measurable party system aggregation as a general principle, even in western democracies. Rather, he confines himself to an assertion of a tendency of unspecified scope buttressed by the discussion of a few illustrative examples. It is one of those impressionistic claims impossible to falsify in any definitive sense.

Nonetheless, if the transformation of western party systems is to be taken seriously as even a descriptive generalization, a degree of aggregation should be observable in the class of nations examined here. Further, such an expected aggregation appears to be a logical entailment of the end of ideology thesis.

Party aggregation may be measured by an index developed in Chapter 13. This index posits two dimensions to the concept: the number of parties and the relative strength of government parties in terms of percentage of seats held in the lower house. The index is justified on logical grounds (face validity) and in terms of predictive validity. The first criterion is essentially a judgmental, intuitive one. The second also involves a judgment, namely, that the concept of party system aggregation has largely been invoked to account for variations in cabinet stability in parliamentary democracies.

On the impressionistic level, it is intuitively plausible that, other things being equal, a party system with many parties better fits what is commonly understood by the term fragmented than a system with fewer parties. Further, it has been suggested that, *ceteris paribus*, the number of parties is related to cabinet stability (Hermens, 1951; Milnor, 1959). Yet, it seems equally apparent that the number of parties in and of itself constitutes an inadequate conception of aggregation or explanation of cabinet stability. For example, small splinter parties do not generally change the essential character of the party system as a whole. Arian and Barnes have shown how a dominant party can provide a stable government despite weak coalition partners or a fragmented opposition (Arian and Barnes, 1974). This dominant party thesis as an explanation of cabinet stability would logically apply to the government coalition; a fragmented opposition would be less of a destabilizing force than a strong, cohesive opposition. It seems intuitively reasonable to conclude that the relative size of the strongest party in the government is another important dimension in a conception of party aggregation.

Such an index would have an advantage over Douglas Rae's oft-cited index of party "fractionalization" (Rae, 1968). Although Rae's index is a continuous variable that avoids the simplistic artificiality of a two- and multiparty categorization, his index does not distinguish between the fragmentation of the government and of the opposition. For example, according to Rae's index, Israel had one of the most highly fractionalized party systems: yet, the domination of its Labor party until 1977 has rendered Israel remarkably stable.

Thus, an index of party aggregation is calculated as $A = 100(S/L)/P$, where $A =$ the aggregation index, $S =$ the seats held by the largest party in the government coalition, $L =$ the total number of seats in the lower house of the legislature, and $P =$ the number of parties holding at least one seat in that house. The higher the score, the more aggregated the party system.

This index was found to correlate far more strongly with a measure of cabinet stability than in any previous attempt to explain such stability (e.g., Taylor and Herman, 1971). Therefore, the measure of aggregation used here possesses predictive as well as face validity. If the party systems of parliamentary democracies were to fragment significantly, this would constitute concern for the subsequent cabinet stability of such nations.

The aggregation index is presented for each of the 18 nations under consideration for each of the two time periods in Table 18–1. It can be seen at a glance that, in 17 of the 18 nations, the aggregation index *lowered* between the two points in time, a result that seems to refute any reasonable interpretation of the Kirchheimer thesis. One may even have a little less confidence in the validity of the concomitant deideologization assumptions that underlie his aggregation thesis. Furthermore, a t test of the difference between the mean aggregation levels during the two time periods yields a critical value of 1.73, a value that is on the border line of statistical significance at the .05 level for the one-tailed test. In other words, the data provide grounds for positing a tendency of such party systems to fragment, not to aggregate. One suspects that these tendencies would be more apparent if the data were drawn for the past year, a year that has seen the electoral vulnerability of one apparently dominant party after another (e.g., Sweden, India, Israel, and possibly Italy) and the increasing rise of regional parties of cultural defense.

TABLE 18–1.   Aggregation Indices

	1965	1973
Austria	16.3	16.9
Belgium	7.4	3.9
Denmark	7.2	2.6
Finland	4.8	3.4
France	7.1	3.7
West Germany	16.4	15.4
Iceland	10.0	7.3
India	13.7	6.2
Israel	5.1	4.7
Italy	5.2	4.7
Japan	15.7	9.2
Luxembourg	10.2	9.4
Netherlands	3.3	1.8
Norway	7.5	4.8
Sweden	9.8	8.9
Switzerland	3.3	2.4
Turkey	8.9	5.1
$X =$	9.33	6.81
variance =	20.17	18.133
$t =$	1.73 (a)	

(a) The critical value of t at .05 is 1.734.

These findings would not be significantly altered if one were to rely on the aforementioned and oft cited index of fractionalization developed by Douglas Rae (Rae, 1968). Rae's index measures the conceptual antonym of aggregation; hence, the logical entailment of the Kirchheimer thesis would be a significant lowering of the index in the latter time period. Rae's index may be less reflective of the trends of which we are speaking, however, since it is only sensitive to the relative size of parties in the legislature and not to numbers of parties as such; very small parties do not even register on the fractionalization index. The computing formula for Rae's index (where F = fractionalization) is $F = \Sigma_{i=1}^{m} (1 - t^2)$, where t = proportion of seats held by ith party and m = number of parties.

Table 18–2 shows that the fractionalization index not only did not lower over the eight-year period in question; the index increased in 16 of the 18 nations examined. Furthermore, the increasing fractionalization of the party systems was not far from statistical significance. The value of t for the data using the Rae index is 1.38, which is significant at the .10 level (using a small sample one-tailed difference of means test). Thus, a tentative conclusion that fractionalization may be a more normal trend than aggregation for the foreseeable future in the party systems in question does seem to be supported by the data.

TABLE 18–2. Rae's Fractionalization Indices

	1965	1973
Austria	.548	.549
Belgium	.643	.780
Denmark	.709	.857
Finland	.769	.822
France	.703	.781
West Germany	.581	.573
Iceland	.701	.742
India	.319	.523
Ireland	.604	.613
Israel	.761	.702
Italy	.706	.718
Japan	.355	.628
Luxembourg	.688	.708
Netherlands	.781	.844
Norway	.718	.725
Sweden	.673	.703
Switzerland	.844	.820
Turkey	.689	.700
$X =$	.65511	.7104
variance $=$	.01749	.0095
$t =$	1.38[a]	

[a]The critical value of t at .10 is less than 1.31.

It remains to try to account for these findings. Some substantial portion of the increased fragmentation comes from the rise of new parties with claims or views of reality that cannot be reconciled with those of existing parties. The aforementioned geographically defined parties of cultural defense (e.g., the Volksunie in Belgium, Tyrolean People's party in Italy, etc.) constitute examples of such new parties. Parties representing new interests arising out of new lifestyles (e.g., Democrats '66 in the Netherlands), out of new issues (e.g., Komeito in Japan), or out of perceived threats to old values (e.g., the Evangelical People's party in Switzerland, the Anti-A.E.C. Liberals in Norway) have all contributed to this proliferation.

The greatest threat to aggregated party systems on the horizon, however, may be the apparent increasing electoral vulnerability of elites in modern democracies. This vulnerability may be due to the increasing inability of such elites to produce workable solutions to the problems of their societies. This insusceptibility of problems to amelioration by public policy may be due in turn to the increased complexity of modern society; hence, the vulnerability of elites may be most clearly an attribute of mature industrial societies (Mayer and Burnett, 1977). Yet, the increasing interdependence of the modern world order does not leave less highly industrialized societies (such as India and Turkey) immune from the insoluble social, political, and economic dislocations of the modern world.

The conclusion of this note, then, is a pessimistic one. The imperatives of an increasingly interdependent and complex socioeconomic order are likely to produce an increasing fragmentation of those party systems where structural arrangements permit such fragmentation. (One may wonder what the relative strength of the Scottish and Welsh Nationalist parties in Britain would now be under some form of proportional representation.) Concomitant to this fragmentation is an increasing vulnerability of elites in such systems and a greater potential for cabinet instability.

The observed fragmentation of the party systems under consideration suggests the possibility that the relevance of ideology in general for interparty conflict has not declined; rather, the content of the principles has changed. Cultural and linguistic defense, for example, is not a manifestly more pragmatic and flexible doctrine than the now atavistic *Weltanschauungen* of the nineteenth and early twentieth centuries. The data presented in this note clearly do not support the widespread assumption of a decline in the political relevance of irreconcilable principles. The implications of these findings for the prospect of the peaceful resolution of issues in modern society are not encouraging.

References

ARIAN, ALAN, and BARNES, SAMUEL. "The Dominant Party System: A Neglected Model of Stability," *Journal of Politics,* 36 (August 1974), 592–614.

BELL, DANIEL. *The End of Ideology*, New York: Free Press, 1962.

LAPALOMBARA, JOSEPH. "The Decline of Ideology: A Dissent and Interpretation," *The American Political Science Review*, 60 (March 1963), 5–16.

LIPSET, SEYMOUR. "The End of Ideology," in *Political Man*, Garden City, N.Y.: Doubleday-Anchor, 1963, pp. 439–456.

HERMENS, F. A. *Europe under Democracy or Anarchy*, Notre Dame, Ind.: University of Notre Dame Press, 1951.

KIRCHHEIMER, OTTO. "The Transformation of the Western European Party Systems," in Joseph LaPalombara and Myron Weiner, eds., *Political Parties and Political Development*, Princeton, N.J.: Princeton University Press, 1966, pp. 117–200.

MAYER, LAWRENCE with BURNETT, JOHN. *Politics in Industrial Societies: A Comparative Perspective*, New York: Wiley, 1977.

MILNOR, ANDREW. *Elections and Political Stability*, Boston: Little, Brown, 1964.

RAE, DOUGLAS. "A Note on the Fractionalization of Some European Party Systems," *Comparative Political Studies*, 1 (October 1968), 413–418.

CHAPTER 19

PARTIES, CLEAVAGES, AND THE SHARPNESS OF CONFLICT

Sten Sparre Nilson

THE PARTY SYSTEM OF NORWAY, as described in Chapter 8, is characterized by more than one dimension of conflict. The parties have been arranged according to their stands on different issues, and more than one kind of issue has been of importance during the last few decades. The role of the dimensions has been studied systematically at the level of the voters, and research has also been done at the parliamentary level. But the question of the interplay between leadership and electorate is an intricate one, which makes it desirable to discuss some theoretical questions.

The shifting salience of dimensions constitutes a problematic phenomenon from the point of view of empirical theory. The sociologist Edward Alsworth Ross once enunciated the principle that a society is "sewn together" by its inner cleavages. If it is ridden by several oppositions, he said, there is less danger of its being torn with violence or falling to pieces than if it is split just along one line: ". . . different oppositions in society are like different wave series set upon opposite sides of a lake, which neutralize each other if the crest of one meets the trough of the other. . . ."[1] This was a beautiful and striking metaphor, and it also looked like a plausible hypothesis. Ross, writing in 1920, pointed to the weakness of class conflict in the United States compared with Europe in the years after World War I. Later the same theme was elaborated by others. E. E. Schattschneider, for example, emphasized the role which urban/rural antagonism had played in limiting the importance of sharp conflict between workers and capitalists in America.[2]

In recent years, however, doubts have been expressed about the validity of Ross's basic proposition. Robert A. Dahl, who used to regard bipolarity as a main danger, reversed himself in a paper presented at the meeting of the International Political Science Association in Edinburgh, 1976. In most countries today there exist a number of different lines of cleavage, and the intersection of such lines has produced a pattern of conflictive pluralism. Bipolarity along a cleavage dimension formed by social class tends to exist only in highly homogeneous countries where other differences, as of language, religion, race, or ethnic group are not sufficiently salient to disturb the effects of differences in social class. Ironically for orthodox theory, however, it is precisely such countries which "manage to deal rather easily with conflicts arising from class cleavages," Dahl asserted.[3] An author like Gordon Smith, in his *Politics in Western Europe*, reached a similar conclusion. He argues that in countries where there is "a simple polarization around one variable, social class," only a "muted" antagonism will result.[4]

It can be asked whether it is possible to reconcile the different points of view. I would indicate the following proposition: *The cross-cutting of cleavage lines can have the effect of either moderating or intensifying conflict, depending on whether a mildly or a sharply polarized dimension constitutes the more salient cleavage line.*

The concepts used in the proposition need to be defined in operational terms, but reference can be made to authors who have provided at least certain tentative definitions. Douglas Rae and Michael Taylor, in their *Analysis of Political Cleavages*, define a cleavage as a division of a community into two different sets of individuals, whereas cross-cutting is "the extent to which individuals who are in the same group on one cleavage are in different groups on the other cleavage."[5] Rae and Taylor also touch on the question of *intensity* of conflict, but declare it to be outside the scope of their monograph.[6] It has been discussed by others, however. E. E. Schattschneider regards it as a great weakness in E. A. Ross's hypothesis that the latter writes as if all cleavages were equally important. They are not. People are seldom equally excited about all issues, says Schattschneider, and it seems reasonable to suppose that the more intense conflicts are likely to displace the less intense.[7] But this is not always what happens. It is sometimes possible for politicians to set the agenda in such a way that they actually determine what kind of issues will become politically relevant.

Alvin Rabushka and Kenneth A. Shepsle have discussed the matter more fully in their *Politics in Plural Societies: A Theory of Democratic Instability*.[8] They distinguish between intensity and salience. A less intense cleavage will take precedence over a more intense one if the former is more *salient* than the latter. And salience in turn depends on the political entrepreneur, "the person who manipulates natural social cleavages, who . . . exploits, uses, and suppresses conflict." Rabushka and Shepsle add, however, that salience does not depend on the politician alone, as he does not have a free hand in the activation of social cleavages. And they end by pointing out the desirability of a further study of the interplay of forces which determines the increasing or decreasing political salience of a given cleavage. In particular, a theory of political entrepreneurship is needed.

As for tendencies in the contemporary world, Rabushka and Shepsle are pessimistic; they do not believe that political entrepreneurs have much chance of suppressing conflict, and they see increasing instability as the future trend. An author like Gordon Smith, on the other hand, optimistically regards the dampening of conflict as the main trend, at least in the Western World. A similar point of view was expressed by Otto Kirchheimer when he argued that the evolution in Western Europe is unmistakably in the direction of pragmatic and moderate "catchall" parties.[9]

Three of the research notes contained in this volume contribute to the discussion. Stephen Fisher, who thinks that there can easily be too much pragmatism in politics, welcomes the bringing of controversial issues before the public. An increase in the sharpness of policy alternatives will do no more, he seems to believe, than provide voters with the opportunity of making a meaningful choice. Consequently, he also welcomes the resurgence of cross-cutting cleavages, thinking that they will tend to increase the sharpness of conflict.[10]

Lawrence Mayer's two papers are based on value premises different from those of Fisher. Mayer notes the recent resurgence of cultural and linguistic movements cutting across the left-right cleavage line, and the resulting increase in the sharpness of conflict. In other words, he too questions Otto Kirchheimer's assumption of a decline in the political relevance of irreconcilable principles. Unlike Fisher, Mayer values pragmatism highly and looks on the tendency of fragmentation and increasing conflict as a great danger for the future.[11] But however different their value premises, they both seem to support the proposition that cross-cutting cleavages, far from moderating conflict, have the opposite effect of sharpening it.

Lawrence Mayer in addition presents indices of party aggregation which show an increasing fragmentation between 1965 and 1973 in 17 different countries. Mayer contends that there was a measurable tendency in the direction of fragmentation, or conflictive pluralism, to use the term quoted earlier from Robert A. Dahl. But it is not quite clear in what way fragmentation is related to sharpness of conflict. Mayer draws a distinction between aggregation of the governing coalition and of the opposition. He asserts that fragmentation of the opposition will enhance stability; aggregation of the opposition will undermine government stability and presumably increase the sharpness of conflict. This seems to be true if the cabinet's opponents represent an antisystem opposition, but scarcely if the opposition is loyal and moderate, offering a credible government alternative. It can be argued, with reference to Denmark, Norway, and Sweden, that the unity of the Social Democratic opposition party has contributed to keeping a nonsocialist coalition cabinet together for a considerable time in each country. The coalitions were not able to afford much internal disagreement; the alternative was a probable long-term Social Democratic rule. In this respect Scandinavia presents some parallels to the party system of a country such as Australia where, as Lawrence Mayer notes, the system has operated "with great similarity to the two-party model."[12] For example, in Norway a coalition cabinet of Conservatives, Agrarians, Liberals, and Christian Democrats governed for five and a half years, opposed by the Social Democratic Labor party. It is true that the Norwegian coalition broke apart in the end because of the Common Market cleavage, but the latter was serious enough to produce a split within the Labor party as well.

With regard to both Denmark and Norway it might be of interest to extend Lawrence Mayer's index series by including data from the latest elections, which were held in February and September of 1977, respectively. Denmark is still characterized by great fragmentation. In Norway, however, there has been a movement in the opposite direction. Actually the Norwegian development during the last two decades exhibits a cyclical pattern, with alternating phases of aggregation and fragmentation, a cycle which is not registered by Mayer's indices, as these refer to only two points of time, September 1965 and September 1973.

When the mild dualism of right versus left became salient in Norway, it cut across the center-periphery cleavage, relegating it to the background. Aggregation of parties and mildness of conflict was the result. When the EEC dimension became salient, it cut across the left-right cleavage, the result being an intense struggle, unusually acute by Norwegian standards. People even talked about "a civil war atmosphere." This was a great exaggeration, of course. The whole controversy could rather be called a tempest in a teacup. But according to physicists there are laws of hydrodynamics which can be studied quite as well in a small cup as in a great lake. Norwegian experience seems to show that, while a process of fragmentation, in the sense of cleavages cutting across one another, is sometimes a prelude to conflictive bipolarity, at other times it represents the transition to a bipolarity characterized by only the mildest of opposition.

To be sure, political fragmentation always entails a certain amount of disharmony. However, as long as disharmony is kept within bounds which a given author considers tolerable, he will be positively inclined towards fragmentation. In that case he may prefer to give it the label of "pluralism." But there is also the possibility that a bipolar situation is distinguished by considerable harmony. If so it will compare favorably with pluralism, at least in the eyes of some, who then tend to speak about the latter as "fragmentation" or "conflictive" pluralism. In such a case Edward A. Ross's dictum, to the effect that cross-cutting cleavages tend to moderate conflict, is not applicable.

It must be added that the fragmentation of a party system is not necessarily caused by cross-cutting cleavages in society. Other factors may be at work, for example, complex and unstable economic conditions, as mentioned by Lawrence Mayer. Contemporary Denmark illustrates the possibility of political fragmentation occurring without the presence of any cross-cutting cleavages in the ordinary sense of the term.

Notes

1. Edward A. Ross, *The Principles of Sociology*, New York: The Century Co., 1920, p. 165.
2. E. E. Schattschneider, *The Semi-sovereign People*, New York: Holt, Rinehart & Winston, 1960, p. 73.
3. Robert A. Dahl, "Pluralism Revisited," IPSA Paper (mimeo), Edinburgh, 1976.
4. Gordon Smith, *Politics in Western Europe*, New York: Holmes & Meier, 1973, p. 16, esp. p. 37.
5. Douglas W. Rae and Michael Taylor, *The Analysis of Political Cleavages*, New Haven, Conn.: Yale University Press, 1970, p. 23, esp. p. 92.
6. Ibid., p. 112.
7. Schattschneider, op. cit., p. 67.
8. Alvin Rabushka and Kenneth A. Shepsle, *Politics in Plural Societies*, Columbus, Ohio: Charles Merrill, 1972, pp. 60–61.
9. Otto Kirchheimer, "The Transformation of the Western European Party Systems," in Joseph LaPalombara and Myron Weiner, eds., *Political Parties and Political Development*, Princeton, N.J.: Princeton University Press, 1966, pp. 177–200.
10. Stephen L. Fisher, Chapter 24 of this volume. E. E. Schattschneider's value premises were similar to Fisher's. Kirchheimer seems ambivalent as to the positive and negative implications of "catchall parties."
11. Lawrence C. Mayer, Chapter 18 of this volume.
12. Lawrence C. Mayer, Chapter 13 of this volume. It is to be regretted that Mayer did not include Britain and Canada in his index of aggregation. He excludes them because, he says, a single-member district plurality electoral system constitutes a structural impediment to fragmentation. However, as recent history shows, the impediment is a weak one, and under certain circumstances it becomes the opposite of an impediment. Mayer wonders what the relative strength of the Scottish and Welsh nationalist parties would now be under some form of proportional representation. It seems that proportional representation would at least constitute a strong obstacle to their further growth. See J. H. Proctor, "Party Interests and the Electoral System for the Projected Scottish Assembly," *The Political Quarterly*, 48 (April–June 1977), 186–200. See my review article, "The Consequences of Electoral Laws," *European Journal of Political Research*, 2 (1974), 283–290. In regard to fragmentation, the contrast is rather between parliamentary systems on the one hand and a presidential system like that in the United States on the other. See Seymour Martin Lipset, "Radicalism in North America: A Comparative View of the Party Systems in Canada and the U.S.," *Transactions of the Royal Society of Canada*, 14 (1976), 40.

CHAPTER 20

SOURCES OF PARTY TRANSFORMATION: THE CASE OF FRANCE

Frank L. Wilson

ONE MAJOR CONCERN of those who study western democratic political parties has been the nature of party system change. Three types of party change have received attention: (1) the development of modern parties in countries which previously lack them;[1] (2) the evolution of coalitions of voters supporting the various parties;[2] and (3) the transformation of the nature of already existing parties. Scholars treating the first two types of party change have gone beyond the simple description of the changes to offer explanations of how and why the changes occurred in the ways they did. However, the causes of the third type of change, namely, the transformation of existing parties, often are not the same as the forces producing the original party system, nor can this type of party change always be explained by studying the sources of shifts in coalition of party supporters. Nevertheless, there have been few efforts to move beyond the description of the transformation of existing parties to provide explanations for why the changes occurred. It is the purpose of this chapter to explore the sources of party transformation in France in the hope of gaining a better understanding of the causes of party transformation in western democracies.

By party transformation is meant change in the very nature of the individual parties. For Maurice Duverger, party transformation was the evolution of cadre parties into mass or devotee parties. For Otto Kirchheimer, party transformation was producing catchall parties. And Leon Epstein argued that the process was leading to the "Americanization" of western political parties.[3] Party transformation is that type of party change that produces new styles, organization, tactics, and interparty relations. Changes in party style may involve alteration in the degree of attachment to an official ideology, in the rhetoric of political communication within the parties as well as between them,

526

in the symbols used to unify the parties' members and followers, and in the breadth of the parties' electoral appeal. Organizational changes include new party organs, new channels and directions of internal communication, decreases or increases in party discipline and hierarchical control, alteration in the balance between the party structures in and out of parliament, and so on. Tactical changes include new activities and practices used by parties in political campaigns and in interelection periods to mobilize, indoctrinate, or encourage their supporters. Changes in interparty relations refer to shifts in the attitudes of the leaders and followers of one party about other parties in the same system, in the nature and intensity of party rivalries, and in coalitional or competitive ties among parties. Interparty relations also include the number of parties and their alignments with or against each other. Because our primary concern is seeking the causes of this type of party change, the historical pattern of party development in France and the evolution of voter coalitions supporting the various French parties are beyond the scope of this chapter.

Although a large body of literature has developed on the nature of party transformation in western democracies, little attention has been devoted to the sources or causes of the transformations. In most studies, one or more possible causes of party transformation are briefly noted. Among those sources of party transformation often mentioned are (1) socioeconomic change, (2) change in the political culture, (3) constitutional or institutional change, (4) change in the terms of party competition, and (5) the impact of party leaders or reformers. Beyond brief reference to these sources of transformation, few scholars have evaluated the relative importance of the causal factors they mention or elaborated on how these causes in fact produce transformation in parties' styles, organizations, tactics, and interparty relations.

On the basis of recent transformations in French parties, this paper proposes a model of party transformation which seeks to show the relative importance of various causal factors and to explain how these factors produce party transformation. This model is presented in Figure 20–1. On the basis of French experience, it appears that there is no single source of party transformation but rather several sources which have some direct or indirect effect on party transformation. As indicated in Figure 20–1, based on the experience of party transformation in France, change in the socioeconomic environment appears far removed from the party and unlikely to do more than contribute to a favorable milieu that might support party transformation. Socioeconomic change also might have an indirect effect on political parties by altering the competitive situation as, for example, the rise and decline of various occupational or generational groups affect parties' electoral strength. Changes in the political culture are only slightly closer to the parties in terms of their likely effect on party transformation. Both socioeconomic and cultural changes are more likely to be valuable in understanding long-term evolution in voter alignments than in explaining more dramatic and rapid shifts in party styles, organizations, or tactics. Changes in political institutions have a more

Figure 20-1.   A Model of Party Transformation

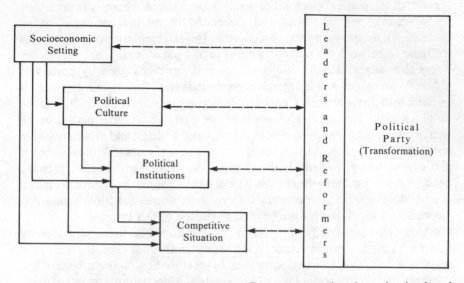

direct impact on party transformation. But, once again, these institutional changes have a most pronounced effect when they alter the competitive situation—as they did in France after 1962. It is changes in the competitive situation which seem to have the most decisive effects on party transformation. Entry of new competitors, discovery of new tactics and approaches by one or more of the competitors, change in the rules of competition, and addition of new "prizes" awarded through the competition are most likely to lead to party transformation. Such changes in the terms of party competition are usually the most immediate motive for party transformation. The commitment to vote maximization, which Anthony Downs identified in western democratic political parties,[4] leads parties to transform their styles, organizations, strategies, and tactics in response to competitive pressures.

The model also indicates that parties are not simply passive recipients of pressures from their socioeconomic, cultural, institutional, and competitive environment. At times, the parties decisively affect their environment by the policies they implement and by the nature of their competition. The model places party leaders and reformers as the key intervening variable that determines whether or not the parties will in fact respond to any of these factors that make transformation possible or desirable. Given the manipulative and conscious nature of party reform, the perceptions, skills, and actions of the leaders are crucial to understanding party transformation.

The Extent of Party Transformation in France

Before exploring the sources of party transformation in France, it is useful to note the extent of these transformations. Unlike parties elsewhere in

Western Europe, the French parties did not begin the process of transformation in the first few years after World War II. Despite conditions seemingly favorable to party transformation—the discrediting of prewar parties, their wartime dissolution, and rapid socioeconomic change—the immediate postwar period saw the reestablishment of basically the same type of parties that had first emerged as part of the French political landscape late in the nineteenth century. The new parties of the immediate postwar era, which at first seemed likely to alter the old party system, either adopted the traditional styles, organizations, and tactics (viz., the Christian Democratic MRP and the Resistance-born UDSR) or disappeared (viz., the Gaullist RPF) as the parties of the Third Republic (the Socialists, Radicals, and various conservative Independents) regained their dominant positions in the party system and government. It was not until 17 years after the war, when the process of transformation had been completed by parties in most other European democracies, that the French parties finally began evolving toward the modern catchall type.

Once begun, the process of party transformation in France affected most major parties and created a substantially different party system by the mid-1970s. A full description of these changes has been given elsewhere.[5] In brief, the transformation of French parties between 1962 and 1977 resulted in the following new features: (1) the emergence of a dominant majority coalition composed of Gaullists and their allies; (2) the reintegration of the Communist party into French politics,[6] the renewal and radicalization of the Socialist party,[7] and the formation of a durable Socialist-Communist alliance;[8] (3) a trend toward a dualist party system composed of two multiparty coalitions and the demise of parties outside these coalitions, (4) renewed citizen interest in the parties demonstrated by higher levels of party identification[9] and growing party memberships; (5) the nationalization and personalization of parties and election campaigns; (6) heightened party discipline and hierarchical control evidenced by greater cohesion in legislative voting[10] and centrally imposed limitations on options in local politics; and (7) a movement toward the clear-cut government/opposition dialogue characteristic of "party government."

There are limitations to these changes. One respected observer of French politics compared the 1962 and 1973 election campaigns in the same districts and found few differences.[11] And the French parties have resisted the decline of ideological commitment that has been a major dimension of party transformation elsewhere in Western Europe. However, it is undeniable that important party transformation has occurred in France since the mid-1960s.

For the past decade, observers of French politics have noted changes but have often concluded with the warning that they may be only temporary changes that would vanish when de Gaulle left politics, or when the Left takes power, or when the traditional legislative political practices of the Third and Fourth Republics inevitably reassert themselves. However, it is time to admit that most of these changes should now be regarded as permanent. Some of these changes are now 15 years old and have already proved themselves against attempts to revert to older patterns. The trend toward a dualist party configuration is now 15 years old and is likely to continue despite periodic tensions and adjustments in the two coalitions. The new party styles, structures, coalitions, and tactics have acquired legitimacy in the eyes of the public, and attempts to reverse them now would disorient the parties' members and voters. The partisan realignments produced by these changes are likely to endure if only out of habit. Finally, party leaders and members have become used to these new practices and styles and will be loath to break with these now familiar routines.

Whether these changes are desirable is an open question, and by no means is it clear that the modernization of French parties will contribute to stable democracy. The new party forms often tend to discourage close ties between the electorate and the party thereby hampering the parties' abilities to link the people with the political process. In a democratic society where the government's role is great and growing steadily, this failure of parties to link the people with politics is a serious one. A second danger in France is the increasing polarization between the Gaullists and the Left. In most countries, the aggregation of parties into dualist systems is accompanied by their moderation or convergence near the political center. But this has not been the case in France. The ideological distance between the two blocs is large with each promising an entirely different socioeconomic and political order. Perhaps more importantly, the psychological distance between the two sides is great. Relations between them are devoid of civility and mutual respect. Indeed, the dualist nature of the current party system may be worse for long-run stability than the multiparty system of the past given the polarization of the two sides. The old multiparty system permitted the separation of the extremes and placed government in the hands of the centrist "Third Force." Under the Fifth Republic, the elimination of the Center has left the direct confrontation of two extremes, one of which must govern, despite the apprehensions of the other.

Whether or not party transformation in France appears desirable, it has occurred and it is important to understand what forces produced the transformation. To elaborate on the model of party transformation presented earlier, it is useful to assess the relative impact on French parties of several purported sources of party transformation: socioeconomic forces, political culture, political institutions, the overall competitive situation, and the action of party leaders and reformers.

Socioeconomic Change as a Source of Party Transformation

One explanation for party change that is often suggested is the effects of socioeconomic change. Some have pointed to the cleavages produced by the socioeconomic system as the explanation of party origins and of changes in party support.[12] Even party goals and techniques of action are seen by some as closely related to the social and economic environment in which the parties operate.[13] As this environment changes, the parties too are expected to change. For example, it is argued that socioeconomic change in Western Europe has reduced social class tensions and produced a broad-based social and political consensus. This in turn has led to the reduced importance of the ideologies espoused by the parties in these societies.[14] Similarly, it is argued that parties have been changed by the communications revolution. Modern communications lead to a nationalization of politics as local political notables are eclipsed by televised national political figures.

However compelling these arguments may seem in abstract, the process of party transformation in France suggests that the impact of socioeconomic change on political parties is neither direct nor automatic. First, some of the changes in party style that have been most closely linked in the literature with socioeconomic change have simply not taken place in France. Specifically, the decline in ideological fervor supposedly linked with long-term economic prosperity and expansion and with the changing class structures of post-industrial societies has simply not occurred in France. Attempts by the French Communist party to modify its doctrine have in no way reduced its fundamental commitment to Marxist-Leninist principles. It is not unusual to find a communist party that remains faithful to its ideology as is the case with the French Communist party. It is somewhat unusual to find a contemporary socialist party that remains as rigorous in its commitment to orthodox Marxism as does the French Socialist party. Indeed, the French Socialist party has deepened its ideological commitment at the same time that other western socialist parties are abandoning their ideologies. It is even more unusual to find in the 1970s, the high degree of commitment to nationalism and doctrinaire anticommunism that is found among the French Gaullists. The prevalence of ideology in French politics is well demonstrated by the fact that a sitting president recently took time to produce a theoretical treatise designed to redefine and defend neoliberalism.[15] Thus, despite socioeconomic change which in theory ought to lead to decreasing attention to ideologies, French parties remained preoccupied with ideological concerns.

Second, there is a long time gap between the advent of socioeconomic change and the era of party transformation. It is clear that socioeconomic changes of the type expected to bring party transformation did take place in France. The successive changes introduced by Vichy and the Resistance between 1940 and 1946 brought about a veritable revolution in the social and economic spheres in France.[16] This revolution seriously undermined the "stalemate society" that had provided the basis for political party activities and rivalries in the past. The socioeconomic milieu was thus ripe to support change in the political party system. However, the French party system reemerged after the war unreformed and assumed the same characteristics that the parties had acquired 50 years earlier.

The period of intense party transformation (1962–1976) came nearly two decades after the wartime socioeconomic changes. To be sure, socioeconomic change continued through the period of party transformation. Indeed, there is reason to believe that government policies and stability imposed by the Gaullist political hegemony greatly contributed to economic growth and the strength of the French monetary system after 1958. But the long gap between the major wartime and immediate postwar socioeconomic changes and the onset of party transformation suggests the absence of a direct causal relationship between socioeconomic change and party transformation.

Once established, parties are durable institutions resistant to change even when changes alter the socioeconomic foundations on which the parties were originally based. This is due to their institutional strength in the form of bureaucratic inertia and resistance to change. Other things being equal, parties rely on existing structures, traditional practices, and tactics, and past strategies rather than on experiment with new modes of organization or campaigning made possible or desirable by socioeconomic change. It is also due to the fact that parties have established clienteles that vote for them out of habit. Abrupt changes may disrupt these loyalties by eliminating the traditional symbols and messages that the party's established clientele expects. Rose and Urwin argue that "parties persist and, for the pragmatic reason of maintaining internal cohesion, tend to maintain preexisting social divisions by socializing their supporters into commitments to their distinctive claims, be they numerous or none."[17] The society, economy, and political regime may change, but traditional patterns of voting and political behavior continue. Parties, thus, are shielded from the impact of a changing environment by the force of tradition.

What seems likely is that socioeconomic changes, such as the decline in intensity of social class distinctions, the diminished salience of religion in politics, the communications revolution, prolonged economic prosperity and growth, and demographic changes, produced a congenial environment for party transformation in France but did not produce the transformation itself. The relationship was by no means deterministic as socioeconomic change permitted but did not mandate change in the party system. In short, socioeconomic change in France made possible party transformation but was not sufficient to bring about the changes by itself. Other intervening variables are more important to an understanding of party change in France.

Political Culture as a Source of Party Transformation

For some, the key to party transformation is found in changing political attitudes and values in the general public. Party forms are seen as reflecting the degree of secularization, polarization, and heterogeneity of the political culture. Thus, Frank J. Sorauf noted that "the political culture sets norms and goals for the specifics of party organization and operation and differences in political cultures, or among the subcultures within one system, beget differences in party style and modes of operations."[18] Walter Dean Burnham contends that the key to the nature of the American party system is found ". . . fundamentally within the American political culture itself."[19] In France, the disorganized, fragmented, and undisciplined nature of traditional political parties has been attributed to the high degree of individualism in the prevailing political culture.[20] Furthermore, a "delinquent community" of reciprocal suspicions, nonparticipation, and predilection for protest and opposition are seen as contributing to and in some cases as producing the traditional party system.[21]

There are some problems in assessing the impact of the changes in political culture on party transformation that need to be noted. There is first the problem of identifying the political culture and subcultures in a country. Inevitably, the description of a country's political culture is based on impressionistic conclusions drawn from the observer's long experience with the country, from content analysis of leading newspapers or political documents, from survey research, or from other more or less reliable sets of data. Often, different observers using different data and approaches, and sometimes even the same data, come to diametrically opposed conclusions about the political attitudes and values in a given country. The problems are whether or not there is *a* French political culture that might shape political parties, and, if there is, how to find it.

These difficulties are compounded when trying to gauge the effects on parties or other political phenomena of *changes* in political culture. In most cases, and this is true of France, we lack data on political attitudes and values in the past to compare with data on contemporary attitudes and values, making it difficult to test the accuracy of claims about a changing political culture. For example, it is often argued that the recent development in France of a consensus on basic issues permits broader electoral appeals, catchall parties, and a more moderate party system than was possible in the past. However, the paucity of public opinion data from the period before 1945 makes it difficult to judge whether the presumed lack of consensus during the 1930s was a mass phenomenon or simply a feature of the French political elite. It is entirely possible, even likely, that the basis for a political consensus was present among French citizens in the 1930s just as opinion surveys suggested it existed in the 1960s. Finally, political culture explanations of party transformation are also vulnerable to the problem of determining which is the dependent and independent variable. As Sartori points out, "If they interact—and everybody seems to pay at least lip-service to this formula—then one of the two actions must be the action of the party system upon the political culture."[22]

In assessing the impact of the political culture on French party transformation, it is important first to note the great continuity of basic political attitudes and values. And this is especially true of the key concept of political power and attitudes toward authority which affect the citizens' political activities in and out of political parties. In their study of French political socialization, Charles Roig and Françoise Billon-Grand argue that the same concept of power passed from generation to generation by the family and schools explains both the authoritarian political structures and the parliamentary structures that have alternated in France the past two centuries.[23] For Stanley Hoffmann, the authority relations that lead to the distinctive French political style of negative protest not only persist but in some ways have hardened and expanded.[24]

Despite this continuity in notions of authority, several apparent changes in the French political culture might be expected to have important consequences for party transformations. One of the most frequently noted changes in the political culture has been the purported emergence of a broad-based consensus on political and socioeconomic issues which supposedly divided the French.[25] This claim is supported by public opinion surveys that reveal far less polarization on supposedly divisive issues than had been anticipated.[26] This change in the political culture is expected to affect the style of parties by reducing their commitment to ideologies as the old issues which supported these ideologies are replaced by consensus or rendered irrelevant by time. This new political consensus is also expected to transform the relationship between parties by reducing polarization and promoting moderation as the parties' positions converge upon the popular consensus.

None of this anticipated party transformation has occurred in France. While the general political culture may have changed in such a way as to permit party transformation to reflect the consensus that appears to exist among the general public, the expected transformations did not occur. If anything, the French parties are more deeply committed to their ideologies than they were a decade ago. Polarization between the Gaullist majority and the leftist opposition is as great or greater than ever. The two camps defend entirely different socioeconomic orders and advocate sharply different relationships among political and social institutions. More importantly, the left and the Gaullist coalition are emotionally polarized. They do not view each other as friendly rivals but as bitter enemies. For the Gaullists, rule by the Left would mean totalitarian communism in France; for the Left, rule by the Gaullists was fascist and authoritarian. In the past, it was possible to attribute this polarization to the aloof and authoritarian political style of Charles de Gaulle. However, the recent efforts of President Valéry Giscard d'Estaing to *décrisper* partisan tensions have failed to produce meaningful dialogue between the majority and the opposition. If it is assumed that the reported movement of general public attitudes toward a consensus is accurate,[27] then the changing political culture does not automatically lead to the anticipated party transformations in the case of deideologization and depolarization.

A stronger case for the influence of changing political culture on party transformation can be made in the case of changed attitudes toward the French

Communist party (PCF). During the 1960s, public opinion toward the PCF gradually shifted to a more positive evaluation of the Communists' role in French politics and to acceptance of possible Communist participation in government coalitions.[28] Such changing attitudes might be expected to encourage the transformation of interparty relations by integrating the Communists into the political system and making them available as possible allies with other left-wing parties.

In fact, these transformations have taken place. The problem here is determining whether the changing public attitudes produced the integration of the PCF or whether the PCF's new role brought new public attitudes. On the one hand, the changes in public attitudes preceded the PCF's internal and doctrinal changes and the establishment of any formal ties with the non-Communist Left. By 1964, the first indication of the new public attitudes had appeared despite the fact that the PCF was still under the hard-line Stalinist leadership of Maurice Thorez.[29] On the other hand, it is clear that the changing public attitudes alone are insufficient to explain the PCF's new position in the party system. A number of other factors must be considered: the leadership of the PCF and the non-Communist Left, the overall constitutional and electoral systems, the bipolarization of politics, the decline of Cold War tensions, French foreign policy toward the Communist world, and so on. Many of these factors can be of equal or greater value compared to public attitudinal changes in explaining the integration of the PCF into the party system. What seems most likely is that the more positive public attitude toward the PCF was both supportive of and the product of party transformation.

One other set of changing attitudes which might be associated with party transformation is the emergence of a public attitude favorable to a bipolar party configuration. In the past, French voters seemed reluctant to accept a twofold political division, insisting on a full range of political options not only to express a variety of political beliefs, but also to avoid the direct confrontation of only two political blocs. A recent study by Bruce A. Campbell suggests that the French are now coming to view political competition in bipolar terms.[30] He shows a steady bipolarization of political attitudes between 1958 and 1969. This attitudinal change coincides with the actual simplification of the party system into two relatively cohesive political blocs.

In this case, the evidence suggests that the attitudinal change came after the party transformation and thus is not likely to have caused the simplification of the party system. In the mid-1960s, a group of French political scientists assessed the party system and concluded that there did seem to be a definite trend in party activity toward bipolarization.[31] But they expressed doubts about its permanence, arguing that French historical traditions obstructed an enduring dualist party alignment. The French, they felt, like to differentiate themselves more than would be possible in a two-bloc party system. Assuming that the perceptions of these observers were accurate gauges of public attitudes at the time, this would suggest that the simplification of the party system was taking place before favorable attitudes toward bipolarization had developed. Campbell's study also provides support for this since he found that younger voters have a stronger tendency toward bipolar attitudes than do older voters. This would suggest that the attitudinal change was the product of the socialization of younger voters taking place in a bipolar political configuration. Older voters, who grew up in the multiparty system, are less likely to have developed attitudes favorable to a bipolar party system. Here, again, it appears that the new political attitudes resulted from the party transformation rather than produced it. Thus, Campbell concludes that the institutions of the Fifth Republic "have imposed a bipolar element on French political thinking."[32]

Clearly, party transformation in France gives little indication of cultural determinism. Evidence of a changing political culture is limited and where it exists it often appears to be the result of rather than the cause of party change. The same political culture may be manipulated to sustain a variety of political party types and activities. The most that can be said regarding the impact of political culture is that some changes in political attitudes may create a possibility of party transformation that party leaders may or may not exploit.

Constitutional Changes and Party Transformation

There is general agreement among those studying party forms and party change that there is a strong interdependence between the political framework and the political party system. For some, parties are the products of the political institutions and structures within which they operate. Epstein contends that the constitutional structures must be taken as "givens" in explaining party development since the constitution typically existed before the parties and compelled the parties to adapt their organizations and electoral efforts to it.[33] In the case of the United States, some claim that federalism and the separation of powers are responsible for the presence of fragmented and poorly disciplined parties.[34]

In assessing the impact of institutional changes on the French parties it is useful to separate those institutional changes that reallocated political power and those changes that altered the terms of party competition by changing the electoral system or creating new electoral opportunities. Those institutional changes that affected the terms of party competition—such as the introduction of direct popular election of the president—had profound consequences for the party system, and they will be explored fully in the next section. But the reallocation of power among the branches of government also had important effects on the parties.

The 1958 constitution altered dramatically the allocation of political power in France, shifting from a parliamentary system to a mixed presidential and parliamentary system. In practice, de Gaulle and his successors have enlarged the presidential powers far beyond those of the arbiter envisaged in the 1958 constitution to make the president the chief policy maker in any policy area selected by him. Associated with this growing presidentialism has been the sharp curtailment of the powers, prerogatives, and activity of Parliament. In sum, the emergence of a powerful and stable executive operating in a democratic context placed French parties in an alien and unfamiliar political setting. Under the Third and Fourth Republics, the center of political power was in the National Assembly where the bargaining and voting of the parties determined major national policy. Under the Fifth Republic, this traditional forum for the parties lost its importance as the crucial decisions were made elsewhere, especially in the Elysée Palace. Political attention was inevitably diverted from parliament and the parties to the president. The presence of the powerful president and the diminished influence of Parliament meant that the parties needed to develop new strategies to influence policies and particularly needed to find ways to win access to the presidency. The political parties' old orientation toward notables with firm local support who, once elected to Parliament, served as a collective body of national leaders, had to be changed to permit the parties to focus on a handful of national figures who might be regarded as presidential contenders.

While the impact of presidentialism has had the greatest impact on parties, other reallocations of power during the Fifth Republic have also affected parties. The decline of Parliament led parties to reorient much of their efforts toward local politics with the consequent partisanization and nationalization of municipal government. Parliamentary rules requiring a minimum of 30 deputies for the formation of a parliamentary group promoted coalitions among smaller parties to meet this requirement and dissuaded potential schismatics within parties from splitting off to form new parties. The attempts to depoliticize the Council of Ministers by bringing into government technical experts without prior parliamentary or political experience also affected the parties, as many of these technocratic ministers soon became involved in partisan politics. They associated themselves with one of the majority parties and ran for local or national offices. This provided the majority parties with new leadership—including individuals like Pompidou, Couve de Murville, and Messmer who served as prime ministers—and developed an important new method of political recruitment. The importance of this new source of political talent is seen in the growing number of civil servants elected to the National Assembly and other public offices. In opposition, the Socialist party too sought to attract technical experts from outside the party structure to aid the party leadership in defining alternative policies. The overall result was to alter the social composition of the parties' memberships to include more technocrats and to reduce the importance in number and influence of traditional local notables.

In the case of Fifth Republic France, there can be little question of the direction of the causal relationship between institutional change and party transformation. The constitutional structures of the Fifth Republic were designed outside the traditional parties and grudgingly accepted by them in exchange for de Gaulle's return to power to avert possible civil war. The ideas and institutions of the constitution were those of de Gaulle and a few close supporters.[35] They reflected de Gaulle's antiparty attitudes and his severe critique of the *régime des partis*. The influence of his own political party was limited both during the drafting of the constitution and during its implementation. The Gaullist party simply provided the political and parliamentary support for de Gaulle's decisions. In some cases, for example, in the choice of the electoral system, de Gaulle chose constitutional options that were designed to disadvantage his own supporters. The traditional parties had even less say over the shaping of the new constitution in its practice. The presidency became the dominant political institution against their will; parliamentary powers were eroded beyond their expectations without their having the means to reverse this trend. Popular election of the president was forced on them in 1962 through a national referendum that was also a poorly disguised means for de Gaulle and his supporters to directly confront and do battle with the traditional parties. In the immediate aftermath of this successful referendum, de Gaulle and his forces consolidated their victory over the old parties by winning an absolute majority in the National Assembly.

It is likely that the limited role of parties in shaping the institutions of the Fifth Republic is atypical, and the result of special circumstances not likely to be recreated: de Gaulle's political philosophy, his hold on the French people, and the discredited state of traditional parties in the wake of the Fourth Republic's collapse. In other settings, scholars have found that parties have had important effects on shaping political institutions. Morton Grodzins argued that, instead of being determined by federalism and the separation of executive and legislative powers, American parties have been among the most important forces that have perpetuated decentralization and dispersion of power in the United States.[36] Theodore J. Lowi acknowledges the importance of constitutional factors in party development but argues that "in the United States the stronger influence has been the other way around."[37] Even in France, during earlier democratic eras, the party system seems to have shaped the political institutions as much or more than it was shaped by them. The Third Republic emerged slowly in the 1870s with the parties dominating the constitution-making process and ultimately imposing their will in the constitutional crisis of 1877. After World War II, the parties reemerged from wartime disgrace and dissolution to control the drafting and adoption of a constitution that reestablished the old unreformed parliamentarism in which the parties felt comfortable. There was, as we have noted already, little or no party transformation at that time despite the trauma of the conflict between Vichy and the Resistance.

Indeed, parties can prove resistant to constitutional and institutional changes. To some extent they have done so in the Fifth Republic. Parties often succeed in continuing past practices or maintaining traditional features by modifying or evading the new political rules. But in searching the sources of party transformation, it is also important to check for the effects of changes in the allocation of power among political institutions. In Fifth Republic France, such changes must be regarded as among the most important causes of party transformation. The reallocation of political power from the Parliament to the presidency has created a new political setting in which several parties have sought to find new styles, organizations, and tactics.

Party Transformation as a Competitive Phenomenon

The effects of institutional changes on the parties in France have been magnified since these changes involved not only a reallocation of power but also the introduction of new forms of party competition. Parties in western democracies exist in a competitive setting where they must compete with other parties—and indeed with interest groups, political clubs, and other political movements—for activists, leaders, money, public attention, and especially votes.[38] The primary objective for nearly all major democratic parties is to get their candidates elected.[39] Therefore, changes outside the party that affect the terms of competition are the ones most likely to stimulate party transformation.

Several of the most perceptive observers of political parties have pointed to competitive pressures as the most important motivating force for party transformation. Thus, Duverger expected a transformation from the cadre-type parties to mass and perhaps devotee-type parties because of the superior organizational strength of the latter two types of parties. The transformation was to occur because the conservative cadre parties would recognize the political challenge of the better organized left-wing mass and devotee parties and would seek to adopt their characteristics through what Duverger labeled "contagion from the Left."[40] Kirchheimer argued that there is a trend toward catchall parties furthered by the general "acceptance of the laws of the political market"[41] and by changes adopted in "hope of benefits or fear of losses on election day."[42] Epstein, too, saw the causes of party transformation in the desire to maximize votes. For this reason the leftist parties would adopt the electoral techniques of the centrist and rightist parties by increasing use of mass media, public relations, election campaign approaches, opinion surveys, and so on. Thus, Epstein argued that, instead of the contagion from the Left that Duverger foresaw, modern parties are actually experiencing "contagion from the Right."[43]

Changes which affect the terms of party competition are likely to have a more immediate and direct impact in promoting party transformation than are changes in the socioeconomic setting, political culture, or even the political framework. Because elections are so vitally important to the success of democratic parties, alteration of electoral rules or opportunities can be expected to produce transformation of the parties' organization and tactics to respond to the new electoral realities. The challenge of a new, successful party is likely to lead its rivals to adapt its strategies to compete with it. The use of new tactics by one party which give it an advantage over its competitors will encourage the other parties to alter their own practices. This is the logic behind Duverger's "contagion from the Left" and Epstein's "contagion from the Right."

Because of the central importance of their competition, democratic parties are particularly sensitive to institutional changes that alter the terms of competition. This is evident in the case of France where the introduction of national presidential elections had profound consequences for the parties. It was not only the powers of the president but more importantly the popular election of the president that made transformation a virtual necessity for a party's survival. When the presidency became the chief prize of political competition, the entire party system was affected. No longer could small parties hope to play key role in politics by holding a strategic center position, as the Radical party had done throughout the Third and Fourth Republics. Instead, parties had to generate national electoral support for one candidate in order to control the government.

The new presidential election in effect expanded the French electorate. In the nineteenth century, the gradual extension of the vote to formerly disenfranchised groups had encouraged the development of new political parties to organize and represent these groups. The popular election of the president opened up similar opportunities. For the first time since 1848, a majority of the entire French citizenry could choose directly the most important government official. Instead of working for a series of small majorities in 490 electoral districts, the parties now had to organize the electorate for a majority in all France. For the parties to compete effectively in the presidential elections, they needed new structures and strategies.

The direct galvanizing effect of presidential elections on efforts at party change is evidenced by the fact that all major attempts to reform the parties originated either in preparation for a presidential contest or in the wake of disappointing performances in presidential elections. There were three efforts to reform the democratic Left prior to the 1965 presidential election campaign.[44] And formal cooperation between the Communist and democratic Lefts began in that same election. After De Gaulle was embarrassed by failing to win on the first ballot in 1965, his supporters took the first steps toward institutionalizing the Gaullist party to be ready for a future presidential election without De Gaulle.[45] The Socialist party began its renovation only after the humiliation of the Socialist candidate in the 1969 presidential election. Other ventures in party transformation were designed to provide political vehicles for the presidential aspirations of Jean-Jacques Servan-Schreiber, Jean Lecanuet, Valéry Giscard d'Estaing, and Jacques Chirac.

A second institutional change that altered the competitive rules was the change in electoral system. In France, electoral laws have changed often, always with the object of benefiting the parties successful in pushing the reform through parliament.[46] The Fifth Republic returned to the system used in the Third Republic: single-member districts with two ballots. For some this electoral system helps to explain the reduction in the number of parties, the fostering of electoral alliances in anticipation of the second ballot, and the division of the parties into two camps. However, the influence of the electoral system should not be overstressed, because the system also encouraged the candidacies of small parties and of local notables with strength in a particular region. Under the Third Republic this same electoral system did not lead to a reduction in the number of parties or long-term second ballot electoral alliances. Certainly the effects of the electoral system have not been as great as some anticipated.[47]

There was a third change in the competitive situation which was not linked directly to institutional changes but to the dynamics of interparty competition, and this was the emergence of a cohesive right-of-center party with a majoritarian bent. De Gaulle's charismatic appeal aggregated a broad section of society into a potential political clientele. Personally, De Gaulle could gather electoral majorities in referendums and presidential elections and his supporters were also able to channel most of this support into votes for the Gaullist coalition in legislative elections. As De Gaulle's personal appeal was routinized into support for the UDR and its allies,[48] the advent of a near majority party prodded other parties to change in response to a new competitive situation. Confronted by a united Gaullist party capable of maintaining a stable majority with its allies in the National Assembly, the opposition parties were handicapped more than ever by their many divisions and rivalries. The threat posed by the Gaullists was especially severe because they represented a new type of progressive catchall party capable of attracting reform-minded voters from the Left as well as from the Center and Right. Furthermore, the Gaullist party's ability to win a majority in parliament—it did so in 1968 marking the first time a single party had done so in five French republics—and to maintain disciplined voting in the National Assembly augmented the challenge posed by this new type of party.

As the new dominant party, the Gaullist party set the style and issues which the other parties needed to adopt or adapt for their own use in order to compete effectively. The discipline of the Gaullists fostered disciplined voting of their allies and rivals in the National Assembly. The Gaullist party's nationwide organization and electoral strength encouraged rival parties to form *regroupe ments* or federations to compete more effectively. Its use of public relations firms and gimmickry were copied by its opponents. In short, much of the transformation in the French party system can be traced to reactions to the competitive challenge of a new and potent entry into the circle of French political parties. For a while it was possible for the French parties to avoid reform by hoping for a return to the old order and a collapse of the Gaullist party once De Gaulle had departed the political scene. But, ultimately, the need to compete in the new game and with the Gaullist majority led to transformation of the traditional parties.

Thus, in the case of recent party transformation in France, the major impetus for change came from alterations in the competitive situation. A new and successful party, a different electoral system, and, most important, a new electoral prize in the popularly elected presidency compelled parties to respond through change or risk extinction. Changes in the socioeconomic setting, the political culture, and the institutional framework may have created a favorable milieu for party transformation but the need to respond to new terms of party competition was the most important and the most direct motivation for change.

The Key Role of Party Leadership

Even in the case of changes in the competitive environment, where failure to adapt may be evidenced more quickly in poor election results or parliamentary ineffectiveness, parties may not respond with appropriate adjustments in their style, organization, tactics, or external relations. The reason is that the key role in the process of party transformation is played by the party leaders. Parties do not make the transformations associated with party modernization unless their leaders will them. In France, party transformation has been delayed and sometimes avoided entirely because party leaders opposed change or were unable to win support for change despite developments favoring party transformation in the socioeconomic setting, political attitudes, political institutions, and competitive situation.

An organized party, even a faltering one, is remarkably resistant to casual attempts to change it. As a result, party transformation is usually the product of conscious effort rather than of unseen forces. Before a change in the socioeconomic or political environment can be translated into change in the parties, the party leaders must perceive the socioeconomic or political change and realize that the party will be better able to achieve its goals and improve its voting strength by adapting to the change. If the leaders do not perceive these changes, if they perceive them incorrectly, or if they decide that the changes are temporary, party transformation is not likely to occur, however much it is needed. And even when the need to change is recognized, the party leaders must have the ability to overcome the internal resistance of the established party bureaucracy and the potential revolt of the party faithful attached to traditional ways.

French experience with party transformation demonstrates the importance of party leaders. All the party transformation that has occurred in France has been the result of deliberate acts by party leaders or reformers. For example, the trend toward a dualist alignment of party blocs was sought by leaders of the principal parties. The Gaullists deliberately sought to structure a dualist party system in which voters would have to choose between them and the Communists in the belief that the French would then prefer them over the Communists and their allies. This dualism was fostered by Gaullist rhetoric and strategy and by altering the electoral system slightly to the disadvantage of small centrist parties. The leaders of the Left also opted for this dualist pattern. Communist leaders worked for an alliance and common program with the Socialists and for internal doctrinal changes to make themselves more attractive to the voters and their allies. The leadership of Waldeck Rochet, Communist party leader from 1964–1969, was important in the de-Stalinization of the French Communist Party and in promoting cooperation with the non-Communist Left. More recently, Georges Marchais has led the French Communist party in renouncing the Leninist doctrine of the dictatorship of the proletariat and pursuing independence from Moscow. Socialist leaders, notably François Mitterrand, worked to achieve the union of the Left and to convince hesitant party militants of its virtues.

Another illustration of the importance of the leadership in party transformation can be found in the nationalization of party activities. This was not simply the product of socioeconomic centralization or of the communications revolution although these developments certainly prepared the way for party reform. French parties were centralized by the efforts of leaders, often driven by presidential ambitions,[49] who sought to develop a nationwide base of support. This nationalization of the parties was achieved through the leaderships' efforts to parachute suitable candidates into key districts, to harmonize their parties' local and national strategies, and sometimes to impose certain leaders on the local party units.

The central importance of capable leaders in pursuing party reform and maintaining the party is evident in the Gaullist party. De Gaulle's personal appeal and electoral drawing power made possible the emergence of a near-majority party. Georges Pompidou's energetic leadership in the mid-1960s enabled the Gaullist party to prepare itself for survival after De Gaulle and to institutionalize its structure and following. He endowed the Gaullist party with a nationwide organization and a mass membership. He shaped its style to fit his own perception of its electoral needs and potential. He managed the majority coalition and later expanded it to take in most of the centrists. But Pompidou's failure to permit the Gaullist party to develop a new leader to take his place left the Gaullists in disarray and defeat when he died. Jacques Chirac's intervention into the declining Gaullist party in late 1974 and his molding of it to support his presidential ambitions have been crucial in the revival of the Gaullist party and in its adaptation to its loss of the presidency.

Not all would-be party reformers are successful as the obstacles to reform are often high. The force of tradition, bureaucratic inertia, ideological blinders, and sometimes leadership ineptitude make party transformation difficult to achieve even when there are leaders or reformers who want change. Socialist Gaston Defferre's attempt to create a Center-Left federation in 1964–1965 failed due to the ideological intransigence of Socialists and Christian Democrats. The political club movement of the 1960s ultimately fell victim to the same vices that the clubs condemned in the older parties: disunity, domination by discredited leaders left over from the Fourth Republic, excessive ideological commitments, personal rivalries, individualism, and suspicion of the Catholic Left.[50] Servan-Schreiber's efforts to reform the moribund Radical party were initially furthered but ultimately checked by his own powerful ambition. And Valéry Giscard d'Estaing's attempt to convert his presidential majority into a new political force failed due to personal rivalries and ideological differences among his followers as well as important mistakes by his chief lieutenants.

The key factor in party transformation is the action of party leaders—and of reformers outside the parties, who sometimes intervene when there are no reform-minded leaders within the parties. The notion that parties are transformed by unseen socioeconomic, cultural, or political forces while their members and leaders remain unaware is misleading. Parties change primarily because their leaders and members see the need to change and make efforts to change them. It may appear simplistic to say that parties change because their leaders change them. But it is important to stress the conscious, manipulative nature of party key variables in transformation.

Of course, if party leadership is the *sine qua non* for party transformation, it alone is not sufficient. Perceptive and capable leaders may be unable to transform parties if the socioeconomic setting, political culture, political institutions, or competitive situation is not conducive to the desired transformations. This may explain why party reformers during the French Fourth Republic failed to succeed in changing their parties. Just as alert and capable leaders are essential to party transformation, so is a favorable political milieu. Successful party transformation requires leaders who perceive the changes in the socioeconomic and political environment, who recognize the potential competitive advantages in adapting to the new environment, and who are capable of overcoming the inertia and other obstacles that block party change. France has had several such leaders since 1958.

Toward a Model of Party Transformation

In a recent book on party reform in America, Austin Ranney concludes that "... party reform is one of the easier forms of social engineering."[51] However accurate this may be of parties in the United States, it does not appear to be true in France. Attempts to reform the party system failed during the Resistance and the immediate postwar period. Pierre Mendès-France's efforts to modernize the Radical party during the 1950s also failed. Despite socioeconomic, cultural, institutional, and competitive pressures for party transformation, party reform came late and even then was thwarted in several parties. One French political scientist noted the difficulties of reforming French parties:[52]

> If it is one of the most fundamental facts—almost a banality—that the party system is at least as important as the letter of the constitution, it is unhappily much easier to write a constitution than it is to establish and maintain a party system that meets the need of a modern society.

Though there are parties that have resisted reform, there has been extensive party transformation in France. Four conclusions can be drawn from both the successful and the unsuccessful ventures in party transformation in France. *First*, party transformation is manipulative in the sense of being the product of conscious efforts of leaders to reform their parties rather than of automatic evolution due to socioeconomic or attitudinal changes. Socioeconomic and cultural influences on French party transformation seem indirect in that they make possible but do not dictate party transformation. *Second*, the trend toward catchall parties or the Americanization of democratic parties discerned by Kirchheimer and Epstein is not inevitable or irreversible. French parties were late in starting movement in this direction and might never have done so were it not for the imposition on the reluctant parties of a new set of political institutions and leaders. Some of the French parties that failed to transform themselves have perished. Notably, the Christian Democratic MRP—one of the most important parties during the Fourth Republic—officially ceased operations in 1967. But other parties avoided or aborted transformations and still retain political influence. The Radical party, for example, resisted the determined efforts of two sets of reformers (the first led by René Billeres, the second by Jean-Jacques Servan-Schreiber) and now once again has a role in government despite its small parliamentary delegation and unreformed condition. *Third*, those changes which seem to have had the most direct effect on party transformation were those that altered the terms of party competition. The introduction of the presidential election by popular vote created a new competitive situation which the old parties were unable to meet without major reforms in their styles, organizations, and tactics. Likewise, the need to compete with a disciplined party having a real majoritarian potential also promoted change in the traditionally small and divided parties. *Fourth*, the key factor in successful party transformation has been the presence of competent leaders or reformers who could recognize the advantage of changing and force through needed changes despite organizational inertia and the often determined resistance of those attached to the status quo. The presence or absence of capable leaders explains why party transformation took place so soon in some parties, so late in others, and not at all in still others.

On the basis of this case study, a model of party transformation was presented in Figure 20–1. French experience points to the competitive situation and the role of leaders as the key factors in party transformation. Corroborative evidence in support of this model is found in case studies of party transformation in other western democracies. Sidney Tarrow probed the possible correlation between economic development and the strength of moderate factions in the Italian Socialist and Christian Democratic parties. He concluded[53]

> There is no necessary connection between objective economic conditions and the strategy of a party, for political strategy is the subjective product of a party elite that does more than simply respond to its environment. It is the response of these leaders to a variety of signals in the environment, in their institutions, and in their own socialization.

A recent study by Raphael Zariski and Susan Welch reexamined this same problem.[54] Like Tarrow, they found little evidence of a correlation between socioeconomic development and political moderation in Italian parties. Instead, they found a strong correlation between political factors and especially party competitiveness on the one hand and the strength of moderate factions on the other.

Gerhard Loewenberg also pointed to the importance of political change rather than social or economic change in explaining the reform of the German party system after World War II.[55] He stressed the importance of the new ground rules for party competition imposed on the parties by outside reformers (in this case, by occupation regimes) in the transformation of the German party system. But the German party leaders themselves were crucial to party transformation over the long run as they "read the signs of social change" and consolidated the new party system.

Finally, support for this model of party transformation is found in the American party system. One of the foremost scholars on party development in the United States emphasized the manipulative nature of party change:[56]

> . . . [M]odern parties and the party system in the United States were indeed the products of a labor of Hercules, and not "natural," unintended flowerings from the soil of independence and popular government. Rather, parties were ingeniously shaped "artifacts," in the sense of structures built up over the years by the industrious, if often groping, activities of men.

In an era when important questions are raised about the suitability and viability of existing party forms in democratic societies,[57] it is important to understand how further transformations may occur. Despite the social, economic, and political changes accompanying the emergence of postindustrial societies, parties will not adapt automatically to the new setting. The value of this model is that it identifies the key variables in party transformation—party leaders and reformers—and suggests which kinds of outside pressures are most unlikely to lead to party transformation—changes in the competitive setting. With the French parties transformed from their pre-1962 condition but seemingly not yet supportive of democratic institutions and with parties in several other western democracies also seemingly ill-adapted to postindustrial democracy, it is as important to probe the processes of party transformation as it is to propose the content of party reforms.

Notes

1. For examples, see Seymour M. Lipset and Stein Rokkan, "Cleavages, Structures, Party Systems, and Voter Alignments: An Introduction," in Seymour M. Lipset and Stein Rokkan, eds., *Party System and Voter Alignments*, New York: Free Press, 1967, pp. 1–64; Stein Rokkan, *Citizens, Elections, Parties: Approaches to the Comparative of the Process of Development*, New York: David McKay, 1970; William N. Chambers, *Political Parties in a New Nation: The American Experience, 1776–1809*, New York: Oxford University Press, 1963; Joseph LaPalombara and Myron Weiner, "The Origins and Development of Political Parties," in Joseph LaPalombara and Myron Weiner, eds., *Political Parties and Political Development*, Princeton, N.J.: Princeton University Press, 1966, pp. 3–42; and William Nisbet Chambers and Walter Dean Burnham, eds., *The American Party Systems: Stages of Political Development*, 2d ed., New York: Oxford University Press, 1975.

2. For examples, see Richard Rose and Derek W. Unwin, "Persistence and Change in Western Party Systems Since 1945," *Political Studies*, 18 (1970), 287–319; V. O. Key "A Theory of Critical Elections," *Journal of Politics*, 17 (1955), 3–18; V. O. Key "Secular Realignment of the Party System," *Journal of Politics*, 21 (1959), 198–210; Paul R. Abramson, *Generational Change in American Politics* (Lexington, Mass.: Lexington Books, 1975); David Butler and Donald Stokes, *Political Change in Britain*, 2nd coll. ed., New York: St. Martin's 1976; Everett Carll Ladd, Jr., *American Political Parties: Social Change and Political Response*, New York: Norton, 1970; and Everett Carll Ladd, Jr. with Charles D. Hadley, *Transformation of the American Party System: Political Coalitions from the New Deal to the 1970's*, New York: Norton, 1976. See, also, Kevin Phillips, *The Emerging Republican Majority*, New Rochelle, N.Y.: Arlington House, 1969; and Ben Wattenberg and Richard Scammon, *The Real Majority*, New York: Coward and McCann, 1970.

3. Maurice Duverger, *Political Parties*, trans. by Barbara and Robert North, New York: Wiley, 1954; Otto Kirchheimer, "The Transformation of the Western European Party Systems," in LaPalombara and Weiner, eds., *Political Parties and Political Development*, pp. 177–200; Otto Kirchheimer, "The Waning of Opposition in Parliamentary Regimes," *Social Research*, 24 (Summer 1957), 127–156; and Leon Epstein, *Political Parties in Western Democracies*, New York: Praeger, 1967.

4. Anthony Downs, *An Economic Theory of Democracy*, New York: Harper & Row, 1957.

5. Frank L. Wilson, "Change in the French Party System Since 1958," paper delivered at the 1975 Annual Meeting of the American Political Science Association, San Francisco, September 2–5, 1975.

6. Frédéric Bon, et al., *Le Communisme en France*, Paris: Armand Colin, 1969; Ronald Tiersky, *French Communism 1920–1972*, New York: Columbia University Press, 1974; and Donald L. M. Blackmer and Sidney Tarrow, eds., *Communism in Italy and France*, Princeton, N.J.: Princeton University Press, 1975.

7. Howard Machin and Vincent Wright, "The French Socialist Party in 1973: Performance and Prospects," *Government and Opposition*, 9 (Spring 1974), 123–145; Jean-François Bizot, *Au Parti des socialistes: plongée libre dans les courants d'un grand parti*, Paris: Grasset, 1975; Pierre Guidone, *Histoire du nouveau parti socialiste*, Paris: Editions Téma, 1973; and Machin and Wright, "The French Socialist Party: Success and Problems of Success," *Political Quarterly*, 56 (January 1975), 36–52.

8. Frank L. Wilson, "The Left in French Politics: Prospects for Union," *Contemporary French Civilization*, forthcoming; and Howard Machin and Vincent Wright, "The French Left Under the Fifth Republic: The Search for Identity in Unity," *Comparative Politics*, 10 (October 1977), 35–68.

9. David R. Cameron, "Stability and Change in Patterns of French Partisanship," *Public Opinion Quarterly*, 36 (Spring 1972), 19–30.

10. Frank L. Wilson and Richard Wiste, "Party Cohesion in the French National Assembly, 1958–1973," *Legislative Studies Quarterly*, 1 (November 1976), 467–490.

11. William G. Andrews, "Presidentialism and Parliamentary Electoral Politics in France: A Case Study of Evreux, 1952 and 1973," *Political Studies*, 21 (October 1973), 311–320.

12. See Lipset and Rokkan, "Cleavages, Structures," and Ladd, *American Political Parties*.

13. Samuel P. Hays, "Political Parties and the Community-Society Continuum," in Chambers and Burnham, eds., *American Party Systems*, pp. 152–181.

14. See esp. Seymour Martin Lipset, "The Changing Class Structure and Contemporary European Politics," *Daedalus*, 93 (Winter 1964), 271–303.

15. Valéry Giscard d'Estaing, *French Democracy*, Garden City, N.Y.: Doubleday, 1977.

16. See Stanley Hoffmann, "Paradoxes of the French Political Community," in Stanley Hoffmann et al., *In Search of France*, New York: Harper, 1965, pp. 26–41.

17. Richard Rose and Derek Urwin, "Social Cohesion, Political Parties, and Strains in Regimes," *Comparative Political Studies*, 2 (April 1969), 7–67. See, also, Mattei Dogan, "Political Cleavages and Social Stratification in France and Italy," in Seymour M. Lipset and Stein Rokkan, eds., *Party Systems and Voter Alignments*, New York: Free Press, 1967, pp. 129–195.

18. Frank V. Sorauf, *Political Parties in the American System*, Boston: Little, Brown, 1964, p. 149.

19. Walter Dean Burnham, "Party Systems and the Political Process," in Chambers and Burnham, eds., *American Party Systems*, p. 281.

20. André Siegfried, *France: A Study in Nationality*, New Haven, Conn.: Yale University Press, 1930, pp. 12–22.

21. See Jesse Pitts, "Continuity and Change in Bourgeois France," in Hoffman et al., *In Search of France*, pp. 235–304; Michel Crozier, *The Bureaucratic Phenomenon*, Chicago: University of Chicago Press, 1964, pp. 203–208, 251–263; and Alfred Grosser, "France: Nothing But Opposition," in Robert A. Dahl, ed., *Political Opposition in Western Democracies*, New Haven, Conn.: Yale University Press, 1966, pp. 284–302.

22. Giovanni Sartori, "European Political Parties: The Case of Polarized Pluralism," in LaPalombara and Weiner, eds., *Parties and Development*, pp. 166–167.

23. Charles Roig and Françoise Billon-Grand, *La Socialisation politique des enfants*, Paris: Armand Colin, 1968, p. 102.

24. Stanley Hoffmann, *Decline or Renewal? France Since the 1930's*, New York: Viking, 1973, p. 136.

25. See, for example, Harvey Waterman, *Political Change in Contemporary France: The Politics of an Industrial Democracy*, Columbus, Ohio: Charles E. Merrill, 1969.

26. See Eméric Deutsch, et al., *Les Familles politiques en France aujourd'hui*, Paris: Editions de Minuit, 1966.

27. Public opinion polls show continued evidence of a political and socioeconomic consensus on specific issues which once divided the French. The cataclysmic events of May 1968 do not appear to have radicalized the general public to the extent that they radicalized portions of the political elite.

28. See Monique Fishelet et al., "L'image du Parti communiste français d'après les sondages de l'IFOP" and Alain Lancelot and Pierre Weill, "L'Attitude des français à l'égard du Parti communiste en février 1968 d'après une enquete de la SOFRES," in Frédéric Bon et al., *Le Communisme en France*, Paris: Armand Colin, 1969.

29. See "Les Français n'ont plus peur du communisme," *L'Express*, July 16, 1964, pp. 17–18, and *Sondages*, 1964 (no. 3), 44–48.

30. Bruce A. Campbell, "On the Prospects of Polarization in the French Electorate," *Comparative Politics*, 8 (January 1976), 272–290.

31. Maurice Duverger and Jacques Fauvet, *Le Bipartisme est-il possible en France?*, Association Francaise des Sciences Politiques, Entretiens du Samedi, No. 3, February 1965. See also François Goguel, "Bipolarisation ou renovation du centrisme?" and Maurice Duverger, *La Démocratie sans le peuple*, Paris: Seuil, 1967.

32. Campbell, "Prospects of Polarization," p. 288.

33. Epstein, *Political Parties*, pp. 31–36, 45.

34. See Frank J. Sorauf, *Party Politics in America*, 2nd ed., Boston: Little, Brown, 1972, pp. 22–23; and David B. Truman, "Federalism and the Party System, in Arthur W. Macmahon, ed., *Federalism Mature and Emergent*, New York: Russell and Russell, 1962.

35. See Nicholas Wahl, "The French Constitution of 1958: The Initial Draft and Its Origins," *American Political Science Review*, 52 (June 1959), 358–382; and François Goguel, "L'Elaboration des institutions de la République dans la constitution du 4 octobre 1958," *Revue Française de Science Politique*, 9 (March 1959), 67–100.

36. Morton Grodzins, "American Political Parties and the American System," *Western Political Quarterly*, 13 (December 1960), 974–998.

37. Theodore J. Lowi, "Party, Policy, and Constitution in America," in Chambers and Burnham, eds., *American Party System*, p. 241.

38. Frank J. Sorauf, "Political Parties and Political Analysis," in Chambers and Burnham, eds., *American Party Systems*, pp. 44–45.

39. Downs, *Economic Theory of Democracy*, pp. 21–35.

40. Duverger, *Political Parties*, p. xxvii.

41. Kirchheimer, "Transformation," p. 184.

42. Ibid., p. 188.

43. Epstein, *Political Parties*, pp. 257–260.

44. Frank L. Wilson, *The French Democratic Left: Toward a Modern Party System*, Palo Alto, Calif.: Stanford University Press, 1971.

45. Jean Charlot, *Le Phénomène gaulliste*, Paris: Fayard, 1969; and Frank L. Wilson, "Gaullism without de Gaulle," *Western Political Quarterly*, 26 (September 1973), 485–506.

46. See Peter Campbell, *French Electoral Systems and Elections since 1789*, 2nd ed., Hamden, Conn.: Archon Books, 1965.

47. Lipset viewed the French two-ballot system as a functional equivalent to U.S. primaries and expected the French parties to become more like their American counterparts. Seymour Martin Lipset, "Party Systems and the Representation of Social Groups," *Archives Européens de Sociologie*, 1 (1960), 50–85.

48. Campbell, "Future of the Gaullist Majority," and Cameron and Hofferbert, "Continuity and Change in Gaullism."

49. On the importance of the relationship between leaders' ambitions and party organization, see Joseph A. Schlesinger, "Political Party Organization," in James G. March, ed., *Handbook of Organizations*, Chicago: Rand McNally, 1965, pp. 764–801.

50. Frank L. Wilson, "The Club Phenomenon in France," *Comparative Politics*, 3 (July 1971), 517–528.

51. Austin Ranney, *Curing the Mischiefs of Faction: Party Reform in America* (Berkeley: University of California Press, 1975), p. 210.

52. Alain Lancelot, *La Participation des francais à la politique*, 3d ed., Paris: Presses Universitaires de France, 1971, pp. 120–221.

53. Sidney Tarrow, "Economic Development and the Transformation of the Italian Party System," *Comparative Politics*, 1 (January 1969), 181.

54. Raphael Zariski and Susan Welch, "The Correlates of Intraparty Depolarizing the Tendencies in Italy: A Problem Revisited," *Comparative Politics*, 7 (April 1975), 407–433.

55. Gerhard Loewenberg, "The Remaking of the German Party System: Political and Socioeconomic Factors," *Polity*, 1 (Fall 1968), 86–113.

56. William Nisbet Chambers, *Political Parties in a New Nation*, New York: Oxford University Press, 1963, p. 10.

57. For example, see Samuel P. Huntington, "Postindustrial Politics: How Benign Will It Be?," *Comparative Politics*, 6 (January 1974), 163–192; and David S. Broder, *The Party's Over: The Failure of Politics in America*, New York: Harper & Row, 1971.

CHAPTER 21

PAN-EUROPEAN PARTIES: PROSELYTES OF THE EUROPEAN COMMUNITY

Zelime Amen Ward

A JOINING OF FUTURES is imminent. Challenged by expanding public allegiance to nonparty groups and institutions, the political parties of Western Europe are reaching a crossroads. At the same juncture in time, the nine nations of the European Communities (EC) also are facing a portentous crossroads: the initiation of direct popular elections to the European Parliament. The elections may signal the transition, beyond the original movement toward economic integration, to cross-national political alignment, eventually even political unity.

The intertwining of the questions of party influence and European unity has become inevitable—but is it fortuitous? What does the waning influence of political parties bode for the furtherance of EC goals? More importantly, what does the fledgling promise of modified political integration among the nine EC nations portend for the wizened party systems of Western Europe?

The immediate consequences of spillover are obvious. Levels of public awareness and participation in EC politics will be heightened. As national parties coopt candidates for the EC Parliament, for example, they will be selecting persons whom the parties were prepared to list at home.[1] The strong national power base would guarantee also a strengthened Community Parliament. In juxtaposition, the national political parties will become open to an expanded mandate, as growing public reliance on party structures for EC representation (or, if the parties abdicate, on the competitive extraparty groups) develops. The expanded network of integrative structures within the EC may serve either to add a new vitality to the national party systems or to hasten the demise of the parties.[2]

552

When the initial period of transition to political integration through a strengthened Parliament is completed, expectations will shift from a change-directed approach to a focus on consolidation. The political alignments that are current will receive fewer challenges and become more secure in their established positions as power brokers. Whether the present system of political parties or a system based on nonparty groups ultimately becomes ensconced in this sunny position will be determined in part by the effectiveness and quality of party responses to the EC direct elections across the next decade.

Cross-National Party Alignments: An Overview

Cross-national party groups have been a central consideration since discussions of European integration were formally initiated after World War II.[3] The party groups were present on an informal basis in the Consultative Assembly of the Council of Europe and in 1953 received formal recognition in the Common Assembly of the European Coal and Steel Community.

Today the party groups are weak but are exercising an influential role in the Parliament of the European Communities. Essentially they are not cross-national parties but rather cross-national parliamentary *Fraktionen*, limited by their own functional difficulties as well as by the weaknesses of the Community Parliament. At present, parties within the Parliament are stratified among six groups: the Christian Democrats (which is the largest group within the EC Parliament), Socialists (the second largest group), Liberals, Conservatives, DEP (primarily Gaullists), and the Communists.

The stratification of party support within the Community electorate provides an indication of the basic alignment pattern if most of the voters were mobilized. Indicators include a 1977 public opinion survey and a compilation of the results of the most recent national election in each of the nine EC nations. The survey and the electoral results yield highly similar proportions, implying a fairly stable pattern of voter alignment. Support for the Socialists is strongest (33% according to the opinion survey, 31% in terms of the summed national elections), followed by the Christian Democrats (23%, 26%), the Liberals (14%, 11%), the Conservatives (10%, 8%), the Communists (9%, 12%), and the parties of the DEP (5%, 5%). Support for other parties was 6% and 7%, respectively. Public willingness to accept other parties (if the first choice were not represented) would benefit primarily the center, that is, the Liberals and Christian Democrats. The party group that is unequivocally rejected most frequently, that is, for which the individual would refuse to vote under any circumstances, is the Communist party.

Despite differences among parties, there is not a strong relation for the general public between party choice and attitudes supportive of a directly elected European Parliament. Communist supporters reflect a somewhat weaker tendency (71%) than do the supporters of other parties (76% to 81%) to favor the direct election; both Communists (21%) and Conservatives (17%) demonstrate a stronger tendency to oppose the election than do the supporters of other parties (7–13%).[4]

The Dilemma of Waning National Party Strength

Waning party influence was noted early by analysts of voting behavior in Western Europe, who have been forced toward critical reevaluations of their theoretical perspectives:[5]

> [One would be inclined to support a position] that deemphasizes the importance of party identification for the analysis of voting behavior and focuses more on the function of party identification as an element of the individual's political belief system and its capability to reduce information costs as well as to constrain diffuse bits of political perception.

The "civic sulkiness" (*Staatsverdrossenheit*) of West German citizens, for example, that became a political slogan early in 1977 contains several connotative dimensions that are appropriate: resentment and irritability toward what is perceived as government inaction in pressing issue areas, coupled with a lack of political self-confidence by citizens.[6]

Public discomfort with party politics is difficult to measure. Yet it is evident from the number of nonparty groups that are establishing themselves within the political process, as well as from public opinion polls that indicate a declining confidence in the parties and their leadership, that the public political demeanor is in a state of flux. Attitudes toward the established systems of parties are assuming a changed character, representing a cross-national response to the growing complexity and urgency of public issues. These include problems of unemployment and school reform; of social security and health care; of energy supplies and protection of the environment; of terrorism, law and order; of European integration and Eurocommunism; and of détente and coexistence.

The expanded use of "citizens' initiatives," as an incursion upon the political domain of the parties, represents a public demand for the renovation of the national party systems. Electoral reversals also signify a challenge to the parties. The West German SPD, for example, was rudely awakened to public discontent by the March 1977 vote in Hesse.[7]

> [The SPD] had become stale in power, was taking the voters for granted, and had ignored clear warning signals. An ingrown bureaucracy had lost touch with the people.

Talks in July 1977 between the SPD/FDP governing coalition and the opposition parties were held to counter the trend. According to the lead article in the *Frankfurter Allgemeine*, "all participants [at the party talks] appear to be aware that regard for the parties has suffered in the recent past."[8]

Helga Schuchardt, member of the FDP parliamentary *Fraktion*, commented succinctly on the problem:[9]

> We have at present . . . two tendencies. One is in politics itself, that is, in the political parties, no longer to talk at all about co-determination (*Mitbestimmung*). They [the parties] now act as if what has been accomplished on questions of [party-public] co-determination . . . is sufficient. On the other hand, there is a very strong movement among the public to be brought into political responsibility much more extensively than has been the case previously—for example in citizens' initiatives, where people have organized themselves and said "we won't drag along with you" (*"wir schleppen nicht mit"*).

Declining party influence also is attributed to the growing technical orientation of the national parliaments and their constituent parties, for example, "it is not controversial speeches but rather technical legal work that determines the order at the German Bundestag."[10]

A comparative perspective is presented by Walther Althammer, who, as vice chair of the CSU *Landesgruppe*, is third in line within the CSU leadership. For Althhammer, the question of waning party influence is double-faceted: a positive side as a "stimulus for the parties" to recognize that the "citizens in growing numbers" want more realistic party leadership on important issues, a negative side in that there is the "danger" that nonparty groups could be "transformed and misused for radical purposes." In response, the established parties should develop a "sober and constructive" orientation toward the extraparty groups.[11]

Karlheinz Reif terms the process by which nonparty groups are activated to the political process the "relativization of the party state."[12]

> The relative influence of the political parties . . . is diminishing in favor of the relatively increasing influence of: (a) interest groups, (b) mass media, (c) the state as well as the (national and multi-national) industrial bureaucracies, (d) the scientific advisory institutions . . . and (e) the "citizens' initiatives" and similar single-purpose movements.

The Backdrop for the Direct Election

The "relativization" or "waning" of party influence has been signaled by the initiation of nonparty groups to the political process as well as by a declining level of support for the established parties. This presents an enigmatic contrast to the expanding strength of the European Communities. Despite severe political and economic problems at the national level, EC member states have continued to move toward tighter integration within the

Community. The Tindemans report[13] provided a major psychological and theoretical stimulus for progress toward European union; the report was buttressed by the signing, on September 20, 1976, of an agreement to hold direct elections to the European Parliament. Acceptance of the agreement has had direct implications for national party structures and functions, as well as for the loose array of party groups already working within the EC Parliament.

Perhaps the most problematic structural issue for the relation between national parties and the Parliament of the EC is that of the double mandate, which permits a member of the Community Parliament to concurrently maintain his or her seat in the national parliament. There are many contentions that the double mandate is a major source of difficulty in the present Parliament, as the constraints of the dual role affect the amount and quality of work performed in both parliaments. Yet the double mandate serves as an invaluable and necessary link. In particular, it must be recognized that significant political power will rest largely with the individual member nations during the immediate future. Those who are exclusively members of the Community Parliament will be able to rely on only a weak and perhaps nonexistent power base. The possibility of a double mandate, therefore, will be retained in the new directly elected Parliament, so that at least some of its members can provide a direct and continuous accounting of the tenor of the national parliaments.[14]

The double mandate opens a broad area to the political parties for activity and influence, an area of which the parties have not yet become fully cognizant. The present alliances of political parties within the Community are inconsequential beyond the domain of the Parliament. The role of the national political parties has revolved around the context of national politics, with interest in only specific aspects of European integration.

However, there appears to be an expanding awareness among national party elites that precedents for future party involvement at the increasingly strengthened level of European politics now are being set. This awareness is encouraging the parties to improve and extend their functions. Within the framework of the EC, cross-European political parties can serve, at the rudimentary level, to transmit political concerns from the base to the center, and, at a more critical level, to establish the future ideological patterns of the EC. If the national parties were to abdicate this role and allow the present EC party groups to remain at a weak level of political influence, the further sapping of the strength of the established parties by nonparty groups would continue.

Another structural issue derives from the constraints placed on Parliament.[15] Within the EC, power is diffused, with few significant sources of power resting in the Parliament,[16] from which the cross-national party groups derive their *raison d'être*. The major decision-making body for the EC is the Council of Ministers, resting on decisions of the component national governments. There is no conflict within Parliament for control of the executive, as no strong supranational executive exists, nor is activity among party groups highly polarized, as there is no possibility for an alternation in power.[17]

The Parliament is basically a consensual body of Europeanists, itself a broad institution of opposition, directed toward the furtherance of integration. Conflict occurs only in technical administrative areas; there is not a set of issues on which the left and right can diverge. Since the 1962–1963 controversy over agricultural prices, there have been no important roll-call votes. Interest groups, in fact, prefer to lobby not the Parliament but the Commission.

The internal functions of the EC party groups also are a source of weakness. Most party members are national politicians following national political careers. Although the upcoming members of the new Parliament will serve from a direct electoral base rather than as delegates of their national parliaments, the legitimacy of the new members will be founded on national constituencies and thereby on the national party systems rather than on the EC party groups. The struggle for power takes place at the national level. The Dutch deputies are perhaps the least constrained in this respect due to the strong popular support in The Netherlands for the principle of European integration and to the security of their electoral list system. Yet the Dutch deputies also must abide primarily by the national rather than the Community-wide political tenor.

The problems are compounded by pressures of work and time. The schedule of travel between the members' national capital, Strasbourg, where most plenary sessions are held, and Luxembourg, which serves as the seat of the General Secretariat of the European Parliament, is tension filled and exhausting. Membership on parliamentary committees creates the added burden of travel to Brussels two or three times each month. It has been estimated that 25% to 30% of the time allocated by the member to his or her Community responsibilities is spent "en route."[18] The difficulties are expanded by the fact that these community duties are superimposed on an already demanding set of responsibilities—to the member's national mandate, to his or her local constituency, and to a personal profession. Ultimately, the European role suffers most heavily.[19]

The strength of the Parliament, and thereby of the cross-national party groups, is also undermined through checks placed on EC delegates by the national parliaments. West Germany represents the most extreme case; the government is required to inform the Bundestag of all ways in which national interests would be influenced by proposed EC regulations which are analyzed in standing committees of the Bundestag, with the prerogative of required testimony by government ministers.[20] Danish intervention through the national Market Relations Committee, whose 17 members are distributed according to parliamentary party proportions, also promotes rigidity. The Danish minister concerned must assure the Market Relations Committee that there is no majority against support of an EC proposal. In the other national capitals, procedures are somewhat less formal. France, in fact, applies no legislative restrictions.

Above all, it is the problem of nationality that most severely constrains party alignments.[21] Among the Christian Democrats, for example, there is considerable cross-national allegiance to a common political philosophy, in particular to the concept of European integration. Yet voting is frequently sectionalized along national lines. In addition, an individual nationality may establish an overbearing presence within a party group. The two largest EC party alignments, the Christian Democrats and the Socialists, are dominated by the West German delegations, who in turn are accountable to the Bundestag. Within the Socialist group, the influential West German SPD delegates determine nominations for committee chairs. Although somewhat mitigated due to weaker group cohesion, the CDU/CSU exercises comparable influence within the Christian Democratic group.

National pressure is also applied on transportation issues by all party delegations from The Netherlands, on discussions of farm prices by the Dutch Christian Democrats, and on numerous policy initiatives by the Danish Social Democrats and the Italian Communists. Even slowness in translating documents, which impedes progress in general, sometimes provokes outbreaks of antagonism between different nationalities in the party groups.

In sum, within the EC, cross-national party alignments are tentative and weak, in spite of the dominant role played by party groups in the Parliament itself. Beyond the EC, party alignments assist cooperation but are not directed toward party integration or the development of a federal party system.[22] There are strong ideological ties between the PCI and PCF, in particular with the increased visibility and theoretical prominence of Eurocommunism.[23] Links among the Socialists also are particularly strong due to their European Liaison Office and a biennial conference which connect the EC parliamentary group with affiliated parties and with the Socialist group in the Consultative Assembly of the Council of Europe.[24] In 1964, the European Union of Christian Democrats was established, but its meetings are infrequent. The Liberals participate in the Liberal International and the Conservatives in the European Union of Conservatives. Yet none of these broad alliances presages the eventual transfer of national party power to the supranational level. At best, they are treaties of friendship and cooperation, with no discretionary power or independent legitimacy at the top.

It is exclusively within the perimeter of the Community Parliament that some degree of party integration, through the six cross-national party groups, currently is pursued. The enlarged bureau, a politically critical parliamentary body which establishes the procedure of Parliament, is composed of the president and vice presidents of the Parliament, as well as the chairs of the party groups. Administrative questions usually are decided among the party groups, as is the presidency, which is rotated every two years among the groups. Party groups also decide appointments to committee chairs and to other parliamentary offices.

Party groups control the plenary proceedings. For debate on the floor of Parliament, group representatives are allotted more time and have priority over individual party delegates. In the committees, the role of the rapporteur is crucial, as he or she becomes responsible for drafting proposals on a particular issue, leading the committee discussion and presenting the formal proposal at the plenary session. Since the late 1960s, the nomination and appointment of rapporteurs has been decided by the party group secretariats. Rapporteurs are distributed proportionately among the party groups, and the individual rapporteur, in turn, maintains close contact with his or her party group.

Cross-national party groups are financially supported by the general budget of the Parliament, which grants a standard sum to each group, supplemented by a proportionate amount per group member and by a translation/interpretation allowance based on the number of languages used by the party group.

A growing administrative staff also has promoted the strengthening of the cross-national party groups within Parliament. The group secretariats, which are based in Luxembourg, are a significant component of parliamentary routine. They continue to function throughout the year, rather than according to the legislative agenda, and establish the first contact for the party groups with issues of administration and policy. Consequently, they have become sources of specialist information.

During the 1970s, the group secretariats increased in both size and expertise. The staff members of the secretariats, who are formally employed by the Parliament, depend on the chairs of the party groups for their positions, which further strengthens the authority of the group chair.

Public Attitudes

Public attitudes provide one of the more reliable indicators of the strength and composition of future party alignments within the new Parliament. The analysis of variations in public attitudes also may assist the development of cross-national party policy.

From the outset, the nine-member Community has been troubled by discrepancies in support for the EC between the new and founding members, although the expanded media coverage of the EC during 1975 momentarily heightened support in Britain and Ireland. By November 1977, a mean of 63% of the national public in the Original Six, versus 56% in the Community, were favorable toward the EC. Of the new members, the Irish are the most supportive of the EC. Irish respondents characterize the Community as a "good thing" (59%) with about the same frequency as do respondents in the original six nations (63%), although 19% of the Irish (versus only 7% of respondents in the founding nations) define the Community as a "bad thing." The Danes, who during Spring 1977 were equivocal (30% for, 30% against, 40% noncommittal or undecided) increased their support for the EC to 37%

six months later, but this was counterbalanced by a 33% ratio of negative assessments. The British are largely negative toward the EC (35% assess the Community as a "good thing," 37% assess it as a "bad thing," and 28% are noncommittal or undecided). The highest levels of support for the EC occur in The Netherlands and Luxembourg, where support also has reflected the greatest continual increase between 1973 and 1977 (from 63% to 74% in the Netherlands, and from 67% to 73% in Luxembourg).[25]

Attitudes toward progressive strengthening of the Community are more heavily negative in Denmark, Britain, and Ireland than elsewhere. In those three nations, 30%, 23%, and 14%, respectively, of the respondents prefer that progress be retarded, by contrast with similar attitudes among only 4% to 9% of the respondents in the original six nations. A majority of respondents in Italy and Luxembourg favor accelerated progress, as do from 37% to 45% of the respondents in the other four founding nations. However, only 12% of the respondents in Denmark, 24% of the British, and 33% of the Irish favor acceleration.[26]

These same three new-member nations also are more heavily reliant on their own national parliaments and thereby will perhaps prove to be hesitant toward placing allegiance in a strengthened directly elected Community Parliament. If a four-point index is constructed to rank attitudes toward the importance of the national parliament,[27] respondents in Denmark (an index of 3.35), Britain (3.22), and Ireland (3.20) attribute the greatest significance to their national parliaments. In the other EC nations, the index rankings are considerably lower: 3.13 in The Netherlands, 3.05 in West Germany, 2.99 in Luxembourg, 2.95 in Belgium, 2.76 in France, and 2.71 in Italy.

Conjointly, the popular conceptualization of the role of the individual national parliament is narrower in the three new nations. Public attitudes in Ireland (70%), Britain (64%), and Denmark (54%) demonstrate a majority in favor of a national parliament that is oriented toward "controlling the use of public funds," which is, among six alternatives, the least progressive and most change-adverse position to be selected. By contrast, only one in every three respondents in the original six nations favored the narrow definition of the national parliament.[28]

However, changes in public attitudes among the three new nations also are evident. Since 1973, the Irish, British, and Danes have become continually more supportive of the direct election of the Community Parliament, with the Irish now placing at the mean for the Original Six (Figure 21–1).

The role of the directly elected EC Parliament, and thereby of the parties that obtain representation in that Parliament, is construed more narrowly by the respondents in the new EC nations than in the founding nations (Table 21–1). Public attitudes toward the role of the EC Parliament are more heavily national than supranational in Ireland, Denmark, and Britain.

In terms of party campaigns for the direct elections to the Parliament, popular opinion among the Original Six favors cross-national alliances among

Figure 21-1.   Public Attitudes "for" the Direct Election of the Community Parliament, 1973-1977

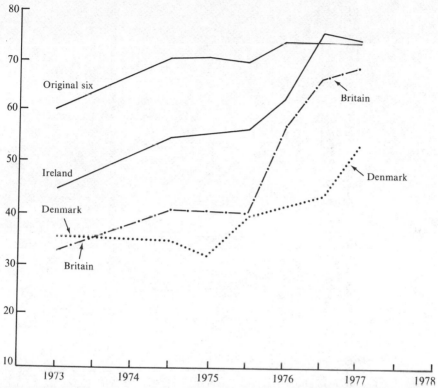

SOURCE: Jacques-Rene Rabier, *Euro-Barometer No. 8: Public Opinion in the European Community,* Brussels: Commission of the European Communities, January 1978, p. 69. Reprinted with permission of the publisher.

parties with similar orientations. In Britain, Denmark, and Ireland, attitudes supportive of campaigning only under the national party label predominate.

Conclusions

If the broad differences between the Original Six and the new EC members, which are basically differences of time and of "socialized" integration within the Community, are applied to an assessment of political parties, a fairly coherent set of conclusions emerges:

1. Effective cross-national party alliances will be more difficult to establish with Britain, Denmark, and Ireland than among the other six EC

TABLE 21-1. Public Assessments of the Appropriate Role for the EC Parliament (November, 1977) (Percent)[1]

	Difference Between National and Supranational Responses	The Immediate National Interest	Interest of the EC as a Whole	Don't Know	Total
	DECISIONS MADE BY THE EC PARLIAMENT SHOULD BE BASED ON:				
The Netherlands	+38	27	65	8	100
Italy	+15	39	54	7	100
West Germany	+13	36	49	15	100
France	+8	40	48	12	100
Luxembourg	+5	43	48	12	100
Belgium	−2	41	39	20	100
Britain	−10	52	42	6	100
Denmark	−16	52	36	12	100
Ireland	−23	58	35	7	100
Total EC[b]	—	45	44	11	100

[a]Jacques-Rene Rabier, *Euro-Barometer No. 8: Public Opinion in the European Community* (Brussels: Commission of the European Communities, January 1978), p. 72.
[b]Weighted average.

nations. In the new member nations, there is an abiding allegiance to the established national parties, coupled with popular disapproval of cross-national party alliances. Among the original six nations, the national publics support the establishment of European party ties (Table 21–2).

2. Time may assist the process of political socialization toward positive public attitudes about party alignments. The maturation of the newer EC members fosters a future of broad public acceptance of strong cross-national parties. In this respect, the postponement of the elections may temper the rise of exclusively national parties for the election and ultimately promote integration among parties.[29]

3. The acceptance of additional new members to the EC, for example, Spain, Portugal, and Greece, will retard cross-national party cooperation.

4. As socialization to the norms of integration proceeds among the new members, the growth of positive public attitudes toward the EC and toward the strengthening of politics at the European level not only will encourage public support of cross-national party systems but also change the character of the national party systems.

5. Public attitudes in the original six nations, by contrast with the three new nations, project a more change-oriented and pivotal role for both the respective national parliaments and the Community Parliament. This may be indicative of a heightened popular willingness to accept a brash and creative restructuring of parties at the national and cross-national levels. It may indeed indicate eventual public support for the strengthening of parties, as integral components of the EC Parliament, at the supranational level. The corollary at the national level could fall to either extreme, that is, either expanded or reduced leverage for the national party systems.

6. The fact that there is less support for strong national parliaments among the Original Six (despite greater support for a pivotal *role* for the national parliaments) may portend a future of waning national party strength. If support for the institution of parliament parallels support for political party structures, public attitudes will become increasingly oriented toward strong cross-national parties that are change oriented and flexible, yet not fully independent of national party prerogatives, which remain subordinate but not insignificant. In short, a federal party system is implied—one that is more heavily balanced in favor of the cross-national entity than is, for example, the U.S. party system.

If attitudes of the political elite are precursors of public attitudes, differences between leaders and nonleaders present significant points of analysis. For the EC, those who are leaders, that is, those who are active participants in the political process, are more supportive of European unification, including cross-national parties, than are the nonleaders.

If leadership is scaled in four categories according to degree of participation in the political process,[30] the level of support for the EC as a "good thing" rises

TABLE 21–2. The Recommended Party Strategy for the EC Parliamentary Campaign, April–May 1977 (Percent)

	BELGIUM	DENMARK	WEST GERMANY	FRANCE	IRELAND	ITALY	LUXEMBOURG	THE NETHERLANDS	BRITAIN	TOTAL EC[a]
Political parties of the same color should unite to campaign in the ensemble of member nations	57	23	47	52	44	66	49	54	38	51
Each national party should campaign under its own banner	21	47	32	30	50	22	39	37	48	33
No response	22	30	21	18	6	12	12	9	14	16
Total	100	100	100	100	100	100	100	100	100	100

Source: Jacques-René Rabier, Euro-Barometer No. 7: L'Opinion Publique dans la Communaute Européenne, Brussels: Commission of the European Communities, July 1977, p. 71.
[a]Weighted average.

from 42% among nonleaders, to 57% among marginal political participants, to 64–65% at the two upper levels of leadership.[31] Similarly, support for acceleration of the movement toward European unification increases according to the leadership level, from 28% among nonleaders, to 39%, 47%, and 58% within each of the higher leadership categories.

The political leaders also demonstrate a strong tendency to aspire for greater prominence of their respective national parliaments (ranging from 44% to 51% to 52% to 63% according to the level of leadership) and to attribute broad significance to the role of the national parliaments.

The national parliament is defined as a body that decides critical contemporary political patterns by 40% of the highest leadership group, to 36%, 32%, and finally 24% of the nonleadership group. By contrast, those who rank lowest in leadership and/or participation have a greater tendency to define the national parliament as merely a problem-solving body (ranging from 36% among the top leadership group to 46% among the bottom leadership group).[32]

In most EC nations, political leaders tend to be more heavily in favor of cross-national party campaigning for the EC election than are the nonleaders. There are exceptions, however, most notably in Denmark, Ireland, and Britain (Table 21–3).

Responses to the question of whether parties of the same political color should unite for the electoral campaign are uniform across all EC nations. In each nation, and in the Community as a whole, support for party alignments increases as the level of political leadership rises. Additionally, support among leaders in each nation has risen over time, averaging a rise among top leaders from 55% to 60% within the EC from November 1976 to May 1977.

Responses to the question concerning each national party conducting its own individual campaign are more variegated. As the leadership level rises, there is no gradual decline in support for that statement, and for the total EC the greatest contrast occurs between the two lower levels of leadership, that is, 30% among nonparticipants in the political process and 36% among marginal participants.

Denmark, Britain, and Ireland, each with over 50% support for the nonalignment statement in either one or both of the two top leadership categories, represent the strongest exceptions to the positive relationship between leadership and support for alignment. In only four nations (Belgium, Ireland, the Netherlands, and Britain) has there been a significant change over time within the top leadership category, in all four cases reflecting decreased support for the nonalignment statement. This is perhaps an indication that with time and increased socialization to the EC, the low level of leadership opposition to cross-national party alignments will decline further in all nations.

The contrast between the patterns of responses to the two statements, in terms of the uniformity of the relationship between level of leadership and support for alignment, is striking. Given, in all nine nations, the gradual rise in

TABLE 21–3. The Recommended Party Strategy for the EC Parliamentary Campaign by Degree of Leadership, April–May 1977 (Percent)

	BELGIUM	DENMARK	WEST GERMANY	FRANCE	IRELAND
Political parties of the same color should unite to campaign in the ensemble of member nations					
Nonleaders (−−)	45	15	30	42	41
(−)	57	23	46	50	43
(+)	70	25	55	57	44
Leaders (++)	73	34	63	60	59
November 1976[a]: Leaders (++)	55	19	63	59	31
Each national party should campaign under its own banner					
Nonleaders (−−)	19	37	28	27	45
(−)	27	46	36	32	52
(+)	19	55	31	30	54
Leaders (++)	16	50	30	30	35
November 1976: Leaders (++)	36	51	28	29	59
No response					
Nonleaders (−−)	36	48	42	31	14
(−)	16	31	18	18	5
(+)	11	20	14	13	2
Leaders (++)	11	16	7	10	6
November 1976: Leaders (++)	9	30	9	12	10
Totals	100 100 100 100	100 100 100 100	100 100 100 100	100 100 100 100	100 100 100 100

	ITALY	LUXEMBOURG	THE NETHERLANDS	BRITAIN	TOTAL EC[a]
Political parties of the same color should unite to campaign in the ensemble of member nations					
Nonleaders (−−−)	55	33	32	33	39
(−)	66	53	51	38	49
(+)	73	50	60	40	56
Leaders (++)	70	59	61	43	60
November 1976[b] Leaders (++)	65	46	56	31	55
Each national party should campaign under its own banner					
Nonleaders (++)	20	41	42	44	30
(−)	22	35	42	49	36
(+)	21	42	33	51	34
Leaders (++)	26	38	33	48	33
November 1976 Leaders (+++)	25	42	40	60	35
No response					
Nonleaders (−−−)	25	26	26	23	31
(+)	12	12	7	13	15
(+)	6	8	7	9	10
Leaders (++)	4	3	6	9	7
November 1976 Leaders (++)	10	12	4	9	10
Totals	100 100 100	100 100 100	100 100 100	100 100 100	100 100 100

Source: Jacques-René Rabier, Euro-Baromètre No. 7: L'Opinion Publique dans la Communauté Européenne, Brussels: Commission of the European Communities, July 1977, p. 72.
[a] Weighted average.
[b] The question was asked only of opinion leaders.

567

support for the alignment statement according to the level of leadership, as well as the rise in support, over time, within the top leadership level, it might be hypothesized that the reverse relationship would characterize the nonalignment statement.

The tendency for top leadership support of the nonalignment statement to decrease over time follows suit, albeit weakly, with the pattern of responses to the alignment statement. Yet there is not, among all nine nations, a uniform decrease in support for the nonalignment statement as the level of leadership rises. In large measure, this lack of uniformity is explained by the high levels of "no response" within the lowest leadership level, which average 31% for the Community as a whole. It appears that there is a dearth of information, which generates a noncommittal response, about the direct elections to the Parliament, particularly among those who are generally nonparticipants in the political process. The nonparticipants, although somewhat weighted toward alignment, divide themselves almost equally among alignment (39%), nonalignment (30%), and "no response" (31%). As leadership level increases, the distribution among the three choices becomes wider. At the third level of leadership, 49% support alignment, 36% favor nonalignment, and 15% do not respond. At the second level of leadership, the respective proportions are 56%, 34%, and 10%; at the top leadership level, 60%, 33%, and 7%.

If the opinion leaders have an effect on the establishment of patterns of political socialization to the EC, and if their own attitudes presage future public attitudes, the future appears to offer growing public acceptance of cross-national alignments among parties for the EC parliamentary campaign. This also implies expanded levels of public support for cross-national party alliances throughout the European Communities.

Conclusions derived from the leadership analysis, therefore, might include the following:

1. It is at the highest level of opinion leadership that there is the strongest support for cross-national party alignment. Moreover, this support is increasing over time.

2. Support for the principle of European unification and the willingness to accelerate the movement toward unification increase in tandem with the degree of leadership. Higher levels of opinion leadership also indicate greater support for a strengthened role for the national parliaments and a definition of that role allocating to the national parliaments the determination of critical national ideological patterns. This stands in contrast to the incremental problem-solving role attributed to the national parliaments by nonleaders.

3. As the leadership level rises, there is a weak pattern of decreased commitment to nonalignment (by contrast with the strong pattern of increased support for alignment). The three new EC nations constitute the major aberrations from the pattern, providing added support to the earlier thesis that

socialization over time to the norms of European unification is a necessary precondition for public acceptance of cross-national alliances among parties.

4. As leadership increases, there is a greater tendency to favor cross-national party alignments as well as to even have an opinion, regardless of its content, on the issue of alignment. Yet the reverse does not hold. Nonleadership does not exclusively indicate an orientation favoring nonalignment but rather also may indicate a noninformed or neutral attitude and reluctance to place oneself on either polar side of the issue. The proportion of replies in the "no response" category is particularly high at the lowest level of opinion leadership, where one of every three respondents is noncommittal.

For the immediate future, it is the lack of information, rather than the specific direction of informed attitudes (as these are continually moving toward positive support of unification and cross-national political processes), that is crucial. There is a serious lack of information that is made readily, broadly, and consistently available to the public. As a consequence, the general public does not perceive EC institutions to be highly salient and thereby often declines even moderate affiliations with Community institutions (e.g., the direct election).

The lack of information about, and socialization to, EC institutions is reflected in attitudes toward voting. Those who attach importance to the act of voting in the direct election tend to explain their vote not in terms of controlling the EC bureaucrats in Brussels but rather with a view toward the significance of electoral participation for the long-term goal of European unification. The reciprocal also holds. Those who do not consider the act of voting for the Parliament to be important are guided not by a fear that the Community Parliament might preempt the powers of the national parliaments but rather by a belief that the act of voting would be a useless endeavor. Again, lack of information about the EC emerges as a crucial variable.

At present, only 47% of the adult populace in the EC nations intends with certainty to vote in the direct elections next spring, although an additional 27% indicate that they "probably" will vote. Youths between 15 and 24 and women over 55 demonstrate the greatest tendency to abstain from voting.

On the issue of information scarcity, there is a cross-cutting of some of the usual cleavages. Regardless of the degree of political leadership and/or participation or the level of education of the respondent, only one in every three persons in the EC nations considers himself or herself to be sufficiently informed about the upcoming direct elections. Where cleavages do occur, it is at the elite level that the dearth of information is realized most acutely. There is a greater tendency to assess one's personal information level about the election as "insufficient" as the level of education rises (i.e., from 53% of those with low educational backgrounds to 57% of those with middle-range educations and 61% of those with a higher education) and as the level of leadership and/or participation is heightened (from 46% at the lowest leadership level to 57% at the two intermediate levels and 63% at the highest level). For the Community, fully 55% of the populace consider themselves insufficiently informed about the election versus only 32% who consider themselves adequately knowledgeable. In Ireland and Britain, two of the three new members, the public assessments of insufficient information are unusually high (64–65%).[33]

The "European Question": A Political Pivot

Attitudes toward cross-national party alignments are explained in part by a scarcity of information. Party strategies for EC electoral campaigns must concern, at present, primarily the broadening of the media coverage of EC events. For the direct election, the parties are facing a two-sided problem: that of information scarcity and, concomitantly, a large proportion of undecided voters, as well as the usual question of ideological cleavages among voters. If waning party strength is to be revitalized and the imprimatur of the European public to be granted to strong cross-national party alignments, the socialization of the public to Community institutions must be encouraged simultaneously with appeals to ideology.

The future prospects for increased public support of the broad principle of European unification, and of cross-national party alignments in particular, are strong. Supportive attitudes appear to be a function of time and of the process of socialization to the EC. Public support of the EC within member nations continues to grow; immediate national interests preempt Community interests primarily in the three new EC nations that have experienced only an abbreviated period of socialization to the EC. Conjointly, opinion leaders demonstrate higher and growing rates of support for processes of further unification, including the cross-national alignment of parties—and it is these leaders who ultimately determine the messages as well as the channels of political socialization.[34] As political leaders belatedly begin to face the dilemma of waning party strength, it may be their response to the "European question" that ultimately decides the future of the national party systems.

Notes

1. There is also a reciprocal effect. If a uniform electoral system, based on proportional representation, is eventually selected for the directly elected European Parliament, the national party organizations would be strengthened considerably, as they would control the EC candidate lists.
2. In general, the development of the EC, which has served, on occasion, to prod parties out of lethargy or political deadlock, has had a positive impact on national

TABLE 21–4. Results of the Elections to the European Parliament 1979: Seats and Some Percentages of the Popular Vote

COUNTRIES (SEATS)	PARTICIPATION		SEATS BY PARTY GROUP (% POPULAR VOTE)						
	EC	Last National Elections	Comm.	Socialists	Liberals	Christian Democrats	Dem. and Progress.	Conservatives	Others
Fed. Rep. (81)	65.9%	91%	—	35 (40.8%)	4 (6.0%)	42 (49.7%)	—	—	—
Belgium (24)	82.0	92	—	7 (23.4)	4 (16.3)	10 (37.7)	—	—	—
Denmark (16)	47.0	70	—	3 (21.9)	3 (14.5)	—	1	3 (14.1%)	4 (17.0%)
France (81)	61.2	85	19 (20.5%)	22 (23.6)	25 UDF (27.8%)		15 (16.3%)	—	7
Gr. Brit. (81)	31.3	76	—	18	—	—	—	60	—
Ireland (15)	58.0	76	—	2	—	5	7	—	1
Italy (81)	85.9	90	24 (29.5)	13 (15.3)	3 (3.6)	30 (36.5)	—	—	11
Luxembourg (6)	85.6	90	—	1	2	3	—	—	—
Netherlands (25)	57.8	80	—	9	4	10	—	—	2
Totals			43	110	20 25 UDF	101	23	63	25

party growth. During the early 1960s, for example, it was Community initiatives that helped eventually to revitalize the calcified West German CDU/CSU. In a 1962 memorandum, the EEC Commission (chaired by West German Walter Hallstein, who was himself a CDU member) proposed long-range economic planning among member states, a goal which threatened the largely antiplanning stance of the CDU under Ludwig Erhard. Yet the strong current of CDU support for EEC institutions carried through the principle of public planning, which quietly began to gain acceptance within the party. The results of formal CDU opposition toward planning became evident during 1966–1968 with the economic recession, the fall of the Erhard government, and the growth of support for the newly founded right-wing NPD. Thereafter, public planning was gradually integrated within party policy and helped to bring the CDU "au courant" with public attitudes.

3. However, the stage was already being set during the war. For a comprehensive documentation of embryonic discussions and strategies for European unification made during the national resistance movements of World War II, consult Walter Lipgens, ed., *Europa-Foederationsplaene der Widerstandsbewegungen 1940–1945*, Munich: R. Oldenbourg Verlag, 1968.

4. Jacques-René Rabier, *Eurobaromètre No. 7: L'Opinion Publique dans la Communauté Européene*, Brussels: Commission of the European Communities, July 1977, pp. 76–82.

5. Max Kaase, "Party Identification and Voting Behaviour in the West German Election of 1969," in Ian Budge and Ivor Crewe, eds., *Party Identification and Beyond: Representations of Voting and Party Competition*, New York: Wiley, 1976, p. 101. Kaase's conclusion that belief systems weigh more heavily than party identification in determining voting behavior may signal not only a new analytic perspective but also waning party strength. The Kaase conclusion provides a contrast with the Inglehart/Klingemann analysis, in which, as a determinant of individual placement on the left-right dimension, "the ideological component tends to be greatly overshadowed by the partisan component everywhere except in the United States." Yet in studying the French case, Inglehart and Klingemann appear to approach more closely the Kaase conclusion. In France "party identification seems to be weaker than in the United States. Important parties have changed their labels repeatedly or disappeared altogether in the last few decades." Consequently, the left-right dimension in France "may serve as a surrogate for party identification. For in France, left-right self-placement is to party identification as party identification is to current party preference." See Ronald Inglehart and Hans D. Klingemann, "Party Identification, Ideological Preference and the Left-Right Dimension among Western Mass Publics," in *Party Identification and Beyond*, pp. 270–271.

6. Note the analyses of *Staatsverdrossenheit* in Eugen Kogon, "Eine grosse Strategie ... /Die Koalitionen und die Parteien," in Walter Dirks and Eugen Kogon, eds., *Frankfurter Hefte: Zeitschrift für Kultur und Politik* 32 (May 1977), 11–16, as well as in *Der Spiegel*, June 27, 1977.

7. George Eckstein, "Germany: The SPD in Trouble," *Dissent* 24, (Summer 1977), 235.

8. *Frankfurter Allgemeine Zeitung*, July 8, 1977, p. 1.

9. Personal interview with Helga Schuchardt, member of the FDP Bundestag Fraktion, June 27, 1977.

10. Michael Hereth, *Die parlamentarische Opposition in der Bundesrepublik Deutschland*, Munich: Günter Olzog Verlag, 1969, p. 32. For a contrasting view, note the positive evaluation of economic and social order, as defined in institutional terms, presented by Heinz Lampert, *Die Wirtschafts-und Sozialordnung der Bundesrepublik Deutschland*, Munich: Günter Olzog Verlag, 1976.

11. Personal interview with Walther Althammer, vice-chairperson of the CSU *Landesgruppe*, July 29, 1977.

12. Karlheinz Reif, "Speculations on the Establishment of Party Government in the European Community," paper prepared for discussion at the 4th Annual Joint Sessions of Workshops of the European Consortium for Political Research, Louvain, April 1976, pp. 17–18. Note also the comments on the weakening of partisanship in Ivor Crewe, "Prospects for Party Realignment: An Anglo-American Comparison," paper presented at the Annual Meeting of the American Political Science Association, Washington, D.C., September 1977.

13. In late 1974, Belgian Prime Minister Leo Tindemans was asked by the heads of government of other EC member states to prepare a report on the future of European unity. The Tindemans report, published on January 7, 1976, proposed continued advanced toward a federalist community, including the beginnings of a common external policy; a "citizen's Europe" incorporating the right of appeal by Community citizens to the Court of Justice when individual rights have been violated by Community institutions; expanded powers for the European Parliament and the Commission; routine majority voting in the Council of Ministers; and renewed initiatives toward economic and monetary union according to a two-tier plan, which would allow lower-tier nations to postpone monetary integration.

14. For expanded detail, see the debate of the issue of the double mandate by national delegates to the EC symposium on the future of European integration held in Luxembourg, May 2–3, 1974: European Parliament, Directorate General for Research and Documentation, *Symposium on European Integration and the Future of Parliaments in Europe: Summary Report*, Brussels: European Parliament No. 36–967, 1974.

15. For a cogent analysis of the implications for cross-national party alignments of the structural strengths and weaknesses of Community institutions, see Geoffrey Pridham, "Transnational Party Groups in the European Parliament," *Journal of Common Market Studies*, 13 (March 1975), 266–279.

16. The 1970 Treaty of Luxembourg granted Parliament control of only a small and insignificant portion of the Community budget. There is indeed a provision in the Treaty of Rome for a parliamentary motion of censure against the Commission, but, as demonstrated by the 1972 attempt of Socialist leader Georges Spenale to introduce censure, the provision is not supported by strong political force and represents at best an opportunity for rhetorical indignation.

17. The dynamism of political parties has been hampered, in part, by the low degree to which conflict is exposed within the Community. If, as Ralf Dahrendorf notes, "conflict is liberty," then a "democratic" European Community must ensure the continual interplay of diverse interests and policies. In a 1978 speech before the House of Commons, Frank Judd, British minister of state for foreign and commonwealth affairs, referred to this problem and stressed the need for integrity

and vigor of debate within the Community rather than "the smooth, manipulative techniques of technocratic government." See Ralf Dahrendorf, *Society and Democracy in Germany* (Garden City, N.Y.: Doubleday, 1967), p. 147; and British Information Services, *Survey of Current Affairs*, 8 (March 1978), 90.

18. Based on a 1971 estimate by Karlheinz Neunreither. See Pridham, p. 277.

19. Not only for legislators, but also for governments, Community responsibilities may constitute a final insurmountable burden that upsets the contrived balance of the political system. The Danish tax revolt during the early 1970s, for example, may be attributed, in part, to the added pressures on the bureaucracy created by Denmark's entry into the EC. See Arnold J. Heidenheimer, Hugh Heclo, and Carolyn Teich Adams, *Comparative Public Policy: The Politics of Social Choice in Europe and America*, New York: St. Martin's Press, 1975, pp. 246–251.

20. In addition, several West German *Laender* maintain their own representatives in Brussels. The Schmidt government, in general, supports the principle of European unification but is critical of disproportionate West German financial commitments that weigh to the advantage of poorer EC members, e.g., Britain and Italy. Note the sketch of West German relations with the EC in David P. Conradt, *The German Polity*, New York: Longman, 1978, pp. 218–219.

21. The socialist parties face an additional internal constraint: an identity crisis in the face of European unity. See W. E. Paterson, "Social Democratic Parties of the European Community," Alastair H. Thomas, "Danish Social Democracy and the European Community," and Peter Byrd, "The Labour Party and the European Community, 1970–1975," *Journal of Common Market Studies*, 13 (June 1975), 415–418 and 454–483.

22. Proposals made by the Dutch labor party for a federal system of parties no longer receive serious attention.

23. Recent studies of the upswing of the Communist Left include Donald Blackmer and Sidney Tarrow, eds., *Communism in Italy and France*, Princeton, N.J.: Princeton University Press, 1975; *Les Partis Communistes d'Europe Occidentale, Etudes Internationales*, 6 (September 1975); Neil McInnes, The Communist Parties of *Western Europe*, London: Oxford University Press, 1975; and Andre Harris and Alain de Sedony, *Voyage a l'interieur du Parti Communiste*, Paris: Editions du Seuil, 1974.

24. Moreover, it is frequently maintained that the Socialists encourage and maintain transnational contacts both within and beyond the party structure to a greater degree than do the members of any other party. See, for example, James May, "Cooperation Between Socialist Parties," in William E. Paterson and Alastair H. Thomas, eds., *Social Democratic Parties in Western Europe*, London: Croom Helm, 1977; and May, "Is there a European Socialism," *Journal of Common Market Studies*, 13 (June, 1975), 492–502. The dilemma of the Socialists' crossnational ties to the working class is discussed as they expose their theory of the mobilization of support for socialist parties, applied to West Germany, France, and Sweden, in Przeworski and Sprague, "A History of Western European Socialism," paper presented at the Annual Meeting of the American Political Science Association, Washington, D.C., September 1977. Yet conflict among the EC socialist parties also is evident, for example, the problematic January 1976 meeting of Socialists in Elsinore, Denmark (*Agence Europe Bulletin*, December 10, 1975).

25. Jacques-René Rabier, *Euro-Barometer No. 8: Public Opinion in the European Community*, Brussels: Commission of the European Communities, January 1978, pp. 48–49 and A6–A7. Britain and Denmark also are distinguished by the low levels of support for European unification within the electorate of several of their parties. Specifically these comprise respondents who identify with the Socialist People's party and Progress party in Denmark (65% and 52% antiunification, respectively) and with the Labour party in Britain (37% antiunification). See Werner J. Feld and John K. Wildgen, *Domestic Political Realities and European Unification: A Study of Mass Publics and Elites in the European Community Countries*, Boulder, Colo.: Westview Press, 1976, p. 70.

26. Rabier, *Eurobarometre No. 7*, pp. 26–27.

27. The role of the national parliament is "very important": 4, "important": 3, "hardly important": 2, "not at all important": 1.

28. Rabier, *Eurobarometre No. 7* pp. 32 and 35.

29. The positive impact of the time dimension on attitudes toward the EC also is indicated, from a contrasting perspective, by public assessments of the near versus distant future. Respondents in a 1958 French public opinion survey evaluated the effects of the EEC on the French economy more highly positive for a future 15-year period than for a 5-year period (*Sondages*, 1972, 1–2, p. 56). In Britain, positive attitudes toward Community membership prior to the 1975 referendum were based in part on respondents' concern for the "future of British children," *Gallup Political Index*, June 1975, no. 179, p. 30.

30. The leadership/participation scale is based on responses to two questions: (1) the frequency with which the respondent engages in political discussion—"frequently," "from time to time," "rarely," "never," "no response," and (2) the frequency with which the respondent, in his or her political discussions, convinces others to adopt the political orientation favored by the respondent—"frequently," "from time to time," "rarely," "never," and "no response." Top leaders (++) were those who both discussed politics "often" and convinced others "often" or "from time to time." Other leadership participation categories were distributed similarly according to the quality and frequency of political discussion. The cumulative distribution for the Community in the spring 1977 survey was comprised of 13% top leaders (++), 31% second-tier leaders/participants (+), 35% at the third tier (−), and 21% at the fourth tier of nonleaders/nonparticipants (−−).

31. Rabier, *Euro-Barometer No. 8*, p. 32.

32. Rabier, *Eurobarometre No. 7*, pp. 28 and 34–35.

33. Ibid., pp. 60–61, 74–75, and 83.

34. A note of caution regarding strong and expanding leadership support of unification also is necessary. The future approach among political leaders may be less evangelical than does the present. "It may be the case that the motives of leaders in new parties are purposive and 'mission'-oriented at first, but shift later, often within the tenure of the original office holders, to a more pragmatic and materialistic approach to political careers." See Kay Lawson, *The Comparative Study of Political Parties*, New York: St. Martin's Press, 1976, p. 231. But are the EC party groups "new parties"?

CHAPTER 22

CITIZEN LOBBIES IN WEST GERMANY

Jutta A. Helm

OBSERVERS OF GERMAN POLITICS in the 1950s and 1960s argued almost uniformly that Germany lacked a participatory political culture. Most Germans shared a subject orientation toward politics, and, while voting was high, more informal modes of political involvement such as discussing public issues or forming political groups were limited.[1] It appeared that most citizens were content to remain on the sidelines and leave politics to those who claimed to possess the required expertise. Even as late as 1968 Edinger concluded that "the contemporary distribution of participant roles is unlikely to undergo major changes in the foreseeable future."[2] As with many earlier prognostications, this prediction was soon overtaken by new developments; the student movement, the extraparliamentary opposition, and, beginning in 1970, perhaps the most far reaching change, the citizen lobby movement.[3] The growth of citizen lobbies is illustrated by some recent opinion polls. In 1973, about 2.0 million citizens were active or had recently been active in citizen lobbies. This figure assumes additional significance in view of the fact that only 1.8 million citizens are members of political parties. Moreover, whereas 12% of all respondents in a representative survey indicated their willingness to be active in political parties, 34% said that they were willing to join a citizen lobby.[4]

The citizen lobbies have already altered the parameters of citizen participation in German politics and, in the process, have left their mark on the political system itself. In the following pages I shall describe the citizen lobbies and their activities, explain their emergence and in conclusion, assess their impact on the German political system.

576

It will become clear that citizen lobbies as such are not new. In the American context especially, but also in Germany, groups promoting various types of public causes and issues have a long tradition. In fact, in democratically constituted polities such groups are protected by civil liberties such as the freedom of assembly and the right to petition. I am not arguing then that citizen lobbies are a new phenomenon in Germany or anywhere else. Rather, my interest is based on their dramatic increase in variety and number during the past seven years in Germany and the very real signs of further development of a participatory political culture.

Citizen Lobbies: Membership and Goals

Citizen lobbies can be defined as more or less loosely organized groups of citizens committed to the promotion of broader goals or, more often, to the realization of specific aims and plans at the local or regional level. The membership of citizen lobbies tends to be middle class. Civil servants, especially teachers, white-collar employees, professionals, and students predominate. Only about 10% of the members are workers. This is true even in the industrial Ruhr area, where blue-collar workers make up the bulk of the labor force.[5] There are a number of reasons for the rather unrepresentative membership structure of citizen lobbies. For one, individuals who are economically well off or even affluent are more receptive, or more committed, to idealistic concerns and values. In a recent cross-national study Inglehart found that respondents from nine countries who enjoyed objectively high levels of need satisfaction were much more likely to express a concern for quality of life issues rather than material well-being and physical security.[6] This is not surprising. Lower-class or working-class individuals devote a comparatively greater share of their energies and time to provide for basic needs.[7] Social psychologists have also emphasized that the lack of individual autonomy in the family, educational institutions, and the world of work tends to depoliticize lower-class individuals and reduces their capacity to empathize with the deprivation and suffering of others.[8] The experience of numerous lobbies further indicates that individuals in the lower class can be mobilized more easily against a deterioration in living conditions that they have experienced personally and directly. Finally, workers, because they are much less aware of their rights as citizens, are more easily intimidated by verbal threats or brash refusals on the part of officials to deal with citizen demands. Middle-class members are more likely to see such reactions for what they are: attempts to demoralize group members who threaten to disturb the officials' ability to do business as usual.

Critics and public officials have attempted to discredit the legitimacy of citizen lobbies and their concerns on the basis of their socially skewed membership. But, if this is a liability, it is one that the lobbies share with virtually every other group or association, including most interest groups and political parties. Data about newly recruited party members show that civil servants, the self-employed, and professional persons are much more likely to join than are workers or low-level white-collar employees.[9] Diederich concluded that "[a]lthough politics in Germany is not a privilege of the wealthy, it can be said that the membership basis of political parties is distorted in favor of the higher strata."[10] The more important question, however, is whether the middle-class basis of the citizen lobbies' membership distorts their activities in favor of the special interests of middle-class groups. Are leftist critics and conservative observers correct when they charge that citizen lobbies are middle-class clubs attempting to obtain special advantages and privileges for their members?[11] To answer this question it will be necessary to take a look at the goals pursued by the lobbies.

The most comprehensive study of citizen lobbies—based on a sample of 1,403 groups—concluded that about 48% of all lobbies pursue social and cultural issues and that 43% devote themselves to environmental issues— broadly defined.[12] A breakdown reveals the following categories:

I. Environmental issues

Environmental protection	17.0%
Traffic	12.0
Urban planning	8.0
Historic monuments	2.5
Urban renewal	3.6

II. Social and cultural issues

Nursery schools and playgrounds	16.0
School issues	8.0
Marginal groups (convicts, slumdwellers, gypsies, foreign workers)	7.0
Tenant issues	5.5
Youth issues	5.0
Communal facilities (swimming pools, etc.)	4.0
Cultural affairs	3.3
III. Narrow groups interests	5.0
IV. Commercial interests	2.0

This list shows that the overwhelming number of lobbies in categories I and II pursue inclusive interests, whose benefits will be available to many citizens. Even where the lobbies deal with the problems of specific groups (such as foreign workers or preschool children), one would be hard pressed to argue that middle-class privileges were being established or protected. This does not apply, however, to the small number of groups in categories III and IV. These lobbies are often cited as examples of the narrow pursuit of group interests. Wealthy homeowners, who oppose building an orphanage in their neighborhood, or the owners of pubs and restaurants lobbying for the repeal of the beer tax, obviously do not fit the prevailing pattern of citizen lobbies oriented to the common good or general welfare.[13] Indeed, as one student of the lobbies puts it, they have as much in common with the typical citizen lobby as the average citizen with the mass murderer.[14]

One of the more fruitful classifications of citizen lobbies divides them into *pro*groups and *anti*groups.[15] Progroups fight for nursery schools, parks, facilities for the handicapped, lower teacher-student ratios in schools, and similar benefits. Their supporters tend to be progressively oriented middle-class persons, often joined by more conservative church groups who are motivated by charitable considerations. Antigroups oppose highways, garbage dumps, urban renewal, or zoning laws that permit the building of industrial plants in or near residential areas. Their membership is also mixed, leftist critics of capitalism joining conservatives who feel that environmental deterioration and destruction of rural communities and neighborhoods are too high a price for economic growth.[16] Often, these groups collide dramatically with established powers and elites over the desirability of technocratic planning decisions which are backed by powerful economic interests and bureaucracies. In the past two years, for example, citizen lobbies opposed to construction of nuclear reactors have forcefully articulated these conflicts over social goals and the unquestioning acceptance of quantitative economic growth.[17] They succeeded in translating these concerns into legitimate social and political issues that are now discussed in policy-making institutions at all levels of government.[18] According to one estimate, investments totaling $8 billion in the energy sector are frozen for the time being, and road construction projects totaling $1.6 billion in the Rhineland alone cannot be completed.[19] Needless to say, at a time of high unemployment and faltering economic growth these "achievements" provoke harsh reactions from construction companies, utilities, and trade unions.

Organization and Activities

How do citizen lobbies manage to force consideration of their goals and objectives? How are they organized and what strategies do they use? It is difficult to describe organization and activities of a "typical" citizen lobby because there is so much variation, depending in part on the resources of the group, its target, and its goals. But some general comments can be made. For one, it is useful to distinguish between loosely organized lobbies and those—amounting to about 70%—that are formally organized either as registered associations or as foundations.[20] Generally, more spontaneous, single-issue lobbies tend to prefer an informal organizational structure, and they often disband after accomplishing their objective. Experience indicates that bureaucrats and spokesmen for government agencies tend to be more responsive to lobbies with a firmer organizational structure, denoting both respectability and continuity. Whatever their organizational status, citizen lobbies have to find members and supporters. It appears that in most cases the impetus originates with a few concerned individuals who try to win support from their friends and colleagues. At the same time some rudimentary publicity activities—posters, newspaper articles, letters to the editor—are organized to attract additional members. The central theme in all these efforts is usually the suggestion that everybody is actually or potentially affected by a certain policy, decision, or omission. Rhetorical excess is not uncommon; clean air lobbies have organized marches and demonstrations in which the marchers wore gas masks. A group protesting the construction of an airport near Munich drove a van through adjoining towns from which a loudspeaker produced authentic landing and take-off noises. The resulting wave of indignation in the latter case was a very effective recruiting device. Such spectacular recruiting efforts are more the exception than the rule, but they illustrate that the initiators of a new lobby often resort to unusual activities to advertise their lobby and win supporters. Once a sufficiently large membership basis has been established, efforts are shifted to holding the members' commitment. This is particularly important if the lobbies are to prevent the estrangement of the group's rank-and-file members from its leadership.[21] An effective group also needs financial resources. Posters, leaflets, newspaper ads, and telephone bills have to be paid for, and, at least initially, most groups rely on their members' contributions. Once established, many groups succeed in receiving material and financial aid from churches, trade unions, and sometimes even public funds. It appears that lobbies which undertake self-help projects, especially those devoted to children and youths, are most likely to receive public support.[22]

As my remarks on recruitment and fund-raising efforts suggest, the activities of citizen lobbies do not deviate significantly from the behavior of more established pressure groups. These parallels carry over into their strategies: reliance on personal contacts to win influential allies in high places, efforts to receive favorable press coverage, and the attempt to secure assistance in the formulation of alternative plans and proposals. All this is part of the familiar arsenal of pressure group activity, and it is not surprising that the success of a lobby is closely related to the concreteness of its goals and to its ability to mobilize those who will be affected by a plan or policy.[23] In important ways, however, citizen lobbies do not fit the mold of typical pressure groups. For one, they operate primarily on a local and regional basis. Increasingly, the major interest groups in industrial systems have shifted their operations to the national level, following the growing centralization of decision-making processes. And, while it is true that in Germany local communities have lost many of their traditional prerogatives, the fact remains that these communities administer and execute a range of policies that affect everybody. Before the emergence of citizen lobbies on a large scale, administrative and executive decisions at the local level were primarily influenced by local business elites.[24]

Their influence was hard to ignore, since they contribute a large share of the local tax revenue (*Gewerbesteuer*). In a very real sense citizen lobbies have served to correct the probusiness bias in local decision-making structures. Citizen lobbies are also distinguished from traditional pressure groups by their mode of operation. In part because of their limited financial resources, but, more largely, because of their commitment to an expansion of participatory opportunities, citizen lobbies are essentially do-it-yourself operations, relying as much as possible on their own members and resources. The Federal Association of Citizen Lobbies for Environmental Protection is a good example, with the association's director, assisted by one full-time staff member, coordinating the activities of 900 environmental lobbies. The 75 to 200 letters which arrive daily are answered by friends and volunteers. In technical matters the association draws on the expertise of 45 scientists that support its aims.[25] Although the reception of citizen lobbies is often mixed, lack of competence or expertise has been a rare criticism. "It is amazing," according to one observer, "how frequently citizen lobbies take on a lot of hard and intensive work to inform themselves, to study all technical, scientific and organizational questions, buy books and find experts . . ."[26]

This survey of the activities and characteristics of citizen lobbies suggests several questions about their emergence. Why this burst of citizen activism in the early 1970s? Why did citizens bypass established political channels to express their demands? In suggesting an answer to this question, three factors will be considered: political values and socialization experiences, dissatisfaction with the functioning of bureaucracies, and the perceived malaise of representative political institutions.

Socialization and Political Values

There is substantial evidence that the citizen lobby movement was facilitated by changes in political values in the 1960s and early 1970s. For example, survey data indicate that interest in politics took a remarkable upswing in the late 1960s (Table 22–1).

TABLE 22–1.   Interest in Politics in Germany (Generally speaking, are you interested in politics?) (Percent)

	JUNE 1952	*FEBRUARY 1960*	*AUGUST 1965*	*OCTOBER 1967*	*NOVEMBER 1969*	*JULY 1973*
Yes	27	37	35	37	44	49
Somewhat	41	40	43	35	40	40
No	32	33	22	28	16	11

Source: Adapted from Juergen Mirow, "Entpolitisierung oder Integration?" in *Zeitschrift fuer Politik*, vol. 23 (1976), no. 11, p. 48.

It is interesting that this rise in political interest coincided with the spread of television in West Germany. Today, virtually every household owns a television set, and four-fifths of all Germans rely on the evening news as a source of information. In addition, television offers a rich and variegated fare of political programs, including frequent panel discussions of controversial issues where critical and opposing viewpoints are presented. It is difficult, however, to assess the impact of television on mass political attitudes, especially participant motivations. It appears that such information as citizens derive from television is more likely to reinforce rather than alter prior beliefs. Moreover, high-ranking white-collar employees and more educated citizens—who tend to participate more—place greater emphasis on newspapers as their primary source of information.[27]

Many observers agree that the student movement made a definite contribution to the politicization of German citizens. By focusing on the need to improve the operation of democratic institutions, in an effort to awaken the broad public to politics, student protesters became an important precursor and impetus for the citizen lobby movement.[28] In a sense, there is a parallel between the student movement and the citizen lobbies: both responded to a new political awareness. The citizen lobbies, however, opened up a whole new array of issues and goals. In 1969 and later the new outlooks received official encouragement from political elites. When Chancellor Brandt presented his legislative program to the Bundestag in October 1969, he promised to "risk" more democracy, to "create an opportunity for every citizen to contribute to the reform of state and society."[29] No wonder the accession of Brandt's social-liberal coalition to political power was often perceived as initiating a process of political change.

In assessing the impact of the student movement and the change of power in national politics in 1969 on attitudes and political values, it is probably fair to classify them as *Zeitgeist* effects, leaving their mark on all German citizens, regardless of age. Because most citizen lobby members are between 25 and 50 years of age, we must also ask whether there is evidence of attitude change among these age cohorts. More precisely, did their socialization experiences instill values and attitudes which fostered a greater willingness to be politically active? To answer this question definitively, we would need panel data. Lacking such data, we cannot be quite sure whether the observed differences between age groups result from unique cohort experiences, from the different composition of the age cohorts, or from life-cycle factors. The following remarks are therefore of a tentative nature.

There is impressive evidence of change in the political values and attitudes of the German public. Conradt, in an analysis of panel data from 16 surveys between 1949 and 1971, documents a dramatic increase in public support for political competition and freedom of expression.[30] The variable that contributed most significantly to aggregate change was age. Those under 30 were considerably more supportive than older respondents. Jennings and

Jansen have demonstrated generational gaps in attitudes toward political change and diversity as well as some data on the differing political priorities of parent-youth pairs in Germany. Of particular interest for our purposes is their finding that younger respondents are more willing to engage in unconventional forms of political participation (petitions, boycotts, demonstrations) to achieve political objectives.[31] The most ambitious effort to trace generational value changes is Inglehart's study of the "post-material phenomenon."[32] Starting with the observation that a large portion of Western populations has been raised under conditions of exceptional economic security, he demonstrates that their values show a greater emphasis on the quality of life, whereas concerns for material well-being and physical security assume a higher priority for older respondents. This shift in values is accompanied by changes in the distribution of political skills. Whereas mass publics have long participated in "elite-directed activities," they are now able to participate increasingly in "elite-challenging" activities taking place outside of established organizations such as labor unions, political parties, and religious institutions[33] (Table 22–2). Inglehart's evidence is quite relevant to an explanation of the German citizen lobby movement. For one, the issues pursued by many citizen lobbies are indeed quality-of-life concerns rather than the more traditional "bread-and-butter" issues. Second, citizen lobbies operate outside of the traditional participatory vehicles such as political parties and labor unions, indicating a broader spread of political interest as well as a wider distribution of potential counter-elites among the public. Considering that Germany has joined the circle of stable and prosperous nations only recently, it is not surprising that the percentage of German respondents choosing postmaterial value priorities over materialist values is only a relatively modest 8%.[34] More important, however, is the fact that younger respondents—whose formative political experiences coincided with a period of relative affluence—chose postmaterial values much more frequently: 19% of the respondents between the ages of 19 and 28 indicated such a value preference as compared with only 10% of the respondents 69 years and older.[35] It can be assumed that, in the last decade, citizen lobbies pursuing environmental and quality-of-life issues have been able to draw on a growing pool of potential members among younger citizens. It is also quite possible, however, that the current economic problems experienced by West Germany and other industrial nations will lead to greater concern with material security among younger age cohorts in the future.

Numerous studies have demonstrated a relationship between education and political attitudes and values.[36] Inglehart's research indicates that in Germany, as well as in other Western nations, preferences for postmaterial values increase strongly with the respondent's education.

These data are interesting for several reasons. For one, they suggest that the greater preference for postmaterial values among younger respondents is not simply due to the higher levels of education that they have received. There is a considerable spread in the value preferences of younger and older

TABLE 22–2. Value Choices of German Respondents by Age Cohort, Controlling for Education (Percentage choosing acquisitive or post-bourgeois values)

AGE IN 1970	PRIMARY			SECONDARY			UNIVERSITY		
	Acquisitive	Post-bourgeois	Number	Acquisitive	Post-bourgeois	Number	Acquisitive	Post-bourgeois	Number
16–24	25	15	(235)	11	36	(47)	7	61	(28)
25–34	36	12	(353)	28	31	(36)	18	47	(17)
35–44	49	6	(330)	29	21	(28)	17	33	(6)
45–54	50	7	(278)	31	3	(29)	18	27	(11)
55–64	63	4	(278)	35	7	(29)	25	25	(8)
65+	59	2	(213)	44	0	(27)	20	20	(5)
Spread: from youngest to oldest cohort	+34	−13		+33	−36		+13	−41	

Source: Ronald Inglehart, "The Silent Revolution in Europe: Intergenerational Change in Post-Industrial Societies," *American Political Science Review*, 65 (1971), p. 1004.

respondents with the same level of educational attainment. Moreover, the data seem to rule out the possibility that the value changes are merely a life-cycle phenomenon. The younger age cohorts do have higher levels of formal education, but these are not going to disappear as the individuals grow older. In fact, evidence from American studies shows that education-related age differences are quite stable over time.[37]

Although we have no data on the educational backgrounds of citizen lobby members, some inferences can be drawn from our knowledge of their social class background and occupational status. As was mentioned above, workers and lower-level white-collar employees are underrepresented, and self-employed professionals, civil servants, and white-collar employees in middle- and upper-level positions are overrepresented. It appears that members are disproportionately recruited from groups with a high level of formal education who are more open to consider postmaterial values. But the high educational level of the membership is significant for another reason as well. Education is related to political efficacy, rates of participation, and the quality of participation. Citizen lobbies depend very much on the motivation and self confidence of their members. Their skills and commitments are needed to compensate for the lack of more traditional organizational resources.

The high level of formal education of citizen lobby members also suggests an answer as to why citizen lobbies exist at all: Why did citizens not opt for the more traditional participatory outlets such as established interest groups, political parties, churches, and cultural organizations? Inglehart implies that individuals who are highly educated and politically well informed increasingly seek a different quality of participation than these traditional organizations have to offer. They prefer a new mode of participation that is more issue-oriented, aiming at specific policy changes rather than simply supporting "our leaders." They opt for ad hoc groups rather than established bureaucratic organizations.[38]

Finally, the introduction of civics courses in the German school curriculum should be mentioned. There has been much speculation about the effects of such direct socialization efforts on the growth of participatory attitudes. After World War II political leaders of all ideological persuasions agreed that such preadult socialization efforts would have a profound impact on the political outlooks of future adults, as well as on the stability of German political institutions. There is some disagreement on the contents of such political instruction, with the result that both quality and quantity of civic education vary from state to state and from school to school. It is also quite unclear what—if any—influence civics courses have on the political orientations of German youths. Some empirical studies have shown little difference in the political knowledge and attitudes of students who had civics courses and those that did not.[39] Especially among students in university preparatory schools, the evidence shows that participant attitudes acquired in the home may be reinforced in schools. But it is comparatively more difficult for schools to counteract apathetic attitudes formed in the home. And the earlier enthusiasm of political elites for civic education waned considerably when it became evident that those students who had the greatest exposure to such courses—students in the university preparatory high schools—were also the ones to supply a generous number of student radicals in the late 1960s.[40]

To conclude, there is a good deal of indirect evidence to suggest that citizen lobbies emerged because of changes in political values and an upgrading of the political skills among younger age groups. Value changes include a heightened interest in politics, greater support for freedom of expression, as well as a higher priority for postmaterial values. In part these changes seem to result from the socialization experiences of younger citizens growing up in a period of relative affluence, in part from increased levels of education, and in part from the impact of the student movement in the late 1960s and the change of political power in national politics. Yet it would be one-sided to attribute the emergence of citizen lobbies to attitudinal and value changes alone; structural factors also played an important role.

The Malaise of Representative Political Institutions

There is evidence throughout Europe that the vitality of representative organizations like political parties and interest groups "has been sapped in part by bureaucratization and in part by the failure of leadership [and] administration . . . to cope with social change."[41] This is not an entirely new development. Twelve years ago, Otto Kirchheimer, in his insightful discussion of party systems in Western European politics, warned that, in the catchall party, the role of top leadership groups is strengthened, whereas the role of the individual party member is downgraded.[42] In the case of Germany, a number of empirical studies have confirmed Kirchheimer's analysis. Political parties have been characterized as oligarchical institutions with deeply entrenched leadership groups and only minimal opportunities for rank-and-file participation in the making of political decisions.[43] Specific charges include the suppression of minority or dissenting viewpoints in party groups, the manipulation of party congresses, preserving the semblance of internal democracy while effectively controlling the discussion of issues or causes that leaders find unacceptable, and leadership recruitment processes that discriminate in favor of establishment candidates.[44] Curiously, this narrowing of party channels has led not to apathy, but to a search for alternate participatory structures.

The very fact that citizen lobbies became popular as an alternative and sometimes in opposition to political parties explains the rather mixed reaction amongst established elites. Especially in the early 1970s, when the lobbies were still a new phenomenon in the German political landscape, it was not uncommon for party politicians to react with biting criticism. Some party leaders even warned that the lobbies were not at all concerned with remedies for concrete problems, but had much more far reaching goals. "They want to overthrow the social order, mobilize prerevolutionary movements and prepare the breakthrough of the pure theory they profess."[45] There was even speculation that the lobbies were incompatible with the system of representative democracy provided in the basic law. Eventually, however, a more sober perspective won out. The parties seemed to realize that it was not good political strategy to denounce and alienate voter groups whose goals were often warmly approved even by less active citizens.

Nevertheless, some tension between political parties and citizen lobbies persists. Many party politicians feel that the lobbies should serve as early-warning systems, alerting decision makers to political problems before they become acute, thus enhancing the efficiency of administrative and political institutions.[46] Others feel that their party should "infiltrate" citizen lobbies and convince the members that their aims can best be accomplished by working through a political party. The CDU, for example, in a manual for party members, encourages them to assume visible and leading roles in citizen lobbies. "Take the initiative, and keep the reins in your hand. Make it clear that correct solutions can only be carried through in cooperation with a political party."[47] Politicians from the Free Democratic party are most consistently supportive of the participatory claim the lobbies articulate. This is confirmed by reports that FDP members are overrepresented in citizen lobbies; in addition, lobbies which maintain contacts with political parties seem to evaluate their relations with the FDP most favorably.[48] It is also interesting in this context that most citizen lobbies do not address their demands to political parties or representative assemblies.[49] Obviously, several factors, such as the nature of the issue, influence the choice of their target, but it appears that their lack of confidence in the responsiveness of representative institutions also plays somewhat of a role. Although the reaction of political parties to the citizen lobby phenomenon is somewhat ambiguous, it is well to remember that the lobbies themselves are somewhat uncertain about their status too. Opinions fluctuate between the concept of direct democracy on the one hand and the narrower view of merely supplementing and improving the somewhat defective representative process on the other.

The dissatisfaction with representative institutions has also colored citizens' evaluation of the more established interest and pressure groups. It would not be unreasonable to suspect that once again the German antipluralist tradition was raising its ugly head. But, as noted earlier, the criticism of interest group activity echoes the themes that are familiar in Anglo-Saxon critiques of pluralism as well. It is difficult for marginal groups to match the political resources of producer groups, and, even more fundamentally, general concerns and interests affecting the entire citizenry are not effectively articulated.[50] In fact, as a German political scientist put it, the chances for the successful articulation of an interest diminish in direct relation to its generality.[51] Mayer-Tasch argues that, due to the growing awareness of environmental deterioration, these critiques of pluralism have become part of public discussion and concern. Citizen lobbies came to fill a widely perceived gap when they began to organize and articulate general interests which the traditional system of interest groups had systematically ignored. Perhaps the most dramatic illustration is provided by the Federal Association of Citizen Lobbies for Environmental Protection. In just four years, the association came to coordinate the activities of 900 citizen lobbies which claim 300,000 members. This strong response would indicate that environmental concerns were not effectively articulated by established representative institutions. The German experience is not unique, however. The success of independent "ecology" candidates in the French municipal election of March 1977 suggests that, in France as well, representative institutions were lagging a growing public concern for environmental issues.[52]

Bureaucracies and Citizens in Germany

While the effectiveness of representative institutions in Western societies declined, bureaucracies expanded their roles. Especially since the end of World War II governments have increasingly intervened in social, economic, and cultural domains. "Having assumed functions as organizer, producer and protector, the state invests, subsidizes, nationalizes, and redistributes."[53] In Germany this implied further growth in the size and complexity of an already formidable bureaucratic structure. For citizens, it meant that individual decisions and choices were increasingly replaced by an all-encompassing network of bureaucratic regulations and controls. Sontheimer and other analysts of German politics report that German citizens have long displayed a divided reaction to bureaucracy. On the one hand, administrators were respected as the bearers of governmental authority. On the other, bureaucracies were resented because of red tape and cumbersome procedures.[54] This second response has become stronger in recent years. Survey data from 1969 and 1971 show that half or more of all respondents complained about bureaucratic practices and the expansion of bureaucratic jurisdictions.[55] Negative evaluations of bureaucracy are not limited to Germany.[56] It appears, however, that attitudinal and behavioral characteristics of German bureaucrats, conditioned no doubt by the continuity of bureaucratic structures in German political development, have intensified public awareness of bureaucratic pathologies. Among these pathologies an often provocative arrogance in the behavior of civil servants, complicated and lengthy procedures, lack of flexibility in the implementation of rules and procedures, and inefficiency have been mentioned frequently.[57] It is not surprising then that over half of all citizen lobbies are directed at bureaucracies.[58] A particular target of the lobbies is the bureaucratic reluctance to consult with groups that will be affected by their decisions. At the same time—and this applies especially to planning decisions—bureaucracies have often developed close relationships with well-organized and articulate economic interest groups. There are several reasons for this bias in the flow of information and communication processes. For one, bureaucracies tend to feel more comfortable with technocratic visions and priorities, and they tend to disqualify as improper "interference" attempts by citizen groups to force them into an open discussion of priorities and goals. It is important in this context that the German bureaucracy has long ceased to play a merely instrumental role, delimited and defined by legislative decisions.[59] Also, the attitudes of bureaucrats toward citizen participation are relevant here. Upper-level administrators in German state governments—especially those over 50—still identify quite closely with antipluralist orientations. The principles of political control and public participation in decision making are at best incompletely reflected in the attitudes of these officials.[60]

These attitudes have also influenced the reactions of local bureaucracies to citizen lobbies. Local administrators are quick to point out the narrow group interests represented by the lobbies, or the high cost of delaying the implementation of community projects. The lobbies defend the delays by arguing that substantial erosions of the quality of the social and ecological environment are an unacceptable price for administrative efficiency and speedy policy implementation. Often, moreover, administrators themselves are directly responsible for these dilemmas when they discourage or rule out public participation in the policy planning stage. As a result, opposition and criticism often surface in the implementation stage when conflicts over basic goals and objectives are much harder to resolve.

It also appears that local administrators have made little effort beyond the verbal endorsement of citizen participation to pursue a policy of active cooperation and communication. Their efforts to collect information about citizen lobbies are haphazard at best; as a result many local governments have only very scanty knowledge about organization, activities, goals, or membership of local lobbies.[61] Moreover, there is usually no effort to coordinate the interaction with lobbies; every agency follows its own policy, thus making government activities even less predictable and transparent. Despite this haphazard approach, many local governments manage to maintain good relations with some citizen lobbies. One study reports that in a few instances local governments have actually organized citizen lobbies. Most of these are active in the social welfare sector, providing services for which the local governments are responsible. Sometimes citizen lobbies receive direct assistance—in the form of material, personnel, or even financial support. These lobbies usually advocate noncontroversial projects for children or youth. But conflicts and confrontations are frequent in such policy areas as environmental protection, urban planning, and urban renewal.[62] This is not surprising. These issues often confront the participants with a choice between economic growth and environmental quality, between technocratic visions of progress and local autonomy. Several observers have predicted that the growing awareness of the interrelationships between economic activity and environmental quality will lead to an intensification of conflicts in these areas.[63] So far the developments support this interpretation.

Citizen lobbies are not entirely dependent on the goodwill of local governments and administrative agencies to open up participatory channels. In some instances, such channels are already available. One such example are revisions of municipal charters in several states, providing new and expanded avenues for citizen participation in local government. In Bavaria, the amended municipal code requires that a public meeting be held if 5.0% of all residents (or 2.5% in larger communities) request the public discussion of a local issue. The law further provides that municipal councils must debate the recommendations adopted at the public meeting within three months.[64] A similar provision in the municipal code of Rhineland-Palatinate requires that mayors submit an issue to the municipal council if 10.0% of all residents approve of the proposed measure. (To prevent the misuse of this provision by radical groups, the code stipulates that the initiative must include a proposal for the financing of the proposed measure.) In Baden-Wuerttemberg, municipal councils are now required to improve communication processes with local residents. Specific measures include the introduction of question periods and public hearings by the councils and the holding of public meetings. In addition, citizens can petition municipal councils to put specific issues on their agenda. Similar provisions have been adopted in Hesse, Saar, and Berlin. Frequently, the new laws explicitly welcome the activities of citizen lobbies, and there is no doubt that the revised procedures facilitate the lobbies' efforts to influence decision-making processes at the local level.

This applies also to several federal laws regulating urban planning decisions.[65] Citizens who will be affected by urban renewal projects are entitled to participate even in the early phases of the planning process when goals and objectives are defined. At this stage, citizen lobbies can be very effective in establishing communication links between citizens and planners. A report on urban planning issued by the federal government explicitly acknowledged that planning decisions must be based on a compromise of conflicting interests. It even went so far as to suggest specific approaches, such as the concept of advocacy planning, to ensure that the concerns of underprivileged groups will be articulated and considered by the planners.[66] On the whole, the report is rather unequivocal in its emphasis on democratic control and participation, even at some cost in administrative efficiency. In practice, however, planners often find it hard to live up to the lawmakers' intent, as I tried to show in the discussion of bureaucratic reactions to demands for citizen participation.

A recent revision of the Federal Planning Act indicates a stronger concern for the efficiency of the planning process. The act provides that planning agencies are not required to grant hearings to each and every individual or group that has entered a similar objection or protest against a planning decision. Instead, the agency may respond to these objections in summary fashion, that is, by publishing hearing dates or final decisions in the local press. This revision—which has since been extended to other federal laws such as the Emission Control Act and the Nuclear Licensing Act—is based on a growing concern among administrators and planners that citizen lobbies or disgruntled individuals can effectively clog administrative channels by encouraging citizens to submit objections to proposed plans en masse. These fears are not entirely unjustified. The agency responsible for the licensing of a planned nuclear reactor in Brokdorf (Schleswig-Holstein) received over 20,000 objections, many of them encouraged by citizen lobbies who opposed the construction of the reactor.[67] What is the trade-off between efficiency and due process? No one will object to procedures which are more efficient in evaluating and weighing the substance of these objections. It is questionable, however, whether this is the intent of recent revisions in licensing laws.

These examples of statutory requirements for citizen participation in local government and planning decisions indicate an awareness that traditional forms of political participation have proven inadequate to the desires of a growing number of citizens to affect government decisions.[68] At the same time, there is a concern for administrative efficiency. But the vast scope of government activity may well require new approaches to ensure that this activity is responsive to citizen concerns and interests.

Conclusion

Many German citizens are no longer content to remain spectators of political events. One might ask, however, whether this growth of political activism is altogether desirable. On the left, observers have criticized citizen lobbies as inadequate to the task of bringing about fundamental political change, especially in the relationships of production.[69] This judgment is certainly correct. But there is no good reason to disregard any political phenomenon simply because it implies reform rather than revolution. On the right, observers cite the basic law in support of their argument that citizen lobbies threaten to undermine the legitimate authority of elected and appointed officials.[70] Do the citizen lobbies really represent a surreptitious entry of plebiscitary formulas into German political life? These fears appear quite unfounded. By and large, the lobbies' activities do not go beyond the articulation and aggregation of political interests. In comparison with traditional interest groups, the lobbies' resources are quite limited and only a few cases of "improper" or "excessive" pressure have been reported.

Mayer-Tasch argues that the lobbies' central contribution consists of invigorating and strengthening representative political institutions.[71] His point is well taken in view of the prevailing meaning of the concept of representation. Accordingly, responsiveness to the preferences of constituents is a vital aspect of representation in a democracy.[72] Whereas this requirement does not rule out disagreement between the representative and the represented, it does mean that when there is such a disagreement, an explanation or justification of the representative's action is called for. In this sense, citizen lobbies are an ideal vehicle for meaningful communication between political representatives and their constituents. Rather than undermining the representative nature of political institutions, the lobbies themselves are in danger of being neutralized by the manipulations of decision makers. There are some examples of lobbies that were coopted into decision processes, whereas planners controlled the agenda and circumvented the consideration of new or divisive issues.[73]

The most challenging interpretation of the growth of citizen participation in postindustrial societies like West Germany is provided by Huntington's "ungovernability thesis." Briefly, it is said that "[t]he expansion of participation could make postindustrial society extraordinarily difficult to govern."[74] This argument—which springs from assumptions about the complexity of policy issues in postindustrial systems—is often used to justify further centralization of decision-making processes. However, it should be noted that decentralized structures have a greater capacity to innovate, to correct mistakes, and to absorb new information. Further, there is evidence that participation, insofar as it creates a willingness to cooperate, may make complexity manageable.[75] Finally, it could be said that Huntington's argument is indicative of a profound difficulty of postindustrial politics: the increasingly central role of values, not means, and the difficulty of integrating conflicting values in decision processes. The experience of many citizen lobbies suggests that decision makers often try to resolve this problem by insisting that no trade-off exists, that there is no conflict between different goals and values. Perhaps the significance of the citizen lobby movement in West Germany is in its contribution to the effort of publicly addressing questions about ends, or value choices.

Notes

1. Gabriel A. Almond and Sidney Verba, *The Civic Culture*, Boston: Little, Brown, 1965, pp. 312–313.
2. Lewis J. Edinger, *Politics in Germany*, Boston: Little, Brown, 1968, p. 195.

3. The German term is *Bürgerinitiative*. It is here translated as citizen lobby.

4. *Infas-Report* of July 23, 1973, p. 1.

5. Barbara Borsdorf-Ruhl, *Bürgerinitiativen im Ruhrgebiet*, Essen: Siedlungsverband Ruhrkohlenbezirk, 1973), p. 80.

6. Ronald Inglehart, "Value Priorities, Objective Need Satisfaction and Subjective Satisfaction Among Western Publics," *Comparative Political Studies*, 9 (1977), 454.

7. Compare the interesting discussion by Hans-Eckehard Bahr, *Politisierung des Alltags—Gesellschaftliche Bedingungen des Friedens*, Darmstadt/Neuwied: Luchterhand, 1972, p. 29.

8. Bahr, p. 19.

9. Some data on the occupational stratification of party members are cited in Bernt Armbruster and Rainer Leisner, *Bürgerbeteiligung: Zur Freizeitaktivität verschiedener Bevölkerungsgruppen in ausgewählten Beteiligungsfeldern*, Göttingen: O. Schwartz, 1975, pp. 100 ff.

10. Nils Diederich, "Zur Mitgliederstruktur von CDU and SPD," in Jürgen Dittberner and Rolf Ebbighausen, eds., *Parteiensystem in der Legitimationskrise*, Opladen: Westdeutscher Verlag, 1973, p. 42.

11. Compare Claus Offe, "Bürgerinitiativen und Reproduktion der Arbeitskraft im Spätkapitalismus," in Heinz Grossman, ed., *Bürgerinitiativen: Schritte zur Veränderung?*, Frankfurt: Fischer Taschenbuch, 1971, pp. 152 ff., who summarized the approach of leftist critics.

12. Paul von Kodolitsch, "Gemeindeverwaltungen und Bürgerinitiativen," in *Archiv für Kommunalwissenschaften*, 14 (1975), 274.

13. For some examples see Wolfgang Hoffmann, "Die grosse Blockade," *Die Zeit*, September 2, 1977, pp. 14–15.

14. Peter Cornelius Mayer-Tasch, *Die Bürgerinitiativbewegung*, Reinbek: Rowohlt, 1976, p. 93.

15. Theo Rasehorn proposed this classification. "Schwarz oder rot, wir schlagen euch tot," *Der Spiegel*, March 21, 1977, p. 42.

16. Reimer Gronemeyer, "Bürgerinitiativen—Die Politisierung des Wetters," in *Frankfurter Hefte*, 31 (1976), 106.

17. For some accounts of the antireactor lobbies, compare Craig R. Whitney, "Ecologists Stall Bonn's Atom Power Plants," *The New York Times*, March 30, 1977, p. 8; Horst Bieber, "Bürgerkrieg in der Wilster Marsch," *Die Zeit*, November 26, 1976, p. 2.

18. On January 26, 1976 the Bundestag finally held its repeatedly postponed energy debate. *Deutscher Bundestag*, Stenographische Berichte, 7. Wahlperiode, 215. Sitzung, pp. 14916 ff.

19. Hoffmann, *Die Zeit*, pp. 14–15.

20. Kodolitsch, pp. 269 ff.

21. Mayer-Tasch discusses the importance of "organization maintenance" for the citizen lobbies, p. 129.

22. Kodolitsch, p. 270; Armbruster and Leisner, p. 175.

23. Armbruster and Leisner, p. 173; Rolf-Peter Lang et al., "Zur Rolle und Funktion von Bürgerinitiativen in der Bundesrepublik und Westberlin," *Zeitschrift für Parlamentsfragen*, 4 (1973), 274.

24. Mayer-Tasch, p. 60.

25. Horst Bieber, "Aufwiegler mit bürgerlichen Skrupeln," *Die Zeit*, February 25, 1977, p. 2.

26. "Schwarz oder rot," p. 44.

27. Lewis J. Edinger, *Politics in West Germany*, 2nd ed., Boston: Little, Brown, 1977, p. 136.

28. Ludwig von Friedeburg, "Youth and Politics in Germany," *Youth and Society*, 1 (1969), 106; Horst Zilleseen, "Bürgerinitiativen im repräsentativen Regierungssystem," in Hans Dietrich Engelhardt, ed., *Umweltstrategie*, Gütersloh Verlagshaus Gerd Mohn, 1975, p. 414.

29. Willy Brandt, "Legislative Program," delivered before the Bundestag on October 28, 1969. Reprinted in Peter Pulte, ed., *Regierungserklärungen, 1949-1973* (Berlin: Walter de Gruyter, 1973), p. 228.

30. David P. Conradt, "West Germany: A Remade Political Culture?," *Comparative Political Studies*, 7 (1974), pp. 230 ff.

31. M. Kent Jennings, Rolf Janse, "Die Jugendlichen in der Bundesrepublik: Der Wunsch nach Veränderung und Meinungsvielfalt in der Politik," *Politische Vierteljahresschrift*, 17 (1976), 319-340.

32. Ronald Inglehart, *The Silent Revolution*, Princeton, N.J.: Princeton University Press, 1977, passim.

33. Ibid., p. 3.

34. Ibid., p. 38.

35. Ibid., p. 36.

36. For evidence on the effect of education on political attitudes, compare Gabriel A. Almond and Sidney Verba, *The Civic Culture*, esp. pp. 315-324.

37. Klaus R. Allerbeck, "Political Generations: Some Reflections on the Concept and Its Application to the German Case," *European Journal of Political Research*, 5 (1977), 127.

38. Inglehart, *The Silent Revolution*, p. 300.

39. This is discussed by Ludwig von Friedeburg, "Youth and Politics in Germany," *Youth and Society*, 1 (1969), 95; and Klaus Köhle, "Ergebnisse einer Untersuchung zum Wissensstand und zur politischen Einstellung von Volksschülern," *Politische Studien*, 22 (1971), 274.

40. Edinger, *Politics in West Germany*, 2nd ed., p. 129.

41. Joint Committee on Western Europe, "New Perspectives for the Study of Western Europe," *European Studies Newsletter*, 5 (1975-1976), 11.

42. Otto Kirchheimer, "The Transformation of the Western European Party System," in Kurt L. Shell, ed., *The Democratic Political Process*, Waltham: Blaisdell, 1969, p. 300.

43. Compare Ulrich Lohmar, *Innerparteiliche Demokratie: Eine Untersuchung der Verfassungswirklichkeit politischer Parteien in der Bundesrepublik*, Stuttgart:

Enke Verlag, 1963, passim; Jürgen Dittberner, "Funktionen westdeutscher Partei-Tage," in Otto Stammer, ed., *Party Systems, Party Organizations, and the Politics of the New Masses*, Berlin, Institute of Political Science, 1968, pp. 116–128.

44. Joachim Raschke, *Innerparteiliche Opposition*, Hamburg: Hoffmann & Campe, 1974, passim; Bruno Zeuner, "Wahlen ohne Auswahl—Die Kandidaten-aufstellung zum Bundestag," in Winfried Steffani, ed., *Parlamentarismus ohne Transparenz*, Köln: Westdeutscher Verlag, 1971.

45. Hans-Jochen Vogel, "Wenn Bürger was wollen—Auch Bürgerinitiativen habe ihre Grenzen," *Die Zeit*, June 6, 1972, p. 58.

46. Horst Waffenschmidt, member of the Bundestag (CDU), quoted in Hanspeter Knirsch and Friedhelm Nickolmann, *Die Chance der Bürgerinitiativen*, Wuppertal: Hammer Verlag, 1976, p. 37; similarly Zillessen, p. 421.

47. Bundesgeschäftsstelle der CDU, "Regiebuch 3", quoted in Knirsch and Nickolmann, p. 38.

48. Lange, pp. 266–279.

49. Kodolitsch reports that only 8% of the lobbies in his study addressed representative institutions, p. 271.

50. Compare the discussion on the growth of public support for political competition and diversity, above.

51. This formulation was introduced by Ernst Forsthoff. Compare *Der Staat in der Industriegesellschaft*, München: C. H. Beck, 1971, p. 25.

52. This was reported in "Leftists Again Gain in French Elections," *The New York Times*, March 21, 1977, pp. 1, 15.

553 Mattei Dogan, "The Political Power of the Western Mandarins: Introduction," in Dogan, ed., *The Mandarins of Western Europe: The Political Role of Top Civil Servants*, New York: Wiley, 1975), p. 5.

54. Kurt Sontheimer, *The Government and Politics of West Germany*, New York: Praeger, 1973, p. 144.

55. The surveys are cited in Mayer-Tasch, pp. 40, 41.

56. For evidence on the attitudes of American respondents toward bureaucracy, compare Daniel Katz et al., *Bureaucratic Encounters*, Ann Arbor, Mich.: Institute for Social Research, 1975, pp. 119–120, 126, 138.

57. Mayer-Tasch, p. 41; Lange, p. 283; Thomas Ellwein, "Formierte Verwaltung Autoritäre Herrschaft in einer parlamentarischen Demokratie," in Winfried Steffani, op. cit., p. 48.

58. Several authors report that most citizen lobbies address the bureaucracy. See Mayer-Tasch, p. 75; Armbruster and Leisner, pp. 181–182.

59. Fritz Scharpf, *Planung als politischer Prozess*, Frankfurt: Suhrkamp, 1973, p. 114.

60. Bärbel Steinkemper, *Klassische und Politische Bürokraten in der Ministerialverwaltung der Bundesrepublik Deutschland*, Köln: Carl Heymanns Verlag, 1974, pp. 68 ff.

61. Kodolitsch, p. 268.

62. Ibid., pp. 273–275.

63. Ibid., p. 276; also Gronemeyer, pp. 102–103.

64. This is discussed by Ulrich Battis, "Bürgerinitiativen als Gegenstand der Gesetzgebung," *Zeitschrift für Parlamentsfragen*, 6 (1975), pp. 140 ff.

65. I am referring here to the *Städtebauförderungsgesetz* and the *Bundesbaugesetz*.

66. "Städtebaubericht der Bundesregierung," reprinted in *Verhandlungen des Deutschen Bundestages*, 6, Wahlperiode, Anlagen Band 144/1970, Dr. 6/1497, especially pp. 51 ff.

67. This example is discussed in Bieber, p. 2.

68. Willy Brandt, "Die Verantwortung der Kommunen für den Ausbau der Demokratie," in *Bulletin des Presse und Informationsamtes der Bundesregierung*, June 10, 1973, p. 1238.

69. Helga Fassbinder, "Bürgerinitiativen und Planungsbeteiligung im Kontext Kapitalistischer Regionalpolitik," *Kursbuch*, 27 (1972), pp. 68 ff.

70. Wilhelm Hennis, quoted in Mayer-Tasch, p. 74.

71. Mayer-Tasch, p. 76.

72. Hanna Fennichel Pitkin, *The Concept of Representation*, Berkeley: University of California Press, 1972, pp. 232–233.

73. This possibility is also discussed by Zillessen, p. 438.

74. Samuel P. Huntington, "Postindustrial Politics: How Benign Will It Be?," *Comparative Politics*, 6 (1974), 177.

75. Armbruster and Leisner, p. 195.

CHAPTER 23

A LEGITIMACY CRISIS OF THE GERMAN PARTY SYSTEM?

Werner Kaltefleiter

THE DEVELOPMENT OF THE GERMAN PARTY SYSTEM after World War II has been a tremendous success for a long time. The transformation of a multi-party system of the Weimar type into a nearly Anglo-Saxon party system with two governmental party coalitions, CDU/CSU and SPD/FDP, alternating in power, characterizes a development, which, according to political observers, began with the "German electoral miracle" in the second general election of 1953. Indeed, the contrast to the development in the Weimar Republic, in which a fragmented multiparty system had collapsed under the burden of the world economic crisis, was remarkable.

This development can first be described by the process of orientation of voting behavior toward the three parties CDU/CSU, SPD, and FDP which gained less than 73% of the total vote in 1949 but 94% in 1961. In the beginning this process primarily favored the CDU/CSU, which increased its votes from about 31% in 1949 to 45% in 1953, which was enough to gain the absolute majority of seats in the German *Bundestag*. One party gained a parliamentary majority for the first time in the history of German parties and parliaments (Fig. 23–1).

Figure 23-1.   The Development of the German Party System

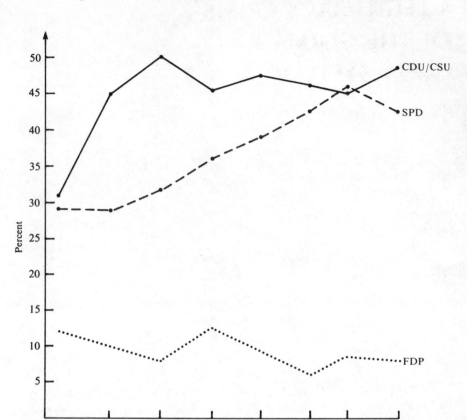

This was more than a large gain in votes. It was the transformation of the party from a minority party in a multiparty system to a majority party in a parliamentary system of the Anglo-Saxon type. The SPD followed this development very slowly. The change in ideology, program, and style of leadership after the party convention in Godesberg in 1959 was the most important precondition for the party's gradual increase in votes of about three percentage points from one election to the other up to the election of 1972, in which the party gained 46% of the total vote.

What were the main reasons for this development? Two main variables have to be mentioned. First was the coalition formation in 1949 in which Adenauer's first government coalition brought together his own CDU/CSU with the FDP and other small bourgeois parties, thereby leaving the SPD in the role of the opposition. In the Weimar Republic, the moderate parties of the center had formed a broad coalition government which gave the right- and left-wing radicals the privilege of the opposition role. This time the moderate Social Democrats fulfilled this crucial role in a democratic system. This decision structured the German party system according to the dichotomy of government and opposition. During the economic miracle this structure was able to integrate the different splinter parties into the CDU/CSU, which explains the large gains of this party in 1953 and again in 1957. After 1958 the slow erosion of consensus within the Adenauer coalition increased the voting support of the SPD over the next 15 years.

The upshot of this development was an asymmetry of the German party system in the late 1950s and in the 1960s which led to the first legitimacy crisis of the party system. After ten years in power, the CDU was unable to renew itself; it offered the formulas of the 1950s to solve the problems of the 1960s. When Erhard succeeded Adenauer in the chancellorship, after four years of internal party struggle in 1963, the change in leadership led only to a short period of perceived innovation. The SPD, on the other hand, had the impression that, given this asymmetry of the party system, they could only gain power by the way of a "grand coalition" with the CDU/CSU. The price for this strategy was a lack of effective opposition in the 1960s that finally led to this coalition in 1966.

The legitimacy crisis of the party system became obvious at that time. Besides numerous opinion poll data that showed, for example, a sharp decline in partisanship, the activities fo the New Left and the electoral success of a new right-wing party, the NPD, in some state elections demonstrated this critical situation. The New Left, referred to as the extraparliamentary opposition (APO), and the success of the NPD were the results of the CDU/CSU/SPD coalition. It is a fundamental rule of a democratic system that the lack of opposition *in* the system leads to opposition *against* the system if dissatisfaction occurs at the same time. This was the case with the economic development in 1966 at which time the highest inflation rate of about 4.0% was reached, followed by economic stagnation and an increase in unemployment to 3.5% in 1967 (Table 23–1). The impact of the combination of these two variables, the lack of opposition and economic dissatisfaction, explains the success of the NPD in the state elections, especially in the state election of Baden-Württemberg in spring 1968, in which it gained 10% of the vote.

The revival of leftist activities was also the consequence of this coalition. These were people from the left wing of the SPD who considered this coalition

TABLE 23–1. The General Election of 1965 (by State) and the State Election from 1966 to 1969 (Percent)

	DATE OF STATE ELECTION	GENERAL ELECTION OF 1965				STATE ELECTIONS 1966–1969			
		CDU/CSU	SPD	FDP	NPD	CDU/CSU	SPD	FDP	NPD
Hamburg	3-27-66	37.6	48.3	9.4	1.8	30.0	59.0	6.8	3.9
Northrhine-Westphalia	7-10-66	47.1	42.6	7.6	1.1	42.8	49.5	7.4	—
Hesse	11-6-66	37.8	45.7	12.0	2.5	26.4	51.0	10.4	7.9
Bavaria	11-20-66	55.6	33.1	7.3	2.7	48.1	35.8	5.1	7.4
Rhineland-Palatinate	4-23-67	49.3	36.7	10.2	2.5	46.7	36.8	8.3	6.9
Schleswig-Holstein	4-23-67	48.2	38.8	9.4	2.4	46.0	39.4	5.9	5.8
Lower-Saxony	6-4-67	45.8	39.8	10.9	2.5	41.7	43.1	6.9	7.0
Bremen	10-1-67	34.0	48.5	11.7	2.7	29.5	46.0	10.5	8.8
Baden-Württemberg	4-28-68	49.9	33.0	13.1	2.2	44.1	29.1	14.4	9.8
Saar district	6-14-70	46.8	39.8	8.6	1.8	a	—	—	—

[a]No state election scheduled between 1966 and 1969.
Source: W. Kaltefleiter, *Vorspiel zum Wechsel. Eine Analyse der Bundestagswahl*, Bonn: Heymanns, 1977, p. 93.

with the old political enemy as betrayal. They had never really accepted the change in the program of 1959. They had considered it as a tactical move, but the idea of a free market economy and other important elements of this program was unacceptable to them.

The change in government in 1969 ended this critical period. In the electorate the CDU/CSU was immediately understood as the alternative to the new government formed by SPD and FDP. The protest vote that had supported the NPD was reintegrated into the party system mainly by gains of the CDU/CSU. This was not for ideological reasons but for the simple fact that this party now fulfilled the role of the opposition. The New Left was integrated into the SPD but partly also into the FDP which led to continued ideological struggle within these two parties.

In the federal election of 1976, the three parties gained about 99% of the total vote and the turnout climbed to 91%. The opposition failed to win the majority by just 1% of the total vote. The SPD/FDP government got a small but arithmetically working majority of six seats, which was confronted by a strong opposition. All indicators seemed to signalize stability.

But this was only the surface of the electorate. As early as 1976, the first indicators showed a growing dissatisfaction in the electorate with the major parties and the party system which became more obvious in 1977 and 1978. The opinion polls showed a remarkable decrease in the sympathy rating of all three parties which was even stronger than during the time of the grand coalition (Fig. 23–2).

Considering this sharp decline over a period of about six years, the question as to which party ranks higher becomes unimportant. The party system itself obviously has lost some attraction. The important fact is that the opposition lost at the same time as the governmental parties did. The fact that governments lose support can be considered as normal but that the opposition is unable to gain from the erosion of the governmental consensus is an alarming signal. This leads to the hypothesis that the CDU/CSU does not adequately fulfill the role of the opposition. It became obvious that just being in opposition is not enough to fulfill the central function of an opposition party, that is, to attract those who are disappointed with the government.

Other indicators showed similar results. In spring 1978, about 20% of the electorate was not able to answer the question of which party they considered best able to handle the problems they mentioned as being important to them (Table 23–2). When people were asked to articulate trust in different political institutions, the opposition was again ranked very low. On the question, Did your trust in these institutions increase or decrease in recent times?, the government and the opposition received negative responses (Table 23–3). Again, these losses of the government can be considered as being normal, but those of the opposition are the problem.

Another indicator is the continued discussion of the need for new parties. This question was raised before 1976 when, under the influence of CSU leader

Figure 23-2. The Sympathy Ratings of Parties, 1961-1978

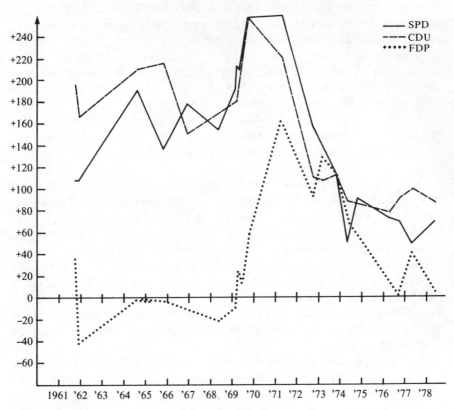

TABLE 23–2. The Competence of Parties in Germany to Handle the Issues That Are Most Important to the Electorate (Percentage of All Respondents)

COMPETENCE OF	MARCH 1978	OCTOBER 1976
CDU/CSU	38	42
SPD	32	37
SPD and FDP	7	9
FDP	3	3
Government	42	49
Opposition	38	42

Strauss, some conservatives argued that only with the help of a fourth party would the CDU/CSU have a real chance to regain power. After the marginal defeat in 1976, the CSU decided not to join the CDU in an united parliamentary party as they always had done since 1949. This was understood

TABLE 23–3.   Rank Ordering of Trust in German Political Institutions

INSTITUTIONS	*MEDIAN RANK*	*TRUST HAS RECENTLY*	*PERCENTAGE CHANGE*	*INDEX*
Chancellor	3.1	Increased	+16	−9
		Decreased	−26	
Federal government	3.5	Increased	+11	−23
		Decreased	−33	
Bundestag	3.7	Increased	+7	−8
		Decreased	−15	
State government	4.5	Increased	+13	−6
		Decreased	−19	
Police	4.8	Increased	+20	+4
		Decreased	−16	
Courts	5.0	Increased	+10	−10
		Decreased	−20	
Opposition	5.0	Increased	+19	−4
		Decreased	−23	
Administration	5.8	Increased	+6	−15
		Decreased	−21	

as the intention of the CSU to give up its geographical restriction to Bavaria and to participate in all state elections, which, of course, would have the implication that the CDU would also campaign in Bavaria. This decision was reconsidered, but the discussion of the CDU's and CSU's running separately in 1980 continued. Above all, this discussion questioned the basic structure of the party system itself and is therefore another indicator for the legitimacy crisis of the party system.

The discussion of a new party received a new dimension in the municipal elections in the state of Schleswig-Holstein in March 1978 in which a so-called Green List, a group of conservationists, was able to exceed the 5% hurdle of German electoral law in the two districts where they had nominated candidates. In the state elections in Lower Saxony in June 1978, a similar group nominated candidates in all but one constituency and gained 3.8% of the total vote. This was not enough to enter the state parliament, but, in a district where the building of a nuclear recycling plant in Gorleben is planned, they received up to 30.0% in some smaller communities. On the same day such a Green List received only 1.0% of the vote in Hamburg, but another more left-wing group of critics with a program involving other political issues also received 3.5%. These results were considered as encouragement to establish conservation parties on a nationwide basis. Among other signs, one CDU member of parliament left his party and founded a new conservation party.

An analysis of the election in Lower Saxony has shown that the support for these lists is much higher than the electoral outcome reveals. A poll led to the following results. About 40% considered the candidacy of these "Green Lists" as useful because the established parties had failed, 30% considered the candidacy useless because of the electoral law, and only 25% considered the candidacy dangerous because it would destabilize the party system. Among the floating voters, the principal support for these groups claimed up to 50% (Table 23–4).

This demonstrates again the potential protest vote. With the exception of some specific regions, conservation is not the issue. But these groups offer the possibility to show the old parties the general trend of dissatisfaction. Those who voted for the Green Lists came mostly from the SPD and FDP, the governmental parties in Bonn. The voting behavior therefore underlined the findings of the opinion polls—that the CDU/CSU opposition has difficulties in attracting those who are disappointed with the government.

In the same period the founding of a tax protest party was discussed by Fredersdorf, the well-known leader of the Union of Civil Servants in the German Internal Revenue Service. In a study in summer 1977, Rudolf Wildenmann revealed that about one-fourth of the German electorate was prepared to vote for a tax protest party similar to the Glistrup group in Denmark. One year later the same question led to a potential protest vote of one-third of the sample. When Wildenmann first published his analysis in 1977, questions were raised as to whether or not the question was poorly worded. This may have been the case because it is unlikely that Glistrup is known well enough in the German electorate so that his name can be used in the wording of opinion questions. Wildenmann also found that one-third of the voters is preparted to vote for a conservation party (Table 23–5).

But what is more important is that so many different approaches led to approximately the same result. There exists a broad dissatisfaction with the present party system in the German electorate and a substantial number of people are principally willing to vote for a new party. This is also demonstrated by the fact that in recent years a kind of inflation of "citizen's initiatives"

TABLE 23–4.   Opinions about the Candidacy of the "Green Lists" for the State Parliament of Lower Saxony (Percent)

CANDIDACY IS	ALL SPONDENTS	SPD IDEN-TIFIERS	CDU IDEN-TIFIERS	POTENTIAL FLOATING VOTER
Necessary because of failures of the estab-lished parties	37	46	18	47
Useless because of the 5% hurdle of the electoral law	38	35	43	37
Dangerous as it would lead to a splintered party system	25	20	39	16

TABLE 23–5.
In Denmark there is a party which wants to abolish high tax burdens. The chairman of this party is Mogens Glistrup. If such a party would exist in the Federal Republic, would you be willing to vote for such a party? (Percent)

	YES	NO	DON'T KNOW	NO ANSWER
1977	25.1	46.5	28.4	0.0
1978	31.5	44.0	24.0	0.5
Interest in politics				
Very strong	23.0	65.0	11.5	0.5
Strong	30.0	53.0	16.5	0.5
Some	34.0	42.0	23.5	0.5
Less	33.0	35.0	31.5	0.5
No	29.5	24.0	46.0	0.5

If citizen's initiatives would form a conservation party on a nationwide level, would you be willing to vote for such a party?

1978	29.0	24.5	14.0	32.5
Interest in politics				
Very strong	28.0	24.5	3.0	44.4
Strong	27.0	23.0	10.0	40.0
Some	30.0	25.0	13.0	32.0
Less	29.5	26.5	19.5	24.5
No	27.0	20.0	35.0	18.0

Source: Capital, 8 (1978), 125.

occurred, in which people organized themselves to protest against or resist measures of public authorities, which was very uncommon in Germany before.

It is doubtful that the Green List will be able to attract this protest movement. Another similar issue for a protest party could be the introduction of the death penalty for terrorists if once again terrorist actions are successful in the Federal Republic of Germany, thereby evoking strong emotions. But the possibility that a well-organized tax protest party can do so is greater because the issue of taxation became a virulent one in the last ten years. In this period, the percentage of all government spending increased from about one-third to close to 50% of the GNP. This led to a situation, in which a wage increase of 1 DM means an increase in net income of only 0.50 DM but an increase of wage costs for the employers of about 1.80 DM. In the last ten years, the development toward a welfare state, together with progressive bureaucratization, has become a permanent source of dissatisfaction.

The German opposition has raised the tax issue repeatedly in the last five years but has not succeeded in transmitting to the voters the image of a convincing alternative to the present government. There are three main reasons for this:

1. Because the CDU/CSU-governed states have had a majority in the Bundesrat since 1972, the CDU/CSU was able to modify the tax laws of the government substantially. Indeed, in this way the party has reduced the burden of the German taxpayer substantially but the procedure is very complicated. First, the majority in the Bundestag passes a law against the opposition of the CDU/CSU, then the CDU/CSU majority in the Bundesrat has to veto the law. Then negotiations start in a joint committee which ends always in a compromise where the CDU/CSU may have to accept some aspects of the law they have opposed in the first round.

Because this is also the case in quite a few other fields, for example, new laws to fight international terrorism, a structural problem of the German political system becomes obvious. If the opposition in the Bundestag is successful in winning enough state elections and gains the majority in the Bundesrat, the principal assumption of the parliamentary system is no longer given. The government cannot pursue its policy, and the opposition adopts the role of a hidden coalition partner. The price for this influence, however, is that the opposition becomes "responsible" and loses its role as the alternative to the government.

2. The structural problem of the political system is aggravated by the confusion resulting from the internal struggles in the government parties and their implications for the relations between the parties. The leftist group in the SPD considers Chancellor Schmidt a betrayer of socialism. On the other hand, Schmidt uses every opportunity to criticize these groups. The voters' view of the position of the party, the chancellor, and other SPD politicians on the right-left dimension gives a very realistic picture (Figure 23–3). Schmidt is located to the right from his own party. The implication is that in some very crucial issues the position of the CDU and that of Schmidt seem to be closer than those of Schmidt and parts of his own party. The same is the case for the FDP, especially on economic issues. Economically, the FDP is closer to the CDU, but the FDP leaders and Schmidt always try to achieve compromises between the FDP and SPD. They also try to use the power position of the CDU/CSU in the Bundesrat to apply pressure to the left wing of the SPD. CDU leader Kohl, on the other hand, attempts to use these rather broad agreements between the CDU and the FDP to come to power by means of a return to the coalition of the CDU and the FDP (Fig. 23–3).

3. Finally, the structural problem of the political system is worsened by a structural problem of the CDU/CSU itself. In recent years, the CDU and CSU have been considered more and more two different parties. On the right-left dimension, for example, the CSU is considered to be much more conservative than the CDU. This image is reflected by the fact that in most issues the two parties articulate more or less different positions, if not in substance at least in style. Especially the tough political approach of CSU leader Franz Josef Strauss is very different from the style of other CDU leaders, especially that of

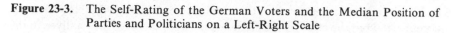

Figure 23-3. The Self-Rating of the German Voters and the Median Position of Parties and Politicians on a Left-Right Scale

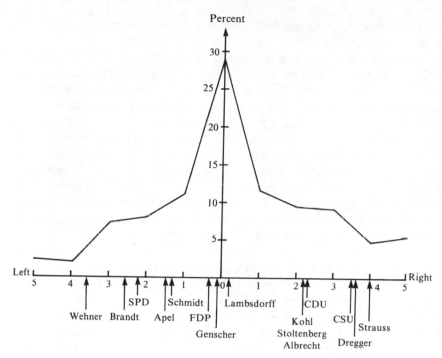

chairman Helmut Kohl. The effect is that the more conservative part of the electorate perceives the CSU as "the" alternative but that the floating vote is reluctant to switch to the CDU for reasons of what they call the "extreme" position of the CSU in general and Franz Josef Strauss in particular. The image of a party speaking with two tongues lames the opposition.

The result of these three variables is a confusing picture of German politics in which the opposition loses its profile. Of course, other variables enforce these tendencies. The rather weak leadership of Helmut Kohl, especially in contrast to Helmut Schmidt, his good personal relations to FDP leader Genscher, the heterogeneous character of the CDU itself have to be mentioned. But these personal variables should not be overemphasized. As Figure 23–2 has shown, the legitimacy crisis of the German party system already started when Willy Brandt was still chancellor and Rainer Barzel leader of the opposition.

Especially the first two variables, the responsibility of the opposition with respect to its majority in the Bundesrat and the confusing distances between the parties and the Chancellor, led to a situation that is similar to the first legitimacy crisis. At that time it was the formal grand coalition that led to the lack of opposition in the system, this time the constituting variables are more complicated but the effect is the same—a lack of perceived alternatives in the system.

Given this situation, the likelihood is high that a change in government would reintegrate the protest vote as did the change in government in 1969. The electorate was prepared for such a change in 1976 at which time the CDU/CSU got 48.6% of the total vote, the second highest percentage a party ever received in Germany. As a result, the party became by far the strongest party in the Bundestag but due to proportional representation fell short of a majority by just six seats. This has demonstrated again that the plurality system is essential for the parliamentary system and has two important implications. It is not only a rather effective safeguard against splinter parties, but, more important, it allows the transformation of changes in voting behavior into a change in the distribution of seats in parliament according to the cubic rule. Under a plurality system or any other type of majority-forming electoral system, the CDU/CSU would have gained a working majority in 1976. The question as to whether a change in government will occur in 1980 is as unpredictable as a change in the coalition behavior of the FDP. Different scenarios can be imagined, but they cannot be discussed here.

As far as the prospects of the protest parties are concerned, again, different scenarios are possible. The Green Lists or other protest parties may fail to exceed the 5% margin as they did in Hamburg and Lower Saxony. If this happened several times, they may slowly fade, and, despite the dissatisfaction in the electorate, the system will survive and can be stabilized by a normal change in government. But, if these groups enter some state parliaments, the likelihood is high that none of the major parties will gain a working majority there, not even in a coalition with the FDP (if this party survives at all). Such a situation would either lead to a new grand coalition with all the destabilizing implications or to a coalition between one of the major parties, most likely the SPD, and these new successful groups. This, of course, would legitimize these groups even more and could lead to a situation where these groups replace the FDP in the German party system.

On the basis of the experience in Hamburg and Lower Saxony, a final and most likely scenario might be that these groups will fail to exceed the 5% hurdle but be strong enough to push the FDP under this margin. This, of course, implies that one of the major parties gets a working majority even if the party fails to receive 50% of the total vote as the CDU did in Lower Saxony. Such a development seems to be more likely in some state elections than in the federal elections of 1980.

CHAPTER 24

THE "DECLINE OF PARTIES" THESIS AND THE ROLE OF MINOR PARTIES

Stephen L. Fisher

IN THEIR comparative analysis of political parties, political scientists have limited themselves, for the most part, to comparative generalizations about the major parties in each political system. This is certainly true in the current debate over whether we are witnessing the decline of Western political parties. Little or no mention has been made of minor political parties and the role that they might play as a result of the major parties' apparent decline.

This lack of attention to minor parties in comparative analysis is easy to understand for at least four reasons. First, by limiting their attention to political parties which have demonstrated a high level of support and stability, analysts can reduce the number of parties to be studied to a manageable level. It would clearly be very difficult to examine all the parties in a large number of countries, even if the examinations were just over a short period of time. Second, by limiting the number of parties to be studied, scholars can focus their research on parties for which information is more likely to be available. In cross-national studies, language is a definite problem; most American investigators, especially when dealing with a large number of countries, must restrict themselves to information published in English or in another language with which they are familiar. Generally, only the programs, manifestoes, and statutes of the major parties in a particular country have been translated into English or another language. Similarly, many of the national studies by American political scientists, studies on which those involved in comparative research often depend, deal only with the larger parties of the country under study. Survey research data are often available only for the major parties. In

609

addition, sources of election statistics frequently provide a breakdown only of the major-party vote, grouping all the votes received by the smaller parties together under the label "other parties." In sum, information on minor parties is just not readily available. A third reason for the concentration on the major parties is that this ensures that the parties under study are those most likely to have measurable consequences on national governments. Whereas a few minor parties may have some effect on government policy, the overwhelming majority do not; thus the safest and easiest method of research is to exclude all the smaller parties from consideration.[1] Fourth, minor parties are often viewed as dysfunctional elements of the political system. For example, a decline of minor-party strength in Western Europe is viewed by most scholars as encouraging, because it contributes to the stabilization of the European party systems. In other words, the two-party system is regarded as functional, the multiparty system as dysfunctional. As a result, those who voice an interest in minor parties in relation to the comparative analysis of political parties are usually concerned with their elimination from, rather than their importance to, the party systems.

Although the exclusion of minor parties from consideration in comparative studies of political parties may be understandable, it is not necessarily justifiable. Leading American political scientists have concluded that some minor parties in American history "must be regarded ... as integral elements of our so-called two-party system"[2] for they have had at times "a long-run influence on the composition, leadership and doctrines of the major parties"[3] and have served as "safety valves" for our party system.[4] My own research indicates that these observations may also be valid for minor parties in Western democratic party systems similar to the United States.[5]

Minor parties face a number of obstacles in the electoral arena. Laws regarding party representation on the ballot are frequently designed to make it difficult for minor parties to participate. Laws regulating the public financing of elections and access to the media during election campaigns usually discriminate heavily against small parties. The system of representation itself can limit the opportunities of minor parties. Winner-take-all, single-member district elections tend to magnify the strength of major parties and the weakness of small ones, thereby reinforcing the idea that to vote for a minor party is to throw one's vote away. Even systems of proportional representation usually have some provisions which make it difficult for minor parties to win legislative seats.[6] Finally, the stabilizing influence of party identification makes it extremely difficult for a minor party to rise suddenly with enough popular support to challenge the existing parties.

The obstacles to minor-party success are significant, but under certain conditions a minor-party movement can attract a large following and play an important role in a party system. Several of the conditions associated with the decline of the major parties in Western political systems appear conducive to increased minor-party activity and success. The economic tensions and frustrations and the increase in sectional and ethnic loyalties present today in several Western political systems are paramount factors in contributing to minor-party successes. Prior political and organizational activities similar to those occurring with the citizen initiatives in West Germany often precede the rise of a significant minor-party movement. The fortunes of minor parties are also enhanced by a decline in traditional party loyalties among voters and a decline in party differences on traditional partisan issues, trends documented in several of the essays in this volume.[7]

The fact that conditions are ripe for the appearance of strong minor-party movements should not necessarily be viewed with dismay. Such parties can cause some temporary instability in a party system, but, as some leading political scientists point out, they can also perform several important functions in a party system that could, in the long run, lead to a more stable situation.

Minor parties, some analysts claim, serve as a testing ground for potential vote-getting issues.[8] A minor party often appears on the political scene when a controversial issue is neglected by the major parties. The minor party takes a clear position on the issue, and if it proves popular it is usually taken over by a major party. This is not to say that minor parties are the primary source of new political ideas or that the major parties embrace certain ideas solely as a result of minor-party agitation. It is maintained only that minor parties play an important role in bringing controversial issues before the public. They serve, in a sense, as trial balloons for the major parties. By popularizing ideas to a point at which major parties can include them in their programs without alienating public support, minor parties perform a valuable educational function.

Some observers believe that minor parties play a "safety valve" role which is important in promoting stability in a party system.[9] Occasionally certain groups may come to believe that the character of the major parties and the structure of society deprive them of a fair hearing for their grievances. Minor parties permit the frustration of their social or economic discontent to be relieved through electoral activity. Regardless of the success, the organization of such a party permits the dissident group to assess its actual strength in the country and provides the satisfaction to members of the group that they are doing something about the sources of their frustration. Thus minor parties perform a useful social function by making it possible for the discontented to find rational expression at the ballot box.[10]

Finally, some analysts believe that minor parties have an important impact on the character of the major parties. V. O. Key, Jr., for example, maintains that a minor-party movement sometimes leads to a sharpening of policy alternatives between the major parties.[11] If a minor party demonstrates a bloc of voters in support of a particular issue or set of issues, a major party frequently will take a stand on the new issues to woo this support. In so doing, policy alternatives between the parties are widened. Key, among others, also claims that minor parties on certain occasions prepare the way for a realignment of party identification within the electorate. The concept of the minor party as a way station during a process of change of loyalties between the major parties is closely related to the idea of the "critical" or "realigning" election.[12] During "realigning" years a minor party often arises because the established parties are not able to adjust quickly enough to the issues bothering the electorate. Having arisen, the minor party provides a "halfway house" for voters who are ready for a change of party identification but who cannot easily move at once all the way into the major party to which they have been opposed. When a minor party serves as a bridge for the movement of people from party to party, it can be regarded as the functional equivalent of various inter- and intraparty processes. For reasons that are by no means self-evident, says Key, on some occasions an outburst of minor-party activity occurs "to realign the parties, to reorient their policies, or perhaps to redirect only one of the major parties."[13] The result is often to stimulate a widening of the differences in the policy orientations of the major parties.

In sum, there is evidence to suggest that conditions are ripe for the rise of important minor-party movements in certain Western party systems and that these parties could perform several interrelated functions which could, on the whole, serve to strengthen rather than undermine these party systems. Furthermore, it appears that minor parties are significant agents of electoral reform. As promoters of ideas, they play an important role in bringing pressing and controversial issues before the public. In serving as vehicles for discontent, they make it possible for those alienated from the system to participate in it. By preparing the way for a realignment of party identification with the electorate, minor parties help to sharpen policy alternatives between the major parties.

Minor parties should no longer be ignored in the comparative analysis of political parties. It is true that there are serious research and analytical problems facing those who attempt to study minor parties comparatively. In addition to the difficulties mentioned at the beginning of this paper, there are definitional and classificatory problems.[14] These problems must be overcome if we are to have a fuller understanding of the dynamics of change in Western democratic party systems.

Notes

1. See the comments by Kenneth Janda, "A Conceptual Framework for the Comparative Analysis of Political Parties," *Comparative Politics Series*, Beverly Hills, Calif.: Sage, 1970, pp. 83–84.
2. V. O. Key, Jr., *Politics, Parties, and Pressure Groups*, 5th ed., New York: Crowell, 1964, p. 279.
3. Judson James, *American Political Parties*, New York: Pegasus, 1969, p. 50.
4. Austin Ranney and Willmoore Kendall, *Democracy and the American Party System*, New York: Harcourt, Brace, 1956, pp. 455–458.

5. Stephen L. Fisher, *The Minor Parties of the Federal Republic of Germany: Toward a Comparative Theory of Minor Parties*, The Hague: Martinus Hijhoff, 1974.

6. A good example is the West German 5% clause, which prevented the National Democratic Party with almost 1.5 million voters (4.3%) from entering the Bundestag in 1969.

7. For a more extensive discussion of these factors, see Fisher, pp. 25–35.

8. Robert Alford, *Party and Society*, Chicago: Rand McNally, 1963, p. 303; Ranney and Kendall, pp. 453–455; C. A. M. Ewing, *Presidential Elections*, Norman: University of Oklahoma Press, 1940, pp. 108–109; William Hesseltine, *The Rise and Fall of Third Parties*, Washington, D.C.: Public Affairs Press, 1948, pp. 9–10; and Daniel Mazmanian, *Third Parties in Presidential Elections*, Washington, D.C.: The Brookings Institute, 1974, pp. 67–68.

9. Ranney and Kendall, pp. 457–458. See also G. DiPalma, "Disaffection and Participation in Western Democracies: The Role of Political Opposition," *Journal of Politics*, 31 (November 1969), 990, 1010; Alford, p. 307; and Hugh Bone, *American Politics and the Party System*, 3rd ed. New York: McGraw-Hill, 1965, p. 141.

10. It should be noted that the chance of a minor party's achieving electoral success in a particular party system may depend on whether there already exists in that system a forum where voters can channel their discontent. For example, the presence of a strong Communist party movement could siphon off many of the protest votes which might normally go to a minor party.

11. Key, pp. 256–262, 280–281. See also Clinton Rossiter, *Parties and Politics in America*, New York: Signet Books, 1964, p. 16; Alford, pp. 303–305; Bone, p. 651; Alan Sindler, *Political Parties in the United States*, New York: St. Martin's Press, 1966, p. 22; and Anthony Downs, *An Economic Theory of Democracy*, New York: Harper & Row, 1957, pp. 127–128.

12. V. O. Key, Jr., "A Theory of Critical Elections," *Journal of Politics* 17 (February 1955), 3–18; Charles Sellars, "The Equilibrium Cycle in Two-Party Politics," *Public Opinion Quarterly*, 29 (Spring 1965), 16–37; and Walter D. Burnham, *Critical Elections and the Mainstream of Politics*, New York: Norton, 1970, pp. 27–31.

13. Key, *Politics*, p. 281.

14. For example, there is a definite need for the development of a universal standard to differentiate between significant and insignificant minor parties and for an explanatory categorization of minor parties. For a discussion of these and other research problems, see Fisher, pp. 448–451.

CHAPTER 25

THE SOCIOLOGY OF EUROPEAN PARTIES: MEMBERS, VOTERS, AND SOCIAL GROUPS

Peter H. Merkl

THE COMPARATIVE SOCIOLOGY of European political parties is a highly developed and sophisticated science to which many of the best names in sociology and political science have made outstanding contributions of one sort or another. There was little need, for that reason, for this volume to go into great comparative details regarding such areas as the development of parties and party systems or the recent advances in the study of party identification. But even this well-developed and data-rich area of study still has some noteworthy lacunae in which the scarcity or incompleteness of the data has held back comparative research. Dennis Kavanagh recently compiled a whole catalog of research-worthy topics on British parties[1] which may well be applied to most other European democracies. Some of the newer democracies—Portugal, Spain, and Greece—are still awaiting the completion of their first stages of basic parties research. But there are also topics such as the study of the membership and internal politics of all European parties, that have barely been initiated.[2]

Party Members as a Political Elite

One of the first things a student of political parties learns is that, outside of the United States and especially in Europe, parties have card-carrying, dues-

614

paying members who play a special role in the political process. Although it is true that only a fraction of the membership, say 10–15% of the Italian Communist party (PCI), could be called activists, formal membership does confer on a person privileged access to the officeholders in his (or her) party and generally the right to participate directly or indirectly in their nomination and election, as well as in policy discussions within the party. The actual practices in most European parties, to be sure, often diminish the exercise of these rights. Considering the near-monopoly of major parties on power and policy-making in most systems, however, we are obviously dealing here with a kind of politically motivated elite that deserves far more attention from parties reseachers than it has received so far. There has been a recent wave of studies of the membership of interwar fascist movements,[3] frequently aiming to demonstrate the "class character" of fascism in New Left perspective. But studies of the membership of contemporary parties are surprisingly rare[4] considering their accessibility, and there is consequently a dearth of easily available data for comparison.

What kind of important comparative questions could be raised given the scarcity of reliable information on many parties? There is, first of all, a descending order of availability of data, which begins with the commonly known size of the membership and its relation to party voters, goes on to the rarer information about the social composition (class/occupation, religion, age, education), and ends with isolated studies on the views and attitudes of party members and public officeholders here and there. As for the member/voter ratios of each party, Maurice Duverger in his classic treatment already explored the subject, comparing European Socialist parties in the late 1940s, an era of massive if declining mobilization among Socialists and Communists. He also commented at length on the cyclical fluctuations in membership growth which often bear little relationship to the electoral fortunes of a party.[5]

Membership/Voter Ratios over Time

After World Wars I and II, in particular, these parties slipped conspicuously from very high membership figures to levels more comparable to some of the right-wing parties opposing them. This drastic decline denoted also changing structural properties within the party and in its relationship to the voting public.[6] Viewed, for example, in the West German context since 1945, the changing ratios not only of the SPD, but also of the CDU/CSU, show the shift from entrenched *Lager* toward cadre party politics as well as the recent retrenchment which was particularly dramatic for the Christian Democrats. Comparing the member/voter ratios of the three German parties, we find that the 1976 relationship between SPD and CDU/CSU is the same as in 1947 if at a lower level. The FDP, a typical cadre party, on the other hand, had a higher member/voter ratio during the years of CDU/CSU dominance than did the CDU/CSU itself. The French figures are even more startling in that they show the Gaullist and Communist wings to be far more mobilized than the middle-of the-road parties, including the Socialists (Table 25–1).

In Great Britain, it has been estimated that about one-fourth of the entire electorate belongs to one of the three major parties, especially to the Conservatives or the Labour party. The Conservatives, with 3 million members, have fluctuated between 22–29% of their voters. The Labour party with about 1 million individual and 5 million union-affiliated members boasts about twice that rate. However, only about 1.5 million of the total of 9 million party members are thought to take part in party activities, and no more than half of these might be considered activists.[7] In Italy today, 4 million are party members chiefly of the Communist PCI (1.7 million), the Christian Democratic DC (1.6 million), and the Socialists (750,000).[8] This gives the PCI a member/voter ratio of 13.5%, the PSI 15%, and the DC 11.4%. These ratios are still substantially higher than those of France and, surprisingly, of West Germany where even the latest surge in participation has as yet to cancel out the posttotalitarian hangover of the first twenty years after 1945.

The ratio of members to party voters or to the adult population varies very considerably from region to region in all systems. In the Italian PCI, for example, the percentage of members per adult population in 1951 and 1961 ranged from as low as 10% to over 25% in many of the provinces of the central "red belt" where the party also polled between 30% and 50% of the popular vote. Together the high membership and vote obviously spoke to the penetration of these areas, their local governments, trade unions, and cooperatives. The Christian Democratic membership in DC strongholds in the Northeast and South instead was between 5% and 10% even where the vote was 50–70%.[9] The national member/voter ratio of the DC, as the party has been pleased to acknowledge, rose from 8% in 1946 to 13% in 1963, the highest point in the curve.

Are the smaller European democracies any less likely to have mass parties with a high member/voter ratio than the four large ones? Certainly not if we consider the size of the Socialist parties of Sweden and Austria which have had member/voter ratios many times as high as that of the German SPD, or Norway and Denmark which have also exceeded it by far. The Norwegian Labour party with a reported 160,000 members had a ratio of 16.6% in 1977, the Conservatives with 77,000 members a ratio of 13.8%, and the agrarian Center party with 70,000 members even 35.7%.[10] The Swedish Social Democrats with 868,000 members had a ratio of 43% in the mid-1960s, the Moderate Unified party 34%, the Center party 20%, the Liberals 11%, and the Left-Party/Communists 10%.[11] A good one-third of the Swedish electorate has held membership in a party although active participation in party activities may be only a small fraction of these numbers.

TABLE 25-1. West Germany and France: Member/Voter Ratios, 1947–1978 (Members in Thousands)

WEST GERMANY	MEMBERS 1947–1948	% OF VOTERS 1949	MEMBERS 1955	% OF VOTERS 1957	MEMBERS 1969	% OF VOTERS 1969	MEMBERS 1976	% OF VOTERS 1976
SPD	875	12.6	585	6.2	778	5.5	1,022	6.3
CDU/CSU	650	8.8	245	1.6	374	2.4	796	4.3
FDP	120	4.1	80	3.5	70	3.7	79	2.6

FRANCE	MEMBERS 1951	% OF VOTERS 1950	MEMBERS 1971	% OF VOTERS (1968)	MEMBERS 1978	% OF VOTERS 1976 (1ST BALLOT)
Gaullists/RPF	1,000	24.2	100	1.0	620	9.6
Republicans/Indep.					90	
Democratic Center/MRP	100	4.2			30	2.9
Radicals/Left	20	1.0			60	
Socialists	116	4.2	75	1.6	160	2.5
Communists	600	11.9	385	8.8	611	10.4

Source: Informationen zur politischen Bildung, no. 171 (1977). "Les Elections Legislatives de Mars 1978," *Le Monde Supplement,* March 1978. Duncan MacRae, Jr., *Parliament, Parties, and Society 1946–1958.* New York: St. Martin's, 1967, and Maurice Duverger, *Political Parties,* London: Methuen and New York: Wiley, 1959, pp. 69, 87–88. See also the figures in Philip M. Williams and Martin Harrison, *Politics and Society in De Gaulle's Republic,* Garden City, N.Y.: Doubleday, 1973, pp. 101, 126, 128, 135, 153.

In the consociational systems of the Netherlands and Belgium, the question of whether there are mass parties takes on a particular significance when we look at the Catholic parties, a major "pillar" of these societies. The Dutch KVP, which since World War I has regularly received the vote of 80–90% of Catholic adults, had a member/voter ratio of 38% in 1925. In 1948, its membership was still 409,000 and its ratio 26.7%. By 1965, however, both membership and ratio had declined, as a result of the process of *ontzuiling*, to 218,000 and a ratio of 15.7%.[12] By that time, the Belgian Christian Social party (PSC/CVP) had only a ratio of 10% but still a particularly strong hold on Flanders where it represented a cross-section of the population and where 70% of its members and a disproportionate share of its electorate could be found.

Changes in Age and Occupation

With the few party systems where membership statistics beyond a dubiously motivated "body count" are kept, we could ask a wide variety of questions about the social composition of the membership and how it changes over time. In the case of the Federal Republic, for example, the changing age composition is a continuing object of curiosity. There is not only the classic example of generational conflict of the Weimar Republic, where the confrontation between the "young" Nazis and Communists, on the one hand, and the "old" Social Democrats, Liberal parties, Catholics (Center), and Conservatives (DNVP), on the other, prepared the way for Hitler.[13] After 1945, there was also a prevalence of older people in all the democratic parties, but this time with a burning desire to reestablish democratic and humane values in politics. In the 1950s and early 1960s, by way of contrast, parties lost much of their older membership by attrition and yet proved unable to attract a substantial following among the young. Since the late 1960s, finally, a new wave of politicized youth has entered first the SPD and FDP, and subsequently the CDU/CSU as well. The available membership statistics on age, unfortunately, are somewhat uneven in their coverage and groupings and for this reason we have represented them in the form of distribution curves (Figure 25–1). From these curves it becomes clear that the CDU of the early 1950s (*A* and *B*) was indeed a rather "old" party with majorities over 50 years of age. We can surmise that the bulk of it, especially in the old Centrist strongholds of Rhineland and Westphalia, were old Center stalwarts who had been in their twenties in Weimar days and rallied again after the debacle of the Third Reich.

The national composition of the SPD (*C*) in 1953 is remarkably similar and leads to the analogous conclusion. These were the young Social Democrats of Weimar whose loyalty had survived the brown years. Only the FDP of 1953 (*D*) had a substantial contingent in their twenties. By 1970, both the CDU (*E*) and the SPD (*F*) had become parties of evenly distributed age groups, with the SPD still somewhat older. The FDP of Berlin (*G*), by way of contrast, already

Figure 25-1. Age Curves of West German Party Members, 1950-1970

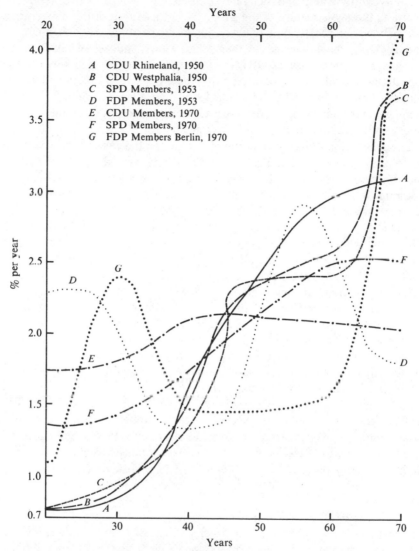

A CDU Rhineland, 1950
B CDU Westphalia, 1950
C SPD Members, 1953
D FDP Members, 1953
E CDU Members, 1970
F SPD Members, 1970
G FDP Members Berlin, 1970

SOURCE: Computed from data in Friedrich August von der Heydte and Karl Sacherl, *Soziologie der deutschen Parteien,* Munich: Isar, 1955, pp. 284-286; *Der Spiegel,* 1970, no. 20, p. 54; and Ossip K. Flechtheim, *Die Parteien der Bundesrepublik Deutschland,* Hamburg: Hoffman & Campe, 1973, p. 406.

showed the new bulge of *gauchiste* youth. On the other hand, more than one out of five Berlin Free Democrats was 65 years or older, corresponding evidently still to the old Weimar generation of Liberals concentrated in the former capital.

For the national SPD and the Berlin FDP, the process of change can be demonstrated even better by contrasting more than two measurements and especially with the help of data on new entries into each party (Table 25–2). Regarding the age structure of the SPD, the composition of the new entries clearly shows the accelerating rejuvenation of the party, already beginning in 1958. By 1972, the new entries by themselves were composed of a majority of those under 30. In the Berlin FDP in the 1960s, the age of the membership also dropped dramatically at the same time that the group over 54 dwindled from a majority of 56.3% in 1963 to 37.4% in 1970. These were obviously years of crucial generational change in the West German parties, even though the top leadership has remained at much higher age levels.[14]

The occupational change in the membership over the years is also dramatic and perhaps even more significant. Naïve conceptions of the SPD as a blue-collar workers' party expect the Social Democratic membership or at least the electorate to have been almost purely "proletarian" at some pristine earlier age, and they profess to see in the conspicuous growth of nonproletarian elements a sign of decay. The membership, of course, never was purely blue collar, although the workers' share was over three-fourths before World War I and about two-thirds after it. Following World War II, as our table shows (Table 25–2), it dropped below 50%. In the 15 years from 1958 to 1972, finally, the trend among new joiners changed from an early reproletarianiza-tion, which evidently followed the social restoration of the 1950s, to a pronounced shift from workers (only 27.6% in 1972) to white collar (25%) and civil service (9%) among the new entries. This trend can be viewed as a kind of "managerial revolution" in a labor party or, more universally, as another manifestation of the increasing prominence of white-collar elements in all parties since the turn of the century.[15] Most importantly, however, it should be viewed as part of the process of *ontzuiling*. The new entries of 1972 in the SPD included far more white-collar and civil service members than workers, also, because proletarian occupations in the Federal Republic have fallen more and more into the hands of foreign workers who are disenfranchised and therefore less likely to join the SPD. The new entries of 1972 also show a surprisingly large share of university students, a category which had not been separately recorded earlier.

The Berlin FDP membership data in Table 25-2 show more clearly the age shifts in the 1960s which brought far larger numbers of young members into the fold than the number of retiring oldsters. In this eight-year span from 1963 to 1970, at least one-third of the members of 1963 and especially those 65 and older must have dropped out.[16] At the same time, 10.0% under 25, 21.4% between 25 and 34, and 7.7% between 35 and 44 had joined to even the balance. At the same time, the already hefty white-collar and public service element—as compared with that of the SPD—increased further and so did housewives and students, whereas the number of independents declined. The shift from independents to employees and civil servants is the significant change here.

Members, Voters, and Deputies Compared

A further dimension worth exploring are the relationships between different levels of this representative process over time. First, we need to separate the "representers" from those who are to be represented. The worker element among SPD voters presumably is supposed to be the element to be represented, or at least, it was at the origins of this workers' party. The SPD party membership is already a part of the medium for representing these working-class voters and hence might include many nonworkers especially among its honorary functionaries. Salaried functionaries by definition already are in a white-collar rather than a proletarian category even though they may be of proletarian origin or serve a proletarian cause. Parliamentary deputies, as in Great Britain, may well include a large share of upper-class, university-educated persons with professional degrees. Still, the processes of socialization and recruitment assure a certain, if declining level of blue-collar workers in the party as we proceed up the ladder.

Comparing the occupational composition of SPD members and voters over time (Table 25–3), for example, we can see not only the considerable differential, say, between the worker or white-collar share among SPD voters and members, but also its changes over the 20 years in question. The drastic social changes between the 1950s and 1970s have reduced the share of workers and increased the white-collar and civil servant share among SPD voters. They brought the white collar/civil service membership more into line with the corresponding element among SPD voters. Thus, we have to amend our earlier conclusion of an increasingly disproportionate white-collar role in the membership and state instead that, so far, it is merely the further underrepresentation of the workers that creates this impression. The growth of white collar and civil service appears to be equally present in the SPD electorate and the population at large. Between 1961 and 1975, the gainfully employed population of West Germany has undergone drastic changes even though its total has not grown:[17]

	GAINFULLY EMPLOYED WEST GERMANS IN	
	1961	*1975*
Blue collar	49.4%	42.9%
White collar	23.3	34.6
Civil service	4.8	8.3
Independents	12.6	9.2
Family helpers	9.9	5.0
	100.0	100.0%

If we compare these percentages with the SPD membership, it turns out that the white-collar element in the SPD is just as underrepresented today as is

TABLE 25–2. Changes in Age and Occupation: New Entries in SPD 1958–1972 and FDP Members in West Berlin 1963–1970 (Percent)

Age	SPD MEMBERS IN 1952–1953	ENTRIES 1958	ENTRIES 1968	ENTRIES 1972	FDP MEMBERS BERLIN	1963	1967	1970
−20		6.0	11.2	19.7				
21–24	(21–35): 13	10.5	10.6	15.6	16–24	2.6	6.4	9.9
25–29		13.2	17.3	15.8				
30–34		14.9	15.3	14.4	25–34	6.6	13.2	24.0
Subtotal		44.6	54.4	65.5		9.2	19.6	33.9
35–39	(36–55): 45	11.6	12.8	9.7	35–44	15.6	15.0	14.3
40–49		19.7	18.5	13.9	45–54	18.9	17.1	14.4
50–59	(56–65): 24	15.9	8.7	6.5	55–64	25.4	23.3	15.8
60–69	(66–): 18	6.2	4.8	3.3	65–	30.9	25.0	21.6
70–		2.0	0.7	1.1				
Total	100	100.0	100.0	100.0		100.0	100.0	100.0

Occupation		1958	1965	1972			
Workers	45	55.0	49.4	27.6	4.2	4.1	5.9
White collar	17	13.2	17.1	25.0	13.6	15.6	15.6
Civil servants	5	7.8	10.4	9.0	20.8[a]	23.1[a]	23.7[a]
Pensioners	12	5.4	4.1	3.7	—	—	—
Independents	14	7.4	10.0	3.9	24.2	21.7	19.2
House-wives	7	11.2	9.0	9.0	30.8[b]	32.2[b]	34.7[b]
Students	—	—	—	15.9			
Other, NA	—	—	—	5.9	6.4	3.3	0.9
Total	100	100.0	100.0	100.0	100.0	100.0	100.0

[a]Includes white collar in public service.
[b]Includes pensioners.
NA – Not available.
Sources: *SPD Jahrbuch* for the years in question, and Ossip K. Flechtheim, *Die Parteien der Bundesrepublik Deutschland*, Hamburg: Hoffmann & Campe, 1973, p. 406.

TABLE 25–3.   Occupational Status of Members and Voters of the SPD, 1952–1973 (Percent)

	SPD MEMBERS 1952	SPD/KPD VOTERS 1953	M/V RATIO	SPD MEMBERS 1966	VOTERS 1967	M/V RATIO	MEMBERS 1973	VOTERS 1969	M/V RATIO
Workers	45 }	75.3	59.7	32	49.4	64.8	26.4	47	56.2
White collar	17 {	14.8	148.6	19 }	25.9	104.2	21.4	22	97.3
Civil service	5	—	—	8 {			9.0	8	112.5
Pensioners	12	—	—	18	18.6	96.8	13.4	11	121.8
Independents and Professions	12	6.4	187.8	5	6.1	82.0	4.8	4	120.0
Farmers	2	3.5	57.1	—	—	—	.4	1	40.0
Housewives	7	—	—	16	—	—	9.9	7	141.4
Students	—	—	—	1	—	—	6.8	—	—
Other, NA	—	—	—	1	—	—	7.4	—	—

NA – Not available.
Source: See chapter on West Germany, Table 2–5, recomputed by party; Horst W. Schmollinger, *Abhaengig Beschaeftigte in Parteien der BRD*, Wiesbaden: Hessische Landeszentrale fuer politische Bildung, 1974; Ossip K. Flechtheim, *Die Parteien der Bundesrepublik Deutschland*, Hamburg: Hoffman & Campe, 1973, p. 63.

the blue-collar worker. On the other hand, SPD civil servants, pensioners, independents, housewives, and students are overrepresented as compared to the SPD voters.[18]

The CDU/CSU, as we have already noted, had three-fourths as many workers and white-collar employees among its voters in 1969 as the SPD, but significantly fewer workers among its membership (Table 25–4). In fact, the member/voter (M/V) ratios given show workers grossly underrepresented, whereas white collar and the civil service are overrepresented among CDU and CSU members as compared with the CDU/CSU electorate.[19] A look at the earlier years in Table 25–4 shows this phenomenon to be rather new. Independent businessmen, professionals, and farmers are another element that is overrepresented today in today's CDU membership, and even more in the CSU and in the CDU/CSU of the mid-1960s. Comparing the CDU/CSU membership to the population averages, furthermore, only this independent element is truly overrepresented in the CDU/CSU which otherwise still deserves the label of a "catchall" party.

The small FDP never claimed to be a workers' party, even though in 1967 it seems to have outdone itself in its understandable efforts at having a few *Renommierarbeiter* (token workers) among its membership. Where then lies its socioeconomic basis? With regard to its electorate, the FDP membership appears to be heaviest in its overrepresentation of civil servants, white-collar employees, and independents (Table 25–5). In fact, it has three and a half times as many independents and more than twice as many civil servants as the general population. If we compare the membership of the three major West German parties, then, the following characteristics stand out:

1. All three appear to have an ample white-collar and civil service element.[20] In the CDU/CSU and FDP, this element is substantially larger today than among the party voters, although only the FDP boasts a white-collar contingent among its members and voters that approaches the population average. The civil service component in the FDP is particularly large.

2. Blue collar is underrepresented in the membership of every one of the three parties in descending order from the FDP to the SPD. Workers still vote disproportionately for the SPD, but not by a very large margin.

3. Independents and professionals are overrepresented in every one of the three parties as compared with their respective voters. In the CDU/CSU and especially in FDP their share is far in excess of the general population.

These findings confirm that the two larger West German parties are catchall parties distinguishable not so much by social class but by matters of style and emphasis better explored in other ways, such as by examining their religious habits, organizational memberships, or politico-cultural attitudes.[21] The FDP, on the other hand, still seems to have sufficient socioeconomic characteristics deviating from the population averages so that here an

TABLE 25–4. Occupational Status of Members and Voters of CDU and CSU, 1953–1976 (Percent)

	CDU MEMBERS 1955	CDU/CSU VOTERS 1953	M/V RATIO	CDU MEMBERS 1964	CSU MEMBERS 1964	CDU/CSU VOTERS 1965	M/V RATIO	CDU MEMBERS 1976	CSU MEMBERS 1975	CDU/CSU VOTERS 1969	M/V RATIO
Workers	15	38.7	38.8	14.6	4.0[a]	31	49.1	11		35	31.4
White collar	18}	24.2	111.6	19.8	7.6	21	94.3	27	48.7	16	168.8
Civil service	9}			10.9	6.6	10	109.0	12	7.5	9	133.3
Pensioners	7	—	—	—	—	10[b]	—	5		12[b]	41.6
Independents }	38	16.9}	102.4	37.1	{22.3	12}	186.0	26	{16.8	13}	130.0
Farmers }	13	20.2}			20.2}	8}			16.8}	7}	
Housewives	—	—	—	—	13.7[a]	7	—	10	4.5	8	125.0
Students	—	—	—	—	1.3	—	—	6	4.0	—	—
Other, NA	—	—	—	17.5[c]	24.3[c]	1	—	3	1.7	—	—
Total	100	100.0	100.0	100.0	100.0	100	100.0	100	100.0	100.0	100.0

[a]Estimates by Alf Mintzel, "Die CSU in Bayern," in Jürgen Dittberner and Rolf Ebbighausen, *Parteiensystem in der Legitimationskrise* Opladen: Westdeutscher Verlag, 1973, pp. 373–374. Otherwise same sources as Table 25–3.

[b]Includes others without gainful employment, such as students.

[c]Includes pensioners.

TABLE 25-5. Occupational Status of Members and Voters of the FDP, 1953–1974 (Percent)

	FDP MEMBERS 1953[a]	VOTERS 1953	M/V RATIO	MEMBERS 1965	MEMBERS 1967	VOTERS 1967	M/V RATIO	MEMBERS 1971	MEMBERS 1974	VOTERS 1969	M/V RATIO
Workers	10.3	28.5	36.1	14	14	11.7	119.7	4.9	5	18	27.2
White collar }	32.5	19.9	163.3	{25	40}	35.6	134.8	{32.7	29	27	121.1
Civil servants }				15}	8}			19.6	13	5	392.0
Pensioners	5.1					12.1			7	18[b]	
Independents }	37.1	{26.0	72.0	36	28	40.6	69.0	31.1	30	22}	115.2
Farmers }		25.6}								5}	
Housewives	7.6								7	5	
Students	7.4								9		
Other, NA	—	—	—	10	10	—	—	11.7	—	—	—
Total	100.0	100.0		100	100	100.0		100.0	100	100	

[a] Averaged from Berlin, Wiesbaden, and Mainz, as reported in Friedrich A. v. d. Heydte and Karl Sacherl, *Soziologie der deutschen Parteien*, Munich: Isar, 1955, p. 292.
[b] Includes students
NA – Not available.
Same sources as Tables 25-3 and 25-4.

occupation/social-class analysis may be worthwhile, although the other approaches mentioned are surely appropriate as well.

To carry the comparison to the higher level of the *Bundestag* deputies of each party, finally, we have juxtaposed members, voters, and deputies (Table 25–6) with regard to age and occupation. As for their ages, the members seem to compare quite well with their respective electorates. If anything, they are younger than the voters, especially in the CDU and in the Berlin FDP. In the Bundestag, on the other hand, those under 35 are very few, whereas the age group over 45 is clearly overrepresented. At the same time, the Bundestag does not have as large a share of those over 60 as are found in the electorate. Deputies of all three parties tend to cluster in the age range from about 35 to 60.

More significant still is the comparison of the occupational composition of the Bundestag parties with their respective membership and voters. The share of blue- and even white-collar voters steeply declines from voters to members and is negligible among the deputies. The proportion of civil servants, on the other hand, rises steeply over the levels and amounts to almost one-third of the Bundestag.[22] The SPD deputies whose civil service share at the member level is the lowest of the three parties, can boast the highest civil service component in the Bundestag, probably including many former local officials. The large number of CDU/CSU civil servants in the Bundestag likewise includes many local officials. By comparison, independents are less frequent among the deputies than among the members, whereas the CDU/CSU and FDP farmers are more so. Finally, there is a sizable category of party and interest group functionaries in all three parties for which we have no comparable information on members and voters.[23] They amount to about two-fifths of the deputies and, probably, a negligible share of voters and members. Even though there are gradations ranging from a total of 45.1% for the FDP to 80.1% for the SPD, this high proportion of *fonctionnaires* of the state, the parties, or the interest groups appears to be typical of modern continental parliaments.[24] They evidently represent the elements of society in a way rather different from the fictions of corporatist theory.

Leaders and Followers in Other Countries

There are several such studies for other European countries, or parts of countries, that show similar features. One of the best, though limited only to the Stavanger area of Norway in 1957, compared the party voters of strong party identification and 149 ward, communal, and provincial party chairpersons and secretaries for the five major parties: Labor, Liberals, Christian People's party, Agrarians, and Conservatives.[25] These local leaders of all but the Liberal and Conservative parties clustered in their ages between 31 and 50, three-fourths of them. The Conservatives had one-third under 30, and the Liberals two-fifths

TABLE 25-6. Age and Occupation of SPD, CDU/CSU, and FDP Deputies, Members, and Voters, 1968–1972 (Percent)

Age

Age	Bundestag Members 1969–1972				Party Members 1970			Voters 1965		
	ALL	SPD	CDU/CSU	FDP	SPD	CDU	FDP	SPD	CDU/CSU	FDP
−34 / −30:	4.7	—f	—	— }	18	23	33.9	20.6	21.5	17.9
35–44 / 31–45:	28.6		—	— }	32	36	14.3	31.1	26.3	28.6
45–49 / 46–60:	21.2						14.4	28.6	28.8	31.8
50– / 61–:	45.5				50	41	15.8	19.7	23.4	21.7
Total	100.0				100	100	100.0	100.0	100.0	100.0

Occupation

	Bundestag Members 1969–1972				Members 1968			Voters 1969		
	ALL	SPD	CDU/CSU	FDP	SPD	CDU	FDP 1971	SPD	CDU/CSU	FDP
Workers	0.2	0.4	—	—	34.5	13.1	4.9	47	35	18
White collar	2.1	3.0	0.8	3.2	20.6	16.9	32.7	22	16	27
Civil servants	30.0	35.3	26.5	12.8	9.9	15.8	19.6	8	9	5
Party functionaries	18.7	22.4	15.1	19.4	—	—	—	—	—	—
Interest group functionaries	21.2	22.4	21.0	12.9	—	—	—	—	—	—
Independents	9.5	3.4	15.1	9.6	5.2	32.8	31.1	4	13	22
[Entrepreneurs]	[5.4]	[—]	[7.5]	[6.4]						
[Small business]	[4.1]	[0.4]	[7.6]	[3.2]						
Farmers	6.4	0.4	10.7	16.1				1	7	5
Professions	9.7	9.7	9.2	22.5				—	—	—
Others, pensioners, housewives	2.4	3.0	1.6	3.2	29.9	21.3	11.7	18	20	23
Total	100.0	100.0	100.0	100.0	100.0	100.0	100.0	100	100	100

NOTE: Data may not add due to rounding.
Source: Kaack (1971), pp. 656–660, Informationen, no. 167, and earlier tables.

over 50. In their occupations, only the Labor party had a substantial number of workers (51%) among its leaders, followed by the Christian People's party with 19%. White collar and party functionaries, on the other hand, made up 40% of the Labor leaders, 73% of the Liberals, 43% of the Christian People's party, and 51% of the Conservatives (mostly in the public service). The typical "pillar elements" were the 51% of workers in the Labor party, the 95% farmers among the Agrarian leaders, and 34% independents in the Conservative leadership, as well as 19% independents among the Christian people's functionaries.[26]

Table 25–7 shows the differential among the Stavanger area party leaders, strong identifiers, and the rest of the party voters. Again, there is the underrepresentation of the working-class voters of each party among the leaders and the prevalence instead of white-collar elements among the latter. As for the educational levels, likewise, the local leadership is better-educated than the voters by a very substantial margin. This goes to show that it is not so much the social status of the white collar, but its upward mobility and ambition that may make it a political elite.

Furthermore, as a result of the in-depth study of the national party leadership of the Italian PCI and DC in the 1950s and 1960s by the Istituto Carlo Cattaneo in Bologna, we can compare this differential between Italian party members and leaders in considerable detail. The leadership samples consisted of 966 Christian Democrats including 798 who had been parliamentary deputies at some time between 1946 and 1963 and of 599 Communists including 465 deputies of the period.[27] In addition, the PCI offered information on its membership and regional and national leadership. In contrast to the West German data, the Italian leadership is classified here (Table 25–8) by the occupational status of the respondents prior to their political careers. As for their ages, the Italian party leaders were born in the following decades (Table 25–9):

This places their bulk during the years in question in the range of 35–55 (PCI) and 40–60 (DC), quite similar to the West German deputies and assuredly older than the average Italian party member or voter. As for the occupational categories, it must be borne in mind that the PCI used to have a much smaller percentage of workers among its leadership before 1951 when new emphasis was placed on the proletarian authenticity of the party. Still, the 1954 figures on Table 25–8 clearly show the underrepresentation of the rural elements and the overrepresentation of white collar and the professions in the leadership. The data on the DC leadership are not as easy to compare with that on the DC membership because of the categories used, but it is clear that neither the sizable share of workers nor the equally strong rural element (not to mention the housewives[28]) are represented in the party leadership. Instead, the bulk is made up of white-collar employees, (including executives), small and large businessmen, artisans, and the professions. The contrast between the DC and PCI leadership is shown tellingly in the juxtapositions by social class and

TABLE 25-7. Occupation and Education of Voters, Strong Party Identifiers, and Functionaries of Five Norwegian Parties in 1957 (Percent)

	LABOR			LIBERALS			CHRISITIAN PEOPLE'S			AGRARIANS			CONSERVATIVES		
	Leaders	Party Identi-fiers	Voters	Leaders	Party Identi-fiers	Voters	Leaders	Party Identi-fiers	Voters	Leaders	Party Identi-fiers	Voters	Leaders	Party Identi-fiers	Voters
Occupation															
Workers	52	83	79	24	25	34	19	36	50	5	3	24	6	8	27
White collar	41	13	13	73	54	39	43	29	21	—	6	8	55	64	36
Farmers	—	1	3	4	13	7	19	16	22	95	91	67	3	4	6
Independents	7	3	5	19	8	20	19	19	7	—	—	1	36	24	31
Total	100	100	100	100	100	100	100	100	100	100	100	100	100	100	100
(n)	42	116	246	26	24	143	26	31	58	19	32	63	33	25	86
Education															
Elementary	50	78	78	24	32	47	39	68	59	27	59	59	6	30	41
Continuation school	24	13	15	8	24	27	22	26	36	63	38	29	3	15	17
High school	7	7	6	20	24	21	9	—	3	5	3	9	27	44	33
Gymnasium, etc.	19	2	1	48	20	5	30	6	2	5	—	3	64	11	9
Total	100	100	100	100	100	100	100	100	100	100	100	100	100	100	100

Reprinted by permission of Norwegian University Press from Henry Valen and Daniel Katz, Political Parties in Norway, 2nd ed., Oslo: Norwegian University Press, 1967, pp. 268–269.

TABLE 25-8. Members and Leaders of the PCI and DC by Occupation and Education, 1946–1968 (Percent)

OCCUPATION	PCI MEMBERS			PCI LEADERS 1954	DC MEMBERS		DC LEADERS 1968	SOCIAL CLASS AND EDUCATION	DC LEADERS	PCI LEADERS
	1946	1955	1963		1955	1961				
Occupations								Social Class		
Workers	52.7	39.8	40.2	40.5	19.4	21.2	1.1	Lower and lower middle	2.2	25.3
Agricultural workers	11.9	17.4	11.3	5.0	6.0	5.5	0.6	Middle	7.7	16.8
Peasants	15.8	16.7	15.6	8.5	17.0	15.6	0.6	Upper middle	22.2	12.4
Artisans and small business persons	5.2	5.2	6.4	16.7	11.3	9.2	58.9	Upper	66.7	32.9
Professions	0.7	0.5	0.7		4.8	5.3	33.1	Political and other		
White collar	3.7	2.2	2.2	15.8	9.4	9.2	a		1.2	12.6
Students	0.6	0.3	0.4	2.7	2.5	2.5 }	0.6			
Housewives	9.4	13.7	13.4	—	24.0	25.5 }			100.0	100.0

							Education		
							None	0.3	4.9
Pensioners and others	—						Elementary or vocational	2.8	25.0
Total	100.0	100.0	100.0	100.0	100.0	100.0	High school	11.5	30.5
	4.3	9.8	5.8	5.6	6.0	5.1	University	85.4	39.6
							Total	100.0	100.0

n = 4,246

[a]Included in small businesspersons.

Sources: Gianfranco Poggi, *L'Organizzazione Partitica del PCI e della DC*, Bologna: Il Mulino, 1968, pp. 372–373, 428, 499, 502; see also the breakdown by regions pp. 456–470. The PCI sample of leaders is computed from Giorgio Galli and Alfonso Prandi, *Patterns of Political Participation in Italy*, New Haven, Conn.: Yale University Press, 1970, pp. 148 and 153 and the DC leaders of 1968 are deputies and local councilors from Samuel H. Barnes, *Representation in Italy: Institutionalized Tradition and Electoral Choice*, Chicago: University of Chicago Press, 1977, pp. 59.

TABLE 25–9.   Dates of Birth of Italian PCI and DC Leaders, 1946–1963

	PCI	DC
Before 1879	.7	1.9
1880–1889	2.4	9.7
1890–1899	14.6	21.1
1900–1909	22.6	26.4
1910–1919	23.5	20.8
1920–1929	35.1	19.4
After 1929	1.1	.7
	100.0	100.0

education in Table 25–8. Except for the one-third of university-educated, upper-class Communist politicians, social class is the chief divide between the two sets of leaders even though it appears hardly very dominant between the two sets of memberships.

A brief comparison between Norway and Italy suggests the following salient differences: Considering the large share of parliamentary deputies in the Italian sample, the number of workers among the PCI leaders is extraordinarily high, whereas its proportion of farmers would indicate that it has been more successful in keeping farmers on its side than has the Norwegian Labor party. In Norway, the Agrarians benefited from the failure of Labor. On the other hand, the high proportion of white-collar persons in nearly all the Norwegian parties (save the Agrarians) had no parallel in the Italy of the 1960s. Independents and professionals evidently ran the Italian DC of 1968. As for the educational levels, moreover, the Italian party politicians are clearly more educated, even in the PCI, which may again reflect only the large number of parliamentary deputies in this breakdown. The university-educated make up a large share of any European parliament.

The Comparison of Occupational Breakdowns

As we have already hinted, we should not necessarily expect the deputies and functionaries of a labor party to be all working-class people. Because most party members are not full-time or salaried politicians but rather amateurs of varying zeal, however, it may still be worth our while to compare their occupational compositions across national boundaries. They tend to have a life of their own. Table 25–10 on the three major Italian parties, at first glance, yields few clues as to the important cleavages dividing the membership. With 28.7% (1965) employed in mining and manufacturing in the general population, their respective shares of industrial workers, to be sure, label the PCI as more of a "workers' party" than the PSI and, especially, the DC. On the other hand, the PCI membership appears to have lost, in the 1970s, the Gramscian image of the sizable rural base it once possessed. The PSI still has it, whereas even the DC can hardly boast enough *coltivatori diretti* to match the 24% of Italians still employed in agriculture in 1965. The real social backbone of the DC membership, apart from the large number of housewives, is hidden in Table 25 10 in the categories of white collar (clerks), the professions (including teachers), and students. Since 1959, every white-collar category, and especially the public employees,[29] has grown among the membership, following the trend we have described for the West German parties (Table 25–11). This growing element is linked to both the urban middle class and the professionals in the Catholic party strain, two of the three traditional components of the DC (the third is that of a peasant party) which used to describe the party in the past.[30] The worker element, which is quite strong in the industrial Northwest, has little representation in the leadership, it will be recalled.

The regional differences in the occupational composition of the PCI are particularly noteworthy in that they show the impact of diverse social structures on the party membership (Table 25 12). Essentially, the PCI is a workers' party indeed in the North, and especially in the industrial triangle of the Northwest where even the DC is composed of about 25% workers.[31] In the central "red belt" where nearly half (46.4 in 1963) the party resides,[32] the urban workers make up little more than a third, whereas there is a substantial number of *mezzadri* (sharecroppers). The DC also has more mezzadri here than elsewhere, but the bulk of its agricultural element in central Italy are again the small farmers. In the rapidly changing South and the islands, finally, the PCI is a party of industrial and agricultural workers: In the South it is a good third workers and over a fifth agricultural workers, in parts of Apulia even approaching one-half the PCI membership in the 1950s.[33] In the islands, the agricultural laborers (36.0% in 1962) outnumbered the workers (23.8%). Even the DC had more agricultural workers in the South and the islands than elsewhere, and relatively fewer small farmers. Thus the two largest Italian parties confront each other in strikingly different fashion in the various parts of the country.

The PCF is rather comparable to the PCI of 1973 which was more than twice as large, far less proletarian (Table 25–9), but had about the same share of women (PCF, 25.5%). By comparison, the PCF had an amazingly large white-collar contingent and, in fact, one-fourth of its members (not counting teachers) were in the public service. To find an equivalent of this, we have to go to the West German SPD of 1966 or 1973 (Table 25–3) or even to the CDU.

The Socialist Parties of Latin Europe

The Italian Socialists (Table 25–13) are not easy to fit into this alignment because the available information is of a different nature. Their membership

TABLE 25–10. Italian Party Members (PCI, PSI, DC) by Occupation (Percent)

	PCI			PSI		DC		
	1946	1960	1973	1961	1973	1955	1961	1971
Workers	52.7	37.4	41.0	30.0	32.1	19.4	21.2	18.1
Agricultural workers	11.9	15.5	6.3	15.3	—	6.0	5.5	3.5
Peasants and sharecroppers	15.8	18.0	7.0	16.2	7.1	17.0	14.4	11.4
Small businesspeople and artisans	5.2	5.9	8.4	6.1	8.7	11.3	9.2	8.0
Clerks and technicians	3.7	1.9	4.2	3.7	12.5	9.4	9.2	12.1
Professionals and teachers	0.7	0.6	1.4	1.8	1.5	4.8	5.3	5.1
Students	0.6	0.3	1.6	0.2	1.5	2.5	2.5	6.0
Housewives	9.4	14.1	12.3	8.1	10.0	24.0	25.5	24.5
Pensioners	—	6.3	16.8	8.9	8.3	2.9	4.5	7.0
Others	—		1.0	9.1	18.3	2.7	1.5	4.3
Total	100.0	100.0	100.0	100.0	100.0	100.0	100.0	100.0

Source: Antonio Landolfi, *Il Socialismo Italiano*, Rome: Lerici, 1968, p. 223; and William E. Paterson and Alistair H. Thomas, eds., *Social Democratic Parties in Western Europe*, London: Croom Helm, 1977, p. 84; official PCI sources quoted by Giuseppe Di Palma, *Surviving without Governing: The Italian Parties in Parliament*, Berkeley: University of California Press, 1977, p. 261; and P. A. Allum, *The Italian Communist Party Since 1945*, University of Reading Graduate School of Contemporary European Studies, 1970, p. 39; Galli and Prandi, p. 123; and calculated from Gianfranco Pasquino, "Crisis della DC e Evoluzione del Sistema Politico," *Riv. Ital. Sci. Pol.*, 5 (1975), 461.

TABLE 25–11.   White Collar, Public Employees, and Students among DC Members, 1959–1971 (Percent)

	1959	1962	1965	1968	1971
White collar	2.1	4.7	5.5	6.1	5.9
Public Employees	8.9	11.7	13.0	13.5	12.7
Students	2.5	2.5	3.0	4.0	6.0
Total	13.5	18.9	21.5	23.6	24.6

has risen from 463,000 to 535,000 (up 15.6%) between 1973 and 1975 alone. Women now make up 13.7% of the membership, a much smaller share than either the PCI (23.6%) or the one-third of the DC. Both those under 30 and over 60, among the members, have decreased, which makes the age structure of the PSI somewhat younger than the West German SPD of 1970 (Table 25–6), at least prior to the wave of young new entries of 1972 (Table 25–2).

In its geographical distribution, the PSI used to have its heaviest concentration (15% members/adult inhabitants) in the central "red belt" of Italy where the PCI membership is still concentrated today (15–20%). In the 1960s, while the PSI began to seek an autonomous course from the PCI, the membership concentrations of the PSI dropped in Central Italy (to 9.1% in 1970) and shifted instead to the South (14.3%) where the DC also happens to have its heaviest concentration of members. Being a DC or PSI member in the South may well be one of the badges tying a person into the party-clientelistic networks of the region.

Because the Italian PCI mostly evolved from (and at the expense of) the Socialists, a comparison with their equivalents in France may reveal more than comparisons with the West German SPD or any other dominant labor party. The French PS emerged from the old SFIO, and some radical elements, at a 1969 party conference to give French socialism a new start. The SFIO had been declining from 336,000 (1946) to 70,000 (1969), whereas its leadership had become superannuated and thoroughly bourgeoisified.[34] By 1973, the new PS could already boast considerable electoral successes, and the attendance at its congress of the same year showed a substantially rejuvenation: 31% of the delegates were under 30, 27% were between 30 and 39, and 23% were between 40 and 49 years old.[35] The voters of presidential candidate Mitterand in 1974, likewise, were substantially younger and more proletarian than the population average and the voters of his opponent, Giscard d'Estaing.[36] The support of the PSU, the CFDT, the FEN, and other groups helped to secure the PS a social base to rival that of the PCF.

Our statistics are for both the pre-1969 and post-1969 Socialists, and they do not appear to differ as much as we might have assumed (Table 25–14). The two grass-roots studies of Mark Kesselman[37] and Jacques Lagroye with Guy Lord[38] have supplied us with fairly representative cross-sections of the PS, in both cases contrasting them to the Gaullists. Kesselman's is geographically

TABLE 25–12. Regional Differences in the Social Composition of the PCI and DC, 1961–1963 (Percent)

	Workers	Agricultural Workers	Share-croppers	Small Farmers	Artisans and Small Businesspersons	Professions, Students, Teachers	White Collar	Housewives	Other	Total
PCI (1963)										
North	54.4	8.3	1.6	3.4	5.3	0.7	2.4	12.5	12.7	100.0
Center	35.7	8.8	18.4	4.3	7.2	0.4	2.3	13.9	8.9	100.0
South and islands	31.5	24.5	6.5	10.3	5.7	1.9	2.1	9.6	7.8	100.0
Total	39.5	12.7	10.7	5.6	5.2	0.9	2.2	12.4	9.8	100.0
DC (1961)										
Northwest	25.4	1.3	0.9	13.7	10.0	6.3	12.8	23.5	6.7	100.0
Northeast	19.2	1.6	2.3	22.0	9.0	5.6	8.0	27.7	4.6	100.0
Center	20.5	1.8	7.6	17.1	9.2	7.8	10.8	19.7	5.5	100.0
South	21.9	7.4	1.1	12.3	9.1	8.8	8.1	25.5	5.8	100.0
Islands	17.6	9.8	1.0	7.8	9.4	7.8	8.4	30.7	7.5	100.0
Total	21.2	5.5	2.0	13.6	9.2	7.8	9.2	25.5	6.0	100.0

Source: PCI, *Dati Sull' Organizzazione del PCI,* 1964; and Poggi, pp. 428, 456–475.

TABLE 25-13. The Italian Socialists (PSI) in 1975: Age, Education, and Status (1963) (Percent)

AGE		PSI	1971 POPULATION
-30		18.5	
31–40		24.0	
41–50		22.9	
51–60		18.2	
61–		16.4	
Total		100.0	
Education			
None or self-taught		34.8	29.0
Elementary only		42.6	47.7
Junior High school		12.8	12.5
High school		7.0	8.4
University degree		2.8	2.4
Total		100.0	100.0
Social Class			
Lower lower		55	
Upper lower		28	
Lower middle		14	
Middle		3	
		100	
		(n = 298)	

OCCUPATION (AREZZO, 1963)	
Agricultural Workers	20.9
Worker	45.1
White collar	8.6
Business and professionals	5.5
Other	19.9
	100.0

Source: "Chi sono gli iscritti al PSI," Almanacco Socialista 1977, Rome, 1977, pp. 186–191; and Samuel H. Barnes, Party Democracy: Politics in an Italian Socialist Federation, New Haven, Conn.: Yale University Press, 1967, pp. 95 and 99.

639

TABLE 25–14. The French Socialists and the PCF, 1966 and 1973 (Percent)

	SOCIALISTS					PCF	SOCIALISTS	
	SFIO 1952		Members SFIO 1966	Members Gironde 1973		PCF 1966 Members	SFIO 1966	PS 1969/1970
	Members	Cadres		PS	PCF			
Age								
–39	30.6	28.2	24.0	23.2	46.3	9.4 (–25)		
40–49	32.3	40.3	50.0	48.4	32.8	33.1 (26–40)		
50–59	37.1	31.5	26.0	28.4	20.1	40.2 (41–60)		
60–						17.3 (61–)		
Total	100.0	100.0	100.0	100.0	100.0	100.0		
Occupations								
Workers and service personnel	24.3	11.4	16.0	17.9	41.3	56.8		
White collar	8.8	13.5	} 53.0	1.6	1.5	(13.5)[a]		
Artisans and small businesspersons	12.3	10.6		8.5	9.7	18.6		
Farmers	7.4	6.8		8.1	5.4	(10.5)[a]		
Agricultural labor	—	—		6.9	6.9	5.8		
Professions, teachers, students }	2.6	10.9	} 31.0	11.4	2.7	3.2		
Cadre moyens	24.9	37.4		26.4	8.9	3.2		
Others (non-employed)	19.7	10.2		19.2	23.6	9.0		
Total	100.0	100.0	100.0	100.0	100.0	100.0		
Education								
Primary only							28	28
Secondary, commercial							31	31
University							41	41
Total							100	100
Religious Practice								
Practicing, occasional church attendance								38
Nonpracticing								62
Total								100

[a]Includes those in public service.

Sources: Jacques Lagroye and Guy Lord, "Trois fédérations des partis politiques," *Revue française de science politique,* 24 (1974), 559–595; Mark Kesselman, "Recruitment of Rival Party Activists in France," *Journal of Politics,* 35 (1973), 2–41; Christiane Hurtig, *De la SFIO au nouveau parti socialiste,* Paris: Armand Colin, 1970, p. 28; and Rapport de M. George Marchais au Dix-huitième Congrès, Paris: PCF, 1967.

more representative of regional PS and UDR militants and leaders, whereas the Lagroye-Lord study surveyed the members of the PCF, PS, and UDR of the Gironde only. Kesselman's findings not only confirm the earlier impression that the French Socialist members and leaders are far better educated and of higher status than those of the PSI, but they even show the generational differential between the 31% of the fathers of his PS respondents who were working-class and the respondents themselves of whom only 16% are still working-class.[39] By the same token, 31% of his PS respondents are now middle class as compared with only 9% among their fathers. This suggests a substantial social upgrading in only one generation as one important reason for the *embourgeoisement* of the French Socialists.[40] Another reason, of course, was the relatively high proportion of older members who joined the Socialists decades earlier. A more accurate assessment of the state of the present PS will have to await more recent data on membership.[41] In the meantime, studies of the attitudes have revealed the character of the new PS better than any social breakdown could. Large numbers of the delegates at the Grenoble Congress considered as most important such issues as the quality of big city life, worker control of industry (*autogestion*), immigrant worker problems, and early retirement. Legalized abortion and opposition to police tapping of telephones rounded out the image of a new kind of socialist party,[42] far removed from the example of the British Labour party or the West German SPD.

Majority Socialist Parties

The membership of the British Labour party, in any case, has received very little attention from researchers since the classic study of Jean Blondel[43] except for some recent studies of constituency party leaders, the National Executive Committee, and Labour members of Parliament. Blondel concluded for the 1950s that the membership of both major parties corresponded in a general way to the social structure of their electorates. In the case of the Labour party, say, according to the Gallup polls of 1955, this would mean that of all working-class members of the two parties (72% of the total), Labour had 56% and the Conservatives 42%, whereas middle- and upper-middle-class members (28% of the total) were 19% with Labour and 79% Tory.[44] The upshot was clearly that the Conservative party was far more heavily influenced by its disproportionate middle-class share than Labour could be by its workers even though definitions of social class vary.[45] For the Labour party of 1955, this would work out to a share of over 80% manual workers.

Among the constituency party leaders, however, the local studies of the 1950s suggest, the working-class element accounted for a mere two-fifths, whereas one-tenth were well to do and one-half were clearly middle-class persons.[46] The study of the constituency parties of Labour by Edward G.

Janosik in the 1960s added to this several further features. The leaders tended to be between 35 and 55 years of age; the M.P.s and constituency party chairmen up to ten years older. Only 26% of the leaders were working class, another 16% salaried trade union or party officials, as compared with 32% business and professional persons, 17% white-collar employees, and 9% housewives. Their educational level was accordingly high and, for those under 45, visibly rising, especially among M.P.s and parliamentary candidates. Their religious affiliations included 19% Methodists and other nonconformists, whereas the lion's share of 66% had none at all. Finally, 84% of them were members of trade unions, including 71% in unions affiliated with the party.[47] This feature, mandated by the Labour party constitution, and the overwhelming role of the unions in the annual conferences of the party, make up much of the difference between the party systems where Socialist or Labor parties are dominant and the Socialist parties of Latin Europe.

The National Executive Committee (NEC) of the extraparliamentary Labour party was examined by Victor J. Hanby who posed the question of whether, in the years 1900–1972, the NEC had not followed the same path of *embourgeoisement* long traveled by the parliamentary leaders and, perhaps, now beckoning the constituency parties as well.[48] Hanby's tabulation of class composition shows indeed the steady decline of the working-class, poorly educated, element on the NEC from nine out of ten before World War I to only five out of ten by 1972. In the last period, 1964–1972, 42% of the new entries were middle class, mostly teachers and journalists, and largely university-educated. Many had evidently moved up from the working-class origins of their parents. The composition of the parliamentary Labour party of 1970, as compared with that of the West Germany SPD of 1969, was the object of another elite study by W. L. Guttsman.[49] Of the Labour M.P.s, 58.7% (as compared with 63% of the Tories) turned out to be university-educated including 25% (Tories, 51.5%) at Oxford or Cambridge. Only 20.6% (Tories, 0.6%) had merely an elementary education, whereas 20.9% (Tories, 74.8%) of the Labourites had even been to a public school like Eton or Harrow. By comparison, the SPD deputies of 1969 included 40.5% (CDU, 64%) with a university education, 5.9% (CDU, 2%) had left school at 14 and another 35.5% (CDU, 19.6%) at 16, and 57% (CDU, 77.6%) had the coveted *Abitur* diploma for graduation from a *Gymnasium* at the age of 19. Guttsman also compared the occupations of M.P.s as well as the social-class composition of recent cabinets. He concluded among other things that the decline of the traditional working-class politicians on the left, in both countries, made for similarities in the elitist character of all major parties there, a situation quite different from the one prevailing at the outset of the period under consideration:[50]

If the political leadership cadres of the two parties in the two countries are thus today possibly more remote from the bulk of the followers this is in Britain largely due to the continuing existence of a wide gulf between the elected and the majority of the electors, while in Germany, where the political elite occupies a somewhat larger spectrum, a complex electoral system and bureaucratic selection procedures are interposed between voter and representative . . .

The Labour party has come a long way from the era when "a closed and solidaristic working-class community sent men with strong local or industrial ties with the community into Parliament." By the same token, today's SPD is very far from the utopian "social ghetto party" (Max Weber) held together mostly by ideology and common suffering. At the same time, their leadership is becoming more and more like that of their bourgeois antagonists.

Let us add to this one more great Socialist majority party on which there is sufficient information. The Austrian Socialists (SPÖ) also have no competition to fear from their left and have repeatedly been in the federal government. Although Austria is a much smaller country, moreover, the size of the SPÖ membership alone puts the SPD, PS, and PSI to shame.[51] Its success in breaking out of the big city "ghetto" into the rural Catholic, female, and young electorate enabled it to gain an electoral majority. The membership too, which used to be concentrated in the Vienna area, had by 1975 no more than a good third (37.2%) in the megalopolis. Its evolution from doctrinaire Marxism to liberal catchall party character is mirrored in its occupational composition (Table 25–15).

A quick glance at the West German SPD in the 1950s and 1960s (Tables 25–3 and 25–6) shows the SPÖ figures to be quite comparable. The SPÖ had more pensioners as indeed some of its age groups (65.2% over 40, including 28.1% over 60) appear to be older. The SPD had a larger share of white-collar, independent, and professional people. As with the Labour party, the worker component in Parliament is difficult to compare across national boundaries as long as we cannot be sure that trade union officials have not been counted as workers. In this case it was supplied to show the great change from 1956 to 1971. The SPÖ also has honorary functionaries called trustees (*Vertrauens-personen*) who make up about 10% of the party. They are somewhat comparable to the figures we had on the SFIO cadres of 1952 (Table 25–4), especially in their large numbers of public employees. The old SFIO as well as the PS of the Gironde resemble the SPÖ in age, but they were always much less proletarian and more attractive to white-collar, independent, and professional people. The Italian PSI, on the other hand, is closer to the SPÖ in these respects with the exception of the strong, if declining, Italian rural base. Despite its electoral inroads in the countryside, the SPÖ has as yet to attract substantial numbers of farmers or even farm workers.

Last but still important is the linkage with the Austrian trade unions. Like in West Germany, after 1945, a single nonpartisan union federation, the ÖGB, replaced the various partisan unions of the First Republic. The free (socialist) trade unions had been by far the largest element of the old unions and literally inseparable from the party. Under the new arrangement, such close ties are no longer feasible, but there is still a large socialist faction in the ÖGB of which

TABLE 25–15. The Austrian Socialists (SPÖ): Occupation of Members, Trustees, and Deputies, 1929–1972 (Percent)

	MEMBERS			TRUSTEES	PARLIAMENTARY DEPUTIES	
	1929	1954	1972		1956	1971
Workers	51.2	39.7	37.3	36.8	60.8	21.5
Agricultural workers	—	—	1.0	—	—	—
White collar	11.8	8.8	13.4	20.7⎫	17.6	40.9
Public employees	8.6	13.6	13.8	20.7⎭	—	—
Professions	1.5	1.5	1.1	—	—	—
Independents	4.3	2.8	2.1	—	—	—
Farmers	—	1.0	0.7	—	—	—
Pensioners	2.2	11.4	16.4	—	—	—
Housewives	16.1	17.3	12.2	42.5	21.6	37.6
Others	1.6	—	2.0	—	—	—
Total	100.0	100.0	100.0	100.0	100.0	100.0

Source: Bericht an den Bundesparteitag 1972, Vienna: SPÖ, 1972; Kurt L. Shell, The Transformation of Austrian Socialism, New York: State University of New York, 1962, p. 50; and Melanie Sully, "The Socialist Party of Austria," in Paterson and Thomas, eds., p. 219.

every member has to join the party. The ÖGB prizes its tactical independence, which even enabled it to have a cabinet post for a Christian trade unionist in a Conservative (ÖVP) government in the late 1960s. Still, there are many direct links to the SPÖ, and, most important, the SPÖ has no real competition for the loyalty of organized labor.[52]

Communist Parties

The subject of the various Communist parties in Western European countries excited interest long before the current vogue of studies of Euro-communism. Although membership figures may be uncertain and the turnover unusually high, it is still possible to compare them in an approximate way (Table 25–16). As we look at the table, we ought also to bear in mind what may well be called the Kriegel thesis on the PCF, namely, that "a party of the working-class," the much-vaunted vanguard of the proletariat, need not be "a party composed of workers."[53] It is the political spirit rather than the vital statistics that make a party Communist. At first glance, these estimated 2.5 million Western European Communists, mostly French and Italian, appear as a formidable force in these not always stable democratic societies. On closer examination, however, their most striking characteristic would seem to be their disunity and uneven role in the various countries rather than the coiled power of the revolutionary left.

As Table 25–16 shows, their member/voter ratios fluctuate wildly from country to country, a sign of their uneven penetration of the electorate. The highest member/voter ratios belong to the anemic British, Irish, Austrian, and West German parties. The latest popular vote of the Communist parties separates the giants (PCI, Iceland, Finland, PCF) and a few runners-up (Portugal, Luxembourg) from the pygmies. The difference becomes clear when we compare the Communist vote with that of the Socialist parties, their chief competitors for the labor and other left-wing and underprivileged votes. Whereas the parties of France, Iceland, and Finland are still competing with Socialist parties of similar strength, most of the others are simply pushed against the wall by powerful Socialist parties that have preempted the political clientele on the left. This can be shown with a simple index composed of the percentage of Communist votes of the combined left (Socialist and Communist) popular vote. This index (Table 25–16, bottom row), indicates the relative significance of each Communist party. Here again, the PCI is in a class by itself (75%) followed by the Icelandic, Finnish, and French parties at a considerable distance (38–51%); the parties of Portugal, Greece, Spain, and Luxembourg still make a respectable showing (20–30%), and the rest is insignificant. The special stature of the PCI also could be demonstrated with

TABLE 25–16. Communist Parties of Western Europe in the 1970s

	West Germany DKP	French PCF	Italian PCI	British CP	Belgian PCB	Dutch CPN	Luxembourg PC	Danish DKP	Swedish Left VK	Norwegian NKP	Icelandic AB	Finland (SKP)	Ireland CPI	Austrian KPÖ	Switzerland (PST)	Spain (PCE)	Portugal (PCP)	Greece (KKE)
Est. Membership (early 1970s)	39,000	611,000	1.6 mil.	28,000	15,000	12,000	500–1,000	7,000	15,000	2,000–5,000	2,000–2,500	48,000	300	25,000	3,000	255,000	30,000	28,000
Est. Member/Voter ratio	34.2	11.8	17.6	84.8	8.8	3.6	0.2	6.3	5.5	15.6		13.8		64.4	40.3	5.9	11.3	6.0
% CP Vote (1974–1978)	0.3	18.6	35.9	0.1	3.2	1.7	10.4	3.7	4.7	0.4	22.9	18.9	0.04	1.2	2.2	10.8	14.4	9.3
Other Socialist party vote (%)	42.6	30.7	12.0	39.3	26.7	33.8	38.1	43.6	42.7	46.5	22.0	24.9	11.5	50.4	25.4	29.8	34.9	25.3
% CP/Combined left vote	0.7	37.7	74.9	0.3	10.7	4.8	21.4	7.8	9.9	0.9	51.0	43.2	0.3	2.3	8.0	26.6	29.2	26.9

Sources: Neil McInnes, *The Communist Parties of Western Europe*, London: Oxford, 1975, pp. 3–4; and Table 1–1.

voting curves since 1945. All the other Communist parties stagnated or declined from their peaks of voting and membership strength since the immediate postwar period.

There are several other points about the membership of Communist parties worthy of comment, especially their age, sex, and religious practices. If we compare what little is known about the present Communist parties with the confrontation between the "old" SPD and the "young" Communists (KPD) of the Weimar Republic, for example, contemporary European communism turns out to be surprisingly "old" (Table 25–17). Despite a rejuvenation campaign throughout the 1960s, the PCF of today is much closer to the allegedly ossified Weimar SPD than to the KPD of that day.[54] Both the old SPD and the contemporary PCF had only 42–46% of members under 40 as compared with 64.5% for the Weimar KPD. And, although the French SFIO and PS may well be older still than the PCF, the Italian PSI, with 42.5% under the age of 40, is at about the same level. The Norwegian, Swedish, Finnish, and Austrian parties are said to be suffering from extreme superannuation, whereas only the Danish party claims to have lowered its average age to a level comparable with that of the Weimar KPD.[55] The decline or stagnation, and sometimes illegality, of Western European Communist parties evidently made for their surfeit of older members[56] and, in many cases, hindered them in their pursuit of the rebellious youth of 1967–1969 who instead preferred more youthful groups of a Trotskyist, Maoist, or anarchist persuasion. Even the Communist youth organizations underwent considerable decline during the 1950s and 1960s.

TABLE 25–17. Age Structures of Weimar KPD, SPD, and Contemporary PCF (Percent)

	KPD 1927	SPD 1930	PCF 1966	PCF GIRONDE 1973
–24	12.3	7.8	—	—
–25	—	—	9.4	—
25–30	19.5	10.3	—	—
26–40	—	—	33.1	46.3
31–40	32.7	26.5	—	—
41–50	21.9	27.3	—	—
41–60	—	—	40.2	32.8
41–60	—	19.6	—	—
51–60	13.6	—	—	—
61–	—	8.5	17.3	20.1
Total	100.0	100.0	100.0	100.0

Source: Richard Hunt, *German Social Democracy 1918–1933*, New Haven, Conn.: Yale University Press, 1964, pp. 106–107; Wienand Kaasch, "Die soziale Struktur der KPD," *Kommunistische Internationale*, 19 (1928), 1066; *Rapport de M. George Marchais au Dix-huitième Congrès*, 1967, Paris: PCF, 1967, p. 269.

With regard to sex, we have seen that the PCI enrolls far more women (23.6%) than the PSI though not nearly as many as the one-third of the Italian Christian Democrats. The PCF today even exceeds the percentage of its Italian confrères and approaches that of the DC. But this was not always so. When the postwar fervor of the PCF still burned most brightly, and rather more youthfully than today, women only accounted for 11.1% of the party. Their percentage rose to the PCI level by the early 1960s, however, and reached 30% in 1972. Even the PCF electorate has become less masculine and, by 1973, was composed of 42% women.[57] Here too, however, the Communist parties of the West, unlike their prewar predecessors, have failed to attract militant young women with appropriate appeals. The timid stand of the PCI on the issue of abortion, motivated evidently by the desire not to abort the "historical compromise," was most unlikely to impress Italian feminists.

The situation is the exact reverse with regard to religious practice. Here the official party policy for more than a decade has been for a reconciliation with the churches, and yet the communist voters and, even more, the members of communist parties have been slow to change. There is a long way, of course, from a policy of tolerating religion—rather than attacking it—to attracting large numbers of practicing, not to mention devout, members of any church. In Catholic countries where the separation of church and state and issues of religious education have long been the source of major divisions, communist anticlericalism had perhaps been too deep-seated to yield to pious homilies overnight. Still, there have been striking changes in a country such as France, when we compare voters' predilections over a period of time.

In a typical survey, although 62% of Frenchmen labeled themselves "practicing Catholics," only 38% claimed to be regular and 36% occasional churchgoers and 26% never attended church.[58] Another recent poll pinpointed the underlying beliefs as 24% firm believers, 12% as "close to" but critical of the church, 38% as merely "peripheral," and 21% as indifferent. Of the regular Catholic churchgoers, only 11% voted for the PCF or PS in 1973, whereas 32% and 31%, respectively, of those who never attend church said they voted for these two parties.[59] Looking from left to right on Table 25-18 the pivotal nature of the religious practices of Frenchmen to their political choices is plain to see. In the Michelat-Simon survey, in particular, the united left turns out to be made up of only 5% regularly practicing and 27% occasionally practicing Catholics as compared with 64% who either never attend or are indifferent to religion. By comparison the Centrists and Gaullists together have 32% regular and 40% occasional churchgoers, and only 25% nonpracticing Catholics or nonbelievers.[60]

The breakdown of the Italian voters by party and religious practice in 1956 and 1968 also fits the pattern of variation from right to left (Table 25-19), although the development over time, if any, remains obscure. Evidently the first row for 1956[61] corresponds roughly to the first two rows of 1968, which would leave no particular evidence of development.

TABLE 25-18. French Voters by Party and Religious Practice, 1952, 1967, and 1978 (Percent)

	PCF	SOCIALIST	RADICALS	CDS/MRP	CONS	GAULLIST	ALL
		SFIO	Rad.-Soc.		Indep./Peasants	RPF	
1952							
Devout	—	9	14	73	56	50	31
Nonpracticing	87	67	60	4	15	24	35
		⎰ PS ⎱		DC		UDR	
Catholics (1971)							
Regular attendance	3	8		40		28	20
Occasional attendance	17	36		37		42	37
Nonattendance	46	41		18		22	28
Nonreligious	30	11		3		4	10
	(1971)		MRG	CDS	Indep. Republ.	RPR	
1978							
Regular	—	—	13	43	27	21	
Occasional attendance	—	—	15	11	20	23	
Nonpracticing	71	50	59	41	25	48	

Source: Stanley Henig and John Pinder, eds., *European Political Parties*, London: Allen & Unwin, 1969, p. 173; *Les Elections Legislatives de Mars 1978, Le Monde* Supplement, 1978, p. 56; Guy Michelat and Michel Simon, "Religion, Class, and Politics," *Comparative Politics*, 10 (1977), 169 which gives no year for its survey.

TABLE 25–19. Italian Voters by Party and Religious Practice 1956 and 1968 (Percent)

	PCI	PSIUP	PSI	PSDI	DC	PLI	MON.	MSI
1956								
Weekly attendance	29	—	41	69	86	75	77	56
Rarely or never	71	—	59	31	14	25	23	44
1968								
Weekly	12	20	29	39	69	53	37	39
Often	16	22	28	17	16	16	21	21
Sometimes	24	30	25	17	10	20	21	30
Rarely	24	16	12	10	4	9	7	6
Never	24	12	6	17	1	2	14	4

Source: Pierpaolo Luzzato-Fegiz, *Il volto sconosciuto dell'Italia 1956–1965*, Milan: Giuffre, 1966, pp. 1285–1289 and Samuel H. Barnes, "Italy: Religion and Class in Electoral Behavior," in Rose, *Electoral Behavior*, p. 195.

The PCI, in any case, seems more religious than the PCF. The comparative voting survey of Richard Rose highlights religion as a major factor of variance in several other Western European countries, such as the Netherlands, Austria, Belgium, and, less so, Western Germany,[62] but this is from an incomplete list which, for example, leaves out Spain, Portugal, Greece, Switzerland, and Luxembourg. Of the countries covered in the book, several show the negative correlation of religious practice with the communist electorate. In Belgium, for example, where church attendance has been rising from 49.6% (1950) to 58.9% (1968), the small PCB/CPB electorate is exclusively composed of nonpracticing Belgians, while the socialist (PSB/BSP) voters have among them 50% of all nonpracticing and only 12% of all practicing Catholics.[63] For the Netherlands, the Labor party (PvdA) in 1956 had no less than 72% of the religiously unaffiliated, although this figure dropped to 55% by 1968. The share of nonpracticing socialist voters was particularly high among the Catholics and Orthodox Reformed.[64] Four-fifths of the communists, according to the 1977 election study,[65] were unaffiliated and the rest were Catholics. The Norwegian Communist and the Socialist People's parties in 1965, and to a lesser degree the Labor party, likewise stand out with a disproportionate share of voters of no or low religious engagement.[66] The same was found to be true of the Swedish Communists, and less so the Social Democrats, in 1968.[67] Unfortunately, all of this information refers to the communist or left-wing voters, even of the PCI and PCF, and not to members.

Conservatives, Liberals, and Christian Democrats

If there is a dearth of empirical information on the membership of left-wing parties, there is likely to be even less on conservatives and other parties to the right of the center. Nevertheless, we have already tabulated some data on the West German CDU, the FDP, the Italian DC, and even some member/voter ratios on the French Gaullists. Some conservative parties, such as the Austrian People's party (ÖVP), make comparison difficult because of their indirect or federal structure. The ÖVP is a federation of the Austrian Workers and Employees Federation (ÖAAB), the Farmers Federation (ÖBB), the Economic Federation (ÖWB), the Women's Federation (ÖFB), and the Youth Federation (ÖJB). Of these, the ÖAAB accounts for 46%, the ÖBB for 38%, and the ÖWB for 16% of the 570,000 members, and an additional 262,000 family members make it 832,000.[68]

As Table 25–20 shows, the ÖVP has a much smaller share of workers among its membership than the CDU or DC, or even the Gaullists or British Conservatives. The membership of the Catholic People's party (KVP) of the Netherlands with 11% workers, 21% small business and farmers, 51% middle class, and 9% upper class may be closer to the Austrian party than any of

TABLE 25–20. Members and Voters of Austrian Parties by Occupation, 1969 (Percent)

	ÖAAB MEMBERS	ÖVP Members	ÖVP Voters	SPÖ Members	SPÖ Voters	FPÖ VOTERS	VOTERS
Workers (including agricultural) (including agricultural)	30.8	9.5	58 (35)	41.2	73 (5)	49 (23)	18
Public employees	42.0	13.0}	29	14.0}	25	40	—
Private employees	17.2	4.8}		10.1}			32
Independent and professions	—		13		2	11	27
Total	90.0	27.3	100	65.3	100	100	77

these.[69] On the other hand, the ÖVP receives a fair amount of working-class votes, especially farm laborers' votes, of which the SPÖ gets very few. Its white-collar membership is not far behind that of the SPÖ, especially among public employees, and its white-collar vote is ahead of that of the SPÖ. By comparison, the right-wing Freedom party (FPÖ) garnered the largest white-collar component among its voters of 1969 and had a surprisingly high labor vote, especially among farm laborers. We have set down the 1969 vote of the West German FDP (omitting pensioners, housewives etc.) for comparison. But, except for the high white-collar vote, the two seem to have little in common.

Do the French Gaullists as a party resemble any other conservative group on which we have information? The Lagroye-Lord study of the Gironde also examined a UDR federation. The UDR there was found to be similar in age to the PS, that is, with 46.6% between 40 and 59, 31% over 60, and 21.5% under 40. The CDU with 23% under 34, 36% between 34 and 50, and 41% over 50 was notably younger. The occupational comparison (Table 25-21) shows up many similarities between the UDR and the DC, although there is no accounting for the housewives, pensioners, and students that appear under "others" for the DC. Unfortunately, the British studies of Conservative constituencies are mostly rather dated. In the 1950s, the white collar component already played a considerable role among Conservative members, but not among constituency leaders who were mostly shopkeepers and business and professional men.[70] The UDR federation in the Gironde also included 29.6% trade union members (PS, 58.5% and PCF, 65.3%); the CDU study by Nils Diederich showed 12% trade union members (SPD, 38%) and another 27% in other occupational and economic interest groups (SPD, 14%). The total membership in various clubs and organizations in the CDU came to 86% (SPD, 79%), which may be quite typical of conservative parties.[71] The DC sample in our German-Italian party members study included 24% members of CISL, the non-Communist labor federation, and another 34.6% in other unions and professional associations. Their share was highest among the public employees.[72]

TABLE 25-21.   Occupations of UDR, CDU, and DC Members

	UDR GIRONDE	CDU 1970	DC 1971
Workers	14.8	13	18.1
Service personnel	4.0		—
White collar	13.5	27	12.1
Cadre Moyens	11.7	18	—
Professions	8.5		5.1
Entrepreneurs	16.6⎱	31	8.0
Farmers (including labor)	6.3⎰		14.9
Others	24.6	12	41.8

Comparing Voting Patterns and Party Systems

This essay would not be complete without a parting glance at the riches of electoral data available on many European countries. Unlike the information on party membership, the information on the voters of the various parties is easily available, and there are few stones that sophisticated social researchers have left unturned.[73] But even there little systematic comparison has as yet been attempted. We have merely scratched the surface of a large area of potential comparative research topics so far. Let us try to turn our attention to some basic research questions without going into further details.

One way to view the voting behavior of major occupational groups is by tabulating the occupational composition of each party to set these breakdowns side by side. This is the way in which *Sondages* periodically publishes its polls, thereby creating marvelous materials for plotting longitudinal curves (Table 25–22). These "vertical" distributions tell much about the nature of each individual party and about the relative weights of each occupational group in it.[74] In Table 25–22, we furthermore have the differentials from party to party and over time to analyze. Consider, for example, the differences between the worker and white-collar elements among PCF and Socialist voters or the amazing shifts between the UDR and Republican electorate of 1968 and the RPR voters of 1978. Similar differences in the sex, age, and size of commune of the individual party electorates also beckon us to analyze their significance. But there is also another "horizontal," or systemic, dimension on which the comparison of electoral data in Table 25–23 is based. Here we are comparing instead the relative partisan shares of the major occupational groups among the voters. The data on France on Table 25–23, in fact, are exactly the same as the 1968 data on Table 25–22, only recomputed horizontally for comparison.

Table 25–23 thus shows how the major parties of our four largest Western European party systems share the vote of such important groups as blue-collar, white-collar, and independent and professional voters. We have also supplied the popular vote of that year or the preceding elections. The tabulation shows, in particular, the similarities and differences between the first two and the second two party systems. Judging from these surveys, West Germany and Great Britain are remarkably similar in the way the major occupational groups are divided politically, the only differences being that

1. the British Conservatives received an even larger share of the white-collar and business and professional vote than the CDU/CSU and
2. the ever-growing pensioner vote inclined toward the CDU/CSU in Germany and toward Labour in Britain.

France in 1968, by comparison, shows a mixed pattern. The Gaullist UDR share of the occupational groups is almost identical to that of the CDU/CSU. The shares of the left, on the other hand, are splintered in idiosyncratic ways, centered around the disunity of Centrist, Radical, and Socialist groups. Eight

TABLE 25-22. French Voters by Party and Occupation (Head of Family), 1968 and 1976–1978 (Percent)

	PCF		PSU	PS	FDGS	CD	UDF	UDR/Rep.	RPR	POPULATION (ADULTS)
	1968	1976	1968	1976	1968	1968	1978	1968	1978	1968
Farmers	8	4	12	8	18	16	10	18	12	17
Independent businesspersons	5	8	8	12	9	15	6	14	8	10
Professions	2		5		3	10	14	6	10	5
White collar	18	15	26	30	16	18	20	18	20	15
Workers	49	52	39	29	34	22	16	25	16	31
Pensioners	18	21	10	21	20	18	34	19	34	22
	100	100	100	100	100	100	100	100	100	100

Source: Sondages, 1968, no. 2, p. 101 and 1976, nos. 3 and 4, p. 41; "Les Elections legislatives de Mars 1978," *Le Monde Supplement*, 1978, p. 56.

TABLE 25–23.   Shares of Occupational Groups of Party Electorates in Major European Countries (Percent)

Country [year of survey (% vote)]	WORKERS	AGRICULTURAL WORKERS	WHITE COLLAR CIVIL SERVICE	TEACHERS	PENSIONERS	PROFESSIONS	INDEPENDENTS	FARMERS
West Germany 1967								
CDU/CSU (47.6)	33		45		45	58		
SPD (39.3)	49		34		36	14		
FDP (9.5)	1		4		2	8		
Great Britain 1970								
Conservatives (46.4)	38		54		36	76		69
Labour (43.1)	51		37		51	18		23
Other (10.5)	11		9		13	6		8
France 1968								
UDR (46.1)	37		46		47	56		54
CD (12.2)	8		12		12	19		13
FDGS (16.6)	18		15		18	12		19
PSU (4.5)	6		7		3	4		4
PCF (20.0)	31		20		20	9		10
Italy 1963								
MSI/PDIUM (6.8)	5	8	8	6			7	5
PLI (7.0)	3	3	10	11			18	8
DC (38.3)	25	21	38	35			32	44
PSDI/PRI (7.5)	11	7	9	9			9	7
PSI (13.8)	25	22	13	18			16	13
PCI (25.3)	29	37	16	17			15	18

Source: Richard Rose, ed., *Electoral Behavior: A Comparative Handbook,* New York: Free Press, 1974, pp. 147 and 502; Gianfranco Poggi, *Le Preferenze Politiche Degli Italiani,* Bologna: Il Mulino, 1968, p. 19; and computed from *Sondages,* 1968, no. 2, p. 101.

years later, with the resurgence of the Socialists and the new Centrist merger of the UDF, the pattern was perhaps clearer, but hardly more similar to West Germany or Great Britain. The major divide between right and left simply does not run around the same percentage point and there is lacking the separate Liberal/Radical force which is typical of the first two systems.

The Italian party system of 1963, by comparison, was even more splintered into seemingly immovable and indissoluble fragments both on the right and the left. At that time, the true nature of the central position of the DC, to speak with Sartori, and the PSI as an obstacle to PCI dominance still stood out. In the meantime, the major generational shifts revealed by the 1972 study of Samuel Barnes and Giacomo Sani[75] and the surge of the vote for the PCI in recent years show that the Italian party system has finally come into motion. Whether this will eventually result in a more simplified system of competition for shares of the major occupational groups remains to be seen. By 1975, the following major groupings were found to characterize the two political poles, the PCI and the DC (vertically).[76]

	PCI	DC	TOTAL ELECTORATE
Big business, executives and professions	10.8	14.5	14.3
White collar, small business, artisans	21.8	22.5	26.5
Skilled workers, farmers	25.8	31.0	26.4
Unskilled and farm workers	41.6	32.0	32.8

The current combination of attraction and fear of seeing the PCI in the government may help the realignment along.

As for the party systems of the smaller European democracies, we have compiled the horizontal breakdowns of the occupational groups as far as the data would permit, in some cases simplifying the excessively splintered systems (Table 25–24). Despite these extremes of splintering, it is amazing to what extent the basic Conservative-Socialist-Liberal scheme will explain the larger shares even though we have not even begun to consider such important factors as religion, regionalism, and age for which there often are sufficient data as many of the country chapters in this book have brought out.[77]

If we group these eight multiparty systems with the sums of the Conservative-Socialist-Liberal share of the two largest occupational groups, there is little left to explain in most cases (Table 25–25). Because our data are in some cases a decade old or older, the unexplained factors sometimes may seem out of phase, as in the case of Denmark's tax revolt which in the meantime has made a showing in Norway and affected other European welfare states as well. The generational roots of the Dutch Democrats '66 similarly disrupted partisan patterns below the surface in most of the other countries in the late 1960s. Perennial problems such as the ethnic question in Belgium or agrarianism in Scandinavia, on the other hand, seem to be as impervious to the obsolescence of these data as are the Conservative-Socialist-Liberal "lion's

TABLE 25–24. Shares of Occupational Groups of Party Electorates in Smaller European Democracies (Percent)

Country/Year of Survey	(% vote)	WORKERS	WHITE COLLAR	MIDDLE CLASS	PROFES-SIONS	INDEPENDENTS	UPPER AND UPPER-MIDDLE CLASS	FARMERS
Belgium 1968								
Catholic CVP	(31.7)	30	33			30		62
Socialist BSP	(28.0)	47	27			14		7
Liberal PVV	(20.9)	11	21			35		23
Flemish VU	(9.8)	8	11			13		7
Walloon RW and FDF	(5.9)	4	8			8		1
The Netherlands 1971								
Catholic KVP	(21.8)	25		27			14	
Socialist PvdA	(24.6)	41		17			13	
Liberal VVD	(10.3)	2		12			31	
Antirevolutionary	(8.6)	6		11			11	
Christian CHU	(6.3)	6		7			6	
Democrats '66	(6.8)	7		8			8	
Others	(21.6)	13		17			17	
Sweden 1968								
Conservatives	(14)	3	15		39	16		19
Social Democrats SD	(50)	75	43		14	31		6
Liberal People's	(15)	7	24		27	22		9
Agrarian Center	(16)	10	14		16	24		61
Communists	(3)	2	1		—	—		—
Norway 1965								
Conservatives	(20.2)	6	21			45		12
Labor	(43.2)	68	49			23		25

658

Liberals	(10.2)	8	15	18	9
Christian CPP	(7.8)	6	4	5	7
Agrarian Center	(9.4)	4	4	6	47
Socialist SPP	(6.0)	7	6	2	1
Denmark 1975					
Center-Right	(21.9)	14	29	28	16
Social Democrats	(29.9)	46	23	9	2
Liberal Venstre	(23.3)	9	22	29	69
Progress	(13.6)	15	14	30	12
Socialist Left	(11.3)	16	12	4	1
Finland 1972					
NC and FCL	(20.1)	10	35	57	15
Socialist SDP	(25.8)	41	26	14	8
Liberal LPP	(5.2)	3	14	10	—
Swedish People's	(5.4)	4	6	9	6
Agrarian FRP	(9.2)	4	3	—	11
Agrarian Center	(16.3)	8	8	5	54
Communist PDL	(17.0)	30	8	5	6
Ireland 1969					
Fianna Fail	(47.7)	41	48	37	43
Fine Gael	(34.1)	17	26	37	39
Labor	(15.4)	28	15	10	3
Others	(2.8)	14	11	16	15
Austria 1973					
Catholic ÖVP	(43.1)	25	45	69	86
Socialist SPÖ	(50.0)	71	46	25	12
Liberal FPÖ	(5.5)	4	9	6	2

TABLE 25–25.   Conservative-Socialist-Liberal Shares of Blue and White Collar Groups (Percent)

	BLUE COLLAR	WHITE COLLAR	REMAINING FACTORS
Belgium 1968	88	81	Ethnicity
Netherlands 1971	67	56	Religion, Generations
Sweden 1968	85	82	Agrarianism
Norway 1965	82	85	Agrarianism, Teetotalism, Leftism
Denmark 1975	69	74	Tax Revolt, Leftism
Finland 1972	54	75	Communism, Agrarianism, Ethnicity
Ireland 1969	86	89	
Austria 1973	100	100	

shares" of the most numerous occupational groups. What is more, there is even a likelihood of some of the remaining parties climbing aboard, or returning to the troika of parties that dominate the field: the amalgamation of religious parties in the Netherlands and the basic kinship of Left Socialists and some right-wing Socialist dissidents (e.g., the Danish Center Democrats) with the great Social Democratic labor parties are cases in point, and this is usually true also of generational revolt movements.

The horizontal divisions of the major occupational groups, of course, can also be used to show the extent to which the parties of a system are limited to a particular such group base or not. A good example of an extremely group-bound party system, as Pertti Suhonen has also pointed out in his essay, is Finland. Here the agrarian parties, CP and FRP, practically monopolize the farm vote, whereas the Socialist parties do the same with the labor vote, and the National Coalition has by far the lion's share of the upper and upper middle class vote. On the other hand, our table is replete with occupational catchall parties, both large like Ireland's Fianna Fail or small like the Netherlands' Democrats '66 which get about the same share—one nearly identical with their popular vote—from every major occupational group. If we had similar "horizontal breakdowns" on religious beliefs and practice, age, education, ethnicity, and region, we could look for the perfect catchall party, one that received the same share from every conceivable group.

The only deviant cases among the smaller democracies, then, would appear to be, on Table 25–24, the Irish parties which really present a pattern of two Conservative parties and a small labor party. In Spain, Portugal, and Greece, it will be recalled, there also appears to be no classical Liberal party, although all three of these systems resemble each other in that they have a basic four-party scheme à la France 1978 with strong Socialist and Center parties, flanked by sizable Communist and Conservative parties. The three most splintered systems, Denmark, Finland, and Switzerland do not deviate all that much from the basic Conservative-Socialist-Liberal scheme except that their Conservative wings tend to be weak or splintered. In the case of Finland, moreover, this weakness is counterpointed by a powerful Communist party.

In this fashion, then, the social composition of voters, members, and leaders of the major Western European parties appears to form surprisingly similar patterns in the different countries of the area. If our cursory comparison has tended to single out cases deviant from the prevalent Western European norm, it has served even more strikingly to show the analogous ways in which the social structures of these countries are linked with their governmental structures through their party systems. The underlying uniformities in the relationship between seemingly different societies and their governmental personnel and policies clearly emerge in the comparative analysis.

Notes

1. "Party Politics in Question," in Dennis Kavanagh and Richard Rose, eds. *New Trends in British Politics: Issues for Research*, Beverly Hills, Calif.: Sage, 1977, pp. 191–219.

2. See esp. Stein Rokkan and Lars Svåsand, "Comparative Data on Party Membership: A Review of Recent Compilations," *European Political Data Newsletter*, 26 (March 1978), 30–40.

3. See esp. Stein Larsen, Bernt Hagtvet et al., eds., *Who Were the Fascists*, Oslo and New York: Norwegian University Presses and Columbia University Press, forthcoming.

4. See Rokkan and Svåsand, pp. 30–31 and Henry Valen and Daniel Katz, *Political Parties in Norway*, Oslo: Norwegian University Presses, 1967.

5. Duverger, *Political Parties*, London and New York: Methuen and Wiley, 1954, pp. 79–101.

6. See now, also, William E. Paterson and Alastair H. Thomas, eds. *Social Democratic Parties in Western Europe*, London: Groom Helm, 1977, pp. 432–436. Member/voter ratios for the Austrian Socialists (SPÖ) were 29.6% in 1975 (37.9% in 1949), the Belgian BSP 17.1% (1974), the Danish SD 15.4% in 1975 (34.9% in 1950), the Finnish SSP 14.6 (1975), the French PS 3.3% in 1973 (8.4% for the SFIO of 1946), the Italian PSI 13.0% (1976) and the PSDI 24.2%, the Dutch PvdA 4.9% in 1972 (9.5% in 1948), the Norwegian Labor party 13.4% in 1973 (25.7% in 1949), the Swedish Social Democrats 44.6% in 1976 (35.5% in 1948), and British Labour 56.5% with and 5.9% without the unions in 1974 (43.1% and 5.5% in 1950).

7. See R. M. Punnett, *British Government and Politics*, New York: Norton, 1968, pp. 79–81; and Jean Blondel, *Voters, Parties, and Leaders: The Social Fabric of British Politics*, 2nd rev. ed., Middlesex: Penguin, 1974, pp. 89–90. The Conservatives trebled their membership in the 1940s and 1950s.

8. The PSI alone had 535,000 in 1977. *Almanacco Socialista 1977*, Rome, 1977. See also the regional differences in the member/voter ratio of the PCI in Sidney

Tarrow, *Peasant Communism in Southern Italy*, New Haven, Conn.: Yale University Press, 1967, p. 318.

9. See Giorgio Galli and Alfonso Prandi, *Patterns of Political Participation in Italy*, New Haven, Conn.: Yale University Press, 1970, pp. 340–343. The national ratio of members to adult population for the PCI was 5.1% in 1961 and 6.6% before the exodus of 1956 when the membership began to decline from 2.1 to 1.6 million (Ibid., p. 110).

10. The membership figures are from Jorolv Moren et al., *Norske Organisasjonen*, Oslo: Grundt Tanum, 1972. For earlier figures see Valen and Katz, p. 70 where ratios of 10% for the Communists, 17.8% for Labour, 16.2% for the Liberals, 15.8% for the Christian People's party, 38.4% for the Agrarians, and 28.3% for the Conservatives are given for 1957.

11. The Social Democrats successfully encouraged whole trade unions to join as units. See M. Donald Hancock, *Sweden: The Politics of Post-Industrial Change*, Hinsdale, Ill.: Dryden Press, 1972, pp. 57–58. During the postwar mobilization period the ratios were even higher for the Center (56%) and the Communists (29%). Already in 1932, over one-fourth of Swedish voters belonged to a party.

12. In the meantime, furthermore, the several religious parties have coalesced into CDA after their votes began to drop. See Jean Beaufays, *Les Partis Catholiques en Belgique et aux Pays-Bas, 1918–1958*, Brussels: E. Bruylant, 1973, pp. 420–422, the chapter by Galen Irwin in this book; Hans Daalder, "The Netherlands: Opposition in a Segmented Society," in Robert A. Dahl, ed., *Political Oppositions in Western Democracies*, New Haven, Conn.: Yale University Press, 1966, pp. 188–236; and Arend Lijphart, *The Politics of Accommodation*, 2nd ed., Berkeley: University of California Press, 1975.

13. See this writer's *The Making of Stormtroopers*, Princeton, N.J.: Princeton University Press, forthcoming.

14. See Table 25–6. The SPD and FDP cabinet ministers including Chancellor Helmut Schmidt in 1978 averaged 54.3 years.

15. This trend already manifested itself very strongly in fascist movements in various European countries in the interwar period, lending further ambiguity to the lower middle class thesis of fascism. See this writer's "Comparing Fascist Movements," in Larsen et al., forthcoming. See also Valen and Katz, p. 271 which shows the prominent role of white-collar occupations among all local Norwegian party leaders.

16. For a rough estimate, leaving aside the balance of older joiners against additional dropouts, we can assume that the 15.6% of the 35- to 44-year-old category of 1963 are almost identical with the 14.4% of the 45- to 54-year-olds in 1970, and so forth.

17. *Gesellschaftliche Daten 1977: Bundesrepublik Deutschland*, Bonn: Presse- und Informationsamt der Bundesregierung, 1978, p. 113.

18. Housewives and independents, of course, are underrepresented with regard to the population.

19. Civil servant members are even overrepresented with regard to the population at large, whereas the white-collar members are not.

20. Among the Young Socialists of the SPD, still, 31% white collar and 22% civil servants together make up a majority and the Young Union of the CDU/CSU has

similar proportions. See Jürgen Dittberner and Rolf Ebbighausen, *Parteiensystem in der Legitimitätskrise*, Opladen: Westdeutscher Verlag, 1973, p. 278.

21. See, for example, this writer's party member study reported in this book and elsewhere.

22. See also the table in Ossip K. Flechtheim, *Die Parteien der Bundesrepublik Deutschland*, Hamburg: Hoffmann & Campe, 1973, p. 408.

23. See also the essay on political professionalization by Dietrich Herzog, "Karrieren und politische Professionalisierung bei CDU/CSU, SPD und FDP," in Dittberner and Ebbighausen, pp. 109–131. Herzog found that this group of party and interest group functionaries had grown from 16% to 40% in the years since 1949. Two-thirds of his sample of 121 professional functionaries began their career by holding local party offices, often for long periods of time. One-third changed over into politics from civil service positions.

24. The percentage of party officials in the Italian Chamber between 1946 and 1958 alone was 44–51% and of union officials an additional 14–24%. Giovanni Sartori et al., *Il Parlamento Italiano, 1946–1963*, Naples: Edizioni Scientifiche Italiane, 1963, pp. 120–121.

25. See Valen and Katz, pp. 265–273.

26. Valen and Katz, p. 276 recorded other features too, such as the politics of the fathers of the respondents. From this, it appears that the local leaders are far more often the children of partisan parents than are the party's voters or those who identify strongly with it.

27. By comparison with the West Germans, only a third or less of these holders of national party office had held local or sectional office, but 84% (PCI) and 70% (DC), respectively, had held a provincial or federation post. See Gianfranco Poggi, ed., *L'Organizzazione Partitica del PCI e della DC*, Bologna: Il Mulino, 1968, pp. 503–504 and Galli and Prandi, pp. 146–148, 157–158.

28. The Carlo Cattaneo survey gives 8.7% for the share of women in the PCI leadership and 2.7% for the DC leaders as compared with a steady one-fourth of the PCI membership (over 50% in the 1960s in Central Italy) with a majority of housewives and to a good one third of the DC membership, consisting to three-fourths housewives, Poggi, pp. 280–281, 355–359, 417–424, 490–491. Being university educated places a person among a mere 2% of the Italian population that is so.

29. See also the table in F. Cichitto et al., *La DC dopo il primo ventennio*, Padua: Marsilio, 1968, p. 175, and the description of P. A. Allum, *Italy: Republic Without Government*, New York: Norton, 1975, pp. 70–73.

30. Raphael Zariski, *Italy: The Politics of Uneven Development*, New York: Holt, Rinehart & Winston, 1972, p. 183.

31. In the Northeast, the much smaller PCI still boasts a majority of workers, but the DC there is dominated by the small farmer element (about one-fifth) outnumbered only by the housewives. See Poggi, pp. 456–475.

32. The population of central Italy is only 18.8% of the national population.

33. See Tarrow, *Peasant Communism in Southern Italy*, p. 207. See also Mattei Dogan, "Political Cleavage and Social Stratification in France and Italy," in Seymour M. Lipset and Stein Rokkan, eds., *Party Systems and Voter Alignments*,

New York: Free Press, 1966, pp. 184–193; and Giordano Sivini, "Le parti communiste, structure et fonctionnement," in *Sociologie du communisme en Italie*, Paris: Fondation nationale des sciences politiques/Colin, 1974, pp. 130–137.

34. The average age of members of the *Comité Directeur* had risen from the early 40s to 54, and professors, teachers, professionals and journalists made up its majority, whereas workers, farmers, and even the white-collar element had a negligible share. Local elected officials constituted the bulk of the membership. See esp. Harvey G. Simmons, *French Socialists in Search of a Role, 1956–1967*, Ithaca, N.Y.: Cornell University Press, 1970, p. 202 and by the same author, "The French Socialist Opposition in 1969," *Government and Opposition*, 4 (1969), 295–296.

35. See Vincent Wright and Howard Machin, "The French Socialist Party: Success and the Problems of Success," *Political Quarterly* (January–March 1975), 40–46.

36. See Alain Lancelot, "Opinion Polls and the Presidential Election, May 1974," in Howard R. Penniman, ed., *France at the Polls: The Presidential Election of 1974*, Washington, D.C.: American Enterprise Institute, 1975, pp. 178 and 192.

37. "Recruitment of Rival Party Activists in France," *Journal of Politics*, 35 (1973), 2–41. The sample was drawn from six different departments of France which present a representative cross-section of militants and leaders.

38. "Trois féderations de partis politiques," *Revue Française de Science Politique*, 24 (1974), 559–595. The Lagroye-Lord sample was limited to the Gironde.

39. See also Samuel H. Barnes, *Party Democracy: Politics in an Italian Socialist Federation*, New Haven, Conn.: Yale University Press, 1967, p. 97 and André Bernard and Gisèlle LeBlanc, "Le Parti Socialiste SFIO dans l'Isère," *Revue Française de Science Politique*, 20 (1970), 557–567.

40. This has to be carefully weighed in the light of the fact that, for example, in comparing the Italian Communist leaders in clientelistic Southern Italy with those of the more developed north, a higher percentage of well-educated professional and upper-middle-class persons were found to be typical of the less developed habitat. Tarrow, *Peasant Communism in Southern Italy*, pp. 230–235. Moreover, the Gaullists in Kesselman's study also showed a substantial difference in middle class status from sons to fathers.

41. The delegates of the 1973 congress of the PS in Grenoble were revealing of several trends: the newness of many members (45% of delegates new since 1971) and the many groups from which they came (only 37% from SFIO, 24% FEN and 18% CFDT members, 1% CGT, and 10% Force Ouvrière). Of the total 60% were under 40 years of age, and very few came from among working class or old white collar, as compared with the 25% teachers and 8% students, Hurtig, pp. 34–35.

42. Robert Cayrol, "L'univers politique des militants socialistes: Une enquête sur les orientations, courants et tendances du parti socialiste," *Revue française de science politique*, 25 (February 1975), 23–52. Despite the abortion issue, incidentally, the PS with 11% women according to the Gironde study has only half an many as the PCF (23.2%) and UDR (23.8%).

43. See Jean Blondel, *Voters, Parties, and Leaders: The Social Fabric of British Politics*, Harmondsworth, Middlesex: Penguin, 1963, who also discusses some of the local studies of British party membership in the 1950s. *Ibid.*, pp. 89–127.

44. Calculated from the figures in Henry Durant, "Voting Behaviour in Britain, 1945–65," in Richard Rose, ed., *Studies in British Politics*, New York: St. Martin's Press, 1966, pp. 122–124.

45. See, for example, Mark Abrams, "Class Distinction in Britain," in *Conservative Political Centre: The Future of the Welfare State*, 1958, cited by Blondel, p. 55, where the working class is said to be 65% of the total and the voting percentages differ accordingly. See also J. Bonham, *The Middle Class Vote*, London: Faber & Faber, 1954, p. 130.

46. Blondel, pp. 96 ff.

47. Edward G. Janosik, *Constituency Labour Parties in Britain*. New York: Praeger, 1968, pp. 11, 14, 17–18, 20–24.

48. Victor J. Hanby, "A Changing Labour Elite: The National Executive Committee of the Labour Party 1900–1972," in Ivor Crewe, ed., *Elites in Western Democracy*, New York: Wiley & Croom Helm, 1974, pp. 126–158. See also B. Hindess, *The Decline of Working-Class Politics*, London: MacGibbon & Kee, 1971.

49. W. L. Guttsman, "Elite Recruitment and Political Leadership in Britain and Germany since 1950: A Comparative Study of MPs and Cabinets," in Crewe, pp. 89–125.

50. Guttsman, pp. 118–119.

51. According to the latest figures, the most recent membership drive has driven the total to over 700,000 from about half that number in 1945. In the 1975 elections, the party polled over 50% of the vote in Burgenland, Styria, and Carinthia. See Melanie Sully, "The Socialist Party of Austria," in Paterson and Thomas, pp. 217–218.

52. See Sully, pp. 223–225.

53. See Neil McInnes, *The Communist Parties of Western Europe*, London: Oxford, 1975, pp. 36–40 on the frequency of turnover (50–66% every four years) and on its significance for the democratic attitudes of current members. Also Annie Kriegel, *The French Communists: Profile of a People*, Chicago: University of Chicago Press, 1968, pp. 95–96, and her detailed account of how the proletarian composition and organization of the PCF have declined since 1936. *Ibid.*, pp. 70–78, 85–86.

54. The aging trend in the PCF was already evident in the years since 1954. See Kriegel, p. 4. The Nazi party (NSDAP) of 1933 was still younger, with 70% under 41 years of age, NSDAP, *Parteistatistik*, Berlin: Reichsorganisationsleiter, 1935, vol. I, 155–162.

55. See McInnes, pp. 46–49. The contemporary SPD, in spite of the recent influx of youth, had only about 31% under 40 in 1970. The Berlin FDP, on the other hand, had 42.5% aged 40 or younger (Table 25–6).

56. See esp. the analysis of the aging process in the PCI 1951–1963, in Poggi, pp. 349–350.

57. *Le Monde*, February 23, 1973. See also the discussion by Kriegel, p. 59. In Sweden, the Communist party claimed 26% female membership. McInnes, pp. 50–52.

58. See also the remarks of Stanley Hoffman et al., *In Search of France*, Cambridge, Mass.: Harvard University Press, 1963, pp. 36–37 and *Sondages*, 24 (1962), 23; vol. 29 (1967), 7; and vol. 35 (1973), 69 ff.

59. See *Sondages*, 35 (1973), 26 and vol. 36, (1974), 54. We have left off the religious minorities for lack of sufficient data on actual practice.

60. In the 1974 presidential contest, the Mitterand supporters had 86% of the religiously unaffiliated and 74% of the nominal Catholics, but only 23% of the devout, whereas Giscard d'Estaing won 77% of the devout, 26% of nominal Catholics, and 14% of the unaffiliated. See SOFRES survey of May 20–21, 1974.

61. The question was whether the respondent had attended church in the previous seven days.

62. Rose, "Comparability in Electoral Study," in Rose, *Electoral Behavior*, A Comparative Handbook, New York: Free Press, 1974, p. 17.

63. See Keith Hill, "Belgium: Political Change in a Segmented Society," in Rose, p. 81.

64. See Lijphart, pp. 246–249.

65. There were only 11 Communists in a sample of 1270. The data were furnished by courtesy of Galen Irwin.

66. Stein Rokkan and Henry Valen, "Norway: Conflict Structure and Mass Politics in a European Periphery," in Rose, pp. 331 and 369.

67. Bo Särlik, "Sweden: The Social Bases of the Parties in a Developmental Perspective," in Rose, pp. 417–420.

68. This information and that on Table 25–20 are from Kurt Steiner, *Politics in Austria*, Boston: Little, Brown, 1972, pp. 145 and 335–336; and Flechtheim, p. 63.

69. See Beaufays, p. 422.

70. See the account and Figure 5 in Blondel, pp. 90, 96–100. The study of Glossop, for example, revealed that three-fifths of the members engaged in nonmanual occupations. Manual workers were two-fifths of the members, and only 8–9% of the constituency leaders. Greenwich was quite similar in this respect.

71. Diederich, pp. 44–45.

72. See this writer's "Partecipazione ai sindacati e ai partiti in Germania Occidentale e in Italia," *Rivista Italiana di Scienza Politica*, 2 (1971), 325–366, esp. 332; and "Party Members and Society," in Rudolf Wildenmann, ed., *Form und Erfahrung, ein Leben für die Demokratie, Zum 70. Geburtstag von F. A. Hermens*, Berlin: Duncker & Humblot, 1976, pp. 153–172.

73. See especially the excellent contributions to Rose, *Electoral Behavior*, and the sources cited there, in particular the comparative chapters by Rose and Philip Converse at the beginning and end of the book.

74. There are major definitional problems in the use of occupational categories which we have chosen to ignore here. For a good discussion of them, see Converse in Rose, pp. 735–738.

75. See also Giacomo Sani, "The Italian Electorate in the Mid-1970s: Beyond Tradition?," In Howard R. Penniman, *Italy at the Polls: The Parliamentary Elections of 1976*, Washington, D.C.: American Enterprise Institute, 1977, pp. 81–122, esp. the materials from the Giovanni Sartori and Alberto Marradi survey of 1975, *ibid.*, pp. 104, 111–112, and Samuel H. Barnes, "The Consequences of the Elections: An Interpretation," *ibid.*, pp. 327–351.

76. From Giacomo Sani, "Le elezioni degli anni settanta: terremoto o evoluzione?" *Rivista Italiana di Scienza Politica*, 6 (1976), 261–288, and "The PCI on the Threshold," in *Problems of Communism*, 25 (Nov./Dec. 1976), 27–51. The data were from the survey of Sartori and Marradi.

77. See also the tree analyses and combinations of factors throughout Rose, *Electoral Behavior*, for most of the countries under consideration.

INDEX

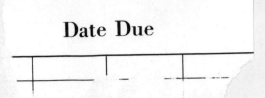

Date Due